Perspectives on Old Testament Literature

PERSPECTIVES
ON OLD TESTAMENT
LITERATURE

Woodrow Ohlsen

Pasadena City College

Harcourt Brace Jovanovich, Inc.

New York   San Diego   Chicago   San Francisco   Atlanta

To the memory of
THOMAS S. KEPLER
teacher and friend

ISBN: 0-15-570484-2

Library of Congress Catalog Card Number: 77-91012

Printed in the United States of America

Picture credits
Page
2 *The Cambridge Bible Commentary: Old
Testament Illustrations,* ed. by Clifford M. Jones,
Cambridge University Press, 1971.

8 The Metropolitan Museum of Art. The Michael
Friedsam Collection, 1931.

40 Harvey Barad/Photo Researchers, Inc.

209 Giraudon, Paris

280 The British Museum

323 The British Museum

367 Radio Times Hulton Picture Library

396 Yale University Art Gallery, Dura-Europas Collection

Maps by Jean Paul Tremblay

PREFACE

As the study of the Bible as literature has expanded rapidly in the past decade, so has the need for an approach to the subject that is both nonsectarian and scholarly. To meet this need, *Perspectives on Old Testament Literature* offers a balanced selection of literary and interpretive readings on the Old Testament. I have chosen the readings with the purpose of presenting a multiplicity of views.

In courses on the Bible as literature, those students already acquainted with the Bible have usually thought of it only as a religious book, and one not subject to literary analysis. Moreover, many students come to class unfamiliar with any but the accepted interpretations of their own religious backgrounds. For these reasons, instructors may find it difficult to elicit from their students the thoughtful and informed opinions that make class discussions fruitful. This book can bring to the classroom a variety of stimulating ideas.

At the beginning of each chapter I have summarized one or more Old Testament books, to introduce students to them and clear the way for an easier understanding of their content. In the Summaries I refer to the translation used in the Revised Standard Version of the Bible, but the chapter and verse references apply to any major translation. Each Summary is followed by a reading on the literary qualities of the Old Testament books and by several selections that give various interpretations of their meaning. Because it is impossible to do justice to all thirty-nine books of the Old Testament in the semester or quarter usually allotted to this subject in a college course, I have selected those that seem to embody the most significant themes and the most representative forms. The nineteen books summarized and discussed (Genesis, Exodus, Deuteronomy, Joshua, Judges, 1 and 2 Samuel, 1 Kings, Amos, Isaiah, Second Isaiah, Song of Songs, Psalms, Proverbs, Job, Ecclesiastes, Esther, Ruth, Jonah) reveal the basic ideas and issues that engaged the Hebrew mind for a thousand years. They portray God and human beings in a drama that is expressed in a variety of literary forms and devices, such as metaphor, simile, personification, meter, rhythm, parallelism, poem, allegory, parable, dialogue, essay, history, folk tale, myth, short story, epic, and saga. These books contain the knowledge and poetic insight that have made the Hebrew vision an illuminating force in our culture for more than two thousand years.

Each chapter ends with a list of Suggested Readings for further study and a set of Questions for Discussion and Writing. In addition to testing the student's comprehension of the Old Testament books and the readings, the Questions allow students to do their own literary analyses of the books and to compare selected biblical passages with other works of literature.

The perspectives in this volume provide a comprehensive, balanced appraisal of the biblical writings. My experience in teaching a course in the literature of the Bible, both in the classroom and on the radio, convinces me that the method implicit in this textbook can be exceptionally helpful to those who want to engage their minds as they read the Bible. Although instructors may find a better way to use this book, I will suggest an approach that has worked well for my students.

1. Read all the summaries at a sitting or two. This preview-overview will dispel any fears you may have that the Old Testament is incomprehensible, or even dull.
2. Beginning with Genesis, read the Summary of each book before reading the Biblical account in an annotated edition such as *The Oxford Annotated Bible* or *The Harper Study Bible.*
3. Read the essay on the literary qualities of the book and reread parts of the book in the light of this analysis.
4. Read the selections under the heading "Interpretations," noting the similarities and differences in the various analyses and points of view.
5. Answer the questions for Discussion and Writing.

I am indebted for information and ideas to the editors and authors of *The Interpreter's Bible, The Interpreter's One-Volume Commentary on the Bible, The Anchor Bible, Harper's Bible Dictionary, The New Westminster Dictionary of the Bible,* and *The New Bible Commentary,* and to the many authors whose works I consulted although I have not selected pieces from their writings. I am grateful to all the authors, publishers, artists, and museums who have granted permission to reproduce their work. I have leaned heavily on *The Oxford Annotated Bible,* edited by Herbert G. May and Bruce M. Metzger, for the historical background and scholarly information stated so succinctly in their introduction and footnotes. The Division of Christian Education of the National Council of the Churches of Christ in the United States of America has graciously permitted frequent use of quotations from the Revised Standard Version of the Bible.

I have been encouraged in my study and teaching of biblical literature by the positive response of students and faculty at Pasadena City College. Leonard Franco and Karen Norris of the Department of English gave me valuable criticism and stimulating insight during our discussions of Old Testament literature for radio broadcast, and Bob Ball and Bill Weitzel of the library Reference Room were always able to find an article or a book that had eluded my search through the card catalogs.

Marie Ohlsen's help as sounding board, critic, and proofreader was indispensable.

The manuscript was reviewed by Charles R. Courtney of Santa Barbara City College, Sidney Gulick of San Diego State University, and Ben Siegel of California State Polytechnic University at Pomona; I appreciate their comments and suggestions. Finally, this book would never have come into being without the diligent, perceptive efforts of several members of the College Department of Harcourt Brace Jovanovich, Inc.: Merton Rapp, Carla Hirst Wiltenburg, Elizabeth Hock, Robert Winsor, and particularly those superb editors, Judy Burke and John Holland.

Woodrow Ohlsen

CONTENTS

CONTENTS

CONTENTS

GENESIS

SUMMARY

Genesis can be divided into two parts: primeval history (Chapters 1–11) and the history of the founders of the nation (Chapters 12–50). As subdivisions of the second part, we have the story of Abraham in Chapters 12–25; the stories of Isaac and his sons Esau and Jacob in Chapters 26–36; and the story of Jacob's family, focusing on Joseph, in Chapters 37–50.

We begin at "the Beginning," when the world was created from preexisting chaos. God orders that a world of land and water, darkness and light, plants and animals, and finally, man and woman come into being. "And God saw everything that he had made, and behold, it was very good" (1:31).

Chapter 2 contains a second account of Creation, one perhaps written by the writer J (see the selection by A. Powell Davies, "Fact and Fable: A Problem for Scholars," pp. 14–20). In this version man is created first; then God plants a garden for him to take care of. Among

1

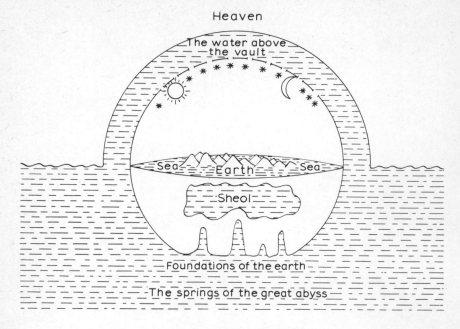

The Hebrew Universe

The Old Testament is not a scientific textbook and nowhere does it describe in precise detail the structure of the universe. From scattered verses, which do not always agree, it is possible, however, to represent in diagrammatic form the view of the universe held by the Hebrews in Old Testament times. "The foundations of earth" (Psalm 18:15) support the universe, and stand in "the springs of the great abyss" (Gen. 7:11), known elsewhere as "the deep that lurks below" (Gen. 49:25). "The vault of heaven" (Gen. 1:14), "spread out . . . like a tent" (Ps. 104:2), and shining like "a mirror of cast metal" (Job 37:18), holds sun, moon and stars, too many to count (Gen. 15:5). The earth is surrounded by sea, described as "the water under the vault" (Gen. 1:17); and Sheol, the abode of the dead, is like "a great chasm" which "opens its mouth and swallows them and all that is theirs" (Num. 16:30). When "the windows of the sky" (Gen. 7:11) are opened the water above the vault pours through them, emptying "the cisterns of heaven" (Job 38:37), and falls as rain on the earth.

The Lord's throne is in "the highest heaven" (Deut. 10:14), the "heaven of heavens" (Ps. 148:4); above the earth, above "the vault of heaven" (Gen. 1:14), and even higher than the "waters above the heavens" (Ps. 148:4).

the trees are the tree of knowledge and the tree of life. Adam and Eve are forbidden to eat of the tree of knowledge, but they nevertheless do so when encouraged to by the serpent. The consequence of their disobedience is expulsion from the garden. Evidently, eating of the tree of life would irreversibly confer eternal life upon them, because God says, " 'Behold, the man has become like us, knowing good and evil; and now, lest he put forth his hand and take also of the tree of life,

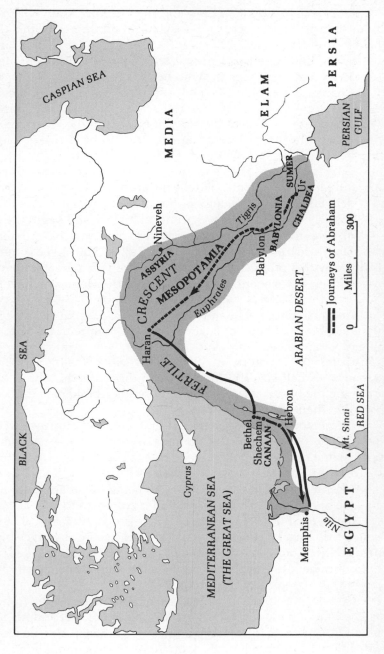

The Fertile Crescent and the Arabian Desert, 2000–1700 B.C.

and eat, and live forever'—therefore the Lord God sent him forth out of the garden of Eden" (3:22).

Eve gives birth first to Cain and then to Abel. Cain kills Abel out of jealousy over the results of their burnt offerings; for this Cain is cursed to wander in the land of Nod, east of Eden. He marries and has a son named Enoch, whose family is traced down to Lamech. Meanwhile, Eve gives birth to Seth, who becomes the father of Enosh.

Chapter 5 is called "the book of the generations of Adam," and in this chapter we are informed of the descendants of Adam down to Noah. Chapters 6–9 present the story of Noah and the Flood. Again, as in the case of the story of Creation, we seem to have two accounts: Compare, for example, 7:1–3 with 6:18–21.

Chapter 10 lists "the generations of the sons of Noah, Shem, Ham, and Japheth." Chapter 11 tells the story of the Tower of Babel and concludes with a genealogy of the descendants of Shem.

With Chapter 12 we leave primeval history and begin the story of Israel. This story begins with the Lord's command that Abraham leave Haran and go "to the land that I will show you." The command is coupled with a promise that "I will make of you a great nation." This promise—a covenant between God and the Hebrews—is repeated in 15:21 and in 17:1–8.

Abraham obeys God and goes to Canaan, taking his wife Sarah and his nephew Lot and Lot's wife. During a famine in Canaan, Abraham and Sarah sojourn in Egypt, where Abraham, afraid for his life because of Sarah's great beauty, passes his wife off as his sister. (In fact, she is his half-sister!) When Pharaoh discovers that she is Abraham's wife, he becomes very angry and sends Abraham and his entourage on their way.

Upon their return to Canaan, Abraham and Lot realize that they cannot support their respective families in the same area. Abraham gives Lot first choice of a place to settle. Lot chooses the Jordan plain, and Abraham goes to the plain of Mamre.

After ten years in Canaan, Abraham and Sarah are without offspring, so Sarah in desperation persuades Abraham to take Hagar as his second wife. But when Hagar becomes pregnant, Sarah abuses her so much that Hagar flees into the wilderness, where she gives birth to Ishmael. Now God tells Abraham and Sarah that Sarah will bear a son. They cannot believe this, but nevertheless Sarah, at the age of ninety, gives birth to Isaac.

God decides to destroy the cities of Sodom and Gomorrah, because he cannot find even ten righteous men there. Lot and his family flee, but Lot's wife is turned into a pillar of salt when she disobeys the Lord's injunction not to look back upon the destruction. Lot's daughters, concerned for the future of humankind, make their father drunk and lie with him. The sons born to them become the ancestors of the Moabites and the Ammonites.

In Chapter 22 we have one of the best known and most master-
fully told stories of the Bible. Eric Auerbach says of "The Sacrifice of
Isaac" that in contrast to the Homeric poems we have here "the ex-
ternalization of only so much of the phenomena as is necessary for the
purpose of the narrative, all else left in obscurity; the decisive points
of the narrative alone are emphasized, what lies between is nonexis-
tent; time and place are undefined and call for interpretation; thoughts
and feeling remain unexpressed, are only suggested by the silence and
the fragmentary speeches; the whole, permeated with the most unre-
lieved suspense and directed toward a single goal (and to that extent
far more of a unity) remains mysterious and 'fraught with background.' "*

Abraham obeys without question God's command to take his
only son Isaac to Mount Moriah and present him as a burnt offering.
At the last moment Abraham's hand is stayed by an angel of the Lord,
and Abraham sacrifices instead a ram that he finds caught in a thicket.
Now God is more pleased with Abraham than ever, and he repeats his
promise that Abraham will have many descendants and that through
them "shall all the nations of the earth bless themselves" (22:18).

When Sarah dies (at the age of 127 years), Abraham seeks a
burial place for her. He chooses the cave of Machpelah, which is located in an area controlled by Hittites. After some dickering, he pays
Ephron the Hittite four hundred shekels of silver for it.

Advanced in years himself, Abraham asks Isaac to promise him
that he will take a bride from among his people in Nahor (a city in
Mesopotamia). He sends a servant there, fearing that if Isaac goes he
may never return. The servant does well for Isaac. He returns with
Rebekah, the daughter of Bethuel, "the son of Milcah, the wife of
Nahor, Abraham's brother." And so, we are told, "Isaac was comforted after his mother's death" (24:67).

Although Abraham is very old now, he takes another wife, Ke-
turah, who bears him six sons. He dies at the age of 175 and is buried
in the cave of Machpelah, where Sarah lies.

Rebekah, wife of Isaac, conceives and bears twin sons, Esau
and Jacob. Esau is born first and is therefore the elder, but Jacob and
his mother manage to hoodwink both Esau and Isaac so that Esau sells
Jacob his birthright, and Isaac gives his blessing to Jacob instead of
Esau.

Frightened of the revenge that Esau has sworn to seek, Jacob
runs away to his uncle, Laban, in Haran. (Haran is also called Pad-
danaram.) On his way, Jacob dreams one night of a ladder going up to
heaven, upon which the angels of God are ascending and descending.
The Lord appears above the ladder and gives to Jacob the same promise that he had given to Abraham. Jacob sets up a pillar on the spot

*Eric Auerbach, *Mimesis: The Representation of Reality in Western Literature*, trans. W. R.
Trask (Princeton, N.J.: Princeton University Press, 1953), pp. 11–12.

and anoints it with oil. He promises that if all goes well with him, he will build a sanctuary here at Bethel and will give a tenth of what the Lord gives him.

Jacob goes on to Haran, meets his cousin Rachel at a well, and falls in love with her. When his uncle, Laban, asks him what wages he wants for working for him, Jacob says he will work seven years to obtain Rachel as a wife. Laban agrees, but when the seven years are up he gives Jacob Rachel's older sister, Leah, instead. Jacob must work another seven years to obtain Rachel. He receives Rachel immediately, however, and soon makes it evident that he loves her and not Leah. We are told that because Leah "was hated," the Lord opened her womb but kept Rachel barren. Leah bears Reuben, Simeon, Levi, and Judah.

Rachel, desperate because she is unable to bear children, orders Jacob to lie with her maid, Bilhah. Bilhah conceives twice and gives birth to Dan and Naphtali. When Leah realizes that she can bear no more children, she tells Jacob to go in to her maid Zilpah. Zilpah bears Gad and Asher.

Now Leah's fortunes change (perhaps with the help of some mandrake roots), and she is able to bear children again. She gives birth to Issachar, Zebulun, and a daughter, Dinah. God then remembers Rachel, and she gives birth to Joseph. Jacob now has eleven sons and a daughter.

Jacob wishes to leave Haran with his family and possessions, but Laban urges him to stay. He agrees to let Joseph have all the speckled and spotted and black sheep and all the speckled and spotted goats. Laban then takes all the sheep and goats with these traits a three-days journey away from Jacob. But Jacob outwits him by setting peeled rods of poplar and almond with streaks in them before the sheep and goats as they breed. They bear striped, speckled, and spotted offspring, and he keeps breeding the strongest of these until he becomes "exceedingly rich."

Jacob learns that Laban and his sons are angry with him, so he leaves with his family and possessions. After three days, Laban catches up to him and asks why Jacob has treated him so badly. Having been warned by God in a dream not to say anything "good or bad" to Jacob, Laban sets up some stones as a witness between them and says "The Lord watch between you and me, when we are absent one from the other" (31:49). Then he and his men depart.

Now Jacob fears an encounter with Esau, the brother whose birthright and inheritance he has taken. On the way to meet Esau, Jacob wrestles with a man who turns out to be God or an angel of God. Jacob's name is now changed to Israel, which means "He who strives with God." Jacob has brought many presents for Esau, and he prevails upon him to accept them. They then go their separate ways without incident.

Lucas Cranach, "Jacob and the Peeled Rods"

Chapter 34 relates one of the less pleasant episodes of biblical legend. Dinah, daughter of Jacob and Leah, is ravished by Shechem, a Hivite. When Jacob protests this behavior, Shechem says that he will gladly marry Dinah. But Jacob's sons deal deceitfully with Shechem and the Hivites. They say that they will accept Shechem and his people if all the men of their city will undergo the rite of circumcision. When they do so, they are massacred by Simeon and Levi "on the third day, when they were sore" (34:25). Simeon and Levi not only slay all the males but plunder the city. This greatly disturbs Jacob, who fears reprisals from the people of the land—the Canaanites and the Perizzites.

God appears to Jacob again at Bethel, and again we are told that Jacob's name will from now on be Israel. God renews the covenant: "The land which I gave to Abraham and Isaac I will give to you, and I will give the land to your descendants after you" (35:12).

On the way from Bethel to Ephroth, Rachel dies as she gives birth to Benjamin. Jacob now has twelve sons. He visits his father, Isaac, at Hebron just in time to see him on his deathbed. He buries him.

Chapter 36 lists the descendants of Esau, who left the land of Canaan to dwell in the hill country of Seir. The name "Edom" becomes identified with Esau (36:8).

Chapters 37–50 recount the story of Joseph, interrupted by the story of Judah and Tamar in Chapter 38.

The history of the family of Jacob is continued in these last chapters of Genesis, which focus on Joseph, the first son of Rachel. At the age of seventeen, Joseph tends the flocks with the brothers born of Jacob and his concubines, Bilhah and Zilpah. His relationship with these brothers is not a happy one, and he does nothing to improve it when he relates dreams in which he is portrayed as superior to them.

7

Biagio di Antonio, "The Story of Joseph" (The Metropolitan Museum of Art, The Michael Friedsam Collection, 1931)

"They hated him yet more for his dreams and for his words" (37:8). When an opportunity presents itself, they throw Joseph into a pit and then sell him to a passing caravan, which takes him into Egypt. Afraid of their father's reaction, they cover Joseph's coat with goat's blood, and Jacob assumes that Joseph has been torn to pieces by a wild beast.

Chapter 38 interrupts the Joseph story to tell the story of Judah and Tamar. Judah's daughter-in-law, Tamar, loses her husband, Er, and his brother Onan will not perform the obligatory function of taking his place to father a son in his name. Judah promises Tamar that his youngest son, Shelah, will do so when he comes of age. But Judah forgets about his promise. Tamar, when she learns that Judah is coming into the area for sheepshearing, covers herself with a veil and sits among the temple prostitutes. Judah approaches her, and she asks for a pledge that he will later pay her with a kid from his flock. Three months later Judah learns that his daughter-in-law is with child. He orders that she be burned, but when she presents him with the signet, the cord, and the staff (the pledge that he had given her), he says, "She is more righteous than I, inasmuch as I did not give her to my son Shelah" (38:26). Tamar is delivered of twins, Perez and Zerah.

We now return to Joseph, who has been sold to Potiphar, a captain of the guard for Pharaoh. Because the Lord is with Joseph, all that he does prospers, so that Potiphar soon entrusts everything in his household to him except (for ritual reasons) the food he eats. Joseph's service to Potiphar is cut short, however, when the captain's wife unjustly accuses Joseph of trying to rape her. In prison, Joseph is as successful as he had been in Potiphar's household, and soon the keeper puts everything in his charge. As a result, when the Pharaoh puts his chief butler and chief baker into prison, Joseph is in charge of them. He interprets their dreams accurately and therefore acquires a reputation that calls him to the Pharoah's attention when Pharoah wants an interpretation of his own recurrent dream. Joseph's interpretation of the dream so impresses the Pharaoh that he makes Joseph second in command to himself. "You shall be over my house, and all my people shall order themselves as you command; only as regards the throne will I be greater than you" (41:40). He then gives Joseph an Egyptian name and an Egyptian wife, the daughter of a priest of On.

In keeping with his interpretation of Pharaoh's dream, Joseph now stores up grain during the seven plenteous years in preparation for the famine that is to follow. During this time, his Egyptian wife bears him two sons, Manasseh and Ephraim. When the famine strikes, people come from everywhere to buy grain from Joseph in Egypt.

When Jacob, up in Canaan, learns that there is grain in Egypt, he sends ten of his sons there. Joseph recognizes them, but they do not recognize him. He accuses them of being spies and gives them grain only on the condition that next time they bring Benjamin with them. He keeps Simeon hostage. When the grain is used up, Jacob agrees to let Benjamin go to Egypt with his brothers, but only after Judah promises to be responsible for Benjamin.

They journey again to Egypt and appear before Joseph, who has difficulty controlling himself when he sees his only full brother, Benjamin. The brothers eat in the same room with Joseph, but not at the same table. When their asses are loaded with grain, Joseph has his steward put their money back in their sacks, as he had done on the previous occasion. And not only the money this time, but a special silver cup of Joseph's is placed in the sack of Benjamin. When the brothers have been on their way only a short time, Joseph sends his steward after them to accuse them of stealing the cup. It is found in Benjamin's sack, so they must all return to the city. They are confronted by Joseph, who accuses them of bad faith. But now Judah steps forward and reviews all that has happened, ending with the plea that he be held prisoner instead of Benjamin so that his father, Jacob, will not die at hearing that Benjamin is in jail. Joseph cannot control himself any longer. He reveals himself to his brothers. They are dumbfounded, but Joseph tells them not to worry, for "it was not you who sent me here, but God; and he has made me a father to Pharaoh, and lord of all his house and ruler over all the land of Egypt" (45:8).

When Pharaoh learns that Joseph's brothers have come to Egypt, he invites all of Jacob's family to come down and sends them plenty of provisions for the journey. On the way to Egypt Jacob is visited by God "in visions of the night" (46:2) and is told not to fear going there, "for I will there make of you a great nation" (46:3). So Jacob and his entire family, with all their possessions, go to Egypt. "All the persons belonging to Jacob who came into Egypt, who were his own offspring, not including Jacob's sons' wives, were sixty persons in all; and the sons of Joseph, who were born to him in Egypt, were two; all the persons of the house of Jacob, that came into Egypt, were seventy" (46:26, 27).

Jacob's family settles in Goshen, where they are free to tend their flocks as they had done in Canaan.

The famine becomes so severe that Egyptians finally sell themselves and their land to the Pharaoh in exchange for food. "So Joseph bought all the land of Egypt for Pharaoh . . . and as for the people, he made slaves of them from one end of Egypt to the other" (47:20, 21). The people now receive seed from Joseph with the understanding that at harvest time they will give one fifth of their produce to Pharaoh and keep four fifths for themselves. The priests of Egypt are the only exception; their land does not become Pharaoh's.

Now Jacob's end approaches. He has been in Egypt for 17 of his 147 years. He blesses Joseph's sons, Manasseh and Ephraim, placing his right hand upon the head of Ephraim, the younger. When corrected by Joseph, Jacob insists that he knows what he is doing: Ephraim shall become greater than Manasseh. Jacob then calls his sons, "that I may tell you what shall befall you in days to come" (49:1).

In Chapter 49 Jacob has something to say about each of his sons: Reuben, Simeon, Levi, Judah, Zebulun, Issachar, Dan, Gad, Asher, Naphtali, Joseph, and Benjamin. Having blessed each "with the blessing suitable to him," and having asked to be buried in the cave at Machpelah where Abraham and Sarah, Isaac and Rebekah, and Leah are buried, Jacob dies.

Joseph orders that his father be embalmed. Then, after receiving permission from the Pharaoh to go up to Canaan, he and a multitude of people, both Hebrew and Egyptian, take Jacob's body to the cave at Machpelah.

Jacob's brothers fear that now that their father is dead, Joseph will avenge himself upon them, so they tell Joseph that Jacob had asked before he died that Joseph forgive them. But Joseph says to them, "Fear not, for am I in the place of God? As for you, you meant evil against me; but God meant it for good, to bring it about that many people should be kept alive, as they are today" (50:19, 20).

Joseph dies, and he is embalmed and put in a coffin in Egypt. But before he dies he prophesies that someday God will bring his people up to the Promised Land again and that his bones will then be taken there.

LITERARY QUALITIES

from "The Literary Form of the Legends"
HERMANN GUNKEL

METHODS OF THE NARRATORS

What means do the narrators use for the representation of the character of their heroes? The modern artist is very apt to explain in extended descriptions the thoughts and feelings of his personages. When one turns from such a modern story-teller to the study of Genesis, one is astonished to find in it so few utterances regarding the inner life of the heroes. Only rarely are the thoughts of even a leading personage expressly told, as in the case of the woman when she was looking desirously at the tree of knowledge, or of Noah, when he sent forth the birds "to see whether the waters were dried up off the earth," or the thoughts of Lot's sons-in-law, who judged that their father-in-law was jesting; the thoughts of Isaac, who feared at Gerar that he might be robbed of his wife (xxvi. 7); or the cunning thoughts with which Jacob proposed to evade the revenge of his brother Esau (xxxii. 9), and so on. But how brief and unsatisfactory even this appears compared with the psychological descriptions of modern writers!

And even such examples as these are not the rule in the legends of Genesis. On the contrary, the narrator is usually content with a very brief hint, such as, "He grew wroth" (iv. 5; xxx. 2; xxxi. 36; xxxiv. 7; xxxix. 19; xl. 2), or, "He was afraid" (xxvi. 7; xxviii. 17; xxxii. 8), "He was comforted" (xxiv. 16), "He loved her" (xxiv. 67; xxix. 18; xxx. 3; xxxvii. 3), "She became jealous" (xxx. 1), "He was filled with fear" (xxvii. 33), "He eyed him with hatred" (xxvii. 41; xxxvii. 4), and elsewhere. But even these brief hints are far from frequent; on the contrary, we find very often not the slightest expression regarding the thoughts and feelings of the person concerned, and this in situations where we cannot avoid a certain surprise at the absence of such expressions. The narrator tells us nothing of the reasons why God forbade man to partake of the fruit of the tree of knowledge, nor of the reasons of the serpent for wishing to seduce mankind. He says nothing of the feelings with which Abraham left his home, or Noah en-

THE LITERARY FORM OF THE LEGENDS From Hermann Gunkel, *The Legends of Genesis* (New York: Schocken Books, Inc., 1964), pp. 58–63. Reprinted by permission of the publisher.

tered the ark. We do not learn that Noah was angry at Canaan's shamelessness, that Jacob was disappointed when Laban cheated him with Leah, that Hagar was glad when she received the promise that Ishmael should become a great nation; we are not even told that mothers rejoice when they hold their firstborn son in their arms. Particularly striking is the case of the story of the sacrifice of Isaac: what modern writer would fail under such circumstances to portray the spiritual state of Abraham when his religious devotion wins the hard victory over his parental love, and when his sadness is finally turned into rejoicing!

THOUGHT EXPRESSED BY ACTIONS

Now what is the reason for this strange proceeding? We can find it in an instance like that of xix. 27 ff. In sight of the city of Sodom Abraham had heard certain remarkable utterances from the three men; they had said that they were going down to Sodom to examine into the guilt of the city. This strange remark he let run in his head; in the morning of the following day he arose and went to the same place to see whether anything had happened in Sodom during the night. And in fact, he sees in the valley below a smoke, whence he must infer that something has taken place; but this smoke hides the region, and he cannot make out what has happened. For the story-teller this little scene is plainly not of interest because of the thing that happens, but because of the thoughts which Abraham must have thought, and yet he does not tell us what these thoughts were. He merely reports to us the outward incidents, and we are obliged to supply the really important point ourselves. This story-teller, then, has an eye for the soul-life of his hero, but he cannot conceive these inward processes with sufficient clearness to express them in definite words.

This is a typical instance for Genesis. In very many situations where the modern writer would expect a psychological analysis, the primitive story-teller simply presents an action. The spiritual state of the man and woman in Paradise and after the Fall is not analysed, but a single objective touch is given by which we may recognise it. The narrator says nothing of the thoughts of Adam when the woman handed him the forbidden fruit, but merely, that he ate it; he does not discourse to us on Abraham's hospitable disposition, but he tells us how he entertained the three men. He does not say that Shem and Japhet felt chastely and respectfully, but he has them act chastely and respectfully; not that Joseph had compassion upon his brethren, but that he turned away and wept (xlii. 24; xliii. 30); not that Hagar, when mistreated by Sarah, felt offended in the depths of her maternal pride, but that she ran away from her mistress (xvi. 6); not that Laban was dazzled by the gold of the stranger, but that he made haste to invite him (xxiv. 30); not that obedience to God triumphed in Abraham over parental love, but that he arose straightway (xxii. 3); not that Tamar remained faithful to her husband even beyond the grave, but that she took measures to rear up children from his seed (xxxviii).

From all this we see on what the story-teller laid the chief emphasis. He does not share the modern point of view that the most interesting and worthy theme for art is the soul-life of man; his childlike taste is fondest of the outward, objective facts. And in this line his achievements are excellent. He has an extraordinary faculty for selecting just the action which is most characteristic for the state of feeling of his hero. How could filial piety be better represented than in the story of Shem and Japhet? Or mother-love better than by the behavior of Hagar? She gave her son to drink—we are not told that she herself drank. How could hospitality be better depicted than in the actions of Abraham at Hebron? And there is nothing less than genius in the simple manner in which the innocence and the consciousness of the first men is illustrated by their nakedness and their clothing.

These simple artists had not learned how to reflect; but they were masters of observation. It is chiefly this admirable art of indirectly depicting men through their actions which makes the legends so vivid. Little as these primitive men could talk about their soul-life, we gain the impression that they are letting us look into the very hearts of their heroes. These figures live before our eyes, and hence the modern reader, charmed by the luminous clearness of these old legends, is quite willing to forget their defects.

SOUL-LIFE NOT IGNORED

But even when the story-teller said nothing of the soul-life of his heroes, his hearer did not entirely fail to catch an impression of it. We must recall at this point that we are dealing with orally recited stories. Between narrator and hearer there is another link than that of words; the tone of the voice talks, the expression of the face or the gestures of the narrator. Joy and grief, love, anger, jealousy, hatred, emotion, and all the other moods of his heroes, shared by the narrator, were thus imparted to his hearers without the utterance of a word.

Modern exegesis is called to the task of reading between the lines the spiritual life which the narrator did not expressly utter. This is not always such a simple matter. We have in some cases gotten out of touch with the emotions of older times and the expressions for them. Why, for instance, did Rebeccah veil herself when she caught sight of Isaac? (xxiv. 25.) Why did the daughters of Lot go in unto him? Why did Tamar desire offspring of Judah? (xxxvii.) What is the connexion of the awakening modesty of the first men and their sin? In such cases exegesis has often gone far astray by taking modern motives and points of view for granted.

A further medium of expression for the spiritual life of the personages is articulate speech. Words are not, it is true, so vivid as actions, but to make up for this they can the better reveal the inner life of the personages. The early story-tellers were masters in the art of finding words that suit the mood of the speakers: thus the malice of the cunning serpent is expressed in words, as well as the guilelessness of the childlike woman, Sarah's jealousy of her slave as well as the conciliatoriness of Abraham (xvi. 6), the righteous wrath of Abimelech (xx. 9), the caution of the shrewd Jacob (xxxii. 9), and the bitter lament of Esau (xxvii. 36) and of Laban (xxxi. 43) when deceived by Jacob. Notable masterpeices of the portrayal of character in words are the temptation of the first couple and the conversation between Abraham and Isaac on the way to the mount of sacrifice.

INTERPRETATIONS

Fact and Fable: A Problem for Scholars
A. POWELL DAVIES

1. WHO WROTE THE BOOKS OF MOSES?

The tradition that Moses was the author of the first five books of the Bible, although tenaciously held, has always been difficult to maintain. How could Moses have written the story of his own death? And if, as some of the ancient rabbis conceded might be possible, this particular passage was supplied by Joshua, what is the meaning of the words, "No man knoweth of his sepulchre unto this day"? (Deut. xxxiv: 6). There is a clear implication here of the passage of time: "*unto this day.*" Surely whoever wrote these words lived long after the death of Moses. Neither Moses himself, nor Joshua, could conceivably have written them.

Moreover, when we read that "there hath not arisen a prophet since in Israel like unto Moses," not only must we suppose that considerable time has elapsed during which such a prophet could have arisen and failed to do so, but if we are well acquainted with the Bible, we remember that the word "prophet" did not come into use until the time of Samuel. ("He that is now called a Prophet was beforetime called a Seer" I Sam. ix: 9). Moses lived in the thirteenth century

FACT AND FABLE: A PROBLEM FOR SCHOLARS From *The Ten Commandments* by A. Powell Davies. Copyright © 1956 by A. Powell Davies. Reprinted by arrangement with The New American Library, Inc., New York, N.Y.

B.C., Samuel in the eleventh. So the authorship must be at least two hundred years after Moses.

It did not pass unnoticed even before the time of modern scholarship that there were disturbing implications in such sayings as "The Canaanite was then in the land" (Gen. xii: 6). Why should such a statement be made if the Canaanite was *still* in the land, as he certainly was at the time of Moses? To draw a comparison, we might ask why an American would say, "There were Indians then on Manhattan Island," if he were living at a time when Indians still possessed it. He would only speak in such terms after—and probably considerably after—the Indians had left.

Again, in Genesis (xxxvi: 31) we read, "These are the kings that reigned in the land of Edom before there reigned any king over the children of Israel." Could this be written *before* there were kings in Israel? For Moses to have been the author of such a statement is as though one of the Pilgrim Fathers had said, "These are the kings that reigned in France before there was any president of the United States." The Pilgrim Fathers had no way of knowing that there ever would be a president of the United States. In the same way there was nothing that Moses could foresee about kings in Israel.

Since the first king of Israel was Saul, who reigned during the last quarter of the eleventh century B.C., this is the earliest date that this passage could have been composed. By this time Moses had been dead for the greater part of two centuries.

A further passage (Gen. xiv: 14) tells us that Abraham pursued his enemies as far as the city of Dan. But we know from the book of Judges (xviii: 29) that this city, the earlier name of which was Laish, did not receive the name Dan until considerably after the time of Moses. Was there any way by which Moses could have foreseen that Laish was going to be called Dan?

Considerations of which these are examples led early scholars to question the tradition that Moses wrote the Pentateuch. Ibn Ezra, in the twelfth century A.D., gave cryptic indications of his doubts but prudently refrained from open statements of them. Spinoza, in the seventeenth century, not only rejected the Mosaic authorship but developed some of the beginnings of the methods of modern scholarship. More outspoken than Ibn Ezra, he was excommunicated from the synagogue.

It is impossible to trace in any detail here the history of Biblical criticism [1] as it applies to the Pentateuch. Suffice it to say that not only was Mosaic authorship disproved but it was discovered that the Pentateuch (actually the Hexateuch, since the book of Joshua is a part of

---

[1] The word *criticism* as used by scholars does not imply anything destructive; it derives from the Greek, κριτικός (criticos), and means (literally) skilled judgment. Scholarly criticism is scientific investigation leading to informed opinion and authoritative evaluation.

the same work) was not written by any one person or even during any one lifetime but is composed of several sources which are plainly traceable and which come from periods as widely separated as the ninth century and the fourth century B.C. A few fragments, chiefly songs, are somewhat older.

We shall now pay some attention to these sources, seeking to discover what light they throw on the general character of the Pentateuch. . . .

2. THE SOURCES OF THE PENTATEUCH

The key to the sources of the Pentateuch might be found in many places; we shall choose, as did Astruc, the early scholar, the sixth chapter of the book of Exodus. Here (vi: 2–3) God says to Moses, "I am Yahweh[2]: and I appeared unto Abraham, unto Isaac, and unto Jacob as El Shaddai, but by my name Yahweh I was not known to them." What this means is that Yahweh is introducing himself by that name *for the first time*. To the patriarchs he had been El Shaddai, their family God from Haran, from which Abraham had come;[3] or simply God (Elohim).

But contrary to the implications of this passage we find the name Yahweh quite freely used in the Pentateuch, almost from the beginning. We find that God does identify himself by that name to the patriarchs. To Abraham he says, "I am Yahweh that brought thee out of Ur of the Chaldees" (Gen. xv: 7). To Jacob he says, "I am Yahweh, the God of Abraham, thy father, and the God of Isaac" (Gen. xxviii: 13). Even as early as the fourth chapter of Genesis, we find it stated that "then men began to call upon the name of Yahweh."

On the basis of the Pentateuch coming from a single author (or even a group of authors, writing in collaboration), these divergences are incomprehensible. One part of the narrative flatly contradicts another and in so flagrant a way that no single author or cooperating group of authors could possibly have overlooked it.

[2] This is the correct name, not *Jehovah*, the name we temporarily used while telling the traditional story. The word *Yahweh* . . . was considered (and still is) too sacred to be spoken aloud and therefore the word *Adonai*, meaning Lord, was substituted. Where *Adonai* was used as a preceding word (the Lord Yahweh), *Elohim*, meaning God (formerly plural, *gods*) was used. There were no vowels in ancient Hebrew, and when, later, they were supplied (as "points" written mostly beneath the line), those for *Adonai* or *Elohim* were used in the case of the sacred name Yahweh, to indicate the pronunciation of *the word to be spoken*, not the word written. . . . Jews understood this, but Christians did not. The latter, therefore, supplied the *Adonai* vowels to YHWH, making YaHoWaH, or *Jehovah*. The word in this conflate form has long been in general use and under ordinary circumstances it is just as well to use it. But in a discussion such as we are embarked upon, it is necessary to indicate quite precisely the "Sinai-Midian" God who was one of many gods but who, in the evolution of Hebrew religion, gradually became the one and only God. We must therefore use the word "Yahweh." In English Bibles, the word *Elohim* is translated "God," *Yahweh* is given as "the LORD" (capital letters), and *Adonai* is translated "the Lord" (*not* capitals).
[3] *El Shaddai* was formerly mistranslated "God Almighty," and this mistranslation appears in all our Bibles.

We have taken a single example. But there are many others. If the reader will turn to the book of Genesis he will discover that chapter one and chapter two down to the word "created" in the fourth verse give a complete summary of the work of creation. With the second half of this verse, however (Gen. ii: 4b), a new story begins and a quite different one. In the first story for instance, God (Elohim) creates man, male and female, on the sixth day. It is the culminating act of creation. But in the second story a single man (no female) is formed by God (Yahweh-Elohim) out of the dust of the earth before there is any vegetation, and God plants a garden for him. Only then does God (Yahweh-Elohim) create the animals, hoping that a species will emerge that will be a fit companion (mate?) for the man. None is satisfactory, so he makes a woman out of one of the man's ribs while he sleeps.

Now, if it is noticed that in the first story the name for God is Elohim while in the second it is Yahweh-Elohim, and if it is observed that as we proceed through the Pentateuch this alternation of passages with first the one name for God and then the other constantly recurs, it gives us a suggestion. Suppose the Elohim passages come from one source, formerly a separate document, and the Yahweh-Elohim passages from another? Suppose these sources in many respects differ in the account they give of the same events? Suppose they have been combined without being harmonized?

Taking this suggestion and applying it to the entire Pentateuch, scholars have long since discovered that it explains completely the many discrepancies. In the one source a single pair of each species of animal is taken by Noah into the ark; in the other source seven pairs are taken of the "clean" animals. In the one source Joseph is sold by his brothers to Midianites; in the other to Ishmaelites. Here, too, we find the explanation of our difficulties with the story of Moses and Mount Sinai. What we were dealing with was a composite narrative, composed of fragments fitted together but not harmonized. What happened according to one source was different from what happened according to another. But the editor, who felt free to combine the fragments, did not feel free to re-write them—or at least not extensively. And so it is throughout the Pentateuch.

Except that this over-simplifies the matter. There are not two sources but four main ones and a number of lesser ones. The four main ones are known as J (Jahvist)[4], E (Elohist), D (Deuteronomic), P (Priestly). They are separated from one another not merely on the basis of the name used for God, but also on that of language, style, and all the indications of internal evidence. We can now see very easily how the passage in Exodus vi can be explained. In one of the

[4] Jahveh is merely the German spelling of Yahweh. The pronunciation is the same. The early pre-eminence of German scholars in Biblical criticism led to the wide adoption of their symbols. Hence J for Yahwist instead of Y.

sources God is never called Yahweh until the moment that he appears to Moses and gives this as his name. In another source, the Jahvist, God is called Yahweh from the beginning. What we have are two different stories from two (or more) different writers.

Although we cannot go into the matter here, the reader should know that these sources have in turn been subdivided and that in certain passages of the Pentateuch there is material from outside them. An important additional source is H, the "Holiness Code" of Leviticus xvii to xxvi. The Biblical scholar, Pfeiffer, one of the foremost in the field, finds an S document (which he subdivides) coming not from Israel but from Edom, which explains passages which are pro-Edomite and hostile to Israel. To this document, revising the views of earlier scholars, he also ascribes the creation narrative generally attributed to J.

D, or the Deuteronomic document, is largely the book of Deuteronomy itself, and we can now see why it has a different version of the Ten Commandments from that given in Exodus. It was originally independent of Exodus. We also know, in the case of Deuteronomy, the date of its publication, 621 B.C., when it became the basis of the reforms instituted by King Josiah. We know, too, that it cannot have been written much before this time and that its author, who had a very distinctive and recognizable style, was much influenced by the prophets of the eighth and seventh centuries who first gave emphasis to God's call for righteousness.

Since detailed treatment is beyond our scope we shall now characterize the main sources of the Pentateuch and give their dates. J, the most picturesque and colorful of the sources, derives its material from folklore tradition with some indebtedness, no doubt, to previous writings and from the history and legends connected with shrines. The emphasis is southern—Judah rather than the northern kingdom. Its date is about 850 B.C. E, which eliminates all appearances of God to mortals, except Moses, idealizes its characters more than J but belongs to the same class of literature. Date: about 750 B.C. J and E were combined by an editor in about 650 B.C.

Of Deuteronomy we have already spoken. The original version, published in 621 B.C., was several times expanded and edited, perhaps for the last time about 550 B.C. It was then combined with JE, producing (with additional material) JED. This was during the Exile in Baylon, after the destruction of Jerusalem in 586 B.C. by Nebuchadnezzar. P, the Priestly Code, was produced entirely during the Exile and it is in this source that we find the Ten Commandments in Exodus xx. About 400 B.C., P was added to JED and the Pentateuch took almost its present form.[5]

---

[5] See Robert H. Pfeiffer, *Introduction to the Old Testament* (rev. ed.). New York: Harper & Brothers, 1948. The most authoritative treatment available (in English), and embodying recent research. S. R. Driver's books are classics but must be largely supplemented by reports of more recent findings.

THE SOURCES OF THE PENTATEUCH
or First Five Books of the Bible

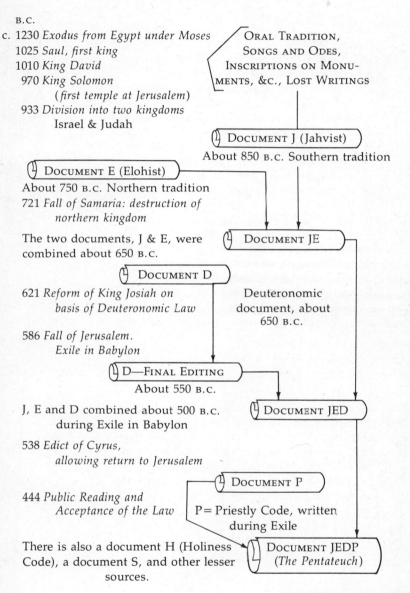

B.C.

c. 1230 *Exodus from Egypt under Moses*
   1025 *Saul, first king*
   1010 *King David*
    970 *King Solomon*
        (*first temple at Jerusalem*)
    933 *Division into two kingdoms*
        Israel & Judah

ORAL TRADITION, SONGS AND ODES, INSCRIPTIONS ON MONUMENTS, &c., LOST WRITINGS

DOCUMENT J (Jahvist)
About 850 B.C. Southern tradition

DOCUMENT E (Elohist)
About 750 B.C. Northern tradition
721 *Fall of Samaria: destruction of*
    northern kingdom

The two documents, J & E, were combined about 650 B.C.

DOCUMENT JE

DOCUMENT D

621 *Reform of King Josiah on*
    basis of Deuteronomic Law

Deuteronomic document, about 650 B.C.

586 *Fall of Jerusalem.*
    Exile in Babylon

D—FINAL EDITING
About 550 B.C.

J, E and D combined about 500 B.C. during Exile in Babylon

DOCUMENT JED

538 *Edict of Cyrus,*
    allowing return to Jerusalem

DOCUMENT P

444 *Public Reading and*
    Acceptance of the Law

P = Priestly Code, written during Exile

There is also a document H (Holiness Code), a document S, and other lesser sources.

DOCUMENT JEDP
(*The Pentateuch*)

Final Form: about 400 B.C.

There are two versions of the Ten Commandments, one in Document D, the other in Document P.

AN EXAMPLE OF THE SEPARATION OF A BIBLE
PASSAGE INTO ITS DOCUMENTARY SOURCES

P   6. *And Noah was six hundred years old when the flood of waters was upon the earth.* 7. And Noah went in, and his sons, and his wife, and his son's wives with him, into the ark, because of the waters of the flood. 8. Of clean beasts, and of beasts that are not clean, and of fowls, and of everything that creepeth upon the ground, 9. there went in *two and two* † unto Noah into the ark, *male and female,*† as *God*‡* commanded Noah. 10. And it came to pass after the seven days, that the waters of the flood were upon the earth. 11.

P   *In the six hundredth year of Noah's life, in the second month, on the seventeenth day of the month, on the same day were all the fountains of the great deep broken up, and the windows of heaven were opened.* 12. And the rain was upon the earth forty days and

J   forty nights. 13. *In the self-same day entered Noah, and Shem, and Ham, and Japheth, the sons of Noah, and Noah's wife, and the three wives of his sons with them, into the ark;*

P   *14. they, and every beast after its kind, and all the cattle after their kind, and every creeping thing that creepeth upon the earth after its kind, and every fowl after its kind, every bird of every sort. 15. And they went in unto Noah into the ark, two and two of all flesh wherein is the breath of life. 16. And they that went in, went in male and female of all*

P & J   *flesh, as God* commanded him;* and the LORD** shut him in. 17. *And the flood was* forty days *upon the earth;* and the waters increased and bare up the ark, and it was lift up above the earth. 18. *And the waters pre-*

J

P   *vailed, and increased greatly upon the earth; and the ark went upon the face of the waters.*

P = the Priestly Document, written during the Exile, sixth century, B.C.
J = the Jahvist (Yahwist) Document, the oldest of the main sources, written about 850 B.C. in Judah, the southern kingdom. The two other main sources, E and D, do not appear in this passage.
† Interpolations from P.
* *Elohim.*
‡ Verses 12 and 16b originally stood after verse 9.
** *Yahweh.*

The Major Themes and Teachings
THE ENCYCLOPAEDIA JUDAICA

The distinctive nature of Genesis within the pentateuchal complex does not mean that it can be understood apart from the other books. On the contrary, it is the indispensable prologue to the drama that unfolds in Exodus. It provides the ideological and historical background for the relationship between God and Israel as it found expression in the events connected with the national servitude and the liberation. Its unique concept of God, of man, of the nature of the world, and of their interrelationships is essential to the understanding of those events.

THE GOD OF CREATION

The external points of contact between the Genesis creation account and the ancient Near Eastern cosmologies are sufficiently numerous and detailed as to leave no doubt about the influence of the latter on the former. Nevertheless, the differences and contrasts are so great that the biblical narrative constitutes a wholly original production. Unlike its pagan counterparts, the theme of Creation occupies a secondary place in the national religion, and the cosmology serves neither to validate the social and political institutions nor to fill the needs of the cult. It does, however, embody the basic Israelite concept of God.

The pagan pantheon inevitably involved a plurality of wills inherent in which was a clash between them. In other words, polytheism did not permit the existence of an omnipotent God whose will was sovereign and who was not capricious. The Genesis creation narrative, on the other hand, presupposes a single God who is totally outside the realm of nature which is His creation and which cannot be other than fully subservient to His will. Creation by divine fiat (1:3, 6, 9, 11, 14, 20, 24) emphasizes just this very concept of the omnipotent, transcendent God Whose will is unchallengeable. In this connection, the external literary form in which the account of cosmogony has been cast is highly instructive. The creative process is divided into two groups of three days each, the first of which represents the stage of preparation or creation of the elements, the second the stage of completion or creation of those who are to make use of them. Each three-

THE MAJOR THEMES AND TEACHINGS From *The Encyclopaedia Judaica* (Jerusalem: Keter Publishing House, 1971), pp. 386–98. Reprinted by permission of the publisher.

day group embraces the same number of creative acts, and in each case the first day witnesses a single deed, the second a bipartite act, and the third two distinct creations. The products of the middle days in the two groups are chiastically arranged. The seventh day is climactic and pertains to God alone. (The human institution of the Sabbath is not mentioned.) This symmetrically arranged literary pattern serves to underscore the fundamental idea that the world came into being as the free, deliberate, and meaningful expression of divine will.

THE PROCESS OF CREATION (GEN. 1:1–2:3)

	Group I	Group II	
Day	Element	User	Day
1	Light (1:3–5)	Luminaries (1:14–19)	4
2	Sky	Marine life (fish)	5
	Terrestrial Waters	Sky life (fowl)	
	(1:6–8)	(1:20–23)	
3	Dry land	Land animals	6
	Vegetation (1:9–13)	Man (1:24–31)	
	(Lowest form of	(Highest form of	
	organic life)	organic life)	

7 *Divine cessation from creativity (2:1–3)*

MAN

Another basic teaching is the exalted concept of man that emerges from the narrative and that is expressed through several unique literary features. The creation of man is the culmination of the cosmogonic process. Only here is the divine act preceded by an annunciation of intention (1:26). Only man is created "in the image of God" (1:26, 27), and to him alone is the custody and exploitation of nature's resources entrusted (1:26, 28, 29). In the second account of the creation of man, his unique position is emphasized by the fact that his appearance constitutes the sole exception to creation by divine fiat and requires, as it were, a special and personal effort by God, from Whom he directly receives the breath of life (2:7). At the same time, the exceptional mention of the material out of which he was formed (2:7) is suggestive of the limitation of his God-like qualities.

EVIL

Another revolutionary departure from polytheism is to be found in the understanding of evil. The sevenfold affirmation of the goodness of God's creative acts (1:4, 10, 12, 18, 21, 25, 31) opposes the pagan concept of an inherent primordial evil in the world. This, too, is the import of the Garden of Eden narrative, which implies that evil is moral, not metaphysical, it being the product of the free, but rebellious, exercise of man's will.

THE MORAL LAW

The divine punishment of Cain for fratricide (4:3–16) and the visitations upon the generation of the Flood for its corruption (6:9–8:22) and upon Sodom and Gomorrah for their wickedness (chapters 18–19) all presuppose the existence of a divinely ordained order of universal application, for the infraction of which men are ultimately and inevitably brought to account.

THE UNITY OF MANKIND

The idea of the derivation of all mankind from one common stock is manifested through the divine creation of a single pair of humans as ancestors to all humanity. It is reinforced by the genealogical lists that illustrate the process of development from generation to generation. This concept of the family of man and the unity of mankind receives its consummate expression in the "Table of Nations" (chapter 10), in which the totality of ethnic entities is schematized in the form of a family geneaological tree deriving from the three sons of Noah and their wives, the only human survivors of the Flood. The attribution of all nations to a primary father serves not only to teach the unity of mankind but also to emphasize God's universal sovereignty. It prefigures the consistent biblical preoccupation with the active role of God in human history.

DIVINE ELECTION

The universal focus in Genesis is gradually narrowed through a process of divine selectivity. Noah is singled out for salvation from the rest of mankind (6:8). Of his sons, Shem is especially blessed (9:26), and his line receives outstanding attention (10:21–31; 11:10–32). His genealogy is continued to the birth of Abraham (11:26) who becomes the elect of God and founder of a new nation (cf. 18:19). Again, of Abraham's two sons, Ishmael is rejected and Isaac chosen (17:7–8, 19, 21; 21:14; 25:6; 26:3–4), and the selective process is repeated in respect of his offspring (35:9–12). The divine blessing of Jacob is the final stage, since at this point the patriarchal period ends and the national era begins. Nevertheless, the universal interest is not neglected entirely for the divine promises involve Israel in the international community (12:1–3; 18:18; 22:18; 26:14; 28:14).

THE COVENANT AND THE PROMISES

One of the most extraordinary features of Genesis is its conception of the relationship between God and man in terms of a covenant by which, as an act of grace, God commits Himself unconditionally to the welfare of man. This is first explicated in the case of Noah (6:18;9:8–17; cf. 1:28–29). With the advent of Abraham, the covenant becomes the dominant theme of the entire book, to which all else is preparatory and which itself becomes prologue to the rest of the Bible. The oft-repeated promises to the Patriarchs consist basically of two parts—a future national existence and the possession of national territory. Abraham is to father a great people destined to inherit the land of Canaan (12:2–3; 13:14–17; 15:4–5, 18–21; 17:2, 4–8; 22:17–18). The same is reaffirmed to Isaac (26:3–4) and Jacob (28:13–14; 35:10–12; cf. 46:2–4; 48:3–4). In fact, most subsequent scriptural references to the three Patriarchs are in connection with these promises, and the measure of their paramount importance may be gauged both by the frequency of their repetition and by the fact that the book closes on this very theme (50:24).

The promissory covenant in Genesis lacks mutuality. It is a unilateral obligation freely assumed by God. The solemnity and immutable nature of the act of divine will is conveyed through a dramatic covenant ceremonial (chapter 15). Abraham's worthiness is indeed stressed (18:19; 22:12, 16; 26:5), and his offspring to come, throughout the ages, are to observe the rite of circumcision as the symbol of the covenant (17:9–14). It should be noted, though, that the idea of a national covenant on Sinai with all its implications for the religion of Israel is beyond the horizon of Genesis, which sees in the promises to the Patriarchs the guarantee of God's eternal grace to Israel and the assurance of eventual deliverance from Egypt (cf. 15:14; 50:24; Ex. 6:4–5).

GOD AND HISTORY

The concepts of God and the covenant in Genesis inevitably mean that the presence of God is to be felt on the human scene. History is thus endowed with meaning. A literary characteristic of the Genesis narratives is the employment of schematized chronology, the featuring of neatly balanced periods of time and the use of symbolic numbers to give prominence to this idea.

The ten generations from Adam to Noah are paralleled by a like number separating Noah from Abraham. The birth of each personality represents, from the biblical point of view, the arrival of an epochal stage in history. It is not accidental that the arts of civilization appear precisely in the seventh generation after Adam (Gen. 4:20–22), through the sons of Lamech who himself lived 777 years (5:31).

Turning to the period of the Patriarchs, it is significant that Abraham lived 75 years in the home of his father and the same number of years in the lifetime of his son Isaac, that he was 100 years of age when Isaac was born, and sojourned 100 years in Canaan (12:4;

21:5; 25:7). Jacob lived 17 years with Joseph in Canaan and 17 years with him in Egypt (37:2; 47:9, 28).

The Patriarchs resided a total of 250 years in Canaan (21:5; 25:26; 47:9), which is exactly half the duration of their descendants' stay in Egypt (Ex. 12:40; according to the Greek and Samaritan versions the correspondence is exact). The important events in their lives are recorded in terms of a combination of the decimal and sexagenary systems with the occasional addition of seven. The idea is clearly projected that what is happening is the stage by stage unfolding of the divine plan of history.

IMPORTANT EVENTS IN THE LIVES OF THE PATRIARCHS

Personality	Event	Age	Source Genesis
Abraham	Migrated from Haran	75	12:4
	Married Hagar	85	16:3
	At birth of Isaac	100	21:5
	At death	175	25:7
Sarah	At birth of Isaac	90	17:17
	At death	$127 = 2 \times 60 + 7$	23:1
Isaac	Married Rebekah	40	25:20
	At birth of twins	60	25:26
	At Esau's marriage	100	26:34
	At death	$180 = 3 \times 60$	35:28
Jacob	At migration to Egypt	130	47:9
	At death	$147 = 2 \times 70 + 7$	47:28
Joseph	At sale to Egypt	$17 = 10 + 7$	37:2
	At rise to power	30	41:46
	At death	110	50:26

"In the Beginning"
The Hebrew Story of the Creation in Its Contemporary Setting
S. G. F. BRANDON

Michelangelo has adorned the walls of the Sistine Chapel with the most majestic presentation in linear art of the Hebrew story of the Creation; and his paintings manifest the mighty influence that this ancient legend had come to exercise on Christian thought. The continu-

"IN THE BEGINNING" from Religion in Ancient History by S. G. F. Brandon is reprinted by permission of Charles Scribner's Sons. Copyright © 1969 S. G. F. Brandon.

ance of that influence and its profundity were again singularly demonstrated, in the very different setting of Victorian England, some three centuries after the great Italian artist had finished his master-piece. The fierce and prolonged public controversy occasioned by the publication of Darwin's *Origin of Species* in 1859 was the natural, if un-fortunate, reaction of Christian believers to the shock they received when the truth of the Biblical account of the Creation seemed to be impiously challenged by the new science.

But, while conflict raged between the representatives of the traditional theology and the new evolutionary thesis, other scholars were quietly at work on the fresh material that the archaeological ex-ploration of the ancient lands of the Near East was providing for a more accurate understanding of the Bible; and their researches supple-mented and confirmed the conclusions that were being reached by the critical literary investigation of the Old Testament documents that had been inaugurated by Jean Astruc, a French physician, in 1753.[1]

This scientifically conducted study of the Bible has persisted. Today we possess an understanding of its origins and contents that has rendered obsolete the earlier dispute; and not only has the con-troversy been shown as to have arisen from a false estimate of the Biblical narrative, but a new appreciation of that narrative has been made possible, which has greatly enriched our knowledge of ancient Hebrew thought. Furthermore, through the development of the com-parative study of religion, we can now evaluate what is unique in this Hebrew cosmogony, when it is seen in relation to the attempts of other peoples of the ancient Near East to account for the origin of the world and of mankind.

Turning first to Egypt, we find in the *Pyramid Texts* (*circa* 2400 B.C.) that the priests of Heliopolis,[2] the ancient center of Egyptian sun-worship, explained the origin of things in terms of the Egyptian environment, and also in the interests of their own sanctuary. No doubt it was the annual inundation of the Nile, when the swollen river obliterates all land-marks in the low-lying valley, together with the spectacle of the boundless horizon of the sea to the north, that caused the Egyptians to picture the primaeval state as a featureless waste of water, which they called *Nun:* and the subsidence of the flood-waters and the gradual emergence of the land also suggested the manner of the beginning of life. In the beginning, taught the Heliopo-litan priests, from the watery chaos of *Nun* a hillock of earth had ap-peared, providing a foothold for the self-created sun-god, Atum-Kheprer. This hillock, of course, was the site of the Heliopolitan temple; which fact, according to the calculations of the Heliopolitan

---

[1] Concerning his work, published in that year under the title of *Conjectures sur les mémoires originaux dont il paroit que Moyse s'est servi pour composer le livre de la Genèse,* Astruc, as a devout Catholic, had some fear lest it should be exploited by free-thinkers.
[2] This is the Greek name for the Egyptian city of *lunu,* which is called On in the Bible.

clergy, should have made it the most revered sanctuary in Egypt; for here, too, the sun-god began his work of creation. In the neighbouring city of Memphis, a rival cosmogony was propagated. The Memphite god was Ptah, and the priests who served his shrine undertook to exalt him above his rival at Heliopolis by designating him the creator of Atum-Kheprer. Their teaching has come down to us in a rather strange form. Inscribed on a large basalt stone, now in the British Museum, is an hieroglyphic text that tells in its preface how the Pharaoh Shabaka (716–701 B.C.) had caused a very ancient writing concerning Ptah to be preserved by carving its text on this slab. The text, which the consensus of Egyptological opinion attributes to about the same period as the *Pyramid Texts*, is a remarkable document. Whereas the Heliopolitan teaching had depicted the sun-god as performing his acts of creation in a somewhat crude physical manner, this Memphite cosmogony represents Ptah as creating by means of his heart (i.e. his mind) and his tongue, or word. Atum acts as his agent—"There came into being as the heart and there came into being as the tongue (something) in the form of Atum."

In these Egyptian creation-myths, there is a curious lack of concern about the creation of mankind. They seem mainly intent on accounting for the beginning of the process of creation and, in particular, on relating the gods to each other in order of appearance. This limitation of interest was undoubtedly due to the rivalry of the priesthoods who composed these cosmogonies. It is especially remarkable, nevertheless, that in the Memphite system, where mankind is mentioned, no clear reason is given for its creation.[3] Indeed, the only clear indication that we have of the Egyptian conception of the creation of man occurs in a monument of Amenhotep III (1405–1370 B.C.), purporting to record the divine birth of the king. In one of the scenes, the god Chnum is represented as making the infant king and his *ka* (i.e. his double) on a potter's wheel, while the goddess Hathor animates them with the *ankh*, the symbol of life.

The apparent failure of Egyptian thought to account for the origin of mankind contrasts notably with the cosmogonies of the contemporary cultures of Mesopotamia, the other great center of civilized life in the ancient Near East. For, even in the period of Sumerian hegemony—before 2000 B.C.—the question of the origin and purpose of the human race had already been asked, and an answer had been given. A broken clay tablet, recovered from the site of the ancient Sumerian city of Nippur, tells how mankind had been created by the wise god Enki (Ea), to act as servants to the gods in building temples for them and supplying them with offerings of food.

The most complete and impressive of the Mesopotamian cos-

---

[3] There is just a faint suggestion in the Memphite Theology that mankind was created to provide temples and offerings for the gods.

mogonies is the great *Enuma Elish*,[4] or Babylonian Creation Epic. The text of this Epic was solemnly recited every year in Babylon, at the *akitu* or New Year Festival, when it was believed that Marduk, the patron god of Babylon, decreed the destiny of the state for the ensuing year. The Epic, in fact, was designed to relate how Marduk came to possess the "tablets of destiny"; and it takes the form of a narrative describing the creation of both the universe and mankind. It begins by envisaging the primordial state, in terms of the Mesopotamian environment, as a watery chaos, made up of Apsu and Tiamat, the personifications respectively of the sweet river waters and the sea:

When on high the heaven had not been named,
Firm ground below had not been called by name,
Nought but primordial Apsu, their begetter,
(And) Mummu-Tiamat, she who bore them all,
Their waters commingling as a single body,
No reed hut had been matted, no marsh land had appeared, . . .[5]

Regarding water as the source of all life, the Epic goes on to explain how the first gods were generated from the commingling of Apsu and Tiamat. These gods and their progeny in time abuse their begetters, and Tiamat determines to destroy them. In the Epic the personification of the sea now assumes the guise of a great monster, which produces other monsters to aid her in her struggle against the gods, who represent the new order as opposed to the former chaos. The gods choose Marduk as their champion—thus the Babylonian version; in its original form their champion was undoubtedly Ea, who appears in the *Enuma Elish* as the father of Marduk. Marduk engages with Tiamat in a titanic struggle, and defeats and kills her. Then from her body, which he is depicted as splitting into two parts "like a shellfish," he proceeds to form the heaven and the earth.

After his creation of the world, the Epic describes how Marduk made the first of human kind. The god is shown meditating on his plan:

Blood will I mass, and cause bones to be.
I will establish a savage, "man" shall be his name.
Verily savage-man will I create.
He shall be charged with the service of the gods
That they might be at ease![6]

To obtain the material for his design, Kingu, one of the monsters of Tiamat, is killed; and from its blood Marduk fashions his new crea-

[4] So called from the first two words of the opening line: "When on high . . ." The Epic probably dates from the early part of the 2nd millennium B.C.
[5] Translated by E. A. Speiser in *Ancient Near Eastern Texts*, ed. J. B. Pritchard (Princeton University Press, 1955), pp. 60–1. "Mummu-Tiamat" probably means Mother-Tiamat.
[6] Tablet VI, 5–9, trans. E. A. Speiser in *op. cit.*, p. 68.

ture, man. This detail of the myth has caused considerable discussion among scholars. Some have interpreted it as an indication of the Babylonians' concern to explain the origin of evil in mankind, in that the substance of man was derived from an evil being. But it seems improbable that such a motive can have operated here since, in this form, the idea does not recur in ancient Mesopotamian literature.

In their cosmogonic thinking, therefore, the inhabitants of Mesopotamia held quite definite views on the *raison d'être* of mankind—namely, that it was to serve the gods. They were equally certain about human destiny. Man, we learn from the great *Epic of Gilgamesh*, has no hope of a happy lot after this life; for, "When the gods created mankind, Death for mankind they set aside, Life in their own hands retaining."[7] In other words, men are mortal because their divine masters have made them such; and with that fate they must be content.

It is against the background of such ideas of the creation of the world and the origin of man that we have to set the Hebrew story of the Creation in the first two chapters of the book called *Genesis*. But first we must notice that, in these chapters, there are really two accounts of the Creation. The first runs from the beginning of chapter i to ii. 4a, and the second starts at chapter ii. 4b and continues to ii. 25. Now, it has long been recognized that these accounts come from different sources of literary tradition. That with which *Genesis* actually begins is not, however, the older account; it derives from what is known as the Priestly source, and critical scholarship dates it at about 450 B.C. The other account is a conflation of two literary traditions, known as the Yahwist and the Elohist; of these the Yahwist is the slightly earlier of the two and is generally dated for about 950 to 850 B.C.

The Yahwist account is the more interesting and, in view of its subsequent influence, the more significant for the history of Western thought. Since it requires extended study, we must first briefly examine the chief characteristics of the Priestly version. The opening verses of this account strongly recall the primordial state as conceived in the Babylonian *Enuma Elish*. "In the beginning," we are told "the earth was waste and void; and darkness was upon the face of the deep: and the spirit of God moved upon the face of the waters." This idea of "the deep" is of considerable interest, because the Hebrew word for it, *tehōm*, is probably a corruption of the Babylonian name Tiamat, which designated, as we have seen, the personification of the chaos of the primaeval waters. In the Priestly account, this *tehōm* also appears as existent before the divine work of creation. But, although the ancient Mesopotamian idea of a primaeval monster of chaos may ultimately underlie the Hebrew story, there is no trace of the primitive mytho-

[7] See Chapter 10.

29

logy concerning the construction of the world from the body of the monster by a victorious god. In the Priestly version, God creates by means of his word alone—"Let there be light: and there was light"— thus reminding us of the creative acts of the Egyptian god Ptah in the Memphite Theology. With the creation of man, the work of creation culminates on "the seventh day," according to the Priestly writer. Nothing is said of the purpose of man, except that he is made in the image of God and is ordered by his Creator to "be fruitful, and multiply, and replenish the earth, and subdue it." On man's nature there is also silence, and the account ends by emphasizing the divine benevolence: "And God saw everything that he had made, and, behold, it was very good."

The older Yahwist-Elohist version is considerably different; but, while its imagery is more naïve, its insight into the problem of human nature and destiny is the more profound. This difference of outlook is apparent at once. Little time is spent on describing the creation of the world, and, in contradistinction to the Priestly account, man is made before the animals—indeed, the *raison d'être* of the latter appears to be that of providing companionship for man, in which they prove inadequate (ii. 18–20).

In his creation of man, Yahweh[8] is depicted as forming his creature from earth, in a manner reminiscent of that of the Egyptian creator-god Chnum. The parallelism with the Egyptian conception is further strengthened by the fact that, after moulding man out of earth, Yahweh animates him by breathing into his nostrils "the breath of life"—the goddess Hathor had endowed Chnum's creatures with life by touching them with the *ankh*. The Yahwist author, however, in depicting man as being created out of the earth, probably did not merely avail himself of a convenient image: he seems to have been preparing for the tragic fate of man that he was soon to describe. Thus there is a significant play on the word for man, *ādām,* and that for the earth, *adāmāh,* from which he is made (ii. 7).

In this Yahwist-Elohist legend of creation, no reason is given for the creation of man. A kind of golden age of primaeval innocence seems to be envisaged. Yahweh places Adam (to give the Primal Man his customary designation) in a beautiful garden, where all his material wants are provided and which he has to tend, apparently, without toil. This garden is located "eastward" (undoubtedly from Palestine); and its name "Eden" is probably derived from the Babylonian word *edinu,* meaning "plain" or "steppe," thus suggesting some Mesopotamian derivation. Here Adam dwells, at first with the animals which are also formed from the earth. An aetiological [etiological—Ed.] motive seems to have inspired this account of the creation of the ani-

---

[8] In the Hebrew text "Yahweh Elohim," which is translated as the "Lord God." "Yahweh" was the personal name of the God of Israel.

mals—they are made as companions for Adam, and from him they receive their names (ii. 18–20). Aetiological interest also seems to underlie the quaint account that follows of the creation of Eve, the First Woman. Her formation from a rib (the Hebrew means "side") of Adam is held to explain the origin of the word *Ishshah* ("woman") which derives from *ish* ("man" or "husband").

The account of Yahweh's placing of Adam in Eden was clearly designed to lead on to the fatal events that were to decide the destiny of mankind. For the Yahwist-Elohist story was not intended only to describe the creation of the world and of mankind; its purpose was to account for the human situation as seen in terms of the Yahwist *Weltanschauung*. This purpose is adumbrated by Yahweh's warning to Adam: "Of every tree of the garden thou mayest freely eat: but of the tree of the knowledge of good and evil, thou shalt not eat of it: for in the day that thou eatest thereof thou shalt surely die" (ii. 16–17).

This warning is of fundamental significance for the proper understanding of the sequel. Its logic is clear: the Yahwist author clearly envisaged Adam as created originally immortal, and, therefore, differed notably from the Mesopotamian view that the gods had withheld immortality from their human servants. But the straightforward theme of the Yahwist narrative—namely, that in the primordial age of innocence mankind was deathless—is somewhat obscured by the brief mention of "the tree of life also in the midst of the garden" (ii. 9). As we shall see presently, however, there is good reason for thinking that the reference here to the "tree of life" is an interpolation made to anticipate the introduction of a different motif later in the legend. What the writer meant by "the tree of the knowledge of good and evil" is not explained; but, as we shall also see, some indication of its meaning may be inferred from the sequel.

The profoundly moving account of the Temptation and Fall of Man that follows in the third chapter constitutes a scene unsurpassed in its drama in the sacred literature of mankind; and its influence has been immense. The primary motive of the Yahwist writer therein was to show that mankind became subject to death through the disobedience of its first parents to the command of their Creator. But this intention was closely linked with the desire to interpret the hard toil of the agriculturist's life as part of the divine curse that fell upon the human race because of its progenitors' fatal sin. This is all made dramatically manifest in the awful doom that Yahweh pronounces upon the fallen Adam, who attempts to excuse himself by blaming his wife: "Because thou hast hearkened unto the voice of thy wife, and hast eaten of the tree, of which I commanded thee, saying, Thou shalt not eat of it: cursed is the ground for thy sake; in toil shalt thou eat of it all the days of thy life; thorns also and thistles shall it bring forth to thee; and thou shalt eat of the herb of the field; in the sweat of thy face shalt thou eat bread, till thou return again unto the ground; for out of

31

it wast thou taken: for dust thou art, and unto dust shalt thou return"
(iii. 17–20). And so the man (*ādām*) is fated to be resolved back into the
earth (*adāmāh*) from which his Creator had moulded him.

This interpretation of the agriculturist's life, as a consequence of
the original sin of mankind, is significant of the Yahwist tradition.
The settlement of the nomadic Hebrew tribes in Canaan had resulted
not only in a change of economy, but also in a disturbance of social
custom and religious belief. By becoming agriculturists, the Israelites
tended to acquire both the arts and the vices of the settled agrarian
communities of Canaan, among which were the worship of fertility
gods and the practice of their licentious rites. Consequently, the Yahwist prophets, who condemned such conduct as disloyalty of Yahweh,
were disposed to look with disfavour upon agriculture and to exalt the
pastoralist's life as the better way—a view that recurs in the Yahwist
story of Cain and Abel (*Genesis* iv. 2–12). Such a denigration of agriculture is notably absent from Egyptian and Mesopotamian mythology; a reminiscence of it does appear in the Greek poet Hesiod (*circa*
8th cent. B.C.), who traces the hard toil of agriculture to some divine
hostility towards mankind; but here the attitude had a different source
of inspiration.

In his account of the consequences of the Fall of Man, the Yahwist writer was able also to explain the origin of a number of other
things. Thus, in the divine punishment decreed for the Woman for her
part in the fall of Man, the origin of child-bearing and its attendant
pain is found: "I will multiply thy sorrow and thy conception; in sorrow thou shalt bring forth children; and thy desire shall be to thy husband, and he shall rule over thee" (iii. 16). How the wearing of clothes
started is similarly explained. After eating of the forbidden fruit,
Adam and his wife become aware of their primaeval state of nudity.
To hide their shame, they had themselves at first resorted to a covering of leaves; later, Yahweh clothed them in garments of skins (iii. 7,
10, 21). An interesting parallel to this attempt to explain the origin of
clothes occurs in the Mesopotamian *Epic of Gilgamesh*. There the wild
man Enkidu represents mankind in its primitive form; when he is
civilized, he learns to wear clothes and eat bread.

The part played by the serpent in the drama of the Temptation
and Fall of Man requires discussion. Owing to the fact that Christian
theology has identified the serpent in *Genesis* with Satan, the personification of evil, the action of the serpent has become invested with
a profound religious significance. In the original story, however, the
character and action of the serpent have no such significance. The serpent is presented essentially as an animal, although endowed with the
power of speech and logical argument. The doom that Yahweh pronounces upon it is clearly designed to explain the serpent's peculiar
method of locomotion; and it also expresses the instinctive fear that
men feel for this insidious creature: "Because thou hast done this,

cursed art thou above all cattle, and above every beast of the field; upon thy belly shalt thou go, and dust shalt thou eat all the days of thy life: and I will put enmity between thee and the woman, and between thy seed and her seed: it shall bruise thy head, and thou shalt bruise his heel" (iii. 14–15). But the introduction of the serpent into the drama of mankind's loss of immortality has a further significance for the comparative study of mythology. The snake's ability to slough off its old skin has fascinated mankind throughout the world, especially since it has often been believed that the snake thereby possessed the secret of self-renewal that man so greatly covets. This concern finds significant expression in the *Epic of Gilgamesh*, where the hero is robbed of the magical plant that makes "the old man as the young man" by a serpent which perpetuates its own youth by devouring it. It is possible that the Yahwist author had this Mesopotamian legend in mind when he related the tragedy of Adam; if he had, he must have adjusted it, so that the serpent became an agent in man's loss of immortality and not the immediate cause of it, as in the Gilgamesh story.

Undoubtedly the most difficult part of the Yahwist legend to explain is the meaning of the tree of "the knowledge of good and evil." The penalty for eating of this tree was death; yet in the narrative the immediate consequence of Adam and Eve's eating of it is the consciousness that they are naked. Now, since the Yahwist writer clearly regarded nudity as shameful (ii. 25; iii. 7, 10, 21), it follows from his account that man only acquired a proper sense of decency by eating of the forbidden fruit. But it is obviously impossible that he could have meant that man acquired moral sensibility by disobeying his Creator. Accordingly, it would seem necessary to conclude that the fruit of the "tree of the knowledge of good and evil" meant knowledge of sex and its dangerous potentialities. Confirmation of this comes from the fact that only after the Fall does Eve conceive and bear children. Moreover, the part that the serpent plays in tempting Eve may be significant, since the serpent was also a symbol of fertility in the worship of the Canaanite deities Baal and Astarte. Herein we may have a further clue to the main purpose of the Yahwist writer. The agrarian rituals of the Canaanites were centred on the principle and process of fertility, which in turn were personified in the relationships of a goddess and her young male lover. The rites, in which these deities were worshipped, were designed to promote fertility and often involved temple prostitution. The tendency of the Israelites, after their settlement in Canaan, to adopt such cults, or to worship Yahweh by such rites, was a danger against which the Yahwist prophets continually inveighed. Hence, it is possible that, in representing sexual consciousness as the immediate result of the eating of the forbidden fruit, the Yahwist author believed that the dangerous knowledge of the means of the procreation of life came through man's primordial disobedience to the command of his Creator.

The problem of "the tree of life also in the midst of the garden" remains to be discussed. As we have now seen, the theme of the Yahwist myth of the creation and fall of Adam is that mankind became mortal through the sin of its first parents. The idea of a "tree of life," which thus logically contradicts that theme, after being briefly mentioned in ii. 9, only appears again in the narrative in iii. 22–4. In this short passage, Yahweh is depicted as expelling Adam and Eve from Eden, saying: "Behold, the man is become as one of us, to know good and evil; and now, lest he put forth his hand, and take also of the tree of life, and eat, and live for ever . . ." The obvious disruption of theme that this passage causes, together with the improbability of there being two trees of unique virtue in the original form of the myth, has led many scholars to conclude that the passage concerning the tree of life was a later interpolation. The motif of a plant that will confer eternal youth, or that of the food of immortality, was well known in Mesopotamian folk-lore. We have already noticed the magical plant of which Gilgamesh was robbed in his quest for immortality; and in another legend, that of Adapa, the hero unwittingly rejects the food that would have made him immortal. It would seem likely, therefore, that, as the story of the Flood was worked into the Yahwist narrative because of its prestige in contemporary Semitic tradition, so the idea of a "tree of life" was incorporated here, despite the obvious disruption of theme that resulted.

The Yahwist story of the creation and fall of Man formed part of the Yahwist philosophy of history. . . . Accordingly, it will suffice to say that the story was designed, in that context, to present the Yahwist view of human nature and destiny. . . .

SUGGESTED READINGS

Anderson, Bernhard W. *Understanding the Old Testament.* 3rd ed., pp. 198–225, "Israel's National Epic." Englewood Cliffs, N.J.: Prentice-Hall, 1975.

Bewer, Julius A. *The Literature of the Old Testament.* 3rd ed., pp. 1–88. Edited by Emil G. Kraeling. New York: Columbia University Press, 1962.

Marks, John H. "The Book of Genesis." In *The Interpreter's One-Volume Commentary on the Bible,* edited by Charles M. Laymon, pp. 1–32. Nashville, Tenn.: Abingdon Press, 1971. (See also the General Articles in this volume.)

Meek, Theophile J. *Hebrew Origins.* Gloucester, Mass.: Peter Smith, n.d.

Neil, William. *Harper's Bible Commentary,* pp. 13–16, "Genesis." New York: Harper & Row, 1975.

Sandmel, Samuel. *The Hebrew Scriptures: An Introduction to Their Literature and Religious Ideas,* pp. 340–70, "Genesis." New York: Alfred A. Knopf, 1963.

Simpson, Cuthbert A. "Introduction to Genesis." In *The Interpreter's Bible*, Vol. 1, edited by George A. Buttrick, pp. 439–57. Nashville, Tenn.: Abingdon Press, 1952. (See also the "General Articles on the Old Testament" in Volume 1.)

QUESTIONS FOR DISCUSSION AND WRITING

1. What development do you see in the covenant relationship as it is described in Genesis 9:8–17 and Genesis 17:1–21?
2. How does the Tower of Babel account in Genesis 1:1–10 qualify as an "etiological" story?
3. What specific qualities of character are displayed by Jacob in the Book of Genesis?
4. What specific accomplishments can be credited to Joseph in Egypt?
5. What characteristics of humankind in general do you find portrayed in Jacob's description of the twelve tribes in Genesis 49?
6. What gives the Book of Genesis its unity?
7. According to Herman Gunkel, how do we learn what characters *feel* in the legends of Genesis?
8. What evidence do you find in Genesis that its writers were "masters of observation"?
9. What reasons does A. Powell Davies give for concluding that Moses was not the author of the first five books of the Bible?
10. What evidence does Davies give for assuming that the Pentateuch is made up of at least two sources?
11. Who are J, E, D, and P?
12. According to the remarks in the *Encyclopaedia Judaica*, what does the Genesis account tell us about the Hebrew God, the Hebrew concept of humanity, and the relationship between them?
13. Why does the writer of the *Encyclopaedia Judaica* selection believe that evil is moral rather than metaphysical in the Genesis account of the fall of man?
14. According to S. G. F. Brandon, what is distinctive about the Hebrew stories of creation as compared with those of the Egyptians and Mesopotamians?
15. To what does Brandon attribute the Hebrew writers' antagonism toward an agricultural society?
16. Compare the Genesis biography of Abraham with that of Jacob. How do they differ, if at all, in structure and development? Is one of them told more dramatically than the other? Is one of them more credible than the other?
17. What characteristics of the modern short story do you find in the Joseph narrative in Genesis 37–50?

EXODUS

Chapters 1–21; 24; 32–34; 40

SUMMARY

The date of the Exodus is assumed by many scholars to be in the thirteenth century B.C., some arguing for as early a date as the beginning of the reign of the Pharaoh Rameses II in 1290, and others arguing that it occurred around 1250. A few hold out for a date one hundred or even two hundred years earlier.

The three strands of J, E, and P persist in Exodus, accounting for discrepancies such as those in Chapter 14, where, for example, Moffatt* allots verses 1–4, 8–9, 15–19a, 20b, 21–23, and 26–29 to P or some other source, leaving the rest to J and E. (For a three-column listing of the J, E, and P passages see Charles M. Laymon, ed., *The Interpreter's One-Volume Commentary on The Bible* [Nashville, Tenn.: Abingdon Press, 1971], p. 34.)

---

*James Moffat, Scottish theologian, translated the Old Testament from the Greek and Hebrew in 1924.

Four hundred years after the Israelites settled in Egypt, a Pharaoh who fears their numbers and strength begins to oppress them. In spite of measures he takes to diminish their numbers, they thrive and multiply.

Moses, a baby born to two Levites, is saved from the decreed drowning of all firstborn Hebrew boys by a daughter of the Pharaoh, who finds him on a riverbank in a basket made of bulrushes. He grows up in the royal household, but his sympathies are with the Hebrew people. When he sees an Egyptian beating a Hebrew, he kills the Egyptian. When this is found out, he flees across the Sinai desert to Midian. There he is taken into the family of Jethro (also called Reuel), who is priest of the country. Moses marries Jethro's daughter Zipporah, and they have two sons, Gershom and Eliezer.

While tending Jethro's flock on Mount Horeb one day, Moses is confronted by God in a burning bush. God commissions him to go to Egypt to bring the Israelites out of captivity. Moses raises all the objections he can but finally agrees to go, with his older brother Aaron to help him. (On the way, Moses is attacked by the Lord but saved by Zipporah, who circumcises their son and touches Moses with the foreskin.)

Arriving in Egypt, Moses and Aaron inform the Israelites of their mission. It is approved, and the brothers gain an audience with the Pharaoh. They ask permission for all the Israelites to go into the desert to sacrifice to their God. Pharaoh will not let them go, so with the help of the Lord they inflict the Egyptians with nine plagues. (We are told that whenever the Pharaoh decides to give in, the Lord hardens Pharaoh's heart, so that the Lord can ultimately show his might and authority to both Egyptians and Israelites.) However, when the Lord begins to destroy the firstborn of the Egyptians, the Pharaoh tells the Israelites to leave. The Lord now establishes the Passover, which the Israelites must observe forever.

The Israelites leave Goshen. They are pursued by Pharaoh's army and are camped by the Sea of Reeds when the army is almost upon them. The Lord parts the waters, the Israelites cross over on dry land, and when the Egyptians follow, the sea washes over them and destroys them. Then Moses and the people sing a song of victory, and Miriam sings a song of triumph.

They arrive at the bitter water of Marah, which is made sweet when Moses throws a tree into it. Here the Lord promises not to visit them with the plagues he had inflicted on the Egyptians—if they will obey him.

In the Wilderness of Sin (Sinai?) the people complain of hunger, and the Lord sends them quail in the evening and manna in the morning. They eat manna for forty years, until they come to the border of Canaan. When they arrive at Rephidim, the people complain of thirst. Angry at their complaint, Moses says that they are putting the Lord to

Hans Holbein the Younger, "Moses and the Burning Bush"

the proof. Nevertheless, instructed by the Lord, Moses strikes the rock at Horeb, and water gushes forth. Next they are attacked by the Amalekites, with whom they fight a long battle at Rephidim. They win, but this is the beginning of the prolonged enmity between Israelites and Amalekites.

In Chapter 18 we again meet Moses' father-in-law, Jethro, who brings Zipporah and the two sons for a visit in the desert. When Jethro learns about the deliverance, he exclaims that Yahweh is greater than all gods and offers a sacrifice. Observing that Moses spends entire days settling disputes, he advises him to set able, honest men over groups of thousands, hundreds, fifties, and tens and to leave all judgments to them except for the most important decisions. Moses takes his advice.

Three months after setting out from Egypt, the Israelites arrive at Mount Sinai, where Moses speaks with God and is invited to the top of the mountain. There he receives the Ten Commandments. Chapter 21 provides examples of the additional laws and ordinances passed on by Moses to the people. These differ from the Ten Commandments in that they are conditional rather than absolute: They are introduced by such words as "if," "when," and "whosoever."

In Chapter 24 Moses again goes to the top of the mountain and returns with ordinances and laws, which the people agree to uphold.

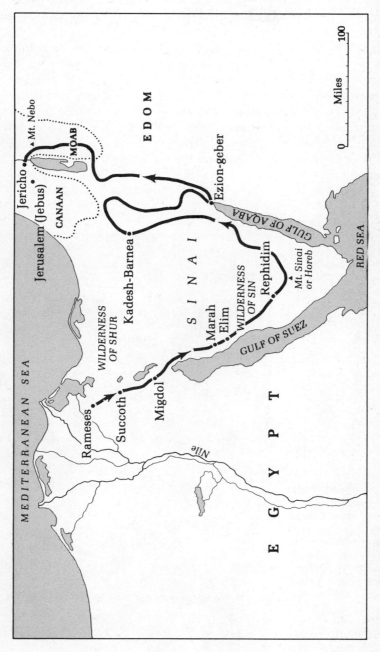

The Exodus from Egypt, *ca.* 1290 B.C.

He ratifies this covenant with the blood of oxen, and then he and three priests and seventy elders go up, "and they saw the God of Israel; and there was under his feet as it were a pavement of sapphire stone, like the very heaven for clearness. And he did not lay his hand on the chief men of the people of Israel; they beheld God, and ate and drank" (24:10–11).

Again Moses goes to the top of the mountain to receive the tablets. After he has been gone for forty days, the people become impatient. They ask Aaron to make them images of gods, and he, taking their gold earrings, fashions a calf, builds an altar, and pronounces a feast day. When Moses finally arrives and asks for an explanation, Aaron lamely says that he threw the earrings into the fire and "out came this calf."

One account of how the Levites became a priesthood is given in

Michelangelo, "Moses" (San Pietro di Vincoli, Rome. Photo by Harvey Barad, Photo Researchers, Inc.). The two horns projecting from Moses' head suggest that Michelangelo took his information from Jerome's Vulgate translation of the Bible, where the Hebrew word is assumed to be *geren* ("horn") rather than *garan* ("shine"). Jerome said, "Moses knew not that his face was horned," but most translators say, "Moses did not know that the skin of his face shone."

Chapter 32, where Moses commands them to kill their brothers, companions, and neighbors. They kill some three thousand men, and thus they are consecrated. Moses asks the Lord to forgive the people's sin in worshiping the calf and to blot him rather than them out of his book, but the Lord answers that he reserves the right to punish sinners, and he sends a plague to punish the guilty.

Again the Israelites are on their way. They take with them the portable sanctuary tent, and every day Moses confers there with the Lord. When he comes out his face shines so brightly that he has to wear a veil.

The last chapter of Exodus describes the completion of the tabernacle tent and the items, including the ark, that are to be kept in it. Throughout their travels the people go on only when the cloud of God's presence is lifted from the tent.

LITERARY QUALITIES

The Epic of the Exodus
LELAND RYKEN

Epic is a particular species within the class of heroic narrative. To begin, epic is long narrative. It is an encyclopedic form—a story with a proliferation of episodes. In fact, epic is so expansive, embodying so many important themes and values, that it can be said to sum up a whole age. Epic has traditionally had a strong nationalistic interest and contains many historical references. In terms of structure, the episodic plot of epic is unified around a central hero who is a political leader. Epic has a strong didactic impulse. It makes much use of what the Renaissance and eighteenth century called "supernatural machinery"—divine beings who participate in the affairs on earth. Many epics have been structured as a quest. And in addition to these characteristics of content, epic has traditionally included certain stylistic techniques that have made it distinctive. These include a high style—a consciously exalted mode of expression that removes the language from the commonplace through the use of epithets (titles for persons or things), pleonasm, repeated formulae, epic similes, epic catalogs, and allusions.

41

With the traditional features of epic providing the standard, it becomes evident that there is only one biblical story that is in the running for consideration as an epic. It is what I shall call the Epic of the Exodus, which occupies parts of the biblical books of Exodus, Leviticus, Numbers, and Deuteronomy. The main narrative sections are as follows: Exodus 1–20, 32–34; Numbers 10–14, 16–17, 20–24; Deuteronomy 32–34. With traditional epic as a measuring stick, it is easy to see to what extent the Epic of the Exodus is conventional.

The story of the exodus from Egypt to Canaan meets the test of long narrative. The story is nationalistic in emphasis, recording the formation of Israel as a nation and depicting the decisive event in the early history of the nation. A great deal of the story is devoted to describing the values and doctrine that can be said to sum up the Hebrew spirit. The story is set in history and is filled with historical allusions. It is unified partly by a normative hero and partly by the quest for the promised land. The Epic of the Exodus displays a strong didactic impulse, and the presence of divine beings is pervasive. The only major way in which the Epic of the Exodus fails to meet the definition of epic is in the area of stylistics. There is virtually a total absence of the high style typical of epic. Instead of poetry there is prose. There is little pleonasm, little use of epithets or epic formulae.

Of all the famous epics, *The Aeneid* of Virgil is the clearest parallel to the Epic of the Exodus. Both epics tell about the formation of an empire and are a call to its readers to contemplate the early history of their nation. Both are quest stories in which a group of people travel from one geographic area to another in order to establish a stable nation in a promised land. Both stories are unified around a hero who is a leader of people and who embodies the normative values of the story. Both epics are religious epics, filled with references to the proper worship of deity. Both epics embody and praise the virtues accepted as being normative in the society from which the epics arose.

The parallels between the Epic of the Exodus and other epics should not be allowed to obscure the important way in which the biblical epic differs from traditional epic. Conventional epic is humanistic in the sense that it exists to praise and glorify a human hero. The conventional epic hero is godlike in his accomplishments; indeed, he may even be of divine parentage, as Aeneas is. Heroes like Aeneas or Achilles or Beowulf merit praise by virtue of their own superhuman deeds. Traditional epics focus on human endeavor and show man accomplishing heroic feats. Their stories are essentially stories of human merit. As John Steadman puts it, "Whatever praise the epic poet might incidentally bestow on the gods, his primary object was to praise men by recounting their laudable achievements."[1]

With this brief survey of the heroic value structure of traditional

[1]*Milton and the Renaissance Hero* (Oxford: Oxford University Press, 1967), p. 196.

epic before us, it is at once apparent that the Epic of the Exodus is, like Milton's epics, an anti-epic. Everywhere we find the traditional epic values inverted. For the praise of men, the writer has substituted the glory of God. Instead of depicting human strength, this epic depicts human frailty and sinfulness. Instead of a story in which a human warrior leads his nation to victory through superhuman feats on the battlefield, this narrative attributes the mighty acts of deliverance to God. Indeed, the human warriors are usually passive spectators of the mighty acts of God. Instead of a human leader who depends on his own qualities of greatness, the storyteller here depicts a reluctant leader who is unsure of his own claims to leadership, inarticulate, of obscure origin, and meek. Instead of exalting the nation about whom the epic is written, this epic continually stresses the imperfections of the Israelites—their rebelliousness, their lack of faith, their tendency to complain. Whereas the traditional epic stresses physical warfare, the Epic of the Exodus places even more emphasis on spiritual conflict. Moral rebellion against God frequently replaces the conventional theme of armed conflict between nations. The usual epic formulae and virtues are attributed to God rather than to a human hero.

A brief look at some key events will document what I have said about the anti-epic. The hero's hesitancy to assume leadership (Exod. 4) is an example of the theme of human inadequacy. Moses' claim that he is "not eloquent" (Exod. 4:10) makes him a contrast to other epic heroes, who are unfailingly eloquent. Similarly, his fear that others "will not believe me or listen to my voice" (Exod. 4:1) is unconventional. Unlike other epic leaders, Moses is without external claim to prominence, being the son of a slave. His only real credential for leadership is that he has been called and equipped by God.

The events leading to the exodus from Egypt, and especially the ten plagues, are solely the result of God's activity. The Israelites themselves remain inactive spectators of the mighty acts of God. At the conclusion of the ten plagues, we read regarding the Jews, "Thus they despoiled the Egyptians" (Exod. 12:36). This is the usual formula in heroic epic, but the usual expectations are completely denied. The conquest has not been won on the battlefield through human effort but has been given to the Israelites by God's miraculous intervention.

The speech of Moses to the people shortly after the departure from Egypt (Exod. 13:3–16) is replete with statements that attribute the epic acts to God rather than a human hero. This anti-epic note comes out in statements such as these: "by strength of hand the Lord brought you out from this place" (Exod. 13:3); "when the Lord brings you into the land of the Canaanites . . ." (Exod. 13:5, 11); "and you shall tell your son on that day, 'It is because of what the Lord did for me when I came out of Egypt' " (Exod. 13:8); "by strength of hand the Lord brought us out of Egypt" (Exod. 13:14); "the Lord slew all the

first-born in the land of Egypt" (Exod. 13:15). In short, the storyteller
reserves his praise for God instead of a human hero.

God is also the epic hero in the events surrounding the deliverance at the Red Sea. In fact, He moves Pharaoh to pursue the Israelites for the purpose of getting "glory over Pharaoh and all his host;
and the Egyptians shall know that I am the Lord" (Exod. 14:4). When
the Hebrew people are terrified by the approaching Egyptian army,
Moses points to their divine deliverer with the words, "Fear not,
stand firm, and see the salvation of the Lord, which he will work for
you today. . . . The Lord will fight for you, and you have only to be
still" (Exod. 14:13, 14). Subsequently we read about how "the Lord
routed the Egyptians in the midst of the sea" (Exod. 14:27), how "the
Lord saved Israel that day from the hand of the Egyptians" (Exod.
14:30), and how "Israel saw the great work which the Lord did against
the Egyptians" (Exod. 14:31). It is small wonder that Moses, instead of
singing a song exalting a human warrior in the manner of classical
epic, leads the people in a song that praises God (Exod. 15). It is also
interesting that God appears in the role of epic warrior, as indicated
by the statement, "The Lord is a man of war" (Exod. 15:3).

The great disparity between God and man is emphasized not
only by exalting God but also by exposing the unworthiness of the
Israelites. The latter are depicted in the story as chronic complainers.
When the Egyptian army approaches, they say to Moses, "Is it because
there are no graves in Egypt that you have taken us away to die in the
wilderness? What have you done to us, in bringing us out of Egypt?
. . . For it would have been better for us to serve the Egyptians than
to die in the wilderness" (Exod. 14:11–12). When they discover the bitter waters at Marah, they are said to have "murmured against Moses"
(Exod. 15:24). Lacking meat, they "murmured against Moses and
Aaron" and hankered after "the fleshpots" of Egypt (Exod. 16:2–3).
When they lack water at Rephidim, they are reported to have "found
fault with Moses" (Exod. 17:2). On another occasion they wept and
said, "O that we had meat to eat! We remember the fish we ate in
Egypt for nothing, the cucumbers, the melons, the leeks, the onions,
and the garlic" (Num. 11:4–5). In short, the Israelites respond to physical hardship by displaying a lack of contentment with what God has
sent, inability to live without luxuries, a complaining spirit, and un-
willingness to postpone gratification until they reach the promised
land.

The consistently unflattering view of the narrator's own nation
involves specifically spiritual sins as well as their complaining spirit.
When God sends quail and manna, making it a test of obedience
(Exod. 16:4–5), the people fail the test by showing themselves guilty of
greed (Exod. 16:20) and desecration of the sabbath (Exod. 16:25–29).
When Moses' return from the mountain is delayed, the Israelites resort
to idolatry (Exod. 32). There are rebellions against legitimate author-

ity, led by Miriam and Aaron on one occasion (Num. 12) and by Korah, Dathan, and Abiram on another occasion (Num. 16). The Israelites' supreme venture in shameful behavior occurs when they display a lack of faith by accepting the report of the ten spies who advise against entering the promised land (Num. 13–14). Even Moses, the highly idealized epic leader, is guilty of pride, impatience, and disobedience when he strikes the rock at Meribah instead of speaking to it (Num. 20:2–13).

As this survey of events suggests, the human record in the Epic of the Exodus is almost uniformly disastrous. At one point God speaks of how the people "have put me to the proof these ten times and have not hearkened to my voice" (Num. 14:22). If one goes back over the story, he will discover ten occasions when the Israelites as a whole are said to murmur against God, against God's chosen leaders, or against the circumstances into which God has brought them. It turns out to be a list of most of the key events that have been recorded.[2] Whatever glory there is in the epic belongs to God, who repeatedly contends with human sinfulness and leads the Israelites to Canaan in spite of themselves. This anti-epic theme reaches its culmination in the song that Moses sings shortly before his death (Deut. 32), a song that praises God's faithfulness and dispraises Israel's waywardness. The song has the whole weight of the previous story behind it and is the logical terminus of the anti-epic motif in the Epic of the Exodus.

The Epic of the Exodus opens on a note of international conflict (Exod. 1). The conflict is precipitated by several things, including the death of Joseph, the ascent of a new Egyptian king, and remarkable growth in the Jewish population. The conventional epic theme of conflict between rival nations takes the form of villainous taskmasters, an oppressed minority, and a monstrous plan of genocide. The midwives' refusal to kill the male Jewish babies is the earliest record of legitimate civil disobedience in biblical literature, and the statement that "God dealt well with the midwives" (Exod. 1:20) alerts us to the fact that from the beginning God is the chief character in the epic.

The birth and early life of the hero are also part of the exposition of the plot. The death-rebirth story surrounding Moses' infancy (Exod. 2:1–10) is the first archetype in a story replete with archetypes.[3] To dramatize the early identity of the hero, the storyteller has chosen two representative incidents—Moses' killing of an Egyptian who was beating a Hebrew (Exod. 2:11–15) and his coming to the aid of the

---

[2] The incidents are as follows: the oppression by the slavemasters in response to Moses' early activity (Exod. 5:20–21); the Red Sea crisis (Exod. 14:10–12); the bitter waters of Marah (Exod. 15:24); the lack of food near Elim (Exod. 16:2–3); the disobedience regarding the gathering of manna (Exod. 16:20, 27); the lack of water at Rephidim (Exod. 17:2–3); the golden calf incident (Exod. 32); the complaining at Taberah (Num. 11:1); the craving for meat (Num. 11:4–5); and the unbelief of the ten spies (Num. 13–14).

[3] Other stories of infants rescued from the water are cited by Theodor H. Gaster, *Myth, Legend, and Custom in the Old Testament* (New York: Harper and Row, 1969), pp. 225–29.

shepherdesses who were mistreated by domineering shepherds (Exod. 2:15–22). These two episodes show the epic protagonist to be a man of decisive action and a champion of oppressed people.

God's call and equipping of Moses (Exod. 3–4) complete the preliminary phase of the action. The appearance of God in a burning bush dramatizes both his immanence and his transcendent holiness (Exod. 3:1–6). The goal of the epic quest is clearly established when God states that he will bring the Israelites out of Egypt "to a good and broad land, a land flowing with milk and honey" (Exod. 3:8; cf. also vs. 17). Scattered references throughout the story to a promised land flowing with milk and honey keep the goal of the quest in the consciousness of the reader. The reluctance of the epic hero to undertake a role of leadership and his total reliance on God invert the usual epic concept of the self-reliant hero. The prominence of God is reinforced by his assertions of authority, such as "I will send you" (Exod. 3:10) and "I will be with you" (Exod. 3:12), and by the use of exalted epithets, or titles, such as "The Lord, the God of your fathers, the God of Abraham, the God of Isaac, and the God of Jacob" (Exod. 3:15; 4:5). God's self designation, "I AM WHO I AM" (Exod. 3:14), keeps alive a sense of His transcendence and mystery.

The crossing of the Red Sea (Exod. 14) is the first major event of the journey and in a number of ways epitomizes the entire trip to Canaan. The episode is centered in a crisis, consisting of the Israelites' precarious position between the Red Sea and the approaching Egyptian army. Faced with a test of their faith, the Israelites fail the test miserably, as they always do, by complaining to Moses. Moses, in turn, calls on God, who effects a miraculous deliverance. This pattern of crisis–complaint–divine deliverance will recur throughout the remainder of the story.

Following the initiation into the rigors of the journey and God's miraculous deliverance at the Red Sea, the story follows the journey motif until the Israelites reach Mt. Sinai. The journey of the Israelites has many similarities to the stories of journeying people in such epics as *The Odyssey* and *The Aeneid*. There are conflicts with the natural environment, with antagonistic countries or tribes, and with elements of rebellion within the traveling community itself. Monotony is the great narrative pitfall that a storyteller must avoid in this kind of story, and the writer of the Epic of the Exodus succeeds magnificently in providing variety of adventure. There are moments of suffering interspersed with moments of relief. Some episodes are narrated briefly, while others are developed more leisurely and in greater detail. Above all, there is the repeated interpenetration of the divine world into the human, earthly realm. All in all, we might say that the journey presents the epic spectacle of man confronting certain elemental aspects of his experience.

The series of crises that comprise the journey illustrates the pervasive theme of biblical literature that man's responses to historical events are the basic issue of his life. Every external crisis presents the Israelites with an opportunity to complain against their predicament or trust God to deliver them. Sadly, in all of the recorded incidents the Israelites repudiate God and resort to complaint. If we keep in mind that biblical writers intend to present the reader with evidence of his own moral tendencies, we will realize that the failure of the Israelites is a comment on fallen human nature.

The incident involving the bitter waters of Marah (Exod. 15:22–26) illustrates these generalizations. The crisis is very dire—not simply disappointment but disappointment after the triumph of the Red Sea deliverance, and not simply the deprivation of water but the presence of water that tantalizes by not being drinkable. The people use the crisis only as an opportunity to repudiate God and Moses, whereas God intended it as an occasion for revelation. The revelation occurs when God makes the waters sweet, after which we read, "There the Lord . . . proved them saying, 'If you will diligently hearken to the voice of the Lord your God . . . I will put none of the diseases upon you which I put upon the Egyptians; for I am the Lord, your healer' " (Exod. 15:25–26). These words establish God's willingness to save, the conditional nature of His salvation, the necessity for obedience, and the status of life as a test. The tragedy is that the Israelites fail to measure up to these realities.

The manna that God sends as bread to the Israelites has symbolic as well as literal significance. As God's provision for the daily physical needs of His people, it symbolizes His providential concern for His earthly creatures. But there is another level of symbolism as well. The manna tasted "like wafers made with honey" (Exod. 16:31). The symbolism becomes apparent when we are also told that "they ate the manna, till they came to the border of the land of Canaan" (Exod. 16:35). The manna was an anticipation which pointed forward to the promised land flowing with milk and honey.

When the Israelites reach Mt. Sinai, the epic is interrupted and all but swallowed up with descriptions of various civil, ceremonial, and moral laws, and the rules governing the tabernacle. This break in the narrative flow is an index to how biblical epic differs from traditional literary epic. For one thing, biblical epic has a far stronger didactic impulse. All epics have some desire to teach and inform, but the Epic of the Exodus carries this all out of proportion, both from the standpoint of traditional epic and the narrative unity. Moreover, the mass of space devoted to the giving of the law reveals the essentially religious nature and purpose of biblical literature. The Bible is above all a religious book. Its literary portions represent literature governed by a religious purpose. Nowhere is a biblical writer bound by what are literary considerations. His devotion is first of all to his religious intention. This explains, I believe, why we find so much obviously religious, nonliterary material embedded in the middle of the Epic of the Exodus.

The experience at Sinai is essentially an encounter with God, and God's appearance is impressive. The people are told to consecrate themselves and wash their garments in awe of God's appearance (Exod. 19:10, 14). God's descent to the top of the mountain occurs initially on the climactic third day (Exod. 19:11). There is a death penalty for touching the mountain (Exod. 19:12–13). The appearance of God is associated with the awesome aspects of nature—thunder, lightning, fire, and earthquake (Exod. 19:16). There is a thick cloud on the mountain (Exod. 19:16), which is also wrapped in smoke (Exod. 19:18), thereby veiling God and distancing Him from direct view. God is also distanced when He tells Moses, "You cannot see my face; for man shall not see me and live. . . . Behold, there is a place by me where you shall stand upon the rock; and while my glory passes by I will put you in a cleft of the rock, and I will cover you with my hand until I have passed by" (Exod. 33:20–22). And when Moses comes down after talking to God on the mountain, his face shines (Exod. 34:29–35). These and other details maintain God's mysterious and awesome transcendence.

Although most of the Mosaic laws are recorded in expository form, the Ten Commandments (Exod. 20:1–17) are written in a highly artistic form.[4] One might well ask, Why have the Ten Commandments been remembered through the centuries, while the mass of Mosaic laws have failed to become embedded in our cultural and religious consciousness in the same way? One answer is that the Ten Commandments are literary in a way the other rules usually are not.

The Ten Commandments are replete with such elements of artistic form as ordered recurrence, variation, balance, pattern, contrast, and centrality. Recurrence according to a discernible order is evident in the series of ten main commandments, each phrased as a command and eight of the ten beginning with the repeated formula, "You shall not." Variation is played off against this recurrence by the interspersing of long and short commands (1 is short, 2 is long, 3 is short, 4 is long, 5–9 are short, 10 is long). Balance is present by virtue of the fact that there are four commands dealing with man's relationship to God and six dealing with man's relationship to his fellow man. Pattern can be seen in the way in which the negative and positive statements unfold in an A-B-A sequence (1 to 3 are negative, 4 and 5 are positive, 6 to 10 are negative). The fact that there is a total of ten commandments conveys a sense of completeness. Contrast is also present, since for each command there is an implied contrast between the pattern of

[4] In addition to the elements of literary form that I discuss, the Ten Commandments display a similarity to the form of international suzerainty treaty, or vassal treaty, found in the ancient Near East. For a complete discussion, see Meredith G. Kline, *Treaty of the Great King* (Grand Rapids: Eerdmans Publishing Company, 1963), pp. 13–26.

conduct described in the command and its opposite. Each command sets up the possibility for choice between two ways of life. The Decalogue employs the artistic device of centrality, much as a painting does, with the concept of law the focal point around which the individual parts are arranged.

There are several important themes in the Decalogue as a whole. One of these is the sovereignty of God. God is the one who gives the laws and who speaks all of the words. The commandments bear the imprint of God's moral character and are a concrete expression of what He is like. The Ten Commandments are presented as a summary of God's will for human life, and they accordingly begin with a call to God-centered living.

A second overriding theme is the moral responsibility of man. The Decalogue is a call to righteous living before both God and society. It is a testimony to the fact that man, in the biblical view, is a moral creature. The Decalogue, moreover, sets up the unavoidable state of human life—a choice between good and evil, which is at the same time a choice for or against God. It is a variation of the great theme of the Bible—the spiritual warfare between darkness and light.

A third theme is what I shall call the beauty of order. The Ten Commandments affirm that life, as it was meant to be lived, is a law-bound life. There are certain spiritual and moral rules inherent in the universe, just as there are physical laws. Personal and social freedom are gained only as man recognizes the moral order that exists and is violated with such miserable results. The very form of the Decalogue, with its clear design and firm sense of structure, embodies the concept of order.

The Ten Commandments are also unified by the theme of love—love to God and love to man. Jesus himself gave this summary of the Old Testament law (including the Ten Commandments) when He said that the "great commandment" is this: "You shall love the Lord your God with all your heart, and with all your soul, and with all your mind. This is the great and first commandment. And a second is like it, You shall love your neighbor as yourself. On these two commandments depend all the law and the prophets" (Matt. 22:37–40).

It is important to realize that the commandments are not presented as the means by which man can be justified before God. They are the response, made in love, to what God has done for His people. The prologue (Exod. 20:2) makes this clear. In it God calls attention to His status as the God of His people and as the one who has already delivered them. This is the context for what follows. Gratitude, not self-justification, is the keynote of the Decalogue.

As is true of most biblical literature, the Ten Commandments display a thrust outward from the particular to the general, from the event or act to a spiritual meaning behind it. Thus, although each commandment speaks directly to a specific act, it implies a general principle that can be applied to any area of life. Like literature generally, it combines the particular and the universal. Thus if one goes down the list of ten commandments, he will find the following principles expressed in shorthand fashion: (1) God's uniqueness and supremacy (the specific command is "no other gods"); (2) God's spirituality and concern for proper worship (no graven image); (3) the dignity of God's name and being (not taking His name in vain); (4) God's claim to the creature's time and His concern with the sabbath as a sign of His covenant relationship (keeping the sabbath day holy);[5] (5) recognition of legitimate authority (honoring of parents); (6) reverence for life (no murder); (7) the sanctity of marriage, the home, and human sexuality (no adultery); (8) respect for property (no stealing); (9) honesty (no false witness); (10) contentment (avoidance of covetousness). The movement from the particular to the general is also evident in the fact that although the commandments are first of all matters of personal living, they have a communal application and are the foundation for a whole society of people as well as for the individual.

Moses' ascent to the mountain to receive supernatural revelation is full of archetypal significance. The mountaintop as a place of encounter with the supernatural is apparently based on the principle that physically a mountain is the point at which earth touches heaven. Other examples of the archetype in the Bible include Abraham's act of obedience on Mt. Moriah (Gen. 22), the deaths of Aaron (Num. 20:28) and Moses (Deut. 34:1–6) on a mountain, Samuel's sacrifice on "the high place" (1 Sam. 9:11–14), God sending of fire on Mt. Carmel and Elijah's ascent to the mountaintop to pray after the event (1 Kings 18:19–42), Elijah's meeting with God on a mountain (1 Kings 19:9–12), the building of the temple on "Mt. Zion," Christ's transfiguration on "a high mountain" (Matt. 17:1–8), and Christ's ascension into heaven from the Mount of Olives (Acts 1:6–12). The initiation of the epic hero into a supernatural realm of experience, from which he returns instructed and equipped to fulfill his mission as leader, is also an archetype. Parallels include Odysseus' journey to Hades, Aeneas' similar journey to the underworld, Dante's journey through the realm of the dead, Red Cross Knight's interlude in the House of Holiness (Spenser's *Faerie Queene*), and Adam's vision of fallen history before his expulsion from the Garden of Eden in Milton's *Paradise Lost*.

The golden calf incident (Exod. 32–34) draws together a number of important concerns in the epic. Moses' delay in returning from the

[5] The following Old Testament passages stress that sabbath observance was a sign of God's covenant relationship with the believing community: "Wherefore the people of Israel shall keep the sabbath, observing the sabbath throughout their generations, a perpetual covenant" (Exod. 31:16); "Moreover I gave them my sabbaths, as a sign between me and them, that they might know that I the Lord sanctify them" (Ezek. 20:12); ". . . hallow my sabbaths that they may be a sign between me and you, that you may know that I the Lord am your God" (Ezek. 20:20).

mountain is another in the series of crises that the Israelites experience. In typical fashion they use the crisis as an opportunity to repudiate God. Special irony stems from the fact that when the people resort to idolatry they violate the very law that Moses is in the process of receiving. Moses' intercession for the people before God confirms his role as mediator between the people and God, much as his breaking of the tables of stone captures in a vivid portrait his impetuousness against spiritual disorder. Aaron, by giving in to the people's evil demand for an idol (Exod. 32:22), emerges as a foil to Moses, the strong leader willing to take an unpopular stand. Finally, the episode shows again God's judgment against evil and His willingness to forgive sins and renew His covenant relationship (Exod. 32:25–33:6).

After a prolonged break in the narrative, the journey motif again comes to dominate the story, beginning in Numbers 10. The rebellion of Miriam and Aaron against the authority of Moses (Num. 12) not only shows God's judgment against a refusal to submit to legitimate authority but is also important to the characterization of Moses. The narrator asserts that "the man Moses was very meek, more than all men that were on the face of the earth" (Num. 12:3). Meekness would seem on the surface to be incompatible with the fact that Moses is so obviously an authority figure who withstands all challenges to his leadership and destroys the forces of evil. The paradox is resolved by the fact that Moses in himself is meek, even retiring, but bold in carrying out God's will and the obligations of his office. God's statement that He speaks with Moses "mouth to mouth, clearly, and not in dark speech" (Num. 12:8) shows Moses' spiritual rapport with God and is an authentication of his heroism.

The sending of the twelve spies into Canaan (Num. 13–14) precipitates yet another crisis of faith. The worthiness of the epic quest is verified when the spies return with the report that "we came to the land to which you sent us; it flows with milk and honey, and this is its fruit" (Num. 13:27). The ten spies who advise against invasion reduce the venture to a physical, military level and ignore their spitirual resources. Thus they conclude, "The people who dwell in the land are strong, and the cities are fortified and very large" (Num. 13:28). A contrast is provided by Joshua and Caleb, who exercise faith in God and realize their supernatural resources: "If the Lord delights in us, he will bring us into this land and give it to us . . . the Lord is with us; do not fear them" (Num. 14:8–9). God's past acts of deliverance are the standard by which the unbelief of the people is exposed, as God Himself makes clear when He says to Moses, "And how long will they not believe in me, in spite of all the signs which I have wrought among them?" (Num. 14:11).

The archetypal death-rebirth pattern comes to dominate the epic when God punishes the unbelieving Israelites by forcing them to wander in the wilderness for forty years (Num. 14:26–35). From the

death of a past nation rises the birth of a new nation, spiritually qualified to enter the promised land. The same motif of a nation reborn appears in Virgil's *Aeneid*.

The Epic of the Exodus, which began with an account of the
hero's birth and early life, concludes with the story of his death (Deut.
32–34). Moses is allowed to see the promised land with his eyes but
does not enter it because of his disobedience at Meribah (Num.
20:2–13). Like the hero in Virgil's *Aeneid*, Moses does not experience
the attainment of the quest.

With the death of Moses, the Epic of the Exodus concludes. Its
story has been unified by the life of its hero and by the single action of
the journey from Egypt to Canaan. The conquest of the promised land,
recounted in the book of Joshua, brings the quest to its fulfillment.
Strictly considered, though, it is not part of the epic, which is the self-
contained story of a journey and the life of a central hero. The story
told in Joshua is additional to this unified narrative, and it has the
more fragmented structure of a historical chronicle.

INTERPRETATIONS

The Book of Exodus stands as a monument to the faith of Israel,
for it records the escape of God's Chosen People from their long bondage in Egypt. It also preserves one of the records of the Ten Commandments (the other is in Deuteronomy 5), which are presumably
the means by which the Hebrews will establish and maintain their
own nation, both now, in their desert wanderings, and later, in the
Promised Land. The life of the book nevertheless depends on the extraordinary character of Moses, who dominates it from beginning to
end. It is with the phenomenon of a hero unexcelled in Hebrew history and literature, but undeified, that Walter Kaufmann concerns
himself in the following selection.

from *The Faith of a Heretic*
WALTER KAUFMANN

One of the most important points about God and man in the
Old Testament involves the person of Moses. . . .

THE FAITH OF A HERETIC From *The Faith of a Heretic* by Walter Kaufmann. Copyright © by Walter
Kaufmann. Reprinted by permission of Doubleday & Company, Inc.

There is ample evidence in the Old Testament—and its authors actually make a point of the fact—that the superstitions and even the idols of neighboring nations often gained a foothold in ancient Israel. No claim whatever is made that all the people from the time of Moses on were pure and dedicated monotheists or that their behavior came up to the highest moral standards. On the contrary, the Old Testament records Moses' epic struggle with his stiff-necked people; and Judges, Kings, and the books of the prophets relate the sequel, which is essentially similar. It took time before the whole people rose, even in theory, to the height of Moses' vision; and, of course, the people never became a nation of Moseses.

Two things, however, are extremely striking. First, in spite of occasional appearances of idolatry, beginning with the golden calf, the theory that objects in this world are gods and merit worship never seems to have gained ground. One gets the impression that some of the people sometimes fell into the habits of the nations among whom they lived and thoughtlessly adopted their practices. What the prophets attack is this unthinking, stupid inconsistency, never a rival creed, and least of all any belief that the traditional religion of Israel either contains or is indifferent to such ideas as, say, that the sun and moon are gods. This fact suggests most strongly that the monotheism of Israel was not derived from that of Ikhnaton,* and that it was not arrived at gradually by way of a slow process of exclusion.

The second point is even more striking. In India, the Jina and the Buddha, founders of two new religions in the sixth century B.C., came to be worshiped later by their followers. In China, Confucius and Lao-tze came to be deified. To the non-Christian, Jesus seems to represent a parallel case. In Greece, the heroes of the past were held to have been sired by a god or to have been born of goddesses, and the dividing line between gods and men became fluid. In Egypt, the Pharaoh was considered divine.

In Israel, no man was ever worshiped or accorded even semidivine status. This is one of the most extraordinary facts about the religion of the Old Testament and by far the most important reason for the Jews' refusal to accept Christianity and the New Testament.

It is extraordinary that the prophets never had to raise their voices against any cult of Moses or the patriarchs. One explanation, theoretically possible but incompatible with the evidence, would be that Moses never lived and was merely the fiction of a later age. But not one of the prophets makes the slightest claim to be an innovator: all remind the people of what they have long known and rebuke them for unthinkingly betraying standards and ideas long accepted. And there is no first prophet: before Amos came Elisha and Elijah and

*Amenhotep IV (1370–53 B.C.), Egyptian Pharaoh who called himself Ikhnaton, worshiped a single god.—Ed.

Micaiah and whole groups of prophets—Kings is full of them—and, before them, Nathan; and, before him, Samuel; and so forth. Yet there is not the slightest evidence that any one of them was the creator of the religion of ancient Israel or even a man who radically changed it. Everything points back at least to the time of Moses.

Why, then, was Moses never deified or worshiped—unlike Lao-tze, Confucius, and the Buddha and the Jina, and the Pharaohs of Egypt? The most obvious explanation is that he himself impressed his people with the firm idea that no human being is divine in any sense in which the rest of mankind isn't.

Being a stiff-necked and critical people, they may have been quite willing to believe that he was not a god, that no Jew is a god, and certainly no Gentile. But it seems clear that Moses himself was unequivocal on this point—as, indeed, the Buddha was, too—and that Moses, unlike the Buddha, succeeded in imprinting it forever in the minds of his followers.

It could not have been hard for a man in his position to suggest to at least some of his most ardent followers that he himself was in some sense divine and without flaw. On the contrary, the image he created of himself was that of a human being, wearing himself out in the service of God and Israel, trying against all odds to wed his people to his God, modest, patient, hard to anger, magnificent in his wrath, but completely unresentful, capable of the deepest suffering, the quintessence of devotion—human to the core.

He went away to die alone, lest any man should know his grave to worship there or attach any value to his mortal body. Having seen Egypt, he knew better than the Buddha how prone men are to such superstitions. Going off to die alone, he might have left his people with the image of a mystery, with the idea of some supernatural transfiguration, with the thought that he did not die but went up to heaven—with the notion that he was immortal and divine. He might have created the suspicion that, when his mission was accomplished, he returned to heaven. Instead he created an enduring image of humanity: he left his people with the thought that, being human and imperfect, he was not allowed to enter the promised land, but that he went up on the mountain to see it before he died.

The Jews have been so faithful to his spirit that they have not only never worshiped him but, alas, have never pitted him against the other great men of the world by way of asking who compared with Moses. To be sure, after relating the story of his death, they added: "There has not arisen a prophet since in Israel like Moses." But they have not confronted the world with this man to stake out a claim for him. One speaks of Jesus, the Buddha, and Socrates, perhaps also of Francis of Assisi, but one does not ask: Does not Moses belong with them? Was he perhaps, man for man, simply as a human being, more attractive, greater, more humane?

What the Jews have presented to the world has not been Moses or any individual, but their ideas about God and man. It is a measure of Moses' greatness that one cannot but imagine that he would have approved wholeheartedly. It would have broken his heart if he had thought that his followers would build temples to him, make images of him, or elevate him into heaven. That he has never been deified is one of the most significant facts about the ideas of God and man in the Old Testament. . . .

There is another strong, outstanding personality in Exodus: Jethro, the priest of Midian (18:1–27). Moses meets him during his sojourn in Midian, and he marries Jethro's daughter Zipporah. In the next selection William Neil considers the possibility that Jethro was a priest of Yahweh and that Jethro introduced Moses to the deity who had been the God of Abraham, Isaac, and Jacob.

The Priest of Midian
WILLIAM NEIL

It is difficult to know quite what to make of the strange interlude involving Jethro, the priest of Midian, father-in-law of Moses, which is inserted after the series of acted parables in 15:22–17:16, and before the great revelation of the Law and the renewal of the covenant at Sinai which is described in 19:1–25.

The caravan has now reached the region of the holy mountain where Moses was called to be a servant of YHWH in the symbolic experience of the Burning Bush (3:1–12). The fact that he has accomplished his mission of leading his people from slavery to freedom is not regarded as a tribute to his own leadership, but to the power of the God to whom he dedicated himself at the end of his exile in Midian (3:12). Now his father-in-law brings his wife and children to meet him and a solemn thanksgiving ceremony takes place.

Many scholars have noted that the impression left by this narrative is that Jethro is represented not so much as a humble convert to the worship of YHWH, moved by the tale that Moses has to tell of the marvellous deliverance that has taken place, but rather as a religious dignitary who is treated with marked respect by Moses (v. 7), and

THE PRIEST OF MIDIAN (pp. 82–84) from *Harper's Bible Commentary* by William Neil. Copyright © 1962 by Hodder & Stoughton, Ltd. Reprinted by permission of Harper & Row, Publishers, Inc.

who acts as the celebrant at the ceremony which follows and at which Aaron, the priest, and the chief laymen of Israel are mere worshippers (v. 12).

It has been argued from this that in effect Jethro is the key to the problem of where Moses derived the new name for God which occurs for the first time, according to E and P, at the Exodus (3:14–15; 6:3). If YHWH was the god of Sinai, worshipped by the Midianites or Kenites (*Judg.* 1:16), and if Jethro was his chief priest, Moses' father-in-law would be receiving no more than his due if he were treated with the utmost respect by all the Israelites, who had by this time learned that this powerful god had been responsible for the events by which they had been enabled to escape from Egypt.

The absence of mention of Moses as partaking in the ceremony of 18:12 would imply that Moses had already, through his encounter with the god of Sinai at the Burning Bush, been incorporated into the cult of YHWH, into which Aaron and the chief representatives of Israel are now formally admitted by Jethro. The subsequent reorganisation of the judicial practice of the fugitives (vv. 14–26) would imply that Israel took not only the name of the god of Jethro but also the judicial system of the Kenites.

It is impossible to dismiss this view as derogatory to the exalted monotheism of the full flower of Israel's faith. We cannot credit Moses with the spiritual insights of the eighth-century prophets, still less with the universalistic faith of Second Isaiah (e.g. *Isa.* 40:28). God discloses the mystery of his being in proportion to the readiness of minds sensitive enough to perceive it. Moses for all his gigantic achievements was a child of his times, and the insights of the later prophets, Jeremiah, Hosea, Isaiah and Ezekiel, were conditioned by the centuries of the experience of the people of God by which their knowledge of his ways and purposes was enriched.

There is therefore nothing inherently impossible in the idea that before YHWH became the God of Israel he was worshipped by the tribe of Midian, among whom Moses in his early days sought refuge from Egyptian justice, and that, in this eighteenth chapter of *Exodus*, the leaders of the Israelites acknowledge that the god whom Moses had come to know had been powerful enough to ensure the defeat of the hosts of Egypt, and was therefore a god well worthy of Israel's allegiance. The fact that in the rest of the Old Testament the part played by Jethro and the Kenites is ignored may simply mean that YHWH had become so closely identified with Israel and the Mosaic revelation that earlier associations were forgotten or regarded as unimportant.

But even if this origin of the name and "identity" of YHWH be conceded, it would still be quite wrong to speak of Israel as having "taken over" the god of the Kenites. There is a radical break between the conception of God as held by the prophets of Israel and developed by priest and psalmist, and that of any other Near Eastern people of which we have any archaeological evidence. Whatever the Kenites meant when they said YHWH, if indeed the above theory is correct, it was certainly not the same as was meant by Israel, even as early as the covenant of Sinai.

On any showing, the Old Testament pinpoints the Exodus as the beginning of a unique faith and singles out Moses as the creative mind which God used to mediate a new conception of himself, albeit under an old name, to the people of his choice. At the Burning Bush, Moses was singled out not by an imaginary tribal deity of an obscure Midianite clan, but by the Lord of Creation and history, the God of Jeremiah, Job, Isaiah and of our Lord Jesus Christ, who used, as he always does, the foolish things of the world to confound the wise (cf. I Cor. 1:18–29).

The God whom the Bible reveals may have entered history as the protector of a now long-forgotten unimportant tribe, but in his providential ordering of man's salvation it was to Moses that he first revealed the dim beginnings of what the name YHWH came to mean. It was to Moses that he revealed that whatever names the patriarchs may have used for God (6:3), it was the same YHWH who had spoken to Abraham, Isaac and Jacob as had now spoken to their dispirited descendants in Egypt, and had laid his hand upon them to make Israel in a far deeper way the bearers of his truth to the nations.

However little even Moses himself may have grasped of the task that was being laid upon his disgruntled followers, nothing less than the renewal of the life of the world, it was clear to him that he had been summoned to a mammoth assignment, and that the God who had summoned him was no circumscribed local godlet but a living personal power, who could overrule the plans of princes and harness the forces of nature in obedience to his will. In this light we may perhaps best think of the significance of this odd prominence of Jethro, priest of Midian, as symbolising the transformation of Yahweh, god of the Kenites, into YHWH God of Israel, and, in the second half of the chapter, we may see the symbolic handing over of authority by Jethro, whose task it had been to make known the will of Yahweh, god of the Kenites, to his godchild Moses, involving the appointment of Moses as the supreme lawgiver whose role it will be to seek to know the will of YHWH, God of Israel, and to communicate it to YHWH's people.

In his study of Middle Eastern mythology, Samuel H. Hooke discusses various types of myth: the ritual myth, the myth of origin, the cult myth, and the eschatological myth. His introduction of the concept of the cult myth is quoted here as an introduction to his comments on the Passover cult myth and the Sinai Epiphany myth.

The Cult Myth

S. H. HOOKE

In the development of the religion of Israel a new use of myth makes its appearance. The three seasonal festivals prescribed in the Book of the Covenant were celebrated at the various local shrines, such as Bethel, Shechem, and Shiloh, during the early stages of Israel's settlement in Canaan. Offerings were brought, and each of the festivals, Passover, Pentecost or the Feast of Weeks, and Tabernacles, had its own special ritual, preserved and carried out by the priests at the local shrines. On these occasions an important part of the ritual consisted in the public recitation by the priests of certain central events in the history of Israel; the recitation was accompanied by antiphonal responses from the people. One of the most deeply rooted traditions of Israel was that of the deliverance of the people from Egyptian bondage. At the Feast of Passover this event was celebrated with a ritual whose origin was far older than the historical event thus commemorated. Accompanying the ritual was the cult myth describing the event, not in historical terms, but in terms borrowed in part from Babylonian and Canaanite myth. The function of the cult myth was to confirm the covenant relation between Yahweh and Israel, and to magnify the power and glory of Yahweh. In this new use of the myth it was divested of the magical potency which it had possessed in the ritual myth. We can see the cult myth still further developed in the prophetic use of it as a means of presenting the conception of "salvation-history" to Israel. The myth still describes a situation, and still has the function of securing the continuance of the situation, no longer by magical, but by moral force. The function of the myth has been lifted to a higher plane in the cult myth as we see it employed by the prophets of Israel.

The Passover Cult Myth

S. H. HOOKE

While it cannot be doubted that historical events underlie the narrative in Exodus of the sojourn of Israel in Egypt and their escape from it, yet the form in which the story has been transmitted is not history. The account of the ten plagues by which Pharaoh was finally forced to let Israel go, of the dividing of the Red Sea to allow Israel to pass through, of the power displayed by Moses' rod, and of the Pillar of cloud and fire in which Yahweh manifested his presence among his people, is the form in which the mighty acts of Yahweh were preserved and recited in liturgical antiphony at the cult-festival of Passover year after year in the spring. From Exod. 12:24–27 and 13:14–15 it may be seen that the myth accompanying the Passover ritual had been thrown into the form of liturgical responses, and the whole "service," as it is here called, was designed to be the glorification of Yahweh and the memorial of his redemptive activity. While the feast may have begun as a family ritual, it soon developed into a festival celebrated at a central sanctuary, and finally could only be celebrated within the precincts of the Temple at Jerusalem. A careful examination of the details of the ten plagues will show that it is not history which is being presented here. For instance, after Moses has turned all the waters of Egypt into blood, we are told that Pharaoh's magicians did the same, which is obviously impossible since all the water in Egypt, including the Nile, had already been turned into blood. The general pattern of the Passover cult myth is repeated several times in liturgies in the Psalter, for example in Pss. 78, 105, 106, and notably in Ps. 136 where the antiphonal character of the liturgical responses is very marked, the congregation answering each utterance of the priests with the refrain "For his mercy endureth forever." In these Psalms we have the cult myth preserved in its fixed liturgical form, while in Exodus it is used by the editors of the Pentateuch as the basis of the "salvation-history" which records for Israel the redemptive activity of Yahweh.

The Myth of the Epiphany on Sinai
S. H. HOOKE

It has been pointed out that the cult myth which we have described above contains no reference to a most important feature of the "salvation-history" in the Pentateuch, the epiphany of Yahweh on Sinai and the establishment of the covenant with Israel. The suggestion, which has much to commend it, has been made that, underlying the confused narrative in Exod. 19–34, we have a cult myth independent of the Paschal cult myth and attached to another important cultic

THE MYTH OF THE EPIPHANY ON SINAI From S. H. Hooke, *Middle Eastern Mythology* (London: Penguin Books, 1963), pp. 145–47. Copyright © S. H. Hooke, 1963. Reprinted by permission of Penguin Books, Ltd.

occasion. We have already alluded to the fact, established by archaeological evidence, that Israel took over the Canaanite sanctuaries after their settlement in the land, and converted them to the worship of Yahweh. One of the most important of these cult-centres was Shechem, and in the twenty-fourth chapter of the book of Joshua we have an account of a gathering of all the tribes at Shechem, a recital of the Passover cult myth, and the performance of a covenant ritual at the sacred oak at Shechem, "that was in the sanctuary of Yahweh" (24:26). We have also an account in Deut. 27 of a covenant ritual which was to be performed at the twin peaks of Ebal and Gerizim, i.e., at Shechem.

It would seem, therefore, that early in the period of the settlement a covenant festival was celebrated at Shechem at which the cult myth of the epiphany on Sinai and the giving of the Law was recited. In Jos. 8:30–35 we have an account of the performance of this ritual by Joshua at Shechem in the presence of "all Israel," and it is recorded that he read all the words of the law to the people. "There was not a word of all that Moses commanded, which Joshua read not before all the assembly of Israel." We are also told that one of the features of this ceremony was a solemn reaffirmation of the covenant which, according to the tradition, had been established by Yahweh with Israel at Sinai.

What actually took place at Sinai cannot be disentangled from the cult myth in which it has been embodied, neither has the exact site of Sinai ever been determined, but it is clear that all the details of the Exodus narrative, like those of the Passover myth, are intended to set forth the glory and unapproachable holiness of Yahweh. One of the prominent features of the epiphany is the myth of the Presence in the Shekinah, a myth which has been described as peculiar to Israel. The beginnings of the myth are to be seen in the account in Gen. 15 of the first covenant with Abraham. After performing the very ancient ritual of the dividing of slain victims, Abraham in a trance sees Yahweh pass between the divided corpses of the victims in the form of "a smoking furnace and a flaming torch" (Gen. 15:17). Then, at the crossing of the Red Sea, Yahweh appears in a pillar of cloud and fire and comes between Israel and their pursuers. In the cult myth of the epiphany on Sinai, Yahweh descends upon the burning mountain in a cloud and fire. This symbolic element in the myth persists throughout the history of Israel. In the oracles of Isaiah, the presence of Yahweh in Zion as a burning fire is declared by the prophet to be the protection of Jerusalem from her adversaries, as well as destruction for the ungodly (Isa. 31:9; 33:14). The most elaborate development of the myth is seen in the visions of Ezekiel. The prophet sees "a great cloud with fire flashing continually" (Ezek. 1:4); the cloud opens to disclose the vision of the cherubim and the throne of Yahweh, and the prophet sees the whole epiphany of the glory of Yahweh leave the Temple and ultimately the city.

In the New Testament the myth of the Shekinah reappears in the Synoptic account of the Transfiguration where "a shining cloud" overshadows the disciples (Matt. 17:5). In I Cor. 10:1–2 Paul tells the Corinthians that Israel had been "baptized" unto Moses in the cloud, where the myth has become a symbol of Christian baptism.

The myth of the epiphany on Sinai, preserved at Israel's cult-centres, and recited at the festival of the renewal of the covenant, became as deeply embedded in the literary tradition of Israel as the Paschal cult legend. It recurs over and over again in the poetry of Israel. In the very ancient "Song of Deborah," celebrating a victory over the Canaanites, and, according to some scholars, sung at a cult-festival, there is a description of the epiphany of Yahweh on Sinai. It occurs in Ps. 18:9–14, and in many other passages of Hebrew poetry.

On the Babylonian monument known as the stele of Hammurabi, the king is represented as receiving from the god Shamash the ancient collection of laws commonly called the Code of Hammurabi. The sanctity of the code was affirmed in the myth of its reception from the hand of the deity. So in the case of the early legislation of Israel, contained in Exod. 21–3, generally called the Book of the Covenant, the laws are embedded in a narrative framework which is based on the cult myth of the epiphany on Sinai. The laws are represented as inscribed on tables of stone and handed to Moses by Yahweh, thus establishing their sanctity. . . .

SUGGESTED READINGS

Keller, Werner. *The Bible As History,* Sections II and III, pp. 81–143. Translated by William Neil. New York: William Morrow & Co., 1956. 14th printing, fully revised, 1964.

Neil, William. *Harper's Bible Commentary,* pp. 67–111. New York: Harper & Row, 1975.

Rylaarsdam, Coert. "Exodus: Introduction and Exegesis." In *The Interpreter's Bible,* Vol. 1, edited by George A. Buttrick, pp. 833–1099. Nashville, Tenn.: Abingdon Press, 1952. (Includes biblical text.)

Sandmel, Samuel. *Alone Atop the Mountain.* New York: Doubleday & Company, 1973. (This novel about Moses and the Exodus, although now out of print, would be worthwhile reading for students who can find copies of it.)

———— *The Enjoyment of Scripture,* pp. 182–87. New York: Oxford University Press, 1972.

———— *The Hebrew Scriptures: An Introduction to Their Literature and Religious Ideas,* pp. 371–87. New York: Alfred A. Knopf, 1963.

Williams, Jay G. *Understanding the Old Testament,* pp. 96–113. New York: Barron's Educational Series, 1972.

QUESTIONS FOR DISCUSSION AND WRITING

1. How are Moses' difficulties overcome in Chapters 1 and 2 of Exodus?
2. What do we learn about the nature of Yahweh and the character of Moses in Chapters 3 and 4?
3. What explanation is given in the biblical account for God's "hardening the heart" of Pharaoh?
4. What "rational" explanations can be given for the various plagues attributed to God's activity in Exodus 7–12? (See Chapter 3 of Section II of Werner Keller's *The Bible As History*.)
5. How did Moses and the Israelites benefit from Jethro's visit (Exodus 18)?
6. Which of the Ten Commandments name obligations to God, and which name obligations to society and the individual (Exodus 20)?
7. What explanations can be given for the seeming inconsistency in Exodus 24:12–14, where Moses is commanded to go up on the mountain to receive the tables of the law, although in 24:7 he had just read the law to the people?
8. Comment on the character of Moses as it is revealed in his responses to his people and to his God in Exodus 32–34.
9. Compare the account of the consecration of the Levites to the priesthood given in Exodus 29 with the one given in Exodus 32:25–29. What differences between the two suggest that these accounts are from two separate traditions?
10. Evaluate the first two chapters of Exodus as illustrative of Eric Auerbach's observation that the Old Testament writers left much unsaid—that their writing is "fraught with background" and calls for interpretation.
11. Write a character sketch of each of these men: Moses, Aaron, and Jethro.
12. In what ways, if any, are Yahweh's concerns in Exodus different from what they were in Genesis?
13. Do you agree with Leland Ryken that Moses cannot qualify as an epic hero because "the usual epic formulae and virtues are attributed to God rather than to a human hero"? Although God directs the drama of the Exodus and even intervenes with supernatural actions, do you think Moses does enough on his own to qualify?
14. Why does Walter Kaufmann think so highly of Moses? (What basic assumption does Ryken make that seems to be absent from Kaufmann's judgment?)
15. What, if anything, can you find to say about the Israelites in Exodus that is complimentary?
16. How does William Neil answer the argument that Jethro first introduced Moses to Yahweh?
17. What, according to S. H. Hooke, is the value of the cult myth of Mount Sinai for the Hebrew religion?

DEUTERONOMY

SUMMARY

Is Deuteronomy the book referred to in 2 Kings, Chapter 22, verse 8, when "Hilkiah the high priest said to Shaphan the secretary, 'I have found the book of the law in the house of the Lord' "? Many scholars believe that it is—not the entire book as we now have it, but very probably at least Chapters 5–26 and 28. If this is true, then Deuteronomy is a book compiled in the seventh century B.C. from sources already available. It was responsible for a reform carried out by King Josiah in the last quarter of that century, a vivid account of which takes up all of 2 Kings 23.

Deuteronomy begins with an address by Moses to the assembled multitude in Moab shortly before they are to cross the Jordan into Canaan, the Promised Land. They have journeyed for forty years since they left the sacred mountain, Horeb (called Sinai in Exodus), and now Moses recalls for them the important events that took place.

He reminds them of their defeat at the hands of the Amorites

Julius Schnorr von
Carolsfeld, "King Josiah
and The Book of the Law"

when they went into battle without the Lord's blessing and of the
Lord's decision not to let any of that generation except Caleb and
Joshua into the Promised Land. Not even Moses will enter, because he
must bear the consequences of his people's behavior. With the Lord's
help, the Israelites have defeated Sihon, king of Heshbon, and Og,
king of Bashan. Now they are at Mount Pisgah, and although Moses
begs the Lord to let him cross over with his people, he is allowed only
to look at it from afar.

After this brief historical survey, Moses tells the people that if
they worship graven images or heavenly bodies the Lord will "scatter
them among the peoples." He has chosen Israel to be his own, and
Israel must worship only him. Moses sets apart three cities east of the
Jordan to serve as sanctuaries for men who kill their neighbors unin-
tentionally (4:41–42).

Moses repeats the Ten Commandments given forty years before
on Mount Horeb (Sinai), reminding his people that they all heard
these commandments given by the voice of the Lord. And now he will
pass on to them other laws and ordinances that were given to him
on the mountain. Chapter 6 records the great commandment: "Hear,
O Israel: the Lord our God is one Lord; and you shall love the Lord
your God with all your heart, and with all your soul, and with all your
might."

The people are instructed to tear down the places of worship of
other gods when they enter Canaan, and they are to worship the Lord
in a place he shall designate. In *The Literature of the Old Testament*,
Julius Bewer says that "Deuteronomy 12–26 are a law code in which
the demands of religion and life are formulated." He summarizes the
body of laws in a two-page outline, the main headings of which are:
Religious Laws (12:2–16:17), Officers of Authority (16:18–20;

17:2–18:22), Judicial Procedure (19), Military Laws (20), Family Laws (21:10–21), Various Laws (21:22–22:12), Chastity Laws (22:13–30), Exclusion Laws (23:1–8), Various Ritual and Humane Laws (23:9–24:9), Humane Laws (24:1–25:4), Various Laws (25:5–19), and Ritual Formulations (26:1–15).*

Chapters 28–30 enumerate the blessings the Israelites will receive if they keep the Lord's commandments and the terrible things that will happen to them if they do not.

Moses summons Joshua and orders him to write down the song which is given in Chapter 32. This song begins with an appeal to the heavens and the earth that is reminiscent of Homer's invocation to the Muse. His theme, says Moses, will be to "ascribe greatness to our God!" God's work is perfect; his ways are just; he is faithful. When the Lord assigned nations to the jurisdiction of heavenly beings, he chose Israel for himself. He cared for Israel in every way, and the people prospered. Then they forsook their God. "They sacrificed to demons which were no gods." He would have destroyed them had he not "feared provocation by the enemy," that is, feared that other nations would discredit the God of Israel. Finally the other nations will fall and Israel will be vindicated, and then everyone will see that the Lord is the only God.

> See now that I, even I, am he,
>   and there is no god beside me;
> I kill and I make alive;
> I wound and I heal;
>   and there is none that can deliver
>   out of my hand.
>
>   (32:39)

The Lord tells Moses that he will die on Mount Nebo and not enter the land of Canaan, "because you did not revere me as holy in the midst of the people of Israel" (32:51).

Chapter 33 is an echo of Chapter 49 of Genesis. Here Moses, as Jacob had done, "blesses" the children of Israel before he dies. Simeon is missing from Moses' account, but Ephraim and Manasseh are added to it.

As the Lord has instructed him, Moses goes up "to Mount Nebo, to the top of Pisgah," and from there he views the Promised Land. Then Moses dies, and the Lord buries him "in the valley in the land of Moab . . . but no man knows the place of his burial to this day." Joshua takes over, but we are reminded that "there has not arisen a prophet since in Israel like Moses, whom the Lord knew face to face" (34:10).

---

*Julius A. Bewer, *The Literature of the Old Testament*, rev. ed. (New York: Columbia University Press, 1962), pp. 128–30.

LITERARY QUALITIES

from *The Search for God*
MARCHETTE CHUTE

Moses had tried to weld his people into a nation that would hold fast to his vision, and thus be set apart for a greater destiny than any other nation had ever known. Whether they would remain so consecrated he did not know; he seems to have underestimated his own work and believed that he had failed. All he could do for them now was to give them a final reminder of his reason for having brought them out of Egypt, the oration that constitutes the *Book of Deuteronomy* and is one of the greatest and saddest of farewells.

The oration in its present form is not, of course, in the words Moses himself used. What he said was carried many generations in the memory of the people before it was finally put on record, and even the very well trained Eastern memory is not infallible. But in its matchless picture of Moses' terror for his people and his entire loneliness, the *Book of Deuteronomy* is too close to the probabilities to be entirely the work of another man. Additional material was added later; but it would have required more historical imagination than the later Hebrews ever showed to have invented the whole speech of Moses, given as he gazed over an assembly in which there was no one to whom he could speak as an equal. They were only children, his children; and he was reduced to bribing them with promises of reward if they would stay on the path he had opened before them, and to threatening them with disaster if they failed.

Moses began his farewell with a backward look over the past, to remind the children of Israel how consistently they had been protected in their forty years of wandering through the wilderness. He reminded them also how they had been dedicated and set apart from the rest of the world; "for what great nation is there that has a god so near as is the Lord our God whenever we call on him?" (*Deut.* iv. 7) They had also a code of laws unlike the rest of the world; "for what great nation is there that has statutes and ordinances so just as all this code that I am putting before you today?" (*Deut.* iv. 8) This code was a kind of covenant they had made with God as a sign of their faithfulness to him, and unless they obeyed it they would not be worthy to inhabit the land that the Lord had given them.

The root of this covenant was not social morality. It was something much more fundamental to Moses, and much more difficult to obtain.

"Listen, O Israel; the Lord is our God, the Lord alone; so you must love the Lord your God with all your mind and all your heart and all your strength."
(*Deut.* vi. 4–5)*

This command is the beginning and the middle and the end of Moses' discourse, and every word of his oration is designed primarily to drive this fact home into the minds of his audience.

In order to reinforce his command, Moses was willing to appeal even to the childish weaknesses of the people before him. As long as he had known them, they had tried to travel the path of least resistance. They liked comfort, and it was their permanent grievance against Moses that he had taken them out of the rich land of Egypt into a barren wilderness. Moses was orator enough to make capital of this failing. The Lord had now brought them to a land richer even than Egypt, where no irrigation was necessary to produce corn and olives and grapes in abundance. If they were faithful to God the land would remain fruitful; but if they went what might seem to be the easier way and worshipped the fertility gods of Canaan, the land would become barren, and the easier way would be the harder way in the end.

"I am putting before you today a blessing and a curse: a blessing, if you heed the commands of the Lord your God . . . and a curse if you do not heed the commands of the Lord your God, but swerve from the way I am appointing you today, by running after alien gods."
(*Deut.* xi. 26–28)

At this point in the discourse there is inserted a series of extremely humane and reasonable laws. Every seven years all debts shall be forgiven; after seven years the Hebrew slave shall go free, with a reward for his services; judges shall administer real justice and not take bribes; there shall be no accumulation of wealth in the royal treasury; the property rights of others shall be respected; no servant shall be oppressed, especially if he lacks means of redress; the accidental killing of a man shall not be punished as though it were intentional; no man shall suffer for other than his own sins; and so on. This part of the discourse closes with the formula for the ritual that was used to curse the more deadly of the sins, with the people joining in the responses.

As Moses said, he had put before his people a blessing and a

* All quotations from the Bible in this article are from *The Bible, An American Translation* (Chicago: The University of Chicago Press, 1935).—Ed.

curse, life and death. It was their own choice which they would follow. If they obeyed the laws and remembered that their God was One, they would become a great nation; if they did not, they would be destroyed. It was no strange mystery that Moses was enjoining his people to follow.

> "For this charge which I am enjoining on you today is not beyond your power, nor is it out of reach; it is not in the heavens, that you should say, 'O that someone would ascend to the heavens for us, and get to know it for us, and then communicate it to us, so that we may observe it!' . . . No, the matter is very near you, on your mouth and in your mind, for you to observe."
>
> *(Deut.* xxx. 11–14)

All that was required was a willingness to obey the first commandment, and it was this willingness that Moses had done his best to instill.

From the first moment of his revelation on Mount Horeb, Moses had labored with his people to make them a fit instrument to carry on his vision. Yet he was afraid that all his work had not been sufficient, that when temptation came his people would run after alien gods and forget all he had taught them. They had not been faithful while he lived, and he had no reason to believe that they would be faithful after he was dead.

Moses was obliged to leave his people now, and to leave the truth he had discovered to take care of itself. He could do nothing more to make it as precious to his people as it had been to him. He had delivered them from Egypt, he had taught them a code of laws, he had led them safely through the wilderness; but they were still not ready to learn what he was prepared to teach. He was forced to leave them now, to go out of their sight forever; but in the same way that a Hebrew father always gave his sons a blessing when he was about to die, Moses gave each of the tribes a blessing as though they were indeed his children.

Each of Israel's sons he blessed, and then to all of them together he gave a reminder and a promise.

> The eternal God is a refuge,
> And underneath are the everlasting arms.
> *(Deut.* xxxiii. 27)

Then he went up into the mountain and left them alone, to follow the truth if they could.

The Intention and Structure
of the Book of Deuteronomy
J. KENNETH KUNTZ

A brief comment is in order concerning the style of Deuteronomy. Fluid, skillful oratory pervades this book. Instruction and persuasion often go hand in hand. Ordinarily the law is not succinctly given. Rather, it is preached in the hope that its listeners will be moved to obedience. Consequently, such expressions as the following are characteristic of Deuteronomic prose: "Yahweh, the God of your fathers," "to go after (or serve) other gods," "to hearken to (or obey) the voice of Yahweh," "that you may prolong your days in the land." The book appeals to the conscience of the individual listener primarily through such phraseology. Hence, the Mosaic faith is revived and cast in the language of the seventh century B.C. in the hope that the present generation of Israelites will live up to their great calling as the elect people of Yahweh.

Chapters 22 and 23 of 2 Kings are necessary background for an understanding of Robert H. Pfeiffer's essay "Deuteronomy and the Reforms of Josiah," which follows. They are reprinted here for easy reference.*

THE BOOK OF THE LAW
IS FOUND

22 Josi'ah was eight years old when he began to reign, and he reigned thirty-one years in Jerusalem. His mother's name was Jedi'dah the daughter of Adai'ah of Bozkath. ² And he did what was right in the eyes of the LORD, and walked in all the way of David his father, and he did not turn aside to the right hand or to the left.

3 In the eighteenth year of King Josi'ah, the king sent Shaphan the son of Azali'ah, son of Meshul'lam, the secretary, to the house of the LORD, saying, ⁴ "Go up to Hilki'ah the high priest, that he may reckon the amount of the money which has been brought into the house of the LORD, which the keepers of the threshold have collected from the

THE INTENTION AND STRUCTURE OF THE BOOK OF DEUTERONOMY From p. 322 of *The People of Ancient Israel* by J. Kenneth Kuntz. Copyright © 1974 by J. Kenneth Kuntz. By permission of Harper & Row, Publishers, Inc.

people; ⁵and let it be given into the hand of the workmen who have the oversight of the house of the LORD; and let them give it to the workmen who are at the house of the LORD, repairing the house, ⁶that is, to the carpenters, and to the builders, and to the masons, as well as for buying timber and quarried stone to repair the house. ⁷But no accounting shall be asked from them for the money which is delivered into their hand, for they deal honestly."

8 And Hilki'ah the high priest said to Shaphan the secretary, "I have found the book of the law in the house of the LORD." And Hilki'ah gave the book to Shaphan, and he read it. ⁹And Shaphan the secretary came to the king, and reported to the king, "Your servants have emptied out the money that was found in the house, and have delivered it into the hand of the workmen who have the oversight of the house of the LORD." ¹⁰Then Shaphan the secretary told the king, "Hilki'ah the priest has given me a book." And Shaphan read it before the king.

11 And when the king heard the words of the book of the law, he rent his clothes. ¹²And the king commanded Hilki'ah the priest, and Ahi'kam the son of Shaphan, and Achbor the son of Micai'ah, and Shaphan the secretary, and Asai'ah the king's servant, saying, ¹³"Go, inquire of the LORD for me, and for the people, and for all Judah, concerning the words of this book that has been found; for great is the wrath of the LORD that is kindled against us, because our fathers have not obeyed the words of this book, to do according to all that is written concerning us."

14 So Hilki'ah the priest, and Ahi'kam, and Achbor, and Shaphan, and Asai'ah went to Huldah the prophetess, the wife of Shallum the son of Tikvah, son of Harhas, keeper of the wardrobe (now she dwelt in Jerusalem in the Second Quarter); and they talked with her. ¹⁵And she said to them, "Thus says the LORD, the God of Israel: 'Tell the man who sent you to me, ¹⁶Thus says the LORD, Behold, I will bring evil upon this place and upon its inhabitants, all the words of the book which the king of Judah has read. ¹⁷Because they have forsaken me and have burned incense to other gods, that they might provoke me to anger with all the work of their hands, therefore my wrath will be kindled against this place, and it will not be quenched. ¹⁸But as to the king of Judah, who sent you to inquire of the LORD, thus shall you say to him, Thus says the LORD, the God of Israel: Regarding the words which you have heard, ¹⁹because your heart was penitent, and you humbled yourself before the LORD, when you heard how I spoke against this place, and against its inhabitants, that they should become a desolation and a curse, and you have rent your clothes and wept before me, I also have heard you, says the LORD. ²⁰Therefore, behold, I will gather you to your fathers, and you shall be gathered to your grave in peace, and your eyes shall not see all the evil which I will bring upon this place.' " And they brought back word to the king.

THE REFORMS OF JOSIAH

23 Then the king sent, and all the elders of Judah and Jerusalem were gathered to him. ²And the king went up to the house of the LORD, and with him all the men of Judah and all the inhabitants of Jerusalem, and the priests and the prophets, all the people, both

small and great; and he read in their hearing all the words of the book of the covenant which had been found in the house of the LORD. ³ And the king stood by the pillar and made a covenant before the LORD, to walk after the LORD and to keep his commandments and his testimonies and his statutes, with all his heart and all his soul, to perform the words of this covenant that were written in this book; and all the people joined in the covenant.

4 And the king commanded Hilki'ah, the high priest, and the priests of the second order, and the keepers of the threshold, to bring out of the temple of the LORD all the vessels made for Ba'al, for Ashe'rah, and for all the host of heaven; he burned them outside Jerusalem in the fields of the Kidron, and carried their ashes to Bethel. ⁵ And he deposed the idolatrous priests whom the kings of Judah had ordained to burn incense in the high places at the cities of Judah and round about Jerusalem; those also who burned incense to Ba'al, to the sun, and the moon, and the constellations, and all the host of the heavens. ⁶ And he brought out the Ashe'rah from the house of the LORD, outside Jerusalem, to the brook Kidron, and burned it at the brook Kidron, and beat it to dust and cast the dust of it upon the graves of the common people. ⁷ And he broke down the houses of the male cult prostitutes which were in the house of the LORD, where the women wove hangings for the Ashe'rah. ⁸ And he brought all the priests out of the cities of Judah, and defiled the high places where the priests had burned incense, from Geba to Beer-sheba; and he broke down the high places of the gates that were at the entrance of the gate of Joshua the governor of the city, which were on

one's left at the gate of the city. ⁹ However, the priests of the high places did not come up to the altar of the LORD in Jerusalem, but they ate unleavened bread among their brethren. ¹⁰ And he defiled To'pheth, which is in the valley of the sons of Hinnom, that no one might burn his son or his daughter as an offering to Molech. ¹¹ And he removed the horses that the kings of Judah had dedicated to the sun, at the entrance to the house of the LORD, by the chamber of Nathanmelech the chamberlain, which was in the precincts; and he burned the chariots of the sun with fire. ¹² And the altars on the roof of the upper chamber of Ahaz, which the kings of Judah had made, and the altars which Manas'sch had made in the two courts of the house of the LORD, he pulled down and broke in pieces, and cast the dust of them into the brook Kidron. ¹³ And the king defiled the high places that were east of Jerusalem, to the south of the mount of corruption, which Solomon the king of Israel had built for Ash'toreth the abomination of the Sido'nians, and for Chemosh the abomination of Moab, and for Milcom the abomination of the Ammonites. ¹⁴ And he broke in pieces the pillars, and cut down the Ashe'rim, and filled their places with the bones of men.

15 Moreover the altar at Bethel, the high place erected by Jerobo'am the son of Nebat, who made Israel to sin, that altar with the high place he pulled down and he broke in pieces its stones, crushing them to dust; also he burned the Ashe'rah. ¹⁶ And as Josi'ah turned, he saw the tombs there on the mount; and he sent and took the bones out of the tombs, and burned them upon the altar, and defiled it, according to the word of the LORD which the man of

71

God proclaimed, who had predicted these things. [17]Then he said, "What is yonder monument that I see?" And the men of the city told him, "It is the tomb of the man of God who came from Judah and predicted these things which you have done against the altar at Bethel." [18]And he said, "Let him be; let no man move his bones." So they let his bones alone, with the bones of the prophet who came out of Sama'ria. [19]And all the shrines also of the high places that were in the cities of Sama'ria, which kings of Israel had made, provoking the LORD to anger, Josi'ah removed; he did to them according to all that he had done at Bethel. [20]And he slew all the priests of the high places who were there, upon the altars, and burned the bones of men upon them. Then he returned to Jerusalem.

21 And the king commanded all the people, "Keep the passover to the LORD your God, as it is written in this book of the covenant." [22]For no such passover had been kept since the days of the judges who judged Israel, or during all the days of the kings of Israel or of the kings of Judah; [23]but in the eighteenth year of King Josi'ah this passover was kept to the LORD in Jerusalem.

24 Moreover Josi'ah put away the mediums and the wizards and the teraphim and the idols and all the abominations that were seen in the land of Judah and in Jerusalem, that he might establish the words of the law which were written in the book that Hilki'ah the priest found in the house of the LORD. [25]Before him there was no king like him, who turned to the LORD with all his heart and with all his soul and with all his might, according to all the law of Moses; nor did any like him arise after him.

26 Still the LORD did not turn from the fierceness of his great wrath, by which his anger was kindled against Judah, because of all the provocations with which Manas'seh had provoked him. [27]And the LORD said, "I will remove Judah also out of my sight, as I have removed Israel, and I will cast off this city which I have chosen, Jerusalem, and the house of which I said, My name shall be there."

JOSIAH IS SLAIN
AT MEGIDDO

28 Now the rest of the acts of Josi'ah, and all that he did, are they not written in the Book of the Chronicles of the Kings of Judah? [29]In his days Pharaoh Neco king of Egypt went up to the king of Assyria to the river Euphra'tes. King Josi'ah went to meet him; and Pharaoh Neco slew him at Megid'do, when he saw him. [30]And his servants carried him dead in a chariot from Megid'do, and brought him to Jerusalem, and buried him in his own tomb. And the people of the land took Jeho'ahaz the son of Josi'ah, and anointed him, and made him king in his father's stead.

INTERPRETATIONS

Deuteronomy and the Reforms of Josiah
ROBERT H. PFEIFFER

A. THE REFORMS OF JOSIAH

The Deuteronomic Code found in the collection box of the Temple was utterly unknown and was not accepted as a divine revelation to Moses until the prophetess Huldah had vouched for it (II Kings 22:14–17); subsequently the book was read to the elders of Judah and after the people had pledged themselves through a covenant to obey Jehovah's commandments in the book it became at once the law of the land and its prescriptions were enforced throughout the kingdom (23:1–3). The measures taken by Josiah, according to the original sections of II Kings 23, are: cleansing the Temple of Canaanite objects (the Ashera, the house of sacred prostitutes, and vessels made for Baal), and of the altars to the astral deities and the chariot of the sun-god; all sanctuaries of Jehovah throughout the kingdom, except the Temple in Jerusalem, were defiled and their priests put on relief in Jerusalem; all heathen sanctuaries were destroyed; Topheth was desecrated and became the dump heap (*ge-Hinnom*, the Valley [of the sons] of Hinnom, on account of the fire became a name for hell, Gehenna); the Passover was celebrated in the Temple, instead of at home, as one of the three annual festivals in connection with Unleavened Bread.

The single sanctuary and other measures were in a sense a return to the worship of the time of Moses. But the real significance of the reforms was in their unconscious innovations, which formed a bridge leading over to Judaism. How unpopular was the destruction of the village high places outside of Jerusalem is indicated by Jeremiah's experience. After the Book of Moses was found in the Temple, Jehovah ordered Jeremiah to proclaim, "Hear ye the words of this covenant, and do them" (Jer. 11:6). But when he went to preach in favor of the reforms in his home town, Jehovah warned him to desist because the men of Anathoth were planning to kill him (11:21). The feelings of the peasants and villagers, to whom the destruction of the local shrine of

Jehovah must have seemed a shocking sacrilege, are well described by James G. Frazer: "With a heavy heart he may have witnessed the iconoclasts at their work of destruction and devastation. It was there, on yonder hilltop, under the shade of that spreading . . . oak . . . How often had he seen the blue smoke of sacrifice curling up in the still air above the trees, and . . . God himself . . . not far off . . . And now the hilltop was bare and desolate . . . God, it seems, had gone away."*

In spite of such hardships, · the reforms of Josiah must be regarded as providential for the future, in the following respects:

I. PRESERVATION OF THE NATION AND THE RELIGION

Without the finding of Deuteronomy and the reforms of Josiah Judah would have lost its nationality and religion as did the exiles from Samaria, the Northern Kingdom, in 722. Only thirty-five years after the reforms the Judean kingdom, its Davidic Dynasty, and its Temple ceased to exist. Deuteronomy and the reforms were the decisive prerequisites for changing the state and nation into the Jewish community, replacing the unique Temple with innumerable synagogues, substituting for the monarchy the Kingdom of God, and supplanting priests and prophets by scribes and rabbis. The Judeans became Jews, surviving without a state of their own until 1948, except for the brief period of Maccabean independence in 141–63 B.C., being held together by a new national feeling based on observance of the divine law and study of the Scriptures which grew up around Deuteronomy.

II. PURIFICATION OF THE WORSHIP

With the enactment of the law of the single sanctuary (Deut. 12) it became possible to abolish ancient heathen religious practices of an objectionable character and enforce the prophetic requirements. It is true that Deuteronomy unconsciously preserved some ancient Canaanite rites, like sacrifice and festivals, but these were now given a new meaning. Sacrifice became differentiated from butchery, and it became possible to eat meat without a sacrificial rite (Deut. 12:14–15, 20–22; contrast Lev. 17:3–4; I Sam. 14:32–35); the festivals lost their ancient connection with shepherding (Passover) and agriculture (Unleavened Bread, Harvest, Ingathering) and became commemorations of national events (Deut. 16:1) and expressions of joy in the presence of Jehovah (16:11, 14); the royal worship in the Temple of Solomon became national in scope; personal piety soon centered no longer in sacrificial ritual but in the study and observance of the law; cities of refuge for

---

*Folklore in the Old Testament (London, 1919), vol. III, p. 106.

unintentional slayers were established to take the place of the ancient local sanctuaries (19:1–7).

III. THE STATE BECOMES A THEOCRACY

The prophetic oracle of Moses, regarded as the law of God, became the charter of the nation in 621, through a solemn covenant; henceforth the activities of the government were to be ruled by religion. We may compare the temporal power of the popes—a religious government carrying out political functions. As a divinely chosen people, as God's kingdom on earth, the Jewish Congregation regarded itself as divinely protected, and believed that Jehovah would judge the other nations and ultimately establish a Jewish empire: thus prophecy became apocalypse.

B. THE INFLUENCE OF DEUTERONOMY

The publication of the initial and basic prophetic oracle of Moses marks the beginning of the canonization of Holy Scripture. We take a sacred, revealed book for granted, but before 621 no one anywhere had ever heard of a book written under divine inspiration. Deuteronomy is the beginning of the written word of God, as distinguished from the inspired prophetic message which was primarily oral. Strangely the Book of Amos, which purported to contain divine revelations, was not considered Holy Scripture in 621, and was not canonized until about 200 B.C. The notion of inspired Scripture was born when Deuteronomy was received as God's word through a covenant; it was then something new and is a contribution of Judaism. It appears later in Zoroastrianism, Hinduism, Buddhism, and the religions derived from Judaism (Christianity and Islam). The idea of the word of God fixed for all time in a divinely revealed book is patently based on prophecy, God's revelation of his word in oral form. Deuteronomy was written as a prophetic oracle of Moses and was received as such. Henceforth the Jews had in it a permanently valid revelation of God's will and mind, the recognized standard of religion and morals. The whole Hebrew Bible grew eventually around Deuteronomy: the Pentateuch was canonized about 400 B.C., the Prophets (Joshua, Judges, Samuel, Kings; Isaiah, Jeremiah, Ezekiel, and The Twelve) about 200, and the Writings (Psalms, Proverbs, Job, Song of Songs, Ruth, Lamentations, Ecclesiastes, Esther, Daniel, Ezra, Nehemiah, Chronicles) in A.D. 90. The appearance of Sacred Scripture in 621 had far-reaching results, besides the canonization of the Old Testament.

Oral revelation through the prophets gradually came to an end, for the possession of a transcript of Jehovah's initial revelation to Moses tended to make sporadic communications of the deity superflu-

ous. The ancient priestly oracle by means of the lots in the sacred box
had been displaced by the far more articulate prophetic oracle, now at
the height of its importance. But the Book of Moses now became the
charter of the nation and the basic divine revelation. Worship and
law, custom and morals were placed on a new basis; they were no
longer to be determined by ancestral practices or by occasional communications of God through the prophets, but by a sacred book. . . .

The Image of Woman
in the Old Testament Laws
Phyllis Bird

Though the laws of the Old Testament give only a partial view
of the norms of ancient Israel, they are nevertheless a primary source
for reconstructing the ideals and practices of that society. They are
preserved, for the most part, in several large "codes," or collections,
ranging in date from premonarchic (before 1,000 B.C.) to postexilic
(500–400 B.C.) times. Each collection, however, in its own prehistory
has taken up material of different ages, and each combines laws of different types, including both "secular" law (the "law of the [city]
gate"—where deliberation of cases took place) and religious law (the
law of the sanctuary or religious assembly). Despite this variety, however, none of the "codes" can be considered comprehensive. All are
samplers of one kind or another. All presuppose the current existence
of a system that they seek not to formulate but to preserve from disso-
lution and destruction. Thus the laws frequently deal with areas in
which changes have occurred or threaten, while the common assumptions of the society are left unspoken and must often be inferred from
the special cases treated in the collections.

In many respects Israelite law differs little from that of ancient
Mesopotamia and Syria. It is testimony to Israel's participation in a
common ancient Near Eastern social and cultural milieu. Salient features of this shared culture revealed in Israel's laws are patriarchy
(together with patrilineal descent and patrilocal residence as the usual
norm), a more or less extended family, polygyny, concubinage, slavery
(under certain conditions), and the thoroughgoing institutionalization
of the double standard. Israel's laws differ most notably from other

THE IMAGE OF WOMAN IN THE OLD TESTAMENT LAWS From *Religion and Sexism*, ed. Rosemary Radford
Reuther, pp. 48–57. Copyright © 1974 by Rosemary Radford Reuther. Reprinted by permission of
Simon & Schuster, a Division of Gulf & Western Corporation.

known law codes in their unusual severity in the field of sexual transgression and in the severity of the religious laws that prescribe and seek to preserve the exclusive and undefiled worship of Yahweh, the national deity. These two unique features are interrelated, and both had significant consequences for women in ancient Israel.

The majority of the laws, especially those formulated in the direct-address style of the so-called apodictic law (the style used primarily for the statement of religious obligations), address the community *through its male members*. Thus the key verbal form in the apodictic sentence is the second person *masculine* singular or plural. That this usage was not meant simply as an inclusive form of address for bisexual reference is indicated by such formulations as the following:

> Thou shalt not covet *thy neighbor's wife*.
> (Exod. 20:19)

> You shall not afflict any widow or orphan.
> If you do . . . then *your wives* shall become
> widows and your children fatherless.
> (Exod. 22:22–24 [Heb. 21–23])

> You shall be *men* consecrated to me.
> (Exod. 22:31)

Similarly, the typical casuistic law (case law) begins with the formula "If a *man* does X . . ." The term used for "man" in this formulation is not the generic term, *'ādām*, but the specifically and exclusively masculine term, *'îš*. Even if one argues that these laws were understood to apply by extension to the whole community, it must be noted that the masculine formulation was apparently found inadequate in some circumstances. Thus *'ādām* is substituted for *'îš*, or the terms "man" and "woman" (*'îs, 'iššāh*) are used side by side where it is important to indicate that the legislation is intended to be inclusive in its reference.

The basic presupposition of all the laws, though modified to some extent in the later period, is a society in which full membership is limited to males, in which only a male is judged a responsible person. He is responsible not only for his own acts but for those of his dependents as well. These include wife, children and even livestock, in the extended and fluid understanding of household/property that pertained in ancient Israel (Exod. 20:17, 21:28–29). The law addresses heads of families (the family is called appropriately a "father's house" in the Hebrew idiom), for it is the family, not the individual, that is the basic unit of society in old Israel.

But this definition of society as an aggregate of male-dominated households was modified in Israel by a concept of the society as a religious community, a religious community composed in the first instance exclusively of males, or perhaps originally all adult males. This is the understanding of the covenant congregation, or the "people" (ᶜam), Israel, addressed by Moses on Sinai:

> So Moses went down from the mountain to the
> people (ᶜam). . . . And he said to the people
> (ᶜam), "Be ready by the third day; do not go
> near a woman."
>
> (Exod. 19:14–15)

It also coincides with the understanding of the "people" (ᶜam) as the warriors of the community, a usage illustrated in certain texts pertaining to the premonarchic period.

> The Lord said to Gideon, "The people (ᶜam) are
> too many for me to give the Midianites into
> their hand."
>
> (Judg. 7:2)

> Sisera called out all his chariots . . . and all
> the men (ᶜam) who were with him . . .
>
> (Judg. 4:13)

In both cult and war the "true" nature of Israel manifested itself.

The coincidence in Israel of these two male-oriented and male-dominated systems (the sociopolitical and the religious) created a double liability of women, enforcing upon them the status of dependents in the religious as well as the political and economic spheres. Discrimination against women was inherent in the socioreligious organization of Israel. It was a function of the system. And though this systemic discrimination need not be represented as a plot to subjugate women—and thereby liberate the male ego—the system did enforce and perpetuate the dependence of women and an image of the female as inferior to the male.

This is illustrated in the legal material by laws dealing with inheritance, divorce, sexual transgressions, religious vows, cultic observances and ritual purity. One of the chief aims of Israelite law is to assure the integrity, stability and economic viability of the family as the basic unit of society. In this legislation, however, the interests of the family are commonly identified with those of its male head. His rights and duties are described with respect to other men and their property. The laws focus mainly upon external threats to the man's authority, honor and property, though they may occasionally serve to define and protect his rights in relation to members of his own household (slaves: Exod. 21:20–21; children: Deut. 21:18–22; wife: Num. 5:11–31). Only in rare cases, however, are the laws concerned with the rights of dependents (Exod. 21:26–27; Deut. 21:10–14, 15–17 and 22:13–21).

The wife's primary contribution to the family was her sexuality, which was regarded as the exclusive property of her husband, both in respect to its pleasure and its fruit. Her duty was to "build up" his "house"—and his alone. This service was essential to the man in order for him to fulfill his primary role as paterfamilias. It was as a consequence jealously guarded. Adultery involving a married woman was a crime of first magnitude in Israelite law (Lev. 20:10; Exod. 20:14), ranking with murder and major religious offenses as a transgression demanding the death penalty—for both offenders. The issue was not simply one of extramarital sex (which was openly tolerated in certain circumstances). The issue was one of property and authority. Adultery was a violation of the fundamental and exclusive right of a man to the sexuality of his wife. It was an attack upon his authority in the family and consequently upon the solidarity and integrity of the family itself. The adulterer robbed the husband of his essential honor, while the unfaithful wife defied his authority, offering to another man that which belonged only to him—and that which constituted her primary responsibility toward him.

The corollary of the unwritten law that a wife's sexuality belongs exclusively to her husband is the law that demands virginity of the bride. The wife found guilty of fornication is, like the adulteress, sentenced to death. In this case, however, the crime is not simply against her husband but against her father as well.

Extramarital sex is treated quite differently when a husband's rights are not involved. The man who violates an unmarried girl must simply marry her, making the proper marriage gift (*mōhar*) to her father. The only penalty he suffers is that he may not divorce her (Deut. 22:28–29). Prostitution seems to have been tolerated at all periods as a licit outlet for male sexual energies, though the prostitute was a social outcast, occupying at best a marginal place in the society. Hebrew fathers were enjoined not to "profane" their daughters by giving them up to prostitution, and the prophets used the figure of harlotry to condemn Israel's "affairs" with other gods.

Taken together, the various laws that treat of extramarital sex evidence a strong feeling in Israel that sexual intercourse should properly be confined to marriage, of which it was the essence (Gen. 2:24) and the principal sign. Thus the victim of rape, the slave girl or the female captive taken for sexual pleasure, must become or must be treated as a wife (Exod. 21:7–11; Deut. 21:10–14). Polygyny was a concession to the man's desire for more than one sexual partner, with concubinage a modification or extension of this. Perhaps prostitution was tolerated as a poor man's substitute. It must certainly have been strengthened by the increasing institution of monogamous marriage as the general norm.

The laws dealing with sexual transgressions represent a strong statement of support for the family. But they are all formulated from the male's point of view, the point of view of a man who jealously guards what is essential to the fulfillment of his role in the family. Thus a jealous husband who suspects his wife of infidelity, but has no proof of it, may require her to submit to an ordeal. If she is "proved" innocent by this procedure, the husband incurs no penalty for his false accusation (Num. 5:12–31). Infidelity by the husband is not considered a crime.

Divorce was recognized in ancient Israel and regulated by law, at least in the later period of the monarchy. The extent of the practice and the circumstances in which it was sanctioned remain unclear; there is no doubt, however, that it was an exclusively male prerogative. Some scholars have interpreted the "indecency" (ʿerwāh) given as the ground for divorce in the law of Deut. 24:1–4 as a reference to sexual infidelity. If so, it would represent a modification of the more severe law of adultery found in Lev. 20. Others have suggested barrenness. The Israelite man must commonly have understood his conjugal rights to include the right to progeny, especially male progeny. A wife who did not produce children for her husband was not fulfilling her duty as a wife. In early Israel it was apparently customary for her to offer him a female slave to bear for her (Gen. 16:1–3 and 30:1–3); or the husband might simply take another wife (where economically feasible [I Sam. 1:2])—or secure the services of a harlot (?) (Judg. 11:1–3). In the monogamous family of the later monarchy divorce must have been a more frequent alternative. All the Old Testament references to divorce are found in sources stemming from this period or later (Deut. 24:1–4; Jer. 3:8; Isa. 50:1; possibly Hos. 2:2).

The integrity of the family was also secured by inheritance laws that insured against the alienation of family property, that essential property which assured to each father's house its "place" in Israel. The basic inheritance laws are not contained in the Old Testament legal codes, but can be inferred from extralegal references and from a number of laws dealing with special cases in the transfer of family property (Num. 27:1–11 and 36:1–9; Jer. 32:6–8; Ruth 4:1–6). Two of these concern the inheritance of daughters. Since a daughter left her father's house at marriage to become a member of her husband's family, she normally received no inheritance. (Neither did the wife, since property was transmitted in the male line.) By special legislation, however, daughters were permitted to inherit where sons were lacking (Num. 27:1–11). But they were only placeholders in the male line, which was thereby enabled to continue in their children. The rare institution of the levirate (the marriage of a widow to the brother of her dead husband) may also have been designed to preserve the property of a man to his name—that is, for his male descendants.

In the patriarchal family system of Israel a woman had only a limited possibility of owning property, though responsibility for managing it may have been assumed with some frequency. Normally, however, a woman was dependent for support upon her father before marriage and her husband after marriage. As a consequence, the plight of a widow without sons might be desperate. Her husband's property would pass to the nearest male relative, who was apparently under no obligation to maintain his kinsman's wife. She would be expected to return to her own family. The frequent impossibility of this solution, however, is suggested by the special plea for defense of the widow that occurs repeatedly in the ethical injunctions of the Old Testament (e.g., Isa. 1:17; Jer. 7:6 and 22:3; Zech. 7:10; Exod. 22:22).

The laws also illustrate, both explicitly and implicitly, disabilities of women in the religious sphere. As noted above, the oldest religious law was addressed only to men, while the sign of membership in the religious community was circumcision, the male initiation rite. Only males were required by the law of Deut. 16:16 to attend the three annual pilgrim feasts, the primary communal religious acts of later Israel. Consonant with this bias was the assumption of the cultic law that only males might serve as priests (eventually restricted to the "sons of Aaron"). However, in keeping with the understanding of the family as the basic social unit, the priest's whole household shared in the holiness of his office and in the obligations imposed by it. Thus a priest's daughter who "defiled" herself by fornication incurred the sentence of death, since she had also defiled her father by her act (Lev. 21:9; see also 22:10–14).

Women also suffered religious disability that was only indirectly sex-determined. Israelite religion, following widespread ancient practice, excluded from cultic participation all persons in a state of impurity or uncleanness—that is, in a profane or unholy state. Various circumstances were understood to signal such a state, during which time (usually limited) it was considered unsafe to engage in cultic activity or have contact with the cult. Israel's laws recognized leprosy and certain other skin diseases, contact with a corpse, bodily emissions of all types (both regular and irregular, in members of both sexes), sexual intercourse and childbirth as among these factors that caused uncleanness (Lev. 12–15). The frequent and regular recurrence of this cultically proscribed state in women of childbearing age must have seriously affected their ability to function in the cult.

An explicitly discriminatory expression—or "extension"—of the idea of ritual uncleanness is found in the law determining the period of impurity occasioned by childbirth (Lev. 12:1–5). Seven days are prescribed for a mother who has borne a son, but fourteen for the mother of a female child. Another cultic law that gives explicit statement to the differential values placed upon males and females is the law of Lev. 27:2–8, which determines monetary equivalents for vows of persons to cultic service. According to this reckoning the vow of a male aged twenty to sixty years was valued at 50 shekels, while that of a woman in the same age bracket was worth only 30 shekels. Thus it appears that a male of any age was more highly valued than a female.

The reason for this differential valuation must have been in large part economic, though a psychological factor is also evident. As in most premodern, labor-intensive societies, a large family was prized, since it offered a superior labor supply and flexibility and sustaining power when faced with serious threats to its existence. The large family carried more weight in the community and assured honor to its head—and to his spouse. Many descendants also assured the continuity of the father's house and name. But only males could perform this task, and only males remained as primary economic contributors. On both economic (labor value) and psychological grounds the significant size of the family was reckoned in terms of males. Females were necessary as childbearers and child rearers, but they always had to be obtained from outside the family—and at a price. A man's own daughters left his house to build up another man's family. Thus an excess of female dependents was a luxury and/or a liability.

The picture sketched above is not a complete portrait of woman in ancient Israel; nevertheless it does present the essential features. Additions and qualifications are necessary at many points. Most stem from sources outside the legal material and are treated later, but a few, explicit or implicit in the laws themselves, must be noted here.

The ancient command to honor one's parents (Exod. 20:12; Deut. 5:16) recognizes the female as the equal of the male in her role as mother. It places the highest possible value upon this role, in which her essential function in the society was represented—the reproductive function. The welfare of family and society and the status of the husband depended upon her performance of that task. Consequently she was rewarded for it by honor and protected in it by law and custom which "exempted" her (indirectly) from military service and "excused" her from certain religious and civic obligations.

Laws of this type, though positive (or compensatory) in their discrimination, may be classed together with those that discriminate negatively as laws in which the sociobiological role of the individual or his/her social value (= productivity) is a significant factor in the legal formulation. In a society in which roles and occupations are primarily sexually determined, sexual discrimination is bound to be incorporated in the laws. At the same time, however, laws that do not regard the person, but only acts or states, may be "egalitarian" in their conception. This is illustrated in the old laws of Exod. 21:26 and 21:28, which assess penalties on the basis of injury suffered, without regard to the sex of the injured person. Egalitarianism, or nondiscrimination, is characteristic of most of the laws concerning ritual impurity and is a consistent feature of the laws dealing with major ethical, moral and cultic infractions. Thus illegitimate association with the supernatural incurred the same penalty whether the practitioner was male or female (Lev. 20:27; Deut. 17:2–7), and cult prostitutes of both sexes were equally proscribed (Deut. 23:17). Illicit types of sexual intercourse, with their equal and severe penalty (death) for both offenders, may also have been viewed as belonging to this category of offenses—that is, as practices of the surrounding peoples, abhorrent to Yahweh (Lev. 18:6–18, 20:10–21; Deut. 22:30).

The only statements of equal "rights" in Old Testament law are indirect and qualified. They, too, pertain to the cultic sphere. The laws of Num. 6:2 ff. and 30:3–15 (both belonging to the latest of the law codes) indicate that women, as well as men, might undertake on their own initiative binding obligations of a religious nature. Num. 30:3–15 qualifies this, however, by upholding—but limiting—the right of a husband or father to annul a vow made by his wife or daughter (thereby allowing the interests of family to take precedence over the interests of the cult).

The picture of woman obtained from the Old Testament laws can be summarized in the first instance as that of a legal nonperson; where she does become visible it is as a dependent, and usually an inferior, in a male-centered and male-dominated society. The laws, by and large, do not address her; most do not even acknowledge her existence. She comes to view only in situations (a) where males are lacking in essential socioeconomic roles (the female heir); (b) where she requires special protection (the widow); (c) where sexual offenses involving women are treated; and (d) where sexually defined or sexually differentiated states, roles and/or occupations are dealt with (the female slave or captive as wife, the woman as mother, and the sorceress). Where ranking occurs she is always inferior to the male. Only in her role as mother is she accorded status and honor equivalent to a man's. Nevertheless she is always subject to the authority of some male (father, husband or brother), except when widowed or divorced—an existentially precarious type of independence in Israel.

The Law Code of Hammurabi
W. J. Martin

The stele of Hammurabi (c. 1792–1750 B.C.) inscribed with his famous law code was discovered between December and January 1901–2 by V. Scheil at Susa, one-time capital of the Elamites. It is in the form of a boundary stone and stands about eight feet high. The upper part has a relief depicting Hammurabi receiving sceptre and

THE LAW CODE OF HAMMURABI From D. Winton Thomas, ed., *Documents from Old Testament Times* (Edinburgh: Thomas Nelson & Sons; New York: Harper & Row, Publishers, 1961), pp. 27–35. Reprinted by permission of Thomas Nelson & Sons, Ltd.

ring from Shamash, the sun-god. The rest of the surface is taken up with the code; the direction of writing is from top to bottom. Seven columns have been deleted, presumably to make way for a memorial to its captor, most probably Shutruk-Nahhunte, who raided and pillaged Sippar in the early part of the twelfth century. One would have expected such an important stele to have been erected in the capital, Babylon, but it may well be that more than one copy existed.

The language of the Code is already grammatically fully organised and classical in form. The choice of the Akkadian language rather than of the Sumerian may indicate that Hammurabi's reforming activities extended to language as well as to jurisprudence. He must have embarked early on his work of reform, for in the Chronological Lists the designation of his second regnal year is—"He established justice in the land." The reference is probably to the promulgation of the Code, but this copy must have been made much later, as certain events referred to in the prologue belong to the latter part of his reign. Although his father and grandfather bore Semitic names, his own harks back to his Amorite origin. In racial matters, however, his policy seems to have been one of compromise, even down to the matter of dress: he adopted the Sumerian long cloak and headdress, but continued to wear his hair long in Semitic fashion. The compilation of his laws may have been carried out in this same spirit of compromise. In the prologue his avowed purpose is to ameliorate the condition of the weak, presumably including vassals and serfs. There are earlier collections of legal maxims, such as that of Bilalama (?) of Eshnunna. These laws date probably from about a century before Hammurabi. Despite some agreement in terminology, there is no ground for supposing that this or any other collection was utilised by Hammurabi. Responsible as he was for a kingdom composed of former independent states, he could hardly have afforded not to acquaint himself with the contents of their various legislative systems, and the knowledge thus acquired would have brought home to him the need of something approaching universal law. It would be the task, and not the sources, that dictated, if at all, the composite character of his work. One extraordinary fact is that, great as was his prestige as a ruler and his achievement in formulating the laws, the Code seems to have remained merely an ideal lacking practical application. There is no evidence in the contemporary legal documents that the provisions of the Hammurabi Code were ever carried out, and to all intents and purposes it might not have existed for them.

The laws of Hammurabi touch on many matters which are dealt with also in the legal parts of the Pentateuch. Despite many resemblances, there is no ground for assuming any direct borrowing by the Hebrew from the Babylonian. Even where the two sets of laws differ little in the letter, they differ much in the spirit, for instance, in the Babylonian regard for the status of litigants. The explanation of the similarities is obvious: the limitation in the variety of crimes and in the possible forms of punishment. How much both owed to a *jus gentium** would be hard to determine. But perhaps both owe more to a *jus naturale*.* In the Babylonian Code punishments are always stated, whereas in the Hebrew there occurs, as is inevitable in the rules of a theocratic community, the "absolute imperative." Any theory which fails to take into account this and the resulting division of statements of principle from statements of specific provisions, has little to commend it. Perhaps the most remarkable feature of the Hammurabi Code is that such specific provisions should have been formulated in a fully organised legal language as early as the eighteenth century B.C.

In the extracts here presented, the numbers refer to the paragraphs of the Code.

TEXT

1. If a citizen has accused a citizen and has indicted him for a murder and has not substantiated the charge, his accuser shall be put to death.

2. If a citizen has indicted a citizen for sorcery and does not substantiate the charge, the one who is indicted for sorcery shall go to the river and shall throw himself in. If the river overwhelms him, (then) his indicter shall take away his house. If the river exculpates that citizen and he is preserved, the one who indicted him for sorcery shall die, (and) the one who threw himself into the river shall take away his house.

3. If a citizen in a case has borne false witness, and does not substantiate the statement which he has made, (and) if that case is one warranting the death-penalty, that citizen shall be put to death.

. . .

5. If a judge has given a judgement and has passed a sentence and has drawn up a sealed document, and afterwards revises his findings, they shall convict that judge of revising his findings; he shall give the prescribed indemnity which follows from that case twelvefold, and they shall eject him from the council, from the seat of his judicature; he shall not return and he shall not sit with the judges in judgement.

. . .

8. If a citizen has stolen an ox, or a sheep, or an ass, or a pig, or a boat, if it is the property of the temple or of the crown, he shall give thirty-fold, but, if it is the property of a vassal, he shall restore ten-fold, whereas if the thief has nothing to give, he shall die.

**jus gentium:* international law; *jus naturale:* natural law.—Ed.

. . .

14. If a citizen steals the child of a citizen, he shall die.

. . .

22. If a citizen has committed a robbery and is caught, that man shall die.

. . .

117. If a debt renders a citizen distrainable, and he has sold for money his wife, or son, or daughter, or if anyone is sold for service in lieu of debt, they shall work for three years in the house of their purchaser or their distrainer. In the fourth year they shall attain their freedom.

. . .

124. If a citizen has given another citizen silver, or gold, or anything whatsoever for safe custody in the presence of witnesses and he denies it, they shall convict that citizen, and in spite of his denial, he shall restore it twofold.

. . .

128. If a citizen has taken a wife but has not deposited her contracts, that woman is not a (legal) wife.

129. If the wife of a citizen is taken cohabiting with another male, they shall both be bound and cast into the water; if the husband of the wife reprieves his wife, then the king may reprieve his servant.

. . .

132. If the finger is pointed at the wife of a citizen on account of another man, but she has not been caught lying with another man, for her husband's sake she shall throw herself into the river.

. . .

135. If a citizen is carried away captive, and there is no sustenance in his house, (and) before his re-appearance his wife has entered the household of another, and borne children, (and if) subsequently her husband returns and comes to his city, that woman shall return to this her former husband, but the children shall follow their (natural) father.

. . .

148. If a citizen has taken a wife, and intermittent fever attacks her, and if he plans to take another wife, he may do so. He may not forsake his wife who is attacked by the intermittent fever, but she

shall dwell in a house which he has prepared, and he shall support her for life.

. . .

154. If a citizen has known his daughter, they shall cause that citizen to leave the city.

155. If a citizen has chosen a bride for his son, and his son has known her, and he himself (the father) lies in her bosom, they shall seize that citizen and bind him and cast him into the water.

. . .

157. If a citizen after (the death of) his father lies in the bosom of his mother, they shall burn them both.

158. If a citizen after (the death of) his father is seized in the bosom of his foster-mother who has borne children, that man shall be turned out of his father's house.

. . .

195. If a son has struck his father, they shall cut off his hand.

196. If a citizen has destroyed the eye of one of citizen status, they shall destroy his eye.

197. If he has broken the bone of a citizen, his bone shall they break.

198. If he has destroyed the eye, or has broken the bone, of a vassal, he shall pay one mina of silver.

. . .

200. If a citizen has knocked out the tooth of one of equal status, they shall knock out his tooth.

201. If he has knocked out the tooth of a vassal, he shall pay a third of a mina of silver.

202. If a citizen has struck the cheek of his superior, he shall receive in the council sixty strokes with a thong.

203. If one of citizen status has struck the cheek of his equal, he shall pay one mina of silver.

204. If a vassal has struck the cheek of a fellow vassal, he shall pay ten shekels of silver.

205. If the serf of a citizen has struck the cheek of one of citizen status, they shall cut off his ear.

. . .

250. If an ox has gored a citizen, while going along the road, and has occasioned his death, there shall be no penalty attached to this case.

251. If the offending ox belonged to a citizen who has been notified by the authorities of its propensity to gore, and he has not removed its horns, or has not tethered the ox, and that ox gored a man of citizen status occasioning his death, he shall pay a half-mina of silver.

252. If he was the serf of a citizen, he shall pay a third of a mina of silver.

. . .

282. If a serf has declared to his master—'Thou art not my master', his master shall confirm him (to be) his serf and shall cut off his ear. . . .

SUGGESTED READINGS

Gehman, Henry S., ed. *The New Westminster Dictionary of the Bible*, pp. 222–25, "Deuteronomy." Philadelphia: The Westminster Press, 1970.

Gottwald, Norman K. "The Book of Deuteronomy." In *The Interpreter's One-Volume Commentary on the Bible*, edited by Charles M. Laymon, pp. 100–105. Nashville, Tenn.: Abingdon Press, 1971.

Hammer, P. L. "Deuteronomy." In *The Interpreter's Dictionary of the Bible*, Vol. 2, edited by George A. Buttrick, pp. 831–38. Nashville, Tenn.: Abingdon Press, 1962.

Miller, Madeleine S. and Miller, J. Lane, eds. *The Harper Bible Dictionary*, pp. 135–36, "Deuteronomy." New York: Harper & Row, 1973.

Wright, G. Ernest. "Deuteronomy: Introduction." In *The Interpreter's Bible*, Vol. 2, edited by George A. Buttrick, pp. 311–31. Nashville, Tenn.: Abingdon Press, 1953.

QUESTIONS FOR DISCUSSION AND WRITING

1. Why does Marchette Chute believe that Moses originally wrote much of Deuteronomy?
2. What techniques of persuasion are used by the author of Deuteronomy? Be sure to include Chapters 28–30 in your investigation.

3. Comment on passages in Deuteronomy that seem to you to be especially effective in expression.
4. Investigate the assumption that much of Deuteronomy is the book found in the Temple by the high priest Hilkiah. (Compare the text of Deuteronomy 5–26 and 28 with the reforms mentioned in 2 Kings 23.)
5. Why does Robert Pfeiffer credit Deuteronomy with the preservation of the nation and the religion of Judah?
6. Contrast Leviticus 17:3–16 and 1 Samuel 14:32–35 with Deuteronomy 12:14–15, 20–22, as Pfeiffer suggests. What general conclusion does Pfeiffer draw from a comparison of these passages?
7. Why does Pfeiffer say that publication of Deuteronomy in 621 B.C. was the beginning of the "written word of God"? Why not give that credit to the writing prophets of the eighth century B.C.?
8. Give the meaning of the words "patriarchy," "polygyny," and "apodictic."
9. Phyllis Bird says (p. 82) that her sketch of woman in ancient Israel is not a complete one but that it presents the essential features. Describe those features in a paragraph.
10. Do the stories involving Eve, Sarah, Rebekah, Rachel, Leah, Tamar, and Zipporah support Phyllis Bird's thesis that the female "is always subject to the authority of some male (father, husband or brother), except when widowed or divorced . . ."?
11. What does W. J. Martin assume to be the "obvious" explanation for the similarities between laws of the Pentateuch and laws in the Code of Hammurabi?
12. What reason does W. J. Martin give for his assertion that "the Code seems to have remained merely an ideal lacking practical application"?
13. Compare laws from Hammurabi's Code with laws on the same subject from Deuteronomy. What similarities and differences do you find?

JOSHUA

SUMMARY

If we take the approximate time of the Exodus to be the early part of the thirteenth century B.C., then the events related in the Book of Joshua should have occurred in the late thirteenth and early twelfth centuries B.C. Many scholars argue that the Book of Joshua is a logical and historical complement to the first five books of the Old Testament and that it would make sense, therefore, to speak of a "Hexateuch" rather than a "Pentateuch." In this book the several strands of J, E, D, and P are again evident. (For a listing of the J, E, D, and P portions of Joshua, see the chart on pages 69–70 of W. O. E. Oesterley and Theodore H. Robinson, *An Introduction to the Books of the Old Testament* [New York: Meridian Books, 1958].)

The Book of Joshua purports to be a record of the speedy conquest of Canaan by Joshua and his armies, aided by the miraculous intervention of the Lord God of Israel. But the narrative itself reveals that a quick, complete conquest did not in fact occur: The Jebusites

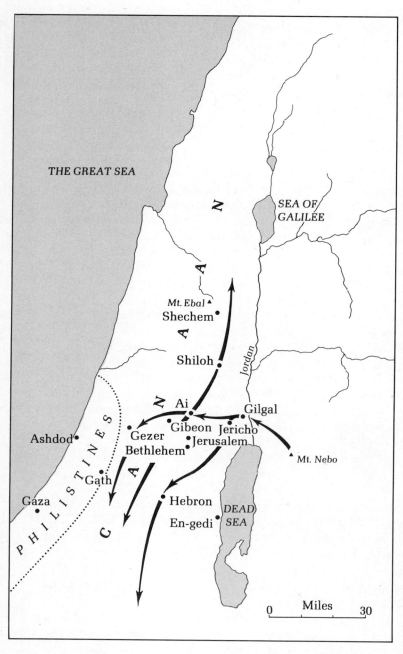

THE GREAT SEA

SEA OF
GALILEE

Mt. Ebal ▲
Shechem •

Shiloh •

Jordan

Ai •
Gibeon • Gilgal •
Gezer • Jericho •
Ashdod • Bethlehem • Jerusalem •
Gath • Mt. Nebo ▲

Gaza •

Hebron •
En-gedi • DEAD SEA

PHILISTINES

CANAAN

Miles
0   30

The Israelites enter the Promised Land, *ca.* 1250–1200 B.C.

still controlled Jerusalem (15:63); Ephraim had not conquered Gezer (16:10); and Canaanites kept the cities of the Plain of Esdraelon (17:11–13). Oesterley and Robinson, who divide the book into three sections (the conquest: Chapters 1–12; partition of the land among the tribes: 13–22; and Joshua's farewell address and death: 23–24), point out that J and E are prominent in Chapters 1–12 but are hardly present at all in Chapters 13–22. They speculate that the Deuteronomic school, which was largely responsible for the editing of Joshua as well as of the Pentateuch, imposed its interpretation upon events. "From its point of view, the supreme peril of Israel from the first had been syncretism [absorption of their religion into that of the Canaanities]. To avoid that, the only safe measure was the complete annihilation of Israel's predecessors. Because, in the view of the Deuteronomists, this ought to have taken place, and was, indeed, enjoined by Yahweh, the whole land must have been given to Israel by Yahweh at once. He would never have demanded the extermination of the Canaanites unless He had also made it possible, and He could make it possible only by giving Israel all the country."*

The Book of Joshua takes up where Deuteronomy left off. After the death of Moses, the Lord tells Joshua that he will be with Joshua as he had been with Moses and that Joshua and the Hebrew people will be established in the Promised Land if they faithfully follow the "book of the Law." The people assure Joshua that they will obey him "just as we obeyed Moses" (1:17). Joshua sends two spies to Jericho, where they learn from a harlot named Rahab that the people of Jericho have heard of the wonderworking power of the Lord and are "faint-hearted" at the prospect of an attack on their city.

The miracle of the Red Sea crossing is repeated when Joshua and his people walk across the Jordan River on dry land. After all the males of Joshua's army have been circumcised and all of the people have celebrated the Passover, Joshua prepares to attack Jericho. Nearby, he meets a "commander of the army of the Lord" (5:14), later referred to as the Lord himself, who instructs him in the way to attack the city. These instructions are followed to the letter, and the wall of Jericho falls. The Hebrews "utterly destroyed all in the city, both men and women, young and old, oxen, sheep, and asses, with the edge of the sword" (16:21).

Their attack on the city of Ai is thwarted at first because a soldier named Achan broke faith at Jericho by taking booty for himself—an act which had been expressly forbidden by the Lord. After Achan and his family are destroyed, the Hebrews successfully attack Ai and destroy it, but this time they are allowed to take cattle and other spoil.

At Mount Ebal Joshua builds an altar for burnt offerings. Then he writes upon the altar stones the entire Law of Moses and reads every word of it to the assembled people.

---

*Oesterley and Robinson, pp. 73–74.

An old engraving showing
the stoning of Achan and
his family.

The kings of the land organize to fight Joshua's forces, but the
inhabitants of one nearby city, Gibeon, use deceit to avoid being
slaughtered. When the deceit is discovered, Joshua cannot retract the
covenant he made with them, but he curses them and dooms some of
them always to be "slaves, hewers of wood and drawers of water for
the house of . . . God" (9:23).

Five kings of the Amorites, frightened by Joshua's successes
against the cities of Jericho, Ai, and Gibeon, attack Gibeon, which is
now allied with the Hebrews. But the Lord helps Joshua again, killing
more of the enemy with hailstones than were killed by the swords of
Joshua's soldiers. The sun and the moon stay their courses when
Joshua asks them to, as we learn from both a poetic and a prose account in 10:12–14. The five kings are imprisoned in a cave where they
had sought refuge, and they are later killed and their bodies returned
to the cave.

Then Joshua moves on to conquer Makkedah, Libnah, Lachish,
Gezer, Eglon, Hebron, and Debir. "And Joshua defeated them from
Kadesh-barnea to Gaza, and all the country of Goshen [in south Pales-
tine] as far as Gibeon" (10:41). Now the king of Hazor summons "a
great host, in number like the sand that is upon the seashore" (11:4),
but "the Lord gave them into the hand of Israel" (11:8). Joshua made
peace with no one but the Gibeonites, "For it was the Lord's doing to
harden their hearts that they should come against Israel in battle, in
order that they should be utterly destroyed, and should receive no
mercy but be exterminated, as the Lord commanded Moses" (11:20).
Finally, Joshua wipes out the giants called the Anakim from the hill
country, leaving only a few in Gaza, Gath, and Ashdod.

Although there is much land still to be conquered (13:1–6), the
people of Israel are assured by the Lord that he will obtain it for them.
Joshua is now told to divide all the land (evidently including that not
yet in their possession) among the "nine tribes and half the tribe of
Manasseh." (As explained in 13:7–8, Moses had already given the

Reubenites, the Gadites, and the other half of the tribe of Manasseh their inheritance east of the Jordan.) Chapters 13 through 21 describe this allotment of territory and list the "cities of refuge," where an accused murderer can have sanctuary until his trial comes up.

Chapter 22 recounts the return of the Reubenites, Gadites, and the half-tribe of Manasseh to their territory on the east side of the Jordan. Before leaving Canaan, they erect a large altar on the bank of the river, an act interpreted by the Israelites as an effort to set up a rival shrine to the otherwise centralized worship of Yahweh. Upon investigation by a priest and ten chiefs of Israel, however, the Israelites are satisfied with the explanation that this shrine is meant only as a witness to the people on the west side of the Jordan and that the Reubenites, the Gadites, and the half-tribe of Manasseh also worship the Lord, the God of Israel. It is meant only as a copy of the altar that stands before the Tabernacle.

The last two chapters consist of Joshua's farewell. Speaking to "all Israel, their elders and heads, their judges and officers" (23:2), he reminds them that it was with the Lord's help that they won this land and that if they obey the Lord they can conquer the rest of what has been promised. "One man of you puts to flight a thousand, since it is the Lord your God who fights for you" (23:10). But if they "transgress the covenant of the Lord" and "serve other gods and bow down to them," the Lord will bring all evil things upon them and destroy them (23:15–16).

Joshua summons all of Israel to Shechem, where he sums up the history of the Israelites from the time they left the territory "beyond the Euphrates" to the present, when they dwell in a land whose cities they have not built and whose vineyards and olive trees they have not planted. He tells the people that they must choose either to serve the gods of their ancestors in Mesopotamia or Egypt, to serve the gods of the Canaanites, or to serve the Lord as he and his house will do. They say that they, too, will serve the Lord. They put away the foreign gods among them and enter into a covenant, which Joshua writes "in the book of the law of God." He also sets up a stone which he declares has heard every word and will be a witness to all that has transpired at Shechem on that day.

Shortly afterward, Joshua dies and is buried in the hill country of Ephraim. Joseph's bones are brought from Egypt and buried at Shechem, and Eleazar the son of Aaron dies and is buried at Gibeah.

LITERARY QUALITIES

Analyses of the Book of Joshua almost always deal solely with its historical value and with the probable identification of the J, E, D, and P material that can be detected in it. It is usually admitted that it is an effective book in terms of its obvious purposes: to show that Yahweh fulfilled his promise to Abraham that his descendants would some day inherit this land, and to remind the Israelites that obedience to the Lord was essential to victory over their enemies. In contrast, the following essay by Mary Ellen Chase considers certain literary aspects of the Book of Joshua other than its structure and purpose.

Joshua
MARY ELLEN CHASE

The book in the Old Testament known as *Joshua* contains the largely legendary story of that warrior, whose name, like that of *Jesus*, another form of the same word, means *deliverer*. Joshua's idea of deliverance, however, bears little resemblance to that held by the later possessor of his name! He has come down to us as the most revengeful character in the Bible, great warrior though he unquestionably was; and his book is most certainly a chronicle of blood and cruelty.

Although this book, which narrates his wars for the conquest of Canaan, was originally thought to have been written by himself, we now know that it is a compilation of material made over a space of many centuries and written by many hands. J, E, P, and D played their several parts in its composition, although it is impossible now to discover the portions originally composed by each nor has the exact form in which they were written been preserved. The book is an interesting, if somewhat horrible, narrative largely because it contains, with all its bloodshed and indiscriminate slaughter, a few excellent and vivid stories and one ancient and beautiful song.

As a matter of fact, we have very little information that can be termed dependable about Joshua himself. In the long cycle of stories concerning Moses, most of which we have found to be largely tradi-

JOSHUA Reprinted with permission of Macmillan Publishing Co., Inc. from *The Bible and the Common Reader*, rev. ed., by Mary Ellen Chase. Copyright 1944, 1952 by Mary Ellen Chase, renewed 1972 by Mary Ellen Chase.

tional, Joshua appears several times. He is commissioned by Moses to choose out fighting men whom he is to lead against the Amalekites; he is chosen to accompany Moses as his "minister" when he goes up into Mount Sinai, the mountain of God; Moses upon one occasion leaves him in charge of the sacred tabernacle in which the Ark of God was housed; and at the approach of his death Moses, under the command of God, gives to Joshua the leadership of the Israelites with the injunction that he is to bring them into the promised land of Canaan. These stories are without doubt largely traditional also, and yet within them there are surely more than grains of truth.

Joshua is by no means an attractive figure. The days are fortunately past when he was extolled as a mighty and saintly hero in Sunday-school lessons. And if he himself is unattractive, the God whom he served and fanatically obeyed is even less appealing. Joshua, unlike Moses, does not stress the mercy and the compassion of God. His God is a God of war, revenge, and bloodshed, who hates the enemies of Israel with merciless and bitter hatred. At one moment He uses the tactics of cruel men, slaying with great slaughter the hosts of the five wretched kings encamped before Gibeon, in Chapter 10, and even "chasing" along the way what remains of their armies; at another, He makes use of His heavenly power and casts down hailstones upon them. He is apparently pleased with Joshua's disposal of the five kings themselves, who, after being confined by force in a cave, lose their heads and are hanged on trees "until the evening." He swears, in fact, in Chapter 7, that He will not be with His people any more unless those who have seized the spoil of battle be immediately slain, stoned with stones, and burned with fire. After the ceremonious circling for seven days of the walls of Jericho in Chapter 6, in which Joshua's God is careful that religious rites be observed, He commands that the city be accursed and that all the inhabitants of Jericho, "both man and woman, young and old, ox, and sheep, and ass," be destroyed by the edge of the sword. This is primitive religion at its worst, and the best that can be said either for Joshua or for his God is that their ferocious methods doubtless seemed necessary for the task they had set out to accomplish, the conquest of Canaan.

In the midst of these chapters of carnage and cruelty the story given in Chapter 2 of Rahab, the harlot, is memorable partly because of its relative freedom from horror, partly because of its lively description of Rahab herself: her clever deceiving of the king of Jericho, her ingenuity in hiding the spies under her stalks of flax, her scarlet cord by which she let them down from her window and which later she bound in the window as the signal of her safety. Likewise there is fine and ironic narrative in Chapter 9, which recounts the ruse attempted by the wily inhabitants of Gibeon, condemned in payment for their desperate trickery to become "hewers of wood and drawers of water."

And lastly, for a moment's poetic relief in so much revenge and bloodshed there is in Verse 12 of Chapter 10 an ancient song attributed to Joshua and yet composed long before his book was compiled or even written. It belongs among those earliest Hebrew writings of which we have record and which were preserved in ancient collections now lost. The names, however, of two of such early collections we know: the *Book of the Wars of Yahveh* and the *Book of Yashar, or the Upright*. This song attributed to Joshua belongs within the ancient poetic material preserved in these collections, originally made probably around 1000 B.C., and was itself included, as the author of the chapter evidently recognized, in the *Book of Yashar*. It may well be of older origin, since it was doubtless part of that folklore and tradition which clustered around the name of Joshua and the conquest of Canaan. It is beautiful in its sharp rhythm, in its simple language, and in its use of old place names:

> Sun, stand thou still upon Gibeon;
> and thou, Moon, in the valley of Ajalon.

It is difficult to think of Joshua paying much heed to the sun or to the moon, even in order to give commands to them. But the poem, considered quite apart from its context, is worth remembering both for itself and for its ancient heritage. Perhaps, indeed, it is the best that we can salvage from Joshua or from his book.

INTERPRETATIONS

If one evaluates Joshua solely on the basis of his achievements as a commander of armies, his leadership deserves praise, even if his conquest of Canaan was incomplete and depended to some extent for its success on Hebrews who had already settled there. Willing as he is to give due credit to Joshua, Fleming James nevertheless presents a strong indictment of Joshua's conception of Yahweh.

Some Thoughts on Joshua's Religion
FLEMING JAMES

If our unsatisfactory sources permit us to say anything of Joshua it is this, that he represents as perhaps no other man in the Old Tes-

SOME THOUGHTS ON JOSHUA'S RELIGION   This excerpt from *Personalities of the Old Testament* by Fleming James is reprinted by permission of Charles Scribner's Sons. Copyright 1939 Charles Scribner's Sons.

tament the conception of Yahweh which we call the War-God. This was inevitable, for no other conception would have answered for the task which he undertook. It was to push into an inhabited and highly civilized district and take possession of it, ousting the present owners. Such an ugly business could be carried out only by group ferocity, and in a fanatical people ferocity can best be produced by the idea of a holy war. It was their enthusiasm for Yahweh that roused in the Hebrews what T. H. Robinson so well calls their "battle-fury"; and Joshua's business was to foster this. He must be full of it himself, and keep his followers full of it. The fact that he exploited the War-God idea to the utmost accounts for his success.

Fifty years ago this gave no offense to Bible readers. Many can remember how Joshua the warrior used to figure as a hero-saint in sermons and in Bible stories for the young. The present writer recalls a picture in a Bible for children portraying the general equipped with Greek helmet and a combination Greek and Roman suit of armour, kneeling before the Prince of the Lord's host in front of a very Roman-looking Jericho. That seemed quite as it should be!

Today however Joshua presents a problem. On the one hand, we ask whether it was right to take part of Canaan from its owners and in the process to fight, kill, destroy. On the other, whether Canaan was not necessary for the future development of Israel's religion; and if so, whether it could have been got in any other way.

Suppose that instead of Joshua the son of Nun the other Joshua whom we call Jesus had been Moses' successor; would he have been as well fitted as his namesake to carry on the religion of Moses? If not, did God need such an agent as Joshua at that moment, just as He needed Jesus later? Are we to say that He sent Joshua to Jericho and Jesus to Capernaum? That there is a "time for everything" in the divine plan? And along with it the whole history of Israel in Canaan?

The present writer holds entirely with those who reject the War-God concept. To his mind God is not, and never was, what Joshua thought Him to be. He never led an armed force into Canaan, and He leads no armed force today. He did not rain hailstones on the fleeing Canaanites nor supply angelic succour to the British at Mons. He did not command the slaughter of the people of Jericho nor bless the starvation of Germans by a blockade. He was not with the American colonists who exterminated the Indian nor with the armies that took Texas from Mexico.

At the same time, Joshua remains fixed in the history of our religion. No longer perhaps a hero-saint, but still a real leader, a link in the chain; raising uncomfortable questions which though answered to some extent are never quite completely answered.

Joshua of course was not alone in his idea of the War-God. Nor is he to be blamed for putting it into practice. Moses had it before him and in pressing it he was but carrying on the Mosaic tradition. If we knew more about him we should doubtless find that he fostered other and more peaceable elements in that tradition also, for it must have been the Mosaic pattern as a whole that he kept going. This, as we have seen, was his most valuable contribution to Israel's religion. A late but credible notice declares that "the people served Yahweh all the days of Joshua, and all the days of the elders that outlived Joshua, who had seen all the great work of Yahweh that he had wrought for Israel." The real test of survival was yet to come, when "all that generation were gathered to their fathers: and there arose another generation after them, that knew not Yahweh, nor yet the works which he had wrought for Israel" (Judges 2:7, 10).

Another view of the "War-God" concept in the Book of Joshua is presented by G. Ernest Wright and Reginald H. Fuller.

God's Gift of a Land
G. ERNEST WRIGHT AND
REGINALD H. FULLER

One of the age-old questions which people have had concerning the Book of Joshua is this: How is it possible to believe in the goodness of God and at the same time to affirm his role of commander in chief in the horrible blood bath of the conquest of Canaan? The Book of Deuteronomy contains a considerable amount of material that has been preserved from the old institution of holy war. The one passage in the Old Testament which attempts to deal with the question of God and war in this connection is Deuteronomy 9:1–6. There Israel is told that the conquest has been carried out by God, not because Israel is more righteous than anyone else. In fact, just the opposite is the case; Israel has been a stiff-necked and rebellious people since the time God first chose them. In the biblical point of view wars exist because of human sin, and God uses human agents to accomplish his purposes in history. When he does so, he does not add up the degrees of righteousness which his agent possesses. The agent is sinful but nevertheless God uses it for his purpose. In Deuteronomy 6 it is affirmed that God is doing what he does in the conquest for two reasons: (1) because of the wickedness of the Canaanites and (2) because of his promises to the fathers of Israel. Now we know not only from the Bible but from many outside sources as well that the Canaanite civilization and religion was one of the weakest, most decadent, and most immoral cultures of the civilized world at that time. It is claimed, then, that Israel is God's agent of destruction against a sinful civilization, for in the moral order of God civilizations of such flagrant wickedness must be destroyed. On the other hand, God has a purpose in the choosing of Israel and in giving her a land, a purpose stated in the promises to the fathers of Israel in Genesis. All this does not mean that Israel as God's agent is free of her responsibility. Later on the prophets saw God using foreign agents as the instruments of his punishment for sinful Israel; yet in time the agents also suffered judgment for their sin (see Isaiah 10:5 ff.). In other words, God has a purpose of universal redemption in the midst of and for a sinful world. He makes even the wars and fightings of men serve his end. In the case of Israel, his purpose as expressed in the patriarchal promises coincided at the moment of the conquest with the terrible iniquity of Canaan. It was a great thing for Israel that she got her land; it was also a sobering thing because with it went the great responsibility and the danger of judgment. . . .

But did God actually tell Joshua to carry on such terrible slaughter, involving even the defenseless elements of the population? It is rather difficult for a Christian to understand how God could be responsible for such a slaughter. From the biblical perspective we may perhaps frame an answer somewhat as follows: In the context of human sin wars and conflicts occur. But God has not withdrawn from the world to heaven. He is not defeated by human sin; even this he uses for his own ends. Unless he did we would have nothing in this earth for which to hope. Yet to say that God is in control, even of our wars and cruelty, does not mean that he is responsible for the way in which men carry them on. It is not God's fault that the Americans dropped an atomic bomb on Hiroshima. Yet no Christian can assume that God had no interest whatsoever in how the last war was to turn out. Two things must be held together in tension here: one is God's control and direction of history to his own ends, and the other is the terrible sin of man for which he is responsible. If we view the conquest in this light, then the Christian may say that God was "fighting for Israel," though his own purposes were larger than Israel understood at that moment. The sovereign goodness of God and the freedom of man must both be affirmed in a biblical understanding of theism. God is thus not responsible for men's atrocities.

An extensive description of Canaanite culture at the time of the conquest can be found in John Gray, *The Canaanites* (New York:

Praeger Publishers, 1964), now out of print. However, the following remarks by Robert H. Pfeiffer present a different view of the Canaanites from the one given in the preceding essay.

Israel in Canaan
ROBERT H. PFEIFFER

In the Canaanitic hinterland occupied by the Israelites, religion was simpler than on the coast. The gods were probably at first divinities of nature (heavenly bodies, storms, mountains, springs, etc.), but in time they became closely associated with human life: the invisible rulers of city-states, the patrons of important human activities, who played a role in the success of human undertakings. There were patrons of agriculture, commerce, law, medicine, war, and so forth. Such a division of labor occurs also in other ancient religions and survives among the Christian saints: St. Anthony of Padua is the protector of domestic animals; St. Barbara is concerned with miners, masons, and artillery; St. Clare is associated with glass and laundry workers; St. Cecelia is the patron of music; and so forth. In Canaan the modern cleavage between religious and worldly activities was unknown, for religion embraced every human activity and interest. Just as a modern farmer needs fertilizers, so the Palestinian peasant needed the favor of his Baal in order to raise crops—a belief based on the everyday experience of generations—for the farmer, having no control over the forces of nature required for the growth of plants, ascribed their favorable or unfavorable action to the gods. We moderns would say that in the traditional art of agriculture these farmers did not distinguish scientific knowledge from superstitious beliefs.

As has been previously noted, religion was the fear of god and worship was the service that supplied the gods with what they needed. It was an activity which was supposedly profitable, a technique which brought practical results; but it lacked spirituality, doctrinal speculation, mystical flights, ethical nobility. The festivals were gay agricultural occasions: sacrifices were offered at the high places, the produce of the fields was presented there, and the worshipers ate, drank, danced, and at times indulged in sexual orgies. Canaan did not have a unified religion any more than a unified government; the local gods were not joined into a pantheon as was the case in Greece. Each town had its local Baal, usually merely called by the name of the local-

ISRAEL IN CANAAN From pp. 61–62 and 64–65 of *Religion in the Old Testament* by Robert H. Pfeiffer. Copyright © 1961 by Harper & Row, Publishers, Inc. By permission of Harper & Row, Publishers, Inc.

ity (Baal Peor, Baal Hermon, Baal Hazor), although the Baal of Shechem was called Baal (or El) Berith (baal or god of the covenant). There
was no Baal or Astarte of all Canaan, there never was a conflict between such a Baal and Jehovah; the Baal of Jezebel was a foreign god,
Melkart of Tyre. Hosea (2:2–13) denounces the worship of the Baals of
Canaan, the supposed givers of agricultural bounty, which he regards
as Israel's adultery against Jehovah, her true husband; it is only in an-
notations added to the book by late readers who had no clear idea of
what Hosea was talking about that an imaginary single Baal of all
Canaan (Hos. 13:lb), alleged to be nothing but an idol (2:8b), was invented. The village shrine was generally a "high place" without a
building: the top of a hill surrounded by a fence and having an altar, a
wooden post, a stone pillar, and at times one or more trees. Temples
housing symbols of the local Baal or his image were found in cities
like Shechem and presumably were in the care of a resident priesthood. Superstitious beliefs in evil spirits causing insanity, in dangerous ghosts of the dead, in the efficacy of magical practices such as
those listed in Deuteronomy 18:10–11, and the like, were current.
The earliest reference to a prophetic oracle (at Byblos) is found in the
Egyptian story of Wen-Amon (or Unamum), dated in the twelfth
century B.C. . . .

The Israelites were not absorbed, but keenly went about learning the arts of civilization from the Canaanites. Except for the products
of their native genius—religion and literature—the Israelites derived
their culture from the Canaanites. The Hebrew language, so brilliantly
used by Deborah (Judges 5) less than a century after the invasion, was
the language of Canaan (Isaiah 19:18), as can be proved from Hebrew
glosses (marginal notes of explanation or interlinear commentary) in
the cuneiform tables from Tell el-Amarna (1411–1358 B.C.). The alphabet used in the days of Ahab (Samaria ostraca, pieces of pottery or tile
on which writing has been found), Hezekiah (Siloam inscription), and
Jeremiah (Lakish ostraca) was the old Phoenician alphabet. The arts of
agriculture, commerce, architecture, pottery, and the like were learned
from the Canaanites. The earliest alphabet of the Israelites was Canaanitic, as shown by some early names of the months which are the
same as the Phoenician: Abib (Exodus 13:4), Ziv (I Kings 6:1, 37),
Ethanim (I Kings 8:2), Bul (6:38); after the Exile the Babylonian names
still in use among the Jews were adopted. The weights and measures
are Canaanitic, and ultimately of Baylonian origin (shekel, mina,
homer, etc.). The ivories excavated at Samaria and Megiddo, as well as
other samples of plastic art, are Canaanitic and show Egyptian and
Babylonian influence (as does Phoenician art). Biblical Hebrew has
numerous words of Babylonian origin (besides names of weights and
measures), notably names of metals, cloths, and commercial transactions.

Even the earliest civil legislation of Israel, preserved in Exodus

21:2–22:17 and in Deuteronomy, is probably Canaanitic, and retains the juristic arrangement of the Code of Hammurabi (about 1800 B.C.). The institution of the monarchy, the administration of government, and the military organization were contributions of the Canaanites and the Philistines.

SUGGESTED READINGS

Bright, John. *A History of Israel.* 2nd ed., pp. 126–130. Philadelphia: The Westminster Press, 1972.

———. "The Book of Joshua: Introduction and Exegesis." In *The Interpreter's Bible,* Vol. 2, edited by George A. Buttrick, pp. 541–673. Nashville, Tenn.: Abingdon Press, 1953. (Includes biblical text.)

Comay, Joan. *Who's Who in the Old Testament,* pp. 235–42, "Joshua." New York: Holt, Rinehart and Winston, 1971. (Contains illustrations and maps.)

James, Fleming. *Personalities of the Old Testament,* pp. 45–57, "Joshua." New York: Charles Scribner's Sons, 1939.

Pfeiffer, Robert H. *Introduction to the Old Testament,* pp. 293–313, "The Book of Joshua." New York: Harper & Row, 1941.

———. *Religion in the Old Testament,* pp. 58–116, "Israel in Canaan." New York: Harper & Row, 1961.

Wright, G. Ernest, and Fuller, Reginald H. *The Book of the Acts of God: An Introduction to the Bible,* pp. 102–112, "God's Gift of a Land (Joshua–Judges)." New York: Doubleday & Company, Anchor Press, 1960.

QUESTIONS FOR DISCUSSION AND WRITING

1. What passages from Exodus and Deuteronomy can be quoted in support of Mary Ellen Chase's statement that Moses stressed "the mercy and the compassion of God"?
2. Compare Joshua and Moses as political, religious, and military leaders.
3. Evaluate the story of Rahab and the spies (Joshua, Chapter 2) as a story using setting, plot, and character to achieve an effect.
4. Which interpretation of Yahweh in the Book of Joshua do you find the more convincing—that of Fleming James or that of Wright and Fuller? Why? If neither is satisfactory to you, propose an interpretation of your own and give evidence to support it.
5. Evaluate Wright and Fuller's comment that "the Canaanite civilization and religion was one of the weakest, most decadent, and most immoral cultures of the civilized world at that time" in the light of the information about Canaan given by Robert H. Pfeiffer.

6. To what extent is the Book of Joshua an account of the fulfillment of the promise that the Israelites will inherit a land "flowing with milk and honey"?
7. For an ambitious essay: Compare the return of the Israelites to Canaan with the return of Odysseus to his home as related in Books 13–24 of *The Odyssey*.

JUDGES

SUMMARY

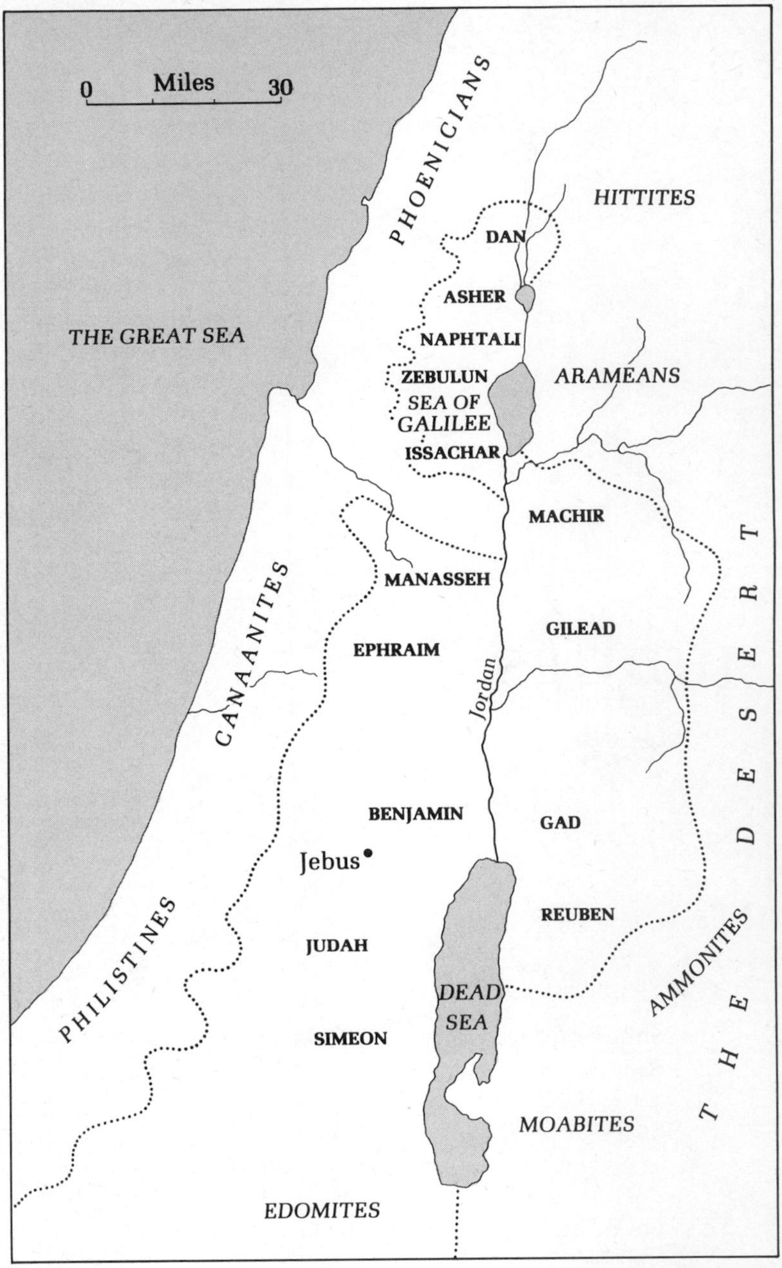
0 Miles 30
THE GREAT SEA
PHOENICIANS
HITTITES
DAN
ASHER
NAPHTALI
ZEBULUN
SEA OF GALILEE
ARAMEANS
ISSACHAR
MACHIR
MANASSEH
GILEAD
EPHRAIM
CANAANITES
Jordan
BENJAMIN
GAD
Jebus
REUBEN
PHILISTINES
JUDAH
DEAD SEA
AMMONITES
SIMEON
MOABITES
EDOMITES
THE DESERT

Israelites entrenched on the central highlands of the Promised Land, 1200–1000 B.C.

9. The Levite and his concubine,
        and the war with the Benja-
        minites (Chapters 19–21)

Our impression on finishing the Book of Joshua is that the land of Canaan had been completely subdued, although even in that book there are passages that suggest otherwise (Joshua 15:63, 16:10, and 17:11–13). The editor of the Book of Judges tells us in the first chapter that many areas were still unconquered and that indeed, at the time of his writing, many Canaanites, Asherites, and Amorites had not been driven out but had been absorbed into the Hebrew population or were being kept in forced labor (1:27–36).

Covering approximately 200 years (from the end of Joshua's conquests to the kingship of Saul), the Book of Judges relates the stories of Israel's continuing battles to maintain the territory promised to them by their God. The tribes were not unified enough at this time to agree to a monarchy such as they later requested of Samuel; they depended on the leadership of "judges"—individuals provided for them by the Lord when they cried out to him for help.

OTHNIEL

The story of Othniel is the first in a series whose purpose is to illustrate the thesis that when "the people of Israel did what was evil in the sight of the Lord" he punished them, whereas when they repented and cried out for help he sent them a deliverer. The episode is really too brief to be legitimately called a story. The Lord had allowed the Mesopotamian king Cushan-rishathaim to oppress Israel for eight years. When the Israelites cry out to him, the Lord raises up Othniel, the son of Kenaz, to deliver them. Othniel defeats the Mesopotamian king and brings peace to Israel for forty years.

EHUD

After Othniel dies, the people do evil again, and they are punished by having to serve Eglon, the king of Moab, for eighteen years. When they finally cry out, the Lord gives them another deliverer, Ehud, a left-handed Benjaminite. When Ehud goes to Eglon in Moab to present the tribute, he takes with him a two-edged sword strapped to his right thigh. After the ceremony of presentation, Ehud manages to be alone with Eglon. "I have a message from God for you," he says, as he plunges the long sword, hilt and all, into Eglon's soft belly. He locks the doors and escapes before Eglon's servants learn what has happened. Then, summoning his forces, Ehud leads them to victory over the Moabites, killing about ten thousand of them. Israel now has rest from enemies for eighty years.

SHAMGAR

A single verse (4:31) accounts for the judge Shamgar, who delivered Israel from an attack by the Philistines.

DEBORAH

When the people again do evil, the Lord allows them to be subdued by Jabin, king of Canaan, whose capital is the city of Hazor. He cruelly oppresses them for twenty years, and the people cry out for help. This time they are saved by a woman, the prophetess Deborah.

Deborah summons Barak and tells him that the Lord Commands him to go up with ten thousand men and confront Sisera, the general of Jabin's army. The tribes of Zebulun and Naphtali provide the men, and Deborah accompanies Barak to the field of battle, where "the Lord routed Sisera and all his chariots and all his army before Barak at the edge of the sword."

Sisera escapes, however, and flees on foot. As he passes through a settlement of Kenites, a tribe at peace with the king of Hazor, he is invited into the tent of Jael, wife of the Kenite king Heber. He asks for water. She gives him milk and covers him with a blanket when he lies down and falls asleep. Then she takes a hammer and drives a tent peg through Sisera's temple. When Barak comes looking for Sisera, Jael invites him into the tent and shows him her victim. After this victory the Israelites continue to attack Jabin until he is destroyed.

Chapter 5, "The Song of Deborah," is a poem that retells the story just given in chapter 4. It contains some particularly poetic and moving passages:

> From heaven fought the stars,
>   from their courses they fought against Sisera.
>
>   . . .
>
> Most blessed of women be Jael,
>   the wife of Heber the Kenite,
>   of tent-dwelling women most blessed.
> He asked water and she gave him milk,
>   she brought him curds in a lordly bowl.
> She put her hand to the tent-peg
>   and her right hand to the workmen's mallet;
> she struck Sisera a blow,

Edwin Austin Abbey,
"Jael and Sisera"

    she crushed his head,
  she shattered and pierced his temple.
  He sank, he fell,
    he lay still at her feet;
  at her feet he sank, he fell;
    where he sank, there he fell dead.

In what must be the oldest example of dramatic irony in Hebrew literature, we are told that Sisera's mother awaits him, wondering why he is so long in returning:

    Her wisest ladies make answer
      nay, she gives answer to herself,
  "Are they not finding and dividing
      the spoil?—
    A maiden or two for every man;
  spoil of dyed stuffs for Sisera,
    spoil of dyed stuffs embroidered,
    two pieces of dyed work
      embroidered for my neck
      as spoil?"

GIDEON

After a peaceful interval of forty years, the people again do evil, and they are given over to the Midianites for seven years. The Israelites are in despair, because Midianites, Amalekites, and other people of the east continually devastate their land and crops. They are informed by a prophet that they are being punished for worshiping the gods of the Amorites.

Nevertheless, the Lord decides to bring them deliverance through Gideon, a young man of the small tribe of Manasseh. The Lord appears to Gideon and tells him to attack the Midianites. Gideon is skeptical; what can he do with his weak forces? He needs a sign. The sign is given, and he is convinced that it is the Lord who has spoken to him.

Lest the people think that they alone have won the battle, the Lord persaudes Gideon to limit the number of his men to 300. These 300 men take trumpets and jars with torches in them and sneak up at night on the vast enemy army. At Gideon's command, they break the jars, reveal the torches, and blow the trumpets. When the enemy army is in flight, other Israelite forces join in the pursuit—"from Naphtali and from Asher and from all Manasseh"— and Gideon sends for more men from the north, from Ephraim. Although the Ephraimites help Gideon by defeating the forces of two Midian princes, Oreb and Zeeb, Gideon and his 300 men are left to pursue the enemy beyond the Jordan. The men of Succoth and Penuel refuse to help him, so Gideon and his small army go on alone. They take the decimated forces of Zeba and Zalmunna by surprise and send them into a panic.

Upon their return with the captured Zeba and Zalmunna, Gideon's men torture the elders of Succoth with briers and thorns, and they knock down the tower of Penuel and kill the men of the city. Then, when he learns from his two captives that they have slain his brothers, Gideon kills them.

The people of Israel ask Gideon to be their king and to found a hereditary dynasty, but he refuses, saying "The Lord will rule over you."

ABIMELECH

Israel enjoys another peaceful forty years, but when Gideon dies his son Abimelech, with a band of hired ruffians, makes himself king after having slain all but one of his seventy brothers. Jotham, the one brother who escaped, goes to Shechem and tells the people there a fable about the trees who sought a leader and found none willing except the lowly bramble. In *The Interpreter's*

Bible Jacob M. Myers explains that "the bramble stands for Abimelech, a worthless fellow, doubtless given the crown in good faith by the Shechemites, but who is in truth unable to furnish what is demanded of a king and may even kindle a fire capable of wiping out not only those who elected him but their neighbors as well."[*]

Jotham then runs away to Beer, because he fears his brother Abimelech.

Aware that they will suffer for their part in the slaying of the sons of Jerubbaal (the brothers of Abimelech), the Shechemites begin to deal treacherously with Abimelech. When he learns of their plans, Abimelech fights back. He destroys Shechem and sows the city with salt; he burns down the tower of Shechem, with a thousand men and women in it. However, when he attacks a tower in the city of Thebez and begins to burn it, a woman drops a millstone on him. His skull is crushed, but he manages to call on his armor bearer to run him through with a sword so that it cannot be said that a woman killed him.

TWO MINOR JUDGES

Two minor judges follow Abimelech: Tola judges for 23 years and Jair for 22. These may have been judges in our sense of the term: men in charge of carrying out the law for the Israelites. They do not seem to have been warriors.

JEPHTHAH

As punishment for serving "the Baals and Ashtaroth, the gods of Syria, the gods of Sidon, the gods of Moab, the gods of the Ammonites, and the gods of the Philistines," the Lord sells the Israelites into the hands of the Philistines and the Ammonites for eighteen years.

Their deliverer this time is Jephthah, the son of a harlot. Although he had been cast out by his "legitimate" brothers, he is such a mighty warrior that the elders of Gilead call upon him now to lead them against the Ammonites. He agrees to lead them only if they will keep him at their head after he has a victory over the Ammonites.

Jephthah negotiates with the Ammonites without success. He therefore attacks and slaughters them, wiping out twenty cities. But he had made a rash vow to the Lord when he solicited his help: He had promised to make a burnt offering of whoever came first to meet him from his house upon his return from battle. The

[*]Jacob M. Myers, "Judges: Introduction," in *The Interpreter's Bible*, Vol. 2, ed. George A. Buttrick (Nashville, Tenn.: Abingdon Press, 1953), p. 754.

first to come out to him is his only daughter. (We are never told her name.) When he explains to her what he has done, she recognizes that he must keep his vow and asks only to be given two months' respite so that she can go away into the mountains with her companions to "bewail her virginity." Upon her return Jephthah makes good his promise to the Lord.

One more of Jephthah's battles is recorded in the Book of Judges, that against the Ephraimites, who attack the Gileadites because they had not been invited to join them against the Ammonites. In the ensuing warfare the Gileadites kill forty-two thousand Ephraimites. After six years of "judging," Jephthah dies and is buried in Gilead.

THREE MINOR JUDGES

Israel is judged for a total of twenty-five years by three minor judges: Ibzan of Bethlehem, Elon the Zebulunite, and Abdon the Pirathonite. "And the people of Israel again did what was evil in the sight of the Lord; and the Lord gave them into the hands of the Philistines for forty years."

SAMSON

This time, when the Lord decides to deliver his people, he also takes special pains to provide a leader for them. An angel tells Manoah and his wife that they will have a son. They are not to cut his hair, for he is to be a Nazirite* from birth and will "begin to deliver Israel from the hand of the Philistines." Samson is born to them, "and the spirit of the Lord began to stir in him."

The first thing Samson does is to marry a Philistine girl named Timnah. We are told that his desire "was from the Lord; for he was seeking an occasion against the Philistines." Seven days before their wedding, Samson poses a riddle to the thirty companions who had been provided him by the Philistines. The riddle depends on knowledge that Samson alone possesses, that he had eaten honey from the carcass of a lion he had killed some days before. Since solution of the riddle would save them each the cost of a linen and a festal garment, the young men prevail upon Timnah to find out the answer. She succeeds, and when Samson learns that she has given them the information, he catches three hundred

---

*"Nazirites: Ascetic individuals who expressed their consecration to God by (1) totally abstaining from products of the vine and all intoxicants . . . ; (2) refusing to cut their hair lest a man-made tool profane this God-given growth; (3) avoiding contact with the dead; and (4) declining . . . unclean food. Laws governing their ideals are stated in Num. 6:1–21." (Quoted from Madeleine G. Miller and J. Lane Miller, *The Harper Bible Dictionary* [New York: Harper & Row, 1973], p. 480.)

Gustave Doré, "The Death of Samson"

foxes, ties them together by their tails, sets fire to their tails, and sends them through the Philistine grain fields and olive orchards. When the Philistines find out what has happened and why, they burn both Timnah and her father. Samson, learning of this, smites them "hip and thigh with great slaughter."

The Philistines seek revenge and persuade some men of Judah (3000 of them!) to help them capture Samson. With their assurance that they themselves will not attack him, Samson lets his

113

countrymen bind him. When the Philistines come to take him, he breaks his bonds, picks up the jawbone of an ass, and slays a thousand men.

Samson goes down to Gaza to visit a harlot. The Gazites go to capture him but decide to wait until the morning light. Samson eludes them by leaving at midnight. He takes the posts and doors of the city gate with him!

When the Philistines learn that Samson is in love with a Philistine woman named Delilah, they urge her to find out where his strength comes from. After three false answers, Samson gives in to Delilah's pleading and tells her that his strength will leave him if his head is shaved. While he sleeps on her knees, she has his locks shorn; and when the Philistines next come upon him, they easily subdue him. They gouge out his eyes and take him prisoner to Gaza, where he is set to grinding at the mill.

When his hair grows out, Samson recovers his strength. Unaware of this, the Philistines command that he be brought to entertain them at one of their great festivals honoring Dagon, their god. After he has entertained them, they make him stand between the pillars of the hall. He prays to God that he can have revenge, and grasping the pillars he brings the building down upon them all, including himself. "So the dead whom he slew at his death were more than those whom he had slain during his life."

We are told that "He had judged Israel twenty years," and since we have had no evidence that he has done any judging in our sense of the word, it is obvious that the term refers very broadly to anyone who gave leadership to the Israelites during the years between the triumphs of Joshua and the establishment of a monarchy under Saul. We now leave the adventures of the judges and turn to two stories that might be considered an appendix to the book.

MICAH AND THE LEVITE

Micah, a man of Ephraim, confesses to his mother that he had stolen some silver pieces that she was missing. She is so happy at his admission that she gives him the silver to make "a graven image and a molten image" (17:3). After a silversmith has made the images, Micah sets them up as part of a shrine in his house. One of his sons serves as priest. That this cultic shrine does not conform with Mosaic religion is perhaps signified by the editor when he says, "In those days there was no king in Israel; every man did what was right in his own eyes" (17:6).

Although his son can and does serve as his priest, Micah is happy to give the position to a young Levite from Bethlehem who is looking for a place to settle. "Now I know," says Micah, "that

the Lord will prosper me, because I have a Levite as priest"
(17:13).

The tribe of Dan is at this time seeking a place to settle, because they are constantly under attack from the Philistines in the
area of the south where they dwell. They travel north and decide
to take the city of Laish, but before doing so they steal not only
Micah's shrine objects (the graven image, the molten image, the
ephod, and the teraphim) but also Micah's priest, who feels hon-
ored to become priest to a tribe rather than to just a family. The
Danites wipe out Laish and then rebuild it and call it Dan.

THE CRIME OF THE BENJAMINITES

A Levite who has been spending some time in Ephraim decides to go to Bethlehem to bring back his concubine, who had
left him and returned to her father's house. Her father greets him
and entertains him for five days. On the fifth day he urges his
guest to stay another night, but the Levite leaves with his concubine, a servant, and two saddled asses. Late in the evening they
look for a place to stay. They are near Jebus (Jerusalem, when it
was still inhabited by enemy Canaanites), and the servant recommends that they spend the night there. The Levite refuses to go
into "a city of foreigners," so they travel on to Gibeah, a Benjaminite town. There they sit in the square until an old man
comes along and offers them the hospitality of his house.

As they are enjoying themselves, some scoundrels from the
city beat on the door and demand that the Levite be given to
them for sexual purposes. The old man refuses and offers them the
Levite's concubine and his own virgin daughter instead. When
the men refuse, the Levite throws his concubine out to them. They
use her all night long, and the Levite finds her dead on the door-
step in the morning.

Taking her body to his home in the hill country of Ephraim,
he cuts it into twelve pieces and sends these pieces out to the
various tribes of Israel. The tribes gather at Mizpah and decide to
attack the Benjaminites. They are defeated twice, but the third
time they destroy the Benjaminites except for six hundred men of
the tribe who are left secluded at the Rock of Rimnon.

These men become a problem. The Israelites had sworn at
Mizpah that no one should ever give a daughter in marriage to a
Benjaminite. But now they repent of their vow, for they do not
want to destroy utterly one of their twelve tribes. They learn that
the people of Jabesh-Gilead had not joined in the fighting, nor in
the vow at Mizpah. They send to Jabesh-Gilead a contingent that
kills everyone but four hundred virgins, whom they bring back as
wives for the Benjaminites. This leaves two hundred of the six

hundred men without wives, so the Israelites propose that these men steal the daughters of Shiloh as they come out to dance at the yearly festival. This they do, and then the Benjaminites return to their towns and rebuild them.

The last verse of the book repeats the editor's earlier comment: "In those days there was no king in Israel; every man did what was right in his own eyes."

LITERARY QUALITIES

The Holy War
T. R. HENN

The tribal wars develop into almost a standard pattern. The land has "rest", for ten or forty or fourscore years, under a strong judge capable, we may suppose, of producing some sort of military coherence in the tribal gatherings:

> Nevertheless the Lord raised up judges, which delivered them out of the hand that spoiled them . . .

> And it came to pass, when the judge was dead, that they returned, and corrupted themselves more than their fathers, in following other gods to serve them . . . they ceased not from their own doings, nor from their stubborn way.[1]

We have therefore the rhythm of prosperity, seduction by the Baals and Ashtaroth, a raid by an enemy, vassalage or slavery, repentance and an outburst of mercy from Jehovah, the emergence of a leader, a battle: and "the land had rest forty years." Perhaps the period is more than a poetic cliché; in forty years a new generation of fighting men, their imaginations fed on the past epics of raids and deliverances, would emerge and cohere: often to fall apart again with internal and personal jealousies. (We recall the quarrels among the Greek allies in the *Iliad*.) There are permanent features of the human situation. We may quote one instance in which the tones of the dialogue are peculiarly vivid:

[1] *Jg.* 2:16, 19. Consider the many references to the "stiff-necked" qualities of the Chosen People: an important aspect of their capacity to survive.

THE HOLY WAR   From *The Bible as Literature* by T. R. Henn. Copyright © 1970 by T. R. Henn. Reprinted by permission of Lutterworth Press and Oxford University Press, Inc.

And Gaal the son of Ebed came with his brethren, and went over to She-chem: and the men of Shechem put their confidence in him.

And they went into the fields, and gathered their vineyards, and trode the grapes, and made merry, and went into the house of their god, and did eat and drink, and cursed Abimelech.

And Gaal the son of Ebed said, Who is Abimelech, and who is Shechem, that we should serve him? Is he not the son of Jerubbaal? and Zebul his of-ficer? Serve the men of Hamor the father of Shechem: for why should we serve him?

And would to God the people were under my hand! then would I remove Abimelech. And he said to Abimelech, Increase thine army, and come out.[2]

This is a particularly interesting episode. The words of Gaal anger Zebul the ruler of the city, who secretly sends word to Abimelech of Gaal's plot. He advises an ambush, and Abimelech arranges a triple one. Men appear on the mountains in the early morning; we can imagine the dramatic moment of the clans gathering in the mist. Gaal thinks that he sees armed men far off. Then Zebul: "Thou seest the shadow of the mountains as if they were men." Now Gaal sees two other bodies of troops "by the middle of the land" and another on the plains converging on Shechem. Scornfully, Zebul recalls Gaal's boast, and bids him go out and fight. (Here the narrative seems to be defec-tive, for verses 39–41 are in the wrong place.) After a day or two Abimelech mounts a three-pronged attack. One company attacks the gate of the city, while two others cut off and slaughter the people who have gone out to work at the harvest in the field. After a day's fighting the city is taken, and its inhabitants massacred. The ruins are sowed with salt. What is left of Gaal's troops retire to the town's fortress, the tower of Shechem. Abimelech makes his troops cut down boughs, and pile them against the tower, and burns it, "so that about a thousand men and women die in it".[3]

Abimelech, flushed with victory, takes the town of Thebez; but in the course of the assault against its citadel, with the same technique of fire, a woman defender throws down a piece of millstone, "and all to brake his skull".[4] Abimelech orders his sword-bearer to kill him, so that it should not be said that he had been killed by a woman.

In these miniature actions of war and intrigue, jealousy and revenge, we have a kind of epitome of all warfare, of the whole human situation. Longinus[5] noted the emotional effects of the "names", whether of heroes, places or battles, ennobling the epic context. We may set out some examples. The first, which is rhythmically clumsy, is

[2] *Jg.* 9:26–29.
[3] *Jg.* 9:30–end. We remember that the same fate overtook the impregnable fortress of Lachish. When the Assyrian siege-engines failed, the troops devastated the country for miles for wood which they piled against the walls.
[4] Note the Middle English of *A.V.*—"all to brake".
[5] *A Treatise Concerning Sublimity,* XXIII.

from Marlowe's *Tamburlaine:* it has, deliberately, a pseudo-barbaric quality of incantation:

> "I left the confines and the bounds of Afric,
> And made a voyage into Europe,
> Where by the river Tyrus, I subdu'd
> Stoka, Podolia and Codemia,
> Then cross'd the sea, and came to Oblia,
> And Nigra Silva, where the devils dance,
> Which in despite of them I set on fire . . ."[6]

Milton reviews the superb troops of Hell with names that reverberate round the world of classical mythology, the Arthurian legend, the long heroic wars that saved Europe from domination by the Turks:

> . . . "though all the giant brood
> Of Phlegra with th'heroic race were join'd
> That fought at Thebes and Ilium, on each side
> Mix't with auxiliar gods; and what resounds
> In fable or romance of Uther's son
> Begirt with British and Armoric knights
> And all who since, baptiz'd or infidel
> Jousted in Ashramont or Montalban,
> Damasco, Marocco, or Trebizond,
> Or whom Biserta sent from Afric's shore
> When Charlemain with all his peerage fell
> By Fontarabbia."[7]

With these examples in mind we may now consider part of the great epic psalm of triumph:[8]

> . . . For, lo, thine enemies make a tumult: and they that hate thee have lifted up the head.

> They have taken crafty counsel against thy people, and consulted against thy hidden ones.[9]

> They have said, Come, and let us cut them off from being a nation; that the name of Israel may be no more in remembrance.

> For they have consulted together with one consent: they are confederate against thee:[10]

> The tabernacles of Edom, and the Ishmaelites; of Moab, and the Hagarenes;

---

[6] I, 2.
[7] *P.L.* 1. 576 ff. *Phlegra* is the home of the giants in Thessaly: *Uther,* King Arthur; *the baptiz'd* are Charlemagne's troops, the *infidel* the Mohammedan Saracens.
[8] *Ps.* 83; of peculiar interest at the time of writing (1967). [The reference is to the political situation in the Middle East in 1967.—Ed.]
[9] The refugees, perhaps in caves (the "pavilions" of *Ps.* 31:20) or in the woods or among the mountains.
[10] The poet exaggerates the amount of co-operation to be expected in the Middle East. There is no historical record of such a confederacy.

Gebal, and Ammon, and Amalek: the Philistines with the inhabitants of Tyre;

Assur also is joined with them: they have holpen the children of Lot: Selah.

Do unto them as unto the Midianites; as to Sisera, as to Jabin, at the brook of Kison:

Which perished at En-dor: they became as the dung for the earth.

Make their nobles like Oreb, and like Zeeb: yea, all their princes as Zebah, and as Zalmunna:

Who said, Let us take to ourselves the houses of God in possession.

O my God, make them like a wheel;[11] as the stubble before the wind . . .

It is a kind of epitome, foreshortened as in a Scottish ballad, of the remembered wars. The "tabernacles" are the tent-dwellers of the no-mads. Edom and Moab were victims of early campaigns, though the Edomites were remote kinsfolk. For eighteen years Israel had served Moab;[12] but then the tables were reversed. Their King Eglon, "a very fat man," was assassinated by Ehud the left-handed Benjaminite,[13] who escaped before the crime was discovered. This was the signal for a popular rising; the Israelites came down from the mountain, and, presumably by forced marches, got to the fords of the Jordan and held them against the routed Moabites:

And they slew of Moab at that time about ten thousand men, all lusty, and all men of valour; and there escaped not a man. So Moab was subdued that day under the hand of Israel. And the land had rest forescore years.[14]

. . .

Of this warfare as literature it is not easy to write; nor, indeed, is it easy to read as a coherent whole. For the narrative is never continu-ous. It doubles back on its track in an exasperating way. Accounts of the same events are often conflated. Details often differ: such as those of the names of Moses' wives. There are obvious instances of wrong sequences of events in the battles themselves. There has been some heavily-biased editing, and there are many suspected interpolations. Everything seems to combine to make the record desultory and epi-sodic. We must constantly remind ourselves of the period that this history covers (say from 1250 to 450 B.C.) and keep in mind standards of comparison from other literatures.

It is a record of war, and the morality behind war, which is con-ditioned as always by the geography and topography of Israel and the great empires that surround it. It is outstanding for its demonstration

[11] The whirling dust-storms.
[12] *Jg*. 3:14. The vividness of the descriptions, the manner in which the poet ranges over the land and its history, is much enhanced by a study of the geography of the land.
[13] The tribe was right-handed; a left-handed assassin has certain advantages in speed and surprise.
[14] *Jg*. 3:29–30.

of the national will to survive in the face of technically impossible odds; both in war and in the captivities. That will is wholly dependent on its belief, however intermittent, partial, subject to human perversions, that the people are under the protection of Jehovah, and that it is His purpose that they should survive. The epic[15] qualities, courage, the great deeds of heroes, are celebrated in poetry, and sustain this Hegelian will. Jerusalem rebuilt and fortified gives a momentary hope of permanence under Solomon. Its power as a symbol may be partly discerned in the report of an Israeli general in the 1967 campaign: "Our men could never have fought as they did if Jerusalem, and the Wall, had not meant everything to them."

We should not underestimate the moral effects on a nation of their own recited histories of adventure and fortitude; it seems likely that, in comparison with the passing of the great empires about them, these memories (incorporated continuously into their daily worship) were the strongest impulses to survival. Nor should we forget, among many examples, the adoption of an Old Testament fixity of spirit by Cromwell's New Model Army: how General Wolfe went to his death after reciting Gray's *Elegy*; nor the memory of that commander who on the Channel Crossing to France in 1944, read aloud to his men from Shakespeare's *Henry V*.

As to strategy, we recognize in history the effect of the positioning of Israel by land and sea. The lessons[16] of its relationship in the warfare of the air have not yet, I think, been fully assessed. History shows us how the invasions, their routes and strategies, have been conditioned by the ground: the lack of any natural harbours from Mt. Carmel to the Delta determine that the invaders must come from the north or south or east until they have secured the plains of Philistia.[17] Jordan remains a permanent and ever-contentious boundary. The campaigns of the Romans, the crusades, of Napoleon and Allenby, follow the ancient routes and the terrain of the battlefields. The basic lessons of surprise, mobility, stratagem and deception, may still be observed and considered in the Old Testament. . . .

. . . It is not, I think, an exaggeration to suggest that, in the present state and temper of the West, these aspects of warfare constitute a serious obstacle to potential readers of the Bible. There are many complicated reasons, into which we need not enter. But among them is the present intense emotional revulsion from war, often most violent in those who have not experienced it, or its direct effects. There are signs that the three recent campaigns in Israel, and the Russian in-

---

[15] I use the word in the sense suggested by W. P. Ker in his *Epic and Romance:* the battle, against odds, as the price of survival: whether of the individual, a tribe or a nation. This is founded in reality, the basic facts of living; and is contrasted with the romance, in which the impulse to action is founded upon the *idea*.

[16] As of June 1967.

[17] An exception is the Allenby Campaign of 1917.

vasion of Czechoslovakia, have brought us a little nearer towards understanding.

The effort to reconstruct in imagination the whole situation of the Chosen People is an intense one; the weapons, the conventions of warfare, the scale, have all to be reconstituted in our minds. Only then can we see the epic in its rise and fall, as an intermittent and heroic struggle first for living room, and then for the merest freedom to survive. . . . Yet the essential elements, the struggle of the human mind against physical and spiritual evil, remain vital in their significance. It is even possible that a future age will return to the historic concept of man's warfare with evil rather than with his irremediable past, and that the imagery linked with the view of morality will, once again, become valid and active. . . .

INTERPRETATIONS

Leaders in Crisis
BERNHARD W. ANDERSON

Israel's invasion of Canaan and her expansion in hill country were made possible, as we have seen, by the lack of political interference by any strong power from Egypt or Mesopotamia. There is, significantly, no reference in the book of Judges to Egyptian intervention. After the death of Pharaoh Merneptah in about 1211 B.C., Egypt lost control of her Asiatic empire and, with the exception of a brief revival under Rameses III (c. 1183–1152 B.C.), lapsed into confusion and political impotence. The Hittites, who had been fought to a standstill by the Egyptians, soon disappeared as a world power as a result of population disturbances in the Aegean at the beginning of the twelfth century. In Mesopotamia, Assyria was beginning to rise to power (about 1250), but as yet she posed no threat to Canaan. Thus Israel's political rivals were confined to Canaan and its immediate vicinity: the new nations in Transjordan, raiders from the Arabian desert, the Canaanite city-states, and the new arrivals known as the Philistines.

The stories in the book of Judges that picture the local conflicts and tribal jealousies of the period are unquestionably derived from very old sources. The Deuteronomic editors have touched up some of

LEADERS IN CRISIS From Bernhard W. Anderson, *Understanding the Old Testament*, 3rd edition, pp. 147–58. Reprinted by permission of Prentice-Hall, Inc., Englewood Cliffs, New Jersey.

the narratives by adding introductory and concluding formulas. But for some reason the narrative of Abimelech and the accounts of the so-called minor judges (Judg. 10:1–5 and 12:8–15) were not altered at all. Similarly, chapters 17–21 show no traces of Deuteronomic editing, and were evidently added to the Deuteronomic edition of Judges (2:6–16:31) by someone else. Thus when the Deuteronomic "frame-work" is removed, we have at our disposal ancient and reliable traditions concerning the period which began with the death of Joshua (c. 1200 B.C.).

When we read these stories by themselves, we gain a clear impression of how loosely organized the Israelite tribes were. The present book of Judges relates how twelve judges, in successive reigns amounting to 410 years, held sway over all Israel. But this is an over-simplification. Actually, tribal leaders arose from time to time in certain trouble-spots in order to relieve the pressure on a specific area. For instance, Ehud was a member of the tribe of Benjamin. Sometimes these leaders were able to appeal to other tribes for support, but by and large their leadership was local in character and was confined to emergency situations.

Nevertheless, there was a sense of participating in a community that transcended the boundaries of any particular tribe. The twelve-tribe confederacy, whose beginnings we have already considered . . ., provided a common basis of worship and social responsibility. Not only did the tribes gather at the common confederate sanctuary of Shiloh for annual religious festivals, as we learn from Judges 21:19 (see also I Sam. 1:3; 2:19),[1] but in times of emergency they were summoned to concerted action in the name of the God of the covenant. A vivid example of such action is given in the story of the Gibeah outrage, related in Judges 19–21. There we read that a Levite, incensed at the rape-murder of his concubine by some Benjaminites, cut up her corpse into twelve pieces and sent the parts throughout "all the territory of Israel." The act of dividing the body into twelve parts (see also I Sam. 11:7) indicates, of course, the twelve-part structure of the Israelite confederacy. The tribal response to this symbolic act was quick and decisive, indicating that the tribes were bound together by a common sense of law and decency, even when one of the tribes was an offender:

> And all who saw it said, "Such a thing has never happened or been seen from the day that the people of Israel came up out of the land of Egypt until this day; consider it, take counsel, and speak."
>
> —JUDGES 19:30

[1] After the central sanctuary was moved from Shechem, apparently Bethel was the confederate center for a time (Judg. 20:26–27) and then Shiloh was selected. During this period Gilgal, near Jericho, was probably visited by pilgrims who celebrated there the crossing of the Jordan and the entrance into the Promised Land. This suggestion has been advanced by H. J. Kraus, "Gilgal: Ein Beitrag zur Kultusgeschichte Israels," in *Vetus Testamentum*, I (1951), pp. 181–99. See also his *Worship in Israel*, [336], pp. 152–65.

So, we are told, all the men of Israel gathered together in the "assembly of the people of God" and resolved to take punitive action, "united as one man."

THE ROLE OF THE JUDGE

Within this framework of the Tribal Confederacy we must understand the role of Israel's judges. The Hebrew word *shofeṭ* is not an exact equivalent of our word "judge," which is restricted to legal functions. In ancient Semitic thought, the role of leadership involved procuring the right of the people either by taking military action or by judging legal disputes. The word *shofeṭ* is close in meaning to "ruler," as we see in this passage from Isaiah 33:22:

> Yahweh is our judge (*shofeṭ*), Yahweh is our ruler,
> Yahweh is our king; he will save us.

Hence the statement that so-and-so "judged Israel" must be taken in a wider sense than the English translation implies. While being primarily a military champion or "deliverer" (Judg. 2:16), the judge did play a part in internal arbitration, as in the cases of the judge Deborah (Judg. 4:4–5) and the last judge, Samuel (I Sam. 7:15–17). The authority of a judge extended beyond the locale of his tribe, and was recognized in the territory of the Tribal Confederacy. It is possible that when the tribes convened at the central sanctuary for covenant-renewal festivals the judge presided as "covenant mediator."[2]

Unlike the dynastic office of the king, which was passed on from father to son, the office of the judge was nonhereditary and rested upon a special endowment of Yahweh's spirit. For this reason the judges have been called "charismatic leaders"—that is, leaders qualified to head the Tribal Confederacy by virtue of the divine *charisma*, or spiritual power, which possesed them. So we read, for instance, that "the spirit of Yahweh took possession of Gideon" or literally "clothed itself with Gideon," empowering him with an authority that was recognized not only in his own clan but in surrounding tribes (Judg. 6:34–35). More vivid examples are found in the legendary Samson stories, where we read that "the spirit of Yahweh came upon him mightily," empowering him to accomplish superhuman feats (see Judg. 14:6). Deborah, too, was a charismatic leader who summoned the tribes of Israel to military action against the Canaanites in the name of Yahweh (Judg. 4–5). Presumably, charismatic success in battle or extraordinary physical prowess encouraged people from

[2] Martin Noth, in "Das Amt des 'Richters Israels' " (*Festschrift A. Bertholet* [Tübingen: J. C. B. Mohr, 1950], pp. 404–17), maintains that the so-called "minor judges" mentioned in 10:1–5 and 12:7–15 were actually legal administrators selected by the Confederacy. But this theory presupposes the dubious view that the book of Judges tells about two different kinds of leaders, whereas the tradition indicates that the two functions—legal and military—were combined in one person.

the various tribes to consult the judge also in cases of legal dispute. In this way, Israel's covenant law . . . was applied to specific cases and was expanded.

Because the judges did not follow one another in chronological succession, contary to the impression created by the Deuteronomic historian, it is difficult to outline the sequence of events between the death of Joshua and the time of Saul, the first king of Israel. However, we do have in these stories vivid vignettes of conditions and crises during the twelfth and eleventh centuries B.C. We shall deal with them in terms of areas of pressure upon the Israelite confederacy.

THE BATTLE OF MEGIDDO

The Israelites, as we have seen, had managed to entrench themselves in the central hill country but could not dispossess the Canaanites on the plains. The most strategic area under Canaanite control was the Valley of Jezreel, through which the main commercial route ran from Egypt to Mesopotamia. Guarding the pass into the valley was the Canaanite fortress of Megiddo, the scene of many decisive battles and, according to religious imagination, the scene of the final battle of Armageddon.[3] So long as the Canaanites were in control of this commercial lifeline, they could throttle Israel's economic life. This was the situation, we are told, during the days of the judge Shamgar (Judg. 3:31):

> In the days of Shamgar, son of Anath,
> in the days of Jael, caravans ceased
> and travellers kept to the byways.
> —JUDGES 5:6

Spurred into action by Deborah and under the command of Barak, the Israelite forces met General Sisera's Canaanite army in the vicinity of the fortified city of Taanach (Judg. 5:19), which provides a commanding view of Megiddo and the whole plain.[4] Apparently only half of the tribes of the Israelite confederacy responded to the summons of Deborah, a charismatic leader. Victory was theirs that day, thanks to a terrific rainstorm that caused the river Kishon, which flows through the plain of Jezreel, to overflow its banks, with the result that the Canaanite charioteers were helplessly trapped in miry clay.

The account of this battle is given in two versions: a poetic version, the Song of Deborah, in Judges 5; and a prose version in Judges 4, which differs somewhat in details. By general agreement, the Song of Deborah is a firsthand, authentic historical witness. It is one of the

[3] Ar-mageddon, referred to in Relevation 16:16, literally means "hill of Megiddo."
[4] Taanach has been excavated under the archaeological direction of Paul Lapp; see *The Biblical Archaeologist*, XXVI, 4 (1963), pp. 130–32.

oldest passages of poetry in the Old Testament, written by one who stood very near the event, perhaps by a participant. Archaeological work at Megiddo has produced evidence for dating the battle and the song that celebrates the event in the latter part of the twelfth century B.C., approximately 1125 B.C.[5]

The meaning of the victory is far more effectively communicated in the poem than in the later prose version. Even in English translation readers are made vividly aware of the spirit of the battle. We sense the quickened pulse beat that responds to the summons to participate in the historic crisis. We are carried along with the "galloping rhythm" toward the climax of victory. We feel the fiercely victorious passion of Jael the Kenite (see 4:11 . . .) and by contrast the bitter pathos of Sisera's mother looking for a son who would never return. The poem deals with history as it was lived, not with history as reported by a detached observer.

To the author of the poem, the event was overwhelming because of its religious meaning. The storm that defeated the Canaanites is seen to be the sign of Yahweh's active presence as the leader and champion of his people. According to the poet's passionate faith, no array of human forces can stand against Yahweh. He is Lord of the heavens and the earth, the Sovereign of history who makes the elements of nature serve his purpose. Even the stars—conceived as Yahweh's heavenly host—join in the battle:

> From the heaven fought the stars,
>   from their courses they fought against Sisera.
> —JUDGES 5:20

Hence his song begins and ends with an exclamation of praise. In the experience of the poet, it was Yahweh's participation in the battle that made the event historic and momentous.

The poem forcefully expresses the cardinal conviction of the Mosaic faith: Yahweh is the "God of Israel" (verses 3, 5) and Israel is "the people of Yahweh" (verses 11, 13). Although there is no reference to the covenant, this close relationship between God and people is the basis of the whole poem. Yahweh is praised as the Leader of his people, who comes in a storm from Sinai through the region of Edom (verses 4–5). The people are exhorted to rehearse his "triumphs," his mighty acts (verse 11: literally, "his righteous deeds"). And since Yahweh goes forth at the head of his people, the tribes are summoned to decision—to come to his side in holy war.[6] Those tribes who did not

[5] W. F. Albright, who argues for this date, points out that the poetry of the Song of Deborah has striking affinities with Canaanite style known from the Ras Shamra literature. See his article "The Song of Deborah in the Light of Archaeology," *Bulletin of the American School of Oriental Research*, LXII (1936), pp. 26–31.
[6] On holy war see especially R. de Vaux, *Ancient Israel* [96], pp. 258–67. An important work in German is Gerhard von Rad, *Der heilige Krieg im alten Israel* (Zurich: Zwingli Verlag, 1951).

answer the summons, who "came not to the help of Yahweh against the mighty" (verse 23), are denounced in the strongest terms, for they were not acting as "the people of Yahweh." Here we see that the basis of Israel was not just political or family ties, but voluntary dedication to Yahweh, the exclusive Lord of the Tribal Confederacy. To the true Israel belong only those tribes who choose to serve Yahweh with their full measure of devotion. They are his "friends," those who love him (verse 31). There is no clearer witness in the Old Testament to the historical character of Israel's faith than the Song of Deborah.

FOES FROM OTHER DIRECTIONS

Israel's decisive victory over Sisera's host marked the end of any united Canaanite resistance against Israel. However, troubles came to Israel from other directions. The newly established kingdoms of Transjordan looked with jealous eyes on Israel's holdings both in Transjordan itself and in Canaan. Moab, under the leadership of a king named Eglon, invaded Israelite territory and took "the city of palms," Jericho. . . . The tide was turned by a deliverer named Ehud, who delivered "a message from God" to Eglon in a left-handed manner with a dagger (Judg. 3:12–30). Later, Israel suffered a series of attacks from the Ammonites, both in Transjordan and in the Canaanite hill country. This threat was met effectively by Jephthah (Judg. 10:6–12:7).

Even more serious, however, was a series of devasting attacks by Midianite raiders who came in from the Arabian desert on camels. The use of the camel was something new in military tactics. The wild tribesmen of Arabia had learned how to use fleets of camels for traveling long distances to make surprise attacks on settled villages. So effective were the raids of these camel-riding nomads that the Israelites had to leave their villages and take to mountain caves:

> For they [the Midianites] would come up with their cattle and their tents, coming like locusts for number; both they and their camels could not be counted; so that they wasted the land as they came in.
>
> —JUDGES 6:5

In the face of these raids, the Israelites could not carry on their farming, and were in danger of losing everything they had gained by the conquest. In this dire emergency the day was saved by a judge named Gideon, otherwise known as Jerubbaal (Judg. 6–8). Gideon's military leadership was based on his charismatic zeal for Yahweh—zeal directed against those, even of his own family, who had turned to Baal. Although Gideon's father, Joash, had a Yahweh name (including the element Yah [Yo]), he erected a Baal altar with a fertility tree, an Asherah, beside it. Gideon destroyed the Baal cult objects and built an altar to Yahweh instead, much to the displeasure of the men of the city of Ophrah (Judg. 6:25–32). This story is important because it shows how deeply Canaanite rites and conceptions had infiltrated, and because it shows how Israel's strength in time of crisis was connected with a revival of a vigorous faith in Yahweh, the God of the Tribal Confederacy. To the surprise of Gideon, and perhaps to the dismay of any person who wants to stand on his own feet, the narrator insists that the victory belongs to Yahweh *alone*, who needs a task force of only 300 men for the huge offensive.[7]

Throughout the twelfth and eleventh centuries, the threat to Israel was increased by the pressure of newcomers known as Philistines. As we have seen, the Philistines were one of a number of "sea peoples" who poured out of the Aegean onto the eastern shores of the Mediterranean. . . . Shortly after 1200 B.C., they swarmed into Canaan by sea and by land, and established a beach-head on the coastal plain. They came during a great transitional epoch which in archaeological terms marked the beginning of the Iron Age (1200–600 B.C.). Their natural aggressiveness was augmented by their skill in making instruments and weapons of iron, a trade in which they achieved a virtual monopoly. From their restricted base on the coast, the Philistines began to move inland, sweeping away Canaanite resistance and coming into contact with the already entrenched and victorious Israelites. In fact, the Philistines came close to making Canaan a Philistine empire. One of the great ironies of history is that the name later given to Israel's land, Palestine, is derived from the name of Israel's archenemies, the Philistines!

Early in the book of Judges we read briefly of the exploits of a certain Shamgar, who slew six hundred Philistines with an oxgoad (3:31). This must have occurred fairly early in the Philistine occupation, for Shamgar is referred to in the Song of Deborah (5:6). Elsewhere we hear of the Philistines only in passing, until we come to the Samson cycle at the very end of the Deuteronomic edition of Judges (chaps. 13–16). It is unnecessary to go into the details of these lusty stories, which have as their theme the discomfiture of the Philistines by an Israelite Tarzan whose fatal weakness was women. The Samson stories are more legendary than any other material preserved in the book of Judges. Although Samson is regarded as a judge, he is unlike the other judges in that he was not a military leader. These stories deal with the marvelous exploits of an individual and are more designed to tickle the fancy than to record history. Viewed theologically, the story of Samson's tragic demise portrays what happens to a man filled with *charisma* when he disregards the guidance of Yahweh in a time of crisis to pursue his own passions.

---

[7] It is interesting to compare the biblical story with a modern interpretation: *Gideon, A New Play* (New York: Random House, 1962), by Paddy Chayefsky.

The Samson tales, however, do give us a valuable picture of the relations between Israelites and Philistines, probably at the beginning of the eleventh century. We see that the Philistines had consolidated their position on the coast and were strong enough to worry the Israelites up in the hill country into spinning yarns that poked fun at their uncircumcised neighbors. But there were no pitched battles, and we find no expressions of despair over Philistine ascendancy. At the most, these stories reflect border incidents that were not sufficiently grievous to disrupt commercial relations between the two peoples. By the end of the eleventh century all this was to change, for the Philistines soon were to be in control of all the arteries leading into the Israelite hill country. As things turned out, this was the first stage in an all-out Philistine offensive that had only one objective: the total destruction, once and for all, of the Israelite confederacy.

THE DECLINE OF THE CONFEDERACY

As political pressure mounted, it became increasingly apparent that the Israelite Confederacy was an ineffective organization for coping with the troubled situation in Canaan. Even in a time of great peril, as we have already noticed, only half the tribes responded to Deborah's charismatic summons and helped to hurl back Canaanite aggression under Sisera. The twelve tribes were bound together, not by a centralized government, but only by a common devotion to Yahweh, the God of the covenant, and by common religious and legal responsibilities. The Confederacy by its very nature encouraged a high degree of tribal independence. Yahweh alone was the ruler of the Israelite tribes. His rule was made known through charismatic judges and through the High Priest who attended the central sanctuary, like Eli at the shrine of Shiloh (I Sam. 1–4). Only when religious festivals were held at the confederate shrine, or when dire emergency arose— such as the Gibeah outrage—did the tribes come together in concert "as one man." This form of organization, at least for a time, spared Israel from the political despotism of the Near East. Moreover, in times of political crisis it threw the people back upon Yahweh, the Lord of history, with the consequent renewal of Israel's distinctive historical faith. For all its merit, however, the Tribal Confederacy was vulnerable to the political forces of the time, as the Philistine menace made clear.

THE SHECHEM EXPERIMENT

The first abortive experiment to establish a centralized government was carried out at Shechem, the very place where the Tribal Confederacy had been established in the time of Joshua. Although the name of Abimelech is connected with this incident, some precedent had been established for it previously in the city of Ophrah. Gideon (Jerubbaal) had been successful in his charismatic leadership against the nomadic raids that had all but ruined Israel. In view of his success in the engagement with Midian, and doubtless in view also of the increasing political tension caused by the Philistine menace, the men of Israel offered to crown him king. "Rule over us," they said, "you and your son and your grandson also" (Judg. 8:22). In other words, they proposed to change the basis of his authority from that of nonhereditary, charismatic judgeship to that of a hereditary monarchy modeled after the kingdoms of Transjordan, notably Moab and Ammon.[8] Gideon firmly replied: "I will not rule over you, and my son will not rule over you; Yahweh will rule over you." His answer was consistent with the foundations of the Israelite theocracy. Yahweh alone was Israel's king, and it was presumptuous for any person to usurp his throne.

Now, besides the many wives of his harem, Gideon also had a concubine in the city of Shechem who bore him a son named Abimelech. Abimelech's career is recounted in Judges 9. After Gideon's death, so we are told, Abimelech went to his mother's kinsmen in Shechem. Pointing out that he was a kinsman of the Shechemites, he persuaded them that he was entitled to rule over them as king. With money furnished him from the treasury of the Baal-berith ("Lord of the Covenant") temple, he hired rascals as his followers and forthwith liquidated his seventy brothers, with the exception of the youngest, Jotham. With these rivals out of the way, the citizens of Shechem crowned him king, possibly near a sacred pillar that can be seen even today in the ruins of the acropolis known as Beth-millo (9:6). . . .

But this incident did not go without rebuke. Standing on Mount Gerizim, Jotham told the famous fable of the trees which, seeking for a king to rule over them, asked the olive, the fig, and the vine in turn, and finally had to settle for the bramble, which still grows abundantly in the area (9:7–15). The implication was that Abimelech's rule, like the inflammable bramble, would be tinderbox for the fires of revolution. In this pointed attack upon Abimelech's kingdom, Jotham was expressing the attitude toward monarchy that prevailed in the conservative circles of the Israelite Confederacy. Abimelech's main support, right from the first, had come from the priesthood of the Baal-berith temple who advocated a kind of government that ran counter to the Israelite theocratic ideal.

For three years (9:22), Abimelech was able to impose his rule over a considerable territory, with Shechem as the chief city of his kingdom. True to Jotham's prediction, however, revolution broke out in Shechem. By means of a strategem of ambush, Abimelech successfully stormed the city and destroyed it, probably about 1100 B.C.

---

[8] According to the list in Gen. 36:31–39, the kingship of Edom was dynastic; apparently the petty kings of the Canaanite city-states did not establish a hereditary line.

(9:45). The revolution must have spread into other parts of his kingdom, for we learn that he met death while attacking the city of Thebez, on the road from Shechem to Beth-shan. Although the Shechem
experiment in monarchy failed, it was a fateful shadow of things to
come. The days of the Tribal Confederacy were coming to an end. A
stronger form of government was needed. . . .

The Period of the Judges
JOHN BRIGHT

The period of the Judges was one of adaptation and adjustment.
For those who had come from the desert the settlement represented
the transition to an agrarian way of life. This transition seems to have
been made rather easily, for the newcomers had not, after all, been
true desert nomads, but people already accustomed to till the soil in a
limited way, many of them the offspring of Hebrews who had experienced long years of settled life as state slaves in Egypt. One must
remember, too, that the Israelite league had absorbed large numbers
of the population of Canaan whose ancestors had been sedentary or
semisedentary for generations and who had, in this regard, no transition to make. These last, however, were for the most part drawn from
the very lowest strata of society and were desperately poor; none of
the feudal aristocracy and very few craftsmen were among them. The
poverty of the people, as well as their lack of technical skill, is illustrated by the fact, noted above, that the earliest Israelite towns were
exceedingly crude and bare of evidences of material culture. Nevertheless, the period of the Judges witnessed a gradual but marked im-
provement in Israel's economy. As skills were learned, material culture
advanced. The introduction of camel caravans for desert transport at
about this time, and the expansion of sea-borne commerce, in which
members of certain Israelite tribes seem to have participated
(Judg. 5:17), undoubtedly contributed to the general prosperity. The
discovery of baked lime plaster for the lining of cisterns . . . enabled
the mountain ridge to support an increased density of population;
numerous towns were built where none had been before. Additional
land was secured for cultivation by clearing the forests that had thith-
erto covered much of the highlands both east and west of the Jordan
(Josh.17:14–18).

But adaptation also went on at deeper levels. As already stated,

THE PERIOD OF THE JUDGES   From *A History of Israel,* by John Bright. © MCMLIX, W. L. Jenkins. ©
MCMLXXII, The Westminster Press. Used by permission.

there was a great borrowing, no doubt chiefly from kindred elements absorbed in Israel's structure, in the realms of legal procedure and sacrificial forms. Ancestral traditions, long handed down in the land, were adapted and made vehicles of Yahwistic faith. Far more serious, however, was the beginning of tension with the religion of Canaan. This was inevitable. Some of those absorbed into Israel were Canaanites, and many more had long lived under Canaanite domination. Though as members of Israel all became worshipers of Yahweh, many of them, we may not doubt, remained pagans at heart. We may suppose, too, that local shrines perpetuated pre-Mosaic practices, many of which accorded ill with Yahwism. Moreover, since Canaan was immeasurably ahead of Israel in material culture, cultural borrowing naturally took place in all areas. It was inevitable that some Israelites should view the agrarian religion as a necessary part of the agrarian life and begin to propitiate the gods of fertility. Others, no doubt, accommodated the worship of Yahweh to that of Ba'al, and even began to confuse the two. The Book of Judges is undoubtedly correct in recording the period as one of theological irregularity.

THE RULE OF CHARISMA

We can add very little to what the Bible tells us of the various leaders, called judges, who arose in the course of this period to save Israel from her foes. Though the order in which they are presented seems to be roughly a chronological one, we cannot assign to any of them a precise date. The judges were by no means men of identical character. Some (e.g., Gideon) rose to their task at the behest of a profound experience of divine vocation; one (Jephthah) was no better than a bandit who knew how to strike a canny bargain; one (Samson) was an engaging rogue whose fabulous strength and bawdy pranks became legendary. None, so far as we know, ever led a united Israel into battle. All, however, seem to have had this in common: they were men who, stepping to the fore in times of danger, by virtue only of those personal qualities (charisma) which gave evidence to their fellows that Yahweh's spirit was upon them, rallied the clans against the foe. . . .

THE TENACITY OF THE TRIBAL SYSTEM

It might seem surprising that the tribal league survived as long as it did, for it was a loose—not to say weak—form of government. Its wars were all defensive; except possibly for Deborah's victory, they gained Israel no new territory. Indeed, Israel perhaps held less at the end of the period than at the beginning. Reuben had been virtually rubbed out, presumably by Moabite aggression. Dan, probably ultimately because of Philistine pressure, had been unable to maintain its position in the central Shephelah (Judg.1:34–36) and had been forced to migrate to the far north and seize new territory there (ch.18). Though Danite clans probably continued to live in the old area, these were, like neighboring Judah, severely restricted by the Philistines. And virtually all the clans continued to have Canaanite enclaves in their midst which they could not master (ch.1).

Nor was the tribal organization able to restrain the centrifugal forces that operated. It could not enforce purity of Yahwism, nor at any time persuade all Israel to act concertedly; nor could it prevent intertribal rivalries from flaring into war (Judg.12:1–6). Moreover, in the case of a crime on the part of members of one tribe against members of another (chs. 19; 20), it had no means of redress in the last resort, the tribe in question being unwilling to surrender the guilty parties, save to call out the clans against the offending tribe. Though a perfectly characteristic procedure, representing the action of Yahweh's loyal vassals against a rebellious vassal, it presents us with the spectacle of the tribal league at war with itself—surely a wasteful way of administering justice!

Yet the league survived for nearly two hundred years. This was partly because the emergencies that Israel confronted, being mostly local in character, were such that the informal rally of the clans could deal with them. But it was also because in circumscribing the actions of the clans only in certain well-defined areas while otherwise leaving them their freedom, the tribal organization expressed perfectly the spirit of Yahweh's covenant which had created it. It was an organization fully typical of early Israel. In all this period Israel made no move to create a state, specifically none (the case of Abimelech being clearly atypical) to imitate the city-state pattern of Canaan. Indeed, the very idea of monarchy was anathema to true Israelites, as both Gideon's rejection of a crown (Judg. 8:22f.) and Jotham's sarcastic fable (ch. 9:7–21) show. Yahweh, the Overlord of his people, rules and saves them through his charismatic representatives.

So matters might have gone on indefinitely had not the Philistine crisis intervened, confronting Israel with an emergency with which the rally of the clans could not deal, and forcing her to a fundamental change.

SUGGESTED READINGS

Gehman, Henry S., ed. *The New Westminster Dictionary of the Bible*, pp. 529–30, "Judges." Philadelphia: The Westminster Press, 1970.
Kraft, C. F. "Judges, Book of." In *The Interpreter's Dictionary of the Bible*, Vol. 2, edited by George A. Buttrick, pp. 1013–23. Nashville, Tenn: Abingdon Press, 1962.

Meyers, Jacob M. "Judges: Introduction." In *The Interpreter's Bible*, Vol. 2, edited by George A. Buttrick, pp. 677–87. Nashville, Tenn.: Abingdon Press, 1953.

Miller, Madeleine S., and Miller, J. Lane, eds. *The Harper Bible Dictionary*, pp. 359–60, "Judges." New York: Harper & Row, 1973.

Smith, Robert Houston. "The Book of Judges." In *The Interpreter's One-Volume Commentary on the Bible*, edited by Charles M. Laymon, pp. 135–37. Nashville, Tenn.: Abingdon Press, 1971.

QUESTIONS FOR DISCUSSION AND WRITING

1. Which narratives in the Book of Judges make effective use of plot, character, setting, and development? Explain.
2. What information does this book give us about the people, their customs, and their problems?
3. Compare the accounts of Jael and Sisera in Chapters 4 and 5 of Judges. Which do you find the more effective? Why?
4. What elements and events in the Samson story suggest that it depends largely on legendary stories passed on by word of mouth?
5. Examine the characters of several of the judges. What qualities do they possess in common?
6. What patterns does T. R. Henn discern in the accounts of the tribal wars in Judges?
7. Support with evidence from Judges T. R. Henn's contention that "In these miniature actions of war and intrigue, jealousy and revenge, we have a kind of epitome of all warfare, of the whole human situation."
8. What was the function of a judge in ancient Israel? How do Bernhard Anderson and John Bright define "charismatic"?
9. What evidence in the Book of Judges itself supports the opinion that Israel was in need of a different political organization?
10. Why, according to Anderson, were the Philistines such a formidable foe?
11. What improvements in Israel's economy does John Bright find in the time of the judges?
12. What reasons does Bright give for the "theological irregularity" that prevailed in the time of the judges?
13. According to John Bright, what made it possible for the tribal league to survive for nearly 200 years?
14. If the Book of Judges did not exist, would the Old Testament be lacking anything of significance? If so, why?
15. For an ambitious oral report or essay: Compare the biblical story of Gideon with the play *Gideon* by Paddy Chayevsky, or the story of Samson with Bernard Malamud's novel *The Natural*.

THE RISE AND FALL
OF ISRAEL

1 Samuel, 2 Samuel, 1 Kings 1–11

SUMMARY

The two Books of Samuel and the first eleven chapters of the First Book of Kings relate events that can well be described as "the rise and fall of Israel." Under Saul the Israelites, although defeated at Gilboa, did win and consolidate most of the territory promised them by the Lord. Under David the monarchy flourished and the territory of the kingdom reached its greatest expanse. Solomon reigned over Israel's most extensive kingdom, and he brought it to its zenith of fame and honor. Unfortunately, however, his practice of forced labor, high taxes, and his betrayal of the Lord brought about a split between Israel of the north and Judah of the south—a division that was never repaired.

Scholars tell us that the duplications (for example, there are two stories of David sparing Saul when he had him in his clutches) and contradictions (for example, Saul does not know who David is when he fights Goliath, although David has been playing the lyre for him for

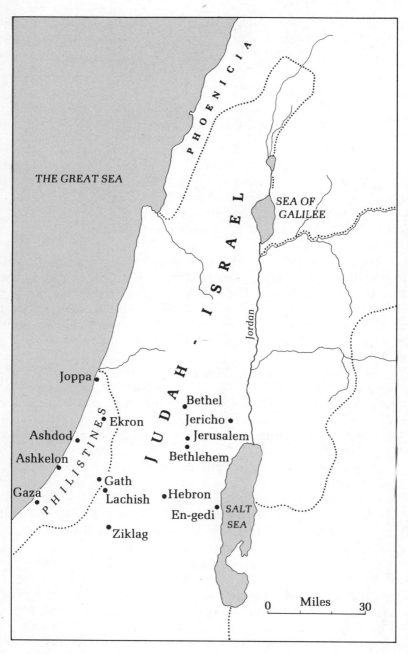

THE GREAT SEA

PHOENICIA

SEA OF
GALILEE

Jordan

J U D A H - I S R A E L

Joppa

Bethel
Ekron   Jericho
Jerusalem
Ashdod
Ashkelon   Bethlehem

P H I L I S T I N E S

Gath
Gaza   Lachish   Hebron
En-gedi   SALT
SEA
Ziklag

0   Miles   30

Judah–Israel under David and Solomon, *ca.* 1000–925 B.C.

some time) can be explained by a reasonable theory that the books are based on two accounts: the Early Source, whose author may have been an eyewitness to events during the reigns of David and Solomon, and the Late Source, written between 750 and 650 B.C.

SAMUEL'S BIRTH AND CALL

A man named Elkanah, from the hill country of Ephraim, has two wives, Hannah and Peninah. Peninah, who has children, makes life miserable for Hannah, who has none. One day Hannah prays to the Lord and promises him that if she can have a son, she will dedicate him to the Lord's service. Her prayer is answered, and when her son is weaned she takes him up to the priest Eli at Shiloh.

In a "song" or poem that may have been written considerably later than the material surrounding it, Hannah "exalts in the Lord." She praises him as the defender and savior of the poor and the weak and sees him as a judge of "the ends of the earth" who "will give strength to his king, and exalt the power of his anointed." (1 Samuel 2:10). The boy, Samuel, is left at the sanctuary with the priest.

Eli's sons, Hophni and Phinehas, are also priests at Shiloh, but they sin against the Lord by stealing parts of the sacrifices and by lying with the women who serve at the sanctuary. Eli reproves them, but they pay no attention. Samuel, on the other hand, continues "to grow in stature and in favor with the Lord and with men" (2:26).

A man of God comes to the priest Eli to tell him that the God of Israel will take the priesthood away from his house because of the behavior of his sons. (There is a suggestion that Eli too is not without guilt in the matter of taking the best part of the offerings.) Hophni and Phinehas, says the man, will die on the same day, and the Lord will appoint a faithful priest.

One night, when Samuel has gone to bed, he hears his name called. Three times he hears the call, and three times he goes to the old priest, thinking it is he who has summoned him. Eli advises that it must be the Lord who is calling the lad. (According to Jewish tradition, Samuel is twelve years old at this time.) So at the next call, Samuel answers, "Speak, for thy servant hears." The Lord tells him that the house of Eli shall be cut off from the priesthood. At Eli's insistence Samuel tells Eli what he has heard. The Lord continues to reveal himself to Samuel, and Samuel's reputation as a prophet is established in "all Israel from Dan to Beer-sheba" (3:20).

WAR WITH THE PHILISTINES

The account of the war against the Philistines begins in Chapter 4. In the first encounter the Israelites are defeated. The elders of Israel, believing that the ark of the Lord may be helpful to them, order that it be brought from Shiloh. In the next battle the Israelites are again defeated; Hophni and Phinehas are killed, and the ark is captured. When Eli learns of the death of his sons and the capture of the ark, he falls dead on the spot. The wife of Phinehas dies in childbirth when she hears the news, but before dying she names her new son Ichabod, saying, "The glory has departed from Israel, for the ark of God has been captured (4:21).

The ark does the Philistines no good. The statue of their god Dagon falls into pieces when the ark is placed in his temple, and the Philistines are afflicted with tumors (perhaps bubonic plague). So after seven months they send it off in a wagon hitched to two milch cows, which they let go to find their own way. When the cows go directly to the Israelites in Bethshemesh, the Philistines know that it is the Hebrew God who has afflicted them. The people of Bethshemesh are afraid to harbor the ark when they find that men looking into it are killed by the Lord. They persuade the people of Keriathjearim to take it, and there it remains for twenty years in the charge of Eleazar, a man consecrated to the task.

Samuel commands the Israelites to put away their foreign gods if they are sincere in their return to the worship of Yahweh. He leads them in a cleansing ceremony, which proves its efficacy when the Lord thunders and scares away the Philistines who are about to attack. The Israelites pursue the enemy and defeat them. We are told that the Lord is with Samuel and that the cities that had been taken by the Philistines are restored.

THE PEOPLE WANT A KING

Samuel's activity as a judge consists mainly of traveling a circuit from Bethel to Gilgal to Mizpah and then back to his headquarters at Ramah. He grows old and turns his work over to his sons, but they are not dedicated to the Lord's service as Samuel has been. "They took bribes and perverted justice" (8:3). The people therefore demand that Samuel appoint a king, a demand that does not please Samuel. Samuel prays to the Lord, who advises him to do what the people want, but also to warn the people of what they can expect from a king.

Regardless of Samuel's unfavorable description of the consequences of monarchical government, the people still demand a king, "that we also may be like all the nations, and that our king may govern us and go out before us and fight our battles" (8:20). The Lord tells Samuel to give them what they ask.

Samuel's search leads him to Saul, the son of Kish, of the tribe of Benjamin. In fact, the Lord points him out to Samuel one day, when Saul has sought the prophet for information about his father's lost asses. "Here is the man of whom I spoke to you! He it is who shall rule over my people" (9:17). Saul is Samuel's special guest that night, and when he leaves in the morning Samuel walks some distance with him to let him know "the word of God." He anoints him king over Israel. But it is a secret anointing, for Samuel sends Saul's servant ahead, and later, when Saul tells his father where he has been, he tells him nothing "about the matter of the kingdom."

Samuel, still resentful that the people have requested a king, calls them together to present Saul. Saul is nowhere to be found until the Lord tells Samuel that he is hiding among the baggage. (If the two-source theory of the composition of the Books of Samuel is valid, this account may be from the Late Source, which seems to be hostile to Saul from resentment that the monarchy was ever established. See *The New Oxford Annotated Bible,* I Samuel, footnote to Chapter 10, verses 17–27.*)

THE CONFLICT BETWEEN SAMUEL AND SAUL

Saul's first test as leader occurs when he learns that the city of Jabesh-gilead is about to be destroyed by the Ammonites. He calls the tribes together, and their armies are victorious. Now that Saul has proved himself, Samuel calls the people together at Gilgal "to renew the kingdom" and to make Saul "king before the Lord" (11:14–15).

Seeing the end of his authority in sight, both because of his age and because the people now have a king, Samuel asks them to acknowledge that he has been a leader of integrity. They do so, and then Samuel reviews their history from the time Jacob went into Egypt to the present. He repeats that they have been wicked in asking for a king, but when they admit their sin Samuel alleviates their fear. He assures them that the Lord will not cast them away as long as they obey him. "But if you still do wickedness, you shall be swept away, both you and your king" (12:25).

Now Saul clashes with the formidable Philistines. His son Jonathan's forces win a victory over the garrison at Geba, and the

*Herbert G. May and Bruce M. Metzger, eds., *The New Oxford Annotated Bible, Revised Standard Version* (New York: Oxford University Press).

Philistines muster a mighty force at Michmash. Threatened by the great army, Saul's men begin to scatter. They run and hide wherever they can. Saul waits the appointed seven days for Samuel to arrive at Gilgal, but when he does not appear Saul performs the religious ritual himself. When Samuel arrives, he is angry that the king has usurped his function, and although Saul protests that he "forced himself" and offered the burnt sacrifice because the men were running away, Samuel says, "Your kingdom shall not continue because you have not kept what the Lord commanded you."

Nevertheless, this first battle with the Philistines is a victory for Saul's army. Encouraged after Jonathan and his armor bearer make a successful raid on the enemy, the Israelites take heart and attack the frightened Philistines. Those of Saul's men who have hidden away come back, and the Philistines would have been even more completely routed had not Jonathan unwittingly broken a vow imposed on everyone by Saul. Saul's impetuous vow, "Cursed be the man who eats food until it is evening and I am avenged on my enemies" (14:24), distresses his men because they need strength for battle, and it almost costs the life of Jonathan, who, not knowing of the vow, eats some honey. When Saul discovers this, he is ready to carry out the threat, but the people ransom Jonathan "that he did not die" (14:45).

Verses 47–52 of Chapter 14 summarize Saul's achievements. We are told that "he fought against all his enemies on every side" as well as against the Philistines and that he "delivered Israel out of the hands of those who plundered them."

Samuel tells Saul that the Lord wants him to utterly destroy the Amalekites: men, women, children, livestock—everything. But Saul and his army spare King Agag and keep the best of the spoil. Then the Lord tells Samuel that he wishes he had never made Saul king. Samuel is angry and "cries to the Lord all night" (15:11). (It is not clear whether he cries in an attempt to change the Lord's mind or out of regret that he ever made Saul king.)

Samuel goes to Saul at Gilgal and upbraids him for not having killed all of the Amalekites and for having taken some of the spoil. Saul argues that he has Agag as a prisoner and that it was "the people" who insisted on keeping the best of the spoil to be used in sacrifice. Samuel answers that the Lord prefers obedience to sacrifice and that

"Because you have rejected the word of the Lord,
        he has also rejected you from being king" (15:23).

Saul admits his sin and asks for forgiveness, but Samuel will do no more than to go with him before the elders. He orders Saul to bring Agag out, and then he "hews Agag in pieces before the Lord in Gilgal" (15:33).

Samuel grieves over Saul, but the Lord stirs him to action. He sends Samuel to Jesse the Bethlehemite and selects Jesse's youngest son, David, to be the new king. Samuel anoints David and then returns to Ramah.

SAUL FEARS DAVID AS A THREAT TO THE THRONE

Saul is tormented by "an evil spirit" (16:14), and to bring him relief his servants recommend that David be called upon to play the lyre. David is so successful that Saul makes him his armor bearer. He goes back and forth between Saul and his own home, where he tends sheep, while three of his brothers remain as soldiers with Saul.

One day, when he is sent by his father to take some provisions to his brothers, David sees Goliath the Philistine giant making the challenge that he has been making for forty days: "I defy the ranks of Israel this day; give me a man that we may fight together" (17:10). David volunteers, although Saul cannot believe that he is serious. He lends David his armor, but David, unable to move comfortably in it, goes to meet the giant clad in his usual fashion and carrying only his staff and sling. He picks five smooth stones from the brook and strikes the giant in the forehead with one shot from his sling. Goliath falls, and David cuts off his head with the giant's own sword. The Philistines flee, with the Israelites in pursuit.

Saul's son Jonathan loves David, and they make a covenant of friendship. Jonathan gives David his clothing, his armor, and his weapons, and David is so successful as a warrior that Saul makes him a commander. But when Saul hears the women praise David as a greater warrior than himself, he becomes angry and fears that David will take the kingdom from him. The next time an evil spirit descends upon Saul and David plays the lyre to soothe him, Saul throws his spear at him twice, intending to kill him. He sends David away as commander of a thousand men, and he becomes increasingly jealous of David's popularity with the people. He offers his daughter Merab to David as a bride, then marries her off to someone else. When his daughter Michal falls in love with David, Saul offers her to him on the condition that he will bring him one hundred Philistine foreskins as a marriage present. When David presents him with two hundred foreskins, Saul gives him his daughter and fears him even more.

David's fame grows, and Saul instructs his son and his servants to kill him. After Jonathan intercedes on David's behalf, David is allowed to return to the household. Then Saul is afflicted by the evil spirit and again tries to kill David, so David runs away. Saul's men pursue him but reach his house too late. His

Ernest Normand, "David Plays the Harp Before Saul"

wife, Michal, has helped him leave by the window and has placed a large image in the bed. This fools Saul's men long enough to allow David to escape.

David goes to Samuel at Ramah, and Saul sends messengers after him three times. Each time the messengers come into Samuel's presence, they begin to prophesy. When Saul himself goes there, he too prophesies, evidently falling into a kind of ecstasy. Jonathan, learning that Saul is determined to kill David, advises his friend to flee. David goes to Nob, to a priest named Ahimelech. The priest is apprehensive at seeing David alone, and David tells him that he is on a secret mission for the king. He says that he is to meet some young men and that he needs provisions. The priest has only some bread from the altar, and David persuades him that it would not be an unholy act to take it. Doeg, the chief of Saul's herdsmen, is nearby and overhears them. David obtains Goliath's sword from Ahimelech and goes to Achish, the king of the Philistine city of Gath. The king suspects him, so David feigns madness. This ruse is of no avail, however, because Achish says that he has enough madmen around him already. Again David flees.

SAUL PURSUES DAVID

David goes to a cave in Adullum, where his family visits him. People in debt or in some other kind of distress collect around him until he has a retinue of four hundred men. He takes

141

his mother and father to stay with the king of Moab and, at the advice of the prophet Gad, returns to Judah.

Saul, hearing that David is at large, speaks sarcastically to his servants about their lack of loyalty to him. This provokes Doeg the Edomite to tell Saul that he has seen David with Ahimelech and that Ahimelech gave David provisions and the sword of Goliath. Saul summons Ahimelech and all his relatives and priests and berates them for helping David. He orders his servants to kill them all; when they refuse, he orders Doeg to do it. Doeg kills eighty-five priests and then kills everyone (including the animals) in the city of Nob. One of Ahimelech's sons, Abiathar, escapes and goes to David. When he tells him what has happened, David takes the blame upon himself.

In spite of the danger from Saul, David and his men deliver the city of Keilah from the Philistines. David and his six hundred men stay in the walled city until their consultation of Abiathar's sacred lots warns them that if they stay they will be trapped. They go to the wilderness of Ziph, where Jonathan joins them. The Ziphites tell Saul that they will deliver David to him, but just as Saul is closing in on David a messenger arrives with the news that the Philistines have launched an attack. Saul and his men withdraw to fight the Philistines.

Later Saul is told that David is in Engedi. He seeks him there, and on one occasion, when Saul goes into a cave to relieve himself, David has an opportunity to kill him but does not, because Saul is "the Lord's anointed." When Saul learns that David spared his life, he is repentant. He says that he knows that David will be king someday and asks David to agree not to kill all his descendants. Saul goes home, but David and his men return to their stronghold.

Samuel dies and is buried.

David sends men to Nabal in Carmel to ask for food. Nabal refuses, and David is angered. His men have for some time associated as friends with Nabal's sheepherders, and they have guarded his flocks and have not touched his property. David prepares to confront Nabal with force, but he is interrupted by Nabal's wife, Abigail, who has heard what has occurred and meets him with a large store of food. David is grateful that she has kept him from slaughtering Nabal and all his workers. When Abigail tells Nabal what she has done, the heart goes out of him and in ten days he is dead. Now Abigail becomes one of David's wives.

Chapter 26 relates another story of David sparing Saul's life. This time David and Abishai sneak into Saul's camp and steal his spear and water jar while the army is asleep. At a safe distance, David calls out and lets Saul know what happened. Although Saul blesses David and predicts that he will succeed in many things, David does not trust him.

DAVID AMONG THE PHILISTINES

David and his 600 men now go to King Achish in the Philistine city of Gath. Achish gives him the town of Ziklag, and from there David and his men make raids on non-Israelite towns, destroying everything in them so that Achish will not be able to find out what David has done.

Achish thinks that David has made himself an enemy of his own people by now, so he trusts him to fight on his side against Israel and makes David his bodyguard. The Philistines line up at Shunem, and the Israelites line up at Gilboa. When he sees the Philistine army, Saul loses his courage. He seeks out a medium—a woman at Endor—despite the fact that he himself has outlawed mediums and wizards in Israel. She brings up Samuel from the depths. Samuel shows no sympathy when Saul questions him.

Gustave Doré, "Saul Visits the Witch of Endor"

"Tomorrow," he says, "you and your sons shall be with me; the Lord will give the army of Israel also into the hand of the Philistines" (28:19). Saul falls to the ground partly from fear and partly from hunger. The woman insists that he and his men eat before they leave, and she kills a fatted calf and bakes unleavened bread for them.

As the Philistines assemble for battle, certain commanders question Achish about David. Although Achish assures them that David can be trusted, they will take no chances, so David and his men return to Ziklag. There they find that the Amalekites have raided and burned the city and have carried off everyone with them. His men are ready to stone David, but he inquires of Abiathar's ephod and is told by the Lord that he should pursue the Amalekites. Leaving 200 exhausted men at the brook Besor, David goes on with the remaining 400.

An Egyptian who has been left behind by the Amalekites leads David and his men to the enemy camp, and there in a battle that lasts for a night and a day they slaughter everyone except 400 men who escape on camels. David rescues his wives and everyone else who had been taken from Ziklag and takes all the spoil left by the enemy. When they meet the 200 men who were left behind, David shares the spoil with them against the wishes of some of those who had gone on to fight. When they arrive at Ziklag, David sends some of the spoil to the elders of Judah, to be distributed by them.

THE PHILISTINES DEFEAT THE ISRAELITES ON MOUNT GILBOA

The last chapter of 1 Samuel tells of the defeat of Saul's army on Mount Gilboa. The Philistines slay Saul's three sons, Jonathan, Abinadab, and Malchishua. Saul himself is wounded and asks his armor bearer to kill him. When his armor bearer refuses, Saul falls on his own sword. Then the armor bearer does the same. When the Israelities see that Saul's army is destroyed, they leave their cities and the Philistines move into them.

The Philistines come the next day and cut the heads off Saul and his sons and nail their bodies to the wall, but at night some men from Jabesh-gilead come and take the bodies down and burn them. Then they bury the bones under a tree in Jabesh.

DAVID SUCCEEDS SAUL AS KING

The Second Book of Samuel begins with a different account of the death of Saul, one in which a young Amalekite slays Saul at Saul's request and then brings Saul's crown and armlet to David.

144

David has the Amalekite killed by one of his soldiers, for he had "slain the Lord's anointed."

David's poetic genius is evident in the moving elegy over Saul and Jonathan: "Thy glory, O Israel, is slain upon thy high places!/How are the mighty fallen!" (2 Samuel 1:19).

With the Lord's approval, David goes up to Hebron, where he is anointed king over Judah (the southern part of the country). In the meantime, Ishbosheth, one of the sons of Saul, becomes king of Israel (the northern part of the country). War breaks out between the two kingdoms, with the northern army led by Saul's cousin, Abner, and the southern led by David's nephew, Joab. Joab's forces defeat those of Abner at Gibeon, but Asahel, one of Joab's brothers, is killed by Abner.

Six sons are born to David at Hebron, each by a different mother.

When Ishbosheth censures Abner for his relationship with Saul's concubine, Rizpah, Abner is annoyed at being treated as an outsider and vows to go over to the side of David. He makes arrangements to meet with David, and he and twenty of his men are given a feast at Hebron. Abner leaves with the understanding that he will bring all of Israel over to David. When Joab learns that Abner has visited David and has been allowed to leave, he is amazed, for he assumes that Abner came only to spy and to deceive David. Without David's knowledge, he sends some of his men to bring Abner back to Hebron, and when they return with Abner he kills him. (According to the narrator, he does so to avenge his brother Asahel, who had been killed by Abner.) David orders everyone to go into mourning, and he himself fasts the entire day when Abner is buried at Hebron. The people are convinced that David had nothing to do with Joab's deed.

Two of Ishbosheth's captains, Baanah and Rechab, steal into Ishbosheth's house and kill him as he lies resting. They bring the king's head to David, expecting gratitude from one who had suffered at the hands of Saul and his family. But David sets his young men upon them, and they are hanged beside a pool at Hebron.

All the tribes of Israel come to Hebron, and David makes a covenant with the elders. He is anointed king of Israel. Now he is the head of both nations—Israel of the north and Judah of the south—and will remain so for thirty-three years. He goes up to Jerusalem and conquers this last city remaining in the hands of the Canaanites. He calls it the city of David and makes it his capital.

DAVID'S ASCENDANCY OVER THE PHILISTINES

Hiram, king of Tyre, builds a house for David. Sons and daughters are born to David from his many wives and concubines.

David defeats the Philistines in two battles, and then with a force of thirty thousand brings back the ark. On the way, however, one of his men is killed when he puts out his hand to steady the ark when the oxen stumble. This frightens David into leaving the ark with a man named Obededom. When after three months it is learned that Obededom's household has been blessed, David takes the ark to Jerusalem with dancing and music. His wife Michal, the daughter of Saul, despises David for dancing scantily clad, and she lets him know how she feels. He replies that the Lord has chosen him over her father to be king of Israel and that he will "make merry before the Lord" (6:21) when it pleases him.

As king of all Israel, David defeats the Philistines, the Moabites, and the Syrians, and he makes the Edomites his servants. His chief of the army is Joab, his recorder is Jehoshaphat, and his priests are Zadok and Ahimelech; his secretary is Seraiah, and in charge of the mercenary army of Pelethites and Cherethites is Benaiah.

DAVID'S POLITICAL AND FAMILY PROBLEMS

David searches for anyone who is a member of Saul's family and learns from Ziba, a servant of the house of Saul, that Mephibosheth, a son of Jonathan, is the only living son. He is a man badly crippled in his feet. David gives Mephibosheth all the property that had belonged to Saul and orders that Ziba and his family serve Mephibosheth and till his land, although Mephibosheth will always eat at David's table in Jerusalem.

David sends some of his servants to Hanun, the new king of the Ammonites, whose father, Nahash, has just died. David means this as a gesture of consolation and friendship, but the Ammonite princes convince Hanun that it is a trick of David's to get spies into the country. Hanun humiliates David's men by having half of their beards shaved off and their garments cut off to the waist. When David learns of this, he sends an army under Joab that defeats both the Ammonites and the twenty thousand mercenary Syrian soldiers hired by them. The Syrians mass extra forces for a subsequent battle, but they are defeated by the army that David leads across the Jordan against them.

Later, while David's army is besieging the Ammonite city of Rabbah, David lies with Bathsheba, the wife of Uriah, one of his captains. When he learns that she is with child, he sees to it that her husband is slain in battle. This greatly displeases the Lord, who sends Nathan the prophet to David with a parable of a rich man who took the only lamb of a poor man to feed to a wayfarer. When David cries out that the rich man deserves to die, Nathan says, "You are the man," and then tells David that he will be punished for his behavior. There will be insurrection in his own house, and other men will lie openly with his wives. However, the Lord will not take David's life.

Soon David's son by Bathsheba is taken ill. David fasts and prays, but the child dies. Then he gets up and goes about his usual ways, telling his servants that there is no point in suffering anymore: The child is dead, and nothing can be done about it. He comforts Bathsheba and lies with her, and she bears him another son, whom they name Solomon.

The city of Rabbah of the Ammonites is about to fall, so Joab tells David to take it lest he, Joab, be given the credit. David takes the city, with much spoil, and enslaves the people in it.

Amnon, an older half-brother of Absalom, has an overwhelming desire to make love to his half sister, Tamar. (Tamar is Absalom's full sister.) Acting on a scheme devised by his good friend Jonadab, Amnon feigns illness and begs his father David to send Tamar to bake cakes for him. When she serves him, he forces her into bed against her protests; when he has finished with her, he hates her and casts her out. Now her brother Absalom hates Amnon for what he had done and bides his time for revenge. Two years later, during sheepshearing, he invites all his brothers to the festivities. Then when Amnon is drunk he has his servants kill him. The brothers flee and so does Absalom, evidently afraid that David will punish him.

Knowing that David grieves over the self-banishment of Absalom, Joab sends a woman to him with a parable that parallels David's treatment of Absalom (for David never communicates with his son or asks him to come to Jerusalem). As a result, Absalom is invited back, but he must live in a separate house. David refuses to see him, so Absalom tries to get Joab to take a message to the king. Joab does not respond until Absalom has his barley field set afire. Then he intercedes, and Absalom is invited to meet David. He bows to the king, and the king kisses him.

THE INSURRECTION OF ABSALOM

Now Absalom collects a band of fifty men to follow him, and he sets himself up in the gate and tells everyone that if he were king they would receive justice. "So Absalom stole the hearts of the men of Israel." Absalom continues to undermine David for four years, and then he goes to Hebron and sends throughout the kingdom messengers who at the proper moment will shout that Absalom is king at Hebron. Learning how strong the conspiracy has grown, David gives instructions to flee Jerusalem, and when he is told that his counselor Ahitophel has gone over to Absalom, he sends another of his counselors, Hushai the Archite, to give himself to Absalom in order to defeat the counsel of Ahitophel. Hushai arrives in Jerusalem just as Absalom is entering the city.

Meanwhile Ziba, Mephibosheth's servant, tells David that Mephibosheth is staying in Jerusalem in the hope that his father's kingdom will be restored to him. Another member of the house of Saul, named Shimei, curses David and the people who are with him. David does nothing to stop him, thinking that the Lord will reward him for being magnanimous.

Absalom seeks advice from both Ahitophel and Hushai, and Hushai's advice prevails. This wins some time for David, and David is not slow in using it. He immediately crosses the Jordan with all his people. Ahitophel, whose advice was rejected, goes home and hangs himself.

Absalom crosses the Jordan, and David organizes his forces with commanders over hundreds and thousands. He sends forth the army under three generals, who forbid David to go with them. He defers to them. They engage Absalom's army in the forest of Ephraim and slaughter twenty thousand men. As Absalom flees on a mule, he is caught by his abundant hair in an oak tree, where he dangles until Joab throws three darts into him. Ten of Joab's armorbearers finish him off, and they throw him into a pit in the forest.

When David hears of Absalom's death, he is so stricken with grief that Joab finally must go and tell him that if he does not come out to the people and resume his role as their king he will be deserted. David goes out and sits in the gate, and the people accept him. After replacing Joab as commander of the army with Amasa, who had been Absalom's commander, David prevails upon the elders of Judah to call him back. There is a division between the people of Israel and the people of Judah, however, because the people of Israel feel that Judah is trying to monopolize the king. The northerners withdraw from David and follow Sheba, the son of Bichri, while the men of Judah follow David to Jerusalem.

DAVID REORGANIZES THE KINGDOM

David decides to pursue Sheba, so he sends Amasa to rally the army. When Amasa delays, David appoints Abishai in his stead. Soon Joab is again in charge, and he kills Amasa when he next meets him. He besieges Sheba in the city of Abel, where a wise woman prevails upon him to spare the city in exchange for Sheba's head. Joab and his army return to Jerusalem.

And now, although David's kingdom is under his control again, he and his people suffer a famine for three years. David consults the Lord, who tells him that the bloodguilt brought upon the house of Saul because Saul put some Gibeonites to death must be expiated. When David asks the Gibeonites what he should do, they request that he give them seven young men from the house of Saul. He gives them, and they are hanged. The bodies lie exposed during the summer until David collects the bones of Saul and Jonathan and buries them with the bones of the seven young men. Thus the bloodguilt is expiated.

In subsequent wars with the Philistines David's men kill four giants descended from the Anakim in Gath.

Chapter 22 is a hymn of praise that was inserted by an Old Testament editor. It is a duplicate of Psalm 18 and praises the Lord for helping David against his enemies.

Another poem appears as the last words of David. He speaks of the everlasting covenant between his house and the Lord. The same chapter contains a list of heroes who fought on the side of David—"thirty-seven in all."

The last chapter of 2 Samuel is an account of David's ordering a census at the Lord's command and of the Lord's punishment of the people because David did so. (In 1 Chronicles 21:1 it is "Satan" who incites David to take the census.) After a pestilence of three days' duration, David is instructed by the prophet Gad to erect an altar on the threshing floor of Araunah the Jebusite. David buys the threshing floor and some oxen for fifty shekels of silver. Then he sacrifices the oxen and thus averts the plague.

SOLOMON SUCCEEDS DAVID

The first eleven chapters of 1 Kings tell of David's decline and death, of the succession of Solomon to the throne after his older brother Adonijah had proclaimed himself king, and of the reign of Solomon.

After Adonijah is put down, Solomon follows his father's orders and sees to it that Joab and Shimei are killed. He banishes the priest Abiathar and has Adonijah slain because he had the effrontery to ask for David's last concubine, Abishag, as his wife. With these four men taken care of, Solomon has firmly established his kingdom.

SOLOMON BECOMES A GREAT KING

Solomon makes an alliance with Egypt by marrying the Pharaoh's daughter. When in a dream the Lord asks Solomon what he would like to have, Solomon asks for an understanding mind. He gets that, and also riches and honor. The story of the two harlots who come to the king for a judgment about who should have the child that they each claim illustrates the wisdom for which Solomon became famous.

Solomon's high officials are named, as well as the twelve men who preside over the districts into which the kingdom is organized. "Solomon ruled over all the kingdoms from the Euphrates to the land of the Philistines and to the border of Egypt; they brought tribute and served Solomon all the days of his life" (1 Kings 4:21).

Solomon's wisdom is praised: He is credited with 3,000 proverbs and 1,005 songs. He had knowledge about trees, plants, beasts, birds, reptiles, and fish, and people came from everywhere to learn from him.

SOLOMON BUILDS THE TEMPLE AND A PALACE

Solomon hires Hiram, king of Tyre, to help him build a temple. He puts thirty thousand men into forced labor to help get the timber from Lebanon. Work on the temple begins in "the four hundred and eightieth year after the people of Israel came out of the land of Egypt, in the fourth year of Solomon's reign over Israel" (6:1), and in seven years it is finished.

Solomon also has a palace and administration buildings constructed, a task that takes thirteen years. Another Hiram from Tyre, not the king, is hired to do all the necessary bronze work, including the "molten sea." When all is completed, Solomon has the ark brought up and put into the inner sanctuary of the temple; he holds a dedication ceremony during which he makes a speech and says a long prayer. After this there is a great feast and sacrifice that lasts for seven days and consumes 22,000 oxen and 120,000 sheep.

SOLOMON'S FAME AND WEALTH INCREASE

The Lord responds to Solomon's prayer of consecration with the promise that he will support the dynasty as long as Solomon and his house keep the commandments and the statutes. If they turn aside and serve other gods, however, "Israel will become a proverb and a byword among all peoples."

When the temple and the palace are completed, Hiram, king of Tyre, seeks repayment for the 120 talents of gold that he had given to Solomon. He is not satisfied with the twenty cities in Galilee with which Solomon presents him.

Chapter 9 gives another account of the forced labor policy of Solomon. In Chapter 5, verse 13, we are told that "King Solomon raised a levy of forced labor out of all Israel; and the levy numbered thirty thousand men." In Chapter 9, however, it is said that he made slaves only of the non-Israelite people in the kingdom—

the descendants of the Amorites, Hittites, Perizzites, Hivites, and Jebusites.

Solomon builds a fleet of ships, which he and Hiram together use to bring gold from Ophir.

The Queen of Sheba comes from Arabia to "test Solomon with hard questions." She is more than satisfied by his answers. "Your wisdom and prosperity," she says, "surpass the report which I have heard" (10:7). She gives him gold, spices, and precious stones, and he gives her all that she desires and more (10:13).

With what his fleet of ships brings him and what is given him by wealthy visitors, Solomon becomes the richest king on earth. He develops a lucrative trade in horses and chariots, importing from Egypt and selling to the Hittites and the Syrians.

SOLOMON BETRAYS THE LORD; THE KINGDOM WILL BE DIVIDED

For all his blessings, Solomon does not keep the Lord's commandments and statutes. Influenced by his foreign wives, he sets up altars to foreign gods, and the Lord despairs of him. Out of deference to David, the Lord tells Solomon that he will not take the kingdom from him, but from his son, and (again because of David) he will allow Solomon's son to keep that part of the nation which is Judah.

Now enemies rise up against Solomon: Hadad the Edomite, Rezon, king of Damascus, and Jeroboam, an Ephraimite. Jeroboam has been advised by the prophet Ahijah that the Lord will take the ten tribes that constitute the northern kingdom, Israel, from the house of Solomon, leaving only Judah, which contains the Lord's city Jerusalem, in the hands of Solomon's son Rehoboam. On learning this, Solomon tries to kill Jeroboam, but Jeroboam escapes to Egypt, where he waits until he hears that Solomon is dead.

After a reign of forty years, Solomon is succeeded by his son Rehoboam, under whom the kingdom is divided, never to be reunited.

LITERARY QUALITIES

The Hebrew Iliad
WILLIAM G. POLLARD

It was in this exhilarating period of national achievement and pre-eminence during Solomon's reign that the first Hebrew written literature was produced. (The Song of Deborah, which is much older, had been preserved by oral transmission.) The authors of this literature were probably priests, since they were then virtually the only learned and literate persons in Israel. One of them who had been an intimate associate and ardent admirer of David in his later years set about writing a connected account of the memorable events that had given his people a new sense of greatness as a nation, and to delineate for them, in a vivid and remarkably unbiased portrayal, the leader whose great prowess, keen judgment, and unfailing good fortune had so decisively influenced the outcome of these events. Just who this author was we do not know, but if we suppose that he himself appeared among the characters mentioned in his narrative, the most likely person is Ahimaaz, the son of David's priest Zadok. . . .

In any event, whoever the author of the Hebrew *Iliad* may have been, he was certainly the true "Father of History." Without his realizing it, the epic story he recorded was the first example of the kind of writing which later ages were to designate as history, and it is moreover one of the finest pieces of prose literature that any age has produced. At precisely what point he began his history is difficult to determine. . . .

The first material that can be identified with reasonable certainty as part of the original epic is that given in the first three chapters of Ahimaaz' history. . . . This material comes from the present books of Judges and I Samuel and consists of stories concerning the beginnings of the struggle with the Philistines as current in tradition during the reign of Solomon. These stories are then followed by a collection of more or less legendary episodes from Saul's youth, his early successes against the Philistines and his later years dominated by an intense jealousy of David. The second half of the history is devoted to David's career after the death of Saul and is told in a way which clearly indicates that the author was an eyewitness and active participant in the events he describes. The history concludes with an account of the accession of David's son Solomon to the throne and the initial steps he took to make his crown secure against rival contenders.

The epic must have been immediately popular and must surely have stirred the souls of hearers privileged to listen to the magic of its prose. For many generations thereafter it was cherished and loved by the people of Israel, in whose national life it became a powerfully integrative, interpretive, and culturally unifying force. In this respect it performed a function . . . similar to that exercised later by Homer's *Iliad* in the life of the Hellenes. But there is one decisive element in the Hebrew epic that has no parallel in the literature of any other peoples. This is the implicitly recognized empowering and determining presence of Yahweh, the God of Israel, in every episode of the story. He is the unseen presence in every event, the source of power and energy for His people in every battle, the One who determines the outcome of every crisis in history, the inescapable Judge of all human actions. Yet for all the pre-eminent role of Yahweh in the narrative, there is nothing of the reflective or speculative element that the experience of the divine in later or more mature stages of culture normally elicits. Yahweh is nowhere in the epic the object of philosophic inquiry or even of pious or moralistic observations. Rather for both the author and his readers he is a living and genuine element in the common experience of all. This characteristic gives the narrative a refreshing directness and simplicity of style that is one of its most engaging qualities.

Here it may be well to pause to consider certain significant parallels and contrasts between some of the major themes in Ahimaaz' epic and Homer's *Iliad*. Both have to do with the stresses and uncertainties in the lives of their respective peoples arising out of a protracted and indecisive period of warfare with a rival contender of superior might and power: the conflict between the Achaeans and Trojans in one epic and between the Israelites and Philistines in the other. Both give expression to a sense of destiny in terms of the intimate involvement of the divine in human history through which the changes and chances of mortal life compound with the weaknesses, defeats, and inadequacies of a threatened people in such a way as to produce an amazing march to triumph. In both epics a central role is played by the god of the storm: Zeus in Homer, Yahweh in Ahimaaz. The march toward victory is in each initiated by a great military leader, Agamemnon in one and Saul in the other, who succeeds in uniting a diverse group of tribes into an effective military force. In each case bitter rivalry and jealousy develop in relation to a younger, more able leader beloved of the people for his daring exploits and commanding personality. Both Achilles and David are long in danger of their lives from the bitter anger of their kings, but in the end, when

153

all seems lost, both lead their followers to the outcome which providence seems to have destined from the first.

It is true that besides these broad resemblances in framework and theme there are equally striking dissimilarities in the details of the two epics. There is nothing in Ahimaaz to parallel the complex fabric of rivalry, jealousy, and scheming among the gods themselves which in Homer accounts for so much of the ambiguities and injustices of the human lot. In Ahimaaz the mystery of the divine will resides solely in Yahweh himself, and the ambiguities of fate and fortune are to be resolved, if at all, on the human rather than divine plane, in terms of sin and righteousness. On the whole, the more one delves into the details of the two narratives, the more one finds that the contrasts outweigh the similarities. In themselves the similarities would not of course justify conferring the title "The Hebrew Iliad" on Ahimaaz' epic. In the final analysis this choice of title must rest, not on internal parallels but, as we have already seen, on the parallel position that Ahimaaz occupies in the literary history of Israel and the parallel function his epic performed in the cultural history of his people.

INTERPRETATIONS

Saul, the Tragic King
DOROTHY F. ZELIGS

Saul, the first king of ancient Israel, is often described as a tragic figure. Classically, the essence of tragedy is a blind and futile struggle against one's destiny. Psychoanalytically, it can be understood as the struggle with unconscious conflicts. In this sense the word fittingly describes the subject of this study.

The personality of Saul is therefore of special interest, for this king of antiquity is clearly portrayed as suffering from an emotional malady, or, in the graphic terminology of the Bible, as being possessed by an *evil spirit*. The purpose of this study is to present a developmental picture of Saul's history and his patterns of behavior to see if there is a psychological consistency in the biblical material concerning him, and to discern, if possible, the specific nature of his conflicts.

SAUL, THE TRAGIC KING From Dorothy F. Zeligs, *Psychoanalysis and the Bible: A Study in Depth of Seven Leaders* (New York: Bloch Publishing Company, 1974), pp. 121–59. Reprinted by permission of the author.

The first monarch of ancient Israel appears upon the scene of Hebrew history in the unassuming role of a farmer's son, who together with a servant is engaged in looking for his father's strayed donkeys. The impression one gets from this situation is that Saul is still quite a young man and, as such, logically subject to parental guidance and control. The Bible, in fact, calls him *young and goodly*. Yet Saul at this time was already the father of a number of children, according to the more convincing of the two possible interpretations of available chronological data. His son Jonathan was evidently old enough to serve as a soldier of unusual courage and strategy only two years later (13:2).[1] Saul therefore must have been a man who had reached the prime of life when we first meet him on his quest for the lost donkeys.

The question that occurs is why Saul, the son of a prosperous farmer, should have been sent upon this rather menial errand. It is true that donkeys were valuable animals. Moreover, in those times even men of substance occupied themselves with the ordinary tasks of their day. But a duty such as this one would seem more suited to a younger man, like Jonathan. Nor is there any doubt whether Saul undertook this obligation of his own free will or was commissioned to do so by his father. The Bible says clearly that Saul was sent by his father upon this mission. Perhaps it is not without significance that Saul's introduction to history is in this role of carrying out a task given to him by his father, as we shall see.

As Saul and the servant wander farther and farther from home in their unsuccessful search, Saul becomes uneasy and says, "Come and let us return; lest my father leave caring for the asses, and becomes anxious concerning us."

The servant replies that they are now in the vicinity of the city where Samuel is residing and suggests that they consult him regarding the whereabouts of the lost animals. Saul's first reaction to this is that they do not have a present to bring the man of God. The servant says that he has a small silver coin which he will use for this purpose and the two proceed to the city gates.

In this brief introductory episode, we see Saul yielding twice to suggestions that come from others, first, his father, and then, the servant. We also see him expressing concern twice about the expectations of a father figure, first, that his father would be expecting them home, and second, that Samuel would expect a gift. It is interesting that the servant has a small silver coin with him but the son of the master does not, thus placing Saul in a position of dependency toward the servant. In fact, when he comments upon his father's anxiety about their absence, Saul puts the servant upon the same level as himself, using the pronoun *us*.

[1] All biblical quotations and references in this chapter, unless otherwise noted, are from First Samuel.

This first view of Saul also suggests a certain incongruity between his physical appearance and his demeanor. We are told that "there was not among the children of Israel a goodlier person than he; from his shoulders and upward he was higher than any of the people." Yet he gives the impression of being modest and unassuming to the point of timidity.

Samuel met the two men within the city gates as if he were expecting them. Without any preliminaries, Saul was invited to be the seer's guest at the sacrificial meal that was about to take place on the hilltop. He was assured that his father's donkeys had been found. Samuel then acclaimed him as the future king of Israel.

Saul was evidently completely unprepared psychologically for this *moment of destiny*. Again, there is an impression of the incongruous in the situation of this princely-looking man, engaged in looking for his father's donkeys, being met by Samuel and elevated at once to a place of high honor. It has a folktale atmosphere of a prince in disguise. But such a person must generally perform some act of unusual merit before the kingdom is bestowed upon him. In Saul's case, the prize was given first and the act of merit had to come later.

Samuel's own reasons for this choice are discussed in the previous chapter. Briefly, he wanted a man who could be a warrior-king but at the same time someone of a submissive and dependent nature, who would offer as little competition as possible to his own power. Perhaps he recognized these qualities at once in a person of Saul's position who was occupied in hunting for his father's lost donkeys.

After the communal feast, Saul was brought to Samuel's house to spend the night. The prophet talked with his guest as they sat upon the house-top in the cool of the evening. Nothing is said of the content of this talk but we can assume that in the course of it, the relationship between the two was more firmly established. Saul must have known of Samuel before but evidently had not met the spiritual leader of Israel in person, for when they first saw each other, Saul did not recognize him.

The next day at sunrise Samuel called Saul, who slept in the guest-chamber on the roof, and accompanied him to the edge of the city. The servant was sent ahead and Samuel secretly anointed Saul king of Israel, pouring a vial of oil over his head and kissing him. Samuel then told Saul of several episodes that would take place on his way home, thus demonstrating his clairvoyant powers.

As Samuel predicted, Saul met a band of prophets coming down from the hill, playing upon their musical instruments and chanting their prophecies. Then "the spirit of the Lord came mightily upon him and he prophesied among them." Saul thus identified himself with the followers of Samuel. That this role was a completely new one for him is made clear by the reaction of the people, who said to one another, "What is this that is come unto the son of Kish? Is Saul also among the prophets?" It seems clear that Saul became a changed man during the period of less than a day that he spent with Samuel. We are, in fact, told that after Saul's anointment by the priest, "God gave him another heart."

What information, if any, does the Bible give regarding Saul's parentage? His father, Kish, is described as a "mighty man of valour." In biblical parlance, this may indicate social prestige rather than physical prowess. Kish was a wealthy farmer and probably regarded as a pillar of society. Except for the one descriptive phrase, which occurs at the very beginning of Saul's history, little more is known about Kish. There is no reference to Saul's mother, not even her name being mentioned.

When Saul returned home, he evidently did not reveal his secret anointment to anyone. Of his public selection as king, the Bible gives two varying accounts. Some biblical critics attribute these seemingly contradictory versions to the work of different editors. However, the traditional point of view that both events occurred as described does not seem to lack either realistic or psychological validity.

In the first account, Samuel calls a national assembly for the purpose of selecting a king. But before the actual choice is made, he expresses his displeasure for the second time at their request for a ruler, saying that this amounted to a rejection of God himself. This was hardly an auspicious way in which to present a future king, and indicates Samuel's reluctance to carry out the will of the people. It presages his ambivalence to the person who is to fill the role. As for the new ruler himself, he was being invited to enter upon his kingdom with feelings of guilt, as a representative of something *bad* that the people had asked of God.

The method that was used to select a king was the casting of lots. The choice fell upon Saul but when they looked for him, he could not be found. With God's help they find him hiding among the baggage. This baggage probably consisted of the saddles and saddlebags left at one part of the assembly grounds by those who had journeyed to the meeting. Saul evidently found himself unable to face this sudden publicity and had sought refuge there. He was brought forth from his hiding-place and received by the people, who shouted, "Long live the king." We are told, however, that "certain base fellows said: 'How shall this man save us?' And they despised him, and brought him no present. But he was as one that held his peace (10:27)."

Perhaps it is not too surprising that Saul was overwhelmed when called upon to take his place as king. Being anointed secretly by Samuel was one thing. Standing up before all the people as their king was another matter, particularly after the doubtful approval of such a figure by the priestly leader himself. Samuel's introduction of Saul was not characterized by effusiveness. He said simply, "See ye whom the

Lord hath chosen that there is none like him among all the people?" He was referring to the fact that Saul stood head and shoulders higher than any of the others. This, then, was his major claim to the kingship, a claim which the spiritual head of Israel found it easiest to accept. Saul returned to his father's farm and continued to live as he had before, except that he now had a small group of retainers with him.

What must have been Saul's thoughts and fantasies as he worked quietly on the farm? No doubt he was wondering when and how his first call to duty would come and if he would be able to meet the challenge. His title to the kingship could have no real meaning until he had proved himself. Saul thus had an opportunity to prepare in fantasy for what might lie before him.

When the call came, it was indeed a dramatic and urgent one. Kinsmen from the city of Jabesh-Gilead, east of the Jordan, were besieged by the Ammonites, a neighboring people. The imperiled city tried to make terms with the leader, Nabash, but he agreed to do so only on the condition that the right eye of every inhabitant of the city be put out, so that it might be a "reproach upon all Israel." The elders of the city asked for seven days respite so that they might send for help throughout the borders of Israel. Nabash agreed, evidently convinced that such assistance would not be forthcoming.

This message was not even brought directly to Saul, so little was he as yet regarded in the role of leader. But as he was guiding the oxen out of the field after the day's plowing, Saul heard the loud weeping of those who had just received the news. When he learned about the terms of Nabash, we are told that

. . . his anger was greatly kindled. And he took his yoke of oxen, and cut them in pieces, and sent them throughout all the borders of Israel by the hand of messengers, saying, "Whosoever cometh not forth after Saul and after Samuel, so shall it be done unto his oxen." And the dread of the Lord fell on the people and they came out as one man.

(11:6–7)

Saul and his army completely routed the Ammonites and saved the people of Jabesh-Gilead. The new ruler had proved his worth as a warrior-king. This victory was the first important move on the part of the Hebrew tribes in this period of history to test their strength, and it stimulated them to the task of regaining the freedom they had lost to the oppressive Philistines, their most powerful foe.

What aspects of Saul's personality does this quick and dramatic response reveal? The man who hid shyly behind the baggage when he was elected king, now becomes a leader of men. He arouses his people to action on behalf of a distant city at a time when lethargy and discouragement tended to separate the tribes from one another. The very boldness of his gesture in sacrificing a valuable pair of oxen, and the imperative quality of his command must have stimulated a responsive boldness in his followers. Here was a man who must be in deadly earnest about his mission. Such a person could be trusted as a leader. This factor, together with the brutal nature of the threat which Nabash had employed, prompted the Hebrews to unprecedented action. It is noteworthy that the intensity of Saul's response to the challenge is in sharp contrast to the modesty and self-effacement with which he had been living since his election.

One wonders why Saul chose the killing of the oxen as a method of stirring up the people. Evidently he was a man of impulsive behavior. The oxen were close at hand when the message for help reached him. Moreover, one reason the people were indifferent to calls from other tribes was that they did not wish to leave their farm work undone while they went off to war. Saul had to show them they could not plow their fields in peace while their kinsmen were in danger. The act was also expressive of his own readiness to give up the life of the farmer for that of the soldier-king.

We may detect further meanings in this symbolic gesture. The oxen, which actually belonged to Kish, may have represented an extension of the father himself. In killing the oxen, Saul might have acted out the conquest of the father who kept him tied to the plow. In addition, these animals may have represented an aspect of Saul's own personality. Oxen are submissive, castrated males who plow the soil in dull routine. By slaying them, Saul may have been overcoming the submissive element in his own personality and rebelling triumphantly against the father, with whom his relationship must have been an ambivalent one. Saul could free himself from the control of Kish, however, only under the influence of a more powerful parental figure, that of Samuel.

After the successful display of his leadership, Saul is publicly anointed king by Samuel. In his earlier election there was no ceremony of anointment. This latter occasion could be understood as the inauguration, the official beginning of his rule. As described in the study about Samuel, this event was used largely by the priest to concentrate attention upon himself and to demonstrate the power he still exercised. He again reproached the people for their wickedness in asking for a king. Not a word of praise or encouragement is extended to Saul from the man who had chosen him. He is exhorted to fear the Lord and to obey his commandments.

The people however express their loyalty to Saul and threaten with death those who had questioned his rule. Saul intercedes for them and the occasion closes on a note of general amicability.

After a period of only two years came the inevitable split between Samuel and Saul. It occurred when Saul intruded into an area which Samuel considered his own—the religious leadership.

Israel was now engaged in a more organized effort, under the leadership of Saul, to defeat the Philistines. The army was encamped at Gilgal, awaiting Samuel's arrival, so that he might perform a sacrifice before the men went into battle. Saul waited the seven days requested by the prophet but the latter did not appear.

In the meantime, the military situation was rapidly deteriorating. Saul's men, frightened by the large hordes of the enemy that were massing against them, were deserting. Finally, on the seventh day, the distraught and impatient king decided to perform the sacrifice himself. No sooner had he completed this act than Samuel arrived. Saul's excuses were in vain. The king was sternly rebuked for his disobedience and told that his kingdom would be taken from him. God would find another to fill his place.

Biblical commentary tends toward the explanation that it was not in the actual performance of the religious ritual that Saul erred, but in the fact that he had failed in a test situation by not obeying Samuel. While it was true that laymen could perform sacrifices themselves, it was customary to have a priest do so when a whole community was involved. This was one of Samuel's chief duties on his circuit tours. On this particular occasion, when the divided powers between church and state were being put to the first test, it must have been of special importance to Samuel that he himself should perform the sacrifice before that important body, the army. He could ill tolerate Saul's usurpation on this occasion. Saul had not only been disobedient but had shown a lack of faith in the man of God, whose prophetic powers supposedly should have been a guiding influence in the military action. Saul thus put his own judgment above that of the leading priest and prophet of Israel. He was again defying the father.

After Saul's unhappy experience with Samuel, the very next military undertaking is initiated by Jonathan, his son, in a spectacular fashion. He and his armour-bearer climb the heights of a rocky plateau at Michmas, where the Philistines are encamped, and boldly attack, killing about twenty men, according to the biblical account. This fierce assault within a small area of land upon the edge of the precipice may have started a landslide, for we are told that an earthquake followed, adding to the terror and confusion among the Philistines. Across the valley, the watchmen of Saul on the heights of Gibeah, see the tumult in the ranks of the enemy. Saul learns that Jonathan and his armour-bearer are not in the camp and makes the correct surmise about what is going on. He and his army hastily move into the battle area and Israel wins a great victory that day.

It is during the course of this long and strenuous day of fighting that Saul again behaves in a rash and impulsive fashion. He imposes a vow upon the people, forbidding them to eat any food until evening as a form of sacrifice to insure God's favor in the outcome of the battle. Jonathan does not hear his father's injunction and when the army enters a forest and the youth sees some honey upon the ground, he extends his rod and lifts some of the honey to his mouth. One of the men then tells him of the ban his father had placed upon eating that day.

Jonathan's reaction was not one of horror or regret although the breaking of the ban carried a curse with it. He expressed a criticism of his father for increasing the hardships which the army had to endure, pointing out that the men would have had more strength with which to win a greater victory had they been permitted to take nourishment.

In the evening, when the battle had been won, the people were faint with hunger. They seized eagerly upon the spoils, slaying the cattle upon the ground without following the prescribed ritual of ridding the animals of their blood. Again Saul shows his concern for religious law and directs the people to slaughter the animals upon a rock. This is the second time within one day that Saul imposes regulations of a religious nature upon the people. Then he proceeds to build an altar to God. The Bible makes a point of stating that it was the first altar Saul built to the Lord.

The king must have been as a driven man that day. He was not content with the victory and with building an altar. He suggested that the battle be continued that night and the fighting go on until morning so that not a man of the enemy would be left. Again the men agree obediently to his wishes, saying, "Do whatsoever seemeth good unto thee." But a priest interposes, suggesting that they consult God first. We are told that God did not respond to Saul's prayer that day. The conclusion the king drew from this was that someone had sinned and God was displeased. Saul then called the chiefs together and questioned them regarding the conduct of their men, declaring that even if it were his own son who was at fault, he would have to die. We are told that "there was not a man among all the people that answered him."

Why should Saul have named Jonathan as the possible sinner? We have no indication that he knew anything about the latter's innocent violation of the ban earlier that day. Was the king only trying to prove to his men that even if someone dear to him was involved, he would still carry out his duty to God as he saw it?

There is something in the way Saul expresses himself that indicates real hostility when he declares, ". . . though it (the sin) be in Jonathan my son, he shall surely die (14:39)." When the chiefs do not reply to his questioning, Saul's next move hardly seems open to any other interpretation than that of deadly anger against his son. Instead of calling for a general casting of lots to discover the culprit, as was customary, Saul asks that all the men of Israel be on one side while he and Jonathan are on the other side, with the choice to be made between these two sides. The father here clearly and unequivocally accuses the son and demands his punishment even before the casting of the lots takes place. We have the impression that Jonathan's sin was committed even before he violated the ban; that the more recent violation was only being used as a substitute for a greater sin of which he had been guilty.

The lots are cast and Jonathan is revealed as the wrong-doer. Saul asks him what he has done and the youth replies that he tasted a little honey. He makes no excuses and asks for no mercy, saying only, "Here I am; I will die." Saul was evidently ready to carry out the punishment, for he repeats his earlier declaration, saying ". . . thou shalt surely die, Jonathan." But the people intervene and save the hero of the day.

On what basis did the people dare to contradict the wishes of their king? All that day they had obediently followed his rather arbitrary orders, saying only, "Do what seemeth good unto thee." But now they act vigorously against his judgment. Their reasoning is given in their answer to Saul, when they declare, "Shall Jonathan die, who hath wrought this great salvation in Israel? Far from it; as the Lord liveth, there shall not one hair of his head fall to the ground; for he hath wrought with God this day (14:45)."

This was indeed the very reason Saul must have felt the need to punish Jonathan. Let us recall the earlier events of the day. Jonathan suddenly takes the initiative from his father by secretly embarking on a military exploit of his own, thus providing the stimulus for a victory that is decisive for the Hebrews.

What must have been Saul's feelings as he learns of the excitement in the Philistine camp and then finds out that Jonathan had departed from Gibeah! His son had acted without consulting him. Jonathan had stolen the show and made himself the hero of the day. Coming as this did, after Saul's rejection by Samuel at Gilgal, the king's vulnerability to being displaced must have been considerably increased.

While the biblical account says nothing of Saul's reaction to all this, his behavior during that entire day can be seen as a response to feelings of hurt, anger, and guilt. The vow of fasting which he imposed upon the army may have represented not only a way of propitiating God but also unconsciously, of punishing the people for accepting Jonathan as a hero. Actually, fasting upon a day of battle was not a customary procedure.

Some may wonder if Saul expressed willingness to sacrifice Jonathan with the hope that the people would intervene, as they actually did, and thus absolve him from this painful duty. But there is nothing in the account to justify such an interpretation. On the contrary, Saul's whole demeanor that day was one of a man possessed. His need for a further outlet of his aggressive energies is indicated by his wish to prolong the battle during the night. His expressed desire not to leave one man alive may have represented an effort to displace his hostility from Jonathan to the enemy. . . .

One gets the impression that Saul is behaving toward Jonathan as Samuel had earlier behaved toward the king himself. Just as the priest had punished Saul for taking the initiative at Gilgal, rejecting the king in the name of God, so Saul was ready to do with Jonathan. His religious fervor is also expressed by acting as a father-priest toward the people. It is possible that Samuel's rejectio1 of him at Gilgal was followed by a period of depression during which he displayed the inactivity manifested at Gibeah. His increased religious zeal and his antagonism toward Jonathan, with whom he must also have identified as the *bad son*, is understandable psychoanalytically. Having lost Samuel as a "good object," he identified with him instead and became a *Samuel* to the projected image of himself in Jonathan.

However, Saul allows himself to be restrained by the people. He does not act out his aggressive impulses and we have no basis for believing that he would have done so under any circumstances. We know how wide is the gap between speech and action. His anger may have dissipated itself in the little scene of the casting of lots which he caused to be enacted, and the episode may have ended as he basically wanted it to.

It is interesting that he gave up his plan to pursue the Philistines further that night. He submits to the will of God, as revealed by the priest, as he had submitted to the will of the people. Thus Saul was able to overcome his impulse of murderous rage and allow his positive feelings for Jonathan and the more normal aspects of his superego to control his behavior.

After the successful battle at Michmas, Saul threw himself with great energy into continuous warfare. We are told that ". . . he fought against all his enemies, on every side, against Moab, and against the children of Ammon, and against Edom, and against the kings of Zobah, and against the Philistines; and whithersoever he turned himself, he put them to the worse. And he did valiantly, and smote the Amalekites, and delivered Israel out of the hands of them that spoiled them (14:47–48)."

One might detect in this energetic and continuous warfare an effort on the part of Saul to externalize his own conflict and to ward off his depression by expressing his hostility in socially approved ways. He may also have learned the danger of inertia, for it allowed others to take over the leadership.

After this period of zealous war-making, Saul's second clash with Samuel occurs and this experience is evidently another turning point in his life. Saul again disobeys an injunction of the head priest and is again rejected by Samuel.

Higher Criticism * theorizes that actually only one such incident took place and that the two accounts are from different sources, giving

---

* Literary-historical study of the Bible.—Ed.

the impression of two separate incidents. For our purpose, however, all of the material has equal psychological validity and we will accept the biblical account as presented.

Samuel commands Saul to make war upon the Amalekites, the most ruthless foes of Israel, who almost wiped out the Israelite tribes in the desert of Sinai when they were fleeing from slavery in Egypt. Saul is adjured to carry out the dreaded *herem* against these people. This meant that every living thing, men, women, children, and animals, were to be utterly destroyed as an offering to God. This primitive procedure was not the usual method of warfare but was performed in certain instances by all the peoples of that area in those times. Scholarly opinion differs about the degree to which the Israelites carried out the *herem* in their conquest of the Canaanites.

We will not enter here into the question of what prompted Samuel to impose such a duty upon Saul on that particular occasion. It is our purpose, rather, to see what its consequences were for the king. Saul first took the precaution of warning the friendly tribe of Kenites, who lived among the Amalekites, to depart from them, in order not to share the same fate. Then the Hebrews made war upon their foes, winning a decisive victory. However, Saul and his men spared the life of Agag, the king, and saved the best of the sheep and oxen.

Samuel learned of Saul's disobedience and, greatly perturbed, set out to confront the king. Saul must indeed have been very fearful of the consequences of his act. He meets Samuel at a short distance from the camp and attempts to beguile him with the greeting, "Blessed be thou of the Lord; I have performed the commandment of the Lord."

Samuel answers sternly, "What meaneth then this bleating of the sheep in mine ears, and the lowing of the oxen which I hear?"

Saul tries to exonerate himself, saying that it was the people who took the animals as spoils for the purpose of sacrificing them to God. Such intent, incidentally, was not indicated earlier when the action took place. Samuel thunders in reply, "Behold, to obey is better than to sacrifice; and to hearken than the fat of rams. For rebellion is as the sin of witchcraft, and stubbornness is as idolatry and teraphim."

It is interesting that Samuel puts the sin of rebellion and stubbornness in the same category as witchcraft and idolatry. To rebel against Samuel was to show a lack of faith in the God he represented. Such an attitude was equivalent to belief in magic and false gods.

Saul then confesses that he has sinned and admits that it was because he feared the people that he followed their wishes. Samuel must have understood well Saul's low sense of self-esteem, for in his denunciation of the king he cried out, "Though thou be little in thine own sight, art thou not head of the tribes of Israel?" Saul pleads for Samuel's pardon but the priest sternly repudiates him saying, "Because thou hast rejected the word of the Lord, He hath also rejected thee from being king."

As Samuel turns to go away, Saul seizes the priest's robe as if to detain him. It must have been a desperate gesture for it was strong enough actually to tear the garment, or perhaps a decorative strip of cloth hanging from the waist. Another interpretation of the unclear text is that it was Samuel who seized hold of Saul's robe and tore it, in order to express symbolically what he then said to Saul, "The Lord hath rent the kingdom of Israel from thee this day, and hath given it to a neighbor of thine, that is better than thou."

This rending of the garment can be seen as a symbolic castration. Perhaps the very ambiguity of whose garment was torn points to a mutual castration. Saul had reduced Samuel to impotence by disobeying him, and the priest, in turn, punished the king by rending the kingdom from him.

The distraught ruler pleads with Samuel to return with him to the camp and perform the sacrifice so that the king of Israel might save face. Samuel finally yields to this plea. Afterwards, the priest commands that Agag be brought before him. Then, in the sight of all the soldiers, Samuel himself hews Agag to death with his sword.

One wonders if Agag served here as the image of the disobedient king of Israel himself, whom the angry priest thus violently destroyed. Samuel then returns to his home in Ramah. He never meets Saul face to face again. . . .

According to some biblical commentators, there are two accounts in the Bible of the first meeting between Saul and David. However, as heretofore, we shall follow the sequence of events as they occur in the text and try to see their psychological significance.

Saul's first encounter with David takes place when the king's retainers suggest that someone be found who could play upon the harp and thus soothe the trouble spirits of the king. David is selected for this purpose. We are told that when the youth stood before Saul, the king loved him greatly and made David his armour-bearer. Thereafter, whenever Saul was troubled by his *evil spirit* the young man played for him and the king found relief.

David is brought before the king in a new role when the youth offers to fight the giant Philistine, Goliath, who has tauntingly challenged the Hebrews as the opposing armies faced each other on opposite hills across a valley. Saul tries to clothe David with his own suit of armour, probably the only one of its kind in the Hebrew camp. But David finds that he is hampered by this apparel and takes it off, explaining that he is not accustomed to it. Then, as the well-known story relates, David selects five smooth stones out of the brook, puts them in his shepherd's bag, and with his sling in his hand, goes out to meet Goliath. David slays the contemptuous challenger of the Hebrews by hurling a stone into the giant's forehead.

It is after this exploit that the king seems not to know David and asks the captain of his host,

> "Abner, whose son is this youth?" And Abner said: "As thy soul liveth, O king, I cannot tell." And the king said: "Inquire thou whose son the stripling is." And as David returned from the slaughter of the Philistine, Abner took him and brought him before Saul with the head of the Philistine in his hand. And Saul said to him: "Whose son art thou, thou young man?" And David answered: "I am the son of thy servant Jesse the Bethlemite."
>
> (17:55–58)

Some commentators think that the king's question refers to David's lineage rather than to the identity of the youth himself. The fact that David answers by describing himself as the son of Jesse without even giving his own first name seems to confirm this interpretation. He assumes that the king already knows him from his earlier role. Why however should Saul suddenly be interested in David's lineage if he has met the youth before? This wish to know more about him is understandable. David is suddenly a hero. The memory of another occasion when a youth suddenly became popular in the eyes of the people must have recurred to the king. This time it is not Jonathan, the son of Saul, who has thus displaced him. Whose son, then, is this young man?

It is significant of the great change in Saul that he did not himself accept the scornful challenge of Goliath. Where now was the spirit of the man who had impetuously carved up his pair of oxen and impelled the people to follow him all the way across the Jordan to save their brethren? Where was the zealous warrior who had defeated Israel's enemies on all sides?

It is possible that Goliath may have represented more than a challenge to physical combat as far as Saul was concerned. The taunting giant may have appeared to the sick king as the very embodiment of the sadistic, destroying father, the evil spirit which tormented him. Had Saul been able to externalize his conflict at this time, had he gone out to meet Goliath and conquered him, the king might have regained his emotional health. But this he evidently was not able to do. The man who felt rejected and abandoned by God, the *Good Father*, and who could not overcome the introjected *bad father*, was not able to meet the terrifying monster in an actual contest.

All we are told about Saul's reaction to David immediately after the latter's victory is that "he would let him go no more to his father's house." This was in line with Saul's policy stated at the very beginning of his reign, that ". . . when Saul saw any mighty man or any valiant man, he took him."

In the first account of how Saul and David meet, however, when the youth stands before him as a minstrel, Saul's reaction is expressed with much more warmth, for we are told that "Saul loved him greatly." His affection was for the skilful player on the harp, but for the hero who slays Goliath, there is only the statement that implies further need for his services.

As David goes on to greater exploits, he becomes increasingly popular among the people. Then there occurs the famous incident when the army is marching home from a victorious battle and the women come out to greet the returning heroes with song and dance. And they chant, "Saul hath slain his thousands, and David his ten thousands." This becomes a turning point in the relationship between Saul and David. We are told that "Saul was very wroth, and this saying displeased him. And Saul said, 'All he lacketh is the kingdom!' And Saul eyed David from that day and forward." This is an apt description of a paranoid reaction, expressing Saul's jealousy, suspicion, and rage.

The very next morning after this incident Saul was again suffering from an onset of his *evil spirit,* and "he raved in the midst of the house." This is the first time that behavior of this type is ascribed to him. The sequence of events is clearly delineated. Saul was hurt by the greater acclaim shown to David by the women. This led to a depression and to *raving,* aggression expressed on an uncontrolled verbal, or oral, level.

The secondary role given to Saul by the women of Israel must have been experienced as a rejection by the mother. This trauma would be especially painful after Saul's repudiation by Samuel, the father-priest. . . .

David's brilliant achievements in war must already have marked him in Saul's eyes as the potential successor to the throne, the *unknown neighbor* of whom Samuel had spoken. Perhaps he recognized in David's bearing the confidence of a man who has been divinely appointed to a mission, one who had a silent pact with Destiny, such as Saul himself had known. He and David would thus share a relationship with Samuel, an unspoken common experience which may have been understood by both of them on a level of nonverbal communication. . . .

Saul's situation at this time was indeed a pitiable one. In reality, he had proven himself a successful soldier-king, accomplishing the purpose for which he had been chosen. As far as the people knew, Saul was the only elected and anointed king of Israel. There is no indication that they were thinking in terms of a successor. And if they were, then Jonathan, the brave and popular young warrior, would be the logical heir to the throne. The shepherd youth's anointment by Samuel was evidently not known to the people. Nor did David in any way contrive against Saul.

David is now an outlaw in the wild terrain of the southern Judean hills. Many followers join him there, especially those who had cause for discontent in the social system of that day.

The king is driven by his obsessive zeal into this remote territory to seek out David for the purpose of taking his life. Several dramatic events are recorded in which the situation is reversed. For it is Saul who inadvertently falls into the hands of David but the king is spared by the very person whose life he seeks. In the first episode, Saul enters a cave for a period of respite. It happens that David and his men are sitting in the deep interior of the same cave. David comes up to the unsuspecting king and cuts off a piece of his robe with a sword. He is then filled with remorse at having performed this indignity against the Lord's anointed, and forbids his men to harm him.

When Saul goes on his way, David follows and calls after him, holding up the fragment of robe. He points out that Saul's life was in the hands of the man he sought to kill. David then makes a moving plea to the king to stop pursuing him. Saul is overcome with emotion and weeps aloud, admitting that David has returned good for evil. He now acknowledges his belief that David will surely inherit the kingdom.

But in spite of Saul's apparent change of heart, David knew better than to take the word of his ambivalent king at its face value. Saul returns home and David remains in his mountain stronghold.

During these events Samuel dies. Some time evidently passes before the old obsession takes hold of Saul again. It is probably stimulated when some men of southern Judea report to the king that David is hiding in their home territory. Saul resumes the chase. But it is David who invades the camp of the pursuing party at night and comes upon the figure of the sleeping king. He removes Saul's sword and the cruse of water at his side. Then he withdraws to a nearby hill and shouts loudly to Abner, captain of the guard, taunting him for not keeping better watch over the king. He holds up his trophies to prove that the king's life had been in his hands. Again David movingly pleads that he has done no evil yet he had been driven out and hunted and not permitted to live among his own people. According to David's complaint, leaving the land of Israel also meant being driven away from the presence of the Lord, as if Saul were saying to him, "Go, serve other gods."

Once more Saul weeps and admits his wrongdoing, crying out, "I have sinned; return, my son David; for I will no more do thee harm, because my life was precious in thine eyes this day; behold, I have played the fool and erred exceedingly (26:19–21)."

But David knows that he will never be safe in the presence of the emotionally unstable king and therefore decides to seek refuge in the territory of the enemy. He secures political asylum from Achish, Philistine king of the city of Gath, and lives in the southern city of Ziglak.

After this, Saul's pursuit of David ends. Realistically, Saul could have followed David into Philistine territory, especially since the fugitive was in a city set apart for him and his followers. The target was clear and defined. It is doubtful whether Achish would have gone to the measure of supporting David in a war against Saul.

Why, then, did the king of Israel abandon his quarry at this point? David must have guessed correctly that only by leaving the land and the people of Israel would he have any real rest from the mad pursuit of Saul. Actually, Ziglak was no farther away geographically than other areas of southern Judea which David had frequented. On an unconscious level, however, by quitting the homeland, David was giving up not only the realities of his land and his people, but the symbolic values for which they stood, the mother and sons for whose love he was a rival. He was also leaving *the presence of the Lord,* and therefore was no longer a threatening competitor to Saul for God's favor.

No doubt, also, the incidents in which David spared Saul's life must have had a profound effect upon the king. David had proven his moral superiority over Saul, who must have been overwhelmed anew by his guilt feelings. Moreover, Saul may have experienced what David did to him on both occasions as partial castrations, warnings of what might happen.

The cutting of the king's robe in the first episode and the removal of his sword and cruse of water in the second, have symbolic significance. The first incident may also have re-activated the earlier experience with Samuel, when the rending of a garment, too, was involved.

The last event in the troubled life of Saul is the dramatic episode that ends in his death. The Philistines are gathered for an all-out attack against the Israelites. When Saul beholds the mighty host of the enemy he is greatly afraid. This is a different Saul from the one who had waged war with such zealous fury.

It seems odd that the account of this battle is prefaced by the statement that Samuel was dead and all Israel lamented him. We had been told earlier about Samuel's death. What, then, was the meaning of this somewhat redundant statement at this point? Psychologically, it might indicate that Saul felt Samuel's absence and abandonment with particular intensity at this crucial moment. This interpretation gains emphasis from the statement that immediately follows, which explains that the king had forbidden the practice of necromancy, the calling up of ghosts or familiar spirits. When Saul was filled with fear and trembling at the sight of the enemy, he tried to inquire of God regarding the outcome of the battle. But God failed to reveal himself to the terrified king. Saul then makes his famous visit to the woman at Endor who, according to the story, brings up the spirit of Samuel for him.

Saul must have had a strong intuitive feeling of what his fate would be in the coming battle and was making a last desperate effort to get a reprieve from the main source of authority in his life—Samuel. He thus refused to accept the finality of Samuel's death, and in spite of his own edict against necromancy, uses this method in his hour of need.

The consequences are inevitable. The spirit of Samuel sternly reproaches him, saying, "Why hast thou disquieted me, to bring me up?" He then prophesies the defeat of Israel and the death in battle of Saul and his sons. Saul falls in a faint upon the floor of the hut. He is restored by the ministrations of the woman who, in a touching scene of motherly concern, kills her fatted calf and bakes bread so that she may feed the king, who has not eaten all that day.

Thus Saul's effort to win forgiveness from the introjected father, externalized in the spirit of Samuel, fails. Actually, Saul fails to forgive himself. His outward channel of aggression in the pursuit of David being closed, Saul yields to his depression. His death on Mt. Gilboa is literally a suicide. The Israelites are overwhelmingly defeated and Saul is relentlessly pursued by enemy archers. We are told that "he was in great anguish by reason of the archers." This anguish must have been mental for there is no statement to the effect that he had actually been wounded. The pursuing archers may have represented vividly the furious father. Saul asks his armour-bearer to kill him, pleading as an excuse that the enemy would do so and then expose him to humiliation. The armour-bearer refuses and Saul falls upon his own sword.

Three of Saul's sons are slain in the battle, Jonathan among them. He is finally united with his father in death. Perhaps his longing for the father, together with his sense of guilt, motivated this conclusion.

The Philistines do as Saul feared. They behead the king and hang his body and those of his sons on the city wall of Bethshan, a half-Canaanite town that had probably quickly surrendered to the Philistines. When news of this reaches the city of Jabesh-Gilead, the men of that town make a midnight march to Bethshan, take down the bodies of Saul and his sons, and bury them with honor in their own land. Thus the people who had been the first to be delivered by Saul in the early days of his rule were the ones who rescued his body from the mockery of his enemies.

Saul had gone into the battle of Mt. Gilboa fully convinced of its outcome. In this last gesture, he did not try to flee from fate. The troubled king of Israel, after a long struggle, submitted to his tragic destiny.

Let us now try to summarize briefly the picture Saul presents in terms of his personality structure and pathology. Saul gives the impression of having been a rather lonely person, suffering from feelings of isolation and withdrawal. There is no indication that he had a particularly close relationship with anyone although he not only had a wife but also a concubine, Rizpah. His personal life with them is never mentioned. Two of the children most involved in his history, Jonathan and Michal, definitely take sides with David, against their father.

Although the people give evidence of loyalty and obedience to Saul for the most part, there is no indication of a strong emotional attachment to him. On several occasions they differ with him and show preference for Jonathan and David. We have seen, too, that Saul feared the people, so his feelings toward them must have been ambivalent. He seemed to inspire neither great friendship nor great emnity. Even in the case of David, the object of so much hostility, little is told of the younger man's real feelings toward Saul. He respected his king for the most part and on occasion pleaded with him for mercy and justice. But neither love nor hate are expressed in David's attitudes toward Saul.

It seems that Saul responded strongly to situations which activated the intrapsychic conflict in a fashion common to a reactive depression. His rage, too, seemed to be in response to definite stimuli and usually followed the period of depression, both being set off by different aspects of the same traumatic experience. Thus, the depressions were responses to instances of rejection or abandonment. When these were also associated with a rival who threatened to displace him and who received the narcissistic supplies such as the love and esteem of others, of which he himself was so badly in need, the depression was followed by rage and aggression against the rival.

Saul could be described as a personality with paranoid trends, a situation which provided a vulnerable background for the depression. The conflict with Samuel was the struggle with a father figure in which the theme of submission and rebellion, with its accompanying undertones of mutual castrative tendencies and defenses against such feelings, played a large role. Saul's long contest with David exemplifies these patterns of behavior, with a reversal of roles for the most part, Saul now being the father.

The repression of sexuality in his social milieu gave an added intensity to the problem of latent homosexuality and its defenses. Saul's pursuit of David, particularly after the latter fled into outlawry, also had a decidedly obsessive-compulsive character. It is common for depression to be associated with symptoms of this type.

Let us try to see more specifically what this pursuit meant for Saul. If the need to do away with his rival had been paramount, the king could have accomplished this aim easily on many occasions. He could have sent a posse into the hills with instructions to find David and kill him forthwith. The fact that Saul had to engage in this activity himself and to fail in it repeatedly shows that the pursuit in itself must have been very important to the king. It is not hard to see why. The conflict with David allowed Saul to externalize his intrapsychic conflict, providing the stimulus for turning the aggression outward, away from his own ego. An important part of therapy in depression is to find a channelized outlet for the introverted aggression. This purpose David served for Saul.

It is likely that on one level Saul first identified with David, as indicated earlier, then projected part of his own ego upon the latter. He could then pursue David with the same sadistic fury which he himself experienced as the target of the punishing, introjected Samuel.

Saul's low sense of self-esteem must have been related to a castration complex. The fear that his kingdom would be taken away from him would assume a greater intensity because of unconscious castration anxiety. This fear was based on an actual threat by a powerful father figure, and Saul had to cope with an actual rival who represented the instrument through whom this dreaded eventuality was to take place.

This leads one to conjecture what Saul's emotional fate might have been if destiny had not called him to the kingship. It is likely that he might then have escaped without a major breakdown. But when the submissive son, ambivalently related to the father, is suddenly chosen by Samuel and given the recognition he must have longed for all his life, something new is added. For a brief period his ego is flooded with unaccustomed strength. He experiences the fulfillment of unconscious infantile wishes in a way that is beyond the scope of reality for most people in a similar psychological situation. His dreams literally come true. The powerful father accepts him and endows him with a God-like omnipotence. At this point Saul may truly have been overcome by *hybris,* a sense of self-confidence so strong that one feels like a god and is therefore immune to the consequences of his behavior. Saul must have experienced this sense of immunity or he would not have dared to ignore Samuel's behests and to disobey his commands. That the son of a farmer, humbly carrying out his father's orders, could reach this point of self-assertion, indicates an unrealistic sense of power. A more reality-minded person would have recognized that Samuel's possible disapproval was not a matter to be treated lightly.

That Saul's new strength was a vulnerable one is shown by the way it yielded quickly to the trauma of Samuel's rejection. The feelings of omnipotence must have suffered a severe collapse and led to a sharp decline in his sense of self-esteem, a process characteristic of depression. The sudden coming to reality of repressed wishes to replace the father must have made Saul more fearful that he would suffer the same fate. In fact, he invited this fate by his behavior toward Samuel so we must infer that strong guilt feelings played a role in his masochistic tendencies.

Saul could not solve his problem of jealousy and rivalry in the simple and primitive fashion that Cain did with Abel. The king had to cope with a moral system, both external and internalized. The fact that he did not kill David but only pursued him, and that he eventually paid with his death as self-inflicted punishment for his aggressive wishes, shows that morality was a potent force in his world of three thousand years ago.

On a reality level, Saul fulfilled the purpose for which Samuel selected him, strengthening the unity of the Hebrew tribes and establishing the monarchy on a sound basis by defeating the enemies of Israel. His personal life might have been a happier one had he not been called to this difficult position of the kingship. But though we see him as a tragic figure, Saul nevertheless has real stature as a historic leader of ancient Israel who served his people well.

from "David"
FLEMING JAMES

PRIMITIVE TRAITS IN DAVID'S RELIGION

The narrative of the ark's removal reminds us that David's religion was by no means free from conceptions of a primitive nature. For one thing, he felt that on occasions Yahweh acted in what we should call an arbitrary fashion (II 6:9). To strike Uzzah dead for steadying the ark was certainly not an ethical action. David attributed the possibility of the same capricious conduct to Yahweh in another situation. When a fugitive from Saul he seems to have wondered at times whether Yahweh was not stirring up Saul against him for some reason David could not fathom. If so, He could be appeased by smelling an offering (I 26:19).

Again, David's dancing before the ark belonged to an ecstatic stage of religion destined to give place to soberer and more ethically coloured manifestations of enthusiasm. We should not forget however that the feeling of utter abandonment to God is something that even developed religion cannot afford to lose (II 6:16ff).

Undoubtedly primitive also was his tying Yahweh to the ark in so mechanical a way. The time was coming when Israel would have to get along without the ark and be better off for the loss. But the idea itself of the sacramental presence of God in a symbol survives with massive power among millions of Christians today. Those to whom it does not appeal may deem it mistaken and injurious, but they can hardly dismiss it as "primitive."

Yet other manifestations of David's religion must be put in this category. Here would fall his belief in the priestly oracle and his crude-

DAVID   This excerpt from *Personalities of the Old Testament* by Fleming James is reprinted by permission of Charles Scribner's Sons. Copyright 1939 Charles Scribner's Sons.

ly anthropomorphic use of Yahweh as the War-God. He also shared the popular idea that it was a sin to number the fighting men of Israel (II 24:10). When a plague followed his census he accepted Gad's interpretation: that it was a punishment for his impiety in trying to find out what Yahweh wished to remain hidden, and that it could be stayed by erecting an altar on a particular spot. Indeed, David seems to have felt that Yahweh actually put the intention to number the host into his mind, in order that He might have cause to vent upon Israel anger which (for some unknown reason) He *already* cherished (II 24). Once more, the story of David's flight from Saul reveals the fact that he and Michal kept a teraphim in their house, evidently an image large enough to look like a man under the bed-clothes (I 19:13ff). What it stood for no one knows. It may have been a representation of Yahweh, or a survival of the household deities used in pre-Mosaic times. In any case it cannot be reconciled with Israel's later religious thinking, or even with Mosaism.

But the most sinister emergence of primitive traits is to be found in David's superstitions concerning blood-guilt. He was convinced that blood once shed would be "returned" somewhere, if not on the head of the shedder then on that of the king and his descendants. This idea worked for rude justice with the man who claimed to have slain Saul and still more with Ishbosheth's murderers. But when Joab killed first Abner, then Amasa David was not strong enough to wipe out the blood-debt by the execution of the murderer. The fact that he had left the score unpaid seems to have troubled him all his life, and on his death bed he commissioned Solomon to bring down Joab's grey head with blood to Sheol in order that David's descendants might not suffer in the future (I Ki. 2:5ff; cf. 2:33).[1] Shimei's curse, in like manner, must have roused his fears. Unless this old Benjamite should die a bloody death the curse would not come back to its sender but would continue to follow its object. David's own hands were tied because in a moment of generosity he had sworn not to put Shimei to death; but since no such obligation lay upon Solomon David left him a charge to clear the matter up! (I Ki. 2:8). In a kind of supplement to the history of David's reign (II 21) we find a peculiarly revolting instance of this superstition. When David "sought the face of Yahweh" to learn the reason of a prolonged drought he received the answer that blood-guilt rested upon the land because of Saul's having put to death the Gibeonites. The Gibeonites, when asked what atonement should be made, demanded the delivery of seven of Saul's descendants for the purpose of "hanging them up unto Yahweh in Gibeah of Saul." David acquiesced and the slaughter took place, followed by the impaling of

---

[1] T. H. Robinson, *HI [History of Israel]*, I, p. 245, following Benzinger and Stade, suspects that these parting injunctions of David have been invented to exonerate Solomon from the guilt of killing Joab and Shimei.

the bodies until the drought was at last broken. In such a circle of ideas did the great king move!

DAVID'S RELIGION AS IT AFFECTED HIS ETHICAL CONDUCT

No survey of the primitive elements in David's religion would be complete without including in it a number of instances in which he displayed an undeveloped ethical sense. We have already noticed his ideas regarding blood-guilt. His cruelty to prisoners of war also shocks the modern reader. So does his readiness to lie if he found himself in a desperate situation. When he made Ahimelech think that he was on the king's business his deceit came very close to downright treachery. What is more, he realized the probable consequences. "I knew on that day," he declared later to Abiathar, "when Doeg the Edomite was there, that he would surely tell Saul: I have occasioned the death of all the persons of thy house" (I 21–22). Yet David showed no sense of having done a great wrong. There was no apparent remorse, no plea for forgiveness. "Abide thou with me, fear not; for he that seeketh my life seeketh thy life; for with me thou shalt be in safeguard." That was all he had to say. Towards Achish king of Gath he pursued a course of systematic perfidy, acting his part with consummate skill. "I know that thou art good in my sight, as an angel of God," his patron acknowledged, when David protested against being sent home from the Philistine army (I 27:8ff; 29:9). David had a wonderful power to win men's trust and he exploited it without scruple. In taking his word Achish took trash. It was different of course with his oath, for that brought in Yahweh as a third party to enforce the engagement. Yet he found a way to evade his oath to Shimei by passing on to Solomon the task of killing him.

Since now we know that David lied in certain situations we have the uncomfortable feeling that he might have been lying in others where we should like to believe him truthful. As one reads his story one cannot shake off the impression that he was always more or less playing a game. Take for example his message to the men of Jabesh-gilead regarding their act of piety towards Saul's dead body: "Blessed be ye of Yahweh, that ye have showed this kindness unto your lord . . . and have buried him. And now Yahweh show loving-kindness and truth unto you: and I also will requite you this kindness, because ye have done this thing. Now therefore let your hands be strong, and be ye valiant; for Saul your lord is dead, and also the house of Judah have anointed me king over them" (II 2:5–7). Was he speaking from a full heart here, or making an astute political gesture? Probably both. In the main, of course, David must have been truthful or he would have lost public confidence. But one could never be sure that policy was not entering in.

We should not indeed blame David for such insincerity, or even for lying. Everyone lied in those days. According to the legend Yahweh showed Samuel how to throw dust in Saul's eyes when he went to Bethlehem (I 16:3). Even Jeremiah lied to the princes of Judah (Jer. 38:27). But in one important respect David seems to have fallen below the standard of truth attained by men like Jeremiah and Samuel. They had after all the fundamental sincerity of unselfishness. They sought, not their own good, but the good of the people. David on the other hand was thinking of himself and his house. Not altogether, but still enough to influence his dealings with others. To him people were never *just* people to be loved and helped, they were to some extent pawns in his game. At least, the reader feels so.

In his family relations David had no very developed concept of duty. Polygamy he practised with a good conscience. Sensuality, so long as it could be indulged within the very wide limits of this institution, was quite legitimate. One cannot forget the revolting picture (drawn in I Ki. 1) of his extreme old age. Towards Michal he acted with harshness, depriving her permanently of her rights of cohabitation because of a single taunt. The concubines violated by Absalom he kept in perpetual widowhood. All quite in conformity with current ideas, of course; but all showing how little right a woman, even a princess, had to live the full life of a woman under polygamy. In fact, throughout the whole story of David's relations with women there is struck not one note of beauty or even dignity, unless it be his words to Abigail (I 25:32ff). His adultery with Bathsheba however need not be included here, for he himself condemned it.

His sons he loved passionately but his affection led him to spoil them. Concerning Adonijah the historian remarks laconically: "His father had not displeased him all his life in saying, Why hast thou done so?" (I Ki. 1:6). What a summary of a boy's bringing up! Apparently the handling of Amnon and Absalom had not been very different. They came to manhood selfish and unrestrained. Even such an outrage as Amnon's crime David left unpunished, merely losing his temper over it (II 13:21). Absalom knew that if he wanted anything done in the matter he must do it himself. He knew also that if he killed Amnon he would probably be taken back into his father's favour after a while. David the resolute was weak as water towards his sons. In this case plainly the failure of David's ethics was not due to low ideals prevailing around him, for public opinion in ancient Israel seems to have been quite awake to the responsibility of a father. His conduct was evidently disapproved of by his biographer.

This painful enumeration of David's deficiencies in ethical insight, however, gives but the lesser half of the story.[2] In our study of Samuel we have reminded ourselves that Israel already possessed in

---

[2] J. M. P. Smith fails to do justice to David when he speaks as if David's finer traits were inconsiderable as contrasted with his "low ideals and attainments." *The Religion of the Psalms* (Chicago, 1922), p. 48

the Mosaic tradition many lofty conceptions of duty. David shared these. What is more, he lived up to them on the whole. "Whatsoever the king did pleased all the people" (II 3:36). How different from Saul, who often shocked them by his deeds of violence.

David was particularly careful not to shed "the blood of war in peace." There are several recorded instances where his religious scruples kept him back from such a step. One is the famous story of his sparing Saul, which has come down to us in duplicate form (I 24 and 26) and must contain some truth, however much legend has been at work on it. Both versions agree that when David got Saul in his power he refused to strike the fatal blow. "Yahweh forbid that I should do this thing unto my lord, Yahweh's anointed . . . for who can put forth his hand against Yahweh's anointed and be blameless?" (I 24:6 and 26:9). On another occasion he held back (under great provocation) from doing harm to Nabal, a private individual, protected by no divine anointing. When the fair and gracious Abigail had prevailed on him to refrain from the bloody deed contemplated David cried out in gratitude: "Blessed be Yahweh, the God of Israel, who sent thee this day to meet me: and blessed be thy discretion, and blessed be thou, that hast kept me this day from blood-guiltiness, and from avenging myself with mine own hand!" (I 25:32–33). Years later when, an old and broken man, he was fleeing before Absalom he responded to Shimei's cursing with a similar forbearance (II 16:11); and on the day of his restoration, in a burst of generosity of which he seems afterward to have repented, forgave him freely. To the remonstrance of Joab and Abishai he replied: "Shall there any man be put to death this day in Israel? for do I not know that I am this day king over Israel?" (II 19:21ff). David plainly had the idea that Yahweh abominated violence towards fellow Israelites, except of course in time of civil war. Joab and Abishai did not agree with him, but, as we have said, most of the people did. Indeed there seems to have been in the Israel of that day a strong aversion from such deeds. Abigail is a good example of this nobler attitude (I 25:26ff).

In other respects likewise David felt bound by his religion to act ethically. He sought out Mephibosheth in order to "show the kindness of God unto him . . . for Jonathan's sake"—thus uniting the religious and the human motive (II 9:3 and 7). "I have sinned against Yahweh," he cried when Nathan brought home to him his crime against Uriah (II 12:13). So the reputation of judging justly must have been earned by David through a long series of decisions in accord with Yahweh's known will: decisions untainted by the suspicion of bribery. Moreover, in spite of his personal and dynastic ambition, David did care for the people. "Lord I have sinned and done perversely," he prayed in the time of pestilence; "but these sheep, what have they done? Let thy hand, I pray thee, be against me and against my father's house" (II 24:17).

Finally, as we have seen, David could love greatly. This trait rightly falls under ethics, for where present it colours a man's whole conduct. Two supreme loves stand forth in his life. The first, belonging to his young manhood, was broken when Jonathan lay dead on mount Gilboa. The other began in the full tide of his vigour and ripened to its tragic close in his old age. "O, my son Absalom, my son, my son Absalom! Would I had died for thee, O Absalom, my son, my son!" (II 18:33). Deplore as we may his fatherly weakness, there is something in that cry that goes very deep. It is akin to what Israel's men of God believed to be Yahweh's own feeling for His rebellious people. "Is Ephraim my dear son? is he a darling child? for as often as I speak against him, I do earnestly remember him still: therefore my heart yearneth for him: I will surely have mercy upon him, saith Yahweh" (Jer. 31:20).

And as he could love, so he possessed an amazing power to win the love of others. Men and women alike were overcome by his charm. This is seen in the beautiful little stories that recall the devotion of his rough soldiery. Joab and Abishai, ferocious and unprincipled though they might be towards others, were true as steel to David. And so were the others. When three of his thirty chief men heard him express a longing in the heat of battle for a drink of water from the well of Bethlehem they broke through the host of the Philistines and got it for him. "But he would not drink thereof, but poured it out unto Yahweh. And he said . . . , Shall I drink the blood of the men that went in jeopardy of their lives?" (II 23:13ff). When advancing years had begun to sap his strength he one day almost fell in battle. Abishai rescued him, and his men "sware unto him, saying, 'Thou shalt go no more out with us to battle, that thou quench not the lamp of Israel' " (II 21:15ff). We have seen how in the hour when the nation seemed to be falling away from him his men stood fast by his side. Ittai the newcomer from Gath refused permission to leave his service: "As Yahweh liveth, and as my lord the king liveth, surely in what place my lord the king shall be, whether for death or for life, even there will thy servant be" (II 15:21). And many others besides his soldiers went with him into exile—or would have gone, had he let them—Zadok, Abiathar, their sons, the aged Husgai, and an unnamed company. Nor must we forget the number who gave their hearts to him when he was young: Michal, Abigail, the men of war, even Saul himself in his lucid moments. But perhaps most of all, Jonathan, whose "soul was knit with the soul of David."

> "I am distressed for thee, my brother Jonathan:
> Very pleasant hast thou been unto me:
> Thy love to me was wonderful,
> Passing the love of women."
>
> (II 1:26)

DAVID'S SIGNIFICANCE FOR ISRAEL'S RELIGION

No reader of the Old Testament (or indeed of the New) can fail to notice how often the name of David occurs in the writings of those who followed him. Why did he bulk so large in the thought and imagination of his successors?

In a real sense David was the founder of the Hebrew nation. Moses had indeed brought the Israelitish people into existence and given them a common faith in Yahweh their God. But not till the days of David did this people take its place as a nation, with a nation's organization and prestige. Saul had begun this work, but his kingdom for all its unity still retained much of the looseness and formlessness of the days preceding it, nor did it win for itself any convincing place amidst its neighbours. David gave it a capital, a court, a government that could be felt. He himself was a king like the sovereigns of important states round about, maintaining equal magnificence, dealing with them as a peer. His kingdom he raised from dependence and insignificance to imperial glory, making it easily the leading state between Egypt and Assyria. Beginning with David Israel was quite a different entity, with a different self-consciousness, a different national life. In spite of the succeeding split between north and south his work remained permanent. Both of the separated members continued to be kingdoms.

The capital that he bestowed upon Israel moreover was something more than a royal residence or a metropolis, however splendid. It was Jerusalem. Now and then in the history of mankind a city has embodied in itself the spirit of a people, becoming the mystic symbol of their achievements and their dreams, taking on in their thoughts something almost of the divine. Such were Athens and Rome. But neither of these meant to its people what Jerusalem meant to Israel. It is well for us to reflect that before David Jerusalem was not; or rather was worse than nothing from the Hebrew point of view, for it remained an unconquered Canaanitish city in their midst. David perceived that it possessed commanding natural beauty and a military situation which rendered it almost impregnable. He saw also that being hitherto alien it could be made his as could no Israelitish city. All his splendour could be poured about it. Finally, it could become the dwelling-place of Yahweh, His earthly home, the religious centre of His people. So he took it and set about shaping its future. He could not of course guess how vast that future would be; but with the intuition of genius he laid the foundation for it. Quite justly was it called thereafter both "the city of David" and "the city of Yahweh."

To David went back also the conception of Jerusalem's temple as Yahweh's home. Though he was not permitted to carry out this idea, David did take thought (as we have seen) for the worship of the

Jerusalem sanctuary, associating with the cult side of Yahweh's religion the influence of his great name. He seems likewise to have fostered the music used in worship, so that the temple singers afterwards looked back to him as their patron. We know how he was regarded as the illustrious prototype of the later psalmists.

But more than all else he became to after ages the Ideal King. As his figure receded into the past its faults were overlooked and its virtues came into their own. People saw in David a king wholly faithful to Yahweh, enjoying a unique place in His favour, able through his merits to avert from the lesser kings that followed and indeed from rebellious Israel itself the full penalty of their sins. Again and again, it was felt, Yahweh withheld His anger "for His servant David's sake." The great king's age appeared in memory as one in which the poor and the oppressed had been protected and justice had flourished on earth. The weakness and humiliation of a later time were contrasted with David's empire, when Israel's hosts went out as conquerors and the heathen round about rendered obedience to Yahweh's anointed.

Thus was born the hope that David would one day come again, in his own person or in a mighty "son" who would deliver Israel and make it head over the nations while at home his reign would bring righteousness and plenty. Too often this dream was tainted with aspirations after military power, and for this we must acknowledge that David himself was responsible. The aspect of his career that appealed to the thirst for material magnificence and military glory was a legacy of doubtful value, keeping alive passions and aspirations which were destined to bear evil fruits. But the other side of David's picture far outshone this. As one traces what we may call the "Davidic expectation" through the Old Testament he finds it in the main charged with aspiration for a better and purer world where the poor shall find a royal friend and God shall be truly known. When blind Bartimaeus heard that Jesus was passing by he "began to cry out and say, Thou son of David, have mercy upon me" (Mk. 10:48). Thus side by side with the memory of the warrior prince of the Psalms of Solomon there lived that of the good king unto whom a thousand years before the needy had "cried" and had not been disappointed.

SUGGESTED READINGS

Articles on "Saul," "Samuel," "David," and "Solomon." In *The Harper Bible Dictionary*, edited by Madeleine S. Miller and J. Lane Miller. New York: Harper & Row, 1973.

Articles on "Saul," "Samuel," "David," and "Solomon." In *The New Westminster Dictionary of the Bible*, edited by Henry S. Gehman. Philadelphia: Westminster Press, 1970.

Bright, John. *A History of Israel*. 2nd ed., pp. 179–224, "From Tribal Confederacy to Dynastic State." Philadelphia: Westminster Press, 1972.

Caird, George B. "I and II Samuel: Introduction." In *The Interpreter's Bible*, Vol. 2, edited by George A. Buttrick, pp. 855–75. Nashville, Tenn.: Abingdon Press, 1953.

James, Fleming. *Personalities of the Old Testament*, pp. 75–165, "Samuel," "Saul," "David," and "Solomon." New York: Charles Scribner's Sons, 1939.

Sandmel, Samuel. *The Hebrew Scriptures: An Introduction to their Literature and Religious Ideas*, pp. 441–70, "Samuel and Kings." New York: Alfred A. Knopf, 1963.

Snaith, Norman H. "I and II Kings: Introduction." In *The Interpreter's Bible*, Vol. 3, edited by George A. Buttrick, pp. 3–18. Nashville, Tenn.: Abingdon Press, 1954.

QUESTIONS FOR DISCUSSION AND WRITING

1. Samuel was the last "Judge" of Israel. What did his work consist of? How effective was he as a leader? Can you find any weaknesses in his character or errors in his judgment?
2. Considering the circumstances under which Saul reigned, argue that he was as good a king as could be expected. What did he accomplish?
3. Find all the reasons you can in 2 Samuel for Absalom's rebellion against David.
4. Review 1 and 2 Samuel and 1 Kings 1–11, looking for instances where the Lord intervenes in the world of humankind. Is the Lord as active in these books as in Genesis, Exodus, and Joshua?
5. Investigate the two-source theory of the composition of 1 and 2 Samuel in several Bible dictionaries and commentaries. Then argue for or against the theory.
6. On the basis of Leland Ryken's definition (p. 41), consider whether 1 and 2 Samuel and 1 Kings 1–11, taken as a unit, can be described as an epic.
7. Which of the three kings—Saul, David, or Solomon—comes closest to being an epic hero in the sense defined by Ryken? Support your answer with evidence from the biblical text.
8. Reread William G. Pollard's essay, "The Hebrew Iliad," and then compare the relationship between Saul and David with that of Agamemnon and Achilles in the *Iliad*.
9. According to Dorothy Zeligs, why was Saul a "tragic king"?
10. What is Saul's basic weakness, according to Zeligs?
11. Argue for or against Fleming James's opinion that to David people were "to some extent pawns in his game" (p. 176).
12. What is Fleming James's final estimate of David? Do you agree? Why or why not?

13. Compare Saul and David as religious men and as politicians. Which man do you admire more?
14. Read D. H. Lawrence's play *David*, and comment on his conception of Saul and David.
15. What evidence is there in 1 Kings 1–11 to suggest that Solomon was not as wise a king as tradition has made him out to be?

AMOS

SUMMARY

[In our treatment of three of the prophets, we have changed the order of their appearance from that in the Bible, where Amos, because his book is short, appears later than Isaiah, among the "Minor Prophets." Historically, Amos's prophesying took place between 760 and 746 B.C., while that of the prophet Isaiah of Jerusalem occurred between 742 and 687 B.C. If, as is assumed by many scholars, Chapters 40–55 of Isaiah were written by an Unknown Prophet (or "Second" Isaiah), the height of his activity would probably be in the year 539 B.C., shortly before Cyrus the Persian conquered Babylon and set the captives free.]

Although we know little about Amos, we do know enough about the political situation in the Near East during his time to assume with some confidence that his prophecies carried the implication that Assyria would be the weapon chosen by the Lord to wreak his vengeance on Judah and Israel. Indeed, it is difficult not to think of

Assyria in Chapter 5, verses 26 and 27, when Amos tells the people that they will take up their images of Assyrian deities in preparation for their exile "beyond Damascus."

As is evident from the accompanying map, Israel and Judah were always vulnerable to the more powerful kingdoms to their northeast, east, south, and southwest. Egypt was not then an active threat; but although Assyria was not yet ready to attack, it was obvious to a person with the world view of Amos that it would not be many years before such an attack would take place—as in fact it did. When invited by Ahaz, king of Judah, to help him meet the threat of the allied kings of Israel and Syria, the Assyrian king Tiglath Pileser III took advantage of this opportunity not only to capture Phoenician and Philistine cities but also to carry away "the Reubenites, the Gadites, and the half-tribe of Manasseh" (1 Chronicles 5:26). Samaria fell to Assyria in 722–721 B.C.

Scholars place the active ministry of Amos between the years 760 and 746 B.C. Beginning with the death of King Adadnirari in 782 B.C., Assyria had settled into a decline that was to last forty years. Egypt too was quiescent, so the small kingdoms on the eastern shores of the Mediterranean enjoyed for a while the peace and prosperity they always longed for but seldom found. The northern kingdom of Israel, particularly, took advantage of the resulting opportunities for the development of its resources and trade with other nations. Ten of the twelve tribes of the Hebrew nation dwelt in the northern kingdom, which had twice the population as well as three times the land area of Judah.

At the height of this prosperity Amos, a citizen of the southern kingdom, suddenly came on the scene. When accused by the high priest of the shrine at Bethel (in the northern kingdom) of being merely a member of the prophetic guild who prophesied for money, Amos denied such membership and claimed that he had been a shepherd and a tender of sycamore trees when the Lord had called him to prophesy the imminent doom not only of Israel's neighbors but of Israel itself. Addressing the people of the northern kingdom at Bethel, one of their holiest places, Amos based his authority on the voice of the Lord as it came from Jerusalem—the city of David, the place also called Zion, which the people of Judah considered the location of ultimate religious authority.

Amos probably wrote his prophecies down after his "retirement," so we possess in his book the essence of his preachings, what we might call his "basic sermon." His introductory remarks identify the time when he preached: "in the days of Uzziah king of Judah and in the days of Jeroboam the son of Joash, king of Israel." Uzziah reigned from 783 to 742 B.C. and Jeroboam II from 786 to 746 B.C. Amos actually pinpoints the time by saying that he spoke these words "two years before the earthquake," but although this must have been

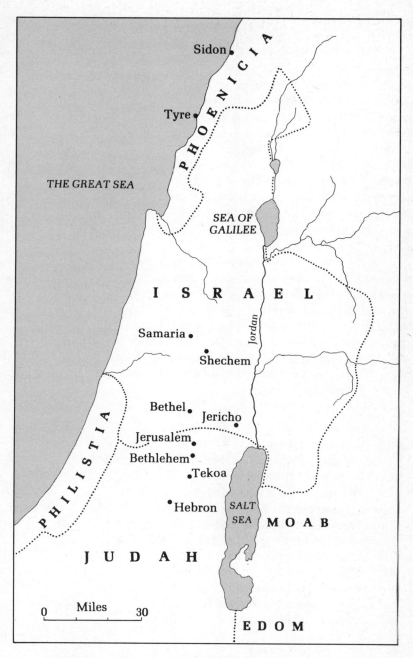

The two kingdoms of Judah and Israel, *ca.* 850–721 B.C.

specific information to his earliest readers, we cannot now be certain of the date of the earthquake he mentions.

Following his brief introduction, Amos first warns Damascus, capital of Syria, that the Lord will destroy Syria. Next he prophesies the doom of four Philistine cities (Gaza, Ashdad, Ashkelon, and Ekron), and then that of the Phoenician city of Tyre and of the old enemy to the southeast, Edom. Other nations that will fall are Ammon (to the east across the Jordan River), Moab (east of the Salt Sea), and Judah, the southern kingdom of the Hebrew nation. Finally, Amos strikes out at Israel. One is soon aware that he has been saving his strongest words for this. The other cities and nations have earned their destruction because of atrocities against their neighbors and warfare against Israel and Judah. But Judah and Israel are especially deserving of punishment, for they have been given the law of the Lord but have failed to observe it.

Now Amos concentrates on the northern kingdom, Israel. It is apparent that the chapter and a half that precedes this indictment has served mainly as a prologue. We can imagine that Amos's listeners approved of his condemnation of their neighbors, who had long been their enemies, but that they were quite unprepared to have the prophet take dead aim at *them*. No doubt many of them had been worshiping regularly, paying their routine homage to the God of the shrine. They had prospered, so wasn't it obvious that the Lord approved of their behavior?

Not so, says Amos:

Thus says the Lord:
"For three transgessions of Israel,
   and for four, I will not revoke the punishment;
because they sell the righteous for silver,
   and the needy for a pair of shoes—
they that trample the head of the poor into the dust of the earth,
   and turn aside the way of the afflicted;
a man and his father go in to the same maiden,
   so that my holy name is profaned:
they lay themselves down beside every altar
   upon garments taken in pledge;
and in the house of their God they drink
   the wine of those who have been fined."

(2:6–8)

Continuing his report of what the Lord had revealed to him (the text says he "saw" the words), Amos reminds his listeners of all the Lord has done for them: He destroyed their enemies the Ammonites; he brought them out of Egypt; he led them through the Wilderness; he helped them obtain the land of the Amorites (Canaanites): and he raised up prophets and Nazirites among them. In response, they

186

Saul Raskin, "Amos,
the Social Reformer"

forced the Nazirites to drink wine (against their vows) and forbade the
prophets to prophesy.

Consequently, the Lord will now punish his people. They de-
serve punishment even more than other peoples, for

> "You only have I known
>   of all the families of the earth."
>   (3:2)

In nature every act brings its own consequences; similarly, the
Lord tells his prophets what he will do, and then he does it. Amos
suggests that Israel invite its enemies the Assyrians and the Egyptians
to come and look at "the great tumults within her, and the oppressions in her midst," and he promises that "An adversary shall surround the land" (3:11). Very likely he has Assyria in mind. Little will
be left of Samaria, the capital city of Israel. The shrine at Bethel will be
destroyed, and the luxurious homes and palaces of the rich will be
demolished.

The wealthy ladies will not be spared. These "cows of Bashan,"
who behave as badly as their husbands do, oppressing the poor and
delighting in their own pleasures, will be taken away by the enemy.
In sarcastic vein, Amos invites the people of Israel to "come to Bethel
and transgress," to bring their usual empty sacrifices and offerings.
Let everyone know about your "freewill offerings"; "publish them,"
he says, "for so you love to do, O people of Israel!" (4:5).

The Lord has tried in more than one way to bend Israel to his
wishes. Not only has he given the nation great benefits; he has also
visited calamities upon them to punish their wrongdoing. But famine,

drought, blight, locusts, pestilences, and warfare have all been to no avail. So now it is time for Israel to meet its God.

Yet Amos is reluctant to say that Yahweh will destroy Israel immediately. In Chapter 5 he tells the people that the Lord wants them to repent and live. It may be that if they will "Hate evil and love good, and establish justice in the gate" (5:15), the Lord will be gracious to them. However, if they do not change their present way of behaving, they should stop looking forward to "the day of the Lord." Contrary to their expectations, the day will bring them not victory over their enemies, but darkness and gloom instead. Their religious feasts, their "solemn assemblies," their sacrifices and peace offerings are not acceptable, nor are their songs of praise. For none of this means anything unless it is accompanied by justice and righteousness. The threat now becomes specific: They will soon be worshiping the Assyrian deities Sakkuth and Kaiwan, because they will be taken "into exile beyond Damascus" (5:25–27).

Those who feel secure and at ease because their fellow men come to ask their advice should be aware of what has happened to the Philistines, and those who indulge themselves in the luxuries of this prosperous kingdom should know that they will be the first to go into exile. The great city of Samaria will fall, and all Israel will be oppressed by the conqueror.

Amos says in the first sentence of his book that he "saw" the words he proclaimed. In Chapters 7 and 8, his "seeing" is made even more dramatic than it has been so far: He presents five "visions" of God's judgment. In the first vision he sees locusts devouring all the produce of the land; in the second he sees a great fire consuming both sea and land. But when Amos beseeches the Lord not to fulfill these visions, the Lord "repents." In his third vision Amos sees a plumb line against which the people are being measured for their uprightness. This time there is no change of mind on the part of the Lord: "the high places of Isaac shall be made desolate, and the sanctuaries of Israel shall be laid waste, and I will rise against the house of Jeroboam with the sword" (7:9).

Now Amos is interrupted by Amaziah, the priest of Bethel, who had reported him to King Jeroboam and then told Amos to leave Bethel forever and go back to Judah to earn his living by prophecy.

It is from Amos's response to Amaziah that we learn the little we know about him besides the fact that he was a native of Tekoa. He is not a professional prophet, he says. He was a herdsman and a dresser of sycamore trees when the Lord ordered him to prophesy to Israel. Presumably Amos leaves to go home, but not before delivering a final denunciation in which he says that the priest's wife will become a harlot, his children will be killed in warfare, the land of Israel will be parceled out, the priest himself will die in a foreign land, and the people of Israel will go into exile.

Then Amos returns to the account of his visions. The fourth

consists of a basket of summer fruit, indicating that Israel is ripe for picking. The Lord has told him in this vision that the end has come and that now the people will bewail their misfortune. They will wait for their usual opportunities to make money and oppress the poor, but they will be disappointed. And although they will call upon the deities of the pagan shrines to help them, "they shall fall and never rise again" (8:14).

In his fifth vision Amos sees the Lord standing beside the altar, giving orders for the destruction of Israel. The people will not escape, no matter where they try to hide, and God will "set his eyes upon them for evil and not for good" (9:4). He will treat Israel as he treats any other nation—Ethiopian, Philistine, or Syrian—if the Israelites are sinful.

Verses 8b–15 of the last chapter are in a different mood from most of what has gone before. They echo verses 1–15 of Chapter 5, however, because they speak of a remnant from the house of David that the Lord will "raise up" and repair and rebuild "as in the days of old." These descendants of David will restore the kingdom of Israel—"the remnant of Edom and all the nations who are called by my name." If Amos is referring only to a remnant that will arise from the kingdom of David in Judah, he nevertheless includes all of Israel in the final rehabilitation that will take place:

> "I will restore the fortunes of my
>   people Israel,
>   and they shall rebuild the ruined
>   cities and inhabit them;
> they shall plant vineyards and drink
>   their wine,
>   and they shall make gardens and
>   eat their fruit.
> I will plant them upon their land,
>   and they shall never again be
>   plucked up
>   out of the land which I have given
>   them,"
>   says the Lord your God.
>   (9:14–15)

LITERARY QUALITIES

Scholars have for some time recognized and praised the effectiveness of Amos's style. The following comment and the accompanying table appear in A Critical and Exegetical Commentary on Amos and Hosea, edited by William R. Harper.

Amos
WILLIAM R. HARPER

The general structure of the book as understood by the present writer is indicated in the table [see page 191]. Its character is extremely simple: a series of judgment oracles; a series of judgment sermons; a series of judgment visions. These various series have each its own unity of thought and its own unity of purpose. . . .

The regular and simple structure of the book exhibits at once Amos' style of thought. What could be more natural and easy than the series of oracles, the series of sermons, and the series of visions? It is unfortunate that some recent critics seem as blind to the simplicity of Amos' style of expression as were the older critics to its refined nature.

This regularity, or orderliness, exhibits itself in detail in the repetition of the same formulas *for three transgressions, yea for four,* etc. in the opening chapters (or, to put it otherwise, in the orderly arrangement of the nations); in the use of the refrain, *but ye did not return,* etc., in the poem describing Israel's past chastisements (4:4–13); in the entire form of the first three visions (7:1–9); in the almost artificial symmetry of form seen in the accusation (7:10–14) and the reply (7:14–17); in the series of illustrations employed with such effect in 3:3ff; in the structure in general, of the several pieces. . . . Moreover, these various series, "while not so long as to become tiresome, are long enough to impress upon the mind of the reader the truths that they are intended to illustrate and justify the use of them by the prophet." There is here the skill, not only of the poet and speaker, but also of the teacher. Every poem in the book is a notable example of this same direct, straightforward orderliness of thought.

The imagery of Amos, like that of Isaiah, is worthy of special study. Tradition has probably been wrong in emphasizing too strongly the prevailingly shepherd-characteristics . . . which mark the figures employed by Amos. But no one will deny that he is especially fond of drawing his language from *nature;* and what, after all, is this but the field of rural life? He not only cites certain facts of agricultural significance, e.g. the recent drought, blasting and mildew (4:7ff), the oppressive taxation of crops (5:11), and the cheating of the grain merchants (8:5), but he finds picturesque illustrations and comparisons in "threshing instruments" (1:3), the loaded wagon on the threshing-

AMOS From "Introduction" in William R. Harper, ed., *A Critical and Exegetical Commentary on Amos and Hosea* (Edinburgh: T. & T. Clark, 1973). Reprinted by permission of the publisher.

Structure	Original	Secondary Sources*	Subject**	Chapter
		1:1	*The superscription*	1
		1:2	The text or motto	1
The Oracles 1:3–2:16.	1:3–5, 6–8, 13–15; 2:1–3.	1:9–10, 11–12; 2:4–5.	Judgments upon neighboring nations, viz. Syria, Philistia, *Tyre, Edom*, Ammon, Moab, *Judah.*	1–2
	2:6–11, 13–16.	2:12.	Judgment upon the nation Israel.	2
The Sermons 3:1–6:14.	3:1–8.		The roar of the lion: destruction is coming.	3–4
	3:9–4:3.		The doom of Samaria.	
	4:4–7a, 8b–12, 13e.	4:7b, 8a, 13 a–d.	Israel's failure to understand the Divine Judgment.	4
	5:1–6.	5:8–9.	A dirge, Israel's coming destruction.	5
	5:7, 10–17.	5:18b, 22b;	Transgressors shall come to grief.	
	5:18a, c, 19–22a, 23–6:1, 3–8, 11b–14.	6:2, 9–11a.	The doom of captivity.	5–6
The Visions 7:1–9:8b.	7:1a–c, 2–7, 8b, 9.	7:1d, 8a	Three visions of destruction.	7
	7:10–17		An accusation and a reply.	
	8:1, 2b–5, 7–10, 11b–14.	8:2a, 6, 11a	A fourth vision, with explanatory discourse.	8
	9:1–4, 7–8b.	9:5–6.	A fifth vision, with a passionate description of the ruin.	9
		9:8c, 9–15.	A later voice of promise.	9

*In his introduction to Amos, William R. Harper argues that these passages were not original with the prophet. He concludes that some may have been quoted by Amos and others probably inserted during the final editing of the book.—Ed. [of Harper's text]

**Titles in italics belong to late sections.

floor (2:13), the height of the cedars and the strength of the oaks (2:9), the roar of the lion in the forest (3:4, 8), the shepherd rescuing remnants from the lion (3:12), the snaring of birds (3:5), the "kine of Bashan" (4:1), wormwood (5:7; 6:14), the lion, bear, and serpent (5:19), the perennial stream (5:24), horses stumbling upon rocks and ploughing the sea with oxen (6:12), swarms of locusts devouring the aftermath (7:1ff), and the "basket of summer fruit" (8:1).

Other features of Amos' style, which may only be mentioned, are (a) its originality (sometimes called unconventionality or individuality), as seen in a certain kind of independence, probably due to the fact that he was a pioneer in the application of writing to prophetic discourse; (b) its maturity, for nothing is more clear than that he had predecessors in this work who had developed, in no small degree, a technical nomenclature of prophecy . . . ; (c) its artistic character, which is seen not only in strophes with refrains, but in the entire strophic structure of the various pieces, together with the measure and parallelism. . . . It is probable that Amos' style, as well as the substance of his message, is to be explained largely by the circumstances of his environment.

INTERPRETATIONS

The Herdsman from Tekoa
Bernhard W. Anderson

We know very little about Amos, for the book that bears his name stresses the "word of Yahweh" spoken by the prophet, rather than biographical facts about the man himself. The heading of the book of Amos (1:1), which was added by a later editor, tells us that Amos came from among shepherds of Tekoa,[1] a village lying a few miles south of Jerusalem, and that he was active during the reign of

---

[1] Some have gone so far as to say that Amos was at home in the atmosphere of traditional wisdom which was esteemed in nomadic clans and small towns like Tekoa. See H. W. Wolff, *Amos, the Prophet* and Samuel Terrien, "Amos and Wisdom," *Israel's Prophetic Heritage* pp. 108–15. Doubtless Amos was influenced by this tradition, as evidenced by his use of literary forms and expressions characteristic of Wisdom. But the wisdom movement exerted an influence upon other prophets too and was undoubtedly a major ingredient in Israelite society (see Jer. 18:18), at least from the time of Solomon.

THE HERDSMAN FROM TEKOA   From Bernhard W. Anderson, *Understanding the Old Testament*, 3rd edition, pp. 270–79. Reprinted by permission of Prentice-Hall, Inc., Englewood Cliffs, New Jersey.

two contemporary kings, Uzziah of Judah and Jeroboam II of Israel. We could date his career more precisely if we were sure of the meaning of the chronological reference, "two years before the earthquake" (see Zech. 14:5). In any case, Amos was active in the Northern Kingdom during the height of the reign of Jeroboam II, some time before Jeroboam's death in 746 B.C. A date of about 750 B.C. fits the conditions reflected in the book.

A clearer picture of Amos' background is given in the prose passage found in Amos 7:10–15, which records the dramatic encounter between Amos and Amaziah, the chief priest of the Bethel temple—the royal sanctuary which Jeroboam I had once established as one of the national shrines of the Northern Kingdom. Here we are told that Amos was a native of Judah where he had been a herdsman and a "dresser of sycamore trees." (The latter expression refers to the puncturing of the fig-like fruit so that the insects that form on the inside may be released.) The appearance of this southerner in the Northern Kingdom points out that the division between Israel and Judah was primarily political, and that the two nations were actually bound together as *one* covenant people with a common religious tradition. Amaziah, assuming that Amos was just another professional prophet who earned his living by his religious trade (see I Sam. 9:8; I Kings 14:2; II Kings 8:8), warned him to return to Judah and there "eat bread"—that is, seek fees for his prophetic oracles. Amos' reply is not transparently clear, but probably the Hebrew should be translated: [2]

> I am not a prophet [nabi'],
> Nor one of the sons of the prophets;
> rather, I am a herdsman,
> and a dresser of sycamore trees.
> However, Yahweh took me from behind the flock,
> and Yahweh said to me:
> Go! Prophesy to my people Israel.
>
> —AMOS 7:14–15

In denying that he was a *nabi'*, Amos did not necessarily intend to disparage the prophetic orders. He believed that Yahweh had raised up prophets to warn the people (2:11; 3:7). And, of course, he himself had striking affinities with such prophets as Nathan, Elijah, and Micaiah.

---

[2] Translation by the author. Some scholars argue that the reply should be translated in the past tense, "I was no prophet, nor a member of a prophetic guild, . . ." implying that Amos was not a member of a prophetic order when Yahweh called him but that he is actually one now by his own admission. See H. H. Rowley, "Was Amos a Nabi?"; this position is also taken by R. E. Clements, *Prophecy and Covenant* pp. 35–38. It is possible to translate the Hebrew that way, although the interpretation curiously inverts the negative statement of vs. 14a into positive agreement with Amaziah. However, this translation makes Amos' statement somewhat awkward as a reply. Amaziah had accused Amos of being a prophet, or seer (hózeh), in the present, not in the past, and Amos' reply to this charge would appropriately express his *present* self-understanding.

Rather, he insisted that he did not understand himself to be a prophet like the professional prophets of the day. He was only a layman, so to speak, whose work had been interrupted by a divine commission which came to him with irresistible power (see 3:8). In other words, this was prophecy of such a different type that the usual terms for "prophet" did not adequately express his understanding of his task.

Amos is the first in an extraordinary series of prophets whose oracles have been left to us in written form. The prophets who preceded him, like Elijah and Elisha, are known to us only through the oral tradition in which the memory of their words and acts was preserved. With Amos, however, we have the actual "words which he saw," as the heading of the book puts it. The book of Amos is a compilation of little units or "oracles," spoken by the prophet on different occasions, and compiled by Amos himself or by the circle of the prophets who treasured them. Amos delivered these oracles in various situations over a fairly brief span of time, during his preaching at Bethel (7:13) and possibly at Samaria (4:1). He directed his message primarily to the Northern Kingdom, but, since he was a southerner, the sister kingdom of Judah was also in his mind (6:1, 2; 8:14). He was concerned about "the whole family which Yahweh brought out of Egypt" (3:1).

YAHWEH'S SOVEREIGNTY OVER THE NATIONS

In reading the book of Amos, we must remember the political situation at the time. As we have seen, in the age of Jeroboam II Israel was able to flex her military muscles and expand because Syria had been weakened and the Assyrian lion was confined to his distant lair. But the whole picture was soon to change with the rise to power of an Assyrian usurper, Tiglath-pileser III (c. 745–727 B.C.). With amazing speed and energy he resumed the Assyrian advance, which had been slowed to a halt shortly after Assyria's crippling attacks on Syria in 805 B.C., and soon he was marching into Palestine, conquering everything before him. These events are clearly reflected in the book of Hosea. But in the time of Amos, Assyria's threat to Israel was still only a little cloud on the horizon the size of a man's hand. With great seriousness, which differed radically from the complacency and self-confidence of Samaria and Judah, Amos saw that trouble was brewing—not just because of Assyria's imperial ambitions, but also because Yahweh was at work in the political arena. Amos shocked his contemporaries with the hard-hitting language of history—of the sword's brutalities, captivity, desolate cities, political collapse. His role as a prophet was to interpret these ominous events in which Yahweh was acting, just as Yahweh had acted in Israel's history in the past.

As the book of Amos opens, we hear that Yahweh is at work among the nations. In the section on "Yahweh's Judgment Against the Nations" (1:3–2:3) Amos may have adopted a cultic "execration" form which was used in the temple to pronounce divine judgment upon the enemies who threaten Yahweh's chosen people.[3] If so, Amos has given the form a completely new twist. The prophet arouses attention by throwing the spotlight of divine judgment upon the small nations that surrounded Israel: Syria, Philistia, Tyre, Ammon, Moab.[4] Amos affirms that Yahweh is sovereign over these enemies and rivals of Israel. Because of their war atrocities a divine fire will break out against their proud palaces and fortifications. But then came the surprise. What Israel least expected or wanted to hear was the prophetic announcement that the same fire would consume the people of Yahweh's choice because of the atrocities committed in peace and prosperity. Thus the climax of the series of divine judgments is the startling announcement that Yahweh's wrath is also directed against his own people, Israel (2:6–8).

It is just at this point, where Amos is affirming the universal sovereignty of Yahweh, that we become most aware of the covenant tradition in which the prophet was rooted. He did not claim to say anything new, although certainly he spoke with a disturbingly new accent. Echoing Israel's confessional affirmation (Deut. 26:5–9; Josh. 24:2–13), he recalled to Israel the memory of events in which Yahweh had made himself known. Just as Americans reflect on the meaning of a world crisis in the light of a common memory of their past, so Amos interpreted Israel's crisis in the light of a common memory of the events that had made Israel Yahweh's people with a special task and destiny. He summoned the people to remember the events of their sacred history: how Yahweh had brought them out of the land of Egypt, had guided them in the wilderness, had enabled them to conquer and possess the "land of the Amorites," and had raised up prophets and Nazirites to keep his people faithful to their God (2:9–1).[5] In short, the prophet was proclaiming the "word of the Lord" within the context of Israel's historical memories. According to his witness, God speaks in the present through the remembrance of the events of a sacred past.

COVENANT PROMISES AND THREATS

This appeal to the past, and to the great convictions that were stamped indelibly on the national epics current in the northern and

---

[3] See especially A. Bentzen, *The Ritual Background of Amos 1.2–2.16*, Oudtestamentische Studiën, VIII (Leiden: Brill, 1950), pp. 85–99.
[4] Scholars question the originality of three oracles—those against Phoenicia (1:9–10), Edom (1:11–12), and Judah (2:4–5)—because they are cast in a somewhat different form and lack a specific portrayal of impending punishment. The oracle against Judah, however, may have replaced an earlier oracle, for it is hard to believe that the prophet would have omitted his own home country.
[5] The Nazirites (literally, "separated ones") were men who took special vows of consecration to Yahweh. Their abstinence from wine was a protest against Canaanite culture in the spirit of Israel's wilderness tradition.

southern kingdoms (J and E), shows that Amos was a vigorous upholder of the Mosaic tradition. That the conclusions which Amos and the people drew from their common convictions were very different, however, is seen in their contrasting attitudes toward Israel's election by Yahweh. The keynote of Amos' prophecy is struck in 3:1–8, a passage which begins by recalling the crucial event of Israel's history: the Exodus from Egypt. It was through Yahweh's action in this event that Israel had become a community, a "whole family" bound together by the bonds of religious loyalty. Israel was "the people of Yahweh." But it was also in that event that Yahweh had bound himself to Israel in covenant relationship. "You only have I known of all the families of the earth. . . ." The verb "know" (yada') refers to the closest kind of personal relationship. In some contexts the verb is used for the intimate union between husband and wife (e.g., Gen. 4:1); but here it reflects ancient covenant (or treaty) language, in which a Suzerain "knows" (that is, enters into covenant relationship with) a vassal, who in turn is obligated to "know" (or recognize) the legitimate authority of the Suzerain.[6] . . . Yahweh, then, was "the God of Israel." As we have seen before, this covenant formula—"Yahweh the God of Israel, and Israel the people of Yahweh"—is the very heart of the covenant faith.

This conviction, however, led the people to an attitude against which Amos protested with all his might. Reasoning from Yahweh's special calling, the people felt that they could go on to say: "Therefore, Yahweh will give us prosperity, victory, and prestige among the nations." After all, they thought, the covenant-renewal ceremonies included Yahweh's promises of blessing! So, flushed with the national revival and economic boom of the age of Jeroboam II, they anticipated the "Day of Yahweh." Apparently this festal Day was celebrated annually during the Fall covenant festival, that is, at the turn of the year. In popular belief this New Year's Day was an anticipation and foretaste of the great Day of Yahweh, a final climax of history when Yahweh would realize his covenant promises and crown his people with glory and honor. This attitude shows through in the oracle found in 5:18–29, where it is said that the people were "desiring" the Day of Yahweh, confident that it would be a day of "light"—that is, a time of victory and blessing. Religion went hand in hand with nationalism. Indeed, in that time there was a great religious revival. Amos paints vivid pictures of a people who were thronging to the shrines to worship (4:4–5; 5:21–23), although they could scarcely wait for the services to be over so that they could get back to their money-making (8:4–6). Over and over again they were saying to one another that they were not really on "the eve of destruction."

[6] See Herbert B. Huffmon, "The Treaty Background of Hebrew Yada'," *Bulletin of the American Schools of Oriental Research*, 181 (1966), pp. 31–37; summarized in Delbert R. Hillers, *Covenant* [182], chap. 6.

According to the Mosaic tradition as remembered in the north, however, the covenant did not give an unconditional guarantee for the future. The covenant rested upon a fundamental condition: "If you will obey my voice and keep my covenant you shall be my own possession among all peoples" (Ex. 19:5, E). It included blessings for obedience, to be sure, but it also included threats in the form of curses upon disobedience. . . .[7] Standing in this covenant tradition, and aware of the serious threats of divine wrath which it held forth, Amos reversed the popular logic of his time, saying: Yahweh has "known" only Israel of all the families of the earth; *therefore,* Israel will be punished for her iniquities. Israel's special calling, said Amos, does not entitle her to special privilege, but only to greater responsibility. In fact, he censured Israel far more heavily than any of the surrounding nations precisely *because* Israel alone had been called into a special relationship with God and had received, through her historical experience, the teaching concerning God's will. Having seen the light, however, she preferred the darkness to cover her evil doings. Consequently, said Amos, "the Day of Yahweh" would prove to be a day of destruction:

> Woe to you who desire the day of Yahweh!
>> Why would you have the day of Yahweh?
> It is darkness, and not light;
>> as if a man fled from a lion,
>> and a bear met him;
> or went into the house and leaned
>> with his hand against the wall,
>> and a serpent bit him.
> Is not the Day of Yahweh darkness and not light,
>> and gloom with no brightness in it?
>> —AMOS 5:18–20; *cf.* 8:9–10

Since Yahweh controlled the movement of all nations, he would raise one of them to be the instrument of divine judgment (6:14).

So critical was Amos of the belief in Israel's election that in one passage he seems to renounce the doctrine altogether:

> "Are you not like the Ethiopians to me,
>> O people of Israel?" says Yahweh.
> "Did I not bring up Israel from the land of Egypt,
>> and the Philistines from Caphtor and the Syrians from Kir?"
>> —AMOS 9:7

[7] R. E. Clements (*Prophecy and Covenant,* pp. 39–44) has an excellent discussion of "the curse of the law" which was rooted in the covenant cult and, under Amos' prophetic interpretation, was transformed into a message of doom. He argues that Amos has taken the covenant threat and radically reinterpreted it to mean not just the purging of sinners within Israel, but the end of Israel absolutely. See further D. R. Hillers, *Treaty-Curses*

Two of the peoples referred to, the Syrians and the Philistines, had been Israel's worst enemies; and yet, says the prophet, Yahweh—the Lord of all the nations—has brought these peoples to their national homelands, just as he brought Israel out of Egypt into Canaan. In this instance the prophet repudiated Israel's notion that Yahweh is a national god, to be mobilized for the service of Israel's interests. Insofar as the doctrine of election meant that God serves Israel, rather than that Israel is called to serve God, it was in error.

The two oracles about divine election just considered (3:2 and 9:7) were undoubtedly delivered at different times. Amos was not a systematic theologian, but a prophet who delivered the word that needed to be heard at the moment. Even so, it is doubtful whether there is a fundamental inconsistency between the two statements. What Amos says in 9:7 is that Yahweh is surely active in the histories of other nations, even though they are not aware that he leads them and judges them. Although they suppose that they are "known" by other gods, they are actually embraced within Yahweh's sovereign control. But with Israel it is different. Israel has been "known" by Yahweh himself in the personal relationship of the covenant. Through her historical experiences she has come to know who God is, and what he demands. Therefore, because she could not plead ignorance, she must stand under a more severe judgment than any other nation.

THE THREAT OF DOOM

Amos spoke in accents of doom. Scarcely a ray of light breaks through the dark clouds he saw on the horizon. So certain was he of the impending catastrophe, which actually took place a generation later when the Northern Kingdom was destroyed by Assyria, that he sang a funeral dirge over Israel. This little lamentation (*qinah*) appears in a special 3–2 qinah-meter, and imitates the dirges that mourners wailed at the scene of death:

> Fállen, no móre to ríse,
>   is the vírgin Iśrael;
> forsáken oń her lańd,
>   with nońe to upraiśe her.
>   —AMOS 5:1–2

The same theme is struck in a series of five prophetic visions, in which everyday objects are transfigured with religious significance. Four of the visions are introduced by the words, "Yahweh showed me." In the first, Amos is shown a locust plague about to consume the crop after the king has taken the first mowing for his tax (7:1–3). In the

---

and the Old Testament Prophecy (Rome: *Pontifical Biblical Institute,* 1964), who points out that the curses of Israel's covenant are paralleled by the curses (e.g., captivity, exile) of ancient Near Eastern treaties.

second, he sees a supernatural fire that has already licked up the sub-
terranean waters which irrigate the earth and is about to consume the
soil upon which man lives (7:4–6). In both cases, Amos is sensitive to
the plight of Israel and intercedes on behalf of the people. So far, there
still seems to be hope for Israel. But not in the remaining visions. A
plumb-line, used by carpenters for construction, becomes the sign of
the destruction that Yahweh will accomplish in the midst of "his people, Israel" (7:7–9). A basket of summer fruit (qáyitz), by a play on
words, becomes a sign that "the end [qētz] has come upon my people
Israel" (8:1–3). And finally a vision of Yahweh destroying the
worshipers in the Temple (which reminds us of Jehu's purge of the
Baal worshipers) fades into the judgment of Yahweh from which there
is no escape, whether in the heights or the depths (9:1–4).[8] The last
clearly authentic word in the book of Amos is one of utter doom:

> Behold, the eyes of Yahweh God
> are upon the sinful kingdom,
> and I will destroy it from the
> surface of the ground.[9]
> —AMOS 9:8

This final prediction of the end of Israel had nothing to do with political fatalism. True, from a purely military point of view, Israel had no
more chance of withstanding the Assyrian colossus than, say, Finland
would have against Russia. But Amos was not thinking of comparative
military strength. Nor did his message of doom spring from social
despair, for the age of Jeroboam II was one of great political confidence. It rested solely on his conviction that although Israel seemed
healthy outwardly, inwardly she was diseased with a spreading can-
cer. Israel was not merely guilty of social crimes; she stood accused of
unfaithfulness to her calling as the people of Yahweh. In the economy
of God, such a society could not long endure.

SYMPTOMS OF SICKNESS

To Amos this unfaithfulness was shockingly evident in the evils
of the flourishing urban society. He pointed out the social injustices of
his day with such severity that Amaziah regarded his message as high

---

[8] Some scholars (e.g., Gerhard von Rad, *Theology*, II, pp. 131–32) believe that the visions
reflect the call of the prophet. After the second vision, he comes to sense the inevita-
bility of divine judgment, and so he goes to Bethel, perhaps in time for the Autumn Festival. The trouble with this interpretation is that none of the visions mentions a
summons to Amos, as we would expect in a "call." See further A. S. Kapelrud, *Central
Ideas in Amos*, pp. 14–16.

[9] Verse 9:8 (beginning with "except I will not utterly destroy") to verse 10, which miti-
gates the force of Amos' word of doom, is usually regarded as a later addition. The
conclusion of the book (9:11–15), which refers to the "fallen booth of David"—that is,
the fall of the Davidic dynasty—seems to come from a later time.

treason and insisted that "the land is not able to bear all his words" (7:10). Wealthy merchants, lusting for economic power, were ruthlessly trampling on the heads of the poor and defenseless. Public leaders, reveling in luxury and corrupted by indulgence, were lying on beds of ease—unconcerned over "the ruin of Joseph" (6:1–7). The sophisticated ladies, whom Amos—in the rough language of a herdsman—compares to the fat, sleek cows of Bashan, were selfishly urging their husbands on. Law courts were used to serve the vested interests of the commercial class. Religion had no word of protest against the inhumanities that were being perpetrated in the very shadow of the temples at Bethel, Gilgal, Dan, and Samaria. To Amos, all these things were symptoms of a deep "sickness unto death": Israel's estrangement from Yahweh and the surrender of her covenant calling. Boldly, the prophet declared that Yahweh "hates," "despises," "abhors" the whole scene:

> Take away from me the noise of your songs;
> to the melody of your harps I will not listen.
> But let justice roll down like waters,
> and righteousness like an ever-flowing stream.
> —AMOS 5:23–24

This passage shows us that Amos was opposed to the forms in which people acted out their worship of God, and other passages strengthen this impression. Turning back to the Mosaic period, Amos asks the rhetorical question (which seems to call for a negative answer): "Did you bring to me sacrifices and offerings the forty years in the wilderness, O house of Israel?" (5:25). He is merciless in his attack on the shrines, especially the royal shrine of Jeroboam II at Bethel (3:14; 7:7–9, 10–17; 9:1). It is very doubtful, however, that he intended a wholesale abolition of the system of worship. Rather, Amos was probably demanding that the cult be purified, for it had become so contaminated by pagan thought and practice that the people had become indifferent to the true worship of Yahweh and the demands of his *torah*. The prophet's standard—Yahweh's revelation in the Mosaic period—demanded that everything be swept away that did not conform to the proper worship of Yahweh. Amos felt that the existing cult was the source of Israel's sickness, and that divine surgery had to be applied radically to the source of the cancerous corruption: the temples and their system of worship (see the vision in 9:1). For the way people worship God, and their theological convictions concerning him, determine the attitudes and the relationships of the community.

A CALL TO REPENTANCE

And yet the divine purpose was not that of mere destruction. Yahweh was active in the midst of his people, said Amos, in order that Israel might turn from her evil ways and "return" to Yahweh. This is the meaning of repentance: it is a return (*teshubah*) to him who is the source of Israel's life, a redirection of the will in response to the jealous claim that Yahweh makes upon people's allegiance, and a corresponding change of life style. In a striking series of oracles, each of which ends with the refrain "yet you did not return to me," Amos affirms that repentance had been the divine purpose behind the calamities that had befallen Israel (4:6–12). But Yahweh had failed in his attempts, for Israel was stubbornly set in her rebellious ways. The prophet warns that even more terrible events could be expected in the near future:

> Therefore thus I will do to you, O Israel;
>   because I will do this to you,
>   prepare to meet your God, O Israel!
> —AMOS 4:12

Amos did not specify when or where this rendezvous would take place, but he was sure that it would take place soon, and in the arena of history. The end of Israel would be a great tragedy, but it would be a *meaningful* tragedy, and Israel herself would be responsible for it. People can choose whom or what they will serve, but they cannot escape the consequences of their choice.

The purpose of Amos' preaching, then, was to give people an opportunity for the reformation and reorientation of their lives. He proclaimed what Yahweh was about to do in the future in order to show how urgent it was to face the demand for covenant renewal—and face it now. Tomorrow, he said, might be too late; *today* is the time for decision, repentance, and change. The end is at hand! Therefore, "seek Yahweh and live"—this was his appeal as the approaching judgment thundered nearer and nearer.

There was little chance, however, that the people of Israel, enslaved by habit and blinded by complacency, would listen to Amos and mend their ways. But the prophet was no fatalist. He admitted that there was a slim possibility that a few (a remnant) might take his warnings to heart and "return" to Yahweh:

> Seek good, and not evil,
>   that you may live;
> and so Yahweh, the God of hosts, will be with you,
>   as you have said.
> Hate evil, and love good,
>   and establish justice in the gate;
> it may be that Yahweh, the God of hosts,
>   will be gracious to the remnant of Joseph.
> —AMOS 5:14–15

This, however, was a "maybe," which rested on the unpredictable response of the people and, above all, on the incalculable grace of God.

Here is a slight indication that the message of doom was not Yahweh's last word, as later prophets recognized more clearly. In making his heavy emphasis upon doom, Amos leaned over backward to counteract the false optimism of his time. Later on, when the desperate political situation drove people to fanaticism or despair, the prophets were to proclaim a message of hope. But the age of Jeroboam II did not need to hear the divine promise, for the people already believed that "God is with us" (5:14).[10] What they needed to hear was the word of divine judgment that would shatter their complacency and false security. Then, perhaps, they would understand that the promise rests, not on political and economic fortunes, but on the gracious dealings of God with his people.

In the short piece that follows, George Adam Smith goes to the core of Amos's teaching as he sees it: Amos's faith "springs from the moral sense; and it embraces, not history only, but nature."

Common Sense and the Reign of Law
Amos. III. 3–8; IV. 6–13; V. 8, 9; VI. 12; VIII. 8; IX. 5, 6
GEORGE ADAM SMITH

Fools, when they face facts, which is seldom, face them one by one, and, as a consequence, either in ignorant contempt or in panic. With this inordinate folly Amos charged the religion of his day. The superstitious people, careful of every point of ritual, and greedy of omens, would not ponder facts nor set cause to effect. Amos recalled them to common life. *Does a bird fall upon a snare, except there be a loop on her? Does the trap itself rise from the ground, except it be catching something*—something alive in it that struggles, and so lifts the trap? *Shall the alarum be blown in a city, and the people not tremble?* Life is impossible without putting two and two together. But this is what Israel will not do with the events of their time. To religion they will not add common sense.

[10] This is the literal meaning of Immanuel—the name that the prophet Isaiah later introduced (see pp. 310–11).

COMMON SENSE AND THE REIGN OF LAW From George Adam Smith, *The Book of Twelve Prophets* (London: Hodder & Stoughton, 1928), pp. 206–210. Reprinted by permission of the publisher.

For Amos himself, all things which happen are in sequence and in sympathy. He has seen this in the simple life of the desert; he is sure of it throughout the tangle and hubbub of history. One thing explains another; one makes another inevitable. When he has illustrated the truth in common life, Amos claims it for especially four of the great facts of the time. The sins of society, of which society is careless; the physical calamities, which it survives and forgets; the approach of Assyria, which it ignores; the word of the prophet, which it silences—all these belong to each other. Drought, Pestilence, Earthquake, Invasion conspire—and the Prophet holds their secret.

Now it is true that for the most part Amos describes this sequence of events as the action of the God of Israel. *Shall evil befall, and Yahweh not have done it? . . . I have smitten you. . . . I will raise up against you a Nation. . . . Prepare to meet thy God, O Israel!* [1] Yet even where the personal impulse of the Deity is thus emphasised, we feel equal stress laid upon the order and inevitable certainty of the process. Amos nowhere uses Isaiah's great phrase: *a God of Mishpat, God of Order* or *Law*. But he means the same: God works by methods which irresistibly fulfil themselves. Nay more. Sometimes this sequence sweeps upon the prophet's mind with such force as to overwhelm his sense of the Personal within it. The Will and the Word of the God who causes the thing are merged in the "Must Be" of the thing itself. Take even the descriptions of those historical crises, which the prophet explicitly proclaims as the visitations of the Almighty. In some of the verses all thought of God Himself is lost in the roar and foam with which that tide of necessity bursts up through them. The fountains of the great deep break loose, and while the universe trembles to the shock, it seems that even the voice of the Deity is overwhelmed. In one passage, after describing Israel's ruin as due to the Word of their God, Amos asks how could it have happened otherwise:—

Shall horses run up a cliff, or oxen plough the sea? that ye turn justice to poison, and the fruit of righteousness into wormwood. [2] A moral order exists, which it is as impossible to break without disaster as it would be to break the natural order by driving horses up a precipice. There is an inherent necessity in the sinners' doom. Again, he says of Israel's sin: *Shall not the Land tremble for this? Yea, it shall rise up in mass like the Nile, and heave and sink like the Nile of Egypt.* [3] The crimes of Israel are so intolerable, that the natural frame of things revolts against them. In these great crises, therefore, as in the simple instances adduced from everyday life, Amos had a sense of what we call law, distinct from, and for moments even overwhelming, that sense of

---

[1] iii. 6*b*; iv. 9; vi. 14; iv. 12*b*.
[2] vi. 12.
[3] viii. 8.

the personal purpose of God, admission to the secrets of which had marked his call to be a prophet.[4]

These instincts we must not exaggerate into a system. There is no philosophy in Amos, nor need we wish there were. More instructive is what we do find—a virgin sense of the sympathy of all things, the thrill rather than the theory of a universe. And this faith, which is not a philosophy, is especially instructive on two points: it springs from the moral sense; and it embraces, not history only, but nature.

It springs from the moral sense. Other races have reached a conception of the universe along other lines: some by the observation of physical laws valid to the recesses of space; some by logic and the unity of Reason. But Israel found the universe through the conscience. It is a fact that the Unity of God, the Unity of History and the Unity of the World, did, in this order, break upon Israel, through conviction and experience of the universal sovereignty of righteousness. We see the beginnings of the process in Amos. To him the sequences which work themselves out through history and across nature are moral. Righteousness is the hinge on which the world swings; loosen it, and history and nature feel the shock. History punishes the sinful nation. But nature, too, groans beneath the guilt of man; and in the Drought, the Pestilence, and the Earthquake provides his scourges. It is a belief which has stamped itself upon the language of mankind. What else is "plague" than "blow" or "scourge"?

This brings us to the second point—our prophet's treatment of Nature.

Apart from the disputed passages . . . we have in the Book of Amos few glimpses of nature, and these under a moral light. There is not in any passage a landscape visible in its own beauty. Like all desert-dwellers, who when they would praise the works of God lift their eyes to the heavens, Amos gives us but the outlines of the earth—a mountain range,[5] or the crest of a forest,[6] or the bare back of the land, bent from sea to sea.[7] Nearly all his figures are drawn from the desert—the torrent, the wild beasts, the wormwood.[8] If he visits the meadows of the shepherds, it is with terror of the people's doom;[9] if the vineyards or orchards, it is with mildew and locust;[10] if the towns, it is with drought, eclipse, and earthquake.[11] To him, unlike his fellows, unlike especially Hosea, the land is one theatre of judgement, but a theatre trembling to its foundations with the drama en-

[4] iii. 7: *Yahweh God doeth nothing, but He hath revealed His secret to His servants the prophets.*
[5] i. 2; iii. 9; ix. 3.
[6] ii. 9.
[7] viii. 12.
[8] v. 24; 19, 20, etc.; 7; vi. 12.
[9] i. 2.
[10] iv. 9.
[11] iv. 6, 11; vi. 11; viii. 8 ff.

acted upon it. Nay, land and nature are themselves actors in the drama. Physical forces are inspired with moral purpose, and become the ministers of righteousness. This is the converse of Elijah's vision. To the older prophet the message came that God was not in the fire nor in the earthquake nor in the tempest, but only in the still small voice. But to Amos fire, earthquake, and tempest are in alliance with the Voice, and execute the doom which it utters. The difference will be appreciated by us, if we remember the respective problems set to prophecy in those two periods. To Elijah, prophet of the elements, wild worker by fire and water, by life and death, the spiritual had to be asserted and enforced by itself. Ecstatic as he was, Elijah had to learn that the Word is more Divine than all physical violence and terror. But Amos understood that for his age the question was different. Not only was the God of Israel dissociated in the popular feeling from the powers of nature, which were assigned by the popular mind to the various Ba'alim of the land, so that there was a divorce between His government of the people and the influences that fed the people's life; but morality itself was conceived as provincial. It was narrowed to the national interests; it was summed up in rules of police, and these were looked upon as not so important as the observances of the ritual. Therefore Amos was driven to show that nature and morality are one. Morality is not a set of conventions. "Morality is the order of things." Righteousness is on the scale of the universe. All things tremble to the shock of sin; all things work together for good to them that fear God.

With this sense of law, of moral necessity, in Amos we must not fail to connect that absence of all appeal to miracle, which is also conspicuous in his book. . . .

SUGGESTED READINGS

Anderson, Bernhard W. *Understanding the Old Testament*. 3rd ed., pp. 270–79. Englewood Cliffs, N.J.: Prentice-Hall, 1975.

Chase, Mary Ellen. *The Bible and the Common Reader*. Rev. ed., pp. 177–231, "Prophecy and the Great Prophets of Israel." New York: Macmillan, 1962.

Fosbroke, Hughell E. W. "The Book of Amos, Introduction and Exegesis." In *The Interpreter's Bible*, Vol. 6, edited by George A. Buttrick, pp. 763–853. Nashville, Tenn.: Abingdon Press, 1956. (Includes biblical text.)

Harper, William R. *A Critical and Exegetical Commentary on Amos and Hosea*, Introduction. Edinburgh: T. and T. Clark, 1973.

James, Fleming. *Personalities of the Old Testament*, pp. 211–28, "Amos." New York: Charles Scribner's Sons, 1939.

Neil, William. *Harper's Bible Commentary*, pp. 289–92, "Amos." New York: Harper & Row, 1975.

QUESTIONS FOR DISCUSSION AND WRITING

1. Summarize briefly what you think is the main thrust of Amos's message.
2. With the aid of William R. Harper's table on p. 191, study the structure of the Book of Amos. Shift the parts around, and consider what would be lost or gained with a different organization of the material.
3. Evaluate the Book of Amos as a satire. What satiric devices does Amos use? What are his targets, and how has he attacked them?
4. What do you think Amos's most effective arguments are in the context of the religious and political situation in the northern kingdom? Which do you consider the most relevant passages for people today?
5. Write a one-act play based on the Book of Amos. You will have to invent some characters, and find a way to handle the visions.
6. Do some research on the so-called "secondary sources." What is the evidence that these passages are probably not original with Amos?
7. According to William R. Harper, what are the outstanding characteristics of Amos's style?
8. Bernhard Anderson says that Amos had "striking affinities with such prophets as Nathan, Elijah, and Micaiah." Reread the accounts of Nathan's role as a prophet in 2 Samuel 12:1–23, 25; 7:2–17, and 1 Kings 1:5–45 and 4:5, and then agree or disagree with Anderson's statement regarding Nathan.
9. According to Anderson, in what way did the people misunderstand their covenant relationship with Yahweh?
10. Why, according to Anderson, did the people need a message of doom rather than a message of hope at this particular time?
11. What support can you find in the Book of Amos for George Adam Smith's opinion that "Amos was driven to show that nature and morality are one"?

ISAIAH

SUMMARY

Many scholars have concluded that Chapters 40–66 of the Book of Isaiah were written by one or two prophets other than the Isaiah whose name is attached to all sixty-six chapters in the Bible. Although there is no universal agreement on this question, I shall follow the judgment of those who hold that only Chapters 1–39 can be assigned (and even then with exceptions) to the eighth-century prophet and that Chapters 40–66 were written in the sixth century B.C., perhaps during the Exile in Babylon. (Chapters 40–55 will be dealt with in the next chapter of this book, titled "Second Isaiah.")

Of these 39 chapters I shall summarize only Chapters 1–12, those designated as Isaiah's "memoirs." The remaining 27 chapters are described by the editors of the *Oxford Annotated Bible* as "oracles against foreign and domestic enemies" (13:1–23:18), the "Isaiah Apocalypse" (24:1–27:13), "oracles generally concerned with Judah's intrigue with Egypt, its implications and consequences" (28:1–32:20), "a collection of post-exilic eschatological oracles" (33:1–35:10), and "an historical appendix" (36:1–39:8).*

Amos had proclaimed his message to the northern kingdom, Israel, some time during the period 760–746 B.C. Isaiah prophesied to the southern kingdom, Judah, between 742 and 687 B.C. Assyria conquered the northern kingdom in 722 B.C., and during much of Isaiah's lifetime Judah had to pay tribute to the rulers of that great empire.

Like Amos, Isaiah also seeks a vision. He sees that under Kings Uzziah, Jotham, Ahaz, and Hezekiah, Judah and its capital city, Jerusalem, have forsaken the Lord—"they have despised the Holy One of Israel." As a consequence the country has been devastated by the Assyrian king Tiglath-Pileser III in 734–733 B.C. and by Sennacherib in 701 B.C. In other echoes of Amos, Isaiah speaks the opinion of the Lord concerning the distinction between sacrificial rites and social justice:

"I have had enough of burnt offerings of rams
    and the fat of fed beasts;
I do not delight in the blood of bulls,
    or of lambs or of he-goats."

(1:11)

"cease to do evil,
    learn to do good;
seek justice,
    correct oppression;
defend the fatherless,
    plead for the widow."
(1:16, 17)

But Judah can still be restored to its former status as "the city of righteousness" (1:26), if its people repent and practice justice. However, the evildoers must be destroyed.

Chapters 2–4 speak of "the latter days" and "that day," as Amos spoke of "the day of the Lord." In that day the Lord will judge between the nations,

and they shall beat their swords into
    plowshares,
and their spears into pruning
    hooks;
nation shall not lift up sword against
    nation,
neither shall they learn war any
    more.
(2:4)

* Herbert G. May and Bruce M. Metzger, eds., *The Oxford Annotated Bible* (New York: Oxford University Press, 1962), p. 822.

Isaiah of Souillac (Giraudon, Paris)

But before that day the idols must be cast out, men must be humbled, and people will flee into the caves and clefts. They will lose their best leaders, and anarchy will prevail. The elders and the princes have exploited the country for their own benefit, and

> ". . . the daughters of Zion are
>   haughty
>   and walk with outstretched necks,
>   glancing wantonly with their eyes,
> mincing along as they go,
>   tinkling with their feet."
>
> (3:16)

In "that day" the Lord will humble these ladies, and their men will battle until so few are left that seven women will be willing to be married to one man.

When the Lord has judged and punished and cleansed, there will be left a remnant of holy people sheltered by the Lord: "In that day the branch of the Lord shall be beautiful and glorious, and the fruit of the land shall be the pride and glory of the survivors of Israel" (4:2).

Chapter 5 is an oracle in the form of an allegory. It describes a carefully planted vineyard, which should have produced fine domestic grapes but yielded only wild grapes. In this allegory Israel is the Lord's vineyard, and its people have perverted the intentions of the Creator. The prophet pronounces doom on those who monopolize the land, those who drink day and night, those who mock God, those who turn morality upside down, those who are conceited, and those who take a bribe from the guilty. The Lord will use the Assyrians to smite his people, to punish them for their wickedness.

According to Mary Ellen Chase, "Readers of Isaiah should begin the book, not with Chapter 1 but with Chapter 6, for it is in this memorable and beautiful story of his vision in the temple about 740 B.C. that Isaiah's great literary and religious work begins. There is no chapter in the Bible more effective and affecting than this one in its account of an overwhelming religious experience granted to a young man who, probably from habit, has gone into the temple for prayer or for some daily service held there."*

Isaiah sees the Lord seated on a throne and hears the seraphim calling one to another: "Holy, Holy, Holy is the Lord God of hosts" (6:3). He is afraid, because he is of "unclean lips," but one of the seraphim touches his mouth with a burning coal, taking his guilt away. When the Lord asks, "Whom shall I send?" Isaiah answers, "Here am I! Send me." He is instructed to harden the hearts of the people, as the Lord had done with the Pharaoh when Moses asked him to let the Israelites leave Egypt.

> "Make the heart of this people fat,
> and their hearts heavy,
> and shut their eyes;
> lest they see with their eyes
> and hear with their ears
> and understand with their hearts
> and turn again and be healed."
> (6:10)

The recalcitrance of the people must continue until they have been almost entirely destroyed and only a small remnant is left.

During the year 734–733 B.C. the northern kingdom (Ephraim†) and the kingdom of Syria make a pact to fight Judah. This frightens

---

*Mary Ellen Chase, *The Bible and the Common Reader*, rev. ed. (New York: Macmillan, 1962), pp. 198–99.
†Another name given to the northern kingdom, after Ephraim became leader of the ten tribes that revolted against King Rehoboam, son of Solomon and last king of the United Monarchy.

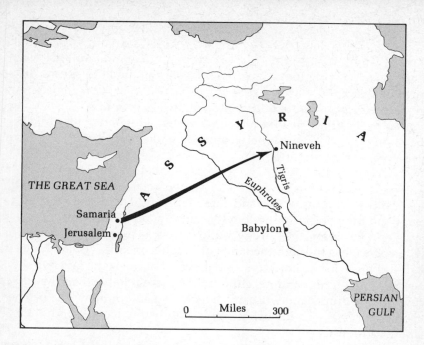

Samaria conquered by Assyria and Israelites taken to Nineveh, 722 B.C.

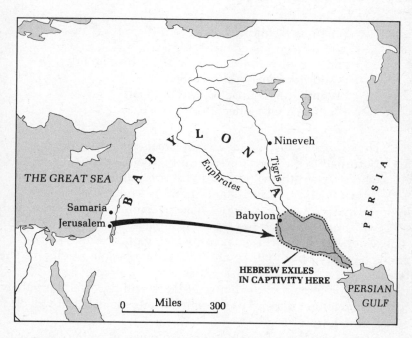

Judah conquered by Babylonia and the people taken to Babylon, 586 B.C.

Judah's King Ahaz, so the Lord sends Isaiah to assure him that whatever those two kingdoms do will not last. Then the Lord speaks directly to Ahaz and tells him to ask for a sign. When Ahaz refuses to do this, Isaiah says that the Lord will nonetheless give him one. A young woman will call her newborn son Immanuel, and before the child is old enough to distinguish between good and evil, the land of Ephraim and Syria will be deserted.

Again Isaiah gives Ahaz a sign to reassure him. This time, Isaiah names his own newborn son Mahershalalhashbaz ("the spoil speeds, the prey hastes") to indicate that Assyria will soon despoil Syria and the northern kingdom. Because Judah is still so afraid of Syria and Ephraim, the Lord will allow Assyria to sweep through Judah as well as through the lands of Judah's enemies. Isaiah himself will still hope in the Lord, for he believes that the signs given to the people through him and his children are more reliable than the advice given by mediums and wizards, "who chirp and mutter" (8:19). The people will finally be in such distress that they will curse both their king and their God.

Suddenly, Isaiah turns to a message of hope (9:1–7). He foresees a time when a messiah will come to Judah, as king upon the throne of David.

> For to us a child is born,
>   to us a son is given;
> and the government will be upon his shoulder,
>   and his name will be called
> "Wonderful Counselor, Mighty God,
>   Everlasting Father, Prince of Peace."
>
> (9:6)

However, because the people of Israel (the northern kingdom) have not turned to the Lord in recognition that it was he, using Assyria, who attacked them, the Lord will continue to punish them.

Assyria does not understand that it is an agent of the Lord. Its king thinks that he and his armies have overcome other nations with their own strength. When the Lord has finished using Assyria against Judah, "he will punish the arrogant boasting of the king of Assyria and his haughty pride" (10:12). He will send a plague among the soldiers, and he will consume Assyria as would a fire.

Then a remnant of the house of Jacob will be left to start anew. They will no longer depend on foreign nations as allies but will depend on the Lord.

Again Isaiah foresees the reign of a messianic king, who will come from the family of David. The Lord's spirit will be with him, and

> He shall not judge by what his eyes see,
>   or decide by what his ears hear.
>
> (11:3)

He will sympathize with the poor and the meek, and "he shall slay the wicked" (11:4). Indeed, his reign will usher in a new order in nature, in which "the wolf shall dwell with the lamb" and "the weaned child shall put his hand on the adder's den" (11:8).

Then the Lord will bring the exiled Hebrews back to Israel. Judah and the northern kingdom will no longer be enemies; they will come together to attack the Philistines in the west and their other enemies in the east. The Lord will make seven channels across the Euphrates River and create a highway for the exiles coming home from Assyria.

The "memoirs" of Isaiah conclude in Chapter 12 with two psalms, one a song of deliverance (12:1–3) and the other a song of thanksgiving (12:4–6).

> "Shout, and sing for joy, O inhabitant
> of Zion,
> for great in your midst is the Holy
> One of Israel."
>
> (12:6)

LITERARY QUALITIES

from "The First Isaiah: Statesman and Radical"
EDITH HAMILTON

As compared with the brevity of Amos and Hosea and Micah, Isaiah is long, and in every respect he is a continuation of them. What he says rounds the others out. He did not go off on any new path of his own as Amos and Hosea did, but he went along the ways they had discovered. He was indeed far from seeing the implications of Hosea's idea of love, not power, constituting God's greatness; but Hosea himself had not seen them and no one was to do so for a long time to come. Nevertheless Isaiah recalls Hosea's God in many a verse. He is "the merciful Lord" who is "like clear heat upon herbs and like a cloud of dew in the heat of the harvest," and in whom "the poor of his

THE FIRST ISAIAH: STATESMAN AND RADICAL Reprinted from *Spokesmen for God* by Edith Hamilton. By permission of W. W. Norton & Company, Inc. Copyright 1936, 1949 by W. W. Norton & Company, Inc. Copyright renewed 1963 by Doris Fielding Reid.

people shall trust." But at the same time there are long chapters about the fury of His anger and the awful power of His vengeance:

> And the hills did tremble,
> And their carcasses were as refuse in the streets.
> For all this his anger is not turned away;
> But his hand is stretched out still.

It was the same conception the men before him had had. The old God of terror had had mercy and love added to Him, but without any modification of the terror.

Not Amos, but both Hosea and Micah looked forward to a day when God would have punished His people enough and would turn His anger away from them, or at the least, from a repentant remnant. Isaiah caught up this idea and expressed it again and again in words which even when translated are as beautiful as any ever written:

> O house of Jacob, come ye and let us walk
> In the light of the Lord.

> For unto us a child is born,
>   Unto us a son is given:
> And the government shall be upon his shoulder.
>   And his name shall be called
>   Wonderful, Counsellor,
> The mighty God, the everlasting Father,
>   The Prince of Peace.

> They shall not hurt nor destroy
> In all my holy mountain;
> For the earth shall be full of the knowledge of the Lord,
> As the waters cover the sea.

It was the goal they all saw. Not to be attained by men when they are dead, but upon this earth by the living. Even in the soaring visions of a far distant future Isaiah kept his eyes fixed upon life.

In general the same outlook and temper of mind mark all four prophets. Fundamental to the thought of each of them was the opposition between what is and what men know ought to be. They saw that life as it is actually lived and the demands of the conscience are antagonistic. The discord inherent in human experience was perceived and felt by all of them with incomparable clarity and intensity, but it was Isaiah who gave it the greatest expression. It has never had a greater. Everywhere and in all ages when men have thought about life they have been brought face to face with the evil they give rise to and their own revolt against it, and now and again they have been able, one here, another there, to put their knowledge into words so profound or so passionate that they could not be forgotten; but among them all

Isaiah is unsurpassed. He had the power to see the depth of the division, the contradiction our life is grounded in—the good that men would, they do not; the evil which they would not, that they do—and he had the power to set it forth:

> Your hands are full of blood.
> Wash you, make you clean.
> Put away the evil of your doings
> From before mine eyes.
> > Cease to do evil;
> > Learn to do well.
> Seek justice, relieve the oppressed,
> Judge the fatherless, plead for the widow.
> Come now, and let us reason together,
> > Saith the Lord;
> Though your sins be as scarlet,
> They shall be white as snow,
> Though they be red like crimson,
> They shall be as wool.

The contrast between the wrong which is and the right which could be goes through the book in one splendid image after another:

> For wickedness burneth as the fire,
> Yea, it kindleth in the thickets of the forest
> And they roll upward in thick clouds of smoke. . . .
> Woe unto them that decree unrighteous decrees.
> To turn aside the needy from judgment,
> And to take away the right of the poor of my people. . . .
> The spirit of the Lord shall rest upon him.
> He shall not judge after the sight of his eyes,
> Neither reprove after the hearing of his ears:
> But with righteousness shall he judge the poor,
> And reprove with equity for the meek of the earth.

Isaiah saw as Amos and Hosea had seen—perhaps even more clearly than they—that men did not want evil even when they did evil. He knew the force of the appeal that hands red with blood could be washed clean, that a man might walk in the light of the Lord instead of the thick clouds of wickedness. He believed it to be stronger than any other and absolutely sure to prevail in the end. Evil would finally be conquered since men were made by God and so were made for goodness and were happy only if they were good.

> The people that walked in darkness
> Have seen a great light.
> They that dwelt in the land of the shadow of death,
> Upon them hath the light shined.

Good and evil he looked at just as Amos and Hosea had, judging them by the way men acted toward each other. To do the will of God was to make human life better.

His thought can be put into a very few simple statements: God is, and He is righteous and omnipotent. The purpose of mankind, the reason they are here, is to carry out God's purpose for the world, and this means to right the wrongs men do. Some day they will all be righted and evil will be at an end. This is not a system of thought. There is no attempt in Isaiah to give a coherent account of God and man and the world. He is not a theologian. He is not interested in explanations, not even of the contradictions he is perpetually emphasizing between what men do and what they want, between God's omnipotence and men's power to thwart Him. He gives no definitions and no formulas. All he does is to assert with the utmost majesty and grandeur of which language is capable, that the purpose behind the universe is good and that men can help or hinder its fulfillment. Therefore Isaiah's words still have meaning. Explanations never hold for very long. The more precise and perfect they are, the more quickly they are discarded. We are so made that when we have achieved a system of thought which explains everything beautifully, we have reached the point where we must begin to give it up. We are contented with it only as long as it is incomplete and we are trying to fit things into it. When it is complete we have got to start on something else. Outgrown explanations and abandoned theologies lie all along the path mankind has gone. But the vision of good and the desire for it remain always, and words that throw light upon either are never tossed aside as unproved and untenable. Light needs no proof. It needs only to be seen.

The prophets were men with extraordinary minds, able to reflect greatly upon human life and to see deep into human nature, but they did not care to analyze or explain what they knew. They never looked at it like that. It did not take the form of consciously thought-out ideas to them. Other, lesser men would get ideas from them and take infinite pains to explain them, but the prophets themselves were not teachers; they were discoverers. Something that had been hidden they uncovered, and it was there for everyone to see. No logical commentary could add force to "What mean ye that ye grind the faces of the poor"; no argument is required to prove the truth in "The burden of the valley of vision"; no one needs to defend the injunction, "Judge the fatherless, plead for the widow."

Such words stand of themselves. They are unassailable and they never wear out. Thousands of years leave them the same; time does not touch them. The book of rational knowledge is being perpetually added to and the earlier pages torn out, but Isaiah is not superseded by Christ or Amos by St. Paul. Their truth is true always and the words in which they embodied what they saw of men's dream and their desire, forever stir the desire and make the dream live.

INTERPRETATIONS

A Virgin Shall Conceive: Immanuel
THEODOR H. GASTER

When Rezin, king of Syria, and Pekah, king of Israel, unite to attack Judah, the latter's king Ahaz receives assurances from Isaiah that the LORD will yet protect his people. A sign of things to come will be that a young woman will conceive and bear a son, and name him Immanuel, i.e., "God is with us." From earliest infancy, the child will feed on curds and honey.

This famous prophecy is susceptible of two alternative interpretations:

1. The reference is purely general, i.e., an era of such prosperity will ensue that any young woman now pregnant will be justified in naming her child Immanuel, "God is with us." This interpretation is supported by the fact that the words "Behold, the young woman (ĝlmt = Heb.: *'almah* of our text) shall bear a son" occur as part of a hymeneal in a Canaanite text from Ras Shamra-Ugarit, suggesting that they were a traditional marriage formula, somewhat like the Italian *fighli maschi!*

2. The reference is to an ancient myth which told of the birth of a Wondrous Child as a presage of the coming of Age of Bliss. This myth—familiar especially from Vergil's *Fourth Eclogue*—was a "projection" of a Seasonal Rite at which the Spirit of the New Year, and hence of returning fertility and increase, was represented as the newborn offspring of a "sacred marriage" between the king (impersonating the god) and a hierodule (impersonating the goddess). This "marriage" is well-attested in the Ancient Near East. It was a recognized element of the New Year festivities at Babylon, and other Mesopotamian cities. Toward the end of the third millenium B.C., the inscription on a statue of Gudea, governor of Lagash, refers to "bringing wedding-gifts on New Year's Day, the festival of the goddess Baú," while a cylinder of

A VIRGIN SHALL CONCEIVE: IMMANUEL From pp. 568–70 of "Isaiah" in *Myth, Legend, and Custom in the Old Testament* by Theodor H. Gaster. Copyright © 1969 by Theodor H. Gaster. By permission of Harper & Row, Publishers, Inc.

the same ruler speaks of the marriage of that divine bride and the god Ningirsu. Similarly, a long Sumerian hymn describes the spreading of the nuptial couch for the "sacred marriage" of Idin-Dagan, third king of the Isin dynasty (ca. 1918–1897 B.C.) and the goddess Innini. Further, a late commentary on the New Year (Akîtu) festivities in Babylon relates how, on the eleventh day of the month of Nisan, the god Marduk "speeds to the marriage," while the same and other documents also describe the nuptials, at Borsippa and Calah, of the god Nabu and the goddess Tahsmetu in the following month of Adar. Lastly, brick couches used in this ceremony have actually been found in the ancient temple at Mari, while the ceremony itself is starkly reproduced on a seal from Tell Asmar.

Egyptian texts give evidence of a similar "sacred marriage" between the god Horus and the goddess Hathor celebrated annually at Edfu on the first day of the month of Epiphi (May–June), and followed three days later by the conception of the younger Horus. So too a feature of the Theban festival of Opet, held annually in the autumn month of Paophi (December–January), was the "sacred marriage" of the god Amon and the goddess Mut; while an inscription in the temple at Deir-el-Bahri, accompanying reliefs which depict the event, describes the mating of god and goddess, impersonated (on the "punctual" and ritual level) by the Pharaoh and his consort.

The rite also obtained in ancient Greece. Aristotle informs us, for instance, that the Boukolikon at Athens was primitively the scene of Dionysus' "sacred marriage" with the king's consort; while Lucian describes a three-day festival, blasphemously travestied by the false prophet Alexander, at which the nuptials of Leto and the birth of Apollo, and those of Koronis and the birth of Asklepios, were celebrated. Moreover, the anonymous author of the *Philosophoumena* relates that at one stage of the Eleusinian Mysteries the hierophant "shouted and exclaimed in a loud voice, 'Holy Brimo hath given birth to a holy child, Brimos' "; while we are told by Strabo that the birth of Zeus was enacted ritually in Crete. Both marriage and nativity survive, albeit in attenuated and garbled form in the modern mumming plays performed in Thessaly, Macedonia, Epirus, and in the Northern Islands of Greece on such crucial seasonal dates as New Year, May Day, and the like; for the leading characters of those plays are often a bride and a groom, and the upshot of the dramatic action is the birth of a prodigious child.

The offspring of the "sacred marriage" was, as we have seen, regarded as divine; and a standard term for a temple-woman in Phoenician was *ǵlmt*, the exact equivalent of the Hebrew word rendered "young woman (KJV: *virgin*)" in the scriptural text. Hence, the prophet speaks of such a woman's bearing a son, who should be named Immanuel, i.e. (on this interpretation), "a god is with us."

The seasonal festival at which the "sacred marriage" was celebrated often coincided with the winter solstice, wherefore the child was identified as the re-emergent sun—an idea eventually adopted (through Hellenistic channels) by Christianity, which came to observe that date as the birthday of him who was regarded as *Lux Mundi.*

If this second interpretation be adopted, the prophecy may be linked to that in 9:1ff. (Unto us a child is given," etc.), and the solstitial background of the underlying rite will lend added point to the words: *The people that walked in darkness have seen a great light; they that dwelt in a land of gloom—over them has daylight shone!*

Isaiah Affirms the *Transcendent* Nature of Israel's Vocation
E. W. HEATON

Not all the perils which the prophets diagnosed in Israel's national life sprang from the soil of Palestine. A glance at a map of the ancient world reminds one how Israel's territory occupied a central and exposed position in a crescent-shaped strip of fertile land. This "fertile crescent" stretched from the Persian Gulf in the east with Babylon at its tip, up through the valleys of the Tigris and Euphrates to Assyria, across to Damascus (an important and prosperous trading centre), and then down along the coast-land of Palestine. It ended with Egypt and the valley of the Nile as its western and most southerly point. Israel's home, therefore, was at once a commercial bridge and a military no-man's-land between the rival civilizations of Egypt and Mesopotamia.

Commercial and political ambitions have always been potential enemies to spiritual integrity and it is clear that Israel caught the infection of both from her more civilized neighbours. She was, of course, never really strong enough for independent action and so she sought trade and military alliances with the great powers on her borders. As part of the same policy, her kings took foreign queens and with them came their gods. When, for instance, Solomon tried to cement the disintegrating fabric of his kingdom by promiscuous marriage, his court admitted a whole spate of foreign cults.[1] When Ahab took the disastrous Jezebel to wife in order to win the support of Tyre, the worship of the Phoenician Baal received royal patronage.[2] Again, the

ISAIAH AFFIRMS THE TRANSCENDENT NATURE OF ISRAEL'S VOCATION   From E. W. Heaton, *The Old Testament Prophets* (Baltimore: Penguin Books, 1958), pp. 73–79. Reprinted by permission of the author.
[1] I Kings II. 1–8.
[2] I Kings 16. 30–3; see pp. 41–4, 71.

almost complete annihilation of the Israelite faith in the reign of Man-asseh two centuries later was a direct consequence of the king's sub-servience to Assyria—just as the religious reformation undertaken by Josiah, his successor, was possible only because Assyria at that time was too weak to intervene.[3]

But such religious syncretism was but one of the many symp-toms of a deeper disorder in Israel's national life. The adoption of many gods betrayed, as the prophets were quick to point out, a radical lack of faith in the sufficiency of the Lord. This was clearly demon-strated by the political factions in the nation, which were always in-triguing for foreign alliances. When Hosea, for example, insisted that

> Ephraim is like a dove,
>> silly and without sense,
>> calling to Egypt, going to Assyria,[4]

he did not mean that Egyptian and Assyrian religion had found their way into Israel. He meant that Israel herself had lost her way. She had mistaken her religious vocation for a political destiny—"like all the na-tions."[5] Her kings, for example, had arrogantly claimed an authority which ran counter to the sovereignty which God had delegated to them. The prophetic diagnosis of Israel's political disease is reflected in the many Old Testament passages which express a profound dis-trust of the monarchy.[6]

The protests of the prophets against the distortion of Israel's vocation by political ambitions and entanglements will best be under-stood from the oracles of Isaiah, the son of Amoz, who prophesied in Jerusalem during the second half of the eighth century B.C. It was dur-ing this period that Assyria overran and re-colonized the northern kingdom (in 721 B.C.) and reduced the southern kingdom to little more than the city of Jerusalem (in 701 B.C.). The background of Isaiah's ministry, therefore, was a constant series of intrigues among the small states of Palestine to form alliances against the Assyrian menace. The most notable of these was that led by Pekah of the northern kingdom and Rezin of Damascus in 734 B.C.[7] The ambition of these two kings was to win the support of Judah against Assyria. When Ahaz, the Judean king, proved unco-operative, this "Syro-Ephraimitic coalition" (as it is called) threatened Jerusalem. The book of Isaiah contains a vivid account of a famous meeting which took place between the prophet and the king, when Ahaz was inspecting the defences of the

---

[3] II Kings 21–3.
[4] Hos. 7. 11; cf. 7.8–9; 8. 8–10.
[5] I Sam. 8. 5; Deut. 17. 14.
[6] Hos. 7. 3–7; 8.4; 9.9 (Gibeah being the home of Saul, Israel's first king: I Sam. 10. 26); 9. 15 (Gilgal being the place where Saul was acclaimed king: I Sam. 11. 15); 10. 3, 9; 13. 10–11; cf. Judg. 8. 23; I Sam. 10. 17–24; Deut. 17. 14–20.
[7] II Kings 16.

besieged city.[8] In abject terror, Ahaz was on the point of appealing to Assyria for help. Isaiah's demand on this occasion for a steadfast faith epitomizes his greatest single contribution to the distinctive religion of Israel:

> Take heed, be quiet, do not fear, and do not let your heart be faint because of these two smouldering stumps of firebrands, at the fierce anger of Rezin and Syria and the son of Remaliah.[9]

> If you will not believe,
> surely you shall not be established.[10]

Only if Ahaz stoof *firm* in God's sufficiency, would he be *confirmed* in his political independence—the pun in the Hebrew for "believe" and "established" cannot adequately be represented in English. Isaiah assured the king that the threat from the northern coalition would be short-lived, that it would, in fact, disappear within two or three years. This is the point of the famous "Immanuel" prophecy. Before a young woman known to the king could marry and see her first child outgrow the baby-stage, the danger would have passed. Therefore, the boy could be named Immanuel, meaning "God is with us".[11] Ahaz ignored Isaiah's assurance and appealed to Assyria.

However we assess the prophet's political sagacity, the true significance of his attitude is to be found in the conviction that God's guardianship of his people was more than equal to all political contingencies. If Israel remained faithful to her calling, she was stronger than these damp squibs in the north and had nothing to fear from the biggest battalions the nations could muster. Throughout the troubled period of his ministry, Isaiah consistently demanded quiet confidence and faith and, in consequence, the refusal of all political entanglements. Those who intrigued with Egypt—a country which had always played the part of the snake-in-the-grass in Palestinian affairs—are frequently denounced in no uncertain terms:

> Woe to those who go down to Egypt for help
>   and rely on horses,
> who trust in chariots because they are many
>   and in horsemen because they are very strong,
> but do not look to the Holy One of Israel
>   or consult the LORD![12]

Isiah tried to teach Israel that she was not called to the dizzy and precarious heights of imperial prestige, but rather to a spiritual and moral service of God—in a serenity like his own:

[8] Isa. 7.1–9.
[9] Isa. 7. 4; the "son of Remaliah" is Pekah, king of Israel.
[10] Isa. 7. 9.
[11] Isa. 7. 10–17.
[12] Isa. 31. 1; cf. 18. 1–7; 22. 15–25; 28. 14–22; 29. 15–16; 30. 1–7.

For thus the LORD said to me:
"I will quietly look from my dwelling
   like clear heat in sunshine,
   like a cloud of dew in the heat of harvest."[13]

For thus said the Lord GOD, the Holy One of Israel,
   "In returning and rest you shall be saved;
   in quietness and in trust shall be your strength."[14]

From first to last, Isaiah's oracles convey an indelible impression of a single-minded man of God standing calm and imperturbable as the conflicts of the world eddy powerlessly about his feet. He upheld the moral and personal conception of Israel's mission which we found in Amos and Hosea, but he gave it stature and a larger perspective by his simple and profound confidence in God at a time when the whole political pattern in Palestine was being shattered by Assyria. He held firm to his faith through the troubled history of his age by interpreting it in the light of his initial vision of God. Israel, like the prophet, had been called by the King whose glory filled the whole earth.[15] Small wonder that her mission transcended the political intrigues of one small corner of it.

His disciples and interpreters, it would seem, have not been content to leave the matter there. They have tried to gild the lily by ascribing to the prophet an explicit promise that God would protect Jerusalem against all the assaults of the enemy:

> Therefore thus says the LORD concerning the king of Assyria: He shall not come into this city, or shoot an arrow there, or come before it with a shield, or cast up a siege-mound against it. By the way that he came, by the same he shall return, and he shall not come into this city, says the LORD. For I will defend this city to save it, for my own sake and for the sake of my servant David.[16]

Isaiah's close connexion with the court and royal family makes it unsafe to deny the possibility that the divine protection of Jerusalem had a place in his teaching,[17] but it is worth noticing that at least on one occasion he denounced the jubilation of its citizens when—physically—the capital was spared:

What do you mean that you have gone up,
   all of you, to the housetops,
you who are full of shoutings,
   tumultuous city, exultant town?

[13] Isa. 18.4.
[14] Isa. 30. 15; cf. 28. 16.
[15] Isa. 6. 3.
[16] Isa. 37. 33–5.
[17] Isa. 29. 7–8; 30. 30–1; 31. 5. . . .

Your slain are not slain with the sword
   or dead in battle. . .
In that day the Lord GOD of hosts,
   called to weeping and mourning,
   to baldness and girding with sackcloth;
and behold, joy and gladness. . .[18]

Flushed with political victory, the people had missed its spiritual meaning: "But you did not look to him who did it, or have regard for him who planned it long ago."[19] If, therefore, we ascribe to the prophet (and not only to his disciples) a belief in the inviolability of Jerusalem, we ought to be clear that what he was concerned to uphold was the inviolability of God's purpose in history:

The LORD of hosts has sworn:
"As I have planned,
   so shall it be,
and as I have purposed,
   so shall it stand,
that I will break the Assyrian in my land,
   and upon my mountains trample him under foot;
and his yoke shall depart from them,
   and his burden from their shoulder."
This is the purpose that is purposed
   concerning the whole earth;
and this is the hand that is stretched out
   over all the nations.
For the LORD of hosts has purposed,
   and who will annul it?
His hand is stretched out,
   and who will turn it back?[20]

Israel's vocation was to bear witness amid the relativities of history to that transcendent purpose by which ultimately it is governed.

[18] Isa. 22. 1–2, 12–13.
[19] Isa. 22. 11.
[20] Isa. 14. 24–7; cf. 10. 5–16; 37. 22–9.

from "Isaiah (Isa. 1–39)"
ABRAHAM J. HESCHEL

PROSPERITY AND POWER

Under the long reign of Uzziah (*ca.* 783–742 B.C.E.), in fame second only to Solomon's, Judah reached the summit of its power. Uzziah built up the economic resources of the country as well as its military strength. He conquered the Philistines and the Arabians, and received tribute from the Ammonites; he fortified the country, reorganized and re-equipped the army. "In Jerusalem he made engines, invented by skillful men, to be on the towers and the corners, to shoot arrows and great stones" (II Chron. 26:15). His success as king, administrator, and commander in chief of the army made him ruler over the largest realm of Judah since the disruption of the Kingdom.

Uzziah's strength became his weakness. "He grew proud, to his destruction," and attempted to usurp the power of the priesthood, even entering the Temple of the Lord to burn incense on the altar, a privilege reserved to the priest. Azariah, the chief priest, followed by eighty priests, "men of valor," pleaded with him:

"It is not for you, Uzziah, to burn incense to the Lord, but for the priests the sons of Aaron, who are consecrated to burn incense. Go out of the sanctuary; for you have done wrong, and it will bring you no honor from the Lord God." This angered Uzziah, and as his anger mounted, leprosy broke out on his forehead. "And King Uzziah was a leper to the day of his death, and being a leper dwelt in a separate house, for he was excluded from the house of the Lord" (II Chron. 26:18–21).

It was about 750 B.C.E. when Uzziah was stricken with leprosy, and his place in public was taken over by his son Jotham, officially designated as regent, though actual power seems to have remained with Uzziah. Under Jotham (d. *ca.* 735), Judah continued to be the most stable, prosperous, and powerful state in the area. Her wealth and military power placed her in the forefront of the anti-Assyrian movement when Tiglath-pileser III of Assyria invaded Syria in 743.

The increasing prosperity of Judah "was not canalized for the exclusive benefit of the aristocracy and the wealthy merchants, as was apparently true of the Northern Kingdom in the eighth century. . . . All private houses so far excavated reflect a surprisingly narrow range of variation in the social scale. . . . In other words, there was no period in Judah during which was such concentration of wealth in the hands of individuals as to destroy the social order."[1] The people made good use of the opportunities for commercial and industrial expansion.

ISAIAH AND THE NORTHERN KINGDOM

The years in which Isaiah began his prophetic activity were the beginning of a most critical period for both Israel and Judah. He received his call to be a prophet in the year in which King Uzziah of Judah died (*ca.* 742), not long after the death of Jeroboam II of Israel (746) and the advent of Tiglath-pileser (745), under whom the Assyrians set themselves the tremendous task of conquering both Babylonia and Syria. Overpowering small states, plundering cities, deporting populations, the Assyrians became a menace that filled Syria and Palestine with terror. Soon Samaria in alliance with Damascus became involved in a treacherous adventure against Judah, which ended in their becoming prey to Assyria's aggression. The relative security of the preceding several centuries was rudely broken.

The future of Judah hung in the balance; Samaria was doomed. The message of Isaiah, particularly as received by him in his great vision, spelled the final judgment.

Amos and Hosea had devoted their ministries to trying to save the people of the Northern Kingdom. They had called for return, but met with no response. What was to be Isaiah's role in relation to Samaria?

Neither the words of the prophets nor the experience of disaster seemed to shake the self-reliance of the people of the Northern Kingdom. In pride and arrogance of heart they boasted:

> The bricks have fallen,
> But we will build with hewn stones;
> The sycamores have been cut down,
> But we will put cedars in their place.
> Isaiah 9:10 [H. 9:9]

All attempts to purify Samaria failed; its final destruction was proclaimed (17:1–11; 9:8–21 [H. 9:7–20]).

> Through the wrath of the Lord of hosts
> The land is burned,
> And the people are like fuel for the fire; . . .
> Isaiah 9:19 [H. 9:18]

[1] W. F. Albright, "The Biblical Period," in L. Finkelstein, ed., *The Jews* (New York, 1949), pp. 39 ff.

The judgment will be carried out at the decree of the Lord.

> He will raise a signal for a nation afar off,
> And whistle for it from the ends of the earth;
> And lo, swiftly, speedily it comes!
> None is weary, none stumbles,
> None slumbers or sleeps,
> Not a waistcloth is loose,
> Not a sandal-thong is broken.
> Their arrows are sharp,
> All their bows bent,
> Their horses' hoofs seem like flint,
> And their wheels like the whirlwind.
> Their roaring is like a lion,
> Like young lions they roar;
> They growl and seize their prey,
> They carry it off, and none can rescue.
>
> Isaiah 5:26–29

The Northern Kingdom was doomed; Ephraim as a people would cease to exist (7:8); Isaiah had no role to play in its destiny (28:1–4). With few exceptions, his message was directed to Judah.

SURRENDER TO ASSYRIA

King Jotham died about 735 and was succeeded by his son Ahaz (735–715 B.C.E.), who at once found himself embroiled in a serious crisis. The western states had accepted the domination of Assyria only at the point of the sword. They hated the conquerors, and yielded only when crushed. The peoples hoped continually for an opportunity to free themselves from the bitter yoke, and the opposition did not long remain dormant. In the Kingdom of Israel a usurper named Pekah (737–732 B.C.E.), leader of an anti-Assyrian movement, came into power. Taking advantage of the Assyrian king's involvement in the east, Pekah together with Rezin of Damascus united against Assyria, and apparently they were joined by Askelon and Gaza, whose independence was threatened by Assyria. King Ahaz, who refused to join the anti-Assyrian coalition, found himself threatened by the allied kings whose combined forces subjected Jerusalem to a state of siege (II Kings 15:37; 16:5; Isa. 7:1 ff.). The object of this undertaking was to depose King Ahaz and to replace him by a friend of their own, probably an Aramaean, who would bring the Kingdom of Judah into the anti-Assyrian coalition. It would have meant the end of the dynasty of David.

The attack by the two superior enemies progressed well. The territory of Judah was devastated, Jerusalem was threatened; the Edomites and Philistines on the south, probably incited by the aggressors, annexed portions of Judah's territory (II Kings 10:5; II Chron. 28:16–18). King Ahaz as well as his people were in a state of panic. As Isaiah put it, "His heart and the heart of his people shook as the trees of the forest shake before the wind" (7:2). There seemed to be only one way to save the Kingdom: to implore powerful Assyria for aid. Assyria would save Jerusalem.

At that critical moment, probably in the year 735, while Jerusalem was besieged by the superior forces of the enemy, Isaiah conveyed the word of God to the king: "Take heed, be quiet, do not fear, and do not let your heart be faint, because of these two smoldering stumps of firebrands" who were planning to conquer Judah. "Thus says the Lord God: It shall not stand, it shall not come to pass." But Ahaz' fear was not allayed. In a final attempt to influence the king, Isaiah offered to confirm the divine authority of his words by a sign. "Ask a sign of the Lord your God; let it be deep as Sheol or high as heaven." But Ahaz said: "I will not ask, and I will not put the Lord to test" (7:1–12).

We have no right to question the king's sincerity. His refusal to ask for a sign was motivated by piety (cf. Deut. 6:16). Besieged and harassed by his enemies, he sent messengers to Tiglath-pileser III (745–727 B.C.E.), king of Assyria, saying: "I am your servant and your son. Come up, and rescue me from the hand of the king of Syria and from the hand of the king of Israel, who are attacking me" (II Kings 16:7).

No other ruler would have acted differently. The state was in peril, so he appealed to a great power for military aid. Isaiah offered words; Assyria had an army. To rely on God rather than on weapons would have been to subordinate political wisdom to faith. The issue was not to let faith in God be a guide in his personal life. The issue was to let faith be the guide in a public life: other people's lives were at stake, the future of the country was in peril. The king would have had to justify to his people a refusal to ask for help.

So Ahaz decided that it was more expedient to be "son and servant" to the king of Assyria than son and servant to the invisible God. He took refuge in a lie (cf. 28:15). The independence of Judah was surrendered to Assyria.

The appeal of Ahaz, accompanied by silver and gold from the treasuries of the Temple and the royal palace in Jerusalem, was accepted by Tiglath-pileser, though he hardly needed Ahaz' request for help as an incentive for his campaigns in Syria and Palestine. Having settled his difficulties in the east, he turned against the Kingdom of Israel and ravaged its northern territory. The whole of Galilee and Gilead together with a strip along the seacoast was made part of an Assyrian province, and the population deported. That was the first act in the Assyrian captivity. Samaria was left intact; the opposition, which presumably favored dependence upon Assyria, did away with

Pekah and placed his assassin, Hoshea (732–724 B.C.E.), upon the throne. Hoshea paid tribute to Tiglath-pileser, and was recognized by him as a vassal king. Thereafter, according to his own account, Tiglath-pileser turned southward, capturing Askelon and Gaza, thus freeing Ahaz from the danger of his other enemies. In 734–732, he ravaged Syria and Palestine to the very borders of Egypt. Damascus was conquered, the king of Syria killed, his chief advisers impaled, his gardens and orchards hacked down, and the inhabitants deported. The whole west was turned into a series of Assyrian provinces.

Ahaz, overawed by the triumphs of the Assyrian king, readily yielded to the glamour and prestige of the Assyrians in religion as well as in politics. In 732, he went to Damascus to pay homage to Tiglath-pileser. There he saw an altar, which he ordered copied and installed in the Temple at Jerusalem (II Kings 16:10 ff.). He also made changes in the arrangements and furniture of the Temple "because of the king of Assyria" (II Kings 16:18). The altar made after the Assyrian pattern carried, it seems, the acknowledgment of Assyria's greatness in the realm of religion and was a public recognition of the power of the alien god.

A COVENANT WITH DEATH

Isaiah asked Ahaz to believe that it was neither Pekah nor Rezin nor even the mighty Tiglath-pileser who governed history. The world was in the hands of God, and it was folly to be terrified by "these two smoldering stumps of firebrands"; those powers were destined for destruction, and even the might of Assyria would not last forever. The right policy was neither to join the coalition nor to rely upon Assyria. The judgment over Judah was inevitable, and it was not to be averted by alliances, arms or strategy. Accompanied by his son Shearjashub—a symbolical name expressing the conviction that a remnant would turn to God and be saved—Isaiah appealed to the king to be calm. He also announced that a young woman would have a son and would call his name Immanuel—God is with us—and that before the boy reached the age of two or three years, the allied kings would have departed from the land. Then evil days would come upon Judah, such days as she had not seen since the secession of the Northern Kingdom. Egypt and Assyria would lay the land waste. But a remnant would return, and a reign of everlasting peace and justice be inaugurated. . . .

A gulf was separating prophet and king in their thinking and understanding. What seemed to be a terror to Ahaz was a trifle in Isaiah's eyes. The king, seeking to come to terms with the greatest power in the world, was ready to abandon religious principles in order to court the emperor's favor. The prophet who saw history as the stage for God's work, where kingdoms and empires rise for a time and vanish, perceived a design beyond the mists and shadows of the moment.

While others acclaimed Ahaz for having gained the most powerful protection, Isaiah insisted that Assyria would bring disaster. "Because this people have refused the waters of Shiloah that flow gently, . . . the Lord is bringing up against them the waters of the River, mighty and many, the king of Assyria and all his glory; it will rise over all its channels and go over all its banks; it will sweep on into Judah, it will overflow and pass on, reaching even to the neck; its outspread wings will fill the breadth of your land, O Immanuel" (8:6–8).

When Tiglath-pileser died in 727, hopes of independence began to stir among the disgruntled vassals in the western part of the empire. Hoshea of Israel, after reaching an understanding with the Egyptian king, stopped payment of the annual tribute. In reprisal, Assyria sent her army against Samaria. Though Egypt failed to offer any aid, Samaria was able to hold out for three years. In 722, the city fell to Sargon II (722–705 B.C.E.); the Israelite monarch was overthrown and the population sent as captives to Assyria. The end of the Northern Kingdom filled the people of Judah with grief and consternation.

JERUSALEM REJOICES, ISAIAH IS DISTRESSED

Ahaz was succeeded by his son Hezekiah (ca. 715–687 B.C.E.) whose marvelous career was predicted by Isaiah when the child was still an infant. Hezekiah was the opposite of his father. No king of Judah among his predecessors or his successors could, it was said, be compared to him (II Kings 18:5). His first act was to repair and to purge the Temple and its vessels, to reorganize the services of the priests and Levites (II Chron. 29:3–36).

Hezekiah must have realized the prudence of Ahaz in refusing to be involved in intrigues against Assyria. To be sure, Judah was a vassal and was paying substantial tribute to the Assyrian overlord. Yet hateful as this condition was, Hezekiah seemed to realize that to throw off the yoke of Assyria would mean to court disaster, and in spite of strong pressure brought to bear upon him by the vassal states in Syria and Palestine to join them in rebellion, he held aloof. He took no part in the abortive revolt instigated by the king of Hamath.

Gradually, however, the people became impatient with the policy of submission to Assyria, which meant perpetual tribute and perpetual strain. In an inscription belonging to the year 711, Sargon II refers to the rulers of Palestine, Judah, Edom, Moab, and others, who had to bring tributes and presents to "my lord Ashur," but who meditated on hostility and plotted evil, and were sending their tokens of homage to the king of Egypt, "a potentate incapable to save them," seeking an alliance with him. . . .

Isaiah could not accept politics as a solution, since politics itself, with its arrogance and disregard of justice, was a problem. When mankind is, as we would say, spiritually sick, something more radical than political sagacity is needed to solve the problem of security. For the moment a clever alignment of states may be of help. In the long run, it is bound to prove futile.

Is it realistic to expect that nations would discard their horses and look to the Lord instead? Indeed, it is hard to learn how to live by faith. But Isaiah insisted that one cannot live without faith. "If you will not believe, you will not abide" (7:9). Faith is not an easy or convenient path. There are frustrations in store for him who expects God to succeed at every turn in history. But "he who believes will not be in haste" (28:16). Enduring strength is not in the mighty rivers, but in "the waters of Shiloah that flow gently" (8:6).

Politics is based on the power of the sword. But Isaiah was waiting for the day when nations "shall beat their swords into plowshares and their spears into pruning hooks." Alliances involve preparation for war, but Isaiah was horrified by the brutalities and carnage which war entails. In his boundless yearning he had a vision of the day when "nation shall not lift up sword against nation, neither shall they learn war any more" (2:4). War spawns death. But Isaiah was looking to the time when the Lord "will swallow up death for ever, and the Lord God will wipe away tears from all faces" (25:8 . . .). Israel's security lies in the covenant with God, not in covenants with Egypt or other nations. The mysterious power of faith maintains: God alone is true protection. Such power will not collapse in the hour of disaster: "I will wait for the Lord, Who is hiding His face from the house of Jacob, and I will hope in Him" (8:17). Never must a calamity shake Israel's trust. . . .

As we have seen, Isaiah's primary concern is not Judah's foreign policy, but rather the inner state of the nation. In the period in which he begins his activity, there is prosperity in the land.

The king is astute, the priests are proud, and the market place is busy. Placid, happy, even gay, the people pursue their work and worship in their own way, and life is fair. Then again appears a prophet, hurling bitter words from the depth of a divine anguish. People buy, sell, celebrate, rejoice, but Isaiah is consumed with distress. He cannot bear the sight of a people's normal crimes: exploitation of the poor, worship of the gods. He, like the prophets before him, has a message of doom and a bitter look. Even things that are pretty are sickening to him.

> Their land is filled with silver and gold,
> There is no end to their treasures;
> Their land is filled with horses,
> There is no end to their chariots.
>
> Isaiah 2:7

What is the issue that haunts the prophet's soul? It is not a question, but a bitter exclamation: How marvelous is the world that God has created! And how horrible is the world that man has made!

The essence of blasphemy is confusion, and in the eyes of the prophet confusion is raging in the world.

The earth is full of the glory of God (6:3), but the land is filled with idols (2:8). Men are haughty and full of pride (2:11), yet "they bow down to the work of their hands, to what their own fingers have made" (2:8). They regard themselves as wise and shrewd (5:21), but are devoid of the simple insight with which even an animal is endowed—knowing whose he is (1:3).

Princes are scoundrels (1:23); judges are corrupt, acquitting the guilty for a bribe and depriving the innocent of his right (5:23). They do not defend the fatherless, and the widow's case does not come to them (1:23). The people are being crushed by the elders and princes, while the mansions of the wealthy contain the spoils of the poor (3:14 f.). And in spite of all this, the knave is called noble, and the churl is said to be honorable (cf. 32:5).

Jerusalem—destined to be the place from which the word of God (2:3), Him Who creates heaven and earth, went forth—even Jerusalem "the faithful city has become a harlot, she that was full of justice! Righteousness lodged in her, but now murderers" (1:21), graven images, and idols (10:10 f.). Indeed, the land that the Lord has given to His people is "filled with idols; they bow down to the work of their hands!" The house of Jacob is "full of diviners from the east and of soothsayers like the Philistines" (2:6–8).

The prophet is struck by man's interminable pride, by his soaring pretension. Things done by man are lofty, high, and brazen, even worshiped, while the exaltation of God is but a hope. . . .

Characteristic of the dreadful intensity of the divine anger is the phrase used repeatedly by Isaiah, describing it when kindled against Ephraim:

As the tongue of fire devours the stubble,
As the dry grass sinks down in the flame,
So their root will be rottenness,
And their blossom go up like dust. . . .
For all this His anger is not turned away
And His hand is stretched out still. . . .
So the Lord cut off from Israel head and tail,
Palm branch and reed in one day, . . .
The Lord . . . has no compassion on their fatherless and widows;
For everyone is godless and an evildoer,
And every mouth speaks folly. . . .
Through the wrath of the Lord of hosts
The land is burned,

And the people are like fuel for the fire;
No man spares his brother.

Isaiah 5:24, 25; 9:14–19; cf. 9:20; 10:4

Grim foreboding, relentless is the account of the anger in action. . . .

Significantly, however, the speech that opens the book of Isaiah, and which sets the tone for all the utterances by this prophet, deals not with the anger, but with the sorrow of God. The prophet pleads with us to understand the plight of a father whom his children have abandoned.

> Hear, O heavens, and give ear, O earth;
> For the Lord has spoken:
> Sons have I reared and brought up,
> But they have rebelled against Me.
> The ox knows its owner
>
> And the ass its master's crib;
> But Israel does not know,
> My people does not understand.

Isaiah 1:2–3

The prophet laments in his own words the children's desertion of their father:

> They have forsaken the Lord,
> They have despised the Holy One of Israel.

Isaiah 1:4

But the sympathy for God's injured love overwhelms his whole being. What he feels about the size of God's sorrow and the enormous scandal of man's desertion of God is expressed in the two lines quoted above which introduce God's lamentation. "Hear, then, O house of David! Is it too little for you to weary men, that you weary my God also?" (7:13.) In different words addressed to the king, the prophet conveys his impression of the mood of God: As happened in the time of Noah and as is happening again, God's patience and longsuffering are exhausted. He is tired of man. He hates man's homage, his festivals, his celebrations. Man has become a burden and a sorrow for God.

> What to Me is the multitude of your sacrifices?
> Says the Lord;
> I have had enough of burnt offerings of rams
> And the fat of fatted beasts;
> I do not delight in the blood of bulls,
> Or of lambs, or of he-goats.
> When you come to appear before Me,
> Who requires of you

232

This trampling of My courts?
Bring no more vain offerings;
Incense is an abomination to Me.
New moon and sabbath and the calling of assemblies—
I cannot endure iniquity and solemn assembly.
Your new moons and your appointed feasts
My soul hates;
They have become a burden to Me,
That I am weary to bear.
When you spread forth your hands,
I will hide My eyes from you;
Even though you make many prayers,
I will not listen;
Your hands are full of blood.

Isaiah 1:11–15

. . .

God's affection for Israel rings even in the denunciations. It is "My people" who do not understand (1:3). It is "My people" who are suppressed by "the elders and princes" (3:14). He is anxious to forgive, to wipe out their sins (1:18). They are His children (1:2), "rebellious children" (30:1).

God is more than Lord and Owner; He is Father (1:2–4; 30–1). But for all His love and compassion, He cannot tolerate the corruption of the leaders who succumb to bribes and run after gifts, who "do not defend the fatherless, and the widow's cause does not come to them" (1:23). "Your silver has become dross, your wine mixed with water" (1:22).

Therefore the Lord says,
The Lord of hosts,
The Mighty One of Israel:
Ah, I will vent My wrath on My enemies,
And avenge Myself on My foes.
I will turn My hand against you
And will smelt away your dross as with lye
And remove all your alloy.
And I will restore your judges as aforetime,
And your counselors as at the beginning.
Afterward you shall be called the city of righteousness,
The faithful city.
Zion shall be redeemed by justice,
And those in her who repent, by righteousness.

Isaiah 1:24–27

There is sorrow in God's anger. It is an instrument of purification, and its exercise will not last forever. "For the Lord will have com-

233

passion on Jacob and will again choose Israel, and settle them in their own land, and the stranger shall join himself to them, and will cleave to the house of Jacob" (14:1). His mercy is not discarded, merely suspended. His anger lasts a moment, it does not endure forever.

> In a very little while My indignation will come to an end. . . .
> Come, My people, enter your chambers,
> And shut your doors behind you;
> Hide yourselves for a little while
> Until the indignation is past.
>
> Isaiah 10:25; 26:20

. . .

In [the] song of the vineyard, the prophet speaks first in his own name (vss. 1–2), then as the voice of God (vss. 3–6), and again in his own name (vs. 7). What personal attitude is reflected in the prophet's words?

It is first the prophet's love of God, Who is called "my Friend" and for Whom he sings "a love song concerning His vineyard." He neither rebukes the people's ingratitude nor bewails their prospect of ruin and disgrace. The prophet's sympathy is for God Whose care for the vineyard had been of no avail. God's sorrow rather than the people's tragedy is the theme of this song.

The song contains a gentle allusion to the grief and the disappointment of God. He feels hurt at the thought of abandoning the vineyard He had rejoiced in, and in which He had placed so much hope and care. In another prophecy we hear the song of God's dream, in which is fondly conceived the preservation of the vineyard, and His joy at the thought of continuing to care for it. . . .

What was the purpose of planting the vineyard (5:1–7), of choosing the people? The vineyard was planted to yield righteousness and justice. Yet the fruit it yielded was violence and outrage, affecting God, arousing His anger.

> Their speech and their deeds are against the Lord,
> Defying His glorious presence.
>
> Isaiah 3:8

Isaiah pleads for the meek and the poor, condemning the ruthless and the scoffers,

> . . . all who watch to do evil, . . .
> Who by a word make a man out to be an offender,
> And lay a snare for him who reproves in the gate,
> And with an empty plea turn aside him who is in the right.
>
> Isaiah 29:20, 21

It is the moral corruption of the leaders that has shattered God's relationship to His people, and in a passage which seems to belong in the context of the parable of the vineyard we read:

234

>The Lord shall enter into judgment
>With the elders and princes of His people:
>It is you who have devoured the vineyard;
>The spoil of the poor is in your homes.
>What do you mean by crushing My people,
>By grinding the face of the poor?
>
>Isaiah 3:14–15

However, it is not only the iniquity of others that upsets the prophet Isaiah. He feels polluted himself! "I am a man of unclean lips, and I dwell in the midst of a people of unclean lips" (6:5). Being unclean (literally: polluted) is a state of estrangement, a state in which one is kept away from the holy.

Isaiah, who flings bitter invectives against his contemporaries, identifies himself with his people (1:9) which are to be "my people" (3:12; cf. 8:10; 7:14). His castigation is an outcry of compassion. He sees his people all bruised and bleeding, with no one to dress their wounds.

>The whole head is sick,
>The whole heart is faint.
>From the sole of the foot even to the head
>There is no soundness in it,
>But bruises and sores
>And bleeding wounds;
>They are not pressed out, or bound up,
>Or softened with oil.
>
>Isaiah 1:5–6

. . .

However, in the face of idolatry and corruption, seeing that his people "have rejected the Torah of the Lord of hosts," and "despised the word of the Holy One of Israel" (5:24), the prophet seems to have lost his sense of compassion. In a moment of anger he utters the astounding words "forgive them not!" (2:9).

Is Isaiah's heart made of stone? Does he feel no pity for the people whose ruin he predicts? Indeed, two sympathies dwell in a prophet's soul: sympathy for God and sympathy for the people. Speaking to the people, he is emotionally at one with God; in the presence of God, beholding a vision, he is emotionally at one with the people. When told of the doom which threatens "this people," Isaiah exclaims with a voice of shock and protest, "How long, O Lord?" (6:11; cf. Jer. 4:14; Ps. 74:10). . . .

Obstinacy in an hour of imminent disaster is uncanny, irrational. Can a people whose plight is so grave remain deaf to the redeeming word of God? How shall one explain such a disposition?

In His effort to bring Israel back to His way, the Lord had tried to call upon the people, to confer favors upon them. Yet, "the more I called them, the more they went away from Me" (Hos. 11:2). "When the wicked is spared, he does not learn righteousness; in the land of uprightness he deals perversely and does not regard the majesty of the Lord" (Isa. 26:10). So He chastised them in order to make them repent, and chastisement proved to be no cure. The people were smitten and continued to rebel (1:5); they did not stop to ponder about the meaning of their suffering nor to "turn to Him who smote them, nor seek the Lord of hosts" (9:12; cf. 10:12). How did the inhabitants of Samaria explain the calamity that overtook their land? They thought it was due to an error in politics rather than to a failure in their relation to God. . . .

Isaiah's primary mission is to his own people. Unlike the nations of the world, Israel is reprimanded not only for arrogance and moral iniquity, but also for idolatry and the abandonment of God. The Creator of heaven and earth is called by Isaiah "the Holy One of Israel." There is a unique and intimate relationship between God and His people, yet the people have gone astray.

A factual description of the state of religion in the time of Isaiah, based upon the data cited in his accusation, would speak of disregard and deviation, of disobedience and evasion. Yet Isaiah speaks of rebellion, rejection, and disdain.

> Ah, sinful nation,
> A people laden with iniquity,
> Offspring of evildoers,
> Sons who deal corruptly!
> They have forsaken the Lord,
> They have despised the Holy One of Israel,
> They are utterly estranged . . .
> They have despised the Torah of the Lord of hosts,
> They have contemned the word of the Holy One of Israel.
>
> Isaiah 1:4; 5:24

There is no contrition, no compunction, no regret. Instead there is pride, conceit, and complacency (32:9 ff.).

"Israel does not know, My people does not understand" (1:3) is, we have seen, the divine complaint with which the book of Isaiah begins. We are told again what Hosea had proclaimed: *"My people go into exile for want of knowledge"* (5:13). The sort of knowledge they lack is alluded to in:

> They do not regard the deeds of the Lord,
> Or see the work of His hands.
>
> Isaiah 5:12

The people do not know how sick they are. Their leaders are "wise in their own eyes and shrewd in their own sight" (5:21). Does the wisdom of their leaders keep them from complete confusion?

Woe to those who call evil good
And good evil,
Who put darkness for light
And light for darkness,
Who put bitter for sweet
And sweet for bitter!

Isaiah 5:20

. . .

Isaiah holds out two hopes for mankind. One is immediate, partial, historical: "A remnant will return!" The other is distant, final, eschatological: the transformation of the world *at the end of days.*

Isaiah had named one of his sons *Shear-jashub,* which means "a remnant will return," as God's living sign for a supreme hope (cf. 8:18). "A remnant will return, the remnant of Jacob, to the mighty God. For though your people Israel be as the sand of the sea, only a remnant of them will return" (10:21–22).

The type of man who will survive the ordeals of history is described by Isaiah as one

. . . who walks righteously and speaks uprightly;
He who despises the gain of oppressions;
Who shakes his hands, lest they hold a bribe;
Who stops his ears from hearing of bloodshed,
And shuts his eyes from looking upon evil.

Isaiah 33:15

But beyond the hope that a remnant will return lies the ultimate hope that the whole world will be transformed.

ZION

Isaiah knew that disaster was bound to come, but also that a remnant would survive, that Zion would endure, and that through Israel and out of Zion redemption for all nations would flow. Unlike Jeremiah, Isaiah never predicted the destruction of Jerusalem.

Over and above all the threats and denunciations uttered by Isaiah rises the more powerful certainty of God's lasting, indestructible attachment to His people and to Zion. His disengagement from Israel is inconceivable. Anger passes; His attachment will never pass. Prophetic messages of doom are ambivalent. He is "smiting and healing" (19:22). Prophecy always moves in a polarity, yet the tension of yes and no, of anger and love, of doom and redemption, is often dissolved in the certainty of God's eternal attachment, as, for example, in the words of a postexilic prophet: "For thus said the Lord of hosts, after His glory sent me to the nations who plundered you, for he who touches you touches the apple of His eye" (Zech. 2:8 [H. 2:12]). . . .

237

SUGGESTED READINGS

Ackroyd, Peter R. *"The Book of Isaiah."* In *The Interpreter's One-Volume Commentary on the Bible,* edited by Charles M. Laymon, pp. 329–32. Nashville, Tenn.: Abingdon Press, Nashville, 1971.

Chase, Mary Ellen. *The Bible and the Common Reader.* Rev. ed., pp. 194–205, "Isaiah." New York: Macmillan, 1962.

Comay, Joan. *Who's Who in the Old Testament,* pp. 167–70, "Isaiah." New York: Holt, Rinehart and Winston, 1971.

Gaster, Theodor H. *Myth, Legend, and Custom in the Old Testament,* pp. 565–80, "Isaiah." New York: Harper & Row, 1969.

James, Fleming. *Personalities of the Old Testament,* pp. 246–69, "Isaiah." New York: Charles Scribner's Sons, 1939.

Scott, R. B. Y. "Introduction, Chapters 1–39, The Book of Isaiah." In *The Interpreter's Bible,* Vol. 5, edited by George A. Buttrick, pp. 151–64. Nashville, Tenn.: Abingdon Press, 1956.

QUESTIONS FOR DISCUSSION AND WRITING

1. What reasons does Isaiah give for preaching a message of hope?
2. How does Isaiah reconcile his ideas of a day of doom, a remnant of the people of Judah, a perfect world, and a Messiah?
3. What echoes of Amos's message do you hear in Isaiah 1–12?
4. Give the best explanation you can for God's command in 6:10 that Isaiah should keep the people from repenting and being healed.
5. Describe and evaluate Isaiah's techniques for putting across his message. Consider, for example, the use he makes of his sons' names. Were his techniques historically successful?
6. Why, according to Edith Hamilton, is Isaiah's superb language of greater value to us than a tightly worked out system of thought would have been?
7. Which characteristics of Isaiah's method of expression does Edith Hamilton consider most admirable?
8. What evidence did Isaiah give that Judah would be better off not making an alliance with Assyria? Did he rely only on faith?
9. What is the nature and the mission of the Messiah described in 9:6–7 and 11:1–11?
10. What illumination, if any, does Theodor Gaster's discussion of the myth of the Wondrous Child shed on Isaiah 7:14: "Behold, a young woman shall conceive and bear a son, and shall call his name Immanuel"?

11. Summarize E. W. Heaton's explanation of the "Immanuel" passage.
12. What, according to Heaton, was Isaiah's interpretation of Israel's mission and God's purpose in history?
13. What was Isaiah's conception of Israel and of God, according to Abraham Heschel?
14. There seems to be nothing good about the people depicted by Amos and Isaiah. Why should even a remnant of them be redeemed?

SECOND ISAIAH

Chapters 24 and 25 of 2 Kings* provide important background for Second Isaiah. They contain accounts of the first fall of Jerusalem to the Babylonians, in 597 B.C., and of the second fall, in 587 or 586 B.C. Approximately ten thousand people were deported to Babylon after the first conquest (24:14 and 24:16 differ about the actual number). According to Jeremiah 52:29, only 832 people were taken after the second conquest.

24 In his days Nebuchad-nez'zar king of Babylon came up, and Jehoi'akim became his servant three years; then he turned and rebelled against him. ² And the LORD sent against him bands of the Chalde'ans, and bands of the Syrians, and bands of the Moabites, and bands of the Ammonites, and sent them against Judah to destroy it, according to the word of the LORD which he spoke

*Reprinted from the Revised Standard Version of the Bible, copyrighted 1946, 1952, © 1971, 1973 by the Division of Christian Education of the National Council of the Churches of Christ in the United States of America.

by his servants the prophets. ³Surely this came upon Judah at the command of the LORD, to remove them out of his sight, for the sins of Manas'seh, according to all that he had done, ⁴and also for the innocent blood that he had shed; for he filled Jerusalem with innocent blood, and the LORD would not pardon. ⁵Now the rest of the deeds of Jehoi'akim, and all that he did, are they not written in the Book of the Chronicles of the Kings of Judah? ⁶So Jehoi'akim slept with his fathers, and Jehoi'achin his son reigned in his stead. ⁷And the king of Egypt did not come again out of his land, for the king of Babylon had taken all that belonged to the king of Egypt from the Brook of Egypt to the river Eu-phra'tes.

⁸Jehoi'achin was eighteen years old when he became king, and he reigned three months in Jerusalem. His mother's name was Nehush'ta the daughter of Elna'than of Jerusalem. ⁹And he did what was evil in the sight of the LORD, according to all that his father had done.

¹⁰At that time the servants of Nebuchadnez'zar king of Babylon came up to Jerusalem, and the city was besieged. ¹¹And Nebuchadnez'zar king of Babylon came to the city, while his servants were besieging it; ¹²and Jehoi'achin the king of Judah gave himself up to the king of Babylon, himself, and his mother, and his servants, and his princes, and his palace officials. The king of Babylon took him prisoner in the eighth year of his reign, ¹³and carried off all the treasures of the house of the LORD, and the treasures of the king's house, and cut in pieces all the vessels of gold in the temple of the LORD, which Solomon king of Israel had made, as the LORD had foretold. ¹⁴He carried away all Jerusalem, and all the princes, and all the mighty men of valor, ten thousand captives, and all the craftsmen and the smiths; none remained, except the poorest people of the land. ¹⁵And he carried away Jehoi'achin to Babylon; the king's mother, the king's wives, his officials, and the chief men of the land, he took into captivity from Jerusalem to Babylon. ¹⁶And the king of Babylon brought captive to Babylon all the men of valor, seven thousand, and the craftsmen and the smiths, one thousand, all of them strong and fit for war. ¹⁷And the king of Babylon made Mattani'ah, Jehoi'achin's uncle, king in his stead, and changed his name to Zedeki'ah.

¹⁸Zedeki'ah was twenty-one years old when he became king, and he reigned eleven years in Jerusalem. His mother's name was Hamu'tal the daughter of Jeremiah of Libnah. ¹⁹And he did what was evil in the sight of the LORD, according to all that Jehoi'akim had done. ²⁰For because of the anger of the LORD it came to the point in Jerusalem and Judah that he cast them out from his presence.

And Zedeki'ah rebelled against the king of Babylon. ¹And in the ninth year of his reign, in the tenth month, on the tenth day of the month, Nebuchadnez'zar king of Babylon came with all his army against Jerusalem, and laid siege to it; and they built siegeworks against it round about. ²So the city was besieged till the eleventh year of King Zedeki'ah. ³On the ninth day of the fourth month the famine was so severe in the city that there was no food for the people of the land. ⁴Then a breach was made in the city; the king with all the men of war fled by night by the way of the gate between the two walls, by the king's garden, though the

241

Chalde'ans were around the city. And they went in the direction of the Arabah. ⁵But the army of the Chalde'ans pursued the king, and overtook him in the plains of Jericho; and all his army was scattered from him. ⁶Then they captured the king, and brought him up to the king of Babylon at Riblah, who passed sentence upon him. ⁷They slew the sons of Zedeki'ah before his eyes, and put out the eyes of Zedeki'ah, and bound him in fetters, and took him to Babylon.

⁸In the fifth month, on the seventh day of the month—which was the nineteenth year of King Nebuchadnez'zar, king of Babylon— Nebu'zarad'an, the captain of the bodyguard, a servant of the king of Babylon, came to Jerusalem. ⁹And he burned the house of the LORD, and the king's house and all the houses of Jerusalem; every great house he burned down. ¹⁰And all the army of the Chalde'ans, who were with the captain of the guard, broke down the walls around Jerusalem. ¹¹And the rest of the people who were left in the city and the deserters who had deserted to the king of Babylon, together with the rest of the multitude, Nebu'zarad'an the captain of the guard carried into exile. ¹²But the captain of the guard left some of the poorest of the land to be vinedressers and plowmen.

¹³And the pillars of bronze that were in the house of the LORD, and the stands and the bronze sea that were in the house of the LORD, the Chalde'ans broke in pieces, and carried the bronze to Babylon. ¹⁴And they took away the pots, and the shovels, and the snuffers, and the dishes for incense and all the vessels of bronze used in the temple service, ¹⁵the firepans also, and the bowls. What was of gold the captain of the guard took away as gold, and what was of silver, as silver. ¹⁶As for the two pillars, the one sea, and the stands, which Solomon had made for the house of the LORD, the bronze of all these vessels was beyond weight. ¹⁷The height of the one pillar was eighteen cubits, and upon it was a capital of bronze; the height of the capital was three cubits; a network and pomegranates, all of bronze, were upon the capital round about. And the second pillar had the like, with the network.

¹⁸And the captain of the guard took Serai'ah the chief priest, and Zephani'ah the second priest, and the three keepers of the threshold; ¹⁹and from the city he took an officer who had been in command of the men of war, and five men of the king's council who were found in the city; and the secretary of the commander of the army who mustered the people of the land; and sixty men of the people of the land who were found in the city. ²⁰And Nebu'zarad'an the captain of the guard took them, and brought them to the king of Babylon at Riblah. ²¹And the king of Babylon smote them, and put them to death at Riblah in the land of Hamath. So Judah was taken into exile out of its land.

²²And over the people who remained in the land of Judah, whom Nebuchadnez'zar king of Babylon had left, he appointed Gedali'ah the son of Ahi'kam, son of Shaphan, governor. ²³Now when all the captains of the forces in the open country and their men heard that the king of Babylon had appointed Gedali'ah governor, they came with their men to Gedali'ah at Mizpah, namely, Ishmael the son of Nethani'ah, and Joha'nan the son of Kare'ah, and Serai'ah the son of Tanhu'meth the Netoph'athite, and

Ja-azani'ah the son of the Ma-ac'athite. ²⁴And Gedali'ah swore to them and their men, saying, "Do not be afraid because of the Chalde'an officials; dwell in the land, and serve the king of Babylon, and it shall be well with you." ²⁵But in the seventh month, Ishmael the son of Nethani'ah, son of Eli'shama, of the royal family, came with ten men, and attacked and killed Gedali'ah and the Jews and the Chalde'ans who were with him at Mizpah. ²⁶Then all the people, both small and great, and the captains of the forces arose, and went to Egypt; for they were afraid of the Chalde'ans.

²⁷And in the thirty-seventh year of the exile of Jehoi'achin king of Judah, in the twelfth month, on the twenty-seventh day of the month, Evil-mero'dach king of Babylon, in the year that he began to reign, graciously freed Jehoi'achin king of Judah from prison; ²⁸and he spoke kindly to him, and gave him a seat above the seats of the kings who were with him in Babylon. ²⁹So Jehoi'achin put off his prison garments. And every day of his life he dined regularly at the king's table; ³⁰and for his allowance, a regular allowance was given him by the king, every day a portion, as long as he lived.

SUMMARY

Chapters 40–66 of the Book of Isaiah are usually considered the work of other prophets, not the Isaiah of Chapters 1–39. Chapters 40–55 are generally attributed to an anonymous prophet living with the Jewish exiles in Babylon, who probably did most of his prophesying around the year 540 B.C. This prophet, known today as the Second Isaiah, knew the reputation of the Persian conqueror Cyrus, who had defeated Croesus of Lydia in 547 B.C., and he anticipated that Cyrus would soon take Babylon, an event that actually occurred in 539 B.C. The prophet was correct in assuming that Cyrus would release peoples held captive by the Babylonians, but if he expected the conqueror to embrace the religion of the Jews, he must have been disappointed. Certainly, he could argue that Cyrus's action in allowing the exiled Judeans to return to their homeland suited the purposes which the prophet identified with the designs of Yahweh.

"Comfort, comfort my people, says your God. Speak tenderly to Jerusalem, and cry to her that her warfare is ended, that her iniquity is pardoned, that she has received from the Lord's hand double for all her sins" (40:1, 2). So the Prophet begins his message to the exiles. God's people have suffered for their sins, and now God will show his love extravagantly: "Every valley shall be lifted up, and every mountain and hill be made low; the uneven ground shall be made level, and the rough places a plain" (40:4) to smooth the way for the exiles' return.

Tomb of Cyrus

This prophet's mission is given him in a much less spectacular way than that described by the First Isaiah in Chapter 6. The Second Isaiah simply wrote, "A voice says, 'Cry!' And I said, 'What shall I cry?' " (40:6).

The prophet sees that "all flesh is grass," and he emphasizes that the princes of the earth are as much victims of decay and death as are their subjects. Scarcely have the kings begun to rule "when he blows upon them, and they wither, and the tempest carries them off like stubble" (40:24). Compared with the everlasting power of God, the rulers of the earth are as nothing. If the exiles could grasp this vision of things, they could be patient for the day of deliverance: "They who wait for the Lord shall renew their strength, they shall mount up with wings like eagles . . ." (40:31). Not only are the rulers as nothing in the long run; even the gods they worship are nothing: "Behold, they are all a delusion; their works are nothing; their molten images are empty wind" (41:29).

In the "First Servant Song" (42:1–4) the prophet says that at God's behest Israel will "bring forth justice to the nations." Here we glimpse the intention of the Lord, later elaborated by the prophet in Chapter 53, to teach the rest of the world justice by means of his servant, Israel. "I have given you as a covenant to the people, a light to the nations, to open the eyes that are blind" (42:66). Having restrained himself for a long time, the Lord will now restore his own people and will "utterly put to shame" those "who trust in graven images" (42:17). He has redeemed Israel and will gather his people from Africa and Arabia. He is "doing a new thing," in that he has now forgiven the Israelites for their sins and will free them to go back to Jerusalem, where they will rebuild the city and the temple.

Using Cyrus as his anointed one, the Lord says to him, "I gird you, though you do not know me, that men may know, from the rising of the sun and from the west, that there is none besides me; I am the Lord and there is no other" (45:5b, 6). To those who would question him, the Lord states that it was he who created the earth and man, and now he will use Cyrus to "build my city and set my exiles free" (45:13). The nations will pay tribute to Israel, and they must all come to the Lord to be saved (45:22). For to compare him with the gods of other nations is nonsense. Other peoples make their gods of precious metals and then must carry these idols about and set them in place to worship (46:7). The Lord used Babylon to punish his people, but the Babylonians became arrogant and merciless. They went far beyond the wishes of the Lord. "On the aged you made your yoke exceedingly heavy" (47:6). The prophet taunts the Babylonians with the ineffectiveness of their sorcerers, "who divide the heavens, who gaze at the stars, who at the new moons predict what shall befall you" (47:13b). Babylon will fall because of its wickedness, and no one can save that nation.

Although the prophet has already said that Israel has suffered double for its sins, he now is reminded how unworthy the Lord's chosen nation has been from the beginning. According to him, Israel has always been a rebel, but nevertheless the Lord will save it for his own sake: "For how should my name be profaned? My glory I will not give to another" (48:11). So the captives will go free. In the "Second Servant Song" (49:1–6) the prophet reaches a conception new to Old Testament thought. He sees that the Lord selected Israel "from the womb" and polished that nation as one would an arrow to accomplish his purpose. That purpose, however, was not only to save Israel, which would be "too light a thing"; the Lord also intended to give Israel "as a light to the nations," so that his salvation might be for everyone (49:6). Giving thanks for their salvation, kings and queens will bow down to Israel and will recognize the Lord as the only God.

In the "Third Servant Song" (50:4–11) the prophet seems to identify himself with the servant, Israel. He says that he has brought the Lord's word to his people and has suffered the shame of being smitten and spat upon without rebelling. The Lord God will vindicate him, he is certain, but those who live by their own light rather than by the teachings of the Lord will "lie down in torment" (50:11).

Reminding his captive people that they are descended from Abraham and Sarah and that he redeemed them from their captivity in Egypt, the Lord promises the Israelites a new Eden when they return to their homeland after their exile in Babylon. The prophet urges the people to stand up and take courage from the knowledge that their enemies are mere human beings who die, whereas the Lord, who is their support, is everlasting. And he will now take the bowl of his wrath from them and give it to their tormentors to drink (51:22, 23).

In the passage beginning with 52:13 and ending with 53:12, which is known as the "Fourth Servant Song," the prophet returns to the theme first stated in 49:6: that Israel serves the Lord as "a light to the nations," as an instrument for the salvation of the entire world. The servant now is "lifted up," but he is battered almost beyond recognition. The kings of the nations are startled when they realize that the servant serves them as well as Israel. "Who has believed what we have heard?" they ask. "And to whom has the arm of the Lord been revealed? . . . Surely he has borne our griefs and carried our sorrows; yet we esteemed him stricken, smitten by God, and afflicted" (53:1, 4). Although personification of the nation is common in the Old Testament (Jacob = Israel), the details used by the prophet to describe the servant in this fourth song make it difficult not to visualize the servant as a particular individual. Who is he, then? The prophet who is speaking in this song? Another prophet? Christians have seen the servant in Second Isaiah as the image of their Savior; indeed, some have seen him as a foretelling of the actual Christ.

In a paean of optimism for the future, the prophet speaks in terms of family relationships to describe the overflowing love that the Lord has for His people: "For your Maker is your husband . . . for the Lord has called you like a wife forsaken and grieved in spirit" (54:5, 6). Although in anger he forsook them "for a brief moment" and hid his face from them, the Lord will now show compassion. As in the days of Noah, when he swore never to bring a flood again, so now he promises that he will never be angry with them again. "For the mountains may depart and the hills be removed, but my steadfast love will not depart from you" (54:10).

In Chapter 55, echoing the ecstatic poetry of Chapter 40, the prophet sings of the release from captivity and the return to the homeland. Believing that now the people will obey his will, the Lord in an extended simile says that as the rain and snow make things grow upon the earth, so his word from now on will be believed and followed. Not only will every valley be lifted up and "every mountain and hill be made low" (40:4); the mountains and hills also "shall break forth into singing, and all the trees of the field shall clap their hands" (55:12). The cypress and the myrtle, springing up in the place of the thorn and the brier, will be as the rainbow in Noah's time: "And it shall be to the Lord for a memorial, for an everlasting sign which shall not be cut off" (55:13).

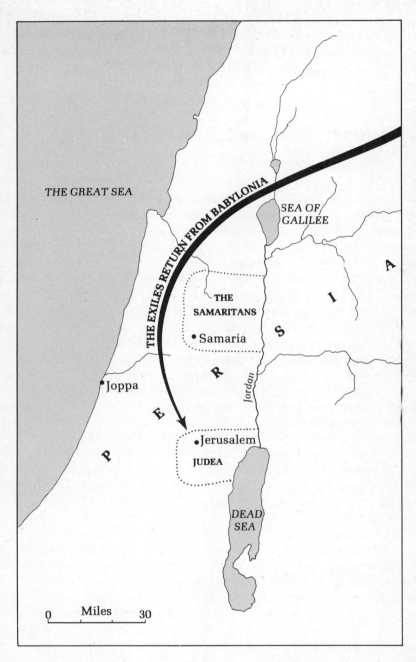

Return of the exiles to Jerusalem, *ca.* 536 B.C.

LITERARY QUALITIES

Literary Form and Structure
John L. McKenzie

Second Isaiah differs sufficiently in its form and structure from the books of earlier prophets to raise a number of questions. The collection exhibits a unity which is in evident contrast to the disarrangement characteristic of most prophetic books. The unity of themes and the progression of thought is not as strict as we find in modern writings of comparable length; but the reader recognizes in Second Isaiah a single work of a type which is not usual in the Bible. It is not merely a collection of detached oracles arranged according to such extrinsic principles as the catchword, that is, the connection of two passages by recurrence of the same word, especially at the end and beginning of the passages. How was this unity achieved? How much of it is due to the author, and how much to his editors?

Within this unity, critics distinguish separate utterances; but there is no general agreement on their number nor on the points of division. Either in the original composition or in the editing the sayings have been arranged so that one flows into another. There are, it is true, repetitions of themes and returns to points already made; the unity is sometimes jerky. But the arrangement makes it more difficult to isolate separate sayings than it is in Amos, Hosea, or Isaiah. Most critics now count about fifty to seventy separate sayings in Second Isaiah. . . .

. . . The poems of the first part [xl-xlviii.—Ed.] are addressed to a group most frequently addressed as Jacob or Israel; this group is most easily identified with the exilic community of Babylon. The themes of these poems are varied, but the promise of return and restoration is the dominant one. The prophet elaborates a presentation of Yahweh as the one God, the Lord of creation and the Lord of history, which is original. . . . The second part [xlix–lv.—Ed.] consists of the Zion poems, together with the three Servant Songs. It is Jerusalem or Zion which is addressed; the city is ruined and abandoned, but it awaits a glorious restoration. This is not a real change of theme and still less of basic theological thinking, but it is a change of perspective; and critics

LITERARY FORM AND STRUCTURE From *Second Isaiah* by John L. McKenzie. Copyright © 1968 by Doubleday & Company, Inc. Reprinted by permission of the publisher.

have good reason for supposing that the Zion poems, with their vivid imagery and note of taut expectation, are later than the Jacob/Israel addresses and reflect the heightened expectation which was excited by the victories of Cyrus. They may indeed represent two collections, as they certainly represent two series of utterances; but critics are very widely agreed that they do not represent two authors.

Otto Eissfeldt notes that the prophet uses the typical forms of prophetic utterance: [1] the vision and hearing narrative, the word of comfort, the promise, the rebuke, the admonition, the speech of the messenger, the taunt-song. Of particular interest is the prophet's use of the plea or charge (see xli 20–29, for example) and the fragments of hymns scattered through the work (xlii 10–13, xliv 23, for example). These echo the forms of earlier prophets, but they are given a personal turn by Second Isaiah; his style and transitions are generally smooth compared to Amos or First Isaiah. The weaving of separate sayings into a single movement of discourse can be seen easily in xl 1–11, which we have entitled "The Call of the Prophet." There are three speakers (Yahweh and two voices) in verses 1–8, and three separate sayings; and in verses 9–12 the prophet addresses "the messenger," another saying. But all these sayings are concerned with the call of the prophet, and in each saying his message is developed from an announcement of forgiveness in the first saying to the coming of Yahweh in the final saying. This introduction is followed by the poem of creation (xl 12–31), which can scarcely be subdivided into separate sayings; it is a literary unity in conception and in execution.

We notice . . . that the mood and tone change, at times rather sharply, from one poem to another. Thus a pleasing alternation of promise and rebuke is maintained; and these two themes are merged in the final chapter (xlviii) of the first part in a way which makes it almost impossible to handle this chapter in any other way than as a single poem. As each theme is brought to a climax, it elicits the next theme in response. There is more conscious art here than one is accustomed to find in materials assembled by compilers. The alternation of themes in this poem can be contrasted with the three poems of chapter xliii, in which two utterances of promise are followed by a rebuke; the rebuke in turn is followed by another poem of promise.

The Zion poems have an even more evident structure, and we have not broken them down into separate sayings. Here the tone is almost entirely a tone of promise; the flow of the poem is sustained by the brilliance of the imagery, the allusions to past history, and the frequent use of dialogue and apostrophe. These devices give the poem an intense tone, almost breathless in its urgency; as the promised salvation approaches, the poet creates an atmosphere of excitement. We have already noted that the final Zion poem (ch. lv) resumes the

---

[1] *The Old Testament: An Introduction*, p. 339.

themes of the introduction; the prophet merges hope and fulfillment. . . .

The unity of Second Isaiah led Paul Volz to suggest that Second
Isaiah himself was the collector and editor of his discourses. This is
connected with another question, whether Second Isaiah was primarily a speaker or a writer, which we discuss below. Karl Elliger suggested that it was Third Isaiah, a single author, who edited the
writings of Second Isaiah and added his own contributions. This
opinion is not widely accepted; if it were true, it is remarkable that
Third Isaiah produced a much more unified work in his edition of Second Isaiah than he did in his own writings. Furthermore, as we have
seen, the existence of Third Isaiah as a single author is highly doubtful. Voltz's opinion does give an explanation of the remarkable unity
of Second Isaiah; if the collection was made by an editor, the editor
had a better understanding of his material than any other editor whom
we encounter in the Old Testament. It seems we should presuppose at
least that Second Isaiah left his writings in a more organized condition
than any other writer known to us in the Old Testament.

But does this suggest that Second Isaiah was a writer rather
than a speaker? The earlier prophetic books are almost entirely collections of oral utterances, spoken before they were put in writing, and
sometimes written in a summary form. These oracles are collected
without any context and arranged according to principles which we
sometimes find impossible to discover. The polish of Second Isaiah
was not achieved by the usual means of collection and edition. Eissfeldt thinks that he wrote his discourses to be circulated in copies.
This would be not only a different manner of publishing the prophetic
word, it would also be a different conception of the prophetic mission.

If Second Isaiah was a prophetic speaker, in what situation did
he speak? The same question can be asked about the pre-exile
prophets, and it is not always easy to answer. We know that prophets
spoke in sanctuaries, and the existence of the cultic prophet, who pro-
nounced oracles in the cult, is fairly well assured. Prophets spoke in
the audience halls of kings and in the market places of the cities and
towns. Actually we can hardly think of many other places in which the
prophet could have assembled a sufficient number of people to make it
worth his trouble to speak. Second Isaiah could have spoken in the
market places of the towns of Babylonia; but a number of interpreters
have suggested that his discourses were spoken in cultic assemblies.
Some have even suggested that they can identify the festivals which
were appropriate for his discourses. The themes of creation and the
kingship of Yahweh, for example, would have been appropriate to the
the New Year festival. A New Year festival of Yahweh king and creator
in pre-exilic Israel has been postulated by a number of scholars, although there is no direct evidence for this festival. The exiles may
have commemorated the anniversary of the fall of Jerusalem by a day

of lamentation; in this case, the oracles of promise of Second Isaiah would have been the liturgical response to the lamentation. Of these suggestions one can say only that they are not without probability. It is not necessary to identify the utterances of Second Isaiah with any particular festivals in order to accept the view that he spoke in the cultic assembly. One has to suppose that prayer for the restoration of Jerusalem and the temple must have been a part of the cult of the exilic community; Second Isaiah delivers what would be oracular responses to such prayers. He does not reflect to any notable degree a ritual of lamentation and repentance; his theme is that the judgment was merited, but that the time of forgiveness and liberation has arrived. He proclaims the rise of a new Israel through a new Exodus. If one thinks of festivals at which he might have spoken in the cult, Passover is one such festival which comes to mind.

It seems probable that Second Isaiah, like his predecessors in prophecy, was a speaker first and a writer second; and as a speaker he is best located in the cultic assembly, and perhaps as an officer of the cult. If this is correct, then we must suppose that his discourses were more carefully written and revised before they reached their present form than the discourses of other prophets. There must have been a rising tension in the Israelite community as they watched the career of Cyrus moving toward the salvation Second Isaiah promised; but the progress of thought and feeling in the composition is the result not only of the movement of history but of literary craftsmanship. Thus one is inclined to accept the hypothesis of Volz that Second Isaiah himself revised and collected his discourses. The collection was a striking witness that the prophetic word had not lost its power in the fall of Israel; and Second Isaiah himself was the last in the series of prophetic witnesses he invokes in his discourses (see xli 21–29). . . .

INTERPRETATIONS

A Job to Do—a Mission
SHELDON H. BLANK

There are two kinds of hoping. Men can hope with a serene and perfect faith, and simply wait supine and open-mouthed for the realization of all desires. Apocalypse and messianism have served as illus-

A JOB TO DO—A MISSION From Sheldon H. Blank, *Understanding the Prophets* (New York: Union of American Hebrew Congregations, 1969), pp. 117–28. Reprinted by permission of the publisher.

trations for this first kind of hoping. But men can also hope with a determined hope, and move with a sure tread towards a desired goal. We turn now to this kind of hoping—and our key word is "mission."

If I am sent to do a job I am given a mission. If I have been given a job to do I have become a missionary. A people with a job to do is a missionary people. A religion that includes a mission is a missionary faith.

In a block of sixteen chapters in the Book of Isaiah, and in another interesting little book called Jonah, we find the best examples of those features of prophetic thought which we associate with the idea of a mission.

THE SECOND ISAIAH

The block of chapters is the sixteen that begin with Isaiah 40 and extend through Isaiah 55. The author of these chapters held out to the Judean captives the hope that Cyrus the Persian would break the power of Babylonia and send those captives home. Centuries ago it was recognized that the author of these sixteen chapters was not the prophet Isaiah who lived in the eighth pre-Christian century and threatened Jerusalem with destruction at the hands of Assyria. The author of the sixteen chapters lived no less than two-and-a-half centuries later than that first Isaiah, and under a wholly different political constellation; also, he lived not where the first Isaiah lived, not in Jerusalem, but in Babylonia. He is not the same person; we know very little about him; we do not even know his name. For convenience we call him the "Second" Isaiah—by which we simply mean Chapters 40–55 of the Book of Isaiah. And we call him "Isaiah" simply because his writings were included in the Isaiah scroll.

What this so-called Second Isaiah said to his people was, like all genuine prophetic words, relevant to the then current human situation. As with other prophets this one did not speak in a vacuum; he brought a word of God which answered to a people's present need. The people of Israel were in need of comfort and he comforted them; they were as refuse and he came to rehabilitate them. And what better way to rehabilitate persons or a people than to provide them with a worthy goal, a purpose for their life, a job to do! This was the time for a mission and it was probably the prophet whom we call the Second Isaiah who conceived and propagated the idea of Israel's mission. It seems to have sprung from the historical context of his place and time.

THE MEANING OF "MISSION" AND "SALVATION"

Persons can use the same words in a conversation and woefully fail to communicate, talking right past each other. This is particularly true of theological terms, and all readers may not mean the same thing when they use words like "mission"—or like "salvation," which also we will refer to in this context. It may be well therefore to clarify the meaning of these two words before we go on, so that we may not seem to be thinking of quite different concepts, and may doubt that we should be calling them "missions" and "salvation" at all. When we are dealing with the thinking of the Hebrew prophets it is proper to use these words as we will. We will use them with the meaning the words had in the days of those prophets; what other meanings they have now have been added since the time of the prophets in a culture predominantly Christian.

When the Second Isaiah sent his people on a mission he sent them to give to all men a religion to live by. His people's goal was a reconciled humanity. Their mission was to the society of men for its earthly good. Their interest was in the quality of men's lives here and now, and in the kind of world they could leave for their children's children. They were not interested in the fate of their own souls in an afterlife. They did not think of achieving heavenly bliss or escaping the torments of hell. They did not think of such matters because the time had not yet come when Jews thought in those terms. The fate of men's souls in an afterlife did not occupy a place in the thought of biblical man. He had this life to live; he did not know anything about life after death and made no provision for it.

We speak here of what did *not* concern men in the time of the prophets in order to make more obvious by comparison what *did* concern them. The term "salvation" as, for example, the Second Isaiah used the term, had none of the associations with eternity which have subsequently gathered round it. In the Bible salvation is not a second chance at life. This is a man's life; and if it is lived in hunger and misery and hurt, in anxiety and servitude and lonely grief, it may be only a fragment of a life—one may not call it living—but this is it. There is no life to save but this life, and salvation is in essence the rescue of the huddled masses from present terror and want.

The Hebrew nouns which mean "salvation" are all derived from a verb which means "to help, to save or deliver." Often, according to the context, the verb means no more than "to deliver persons or armies, cities or nations from danger," from an enemy or from any other threat to their safety. The word does not always have theological implications; one man may save another from peril, one army may save another from defeat. Nor does it always have negative overtones; it does not always mean "deliverance *from*." It can have a positive sense and refer to a bestowing on, a giving to. It can include all that a man may wish—all that one may expect in this life from a benevolent God, whose generous will is unopposed.

Salvation is both: security *from* and enjoyment *of*. It is first of all security—security from the sword, from pestilence, from famine; but it is also blessing, the blessing of the womb, of the field, of the barn;

and it is life and length of days. It is these earthly and homely bless-ings, for, as we have noted, the age had not yet come when Jews thought in terms of heavenly reward.

For the Second Isaiah, salvation meant something more. His spirit was expansive, his horizon broad. His God was the one, unique world-God, universal in time as well as in space. To such a prophet, representing such a God, salvation must be something more, some-thing commensurate with his spirit. According to this prophet salva-tion is world-wide. It is the goal God has set for mankind, the realization of the divine purpose in human society.

Out of chaos God created the world. Creation is purposive, and it is not to be reversed—creation should not revert to the *tohu va bohu* which it was before God spoke.

> Not to be an empty waste did He create it
> > [the prophet said];
> to be inhabited He formed it.
>
> > > (45:18)

Once because of human depravity He had been constrained to destroy with a cosmic flood all flesh and start anew with the family of Noah. Again, for men's arrogance, he had found it necessary to divide man-kind into a Babel of unrecognizable tongues and scatter them over the earth. But both events were a slipping back, and what ground was lost was yet to be regained. Mankind divided into warring tribes, hope-lessly unable to reach an understanding because their words have lost all meaning and so communication is cut off—such a society was not the goal of God's desires for humanity. Eventually the family of man must again be united. Their reunion is the goal; a reconciled human-ity, this is salvation.

And it is the same as the messianic hope, the Utopian ideal which we have considered, God's kingdom on earth: when swords will be beaten into plowshares and spears into pruning hooks, when people will not raise sword against people or learn war any more, when each man may sit under his vine and his fig tree with none to make him afraid.

It is the hope that the lion will lie down with the lamb, that men in power will abandon their rapacious, predatory drives, and learn to live with the weak and the humble in active harmony. It is the hope for that beckoning time when men will "not hurt or destroy" in all God's holy mountain—in all this world which He made.

Now one may want to ask where we have got to and where we are going. We seem to have returned to themes which we have already considered, themes which we classed with the kind of faith that only accepts. And here we are, citing those shapes of hope that belong to that sort of faith, when we claim to be speaking of the products of the other kind of faith—the kind that requires doing.

THE MISSION OF THE SERVANT

But we have not wandered from the subject. The goal is the same for faith of both sorts; it is only a question of man's role in achieving the goal, whether he simply accepts or whether he has a job to do. According to the Second Isaiah he has a job to do. Or must we be more precise and say: "*Israel* has a job to do"? If we are speaking of the Second Isaiah this is what we should say; he assigned to *his people* a task, a role in the process of deliverance. That is the meaning of the figure known as "the servant of the Lord." It has broadened since his time, but when the Second Isaiah spoke of the servant of the Lord he spoke of Israel.

Consider this conception: "the servant of the Lord." Not every scholar will agree on the meaning of the servant. Not every Jew will agree. There is no single Jewish interpretation, nor any single Christian interpretation, either. Many will agree with the interpretation offered here (for the reasoning behind it, see Blank, *Prophetic Faith in Isaiah*, pp. 77–104), but it still is *an* interpretation, not *the* interpretation.

In the passages which interest us here, in all of them, even in the famous fifty-third which describes the "passion" of the servant, the servant is a personification of the people Israel. The servant was not understood in this way when the New Testament was written. To the authors of the New Testament the servant was not a people but a person, he was the hoped-for messiah. And to the extent that the life and fate of Jesus followed the pattern of the servant, Jesus was identified as this messianic servant of the Lord. The Jewish interpretation of the Isaiah material current at the time of Jesus no doubt facilitated this identification. Jewish thinking had been moving in that direction. But the prophetic author of the sixteen chapters had no such meaning in mind.

Wherever we look in Isaiah 40 to 55 the servant is the people of Israel, chosen by God to serve Him, commissioned by God to bring witness. Let us reread a few passages quoted from there and decide for ourselves who the servant must be, setting aside while we read, if we can, any interpretation we are familiar with, in the New Testament, or in Jewish tradition, or elsewhere, and simply listening and judging for ourselves who the servant is. In the following three passages God is speaking. To whom is he speaking?

> You, Israel My servant,
>   Jacob whom I chose,
>   seed of Abraham, My friend,
> You whom I took from the ends of the earth,
>   summoned from its distant parts

Saying to you: "You are My servant,"
  I favor you and I have not rejected you.
Do not fear for I am with you. . . .
                                    (41:8–10a)

Now hearken Jacob My servant,
  Israel whom I have chosen.
Thus says God your maker,
  He who formed you at birth, who will help you:
"Fear not, My servant Jacob,
  Jeshurun whom I have chosen."
                                    (44:1f.)

Remember these things, O Jacob,
  O Israel, for you are My servant.
I formed you; you are a servant to Me.
  O Israel, I will not forget you.
                                    (44:21)

In another passage God speaks to the conquering Cyrus, His agent, about His chosen servant:

For the sake of My servant Jacob,
  Israel My chosen one,
I summoned you by name,
  naming you though you know Me not.
                                    (45:4)

It would be less than honest to say that there are no problems at all, but certainly these and about a dozen other passages make a fairly uniform impression; the servant of the Lord is Jacob, Jeshurun, the chosen one, Israel—personified.

Personification is a literary device, a figure of speech. The Second Isaiah was a master at personification. He could develop a figure until his figment lives and we seem to have a real person before us. And it is perhaps no wonder that later times had trouble with his servant figure. He made it so lifelike that it could easily seem that he had a known person in mind. If he had been less skillful the many volumes written about the identity of the servant would not have been written. Everyone would have known: he meant Israel.

Now we could properly devote several chapters to this servant figure and even then have barely touched the subject. But in order to preserve reasonable proportions we will limit ourselves here to three observations. The first is brief, the others longer.

The first focuses on the word "servant." The Second Isaiah thinks of Israel as a servant. A servant serves, has a task, a job to do. If we seem to be repeating this thought, saying the same thing again and again though in different words, that is done in order to make the point. In personifying Israel as the servant of the Lord, the Second Isaiah assigned to his people not a passive but an active role, asked of his people the faith that requires doing. The very word he used, *'eved*, "servant," implies as much. It distinguishes the thought of the Second Isaiah from the thought of those authors of the messianic or apocalyptic passages which we have already reviewed. He goes along with those authors some of the way but then he parts with them. His goal is the same as that of the messianists, as we shall yet see, but attaining the goal will not be God's work alone; man has a role to play, a role in the redemptive process—a mission.

THE "SUFFERING" SERVANT?

What is this role? It is not martyrdom; that is the second observation and it can not be stated as briefly as the first. When they speak of "the servant" in these chapters Jews are inclined to toss in an adjective and to say, without even thinking: "the *suffering* servant." And Jews are not alone in this misconception. At first glance the description of the servant in Isaiah 52:13–53:12 gives reason enough for this view:

> . . . His looks were inhumanly marred,
>   his appearance unlike a man's.
>
>   (52:14)

> He was despised and ignored by men,
>   a man of pains, familiar with sickness,
> One to look away from . . .
>
>   (53:3)

> He was driven and was meek,
>   not opening his mouth—
> As a sheep led to the slaughter,
>   as a ewe is dumb before her shearers—
>   not opening his mouth.
>
>   (53:7)

There is quite enough in this chapter to account for the image of Israel the suffering servant.

Nevertheless it is a false and a profitless image. It is false because the chapter speaks not of a people destined to suffer but of a people which has suffered. In the tense lies the error and the misconstruction. All the verbs in the verses just quoted are in the past tense. "His looks were . . . marred." "He was despised." "He was driven." That Israel had suffered was, of course, undeniable. Defeat, destruction, captivity had been its lot—were still its lot. There had even been meaning in their past suffering. The kings of the nations knew well what it meant. "Suffering which could lead to our welfare," they called it.

> Indeed, he has borne sickness for us. . . .
> He was [in fact] wounded because of our
>   transgressions,
> crushed because of our iniquities.
> He experienced the suffering which might
>   lead to our welfare,
> and there was healing for us in his bruises.
>   (53:4a, 5)

This is a somewhat unusual and difficult thought but it is not unique in the Bible. Perhaps the most graphic parallel is one in Exodus, in 14:30f. Israel had just crossed the Red Sea. "So God delivered Israel from Egypt on that day," we read. And then the suffering which might lead to this people's welfare: "And Israel saw Egypt dead on the shore of the sea. And Israel [thus] experienced God's great might, employed against Egypt, and the people both feared God and believed in God and His servant Moses." From what Egypt had suffered Israel learned and might derive profit. So from Israel's experience others might learn and profit.

According to the Second Isaiah there had been that much meaning in Israel's pain—there *had* been—in the past. Here the prophet stopped. He did not go on to say that for such a purpose Israel was yet to suffer, through future untold ages. He did not think of grief as Israel's destiny; he made of it neither a project nor a program. Quite the contrary! He spoke consistently of the suffering as over and past; a servant who had suffered, yes; a servant destined to suffer, no; the future is only radiant. Speaking for God, the prophet has this to say of Israel's future:

> Lo, My servant shall prosper,
>   shall rise, be lifted up, be greatly exalted
>   (52:13)

[That is the prophet's expectation.]

> Even as many were appalled at him
>   because his looks were inhumanly marred
>   and his appearance unlike a man's
>   (52:14)

[That is the misery and disgrace of the past, but it is followed by what shall yet be, namely:]

> Even so many will be aghast at him;
> > kings will be dumbfounded,
> Having seen what had never been told them,
> > having considered what they never had heard
> > > (52:15)

[That is to say, unheard-of glory is in store for the servant of God, for Israel—such future glory that the kings of nations shall be aghast.]

The key words for the understanding of this chapter, the words revealing the prophet's original intent, are words which he himself speaks of the servant in a climactic position in the fifty-third chapter (vs. 10): "God's desire shall succeed through him." This is an exciting thought about which we shall want to say more.

This has been our observation about the idea of the "suffering" servant: that the Second Isaiah never meant to assign to Israel, the servant of God, the role of a scapegoat, a vicarious sacrifice. He never suggested martyrdom as his people's future lot. We do not find in the servant image the idea of a people by nature defeated before it begins.

A PEOPLE OF PROPHETS

What, then, is the role of the servant Israel according to the Second Isaiah? The servant has the role of a prophet; and this is the third observation, and it is not to be misunderstood. It does not mean that the servant is any one prophet, known or unidentified, past, present or future—the servant is, as we have been saying, the people Israel, drawn in personification to look like a prophet, with the features of a prophet—a people sent to serve as a prophet must serve, and to accomplish what, ideally, a prophet may accomplish, sent to save from ruin not a people (Israel) but mankind, sent to realize God's wider purpose. "God's desire shall succeed through him"—"through him"—that is what the Second Isaiah says of the servant: "God's desire shall succeed through him"; and this also is contained in that fifty-third chapter. Elsewhere too the Second Isaiah represents God as saying:

> Here is My servant whom I uphold.
> > My chosen one in whom I delight.
> I have put My spirit on him;
> > he will publish truth among the nations.
> > > (42:1)

That is his activity: publishing the truth.

God could say most of that about any of His other prophets: I have put My spirit on him; he will publish the truth. The difference is in the last phrase: "among the nations." God put His spirit on single prophets and sent them to publish the truth among His people Israel.

He sent His servant Israel, a whole prophet-people, according to the Second Isaiah—He sent this servant to publish the truth among the nations.

> He will not fade nor be broken [the passage continues],
>   until he establishes truth on earth.
> The coastlands wait for his teaching.
>
> (42:4)

And in a similar passage God says:

> So I make you a light to the nations,
>   that My salvation may reach
>   to the ends
> of the earth.
>
> (49:6b)

These are the words that draw it all together—Israel, the job, salvation, all that we have been talking about in this chapter—all in the words here spoken to Israel, the "servant": "I make you a light to the nations, that My salvation may reach to the ends of the earth."

Let the name Israel stand for all men who have a sense of dedication, commitment. Think of salvation as a state of blessedness and security *here*. Then listen again: "I make you a light to the nations, that My salvation may reach to the ends of the earth."

Combine a faith that requires doing with an orientation towards life here, and the result is: human efforts to improve the human state, the service brought by persons dedicated to the achievement of the messianic goal, that every man may enjoy freedom from fear and from want, and enjoy that freedom here.

The Suffering Servant
Theodor H. Gaster

The prophet comforts his oppressed compatriots by reminding them of a certain character who, though traduced, smitten, tortured, and vilified, bears all this in equanimity, as a kind of human scapegoat serving to make expiation for public sin and wrongdoing. A feature of this martyr is that he is of unsightly appearance, like "one from whom men turn their face."

We need not enter here into the vexed question of who the Suffering Servant was intended to be—a problem as chronic and as seemingly

THE SUFFERING SERVANT From pp. 580–82 of "Isaiah" in *Myth, Legend, and Custom in the Old Testament* by Theodor H. Gaster. Copyright © 1969 by Theodor H. Gaster. By permission of Harper & Row, Publishers, Inc.

insoluble as the identity of the Dark Lady of the Sonnets. Our concern is solely with the folkloristic background of this image.

The picture is drawn, we suggest, from the widespread institution of the *human scapegoat,* usually a misshapen person or one already under sentence of death, upon whom is saddled the taint of all sins and offenses which might otherwise be visited on the community, but precise responsibility for which cannot be placed, for one reason or another, on any particular individual.

In Babylon, a condemned felon (*bêl ḫiṭṭi*) was paraded through the streets, scourged and expelled at the New Year (*Akîtu*) festival. At Athens in times of drought or calamity, a misshapen man and woman were driven out of town as a public expiation; they were called *pharmakoi.* At Chaeronea, during a famine, a slave was ceremoniously beaten with twigs of *agnus castus* (a kind of willow); and at Marseilles, this was done in time of plague. At Ephesus, Apollonius of Tyana, the shamanistic "prophet" and charlatan, had a beggar stoned to relieve pestilence, and a similar use of human scapegoats is recorded from Abdera. In Athens, a misshapen man and woman were scourged with squills; while similarly in Rome, an old man known as Mamurius Veturus was clad in skins and beaten with white rods annually on the Ides of March, evidently an ancient method of forefending evil at the beginning of the year. At Oritsha, on the Niger, two sickly persons act as human scapegoats in moments of public crisis; while in Thailand, purification is effected by parading on a litter a woman broken down by debauchery, pelting her with offal, and subsequently throwing her on a dunghill. Among the aboriginal tribes of China, a man of great muscular strength is expelled in times of crisis, his face having first been disfigured by paints. In Switzerland, a lad disguised as a witch, goat or ass is driven out of town on the second Thursday before Christmas; and at Munich, Germany, the same custom used to prevail on Ascension Eve.

Now observe how perfectly all this chimes with the prophet's description of the Suffering Servant. He is disfigured and sickly (Isa. 52:14; 53:2–3). He bears physical sickness and pain on behalf of the community (53:4, 10). He is expelled, "cut off" (53:8). He is treated as a felon (53:9). He is subjected to stripes, i.e., trounced (53:5).

The Suffering Servant is described also as *one from whom men hide their face.* On this expression too Comparative Folklore sheds interesting light.

The Servant is a sick man, and, in ancient and primitive thought, sickness implies possession by a demon; indeed, he is said expressly (53:4) to be "smitten of God (i.e., demon-struck) and afflicted (i.e., plagued)." Now, such demonic influences can be relayed to others by a mere glance. Hence, those who wish to avoid being so "infected"—especially persons possessed of some special or divine power—customarily veil their faces. Moses, we are told (Exod. 34:33), veiled his face when addressing the people after his descent from Mt. Sinai. However it may later have been re-interpreted, the real purpose of this action was to protect from untoward and demonic glances that divine glory with which he had become suffused. In the same way, the kings and sultans of several African peoples often keep their faces veiled; and in ancient Persia only the seven highest courtiers were normally permitted to look upon the countenance of their sovereign at all times.

Alternatively, the person who is demonically possessed had to keep *his* face covered, lest he pass the evil to others. In ancient Greece, for example, a man guilty of unwitting homicide had to keep his head covered; and among West African primitives, human sacrifices are often veiled. Not improbably, this is also the true basis of the law which anciently required lepers to wear hoods. Sometimes too, as in the case of the human scapegoats described above, the necessary disguise is effected by *whitewash.*

SUGGESTED READINGS

Bewer, Julius A. *The Literature of the Old Testament.* 3rd ed., edited by Emil G. Kraeling, pp. 100–117, "Isaiah and Micah." New York: Columbia University Press, 1962.

James, Fleming. *Personalities of the Old Testament,* pp. 360–89, "Second Isaiah." New York: Charles Scribner's Sons, 1939.

McKenzie, John L., ed. *The Second Isaiah.* The Anchor Bible Series, No. 20. New York: Doubleday & Company, 1968.

Muilenburg, James. "Introduction, Chapters 40–66, The Book of Isaiah." In *The Interpreter's Bible,* Vol. 5, edited by George A. Buttrick, pp. 381–419. Nashville, Tenn.: Abingdon Press, 1956.

Sandmel, Samuel. *The Hebrew Scriptures: An Introduction to Their Literature and Religious Ideas,* pp. 167–93, "Second Isaiah." New York: Alfred A. Knopf, 1963.

QUESTIONS FOR DISCUSSION AND WRITING

1. Summarize the message of Chapters 40–55 in a short paragraph.
2. Review the history of Israel as presented in the Bible from the time of Abraham to the time of the Babylonian Captivity, and then judge whether the nation can qualify as a "servant." *How* has it served, and *whom* has it served?

3. What evidence does John McKenzie find in Chapters 40–55 to support the thesis that these chapters constitute a separate unity in the Book of Isaiah?
4. What evidence can you find in the text of Second Isaiah to support McKenzie's opinion that the prophet "proclaims the rise of a new Israel through a new Exodus"?
5. How, according to Theodor Gaster, does the folklore background of the image of the "suffering servant" shed light on Second Isaiah's portrayal of the servant?
6. What features of the servant in Second Isaiah might qualify him as a "scapegoat"?
7. What does "salvation" mean in Second Isaiah, according to Sheldon H. Blank?
8. How, according to Blank, is it possible for a nation—for Israel in this case—to be a "servant"?
9. Does the covenant made with Abraham recorded in Genesis 12:1–3 and 17:1–8 substantiate Blank's interpretation of Israel's mission of servant as depicted in Second Isaiah?
10. What arguments can you bring from Chapters 40–55 against Blank's opinion that the servant is Israel?
11. Comment on Blank's observation that if the Second Isaiah "had been less skillful" and had not made the servant figure seem so lifelike, we would have no trouble recognizing the servant as the nation Israel.
12. Note that Chapters 40 and 55 serve as a frame for the message of the prophet. How does the ecstatic poetry of these two chapters enhance the message?
13. Compare Second Isaiah's mission with that of Amos.

VERSE AND POETRY

INTRODUCTORY NOTE

Our readings so far, especially Amos, Isaiah, and Second Isaiah, have revealed the Hebrew bent for poetic communication. There are poems in Genesis (2:23; 3:14–19; 4:23–24; 9:25–27; 14:19–20; 25:23; 27:27–29; 27:39–40; 48:15–16, 20; and 49:3–27), Exodus (15:1–18, 21), Deuteronomy (32:1–43; 33:2–29), Joshua (10:12–13), Judges (5:2–31), 1 Samuel (2:1–10; 15:22–23), 2 Samuel (1:19–27; 3:33–34; 22:2–51; 23:1–7), and in 1 Kings (8:12–13).

Now, however, as we study the Song of Songs, Psalms, Proverbs, and the Book of Job, we will be reading poetry almost exclusively. Some information about Hebrew poetry will therefore be helpful, and Samuel Sandmel provides it in the selection that follows. The first six paragraphs—on verb forms—may seem too complicated to those of us who know no Hebrew, but we don't need to understand all the details. "Why should we spend this space on the verb forms?" asks Sandmel. "To make the point that the Hebrew language, despite its paucity of tenses, is able to express subtleties in meaning."

Verse and Poetry
SAMUEL SANDMEL

We have seen in passing some random specimens of Hebrew verse and poetry. Now we shall look more closely, recalling the essential differences in any literature between verse and prose. Verse is a form of writing which conforms to certain external characteristics, normally either meter or rhyme; in biblical literature it is meter, never rhyme, which distinguishes verse from prose. There are a number of distinctive meters which we shall notice.

Poetry, even while adhering to the form of verse, rises above prose and verse by its heightened expression, through capturing some intensely emotional mood or feeling, often expressed through felicitous words and phrases, such as figures of speech. (Naturally, there are passages which to some tastes would be verse and to others poetry, for the line of demarcation is not always clear-cut.)

Because verse and poetry conform to a metrical pattern, there is often, or always, a potential artificiality in them, but the better the versifier or the poet, the less evident the artificiality. We tend to tolerate the artificiality in verse and poetry because the greater effectiveness of the total compensates for the departure from prose. The nature of the Hebrew language, and of Hebrew syntax, tends to reduce artificiality to the vanishing point. For example, what we call a verb in Hebrew can contain the action, the subject, and the object; thus, re'ītikā, a single word, means "I have seen you." Hebrew verse, accordingly, is relatively free of glaring disruptions of word order or of syntax, as when a poet writes, in English, "Him I saw." In Hebrew the usual word [order] of a sentence, even in prose, is normally the verb, the subject, and then the object. Thus, "God remembered Noah" (Gen. XIII:1) is: "remembered God Noah." In Hebrew, where the writer desires to indicate an emphasis, he accomplishes this by putting that word first in the sentence or poetic line, so that the Hebrew, "Noah remembered God" would denote that it was Noah, *not somebody else*, whom God remembered. On the other hand, the order, "God remembered Noah," would denote that God, *not somebody else*, did the remembering. The flexibility available in Hebrew word order dissolves the artificiality.

A peculiarity in Hebrew (and in some other languages) is the

VERSE AND POETRY From *The Enjoyment of Scripture: The Law, the Prophets, and the Writings* by Samuel Sandmel. Copyright 1972 by Oxford University Press, Inc. Reprinted by permission.

ability to dispense with the verb "to be" in the present tense. In Psalm XXIII, the best-known of the Psalms, the literal rendering is: "Yahve my shepherd," though the meaning is inescapably "Yahve *is* my shepherd." Grammarians of Hebrew call this kind of construction a "noun clause," simply because no verb is directly expressed. Indeed, we must note the verb tenses in Hebrew. An English verb has six tenses: I see; I saw; I shall see; I have seen; I had seen; I will have seen. A Hebrew verb has only two. We give the two tenses names comparable to those some grammarians have given Indo-European tenses, calling them "imperfect" and "perfect." However, a Hebrew verb, whether "imperfect" or "perfect," lacks a clear and definitive sense of time, such as past or future; the two Hebrew tenses express the completeness or incompleteness of the action, without respect to time. Thus, "I *went* to the store yesterday" would in Hebrew mean that I went there and finished my going; in such a case one would use what is called the perfect tense. But suppose that yesterday, on my way to the store, I met a friend, stopped to talk, and forgot to go on to the store; that is, I left the going uncompleted. In such a case, the Hebrew, in saying, "as I *went* to the store yesterday," would use the imperfect tense, not the perfect, and mean, "as I *was going.*" It follows, then, that there is a certain suppleness in the tenses of the Hebrew verb, despite the lack of a full system of tenses.

Psalm XLI:2 reads, "Happy the considerer of the poor," meaning, "Happy is he who considers the poor." Analysts call the Hebrew form for the word "considerer" a participle. In Hebrew, a participle is part verb, part adjective, and part noun. When a participle is used along with a noun, it is an adjective; for example, "The man, *seeing* the cloud, knew it would rain." As a noun it denotes "the one seeing" or even "the see-er." We can translate a participle by a noun like "see-er," or even use a roundabout English expression, "the one who sees . . . ." There are times—for instance, in our use of the present tense—when the Hebrew participle acts like a verb. We might illustrate this from the well-known verse: "Yahve *visits* the sins of fathers on the children." In the sentence, a perfect tense ("visited") would mean that the action was completed, as if, "Last year, God *visited* the sins . . ."; an imperfect would mean, "Yahve was *in the act of visiting* the sins . . ." but did not complete the act. The sense of the participle is that "Yahve *continually* (or *customarily*) visits the sins. . . ."

The time factor (past, present, or future) of a Hebrew sentence is dictated largely by context. A kind of convention has existed among earlier translators whereby an imperfect has come to be rendered into English as a future; often this is right, but just as often it can be wrong. The sentence, "Yahve is my shepherd, I *shall* not *want*" (understanding "want" as "lack") illustrates in "shall . . . want" the way in which an imperfect can become a future in English. It is just as accurate to render this, "I *do not* want." Had the verb been a perfect, it would have meant, "I did not lack"; had it been a participle, "Yahve is my shepherd, I *continuously* do not lack." The Hebrew imperfect means, "now, at this time, I do not lack."

Why should we spend this space on the verb forms? To make the point that the Hebrew language, despite its paucity of tenses, is able to express subtleties in meaning.

The opportunity for subtlety is increased by a characteristic Hebrew mannerism, used both in prose and in verse. The usual Hebrew sentence is composed of two parts, so that we speak of an A and a B part of a verse. In prose, this is a typical sentence: "In the beginning God created heaven and earth" (the A part); and "the earth was waste and void" (the B part). While there are some occasional short sentences which are not in two parts, most Hebrew sentences are, even in prose.

In verse, where meter enters in, the two parts are ordinarily of the same length metrically, consisting, in the most usual pattern, of two three-beat half-sentences:

$$— — — \ / — — —$$

Whereas in prose, devoid of meter, the two half-sentences are only loosely tied to each other, in verse they are intimately bound together.

For example:

Le-yáhve hā-áretz u-melóāh / tēvél ve-yóshevé-hāh
(A:) The earth is Yahve's, and its contents; (B:) the world
and those who inhabit it.

(Ps. XXIV:1)

Here B essentially repeats A, extending it somewhat. Again:

(A:) He has me graze in grassy fields; (B:) He leads me
beside tranquil waters.

(Ps. XXIII:2)

Here, too, B extends A.

But there are instances in which B adds to A by providing a contrast:

(A:) Sons have I reared and raised; (B:) but they have
sinned against Me.

(Isa. I:2)

So close, then, is the relationship between A and B in verse that the sense of A carries over into B, and without A, B is often incomplete or unintelligible or absurd. Here is an example:

(B:) And righteousness like a mighty stream.
(Amos V:24B)

This is fragmentary; it lacks a verb. The verb, though, is in A; it carries over to B.

(A:) But let justice flow like water.
(Amos V:24A)

Putting A and B together, we have: "But let justice flow like water, and righteousness like a mighty stream." ("Mighty" is the figure for a watercourse which, when the dry season is over, fills and rushes.) A and B are so tightly intertwined here that they are in effect inseparable.

The term for the relation between A and B in verse is "parallelism." Sometimes in scholarly analysis adjectives are added to modify the term, such as "balancing" parallelism, or "intensifying" parallelism, or the like. It is sufficient for us to know the basic term without these various shadings. More important is our grasp of the utility of parallelism. Hebrew lacks all but a few adverbs, and its stock of adjectives is not abundant. It possesses only a few synonyms in its verbs. Moreover, Hebrew has no common words that are compounds, as do Indo-European languages. (In Hebrew only proper names are compound.) Thus, in English (from Latin), we can say transfer: to carry across; refer: to carry back; prefer: to carry in advance; confer, to carry with. That is to say, compound words, especially when prepositions are joined to verb roots, can lead to the expression of a precise meaning, or a subtlety in meaning; in this sense both Greek and Latin (and thus English) are richer than Hebrew. But in many ways parallelism gives a comparable subtlety to the Hebrew, for the A and the B combine to provide precision and shade of meaning. Parallelism also helps make good the lack of adverbs.

Most of us would, I think, regard what we find in Proverbs as verse, rather than poetry, for the figures of speech are more restrained and the emotion less intense than they would be in poetry. Indeed, the proverbs usually possess the parallelism of verse, while they do not always have the usual or expected metrical regularity. The following, though, exhibit both the 3/3 meter and the parallelism:

A soft answer turns wrath away,
A paining word raises anger.
(XV:1)

The memory of the righteous becomes a blessing,
But the fame of the wicked rots away.
(X:7)

Other passages in Proverbs diverge from the 3/3 meter, but almost never from the parallelism:

Hatred stirs up strife,
But love covers all sins. (3/4)
(X:12)

Whoever heeds advice is on the road of life,
But whoever abandons prudent counsel goes astray. (4/3)

(X:17)

Poetry, in contradistinction to mere verse, combines parallelism and elasticity of word order to provide an emphasis which can heighten the poetic expression that is accomplished in other languages by the use of adverbs or adjectives. When verse moves into genuine poetry, these resources are employed to wondrous effect, as we shall see. Indeed, the resources of Hebrew can turn even unlikely passages into high poetry. The form of verse called an alphabetical acrostic, in which the first line begins with A, the second with B, the third with C, and so on, is in other languages highly artificial, and almost always wooden; in Hebrew the use of the acrostic is no barrier to poetic eloquence:

A. Aleph
Whoever finds a worthy woman, beyond pearls is her value.
B. Beth
Her husband's heart relies on her, and he does not lack gain.
C. Gimmel
She requites him with good, not evil, through all the days of her life.

(Prov. XXXI:10–12)

The poem continues, as do many Hebrew poems, through all twenty-two letters of the Hebrew alphabet.

Without figures of speech, metaphor, simile, or personification, there can seldom be poetry. Hence, figures of speech are abundant in Hebrew poetry. Personification is what makes Psalm XXIII so vividly beautiful:

Yahve is my shepherd, I lack nothing
He has me graze in grassy fields, He leads me beside
tranquil waters.

Both simile and metaphor are exemplified in the allusions to the adversaries normal in life:

Who have sharpened their tongues *like a sword,*
They aim *their arrow,* a bitter word

(Ps. LXIV:4)

Or:

Would that someone would give me the *dove's wing;*
I would flee away and [there] settle down.

(Ps.LV:1)

Or:

> The heavens tell of God's glory, the sky relates
>   His handiwork.
> One day tells it to the next, and night hands on the
>   tidings to the next night.
> There is no telling, there are no words, no voice at
>   all is heard.
> Yet the sound of these permeates all the earth, and the
>   words reach to the end of the world.

(Ps. XIX:2–4)

The figures of speech are normally strong and vivid:

> After Israel came out of Egypt, the house of Jacob from
>   the foreign land,
> Judah became His sanctuary, Israel the seat of His reign. . . .
>
> The sea observed—and fled; the Jordan flowed upstream.
> The hills danced like rams, high places like kids.

The poet now turns to the second person:

> What has happened to you, O sea, that you flee,
>   O Jordan, that you flow upstream?
> You hills that you dance like rams, you high places
>   like kids?

(Ps. CXIV:1–4)

Such shifts in person are not infrequent in Hebrew poetry. The Hebrew grammar, with different forms for singular and plural, and for first, second, and third person, is the clue that such a shift in person is occurring; that is, the poem itself lacks the direct stage direction; it is the sense of the poem, as buttressed by the unobtrusive grammatical forms, which reveals such shifts. This shift occurs in individual Psalms. In a long poem or group of poems such as Canticles, it occurs to the point that we are not told who, of a range of possibilities—the boy, the girl, the friends—is speaking; we ourselves must supply this from the content.

Scripture tells us virtually nothing about the poets; there are allusions to David, and there are references to what we might call certain "guilds" of poets, such as is likely meant in allusions in Psalms to "Asaph" and "the sons of Korah." An ancient book of poems is mentioned, and even quoted from, and in a way this causes a problem, for the title given is at times "The Book of yšr" (II Sam. 1:18), but at one point the Greek translation (there, I Kings, VIII:54, diverging from the Hebrew) suggests that the word should be šyr; if the latter, the title was "The Book of the Song," but if the former, "The Book of the Upright." We do not know what "Upright" connotes. Elsewhere (Num. XXI:27) mention is made of mōshlîm, for which a possible translation might be "minstrels." In the absence of any direct information about poets, we are left completely dependent upon the poems.

That some of the verses are alphabetical acrostics clearly reveals some conscious intent on the part of someone to write a poem; on the other hand, there are bits here and there, like the song of Lamech . . . and an incantation to a well (Num. XXI:17–18) which suggest folk poems. A single short citation is made from a book called "The Wars of Yahve" (Num.XXI:14); we know nothing about this book. The citation seems to come from a folk poem, describing briefly the boundaries of Moab. Perhaps ultimately every folk poem was created by a person, and hence some poet lies behind a folk poem too, but Scripture gives us no information to help us. Other types of poems, some seemingly liturgical hymns, and some reviews of Israel's history, appear to have been composed deliberately. Meter and parallelism suggest that these poets were craftsmen. One would need to conclude, too, that the people were receptive to the poems; some high status of the poet is certainly to be inferred from the epithet applied to David, that he was Israel's sweet singer.

A Literary Analysis of Genesis 49:22–26

The following analysis of some of the literary characteristics of Genesis 49:22–26, a poem about Joseph, illustrates the way stylistic devices are used in Hebrew poetry.

Jóseph is a fruítful boúgh,
  a fruítful boúgh by a spríng;
  his bránches run óver the wáll.

[Metaphor of Joseph as bough repeated and expanded to emphasize the growth of the tribe of Joseph.]

The árchers fiércely attácked him,
  shót at him, and hárassed him sórely;

[Parallelism: repetition of thought units in similar grammatical structures; "attacked him," "shot at him," "harassed him" intensify his peril.]

Note: The rhythm of three stresses to a line occurs very frequently in Hebrew poetry.

yet his bów remáined unmóved,
   his árms were máde ágile

by the hánds of the Míghty One of Jácob
   (by the náme of the Shépherd, the Róck of Iśrael),

by the Gód of your fáther who will hélp you,
   by Gód Almíghty who will bléss you

   with bléssings of heáven abóve,
bléssings of the deép that coúches beneáth,
   bléssings of the breásts and of the wómb.
The bléssings of your fáther
   are míghty beyond the bléssings of the etérnal moúntains,
   the boúnties of the éverlasting hílls;
may they bé on the heád of Jóseph,
   and on the brów of hím who was séparate from his bróthers.

[Metaphors of "bow" and "arms" represent physical prowess.]

[Three metaphors for God.]

[Parallelism of "who will help you" and "who will bless you" stresses God's love.]

[Repetition: "Blessings" used five times in structurally parallel phrases; comprehensiveness of the "blessings" pictured with the words "heaven," "deep," "breasts," and "womb".]

[Parallelism: "blessings . . . mountains" and "bounties . . . hills"; "head of Joseph" and "brow of him."]

    The simple but concrete images lend solidity and reality to the description of Joseph and the blessings: "bough," "spring," "branches," "wall," "archers," "shot," "bow," "arms," "Shepherd," "Rock," "heaven," "deep," "breasts," "womb," "mountains," "hills," "head," "brow."

THE SONG OF SONGS

INTRODUCTORY NOTE

My practice has been to summarize each book of the Old Testament or that portion of a book with which we are dealing. For the Song of Songs and Psalms, however, this would not be practical. Instead, I have chosen essays by the biblical scholars Theodore H. Robinson and Theodore G. Soares to summarize and analyze the selections.

LITERARY QUALITIES

The Song of Songs
THEODORE H. ROBINSON

In I Kings 4:32 it is said of Solomon "And he spake three thousand proverbs, and his songs were a thousand and five." Like his father, then, Solomon won from his contemporaries a great reputation as a poet, and it is not surprising that later generations were inclined to attribute to him, not only the proverbial sayings of the whole nation, but also a certain amount of its poetry. True, only one Psalm was ascribed to him (Ps. 72), and it is clear that men never thought of him as they did of David, but it was easy to regard him as one of the great figures in the story of Israel's secular poetry. Little enough of that poetry has survived; we have an occasional snatch here and there, but the men to whom we owe the preservation of that fraction of Hebrew literature which has come down to us were interested in religion first, last, and all the time. A piece of prose or verse had to prove its title to be called religious to justify its inclusion in the enduring corpus of ancient Israelite writings.

The matter was simpler in the case of the "Song of Songs," because the name Solomon occurs in the book some half dozen times. There was nothing strange to the ancient mind in a man's writing in the third person about himself, and who should be able to write better about the king than Solomon himself? But a close study makes it practically impossible for us to accept this tradition, for reasons into which we may enter later. We shall do well first of all to see what the book actually contains, and then we shall be in a better position to discuss matters of authorship and interpretation.

On the surface the book is composed of a number of short poems, some of them clearly mutilated, and others showing serious corruptions of text. They are all love poems, of that there can be no doubt, and in differentiating them we are guided by an important grammatical factor. Hebrew, like all Semitic languages, distinguished between the masculine and the feminine of the second person in its

THE SONG OF SONGS   From Theodore H. Robinson, *The Poetry of the Old Testament* (London: Gerald Duckworth & Company, 1947), pp. 192–204.

274

pronouns and verbs. It is thus in a large number of cases, possible for us to see whether a poem, or even a sentence, is addressed to a man or a woman. The sex of the speaker is often easily determined, and from time to time we have language put into the mouth of a group of people, though it is not necessarily clear whether they are male or female. We may analyse the book as follows:

1. 1:2–4.   A woman speaks to a man.
2. 1:5–6.   A woman speaks to a company, probably of women.
3. 1:7–8.   A woman speaks to a man, and is answered by him.
4. 1:9–11.   A man speaks to a woman.
5. 1:12–14.   A woman speaks to a man.
6. 1:15–17.   A man speaks to a woman, and is answered by her.
7. 2:1–7.   A woman speaks to a company of women.
8. 2:8–14.   A woman speaks.
9. 2:15.   A man speaks (?) (apparently a fragment only).
10. 2:16–17. A woman speaks to a man.
11. 3:1–5.   A woman speaks to a company of women.
12. 3:6–8.   A short piece describing a woman coming in state from the wilderness.
13. 3:9–11.   A company of women is summoned to look at Solomon, coming in procession.
14. 4:1–7.   A man speaks to a woman (probably there are two pieces here).
15. 4:8–11.   A man speaks to a woman.
16. 4:12–5:1. A man speaks to a woman, who replies in the latter part of 4:16.
17. 5:2–6:3. Dialogue between a woman and a company of women.
18. 6:4–9.   A man speaks to a woman.
19. 6:10.   A company speak (?) (apparently a fragment).
20. 6:11–12. A woman speaks.
21. 6:13–7:5. A company (of women?) speak to a woman.
22. 7:6–9.   A man speaks to a woman.
23. 7:10.   A woman speaks (a fragment?).
24. 7:11–13. A woman speaks to a man.
25. 8:1–3.   A woman speaks to a man. (8:4 probably introduced by accident.)
26. 8:5–7.   A woman speaks to a man, following on an enquiry by others.
27. 8:8–10.   Brothers speak of their sister, who takes up their last remarks.
28. 8:11–12. Solomon's vineyard.
29. 8:13–14. A man speaks and is answered by a woman.

On the surface, then, the book consists of a number of love poems, or parts of love poems. Two questions naturally arise. One is as to whether it is to be regarded as a single whole, into which all the parts fit, or whether it is only an anthology. The other is as to the interpretation to be placed on the whole. In part the two questions may overlap; if it be a consistent unity, then the interpretation will necessarily be affected.

As we read this book, we feel that we fully understand the difficulty the Jewish Rabbis are said to have met when they sought to give it a place in Scripture. Tradition says that it, together with Ecclesiastes, was admitted only after the fall of Jerusalem in A.D. 70. The name of Solomon gave it a certain title, but the saints and sages of Judaism could hardly include in their sacred literature a work which dealt wholly with secular love. The problem was solved by the theory that it was an allegory from start to finish, and that it really gave a picture of the love existing between Yahweh and the ideal Israel. The same problem faced the Christian Church, and it was not alleviated by the tendency to monasticism, which placed love between man and woman on a comparatively low level, and regarded marriage as an inferior state to celibacy. The example of Jewish scholars, however, afforded a precedent, and for centuries the book was held to be a parable of the mutual love between Christ and His Church—a view which is still represented in the chapter headings of many modern Bibles.

The general outlook of modern scholarship, going back to the earlier part of the nineteenth century, was unable to accept an allegorical explanation of the book, and tried to explain it as a purely secular poem. It was still held to be a unity, due to a single author, and the favourite method of treatment was to describe it as a drama. Solomon, the great lover, was on royal progress through northern Israel, and, passing through the village of Shunem, observed a maiden of extraordinary beauty. He wooed her in the guise of a shepherd and had her brought to his harem, eventually winning her love. This scheme left certain points unexplained, and seemed in some ways to be forced until it was modified by the introduction of a third character. The new view followed the old up to the point at which the maiden was taken to Jerusalem, but it gave her a rustic lover in her old home to whom she had been betrothed. The king used all his arts, but in vain; the girl remained true to her old love, and in the end Solomon yielded, and generously sent her back to her home, where the faithful couple were reunited.

It would be going too far to say that a romantic story of this kind would have been quite impossible in ancient Israel. We have too small a fragment of Israelite literature in our hands to make so dogmatic a statement. But we can say that, apart from this book, there is not the slightest evidence for its existence. There are plenty of instances of deep affection and even of passionate love between men and women—who can forget the story of Hosea? But we have nowhere else any suggestion of a literature surrounding this aspect of human relations. Matrimony is usually much more a *mariage de convenance*, and where it is described it is cited because of its influence on family or national fortunes. It may, however, be fairly answered that such a literature, if it existed, would hardly have been likely to survive.

The case against the dramatic form is more serious. We have good reason to believe that drama did exist in ancient Israel, as among the surrounding peoples. We have abundant evidence for it both from Babylonia and from northern Syria, and from time to time we meet with passages in the Old Testament which suggest very strongly that similar drama was to be found in Israel also. But this drama was always essentially religious, and was, indeed, intimately bound up with the cultus. The New Year festival, for example, in Mesopotamia involved a mimic representation of the great war among the gods which preceded the foundation of the earth as we know it. Its leading characters were Tiamat and Marduk, and the so-called Creation epic formed a part of it. So in northern Syria we have the annual representation of the death, rebirth and marriage of the fertility-god, forming a ritual whose magical effect is to secure prosperity for the coming year. But nowhere have we any evidence of a drama outside the cultic system. It is true that our Israelite literature is very scanty, but that of Mesopotamia is abundant, and we should almost certainly have found some reference to secular drama if it had existed in Babylonia or within the knowledge of the Babylonians. Drama developed in Greece from a rude form of cultus, but we can trace the process, and we have no right to assume that a parallel course was followed in the Semitic world. Compared with this objection the entire absence of anything approaching stage directions is a minor difficulty, though it leaves room for a high degree of imagination and, possibly, of ingenuity.

The theory of a secular drama, then, has been largely abandoned. But an interpretation has been offered which brings the Song of Songs into close connection with the religious drama of the ancient world. It has been noted that many of the phrases used and of the ideas involved are characteristic of the fertility cult common to practically all western Asia in ancient times. In particular the worship of Ishtar is cited for parallels—the dove, for example, is the bird sacred to this goddess. She was known in many parts under different names—Ishtar, Astarte, Ashtoreth are all forms of the same word. She is also the Aphrodite of Cyprus and the Levant generally, and the Artemis of Ephesus. No cult was more widely spread in the ancient world than hers, especially after her identification with the Egyptian Isis. Normally her worship involved the sacred marriage to which reference has already been made, and room was often left for gross and licentious rites. It has been suggested that we have in the Song of Songs a Hebrew version of the libretto for a ritual performed in honour of Ishtar. Naturally it could not have been accepted as such by correct post-exilic

Judaism, but it might have survived in northern Israel, and copies of the text might have found their way to the south long after the original meaning and purpose had been forgotten.

A hypothesis of this kind is as difficult to refute as it is to demonstrate. The list of words known to be common to the Ishtar cult and to the Song of Songs is impressive, though most of them may quite well have been used in other connections. All we can say for certain is that if this view be correct, the origin of the book must have been long forgotten before it could even have been considered in the orthodox Judaism of the post-exilic age.

One other line of interpretation deserves mention. It is held in some quarters that the marriage customs of modern Syria (which may go back to very ancient times) afford a clue to the nature and purpose of the book. The festal season lasts for a week, and during that time the bride and bridegroom are hailed and treated as king and queen. Their throne is the threshing-sledge, a heavy structure of wooden boards forming a small platform, studded with nails and stones on its under side. Its normal use is to be dragged by oxen over the corn on the threshing floor. It was certainly one of the implements in common use from the earliest times, and we hear of it in II Sam. 24:22, Is. 28:27, 41:15, Am. 1:3. A seat is placed on it for the wedding ceremony, and the young couple are drawn in state wherever they have to go. The ritual is sometimes elaborate, and includes various interludes such as a sword dance, in which the bride protects herself against her lover by whirling a sword before her. She may sometimes cut him severely with it, though as a rule she is not too severe in her defence. It is at least possible that similar procedure was current in ancient Palestine, though direct evidence is lacking. But practically every piece contained in the Song of Songs can be fitted into the scheme. At the same time, such attempts as have been made to reconstruct the ritual from the Song have to place the various portions in a different order from that in which the book itself presents them.

The plain fact is that any attempt to find a consistent thread running through the book, with whatever interpretation we may seek to place on it, must depend to a large extent on imaginative conjecture. All we can say for certain is that we have a collection of erotic lyrics, most of them short and some mutilated—in a few instances we seem to have only a single line. The same phrase or sentence may occur more than once;

> "I adjure you,
>> Ye daughters of Jerusalem,
>>> By the roes and by the hinds of the field,
>> That ye stir not up, nor awaken
>>> Love till it please."

This is in 2:7 and 3:5, and, with slight variation, in 8:4, though it is hardly in place in this last context. The last verse of the book runs:

> "Flee, my beloved,
>   And be like a roe,
> Or a young hart
>   On the mountains of spices."

Here we have a verse which is almost identical with 2:17; the differences may easily be explained by textual corruption. These and similar facts suggest the same kind of structure which we find so often in the prophetic books, a collection of independent short pieces, sometimes put together almost haphazard, though there are instances where the compiler's motive may be guessed. Thus the picture of the woman coming attended by a stout company of swordsmen (3:6–8) is immediately followed by a description of "Solomon's" gorgeous travelling litter. The two pieces 6:13–7:5 and 7:6–9 both speak of a woman's beauty, though the speakers are not the same.

The pieces are of varied character. Some are descriptions of the physical beauty of the beloved, man or woman. In 4:1–7, for example, and in 7:6–9 the suitor gives pictures of the woman he loves, while in 6:13–7:5 we have a more intimate account of her charms. Here the girl has been asked to reveal herself to a company of people, almost certainly other women, and they find no fault or blemish of any kind in her. If the marriage theory be correct, this may indicate one feature of the proceedings; such inspection of a bride by older women has parallels elsewhere, though we should have to go far before finding anything exactly similar. In 5:10–16 the position is reversed, and the woman gives a description of her lover, in answer to a request by a company of women. This piece forms a part of a longer poem, and it is possible that originally those already mentioned may have been extracted from more extensive narratives. In a few cases we have little idylls. In 1:7–8, for instance, the fair shepherdess—or rather goatherd—seeks to enjoy her swain's company during the noonday rest. But she wishes to avoid the possibility of being insulted by his ruder fellows, and he gives her directions as to how he may be found. Twice we have stories of nocturnal adventures, which may be regarded rather as dreams than as records of actual events. The two are in some ways similar, though they end very differently. In the one case (3:1–5) the girl rises to seek her lover, asks the city watchmen if they have seen him, and soon afterwards finds him and brings him to her mother's home. In the other (5:2–8)—which is more obviously a dream—he himself comes to the house and asks her to come out with him. After a protest against being taken out she consents, but when she leaves the house the man is gone. Again we have the watchmen, but this time they maltreat her, and she appeals to a company of women for help in finding him. The form of the poem suggests that she may have been telling them her dream, for it is somewhat strange to meet a company of women in the streets of an eastern city by night. They ask her to describe him and she gives the account which we have

This reproduction of one of the reliefs from Gozan (Tell Halaf), dating from the ninth century B.C., shows a man climbing up a palm-tree on a wooden ladder. (The British Museum, London.) "I say I will climb the palm tree and lay hold of its branches. . . ." (Song of Songs 7:8)

already mentioned. Then they ask what are his habits, that they may know where to look for him, and are told that he feeds his flock among the "lilies," a word which probably indicates the scarlet anemone so common in Palestine.

Many of the pieces are concerned with the delight the lovers have in one another's society. Particularly noticeable is their pleasure in being together in the outdoor world. The songs carry us into the springtime of the year, into lovely mountain scenery, and into gardens beautiful with flowers and fragrant with spices. The background is that of a people whose work lies primarily with flocks of goats and sheep, and we have only occasional references to agriculture proper. We miss any mention of the cornfields, and only once does wheat appear. On the other hand the lovers' world is rich in fruits; we hear much of vineyards, of figs, of apples and pomegranates. These imply a settled community, and the impression is borne out by the fact that the houses are solidly built, and not mere tents or booths. People know, too, what royalty is like, though it may be only from hearsay, for we get the impression that the gold, silver, ivory, costly woods and rich Tyrian dyes must have been a little remote from the ordinary life of the people who sang and heard these songs. In the exultation of his spirit the lover may feel himself to be a king, and the girl to be a queen. Indeed, there are good grounds for supposing that the title "Shulamite" does not refer to the village of Shunem, as is so often said, but is really no more than a feminine of Solomon. What can love not do? Many waters cannot quench it and it is stronger than death; it is not too much to expect that it should give the lovers the entry into an empire of the soul. It sheds a radiance over the one-storey cottage and the muddy village street, over the burning noon-day sun and the watchful toil of the shepherd's life.

To what date, or rather to what period are we to assign these lyrics? It may be said at once that there seems to be no valid ground for connecting them with Solomon. On the contrary, there are features which suggest a comparatively late date. The vocabulary is unique; a large proportion of the words used are found nowhere else in the Bible. This may be due in part to the objects mentioned in some of the poems, e.g. the henna and nard which are symbols of fragrance. These might be explained as words common in ordinary speech which by accident have not been preserved elsewhere. But we notice that among them we find quite a number of foreign origin. Most of these appear to have come into the Hebrew vocabulary from Persian, and it is difficult to place their introduction before the time of Cyrus. The word describing Solomon's palanquin in 3:9 may be Persian but is equally likely to have been Greek in origin, and even in that language it is not known before the latter part of the fourth century B.C. One curious feature is the relative pronoun. That which is normal in Biblical Hebrew appears only in the title to the book, 1:1; elsewhere the form used is that which is almost invariable in post-Biblical Hebrew and common only in Ecclesiastes in the Bible itself, though it appears in a number of late Psalms. It is not, however, necessarily late, for it occurs in one of the oldest monuments of Hebrew literature, the song of Deborah in Jud. 5. It may be dialectal, and be characteristic of northern Israel, for it is similar to the common form in Phoenician. Even this, however, is not a decisive clue, for it is found three or four times in Lamentations. Allowing for all considerations, we cannot place the compilation, and probably for the most part of the composition, of these poems earlier than the third century B.C.

Whenever they arose, for sheer literary beauty there are few parallels to these snatches of Hebrew lyric to be found elsewhere in the world's poetic store. Quaint conceits are not lacking; who can fail to be delighted with such a passage as 8:1 ff? The girl wishes that her lover were as her brother, that she might freely ignore conventional restraints—kiss him in public, and take him when she would to her own home. The picture of Solomon's marvellous vineyard in 8:11 f, the vineyard which is worth less to the true lover than his little rustic farm, offers us a *motif* which recalls the old French lyric:

"Si le roi m'avoit donné
Paris sa grand'ville . . ."

and the Hebrew will not suffer by comparison.

Simplicity and a fresh beauty are outstanding characteristics of these poems. We, too, cannot but delight in the cool dew of early morning, in the flowers which make the pastures so rich in colour, in the fragrance of fruit and blossoming tree, in the delicate shades of gold and pink that spread over the ripening fig. Against this background, Theocritus, Vergil and even the Italian sonneteers seem artificial and stilted, and it is, perhaps, only in the cavalier poets, in Burns and at times in Heine, that the modern reader will find anything approaching the charm of these ancient Hebrew lyrics. But there is more than freshness, there is also passion, deep and intense, such as that which inspired the best of the Shakespearean sonnets. The lover and his lass shew us their inmost soul, without shame and without reserve. It may be that it is only in Sappho that we shall find a combination of qualities which we may compare with what is so justly entitled the "Song of Songs."

Commentators and expositors may have been justified in seeking a spiritual interpretation for this book. But to many readers this will be forced, unnatural, and even impossible. The book remains to them an anthology of secular love poems. What, then, is its place in Holy Scripture? Can we justify to ourselves its inclusion in a body of literature which is essentially religious, and deals primarily with our relation to God? We may well be grateful to the ingenious Rabbinic scholarship which secured its preservation, even if we are unable to accept its views, for the world could ill have spared the book. But we may go further still, and find a valid reason why we should gladly accept these poems in a corpus of writings whose function is above all things to help men into fuller communion with God. That love which culminates in marriage is the deepest and holiest element in human physical nature. Sex is capable of extreme abuse, but that is just because it is capable also of the greatest heights of earthly experience. What this book has to tell us, more than anything else, is that this element in mankind is not outside the range of God's interest in us, that it may be and should be employed in accordance with His will in the concentration for a lifetime on a single human object. "Threescore queens and fourscore concubines and virgins without number"? No; "My dove, my undefiled, is but one."

INTERPRETATIONS

The Song of Songs
HARRY RANSTON

THE THREE MAIN CHARACTERS THEORY

The defenders of this view to be specially named are Jacobi, Ewald, Rothstein, and Andrew Harper, and of all the dramatic explanations it is the most popular. The first-named thought of Solomon, a young Shulamite wife, and her peasant husband. All later exponents think of the Shulamite as unwedded, and the shepherd as her betrothed lover. A. Harper,[1] our best English commentator, describes the book as "a series of lyrics, in varying form and rhythm, each representing a scene in a woman's life, and containing the history of love's triumph in it." Not a fully developed drama, it yet has real dramatic elements, and is, in fact, a rudimentary drama. Some students (Ewald, Böttcher, S. R. Driver) believe it was originally intended to be acted, but Hitzig and his followers have adduced sound reasons to the contrary. It seems that the author has either actually incorporated in his work, or modelled some of his poems on, such songs as are known among the modern Syrian peasants as *wasfs*, i.e. descriptions of the bodily perfections or personal ornaments of bride and bridegroom or other beloved person.

The following is a common outline of the plot, from which individual interpretations somewhat vary: A beautiful virgin of the rustic village of Shulem (vi. 13), an only daughter (vi. 9), was forced to guard the vineyards (i. 5 ff.) by stern elder brothers very jealous of her good name (viii. 8–9). She had won and reciprocated the affections of a young shepherd (v. 16). Wandering one day in the garden to admire the opening loveliness of spring, she suddenly meets a company of Solomon's courtiers, and is either compelled or persuaded to come to the king (vi. 11 ff.), at first in Jerusalem (i. 1–ii. 7) and then near Lebanon (ii. 8 ff., iv. 8 ff.). The women of the Court, the daughters of Jerusalem, endeavour to win her affection for the king (i. 1 ff., vii.

---

[1] *Cambridge Bible for Schools and Colleges.*

THE SONG OF SONGS   From Harry Ranston, *Ecclesiastes and the Early Greek Wisdom Literature* (London: Methodist Publishing House, Epworth Press, 1925), pp. 192–95 and 227–31. Reprinted by permission of the publisher.

1 ff.), who himself declares his passion (i. 9 ff., iv. 1 ff., vi. 4 ff.). But she turns away, affirming that she belongs to her shepherd-lover alone (i. 7, 12–14, i. 16–ii. 1, ii. 3–7), of whom at night she dreams (iii. 1–4, v. 2–8). He appears in person, and entreats her to flee with him from her dangerous position (iv. 8 ff.). Moved by her continued resistance and her steadfastness to her friend, Solomon magnanimously permits her to depart, and with her beloved she returns home (viii. 5 ff.). Then comes the culminating point of the little drama—the magnificent praise of true love intended as the interpretation of the whole series of lyrics:

> Set me as a seal upon thine heart,
> As a seal upon thine arm;
> For strong as death is love,
> Cruel as Sheol is jealousy;
> The flashes thereof are flashes of fire,
> A very flame of the LORD.
> Many waters cannot quench love,
> Neither can rivers drown it;
> If a man would give the whole substance of his house for love
> He would be utterly despised.
>
> (viii. 6–7)*

This exposition is much to be preferred to that of Delitzsch. (1) It is far more likely that a country maiden would be represented as loving a real shepherd than a king masquerading as one—a very improbable action on the part of the Solomon of history. (2) A far higher ethical significance is attached to a story of trothed love rising superior to worldly blandishments than to a series of expressions of mutual admiration between two. The song just quoted (viii. 6–7) forms a fitting climax. (3) To Solomon are given i. 9–11, ii. 2, iv. 1–7, vi. 4–10, vii. 7–9, &c.; to the shepherd, ii. 10–14, iv. 8–15, v. 1, viii. 13, &c. It is held that a difference in tone between these can be detected. Those of the king are coarse and earthy in merely human passion. With no real genuine feeling in them, they reveal a voluptuary whose heart has become so dried up by sensuality that his love-making is called forth by physical charms alone, and couched in the extravagant language of stereotyped and conventional courtship. On the other hand, those of the rustic lover are said to be genuine expressions of the heart, warm with an ideal and devoted affection. (4) The daughters of Jerusalem (i. 5, ii. 7, iii. 5, 10, v. 8 f., 16, vi. 1, vii. 1 ff., viii. 4) are held to be a kind of chorus, as in a Greek play. (5) Rothstein (Hasting's *D. B.* [Dictionary of the Bible.—Ed.], vol. iv., pp. 589 ff., a very important article) points out the close resemblances to the Arabian story of Habbas

---

* The last two lines read as follows in the RSV: "If a man offered for love all the wealth of his house, it would be utterly scorned."—Ed.

and Hamda, and thinks that the poem is based upon a popular story that Abishag the Shunammite (cf. 1 Kings i., ii.) had refused to become Solomon's wife because of her love for a youth in her native district. But, if not concerning Abishag, the foundation of the Song is, Harper believes, some current tale of Solomon and a beautiful girl of Shulem. (6) Great stress is laid by the advocates of this theory on the unity they find in the Song. Throughout, the language and imagery, the feeling and spirit, are similar. Phrases are used which send the thoughts of the reader from one part of the book to another (i. 7, iii. 1–4; ii. 7, iii. 5, viii. 4; ii. 17, iv. 6, viii. 14; ii. 16, vi. 3; ii. 5, v. 8; i. 6, iii. 4, viii. 2, 5). The narrator is one of the actors (iii. 1 ff., 6, v. 2 ff., viii. 8 ff.), and the poet nowhere appears. There are voices of several recognizable characters. One constant thread runs all through; the beautiful portrait of the maiden is the same everywhere.

On the contrary, opponents urge: (1) The unity has been considerably exaggerated by its exponents, and, if not actually assumed, certainly not proved. . . . (2) The fact that on the three-character hypothesis the book has a higher ethical significance than on some others does not necessarily prove it correct. (3) Some (e.g. Delitzsch, N. Schmidt) can see no perceptible difference between the language of Solomon and the shepherd, and the responses of the maiden assigned to one or the other. The former scholar pertinently asks "whether words such as iv. 13 are less sensuous than iv. 5, and whether the image of the twin gazelles is not more suitable in the mouth of the shepherd than the comparison of the attractions of Shulamith with the exotic plants of Solomon's garden." . . .

THE SONG AS LITERATURE

The Song is the most exquisite pastoral poetry. Many are the lovely pictures and charming imagery, felicitous and graceful expressions, picturesque and striking figures. The author was a literary genius, and produced a wonderful work of art. His words breathe of nature. Not wanting are descriptions of the pomps and luxuries in palaces, but he is most at home in the country. The loveliness of nature delights him. He names nearly a score of plants and over a dozen animals. The reader walks in the open air amidst gardens, woods, vineyards, mountains, streams, and orchards. He is led to think of flowers, trees, doves, gazelles, and incense-laden breezes. The poetry is that of spring: songs graceful and tender, passionate and appealing, ringing with intense yet simple joyousness. Of course, to us Westerners the imagery is too glowing and highly coloured. The frankly sensuous descriptions of physical charms and the luscious, amatory pictures are distasteful. Yet it is to be remembered that it was written for Eastern readers, to whom such expressions, as many parallels show, were thoroughly harmonious with their disposition. The *wasfs* are the least pleasing parts of the Song, being undoubtedly artificial and stereotyped.

THE TEACHING

(1) The ethical and religious significance will depend upon the answer to the question, What is the Song? A drama? An allegory? A fertility-cult liturgy? An anthology of love-lyrics? Or what? On the meaning, for those who have *allegorized*, enough has been said in the previous chapter. All such teaching is put into the poem by the interpreter. Very much the same judgement can be passed on the efforts of scholars who have accepted the *Typical Theory*.* Yet the present writer thinks it very possible that, like other Eastern poets, ours had the intention of adumbrating a higher spiritual passion in the expressions of human and natural love. The trivialities of ingenious exegetes do not disprove this. The fact that the early Jewish allegorizers identified Solomon with Yahweh, and the Shulamite with His beloved people, the whole setting forth their love-relation, suggests the same as the spiritual meaning originally intended to be read along with the primary one of human affection. But to enter into greater detail as to the religious significance of particular figures would lead, as it has in the past, into a maze of profitless speculations. On the *Tammuz-Liturgy Cult Theory* of Meek it is argued that the religious import of original Canaanite ritual became very early changed to satisfy the demands of the higher religion. The Song always was religious. At first it was two lovers who represented Tammuz and Ishtar, but soon it was adapted to express the mutual affection of Yahweh and His bride, the Jewish people. And, whatever was the first significance, this is the teaching of the Song in the form we have received it.

(2) Most modern students agree—even those who are inclined to accept a hidden spiritual meaning as well as the more obvious natural love one—that the latter is primary. (a) Exponents of the *Three-Figure Dramatic Interpretation* rightly show that it gives to the Song a most noble meaning. The climax is the splendid eulogy of love in viii. 6–7.

Two kinds of human love are exhibited. One is that of Solomon and the daughters of Jerusalem—polygamous, sensual, coarse, merely physical and degrading. The other is that of the Shulamite and her shepherd. It is affection strong and pure; the real thing; the love of one for one which absolutely excludes polygamy, superior to mere sense, faithful amidst trials and the seductions of wealth and worldly splendour, contemptuous of the dazzling attractions of Court life. The maiden's character appeals to all, so instinct with purity, sincerity,

---

Typical Theory: The story typifies the mutual affection between Yahweh and his people.—Ed.

simplicity, dignity, fidelity, chaste and holy womanhood. Here is a story of the sorrows and longings of two loving hearts, their fiery trials and final triumph. The deliberate intention of the poet is to counteract slack morality and protest against debasing practices, to undermine and censure polygamy, and to set forth the ethical foundation of marriage. True marriage is a bond between two only, a love-knot; not something bought by worldly price, but a free, spontaneous, and exclusive affection. He aimed at polygamy and concubinage, and a system of marriage in which the woman was contracted for at a price and so often used as a plaything. Such lessons are not without need, even to-day. Are loveless marriages, in which wealth and social position are the main factors, unknown among us?

(b) On the *Anthology of Love-Songs View* the author has simply given expression to the glory of love, man for woman and woman for man, setting it amidst all the loveliness of spring. He sings of love—its intense longings, its joys and sorrows, its strength and everlastingness, its freeness and spontaneity, its tenderness and beauty—and thus finds a fitting outlet for one of the deepest instincts of human nature.

(3) Yet more must be said if we accept any theory which takes the view that human affection is exclusively or primarily in the mind of the author of the Song. Love, sings the poet, "is a very flame of the Lord" (viii. 6).[2] It is a flame divine. Human love is an inextinguishable blaze kindled and sustained in the heart by God Himself; in its primal purity a radiation from His own love, not something essentially different from it. True human affection means the presence of the living God in human life. The burning passion, purely human, of a Sappho, an Anacreon, an Ovid, is of an infinitely lower order. Genuine human love is not merely earthly; it is heavenly. The seal of God is set upon it by His presence in it. Hence it ennobles and transfigures and exalts the whole being of the man or woman warmed by its flame. Love is canonized as at the bottom religious. As Robert Browning sings in "Any Wife to any Husband," it is

> the spark
> He gave us from His fire of fires, and bade
> Remember whence it sprang, nor be afraid
> While that burns on, though all the rest grow dark.

(4) But, even if our interpretation of viii. 6 be wrong, . . . the presence of a book of love-poems in the Sacred Canon is fully justified. Think how much depends upon the purity and strength of the love of husband and wife. Is it not the strongest factor in the welfare of the

---

[2] Lit. "a flame of Yah." Many scholars think, however, that the reference is to the lightning flashes, or simply means "a most vehement flame." It is the only direct reference to God in the book.

family, and hence the most powerful force in society and civilization? Surely Niebuhr was right when he wrote: "As for me, I should feel that something were missing in the Bible if there were not in it some expression of the profoundest and strongest of human sentiments." God has put the stamp of His approval upon the love of man and woman. It is claimed as wholly within the sphere of religion. Marriage in its truest sense is no mere concession to human weakness, but a divine purpose, a sacrament of life consecrated to ends regarded, not as only secular, but definitely religious.

(5) Origen and Jerome inform us that the ancient Jews prohibited the reading of the Song until the age of thirty had been reached. It must be granted that it is not suitable for the young and immature. Matters are frankly dealt with which we are accustomed to hide by our conventions, and expressed in language far too unreserved for our Western minds. Nevertheless, this book, which sings of love, an affection pure, devoted, sincere, giving itself without reserve, constant, rising above the sphere of barter and family arrangement, spontaneous and unfettered as the gazelles and the hinds of the field, the free boon of the heart—this book needs no apology for its presence in Sacred Writ. Its theme is the Flame divine.

from "The Offering Lists in The Song of Songs and Their Political Significance"
WILFRED H. SCHOFF

I concur with the view that there are only two figures in the Song; that they are described under various characteristics in accordance with some ceremonial to which we no longer have the key. In every chapter, analysis of the substances mentioned leads to the same conclusion. There was an original list in which there were mentioned only the things connected with the Tammuz–Ishtar cult. To this there were additions that tied the cult in some sort of way to the accounts of the tabernacle and first temple as they appear in Exodus and I Kings, and to this finally were added things connected with the second temple* . . . . It is an arbitrary adaptation.

*"*The Second or Zerubbabel's Temple* was completed c. 515 B.C., at the insistence of the prophets Haggai and Zechariah, while Jeshua was high priest and Zerubbabel, grandson of the exiled King Jehoiachin, governor of Judaea." *Harper's Bible Dictionary*, Rev., Madeleine S. Miller, Harper and Row, N.Y., 1973, p. 734.—Ed.

THE OFFERING LISTS IN THE SONG OF SONGS AND THEIR POLITICAL SIGNIFICANCE From Max L. Margolis et.al., *The Song of Songs* (Philadelphia: The Commercial Museum, 1924), pp. 99–113. Reprinted by permission of the Museum of the Philadelphia Civic Center.

In the first chapter there is a groundwork of wine and vine-yards, flocks and doves, and the like. To this are added the tents, curtains, chains, borders and studs of the tabernacle, the ointments, veils (if we follow the Septuagint which here, as elsewhere, probably gives a less fluid text in details of this kind), horses, chariots, jewels and myrrh. The Tammuz cult was one of gardens and groves, with the sun, moon and stars as witnesses. How arbitrarily this was transferred to a public building is indicated in the closing passage "our couches are leaves, the beams of our house are cedar, and the panels are cypress." To this account are added the spikenard and henna of the post-exilic temple. Here I assume that the unidentified plant, *kippath*, of the Talmud is the same as *kopher*, henna, which involves the slightest possible change in the manuscript.

In the second chapter the Rose of Sharon, or more correctly, the flower of the plain, or the lily of the valleys, is connected as she should be, with the flagons and apples of the Tammuz cult, but she is covered with the banners of the tribes about the tabernacle and located in the banqueting house that stood next to the temple.

The third chapter is almost entirely of the fabrics and ornaments of the temple, with the royal couch and chariots and the swords of the guard.

Chapters four to seven contain the personal descriptions of the figures in the ritual. In the fourth chapter the origin of the cult in Lebanon and Damascus clearly appears, and we have again the doves, the honey, the garden, springs and vineyards, pomegranates and other natural fruits that are connected with this cult wherever it appears, whether in Syria or Asia Minor, or in the pages of Homer, Theocritus or Ovid. One wonders whether the honey and raisin cakes of Ishtar did not sometimes find their way into the sanctuary as sacred offerings,[1] and whether the insistence upon unleavened bread and the barring of honey in the Jewish ritual did not reflect some party disagreements on that score. But if we examine the female figure in the fourth chapter, she has dove's eyes it is true, but according to the Septuagint they are within the veil; she has the goats' hair and fleece of the tabernacle; her lips are like the vermilion which was specified for the heave-offering, she is likened to the tower of David with its bucklers and shields, and is perfumed with the myrrh, frankincense and ointments of the sacred oils and incense; and then to this are added the spikenard, saffron, aloes, and henna of the second temple. Search as you may, you will find no material detail that goes beyond these four institutions—the original cult, the tabernacle, and the first and second temples.

In the fifth chapter the male figure is described. He begins as before with the garden, honeycomb, wine and milk, dove's eyes,

[1] Cf. Ezek. 27:17; Hos. 7:8; Jer. 7:18; 44:19.

sweet flowers, lilies and Lebanon; but he acquires the myrrh, spices and frankincense of the temple, the coat and the golden chains and the washed feet of the priests, and enough of its jewels to suggest the breastplate. Again removal from the great outdoors to the public building is suggested by the closing reference to cedar. An interesting detail is the rivers of waters which the Septuagint renders "bowls of spices", and which may represent a transfer of the ritual from the Syrian stream of Adonis to the lavers and basins of the temple.

In the sixth chapter we have again the gardens and lilies, with a reference to the sun and moon and the misleading passage rendered Tirzah and Jerusalem,[2] which more probably contains names of the ceremonial actors; once more the garden, with its nuts, fruit, wine and pomegranate and the Shulamite who, like Jerusalem, began probably as Shulmanitu; but these figures gather to themselves the army with banners as it camped about the tabernacle, the goats' hair and the fleece of the tabernacle and the sanctuary; once more the vermilion; once more the army with banners and the chariots of the kings.

In the seventh chapter we are introduced to the Prince's daughter, who was certainly the Daughter of Jerusalem—that is, the national figure who gradually replaced the original figure of the ceremony. Here we have the groundwork of wine, wheat, lilies, deer, palm tree, grapes, apples, vine, vineyards, pomegranates, mandrakes and pleasant fruits both new and old, with the same significant additions. Her feet are shod with shoes; probably, as on the feet of Ezekiel's foundling, the leather is the sealskin of the tabernacle.[3] She is adorned with the chains and jewels of the sanctuary, and likened to the house of Lebanon that adjoined the temple; her hair is purple like the hangings and the fabrics of the priests' garments. To the objection that this is a general phrase that has its parallel in Homer and many poets, it may be answered that it is but one detail in a list, all of which is taken from the sanctuary. The king is said to be held in the galleries, a *motif* of the cloister that connected the temple with the royal palace.

In the eighth chapter, to the spiced wine of pomegranates and the deer are added the seal of David and the wall and bulwarks of the palace, the door and cedar boards of the temple. An interesting bit of the law of offerings seems to survive in the passage about the thousand to Shelem and the two hundred to the keepers—perhaps the priests. And in the remark, "many waters cannot quench love", what have we but the "waters under the earth" into which Tammuz descended and from which Ishtar rescued him?

In recapitulation, and subject, of course, to generous correction, there appear to be in the eight chapters of the Song of Songs 134 references to things suited to the ancient Tammuz cult, 126 to things speci-

[2] Tirzah is literally "pleasure giver"; Jerusalem, we have seen, may be Uru-silim-ma, "stronghold of Shelem".
[3] Ezek. 16:10.

fied of the tabernacle, the first temple and palace, and 7 to things of the second temple. Of the things added to the original list, most are foreign in nature and use and would have had no place in an original Tammuz ritual, nor in the markets and trade of its time. Nor had the Tammuz cult offerings any place in the ceremonial of the sanctuary as specified in the Pentateuch. As adapted, however, to a ceremonial use, perhaps only occasional and in recognition of a Tammuz party existent within the state, and always numerous, they appear to reflect an effort to make the earlier cult suitable in some way to the later conditions. Ezekiel tells us of the women of Jerusalem who mourned for Tammuz,[4] and there is no reason to suppose that the cult ever entirely died out. A passage in Zechariah, usually regarded as late, speaks of it as persisting at Megiddo[5] and, by no means impossibly, at Jerusalem. As I have shown elsewhere, it was sufficiently widespread in the reign of Tiberius for a ship pilot to be confused by it off the coast of Epirus, perhaps because of the presence of Syrian colonies there.

> "Jerusalem the golden
> With milk and honey blest"

was how Bernard of Cluny figured the mystical Paradise of the future; but he began by emphasizing features of the Jerusalem of the land of Canaan "flowing with milk and honey" which were barred, as idolatrous, from the Jewish sanctuary.

It may be a far cry from an Oriental Goddess of Love with her many names, Ishtar, Shulmanitu, Aphrodite, Venus, to the Daughter of Jerusalem, the bride of Yahweh, or the Holy Catholic Church. It is a far cry also from Tammuz or Adonis to Yahweh himself, or to the bridegroom of the Apocalypse with his "Behold, I stand at the door and knock,"[6] so well conceived in the beautiful painting by George Watts; but the connection of both with the original types is unbroken and unmistakable.

When the Song of Songs acquired its later additions cannot perhaps be determined from its text. It could have been written as it stands by someone familiar with the development of the tradition, just as Josephus wrote his histories. On the other hand the fact that it was written in Hebrew and not in Aramaic, in a northern dialect, and that its incorporations of new matter with old are so obvious and sometimes so clumsy, rather seems to point toward a progressive development of the text, and toward an original form quite as old as the time of David and Solomon with whom it is connected. The treatment of

---

[4] Ezek. 8:14.
[5] Zech. 12:11.
[6] Rev. 3:20. Contrary to the view of Dr. Montgomery, as expressed in this volume, I regard this passage as a direct citation from the Song, 5:2. The Apocalypse is too full of intentional citations from the Hebrew Scriptures to regard any identity in expression as accidental. Cf. Grinfield's Hellenistic New Testament *ad loc.*

details points in the same direction. Most of the passages in it which would offend the taste of a later and more conventional day, have been carefully covered over with references to things of the sanctuary in such a way as to conceal or weaken their original meaning. The breastplate has been substituted for the fig leaf. . . .

Jastrow balked at the rabbinical musings on the sacred significance of the substances mentioned in the Song, and regarded them as mystical and unreal;[7] but he did not distinguish between the various lists that are incorporated in the book. Once we grasp the idea that the original Tammuz nature-list has been overlaid with a second list embodying the most sacred symbols of the Jewish state from tabernacle through temple and palace to second temple, their meaning becomes clear. They have a sacred significance because they were inserted there for that very purpose—not because the original list included them. It did nothing of the sort. And their sacredness is on the political side.

The list of the Therumah or heave offering in Exodus must have been the starting point of the national political philosophy. Go into that golden land flowing with milk and honey, that Tammuz land, said Yahweh, and if you will make me a dwelling place of these certain things, I will come into it and abide with you and give you power and riches. Such was the covenant as taught to the school boys of Jerusalem. It must have been made as familiar to them as the Declaration of Independence to American boys. Perhaps in each case only the opening lines were ever thoroughly memorized. "When, in the course of human events, it becomes necessary for one people to dissolve the political bands which have connected them with another, and to assume, among the powers of the earth, the separate and equal station to which the laws of nature and of nature's God entitle them, a decent respect to the opinions of mankind" etc. etc., would thus parallel "of every man whose heart maketh him willing, ye shall take My offering. And this is the offering which ye shall take of them: gold, and silver, and brass; and blue, and purple, and scarlet, and fine linen, and goats' hair; and rams' skins dyed red, and sealskins, and acacia-wood; oil for the light, spices for the anointing oil, and for the sweet incense; onyx stones, and stones to be set, for the ephod, and for the breastplate. And let them make Me a sanctuary, that I may dwell among them."[8] How readily in such case would any allusion to those items, however fleeting, bring to the mind of the hearer the institution of the state erected on that foundation! When the state is personified as a female character, clothed and adorned with these same substances, the sex symbolism readily follows. The coming of Yahweh is then to the woman, rather than to the sanctuary. The idea is the same as that of Ezekiel's faithless foundling and wanton sisters differently applied.

[7] *The Song of Songs*, Lippincott 1921, Ch. III.
[8] Ex. 25.

The Song of Songs in its final form must have made a strong appeal politically to its generation. It was addressed to people still more or less familiar with the ancient Tammuz cult, especially to the substantial element still surviving among them who, because of earlier racial affiliations, would have been under strong pressure from the governing power to abandon Judaism and embrace the Hellenistic cults of Adonis and Aphrodite. It strengthened their national spirit by assuring them that the true Adonis was Yahweh and the true Aphrodite the Daughter of Jerusalem. It recognized the existence of a Tammuz or Canaanite party within the Jewish state, for whose defection the Hellenistic administration was bidding. It claimed their allegiance in the language of their ancient spring-festival ritual suitably re-edited to meet the conditions of the time.

The reconstruction of the original text of the Song has often been attempted, but apparently without success. I suggest that the best guess would be to eliminate all the substances of the Therumah and its appendant lists and to restore to its couplets the substances and things connected with the Tammuz cult which they displaced. The resulting text might give us a true picture of the primitive festival; it would also be unprintable and were best left undone. We have early parallels in abundance, for example in the Gilgamesh Epic.

The Song of Songs is an epitome of racial assimilation in Palestine. When the Canaanite was reduced to serfdom his ritual observances were excluded from the sanctuary, but he was too substantial an element in the population to be submerged and his ceremonies had too human an appeal to be permanently put aside. They remained where the sayings of many a priest and prophet were lost. As assimilated by the ruling class they helped to knit overlord and serf together into a body politic. That process was but strengthened by foreign persecutions. Nineveh and Babylon fell before combinations of foreign enemies with discontented elements within their boundaries, but in Palestine Antiochus failed to bring about such division, as had Nebuchadrezzar and Sennacherib before him, and their failure is in part reflected in this survival of one of the most charming ceremonial productions of a youthful world, wherein the Joys had not yet been routed utterly by the Glooms.

SUGGESTED READINGS

Chase, Mary Ellen. *The Bible and the Common Reader*. Rev. ed., pp. 264–68, "The Song of Songs." New York: Macmillan, 1962.

Gaster, Theodor H. *Myth, Legend, and Custom in the Old Testament*, pp. 808–814, "The Song of Songs." New York: Harper & Row, 1969.

Gottwald, N. K. "Song of Songs." In *The Interpreter's Dictionary of the Bible*, Vol. 4, edited by George A. Buttrick, pp. 420–26. Nashville, Tenn.: Abingdon Press, 1962.

Henn, T. R. *The Bible as Literature*, pp. 63–79, "The Imagery." New York: Oxford University Press, 1970.

Meek, Theophile J. "The Song of Songs: Introduction." In *The Interpreter's Bible*, Vol. 5, edited by George A. Buttrick, pp. 91–98. Nashville, Tenn.: Abingdon Press, 1956.

Ryken, Leland. *The Literature of the Bible*, pp. 217–30, "The Song of Solomon." Grand Rapids, Mich.: Zondervan Corp., 1974.

QUESTIONS FOR DISCUSSION AND WRITING

1. How did Jews and Christians interpret "The Song of Songs" so that it would be acceptable as Holy Scripture?
2. What reasons does Robinson give for placing the compilation date of the "Song" no earlier than the third century B.C.?
3. How does Robinson justify the inclusion of this "anthology of secular love poems"—if it is that—in Holy Scripture?
4. If you agree with Harry Ranston that "to us Westerners the imagery [of the Song of Songs] is too glowing and highly coloured," cite two or three examples from the book to illustrate your agreement.
5. Quote some images from the "Song" that you find particularly effective. What makes them effective?
6. List if you can the "score of plants and over a dozen animals" that Ranston finds in the book.
7. What interpretation of the "Song" does Ranston accept? Why?
8. How does Ranston account for the rich imagery of the "Song"?
9. What is Wilfred H. Schoff trying to prove in his essay? What weaknesses, if any, do you find in his argument?
10. Explain what Schoff means in the last paragraph of his essay when he says that "the Song of Songs is an epitome of racial assimilation in Palestine."
11. Using the Song of Songs and the essays of Robinson, Ranston, and Schoff as your sources, write an essay in which you come to some conclusion about the meaning of the book and whether you think it deserves a place in Scripture.

PSALMS

SUMMARY

The Temple Hymn Book
THEODORE G. SOARES

Song is the natural language of emotion. When we are deeply moved we say, "my heart is too full for speech," we are conscious of inability to express our feelings. Hence the need of the poet, who finds words for the inarticulate, words so fitting and beautiful that we are satisfied. Such poetry we call lyric, for it was sung in early times to the accompaniment of the lyre.

The principal emotions that call forth song are joy, love, sorrow, war, and religion in all its varied experiences. The Hebrews had a considerable literature of all these types but most of it, except the religious, has perished. A love poem found its way into the Bible on the mistaken notion that it was written by Solomon and was a symbol of spiritual devotion. Fragments of other poems were also preserved, enough to indicate the place of song in the life of Israel. In that land of the uncertainty of water the digging of a well was an important event. With a kind of incantation they sang:

> Spring up, O well;
> Sing ye unto it:
> The princes digged the well,
> The lords of the people digged it.
> By command of the lawgiver,
> They digged with their staves.

There is abundant evidence of harvest songs. An incidental reference in one of the prophets preserved for us a snatch of a vintage song:

> Destroy it not;
> For a blessing is in it.

And there are many references to the dirge, the solemn chant over the bier of the hero, one of the oldest forms of poetry. Few elegies are more touching than David's lament over Saul and Jonathan:

> The glory of Israel is slain upon the heights:
> How are the mighty fallen!
> Tell it not in Gath,
> Publish it not in the streets of Ashkelon,
> Lest the daughters of the Philistines rejoice,
> Lest the daughters of the heathen triumph.
> Saul and Jonathan were lovely and pleasant in their lives,
> And in their death they were not divided:
> They were swifter than eagles,
> They were stronger than lions.
> I am distressed for thee my brother Jonathan:
> Very pleasant hast thou been unto me:
> Thy love to me was wonderful,
> Passing the love of women.
> How are the mighty fallen!

Perhaps the battle songs should not be included among the secular literature, for the help of Jehovah was always sought even as it is today. Indeed there are references to an early collection of songs and stories called, *The Book of the Wars of Jehovah*. The great battle song, which we have already noted, *The Ode of Deborah*, has a certain religious character, closing with the pious hope,

So let all thine enemies perish, O Jehovah:
But let them that love him be as the sun when he goeth forth
in his might.

There is no space here to discuss the character of Hebrew poetry. A glance at the above selections will show its difference from our own. There is a balancing of thought and a rhythm of sound, which can be fairly reproduced in translation. In addition there are regularities of metrical beats which can only be appreciated in the original.

The great body of Hebrew lyric was religious. Much of this is to be found in the prophets, where it is part of a larger purpose. But there were also through the centuries scores of poets who sang their faith. One hundred and fifty of these songs were finally gathered into a collection, which was called in Hebrew, the *Praises of Israel*, but which we know from its Greek name, the *Psalms*.

We cannot identify any of the psalm writers; David may have written religious lyrics but nothing can be decided from the psalm headings, which are of very late origin. Apparently there was little pride of authorship. Of course there was no copyright and there were no royalties. Nor was there such a crime as plagiarism. A poet used anything from the past that met his need, and expected anyone to use his own work with equal freedom. Moreover the poems were generally unwritten, living long in memory, subject to constant change. At last the scribes would commit them to writing in the form which seemed most satisfactory at their time.

When poems are to be used in corporate worship there is a certain excuse for the editor who thinks he has the right to change an old hymn that it may fit better the needs of his own time. Our hymnody has been subject to many such alterations, as a few examples may indicate. Neale translating a great Latin hymn has the lines,

They stand, those halls of Sion,
Conjubilant with song.

As the strong word "conjubilant" is not modern most hymn books substitute the rather weak, "all jubilant." The old theology approved the thought,

Would he devote that sacred head
For such a worm as I?

Modern editors, without much poetical success, have tried to eliminate the worm. A youth hymn of a generation ago has the line,

Strong men and maidens meek.

Quite impossible now, for there are no such maidens. Many of the great trinitarian hymns have been altered to suit unitarian hymnody. The psalms were constantly subject to this process.

The religious lyric of the Hebrews ran the whole gamut of experience.

It was harvest time. The riches of the fields were being gathered; the young things of the spring were growing up. How good is God who provides thus generously for our needs!

> Thou waterest the ridges abundantly;
> Thou fillest the furrows with rain:
> Thou softenest the earth with showers:
> Thou blessest the springing thereof.
> Thou crownest the year with thy goodness;
> And thy paths drop fatness.
> The pastures are clothed with flocks;
> The valleys are covered over with grain;
> They shout for joy,
> They also sing.

Days of distress and difficulty came to the people. God seemed far away and men were losing their faith. But that is just the time when the servant of God should be hopeful. Many a psalm of peace and reliance was born of just such travail:

> Why art thou cast down, O my soul?
> And why art thou disquieted within me?
> Hope thou in God;
> For I shall yet praise him,
> Who is the health of my countenance and my God.

The loveliest of the psalms, the one which is carried in the memory of us all, breathes that deepest religious mood of utter confidence. It is the song of a poet accustomed to the pastoral scene, as even now one can see the little flock following their shepherd on the Judean hills. Even so,

> The Lord is my shepherd,
> I shall not want.

But in that beauteous and gentle lyric there is reference to enemies. Half of the psalms breathe fear or hatred or defiance of enemies. That is a reflection of the tragic history of the Jew. Egyptian, Philistine, Assyrian, Babylonian, Edomite, Persian, Greek were the oppressors. Brutal soldiery sacked their cities, kings kept them in subjection, heathen mocked their religion. And within their own nation moneylenders and land-grabbers oppressed the poor. Likening these foes to a ravening beast one psalmist prayed,

> Break their teeth, O God, in their mouth:
> Break out the great teeth of the young lions, O Lord.

If that sounds vindictive, unfit for the responsive reading of a Christian congregation, let us read it:

> Stay their bombs, O God,
> And break their engines of destruction.

We can think of peoples who might have used such a prayer without blasphemy. But vengeance is dangerous. It easily becomes hatred. And there are psalms that have all the quality of an oriental curse. Ps. 109 sounds very much like personal vindictiveness,

> Let his days be few;
> And let another take his office.
> Let his children be fatherless,
> And his wife a widow.
> Let the extortioner catch all that he hath,
> And let strangers spoil his labor.
> Let there be none to extend mercy unto him:
> Neither let there be any to favor his fatherless children.
> Let his posterity be cut off;
> And let their name be blotted out.

More often the psalm is not a curse, but a cry for help. Perhaps Ps. 74 comes from those terrible days before Judas the Maccabee saved his people. Note that besides the physical ills there is no prophet to tell the meaning or even to reproach the people for their sins:

> O God, why hast thou cast us off forever?
> Why doth thine anger smoke against the sheep of thy pasture?
> They have cast fire into thy sanctuary,
> They have defiled the dwelling place of thy name.
> They said in their hearts, "Let us destroy them together."
> They have burned all the synagogues of God in the land.
> We see not our signs;
> There is no more any prophet;
> Neither is there any among us that knoweth how long.

Sometimes the help had already been given and the song of deliverance could be chanted:

> If Jehovah had not been on our side,
> Now may Israel say;
> If Jehovah had not been on our side,
> When men rose up against us:
> Then the waters had overwhelmed us,
> The stream had gone over our soul.
> Our help is in the name of Jehovah,
> Who made heaven and earth.

Notwithstanding all the troubles of life the prevailing mood of true religion is thankfulness. The psalms are the praises of Israel:

> Bless the Lord, O my soul:
> And all that is within me bless his holy name.

E. M. Lilion, "With
Voices Stilled"

> Bless the Lord, O my soul,
> And forget not all his benefits.

Or again,

> What shall I render unto the Lord
> For all his benefits toward me?
> I will take the cup of salvation,
> And call upon the name of the Lord.

The essence of paganism is bargaining with God—so much
worship for so much blessing. It is the idea that divine help may be
obtained without moral purpose. It is the repentance of the criminal
who is sorry that he has been detected. Paganism disappears when
ethical penitence enters the heart. A truly repentant and forgiven man
it was who sang,

> Blessed is he whose transgression is forgiven,
> Whose sin is covered.
> Blessed is the man unto whom Jehovah imputeth not iniquity,
> And in whose spirit there is no guile.
> I acknowledged my sin unto thee,
> And mine iniquity have I not hid.
> I said, "I will confess my transgressions unto Jehovah";
> And thou forgavest the iniquity of my sin.

And it was one who had accepted the great prophetic truth that mere
ceremonial observances and propitiatory offerings were not enough,
who testified,

> Thou desirest not sacrifice, that I should give it:
> Thou delightest not in burnt offerings.
> The sacrifices of God are a broken spirit:
> A broken and a contrite heart, O God, thou wilt not despise.

Deepest of all is the mystic experience of complete union with
the Eternal. If one has God he has everything. Things, comforts, blessings, are incidental. He wants only God:

As the hart panteth after the water brooks,
So panteth my soul after thee, O God.
My soul thirsteth for God, for the living God:
When shall I come and appear before God?

When the nature mood becomes religious the world seems instinct with the divine. How wonderful is God! In one sense man is insignificant, and yet God is revealed to him:

When I consider thy heavens, the work of thy fingers,
The moon and the stars, which thou hast ordained;
What is man that thou art mindful of him?
And the son of man that thou visitest him?
For thou hast made him a little lower than God,
And hast crowned him with glory and honor.

Many of the psalms, perhaps most of them, were not written for worship. Like many of our hymns they were spontaneous expressions of the religious mood of the poet. Some however were written directly for the Temple. Ps. 136 is antiphonal. There are twenty-one couplets. The first line of each couplet to be sung by a choir recited a providential event in Israel's history, the second line sung by the responding choir is always the same, "For his mercy endureth forever." One can realize the impressive beat of this refrain as twenty-one times it came from the answering chorus.

Ps. 81 was clearly designed for the Feast of Tabernacles:

Blow up the trumpet in the new moon,
In the time appointed on our feast day.
For this was a statute for Israel.
And the law of the God of Jacob.

Fifteen of the psalms (120–134) have the heading, "Songs of Ascents," referring to the practice of the pilgrims, who sang these hymns as they went up to Jerusalem to the feasts. They were not written for this purpose but were chosen from the body of psalmody for their special fitness to the pilgrim mood:

I will lift up mine eyes unto the hills:
From whence shall my help come?

I was glad when they said unto me,
Let us go unto the house of Jehovah.

As the mountains are round about Jerusalem,
So is Jehovah round about his people.

They that sow in tears
Shall reap in joy.

301

> Except Jehovah build the house,
> They labor in vain who build it.

> We will go unto his tabernacles:
> We will worship at his footstool.

Sometimes the mood of religion is didactic rather than lyric. Notable is the longest psalm. It was intended to stress the meaning of the Law. It has twenty-two stanzas, corresponding to the number of letters in the Hebrew alphabet. Each stanza has eight couplets beginning with the same letter; this is an aid to memory. Each couplet refers to the divine revelation by one of its many names: law, testimonies, ways, precepts, commandments, judgments, statutes, word. To learn the three hundred and fifty-two lines of Ps. 119 must have been a strong exercise for Jewish boys.

There were doubtless choirs in Solomon's Temple, but the great development of sacred music grew out of the ecclesiasticism which had been worked out by the priests in Babylon for the Second Temple. We have noted that the scribes were not only busy with the organization of the Law but also gave attention to the preservation of the prophetic literature. After Ezra had taken the Pentateuch to Jerusalem* there was a sense that nothing could ever be added to it. So far as the Law was concerned the canon of scripture was established. But there was no thought that the prophetic line had run out. At any time a new prophet might declare with authentic voice, "Thus saith Jehovah." And as today anyone may express his faith in song or hymn, so then scribe or priest or layman might sing as the religious spirit prompted him. The test of its value was then the same as now: the song lived if people loved it. And when that was clear the scribes wrote it and added it to their store.

Thus the choirs of the Second Temple found a goodly number of songs available for use and were continually supplied with more, even as in our hymnody today. In course of time the current psalms were carefully sifted and forty-one were found suitable for preservation. These were edited and published with the final doxology:

> Blessed be Jehovah, God of Israel
> From everlasting to everlasting.
> Amen and Amen.

More songs were written and more came out of the memories of the past until an additional forty-eight were combined into a book with the appended doxology:

> Blessed be Jehovah for evermore.
> Amen and Amen.

*Ezra, Chapter 7, especially verses 10, 14, and 25–26.—Ed.

The process went on until sixty-one more were collected. The final psalm took the place of a doxology for it was one paean of praise, culminating in the challenge,

> Let everything that hath breath praise Jehovah.
> Hallelujah.

As the scribes still worked on their sacred literature they came to feel with their sense of precision that as there were five books of Moses so there should be the same division of the psalms. By appending doxologies to Pss. 72 and 106 this arrangement was effected. And so we have it in our Bible today. The final editing may not have been completed until about 100 B.C.

It is often thought that spiritual and liturgical religion are antithetical. Indeed the history of Israel is sometimes written as if Judaism became hard and formal after the prophet had given place to the priest. But when we recognize that the psalter was largely used in the Second Temple, and much of it was written for the Levitical choirs, so that in a certain sense it can be called "The Temple Hymn Book," we see how deeply spiritual may be a worship, which is even so ceremonial as that of the sacrifice of animals upon a burning altar. A worship in which priests and Levites, rabbis and scribes, nobles and people, expressed their hopes and faith, their longings and penitence, their purpose of devotion in the tender and spiritual language of the psalms was something more than a formal sacramentalism. And if the Temple was sometimes the preserve of selfish priests, and the worship too often the mere ritual of a state religion, it was also to many the house of God—"My house shall be called a house of prayer for all peoples"— where the humble worshiper, singing the *Praises of Israel*, could come into the innermost experience of personal communion with God.

LITERARY QUALITIES

The Language of the Psalms
MARK VAN DOREN AND MAURICE SAMUEL

SAMUEL: We closed last time, Mark, with a promise that we'd look into this matter of the psalms for "unbelievers"

THE LANGUAGE OF THE PSALMS by Mark Van Doren and Maurice Samuel, from pages 17–31 in *The Book of Praise*, edited and annotated by Edith Samuel (The John Day Company). Reprinted by permission of Thomas Y. Crowell Company, Inc. Copyright © 1975 by Dorothy G. Van Doren and Edith Samuel. All rights reserved.

or for rationalists. Let's pursue that subject a little because it's one avenue of understanding the power of the psalms. I never cease to be amazed by the frequency with which men who call themselves unbelievers keep on using the psalms as emotional outlets. In one sense, you know, this is a kind of parasitism: they will use religious material as emotional nurture, but deny the source of the nourishment. However, that's by the way. The rationalist who looks upon the psalms as simply emotional material is quite false in his intellectual approach. I was often puzzled, for instance, by Blaise Pascal's approach to the question of belief. Here is this very deep believer making a gamble:

> Let us weigh the gain and the loss in wagering that God is. Let us estimate these two chances. If you gain, you gain all; if you lose, you lose nothing. Hesitate not, then, to wager that He is.

"What have you got to lose by believing?" he asks—as though it were such a simple matter! But, of course, it wasn't and it isn't such a simple matter; and it should be made clear to those who derive from literature of this kind (if one may use the word "literature" without further ado about it) a sustenance in life that there's more involved merely than the emotional side. And yet, I'm very anxious to probe through you—through your poetic insight and knowledge—the actual technical side of the psalms. What is associated technically with this power of expression in the Book of Psalms?

VAN DOREN: You mean this power of expression which is the cause of the very effect that you have been talking about, namely, the usableness of the psalms, even by men who think they do not accept the first principles that are somehow assumed in the book? Well, I don't know that I like the word "technical" too well. In English, we're in the unfortunate position of being able to talk both about "art" and about "technique."

SAMUEL: Yes, the word "art" sometimes leads into "artful," just as the word "craft" leads into the word "craftiness."

VAN DOREN: Exactly! I've always envied the Greeks because they had only one word for "art" and that was *tekhnē*. They talked about the "art" of anything as the knowing how to do it, no matter what it was. However, maybe I could take off from one word that you used in your opening remarks: "intellectual." In one sense, it

seems to me, there's no intellectual operation being conducted in the psalms. That doesn't mean that there isn't a
great deal of mind, a great deal of intellect, if you please,
being used; but it isn't being used, as I said last time, to
"prove" anything. It isn't being used to establish that
God exists, that He is there, and that He is who and what
He is. The Psalmist is able to assume that; he *begins*
there. And then the operation of his mind is that of a
poet's mind. It explores all the possibilities that follow
upon this, all the avenues that are open once belief exists. For instance, the Psalmist's mind goes without any
difficulty into innumerable recesses of the created world
to find images and objects with which to express his faith
and his feeling—not that the creation is anything more
than convenient for him. It is all about us, it is the thing
that we all know, the thing we—both the poet and the
listeners to the poet—live with. It is there, it is our common life. And it has no ultimate value because the Psalmist never forgets that God is greater than His creation.
One must not rest in the creation; and yet, creation is the
mine for his references and his images. As I got ready to
discuss the Book of Psalms with you, I was very much interested in making a kind of list in my mind of the
images and the objects that are always recurring in the
psalms. They are the *body* of the work; the *soul* of the
work is something else. But poetry must have body as
well as soul. "Wings," for instance. Notice how that
word recurs.

SAMUEL: "Hide me in the shadow of Thy wings."   PSALM 17:8

VAN DOREN: ". . . in the shadow of Thy wings do I re-   PSALM 63:8
joice." Wings seem to fill the world of the Psalmist. It's as
if there were nothing but a great pair or set of wings
always there!

SAMUEL: It's an image that keeps reappearing.

VAN DOREN: And then the image of the high tower, the high
rock, the solid rock—which God is. You will agree, I dare
say, that time and time again, we are up against—so to
speak—that rock, that unshakable, immovable mountain.

SAMUEL: Yes, "my Fortress," and "my Rock" are a favorite   *e.g.,*
image with the Psalmist. Do you know, Mark, I almost   PSALMS
went and counted the times that the word "heart" occurs   19:15 AND
in the psalms. It makes the effect of being innumerable.   144:1–2
The Psalmist doesn't refer to the emotion alone: he refers
to the agitation which it sets up in the body, and he uses
that both for feeling and for intellection, to use a rather
barbarous word: "Thou hast put gladness in my heart."   PSALM 4:8

Or in another instance, he speaks of "the upright in heart." Of deceivers, the Psalmist says they speak "with a double heart." Actually, we would say in English that they are "two-faced," or "doubled-faced"; but in the Hebrew, it's *be-lev va-lev*—they speak "with a heart and with a heart." They have two hearts in them! PSALM 7:11 PSALM 12:3

VAN DOREN: I've never forgotten that wonderful line, "The Lord is nigh unto them that are of a broken heart." PSALM 34:19

SAMUEL: Yes, and "a broken and a contrite heart." Or the Psalmist says, "The fool hath said in his heart: 'There is no God.'" PSALM 51:19 PSALM 14:1

VAN DOREN: By the way, Maurice, what is the Hebrew word which is translated "heart"? Is it the same thing that we understand it to be?

SAMUEL: *Lev*—literally, the heart itself.

VAN DOREN: The same organ?

SAMUEL: It is the organ within the body, and it is a very wonderful word because it is put into dozens of forms. For example, you remember that wonderful phrase, "Thou hast ravished my heart." It's one word in Hebrew, *libavtini*, based on *lev*, heart; and it means, "You have taken my heart captive," or "filled my heart," or "given me a new heart." Or there's a phrase which has gone into the daily prayers of the synagogue: "Let the words of my mouth and the meditation of my heart be acceptable before Thee." And by the way, for the parallel to the heart, we have: "Test my reins and my heart." There's another interesting use of that word: "He that fashioneth the hearts of [men]. . . ." That is to say, the ancients had, one might almost say, a modern psychological approach, in that they indicated the depth of an emotion by the response which it actually provoked in the physical being of the man. SONG 4:9 PSALM 19:15 PSALM 26:2 PSALM 33:15

VAN DOREN: By the way, Maurice, a moment ago you spoke of Pascal, who was certainly one of the great psychologists of religion. I think he was a very great man. You remember his famous statement about the mind and the heart. That was not a sentimental statement for him at all.

SAMUEL: He said in his *Pensées*, "The heart has its reasons which reason does not know." It's put very charmingly by a modern and very much neglected poet, Ralph Hodgson, who says:

> Reason has moons, but moons not hers
> Lie mirrored on her sea,

> Confounding her astronomers,
>   But O! delighting me.*

VAN DOREN (*laughing*):   Very fine!

SAMUEL: The Psalmist's compulsive preoccupation with the physical structure of the world as one of the means— I'd say the *supreme* means—of expressing for the ordinary man the attitude toward God *is* what makes the Bible in general, and the Book of Psalms in particular, the intellectual book without intellectuality.

VAN DOREN: That's exactly what I was trying to say! There's no doubt that a beautiful intellect is operating throughout, but it is operating in the way that the intellect of poetry operates: it is searching for evidences, watching for every movement, every sound; it is listening for testimonies that the whole world somehow is uttering. The physical world of the Psalmist is very active, and very vocal: the mountains "skip like rams"—you can PSALM actually *see* the mountains skipping! And of course, there 114:6 are winds. That word "winds" is a very powerful word, wouldn't you say?

SAMUEL: Yes, it has a double force. The word *ruach* in Hebrew means both "wind" and a "spirit." It can be an indwelling spirit, and it can be the physical wind, the winds of Aeolus, if you like, the pagan wind, as it were.

VAN DOREN: If I may, I'd like to go on enumerating some of those images which will recur in our discussions. There are trees, of course, too: the palm tree and the *e.g.* PSALM cedars of Lebanon—trees are of the utmost importance 92:13 here. He who meditates in His law day and night "shall PSALM be like a tree planted by streams of water, That bringeth 1:2-3 forth its fruit in its season, And whose leaf doth not wither"—vigorous, healthy, beautiful trees are the very image of spiritual health here. And not only trees, but water—water in every form, the seas, streams, still waters. . . .

SAMUEL: "He leadeth me beside the still waters."   PSALM 23:2

VAN DOREN: And the deeps. There's a great line: "Thy   PSALM 36:7 judgments are like the great deep."

SAMUEL: And floods, as well as waters: "the flood over-   PSALM whelmeth me"; and *bah-u mayim ad nahfesh*, "the waters   69:3,2 are come in even unto the soul." The Psalmist is always using the physical, the plastic, the "feelable." He talks

*Ralph Hodgson, *Poems.* Copyright 1917 by Macmillan Publishing Co., Inc., renewed 1945 by Ralph Hodgson. By permission of Mrs. Hodgson, Macmillan Publishing Co., Inc., Macmillan London and Basingstoke, and The Macmillan Company of Canada Limited.

about things that you handle, or touch; and in the "handling" of these, there flows into you the feeling of gratitude, appreciation, or whatever you want to call it, of the created world—the created world as itself being a poem, an utterance.

VAN DOREN: It's as if God had made the world almost as a musical instrument upon which we can play. Here are the trees, and here are the winds, and here are the seas and the streams; here is water, here is dry land, and here, of course, are the animals—the creatures other than ourselves—whom we can constantly bring into our speech, playing upon them very much as a great musician might play upon a many-stringed lyre.

SAMUEL: You get that feeling especially in the great lyrical outburst at the end of the Book of Psalms, where *everything* praises God—creeping things, the mountains, the blades of grass, everything that is in the world is a praise of God. In the conception of the Psalmist, the world is a psalm; the commentators dwell with a great deal of insistence on this. Even the dead things, as we see them, are interpenetrated. It's interesting, Mark, that the modern philosopher sometimes talks of matter as being "psychoidal," that is to say, that there couldn't have emerged a thing like "mind" or "psyche" from dead matter if dead matter itself didn't have within itself implicitly the possibility of a psyche. This is what the Psalmist has seen without any of the devices of the modern psychologist, just as he saw—anticipated, really—what the modern scientist has often said: "God is a mathematician." That is putting it, in my opinion, a little bit too baldly; it's like the critic's view of Kipling, who accused the poet of describing God as though He were a Scots engineer steering a boat! God as a "mathematician"—yes, if you see that aspect as occupying its proper place within the setting of all the other attributes of God. The writers of the Bible anticipated that when they talked of God making the world and meting out waters "by measure." But certainly, He made it not merely "by measure," and this is only one of the innumerable forms of appreciation of the diversity and colorfulness of the world.

see PSALM 148

JOB 28:25

VAN DOREN: Maurice, I would make the same protest against anyone who said that God was a poet. He made a world which poets can use to praise Him or to express Him.

SAMUEL: I agree with you, Mark. Poets are great things, but they aren't that good!

VAN DOREN: No!

SAMUEL: I mean, they aren't quite the equivalent of God!

VAN DOREN: No! Poetry is not that important, neither is mathematics. But both are very, very important modes of understanding. That brings me back to a few more of these recurrent images, Maurice. Think of the parts of the body in the psalms, in addition to the heart: the tongue, the lips, the teeth, the bones. "The crushed bones"—in one of the psalms of despair, the Psalmist speaks as if he had been literally torn apart. *see* PSALM 51:10

SAMUEL: "I am poured out like water, And all my bones are out of joint; . . ." PSALM 22:15

VAN DOREN: And the lips which conceal the tongue of the serpent and the venom of vipers. Of course, to go back to more physical things, there's grass: man's "days are as grass." *see* PSALM 140:4 PSALM 103:15

SAMUEL: Yes, "In the morning it flourisheth, and groweth up; In the evening it is cut down, and withereth." You know, Mark, what you've just said is particularly interesting because you reconstituted this image of man as being a kind of cosmos—man as the whole world—and that is the way the Jewish mystics, particularly in the Kabbalah, have seen man. They have taken him, the human being, and turned him into an image of the cosmos. This gets its lead from what you've just observed, that in the psalms particularly, every part of the human being has a religious function, and it is to be used in the attempt at the lyrical appraisal of God's relationship to man. PSALM 90:6

VAN DOREN: I think you're referring to something that used to be called the "microcosm."

SAMUEL: That's right, yes!

VAN DOREN: Man is the cosmos in little; everything in the cosmos is condensed in him somehow, and it's in him, ticketed; and each part of him can be separated out and made to refer to something.

SAMUEL: Let me interrupt, Mark. James Joyce tried to do that also in his *Ulysses*. In the wanderings of his hero through the city of Dublin, he tried to project the image of the wanderings of Odysseus. In various sections, he used the parts of the body almost in a kabbalistic attempt to recreate a cosmos in the man himself. I'm sorry, you were going to say . . .

VAN DOREN: No, I'm glad you interrupted to mention that. Joyce tried to do more of the same thing in his very last book, *Finnegans Wake*—he did more of it more elaborately and almost bafflingly.

SAMUEL: Too elaborately for me, by the way.

309

VAN DOREN: For me, too.

SAMUEL: I've never struggled through that last book.

VAN DOREN: Returning to these images, there's not only water in great variety and great quantity as a most lovely thing in the Book of Psalms, but there are other liquids, too—honey, oil. You remember: "Behold, how good and how pleasant it is/ For brethren to dwell together in unity!/ It is like the precious oil upon the head,/ Coming down upon the beard; . . ." PSALM 133:1–2

SAMUEL: Is this a poetic hyperbole, do you think, or did they literally *pour* it on? Yes, they would anoint a man's head with oil, and even that, I suppose, was a symbolic gesture. But does it mean that they poured it on, until it ran over his beard and his moustache? Was it supposed to be *enjoyed*? That's one of the things that's baffled me, and I don't know how literally it ought to be taken.

(laughter)

VAN DOREN: No, it does sound excessive, although very charming! Of course, there's "night," too, as well as "day." The Psalmist is often lying upon his bed meditating, as he puts it in one place: ". . . I remember Thee upon my couch,/ And meditate on Thee in the night-watches." "Night-watches" is a term that comes in often, too. These are the great fundamental images, by the way, in all poetry: night, day, animals. The animals that are here I shall want to talk about later, but I suppose the commonest symbol of the vicious or dangerous animal is the lion. PSALM 63:7

SAMUEL: The lion keeps on recurring in the psalms. What's interesting, though, is that several Hebrew words are used for that: *aryeh* is lion, and *kephir* is a young lion.

VAN DOREN: I didn't know that!

SAMUEL: It strikes you with an additional force in the Hebrew—as though when the lion has grown from a certain stage to the majesty of completion, it has taken on a new personality.

VAN DOREN: The lion who walks the streets is familiar to us from the Book of Proverbs, but we can find him in the psalms too, preying upon the lamb. Of course, he's the violent man, the vicious man, who victimizes the poor, the needy, and the orphan. The poor and the needy are ever present in the psalms, too, wouldn't you say? see PROVERBS 22:13; 26:13

SAMUEL: Oh, yes! But there's so much to say, I'm a bit perplexed. e.g., PSALMS 9:19; 12:6; 72:12

VAN DOREN: There's just one more, and then I'll stop. I hope I haven't pursued this matter too far.

SAMUEL: You can't! Each of them is very tempting, and can be used with a great deal of illuminative effect.

VAN DOREN: There's the "pit." When we once discussed the Joseph story, we talked about the immense significance of the pit into which Joseph was thrown, the pit into which the soul descended. The image could be used in all sorts of ways. Egypt, for example, was a pit into which the whole people descended, deprived as they were of their own native land. But the pit here often appears as something that has been dug for our hurt; the digger of the pit falls into it himself.

e.g., PSALM 7:16

SAMUEL: Yes! There's always that note: if a man digs a pit, he's going to fall into it himself, and it is the symbol of the wicked man overreaching himself. Wickedness is something which, in the end, is bound to lead to self-destruction. We're going to talk more of this particular image when we come to examine the aspect under which wickedness is presented in the psalms. But while we're on this subject of the use of the sensuous, the "feelable," for the illumination of the intellectual (I must use that word!), the body as the instrument of expression of the mind, I can't help adverting to the tremendous concern which the Psalmist shows with truthfulness to oneself. He pleads with God, "Create me a clean heart." When he speaks of proud people as "Their heart is gross like fat"—the heart got fatted up!—he seems to be continuously aware of the power of self-deception in human beings. What he means by a "clean heart" is—I'm going to use the modern terminology—"Prevent me from rationalizing"; that is to say, "Don't let me mislead myself by giving a false reason and thus covering up some misdemeanor, or claiming a credit to which I'm not entitled." By the way, now that I've mentioned the word, it is one of the oddities of modern terminology that the word "rationalized" is used in an absolutely inverse sense. When we "rationalize" an industry, we put some common sense into it. But when we're "rationalizing" a wish, we're doing the very opposite: we're committing a stupidity! We're being irrational when we rationalize.

PSALM 51:12
PSALM 119:70

VAN DOREN (*laughing*): Exactly! We're fooling ourselves. And of course, one of the commonest forms of this is found in the man who confesses to some kind of shortcoming in himself, with the full expectation that you will say, "But ah, that is after all a virtue!" or "It's the defect of a virtue!"

311

SAMUEL: Yes, he expects you always to say, "Now, *you're* the kind of man I like!"

VAN DOREN: Yes, "You have this weakness."

SAMUEL: Now this is the thing that the Psalmist girds at, and he is tremendously troubled by it. Do you know, there's another way of putting it: some years ago, an English newspaper ran a competition, in which a series of parallels of three were given. For instance: "I am firm. You are obstinate. That fellow is pig-headed." All three meant the same thing—and this is the danger of rationalization!

INTERPRETATIONS

The Book of Psalms
HAROLD H. WATTS

The Book of Psalms is . . . a collection of poems that effect variations on themes suitable for Temple worship. It is thought that *The Book of Psalms* is not one but several collections, made at different times and, perhaps, for different groups of Temple singers, such as the sons of Korah and the sons of Asaph. Hebrew song is very old, as sections of lyric expression embedded in the books of history indicate. Ancient hymns to other gods, such as the Babylonian Ishtar and the Egyptian Aton, Ikhnaton's deity, have survived and suggest that Hebrew poetic compositions might have existed in David's day. However, the level of religious thought in David's day, as we sample it in *I* and *II Samuel*, could hardly have led to the creation of all the Psalms, for some of them display modes of comprehending deity that, so far as we can judge with certainty, were the creation of the prophets (850–500 B.C.). *The Book of Psalms* was probably given its present form in the centuries after the return from exile (537 B.C. onward to about 100 B.C.). It contains, however, a range of religious poetry that may reach back beyond the time of David.

The poetry of the *Psalms* is poetry in service of "the Other." It amounts to a kind of action rather than a leisurely discourse, and tells us a good deal about the Hebrew's awareness of "the Other," on which they were dependent, or judged they were. . . .

THE BOOK OF PSALMS   Abridged from pp. 209–211 in *The Modern Reader's Guide to the Bible*, Rev. Edition, by Harold H. Watts. Copyright, 1949 by Harper & Row, Publishers, Inc. Copyright © 1959 by Harold H. Watts. By permission of Harper & Row, Publishers, Inc.

The form of the story of Hebrew religious awareness offered by *The Book of Psalms* is difficult for an obvious reason. In this anthology of devotional poetry mingle religious attitudes that the more orderly story of the prophets allows us to classify as early and late. Psalm 68 begins thus, and so continues:

> Let God arise, let his enemies be scattered: let them also that hate him flee before him. As smoke is driven away: as wax melteth before the fire, so let the wicked perish at the presence of God (*Psalms* 68:1–2).

It is plainly removed from the kind of religious sentiment that pervades this unwarlike, unparticularist, peaceful Psalm:

> Lord, thou has been our dwelling place in all generations. Before the mountains were brought forth, or ever thou hadst formed the earth and the world, even from everlasting to everlasting, thou art God (*Psalms* 90:1–2).

These and other impressions about deity troop through the 150 songs. What topics are they concerned with? They tell us what God is, without utter unanimity. God is a man-shaped being; he is a spirit. He is the protector of a certain place, Zion; he is the protector of all places since he created all that exists. What is God's character? He is a jealous god; he is a god of mercy. He is a god who holds up before himself and his people a standard of absolute righteousness; he is a god who plays favorites and will permit his chosen people to "get away" with a good deal. How does one please God? By minute observance of all the laws of Moses and by Temple attendance; by turning to him in the quiet of the night and speaking to him without aid of priest and rite. Whom does God favor? His own people and all people.

In the *Psalms*, it is as if an exposed cliffside which had preserved in its strata an orderly account of the successive geological ages had been dynamited and had collapsed into the quarry beneath it. The result? A mass of wonderful and fascinating debris which we can wander over and try to assign to proper places in Hebrew religious history. Indeed, its extreme importance for subsequent Jewish and Christian worship is that it does not record, in terms of poetic wisdom, the religious insights of only one age of Hebrew history—say, of the postexilic theocratic state in which *Psalms* took on its final form. It has, in a popular phrase, "something for everyone." Throughout history, all stages of religious insight persist and are able to find their echo somewhere in *The Book of Psalms*. Less obviously but just as truly, all stages of religious insight are likely at various crises to turn up in the mind and heart of each person. We probably flatter ourselves when we believe that we have put certain religious concepts behind us. Whatever our conscious religious attitudes, there is little in *The Book of Psalms* that at some time does not have power to make us feel

313

that what we read comes not from the collection of songs accumulated around the name of David but from our own hearts.

Death in The Psalms
C. S. LEWIS

Our ancestors seem to have read the Psalms and the rest of the Old Testament under the impression that the authors wrote with a pretty full understanding of Christian Theology; the main difference being that the Incarnation, which for us is something recorded, was for them something predicted. In particular, they seldom doubted that the old authors were, like ourselves, concerned with a life beyond death, that they feared damnation and hoped for eternal joy.

In our own Prayer Book version, and probably in many others, some passages make this impression almost irresistibly. Thus in 17, 14, we read of wicked men "which have their portion in this life". The Christian reader inevitably reads into this (and Coverdale,* the translator, obviously did so too) Our Lord's contrast between the Rich Man who had his good things here and Lazarus who had them hereafter; the same contrast which is implied in Luke 6, 24—"Woe unto you that are rich, for you have received your consolation." But modern translators can find nothing like this in the actual Hebrew. In reality this passage is merely one of the cursings we were considering in the previous chapter. In 17, 13 the poet prays God to "cast down" (in Dr. Moffatt,† "crush") the ungodly; in verse 14, a refinement occurs to him. Yes, crush them, but first let them "have their portion in this life." Kill them, but first give them a bad time while alive.

Again, in 49, we have "No man may deliver his brother . . . for it cost more to redeem their souls; so that he must let that alone forever" (7, 8). Who would not think that this referred to the redeeming work of Christ? No man can "save" the soul of another. The price of salvation is one that only the Son of God could pay; as the hymn says, there was no other "good enough to pay the price". The very phrasing of our version strengthens the effect—the verb "redeem" which (outside the pawnbroking business) is now used only in a theological sense, and the past tense of "cost". Not it "costs", but it did cost, more, once and for all on Calvary. But apparently the Hebrew poet

*Miles Coverdale brought out in 1535 the first complete Bible to be printed in English.—Ed.
†James Moffatt, Scottish theologian, translated the Old Testament in 1924.—Ed.
DEATH IN THE PSALMS From *Reflections on the Psalms*, © 1958 by C. S. Lewis. Reprinted by permission of Harcourt Brace Jovanovich, Inc.

meant something quite different and much more ordinary. He means merely that death is inevitable. As Dr. Moffatt translates it: "None can buy himself off. Not one can purchase for a price from God (soul's ransom is too dear) life that shall never end."

At this point I can imagine a lifelong lover of the Psalms exclaiming: "Oh bother the great scholars and modern translators! I'm not going to let them spoil the whole Bible for me. At least let me ask two questions. (i) Is it not stretching the arm of coincidence rather far to ask me to believe that, not once but twice, in the same book, mere accident (wrong translations, bad manuscripts, or what not) should have so successfully imitated the language of Christianity? (ii) Do you mean that the old meanings which we have always attached to these verses simply have to be scrapped?" . . . For the moment I will only say that, to the second, my personal answer is a confident No. I return to what I believe to be the facts.

It seems quite clear that in most parts of the Old Testament there is little or no belief in a future life; certainly no belief that is of any religious importance. The word translated "soul" in our version of the Psalms means simply "life"; the word translated "hell" means simply "the land of the dead", the state of all the dead, good and bad alike, *Sheol*.

It is difficult to know how an ancient Jew thought of *Sheol*. He did not like thinking about it. His religion did not encourage him to think about it. No good could come of thinking about it. Evil might. It was a condition from which very wicked people like the Witch of Endor were believed to be able to conjure up a ghost. But the ghost told you nothing about Sheol; it was called up solely to tell you things about our own world. Or again, if you allowed yourself an unhealthly interest in Sheol you might be lured into one of the neighbouring forms of Paganism and "eat the offerings of the dead" (106, 28).

Behind all this one can discern a conception not specifically Jewish but common to many ancient religions. The Greek Hades is the most familiar example to modern people. Hades is neither Heaven nor Hell; it is almost nothing. I am speaking of the popular beliefs; of course philosophers like Plato have a vivid and positive doctrine of immortality. And of course poets may write fantasies about the world of the dead. These have often no more to do with the real Pagan religion than the fantasies we may write about other planets have to do with real astronomy. In real Pagan belief, Hades was hardly worth talking about; a world of shadows, of decay. Homer (probably far closer to actual beliefs than the later and more sophisticated poets) represents the ghosts as witless. They gibber meaninglessly until some living man gives them sacrificial blood to drink. How the Greeks felt about it in his time is startlingly shown at the beginning of the *Iliad* where he says of men killed in battle that "their souls" went to Hades but "the men themselves" were devoured by dogs and carrion birds.

It is the body, even the dead body which is the man himself; the ghost is only a sort of reflection or echo. (The grim impulse sometimes has crossed my mind to wonder whether all this was, is, in fact true; that the merely natural fate of humanity, the fate of unredeemed humanity, is just this—to disintegrate in soul as in body, to be a witless psychic sediment. If so, Homer's idea that only a drink of sacrificial blood can restore a ghost to rationality would be one of the most striking among many Pagan anticipations of the truth.)

Such a conception, vague and marginal even in Paganism, becomes more so in Judaism. Sheol is even dimmer, further in the background, than Hades. It is a thousand miles away from the centre of Jewish religion; especially in the Psalms. They speak of Sheol (or "hell" or "the pit") very much as a man speaks of "death" or "the grave" who has no belief in any sort of future state whatever—a man to whom the dead are simply dead, nothing, and there's no more to be said.

In many passages this is quite clear, even in our translation, to every attentive reader. The clearest of all is the cry in 89, 46: "O remember how short my time is: why hast thou made all men for nought?" We all come to nothing in the end. Therefore "every man living is altogether vanity" (39, 6). Wise and foolish have the same fate (49, 10). Once dead, a man worships God no more; "Shall the dust give thanks unto thee?" (30, 10); "for in death no man remembereth thee" (6, 5). Death is "the land" where, not only wordly things, but all things, "are forgotten" (88, 12). When a man dies "all his thoughts perish" (146, 3). Every man will "follow the generation of his fathers, and shall never see light" (49, 19): he goes into a darkness which will never end.

Elsewhere of course it sounds as if the poet were praying for the "salvation of his soul" in the Christian sense. Almost certainly he is not. In 30, 3, "Thou hast brought my soul out of hell" means "you have saved me from death". "The snares of death compassed me round about, and the pains of hell gat hold upon me" (116, 3) means "Death was setting snares for me, I felt the anguish of a dying man"—as we should say, "I was at death's door."

As we all know from our New Testaments Judaism had greatly changed in this respect by Our Lord's time. The Sadducees held the old view. The Pharisees, and apparently many more, believed in the life of the world to come. When, and by what stages, and (under God) from what sources, this new belief crept in, is not part of our present subject. I am more concerned to try to understand the absence of such a belief, in the midst of intense religious feeling, over the earlier period. To some it may seem astonishing that God, having revealed so much of Himself to that people, should not have taught them this.

It does not now astonish me. For one thing there were nations close to the Jews whose religion was overwhelmingly concerned with the after life. In reading about ancient Egypt one gets the impression of a culture in which the main business of life was the attempt to secure the well-being of the dead. It looks as if God did not want the chosen people to follow that example. We may ask why. Is it possible for men to be too much concerned with their eternal destiny? In one sense, paradoxical though it sounds, I should reply, Yes.

For the truth seems to me to be that happiness or misery beyond death, simply in themselves, are not even religious subjects at all. A man who believes in them will of course be prudent to seek the one and avoid the other. But that seems to have no more to do with religion than looking after one's health or saving money for one's old age. The only difference here is that the stakes are so very much higher. And this means that, granted a real and steady conviction, the hopes and anxieties aroused are overwhelming. But they are not on that account the more religious. They are hopes for oneself, anxieties for oneself. God is not in the centre. He is still important only for the sake of something else. Indeed such a belief can exist without a belief in God at all. Buddhists are much concerned with what will happen to them after death, but are not, in any true sense, Theists.

It is surely, therefore, very possible that when God began to reveal Himself to men, to show them that He and nothing else is their true goal and the satisfaction of their needs, and that He has a claim upon them simply by being what He is, quite apart from anything He can bestow or deny, it may have been absolutely necessary that this revelation should not begin with any hint of future Beatitude or Perdition. These are not the right point to begin at. An effective belief in them, coming too soon, may even render almost impossible the development of (so to call it) the appetite for God; personal hopes and fears, too obviously exciting, have got in first. Later, when, after centuries of spiritual training, men have learned to desire and adore God, to pant after Him "as pants the hart", it is another matter. For then those who love God will desire not only to enjoy Him but "to enjoy Him forever", and will fear to lose Him. And it is by that door that a truly religious hope of Heaven and fear of Hell can enter; as corollaries to a faith already centred upon God, not as things of any independent or intrinsic weight. It is even arguable that the moment "Heaven" ceases to mean union with God and "Hell" to mean separation from Him, the belief in either is a mischievous superstition; for then we have, on the one hand, a merely "compensatory" belief (a "sequel" to life's sad story, in which everything will "come all right") and, on the other, a nightmare which drives men into asylums or makes them persecutors.

Fortunately, by God's good providence, a strong and steady belief of that self-seeking and sub-religious kind is extremely difficult to maintain, and is perhaps possible only to those who are slightly neurotic. Most of us find that our belief in the future life is strong only when God is in the centre of our thoughts; that if we try to use the hope of "Heaven" as a compensation (even for the most innocent and natural misery, that of bereavement) it crumbles away. It can, on those terms, be maintained only by arduous efforts of controlled imagination; and we know in our hearts that the imagination is our own. As for Hell, I have often been struck, in reading the "hell-fire sermons" of our older divines, at the desperate efforts they make to render these horrors vivid to their hearers, at their astonishment that men, with such horrors hanging over them, can live as carelessly as they do. But perhaps it is not really astonishing. Perhaps the divines are appealing, on the level of self-centred prudence and self-centred terror, to a belief which, on that level, cannot really exist as a permanent influence on conduct—though of course it may be worked up for a few excited minutes or even hours.

All this is only one man's opinion. And it may be unduly influenced by my own experience. For I (I have said it in another book, but the repetition is unavoidable) was allowed for a whole year to believe in God and try—in some stumbling fashion—to obey Him before any belief in the future life was given me. And that year always seems to me to have been of very great value. It is therefore perhaps natural that I should suspect a similar value in the centuries during which the Jews were in the same position. Other views no doubt can be taken.

Of course among ancient Jews, as among us, there were many levels. They were not all of them, not perhaps any of them at all times, disinterested, any more than we. What then filled the place which was later taken by the hope of Heaven (too often, I am afraid, desired chiefly as an escape from Hell) was of course the hope of peace and plenty on earth. This was in itself no less (but really no more) sub-religious than prudential cares about the next world. It was not quite so personal and self-centred as our own wishes for earthly prosperity. The individual, as such, seems to have been less aware of himself, much less separated from others, in those ancient times. He did not so sharply distinguish his own prosperity from that of the nation and especially of his own descendants. Blessings on one's remote posterity were blessings on oneself. Indeed it is not always easy to know whether the speaker in a Psalm is the individual poet or Israel itself. I suspect that sometimes the poet had never raised the question.

But we should be quite mistaken if we supposed that these worldly hopes were the only thing in Judaism. They are not the characteristic thing about it, the thing that sets it apart from ancient religion in general. And notice here the strange roads by which God leads His people. Century after century, by blows which seem to us merciless, by defeat, deportation, and massacre, it was hammered into the Jews that earthly prosperity is not in fact the certain, or even the probable, reward of seeing God. Every hope was disappointed. The lesson taught in the *Book of Job* was grimly illustrated in practice. Such experience would surely have destroyed a religion which had no other centre than the hope of peace and plenty with "every man under his own vine and his own fig tree". And of course many did "fall off". But the astonishing thing is that the religion is not destroyed. In its best representatives it grows purer, stronger, and more profound. It is being, by this terrible discipline, directed more and more to its real centre. . . .

SUGGESTED READINGS

Barth, Christopher. *Introduction to the Psalms*. Oxford: Basil Blackwell, 1966.

Bewer, Julius A. *The Literature of the Old Testament*. 3rd ed., edited by Emil G. Kraeling, pp. 359–412, "The Psalms." New York: Columbia University Press, 1962.

Chase, Mary Ellen. *The Psalms for the Common Reader*. New York: W. W. Norton & Company, 1962.

James, Fleming. *Thirty Psalmists: Personalities of the Psalter*. Edited by R. Lansing Hicks. Naperville, Ill.: Alec R. Allenson, 1965.

Lewis, C. S. *Reflections on the Psalms*. New York: Harcourt Brace Jovanovich, Inc., Harvest Books, 1964.

Sandmel, Samuel. *The Enjoyment of Scripture: The Law, the Prophets, and the Writings*, pp. 188–207, "Verse and Poetry: Canticles, Lamentations, and Psalms." New York: Oxford University Press, 1972.

———— *The Hebrew Scriptures: An Introduction to Their Literature and Religious Ideas*, pp. 239–58, "Psalms." New York: Alfred A. Knopf, 1963.

QUESTIONS FOR DISCUSSION AND WRITING

1. What purposes did the psalms serve in ancient Israel, according to Theodore G. Soares?
2. Soares says that "The religious lyric of the Hebrews ran the whole gamut of experience." What experiences does he refer to in the psalms in support of that statement?
3. Why does Soares call the Book of Psalms "The Temple Hymn Book"?
4. Maurice Samuel finds it "amazing" that unbelievers use the psalms as "emotional outlets." Selecting some psalms that will support your argument, show how they can be moving and meaningful even to someone who does not believe in God.
5. Explain what Samuel means when he says that the Book of Psalms is "the intellectual book without intellectuality."
6. Elaborate on Samuel's observation that "In the conception of the Psalmist, the world is a psalm." Who is singing it? To whom is it being sung?

7. Try to illustrate, with reference to some of the psalms, Samuel's observation that "in the psalms particularly, every part of the human being has a religious function."
8. List the frequently recurring images mentioned by Van Doren and Samuel. Then list some important images from the Psalms that they did not refer to.
9. Compare two or three psalms that seem to you to support Harold Watts's assertion that the Book of Psalms records the religious insights of more than one age of Hebrew history.
10. Following the lead of C. S. Lewis, comment on all references to Sheol, hell, and the pit in the Book of Psalms. What portrayal of the underworld can you assemble from these references?
11. What is Lewis's personal explanation of the fact that the psalms reveal no belief in a heaven and a hell in the Christian sense?
12. Describe and illustrate what you consider an outstanding aspect of the artistry of the psalms.
13. Complex though it may be, what portrait of God can be drawn from the psalms? What portrait of humankind?
14. Select several psalms that seem particularly appropriate for our time, and explain their significance.
15. What attitude toward *sin* do you find in many of the psalms?
16. What general philosophy of life do you find in the Book of Psalms?

PROVERBS

SUMMARY

Although some of the proverbs derive from the time of Solomon and even from Solomon himself, the Book of Proverbs as we have it very likely dates from some time after the Exile (the fifth or perhaps even the fourth century B.C.). It therefore includes not only the wisdom of Solomon but that of many teachers, accumulated over a period of 500–600 years.

"The wise men were the intellectuals of the ancient world and like all intellectuals sometimes strayed into dangerous, certainly unorthodox, realms of speculation. Ecclesiastes and Job are products of this kind of private, unconventional intellectual activity. Proverbs however—with the possible exception of Chapters 30–31—is a collection of maxims and essays composed by wisdom teachers of unimpeachable orthodoxy. Its component units were designed for practical use in instruction, each one presumably intended to be memorized by the pupil and further expounded orally by the teacher."*

* Robert C. Dentan, "The Proverbs," in *The Interpreter's One-Volume Commentary on the Bible,* ed. Charles M. Laymon (Nashville, Tenn.: Abingdon Press, 1971), p. 304.

This collection is made up of several earlier collections, which are evident to some extent in the arrangement into seven sections given in the *Harper Study Bible*,* an arrangement that I shall use in the following summary.

SECTION I: WISDOM (1:1–9:18)

The purpose of the proverbs is to make available instruction in wisdom and understanding to anyone who wants it—even to those who are wise. And we are to keep in mind that "The fear of the Lord is the beginning of knowledge" (1:7).

Especially compelling in this section are the two poems on wisdom (1:20–33 and 8:1–9:6) and the story of the young man ruined by a harlot in 7:6–27.

In the first poem wisdom, personified, "cries aloud in the street" (1:20). She warns those who refuse to listen to her that when they finally call on her in their distress, she will mock them.

> ". . . they shall eat the fruit of their way
> and be sated with their own devices."
>
> (1:31)

In the second poem wisdom calls again "on the heights . . . in the paths . . . beside the gates" (8:2, 3). Here she makes known her virtues and the rewards that will come to those who listen to her. "Wisdom is better than jewels . . . I love those who love me . . . Riches and honor are with me . . . my fruit is better than gold . . . I walk in the way of righteousness, . . . endowing with wealth those who love me . . ." (8:11, 17, 18, 19, 20, 21).

Wisdom says that the Lord created her "at the beginning of his work, the first of his acts of old" (8:22).

> "When he marked out the foundations of the earth,
> then I was beside him, like a master workman; and I was
> daily his delight, rejoicing before him always,
> rejoicing in his inhabited world and delighting in the
> sons of men."
>
> (8:30, 31)

Those who find wisdom find life, and those who hate her love death.

> "Leave simpleness, and live,
> and walk in the way of insight."
>
> (9:6)

Harper Study Bible, ed. Harold Lindsell (Grand Rapids, Mich.: Zondervan, 1965), pp. 925–26.

The story in Chapter 7 is told from the viewpoint of a man who, looking out his window, sees "a young man without sense" going along the street near the harlot's house. A married woman dressed as a harlot meets him and embraces and kisses him. She tells him that she has meat left over from her sacrifice and that she has ornamented her couch and perfumed her bed. She persuades him to go home with her and make love all night. They need not worry about her husband, who has gone on a long business trip. The young man suddenly follows her "as an ox goes to the slaughter," for "he does not know that it will cost him his life" (7:22, 23).

The narrator warns others that "many a victim has she laid low."

> Her house is the way to Sheol,
>   going down to the chambers of death.
>   (7:27)

Assyrian relief, "The Face at the Window"

SECTION II: THE WEALTH IN WISDOM (10:1–22:16)

These proverbs, attributed to Solomon, are short aphorisms such as

> A wise son makes a glad father,
>   but a foolish son is a sorrow to his mother.
>   (10:1)

Almost two hundred of the four hundred sayings in this section are similar to this one. The two lines are parallel and consist of two thoughts, the first one favorable and the second antithetical and unfavorable. The second line is almost always introduced by the conjunction "but." Many of the remaining approximately two hundred are also antithetical in nature, but they employ other means of signaling contrast. For example, in

> Better is a poor man who walks in his integrity
>   than a man who is perverse in speech and is a fool
>   (19:1)

the words "better" and "than" indicate the contrast. In

> The hand of the diligent will rule,
>   while the slothful will be put to forced labor
>   (12:24)

"while" introduces the contrast.
    Sometimes the signal word is only implied, as in

> One man pretends to be rich, yet has nothing;
>   another pretends to be poor, yet has great wealth
>   (13:7)

where "while" is implied before "another."
    Roughly 170 of the parallel constructions in these 400 aphorisms are of the *repetition* or *addition* type. An example of the repetition type is

> A good name is to be chosen rather than great riches,
>   and favor is better than silver or gold
>   (22:1)

where the second line repeats the thought of the first but in different words.
    An example of the addition type is

> Thorns and snares are in the way of the perverse;
>   he who guards himself will keep far from them
>   (22:5)

where the thought of the second line builds on the first.

SECTION III: SUNDRY SAYINGS (22:17–24:34)

In verse 20 of Chapter 22 the writer mentions "thirty say-ings," a reference to an Egyptian book of thirty chapters attributed to Amenemopet. This section of Proverbs has many parallels to the work of Amenemopet and may in fact be largely indebted to him. (See the selection on pages 341–43.)

Those who "incline their ears" are advised not to rob the poor, nor make "friendship with a man given to anger" (22:22–24). They must not incur debts that they cannot pay, nor should they remove landmarks from other people's property. They are admon-ished not to desire the possessions of others, for wealth is de-ceptive and fleeting. They would also be wise to discipline their children, thus helping to save their lives from Sheol.

A strong warning is given to young men not to become winebibbers. For who has woe, sorrow, strife, complaining, wounds, and redness of eyes?

> Those who tarry long over wine,
> those who go to try mixed wine.
> (23:30)

Verses 3–9 of Chapter 24 praise wisdom as the begetter of riches and the source of might, and verses 13–22 assure the young that wickedness is always punished, whereas "a righteous man falls seven times, and rises again."

This section closes with warnings against unfair judgments of others and with the recommendation of a high ethical standard in the treatment of one's neighbors:

> Do not say, "I will do to him as he has done to me;
> I will pay the man back for what he has done."
> (24:29)

SECTION IV: MISCELLANEOUS SAYINGS OF SOLOMON (25:1–29:27)

These sayings, copied by "the men of Hezekiah king of Judah," tell one how to behave in the king's presence and in the law court:

> A word fitly spoken
> is like apples of gold in a setting of silver.
> (25:11)

They also give advice on treatment of others and control of one-self.

In this book full of wisdom we find frequent castigation of

the fool, who illustrates the consequences of ignoring wisdom. Seven similes in 26:1–12 exemplify the fool's extreme folly.

The sluggard and the liar come in for their share of condemnation in 26:13–28, and the wicked are contrasted with the righteous in 28:1–28. This section concludes with praise of those who rule justly and love wisdom.

Many seek the favor of a ruler,
but from the Lord a man gets justice.
An unjust man is an abomination to the righteous,
but he whose way is straight is an abomination to the wicked.

(29:26, 27)

SECTION V: THE WORDS OF AGUR (30:1–33)

With a touch of humor, Agur reminds us of our insignificance and suggests that we practice humility in the face of our ignorance.

Three things are too wonderful for me;
four I do not understand:
the way of an eagle in the sky,
the way of a serpent on a rock,
the way of a ship on the high seas,
and the way of a man with a maiden.

(30:18, 19)

Agur recommends:

If you have been foolish, exalting yourself,
or if you have been devising evil,
put your hand on your mouth.

(30:32)

SECTION VI: THE WORDS OF LEMUEL (31:1–9)

These words, taught to King Lemuel of Massa by his mother, advise kings to stay away from strong drink, which weakens their judgment. Strong drink should be given only to those who are dying, those in distress, or those suffering the misery of poverty. She advises him further to

Open your mouth for the dumb,
for the rights of those who are left desolate.
Open your mouth, judge righteously,
maintain the rights of the poor and needy.

(31:8, 9)

SECTION VII: THE VIRTUOUS WOMAN (31:10–31)

This poem describes the perfect wife. The demands on her are so great that one wonders if the opening line, "A good wife who can find?" is an admission from the outset that what follows is an impossible dream. She is trustworthy; she works at wool and flax; she buys land, plants it, harvests it, and sells the produce; she stays up late; she spins and weaves cloth; she helps the poor; she clothes herself and her family; she makes clothes and sells them; she is strong, dignified, wise, and kind. Her husband and children praise her, as well they should!

> Charm is deceitful, and beauty is vain,
>   but a woman who fears the Lord is to be praised.
> Give her of the fruit of her hands,
>   and let her works praise her in the gates.
>
> (31:30, 31)

LITERARY QUALITIES

The literary qualities of the Book of Proverbs have to some extent been dealt with in the Summary. In the following essay Fleming James interweaves comment on structure and style with his discussion of ideas.

The Wise Men of the Book of Proverbs [Mainly after 586 B.C.]
FLEMING JAMES

From an early age there existed in Israel men who gave themselves to the study of what was called "wisdom." This wisdom was not peculiar to Israel but was found throughout the ancient east, especially in Babylonia, Egypt and Edom. Solomon, as we have seen, became its patron in Israel and was credited with having attained great proficiency in its pursuit. Partly by the aid of his powerful name it

THE WISE MEN OF THE BOOK OF PROVERBS This excerpt from *Personalities of the Old Testament* by Fleming James is reprinted by permission of Charles Scribner's Sons. Copyright 1939 Charles Scribner's Sons.

won a place in the Hebrew Scriptures, appearing in a number of psalms and in three remarkable books which are popularly called "wisdom books"—Job, Proverbs and Ecclesiastes.

THE SOURCES

Of all the examples of wisdom literature that have come down to us from ancient Israel the most typical are the collections contained in the Book of Proverbs. It is here that we see the *usual* work of the wise men, as contrasted with such unique utterances as the books of Job and Ecclesiastes (Qoheleth). For our study of these teachers it is not necessary to distinguish the several collections nor concern ourselves with their dates. The book may be taken as a whole. In it we have the best sort of primary sources, since here the wise men speak for themselves.

THE WISE MEN SOUGHT TO WIN THE INDIVIDUAL TO WISDOM

The moment one begins to read the Book of Proverbs he is struck by the fact that he is being addressed personally. "My son, hear the instruction of thy father (1:8) . . . My son, if thou wilt receive my words (2:1)." How different from the prophets! There everything was directed to Israel or Judah as a people. The unit was the nation or the city Jerusalem or at times the king, the princes, priests or prophets. Only now and then did some individual receive a message, and then he was singled out for a special reason, as Amaziah, Shebna, Hananiah, Baruch. But in the Book of Proverbs the nation has disappeared from view. Its public functionaries, with the exception of the king, are forgotten and attention is concentrated upon the ordinary citizen. Yet he is no longer regarded primarily as a citizen, or even a Jew. What is said to him is applicable to any one, whether Jew or Gentile, ancient or modern. That is, in the main. Once and again things peculiar to Israel are alluded to; and of course the name given to God is Yahweh. But the whole idea that Israel is in unique covenant relation with God, involving special privileges, responsibility and destiny, lies below the horizon. The reader is nowhere appealed to on the ground that he belongs to a favoured group or has any part to play in the world because of it. He is just a man. The wise men are interested in him for his own sake, because he personally—as every one else—is worth while.

And they really *are* interested. They have no axe to grind, no institution such as the nation or the priesthood to promote, no advantage of their own to seek. They are concerned entirely with the good of the reader, or hearer, as the case may be. To be sure, they look beyond him to other individuals, whose happiness they would foster as well as his own. For while, as Toy says, they show no recognition of society as an ethical cosmos or unified whole, no one can fail to see that they want human relations in general made beautiful and fruitful. They are ever looking at the individual as one of many to whom both he and they have responsibilities. He is a father, a son, a husband, a neighbour, a friend, a business man, a subject; and they would so guide him in all these relations that he may be a blessing to himself and to others.

Their approach to him is fatherly. It is not, "Thus saith Yahweh," as with the prophets. They do not command, like the legislators. The only authority to which they lay claim is that naturally conferred by age, experience and learning. They speak in their own name only, and aim to win the hearer to wisdom by persuasion. They appeal to inherited beliefs, common sense, his own observation and right feeling. They tell him plainly what is best for him, give their reasons, and urge him with all the compulsion of friendliness to follow it. The course to which they would win him they call "wisdom."

WISDOM IS ETHICAL CONFORMITY TO GOD'S CREATION

Throughout most of the Book of Proverbs wisdom is plainly a human quality; but the wise men, being deeply religious, felt the necessity of giving it a higher sanction and origin. For they began their thinking with God. He was the kind of God whom the prophets had declared—a Person, possessing intelligence, character and purpose. He had created the world with a plan conformable to His own nature, and this plan they named Wisdom, looked at from its divine side. In an eloquent passage the author of the first collection introduces Wisdom herself as saying: "Yahweh formed me in the beginning of his way . . . before the earth was. . . . When he established the heavens I was there, . . . when he marked out the foundations of the earth . . . I was by him as a master workman" (8:22–30). Wisdom therefore was wrought into the constitution of the universe. It was independent of men, though in a real sense it existed specially for them. "My delight," Wisdom adds, "was with the sons of men" (8:31).

Man's wisdom was to know this divine Wisdom—plan, order— and attune his ways to it. For him wisdom began by acknowledging the primary reality of the cosmos—God. "The fear of Yahweh is the beginning of knowledge" (1:7). "Trust in Yahweh with all thy heart and lean not upon thine own understanding: in all thy ways acknowledge him and he will direct thy paths" (3:5–6). Like all things else, wisdom came from God. It was apparently conceived, to use Toy's words, as "a life common to God and man, breathed into man by God," and thus is "parallel to the Old Testament idea of 'spirit.' "

In human life therefore wisdom meant conforming to the divine constitution of the world. One must find out what it is, then order himself accordingly. Of course this was but another way of saying that one must do the will of God. But the wise men tended always to look on that will as taking effect in an orderly path of causation. While they spoke at times as if the thought of God watching over each act of man and meting out His response to it were present in their minds, yet in the main they expressed their observations in terms of natural law. They had the strong feeling that whatever runs counter to these laws is unsound, crooked, doomed to collapse—just as Ezekiel called prophecy opposed to God's will "building with untempered mortar" (Ezek. 13:11ff).

Now since God is ethical in His inmost nature the constitution of the universe must be ethical also. We find therefore that wisdom in the Book of Proverbs is largely identical with ethics. To be sure, one occasionally runs across maxims of what we might term mere prudence, but these are rare in comparison with those that have a distinctly moral tone. The fundamental assumption is that virtue is the only sound way of life.

The standard of ethics that they set was high. The divine plan calls for a society in which people work hard, observe each other's rights, respect each other, treat the less fortunate kindly, have concern for the poor, maintain an atmosphere of general friendliness, enjoy the pleasures of moderation, love their families and homes, are sincere, modest, self-controlled, temperate, reliable, chaste, willing to listen and learn, forgiving, considerate, discreet, kind to animals, sweet-tempered, liberal, yet withal prudent and keeping an eye to their own welfare. Such an ideal, though falling short as we shall see in several important ways, is certainly one which if carried into effect would make the world a not unlovely place.

It will be seen from this that wisdom to these men was a very practical thing. It had to do with life more than with thought. Indeed one could hardly call the wise men thinkers in the sense in which we apply that word to Socrates or even to the Hebrew Qoheleth (Ecclesiastes). Certainly they were no philosophers inquiring into the nature of reality and endeavoring to define common-sense concepts. They took over their view of the universe ready-made from their predecessors. Only once was any question raised, and then it quickly died into silence (30:1–4). In their ethical sayings no attempt was made to discuss the nature of right and wrong, or to strike a balance between apparently conflicting duties. All was simple, direct, dogmatic, traditional. Nor can we say that the wise men were even profound observers of human life. They did indeed perceive many truths regarding it; but their vision was so clouded by the inherited dogma of retribution that they simply refused to look at great masses of facts which contradicted it.

This dogma formed a central part of their interpretation of life and it is time that we now consider it.

WISDOM INFALLIBLY BRINGS HAPPINESS

God has so ordered the world, taught the wise men, that the exact reward of each man's conduct is sure to be meted out to him before he dies. There was nothing new in such a belief. Ezekiel had formulated the doctrine that the sinning soul—and no other—would die for its iniquity, while the righteous soul would live (Ezek. 18). Back of Ezekiel the prophets and Deuteronomists had made the same claim regarding God's dealings with the nation. Sin brought doom, repentance delivered from death. The wise men assumed it as a truism which needed only to be asserted over and over again but never to be established by argument. "Behold, the righteous shall be recompensed in the earth: how much more the wicked and the sinner" (11:31).

It is easy to see that this was a corollary to their deep conviction that God is just and that His universe is fundamentally ethical. Since they could not fall back upon a future life in which accounts would be evened, they must posit retribution this side the grave. For that God could be satisfied to allow wickedness to go unpunished and virtue unrewarded was unthinkable.

They developed the dogma of retribution in great detail. One need but open the Book of Proverbs at random to find saying after saying in which threats alternate with promises. "Treasures of wickedness profit nothing; but righteousness delivereth from death." "He becometh poor that worketh with a slack hand; but the hand of the diligent maketh rich." "The memory of the righteous is blessed; but the name of the wicked shall rot" (10:2, 4, 7). Many of these convictions could have been arrived at empirically by noticing the usual results of different kinds of conduct. They do little more than describe the working of ordinary cause and effect. But many of them are pronouncements of faith in the moral order, in the light of which actual happenings are read, and to which they are somehow made to conform. And always behind the sayings based on experience lay the same vigorous faith, ready to reinforce them if at any point they seemed to fail.

WISDOM IS OPEN TO ALL WHO WILL LEARN IT

Along with this retribution dogma went the tacit assumption of free will. Every man had the ability to insure happiness through wisdom, if he would but use it. There was equal opportunity for all. Nothing was said of handicaps of environment and education, of differing temperaments and mental capacities, or of the weakness of the will to which all are so prone. The attitude of the wise men was: "It lies with you. If you pay the price you can live to a good old age in excellent health, gain a competence, rear a family of children in whom

331

you will take pride, enjoy the good will of your fellow men and leave an honourable name behind you."

It need not surprise us therefore to find them harsh towards the man who refused to learn wisdom. In their eyes he was indeed a "fool." When he got into trouble as the result of his ways they wasted scant sympathy upon him. Wisdom had warned him beforehand that such would be the case. "Because ye have set at nought all my counsel . . . I also will mock when your fear cometh" (1:25f). The wise men were not the ones to help a poor fellow out of the ditch.

THE EDUCATIONAL METHOD OF THE WISE MEN

However open wisdom might be to all men, it would not come to any spontaneously. It could be acquired only through education.

Here it was that the function of the wise men came in. They looked on themselves as able and ready to impart wisdom to those who sought it, especially the younger generation. The Book of Proverbs shows us how they went about their task. Not that it tells us much explicitly regarding their method; but viewed as itself the great illustration of their teaching it furnishes rich material from which we can draw inferences.

We see from it that they aimed to carry on and improve a tradition. It did not occur to any one of them to question it or strike out on a new path for himself. Their material was inherited from those who had gone before them. What they had to impart was really the funded experience of mankind regarding human life.

Inherited likewise was the vehicle by means of which this experience was handed on. The "proverb" or aphorism (*māshāl*), as it here appears, was not a genuine folk-saying but the product of conscious and laborious art. By generations of striving there had been worked out a literary form of singular beauty and incisive power into which each writer endeavoured to throw his own contribution. Of course, the aphorism gave place at times to flowing sentences developing a theme at some length, but it remained none the less the unit of style and constituted the bulk of the older part of the book. Evidently the wise men believed in its effectiveness. It challenged the attention, provoked thought, could easily be retained in memory by reason of its poetic rhythm and trenchant brevity, and tended to unfold as the imagination dwelt upon it into a wealth of concrete detail. Its very beauty also acted as a charm to win men. To judge from the perfection attained, the wise men must have laboured very hard over this literary form.

Having made ready the material they desired to inculcate they next set out to find their pupils. These they sought from the general public, making their appeal as wide as possible. It was no esoteric doctrine that they had to reveal, confined to some picked group, but plain and wholesome good sense for the ordinary man. "Doth not wisdom cry? . . . On the top of the high places by the way, where the paths meet, she standeth; beside the gates, at the entry of the city, at the coming in at the doors, she crieth aloud: Unto you, O men, I call. . . . Whoso is simple, let him turn in hither. . . . Come, eat ye of my bread" (8:1–4; 9:4f). Stripped of its poetic personification, this seems to mean that the wise men did not wait till they were visited by inquirers but themselves went out into the "streets and lanes" of the city with a genuine evangelical spirit, teaching on corners and in public squares and uttering impassioned calls to the passing throngs. Theirs was a genuinely democratic enterprise.

Surrounded as a result of these efforts by a group of pupils, they taught by means of maxims. These must have been uttered with all the impressiveness at their command. They would avail themselves of the corporate influence of the class to which they belonged and also of any personal prestige the individual may have acquired. For their aim was to carry the hearer along with them, to convince him and induce him to action, and the weight of the speaker was an important factor in attaining this result. Such a bearing, combined with their genuinely affectionate interest in the individual, would be reinforced by the telling style of their diction and the manifest truth of what they uttered.

Their purpose, as has just been said, was practical. Almost every one of their aphorisms was intended to lead straight to some sort of action. Teaching was tied to life. Therefore they made themselves masters of the art of playing upon motives. What these motives were we shall consider in the next section.

It is a significant fact that the wise men did not argue. Their method was to assert, not to prove. All through the book we get intimations that some of the community repudiated the assumptions on which their teaching was based, but nowhere do we find them disputing with these "scoffers"; they met such opposition only by sweeping denials and a mixture of condemnation and threatening. The idea of the Greek "dialogue," in which the exponents of differing views confront each other as equals and have the right to a full examination of their respective claims in the court of reason, was evidently quite foreign to these sages—as indeed to the men of the Old Testament generally. Similarly, when they were talking to their pupils and others who sympathized with their beliefs, they nowhere sought to establish these on the foundation of reason. If asked why argument was unnecessary they would probably have pointed first to the authority of tradition. All this has been settled long ago, they would have said. Then they would have appealed to men's own observation of the results of various kinds of conduct. But always they would have met any further pressing of difficulties by simple dogmatic affirmations. Such at least was the course of Job's friends, who seem to represent the view-point of the Book of Proverbs very faithfully.

Naturally therefore they required from their pupil an attitude of receptivity. They aimed to promote those mental activities by which the tradition would be passed on most surely and effectively—unaltered. Great stress was laid on the value of attention. In this activity memory played an important part. "My son, forget not my law; but let thy heart keep my commandments. . . . Let not kindness and truth— i.e. the chief element of my teaching—forsake thee; bind them about thy neck; write them upon the tablet of thy heart" (3:1ff). Nothing was further from their desire than to "teach their pupil to think." To be sure, they did provoke thought of a certain sort. They wanted him constantly to revolve in his mind the aphorisms they uttered and enrich them by applications of his own. They would encourage him to produce aphorisms for himself—a strenuous mental exercise. But the search-light of his scrutiny must always be kept away from the foundations upon which the structure of wisdom rested, unless it were to admire and extol. Anything like independence of reflection was anathema. "Seest thou a man wise in his own conceit? There is more hope of a fool than of him" (26:12).

Such a method of education had its obvious drawbacks. It tended to close the mind against new views of truth. It made for rigidity and intolerance. It left its product quite unprepared to meet unlooked for situations, changing needs. If one should find that its dogmas were insufficient to explain his experience, it might lead to a collapse of his whole religious faith. But on the other hand it did succeed in preserving and strengthening a tradition that after all was a noble one. It freed the plain man—so far as it succeeded—from hesitancy and the bewilderment of conflicting ideas. It engendered solidarity, enthusiasm, power.

Nor must we lay too much stress on its dogmatic element. Along with affirmations of dogma we meet in Proverbs an abundance of observations, the self-evident truth of which is as inescapable today as when the wise men first uttered them.

A few other things may be said of their way of teaching. They realized the importance of moulding lives while yet they retained their plasticity. With this in view they called in the aid of parents as teachers of young children, provided them with material, and reinforced their influence with all the means at their disposal. How frequent are the exhortations to young people to heed what they have learned from father and mother! The home and the school thus co-operated towards the common end. Upon fathers they urged what they felt was a wise severity in dealing with their sons. "Withhold not correction from the child; for if thou beat him with the rod, he will not die" (23:13). "Chasten thy son, seeing there is hope; and set not thy heart on his destruction" (19:18). They themselves sought especially the young man, presumably at the age when he would look beyond the home for his ideas. They tried to win him to a life-decision in favour of wisdom, and when that was done to provide for his "increase in learning" through the means outlined above, and also (apparently) by association with wise men. The company of "fools," loose women and others who disregarded wisdom's dictates, was to be sedulously avoided (13:20). Nor did they hesitate to go to him with sharp rebukes if it seemed necessary (17:10).

THE WISE MEN ADDRESSED THEMSELVES TO VARIOUS MOTIVES

Nothing is of more importance in education than the motives which are called into play. First of all, it is necessary to excite motives of some sort if one expects to obtain results in human lives. That was well understood by the wise men, who learned to work constantly upon the desires of their pupils. Another thing that they knew very well was that the mind is swayed by a rich variety of motives, all of which may be called in to promote a given course of action. They avoided in consequence the mistake of over-simplicity in their appeal; and it is not uncommon to find that within the compass of a few aphorisms desires of quite different sorts are stimulated. Let us now ask ourselves into what classes these various motives fall.

1. By far the largest number of direct appeals was made to self-interest. The wise men frankly assumed that a controlling motive in man's mind is and ought to be his desire for personal happiness. Therefore they strove by all sorts of approaches to inculcate in the pupil the conviction that the individual most concerned in his choice between good and evil was himself. "If thou art wise, thou art wise for thyself; and if thou scoffest, thou alone shalt bear it" (9:12). They pictured wisdom as laden with rewards for her devotee. "Length of days is in her right hand, and in her left hand are riches and honour. Her ways are ways of pleasantness and all her paths are peace. She is a tree of life to them that lay hold upon her, and happy is every one that retaineth her" (3:16–18). It is hardly necessary to enumerate the many different goods which they held up to him as obtainable through wisdom. They range all the way from health, money and the satisfaction of hunger, through popularity, good reputation, a blessed memory, the prosperity of one's children after one, power over others, to such things as service, truthfulness, the glory of self-control, the enjoyment of married love, a place in the affection of others, the favour of Yahweh.

This note of self-interest is struck so often in the Book of Proverbs that one might get the impression from a cursory reading that no other incentive is there held out to virtue. But closer examination reveals frequent exceptions.

2. Interest in others was also used as a motive by the wise men. For they realized very well two things: one, that to say "thou alone shalt bear it" is untrue, since every man's life is bound up with that of

others; and second, that people are swayed by a desire to give these others pleasure, not pain. And so they appealed to what we may call natural good feeling, quite apart from self-interest. It is here that we find most of the loftiest utterances of the book. The sages hold out as lovely and desirable such actions as to gladden one's father and mother (23:25), one's husband (12:4) and indeed any one else, to brighten the heavy-hearted (15:23; 12:25), to avoid causing sorrow (12:18), to give life to others (10:11), to feed many with satisfying words (10:21), to prove faithful to the trust of others (11:13), to promote peace and pour forth forgiveness (10:12), to guide one's neighbour (12:26), to exalt one's city (11:11) and one's nation (14:34) by one's character.

Because however motives of this altruistic sort are mingled with others of an egoistic nature, some readers of the book have felt justified in merging the former in the latter, and pronouncing all such appeals as addressed to self-interest. But this does not seem fair. They stand out sharp and clear and should not be confused because of mere proximity with appeals to personal happiness. For the book here is true to life. In any individual motives are generally mixed—that is, different motives co-operate towards the same result. The same may be said of the other two classes of motives upon which the wise men played.

3. One of these was the love of wisdom for its own sake. Who can read the impassioned praise of wisdom in the first section of the book and not feel that altogether apart from any of her external rewards these men loved her with an ardent devotion? She was at once an ideal to inflame the affection and a possession to feed the mind with inner joy. "Then shalt thou understand righteousness and justice, yea, every good path. For wisdom shall enter into thy heart and knowledge shall be pleasant unto thy soul" (2:9–10). "Happy is the man that findeth wisdom, . . . for the gaining of it is better than the gaining of silver, and the profit thereof than fine gold. She is more precious than rubies, and none of the things that thou canst desire are to be compared unto her" (3:13–15). Of course this was not what we should call intellectual curiosity; it was not the love of knowledge of learning for its own sake. It was more akin to ethical and religious passion. But to class it with the desire for money and a long life or any of the external goods that one can get out of the pursuit of wisdom is a confusion of terms.

4. Finally, the wise men appealed to the love of God; or more exactly, the desire to please Him and be loved by Him. This is more difficult to prove by actual citations than even the third class of motive. God is not mentioned often in the book, and comparatively few things are said which would reveal explicitly the deeper attitude of heart which the wise man had towards Him. It is true that He is spoken of a number of times as the rewarder and punisher of men;

and this thought is always present as a background. But there is a background behind that—an ultimate repose in Him as man's guide and friend, who gives meaning to life and the universe, making both good—if one conforms to His purpose. The constantly recurring admonition to trust Yahweh surely had in mind something more than the mere reliance on Him to provide riches and honour and length of days. To trust Yahweh with all one's heart was first of all to feel Him *there* and be glad. The resolve to avoid those things that He abominated and follow what He loved sprang from a deeper motive than the desire to play safe. Once in a great while this longing to be at one with Him found definite expression. "My son, despise not the chastening of Yahweh, neither be weary of his reproof; for whom Yahweh loveth he reproveth, even as a father the son in whom he delighteth" (3:11–12). "His friendship is with the upright" (3:32). But on the whole it was just an atmosphere in which the wise men lived and would have their pupil live also.

PARALLELS FROM OTHER CULTURES

Babylonian Moral Teachings
W. G. LAMBERT

The various documents which portray the Babylonian view on life, spread as they are over more than a millennium, do not, of course, present a uniform picture. Hedonism, pessimism, pacifism are all represented. Yet there is an approach to life which can be considered orthodox. It demands the performance of the proper duties to the gods and to men, and it promises in return a goodly measure of health and prosperity. Instructions in this way of life circulated in several different forms. A compilation of admonitions was connected with the name of the Sumerian flood hero Ziusudra. The Sumerian work is preserved, though not yet published. A small fragment of a Babylonian translation is preserved on a fragment of a tablet written about 1100 B.C. in Assyria. It is not a coincidence that Noah received some admittedly very different instructions on disembarking from the ark, according to Gen. ix.1–7. A better-known Babylonian work of the same

BABYLONIAN MORAL TEACHINGS   From D. Winton Thomas, ed., *Documents from Old Testament Times* (Edinburgh: Thomas Nelson & Sons; New York: Harper & Row, Publishers, 1961), pp. 104–107. Reprinted by permission of Thomas Nelson & Sons, Ltd.

category is the Counsels of Wisdom, which is treated below. Moral teachings are also contained in some hymns, especially in those to gods of justice. In Sumerian a hymn to Nanshe includes a very eloquent ethical section, and a famous hymn to Shamash is the classic of Babylonian preceptive hymns. Selections from this are also given below. The Psalter likewise has examples of didactic liturgy (Pss. xv, xxiv.3–6).

It appears that several of the matters of conduct which receive attention in Babylonian writings were also matters of concern to Hebrew writers, for example, guarding one's speech (Prov. x.19), leaving a neighbour's wife alone (Exod. xx.17), corruption in law courts (Exod. xxiii.6ff.), two standards of weights and measures (Amos viii.5), and injustice towards poor borrowers (Exod. xxii.25ff.). The idea too of promising material rewards for the observance of the injunctions is common to both literatures. There is, however, this difference, that the Babylonians had no god whose holiness was such that his worshippers must conform to his standards. Not even Shamash is extolled for his own virtues, though he was certainly conceived as having them. In the O.T., however, the concept of the holiness of Yahweh results in a deeper moral tone, and more penetrating exhortations. The similarities, when studied in the whole context of the two cultures, are undoubtedly not coincidental, but result from a common heritage on which both are built.

1 COUNSELS OF WISDOM

These are a collection of short sections of moral precepts, distinguished from each other by content and metre. Originally the work extended for about one hundred and sixty lines, of which less than half remains. Both beginning and end are missing, a loss which obscures any literary framework into which the sections may have been fitted. Only the most slender evidence for dating exists. To the writer the feel of the work is that of the Cassite period (1500–1000 B.C.), though an Old Babylonian date (1800–1500 B.C.) cannot be possitively excluded. The copies were all written between 700 and 400 B.C.

Text

31 Do not frequent a law court,
Do not loiter where there is a dispute,
For in the dispute they will have you as a testifier,
Then you will be made their witness,
35 And they will bring you to a lawsuit not your own to affirm.
When confronted with a dispute, go your way; pay no attention to it.
Should it be a dispute of your own, extinguish the flame!
Disputes are a covered pit,

A strong wall that scares away its foes.
40 Though a man forget it, it remembers him and lays the accusation.
Do not return evil to the man who disputes with you;
Requite with kindness your evil-doer,
[Pay] back justice to your enemy,
Be devoted to your adversary.
45 If your ill-wisher is . . . ., nurture him.
Do not set your [mind] on evil [doing.]

57 Do not insu[lt] the downtrodden and . . . .
Do not vent your anger on them as an autocrat.
With this a man's god is angry,
60 It is not pleasing to Shamash, who will requite him the e[vi]l.
Give food to eat, beer to drink;
Grant what is asked, provide for and honour.
In this a man's god takes pleasure;
It is pleasing to Shamash, who will requite him with favour.
65 Do charitable deeds, render service all your days.

72 Do not marry a prostitute, whose husbands are legion,
A temple harlot, who is dedicated to a god,
A courtesan, whose favours are many.
75 In your trouble she will not support you,
In your dispute she will be a mocker;
There is no reverence or submissiveness with her.
Even if she dominate your house, get her out,
For she has directed her attention elsewhere.
80 (*Variant:* She will disrupt the house she enters, and her partner will not assert himself.)

127 Do not utter li[bel, s]peak what is of good report.
Do not say evil things, speak well of people.
One who utters libel and speaks evil,
130 Men will waylay him with the retribution of Shamash.
Beware of careless talk, guard your lips;
Do not utter solemn oaths while alone,
For what you say in a moment will follow you afterwards.
But exert yourself to restrain your speech.
135 Every day worship your god.
Sacrifice and benediction are the proper accompaniment of incense.
Present your free-will offering to your god,
For this is proper toward the gods.
Prayer, supplication, and prostration
140 Offer him daily, and you will get your reward.

339

Then you will have full communion with your god.
In your wisdom study the tablet.
Reverence begets favour,
Sacrifice prolongs life,
145 And prayer atones for guilt.
He who fears the gods is not slighted by . . .
He who fears the Anunnaki extends [his days.]

Notes

Lines 41–5. This is not "loving one's enemies," nor even "heaping coals of fire upon his head" (Prov. xxv.22). The previous lines warn men against becoming embroiled in a lawsuit. These lines offer practical advice on achieving this end. Similar advice is offered to rulers in The Cuthean Legend of Naram-Sin—"Respond to their wickedness with kindness, to kindness with gifts and exchanges, but do not go forth before them" (lines 170ff., translation of O. R. Gurney, *Anatolian Studies*, v (1955) 109). This whole text is written around the moral that pacifism is the best policy for a ruler.

Lines 60, 64. These lines include aphorisms which probably had a very wide oral circulation, as they also appear in the Shamash Hymn (lines 100, 106, 119 below), and in the Aramaic version of the Words of Ahikar (*A.N.E.T.*, 428, vi.92f.).

Lines 72–80. Both street- and cult-prostitutes were exceedingly common in ancient Babylonia, and their activity seems generally to have been accepted as a respectable profession. As worded, this section merely condemns them as unsuitable as wives. Simple observation might well suggest that a woman of this kind will have a strong, self-willed character, but it is still possible that a moral revulsion at this institution may have been rationalised in this thought.

The story of Judah and Tamar (Gen. xxxviii) shows an attitude to prostitution which is very similar to that of the Babylonians and Assyrians; as a class such women were tolerated, though it was a serious offence for a married woman to engage in this practice; serious, because it was an offence against her husband. No restrictions were put on men, however, in this respect, whether married or not. Elsewhere in the O.T. prostitution is fully condemned. A particularly striking warning against it is contained in Prov. vii. In the other similar condemnations found in Prov. i–ix it may be noted that in ix.13 the phrase "knoweth nothing" is probably more correctly translated "is not still" . . . ; the thought is thus similar to that of line 77. From Amos onwards the prophets denounce cult prostitution (Amos ii.7; Hos. iv.11–18; Jer. ii.20). It became indeed a symbol for any debased form of religion.

Lines 127–34. Two other sections of the Counsels of Wisdom not included here also deal with restraint in speech, and it is a common topic in the book of Proverbs (e.g. x.19), and is found also in Egyptian Wisdom literature (e.g. *A.N.E.T.*, 420, iv.1). The basis of the section under discussion seems to be a magic conception of speech as something which cannot be withdrawn once it has been uttered, but remains operative, even if it returns onto the head of the speaker. The account of the blessing of Jacob and Esau (Gen. xxvii), when Isaac was unable to take back the blessing which Jacob had gained by trickery, shows that this same idea of the solemn utterance was known among the Hebrews (cp. Is. lv.11).

Line 147. *the Anunnaki* are the underworld gods.

The Instruction of Amen-em-Opet
translated by JOHN A. WILSON

A general parallelism of thought or structure between Egyptian and Hebrew literature is common. It is,
however, more difficult to establish a case of direct literary relation. For this reason, special attention is directed
to the Instruction of Amen-em-Opet, son of Ka-nakht,
and its very close relation to the Book of Proverbs, particularly Prov. 22:17–24:22. Amen-em-Opet differs from earlier Egyptian books of wisdom in its humbler, more re-
signed, and less materialistic outlook.

ANET, 421-
424

The hieratic text is found in British Museum Papyrus 10474 and (a portion only) on a writing tablet in
Turin. The papyrus is said to have come from Thebes.
The date of the papyrus manuscript is debated. It is certainly subsequent to the Egyptian Empire. A date anywhere between the 10th and 6th centuries B.C. is possible, with some weight of evidence for the 7th–6th
centuries. Some introductory lines have been omitted
here.

HE SAYS: FIRST CHAPTER:
Give thy ears, hear what is said,
Give thy heart to understand them.   (10)
To put them in thy heart is worth while,
(But) it is damaging to him who neglects them.
Let them rest in the casket of thy belly,
That they may be a *key* in thy heart.
At a time when there is a whirlwind of words,   (15)
They shall be a mooring-stake *for* thy tongue.
If thou spendest they time while this is in thy heart,
Thou wilt find it a success;
Thou wilt find my words a treasury of life,   (iv 1)
And thy body will prosper upon earth.

Prov. 22:17–
18a

Prov. 22:18–
19

SECOND CHAPTER:
Guard thyself against robbing the oppressed
And against overbearing the disabled.   (5)
Stretch not forth thy hand against the approach of an
    old man,

Prov. 22:22

THE INSTRUCTION OF AMEN-EM-OPET from "Wisdom, Prophecy and Songs," translated by John A.
Wilson in *The Ancient Near East: An Anthology of Texts and Pictures*, ed. James B. Pritchard (copyright
© 1958 by Princeton University Press), pp. 237–43. Reprinted by permission of Princeton University
Press.

Nor *steal away* the speech of the *aged*.
Let not thyself be sent on a dangerous errand,
Nor love him who carries it out.
Do not cry out against him whom thou hast
    attacked,   (10)
Nor return him answer on thy own behalf.
He who does evil, the (very) river-bank abandons him,
And his *floodwaters* carry him off.
The north wind comes down that it may end his hour;
It is joined to the tempest;   (15)
The thunder is loud, and the crocodiles are wicked.
Thou heated man,[1] how art thou (now)?
He is crying out, and his voice (reaches) to heaven.
O moon,[2] establish his crime (against him)!
So steer that we may bring the wicked man   (v 1)
    across,
For we shall not act like him—
Lift him up, give him thy hand;
Leave him (in) the arms of the god;
Fill his belly with bread of thine,   (5)
So that he may be sated and may *be ashamed*.   Prov. 25:21–22
Another good deed in the heart of the god
Is to pause before speaking. . . .

SIXTH CHAPTER:
Do not carry off the landmark at the boundaries of the
    arable land,
Nor disturb the position of the measuring-cord;
Be not greedy after a cubit of land,
Nor encroach upon the boundaries of
    a widow. . . .   (vii 15)
Guard against encroaching upon the boundaries of the
    fields,   Prov. 22:28; 23:10
Lest a terror carry thee off.   (viii 10)
One satisfies god with the will of the Lord,
Who determines the boundaries of the arable
    land. . . .   Prov. 23:11
Plow in the fields, that thou mayest find thy
    needs,   (17)
That thou mayest receive bread of thy own threshing
    floor.
Better is a measure that the god gives thee
Than five thousand (taken) illegally.

[1] The "hot" man is the passionate or impulsive man, in contrast to the "silent" or humbly pious man.
[2] Thoth was the barrister of the gods.

They do not spend a day (in) the granary or
  barn;   (ix 1)
They make no provisions for the beer-jar.
The completion of a moment is their lifetime in the
  storehouse;
At daybreak they are sunk (from sight).
Better is poverty in the hand of the god   (5)
Than riches in a storehouse;
Better is bread, when the heart is happy,   Prov. 15:16–
Than riches with sorrow.   17

SUGGESTED READINGS

Blank, S. H. "Proverbs, Book of." In *The Interpreter's Dictionary of the Bible*, Vol 3, edited by George A. Buttrick, pp. 936–40. Nashville, Tenn.: Abingdon Press, 1962.

Dentan, Robert C. "The Proverbs." In *The Interpreter's One-Volume Commentary on the Bible*, edited by Charles M. Laymon, pp. 304–19. Nashville, Tenn.: Abingdon Press, 1971.

Scott, R. B. Y., trans. *Proverbs and Ecclesiastes*. The Anchor Bible Series, No. 18. New York: Doubleday & Company, 1965.

"Sumerian Wisdom Text" and "Akkadian Didactic and Wisdom Literature." In *The Ancient Near East*, Vol. 2: *A New Anthology of Texts and Pictures*, edited by James B. Pritchard, pp. 136–67. Princeton, N.J.: Princeton University Press, 1975.

"Wisdom, Prophecy, and Songs." In *The Ancient Near East, An Anthology of Texts and Pictures*, edited by James B. Pritchard, pp. 234–59. Princeton, N.J.: Princeton University Press, 1975.

QUESTIONS FOR DISCUSSION AND WRITING

1. Identify five to ten proverbs that express concern with social problems and justice, and put them together as a single poem. Comment on the theme of that poem.
2. Considering structure, theme, style, and appeal to the emotions, argue that the Book of Psalms represents a higher order of literature than the Book of Proverbs does.
3. Proverbs describes the "good wife." What description of the "good man" or "good husband" emerges from the book? Try to create a "poem" by stringing together proverbs on one or the other of these themes.

4. What are the good things in life, according to the authors of the Book of Proverbs?
5. What striking difference in purpose does Fleming James see between the work of the prophets and the work of the wise men?
6. What is the underlying philosophy of Proverbs, as James sees it?
7. What facts from your own experience and knowledge can you muster to refute "the inherited dogma of retribution" espoused by the wise men?
8. Why, according to Fleming James, is it no surprise that the wise men had no sympathy for the person who refused to learn wisdom?
9. What attributes does James find in the art of the aphorism as it was developed and refined by the wise men?
10. Locate some passages in the Book of Proverbs that illustrate James's observation that "All through the book we get intimations that some of the community repudiated the assumptions on which their teaching [that of the wise men] was based."
11. What, according to James, are the obvious drawbacks of the method of education presented in the Book of Proverbs? What are its advantages?
12. To what motives do the wise men appeal, according to James? Illustrate each of them with a proverb not already quoted by James.
13. Identify some proverbs that parallel those in the "Babylonian Moral Teachings."
14. What parallels do you find between the ideas in Proverbs and those in "The Instruction of Amen-em-opet"? What structural similarities are evident?
15. Sum up the moral code expressed in Proverbs in statements such as "Do not steal." Are there do's as well as don'ts?

JOB

SUMMARY

Many scholars agree that the Book of Job was written by an anonymous poet sometime around 400 B.C. However, some prefer not to give a date more precise than between 600 and 400 B.C.

In a prose Prologue (Chapters 1 and 2), we are told that at a meeting of the Heavenly Court the Adversary (Satan), a divine being who ranged the earth as a kind of inspector for God, provoked God into a test of Job, an "upright, perfect man" from the land of Uz (perhaps Edom). The Adversary saw no reason why God should be proud of the allegiance of a man who had been given every blessing. "Put forth thy hand now, and touch all that he has, and he will curse thee to thy face." Then the Lord gives Satan the power to take everything from Job: sons, daughters, cattle, sheep, barns—his entire property. But Job does not curse God as the Adversary had predicted, so the Adversary asks God to let him go further. His request is granted, and he now afflicts Job with "loathsome sores from the sole of his foot

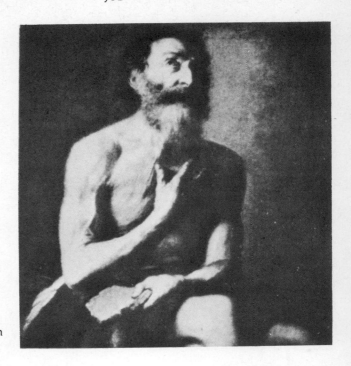

Bartolome Esteban
Murillo, "Job"

to the crown of his head" (2:7). Even though his wife urges him to
"curse God and die," Job still holds fast to his faith in God. "In all this
Job did not sin with his lips" (2:9–10).

As Job sits among the ashes, scraping himself with a potsherd,
three of his friends come to give him sympathy and comfort. Astounded at his appearance and his suffering, they sit for seven days
without saying a word.

When Job at last opens his mouth and curses the day of his
birth, the long poem known as the Dialogue begins. Extending from
Chapter 3 through 40:6, this poem consists of three cycles of speeches
by Job and his friends, five speeches in verse by a young man named
Elihu (perhaps inserted later by an editor), a poem on wisdom
(Chapter 28), which may not have been written by the author of the
Dialogue, and four chapters in which the Lord confronts Job from the
midst of a whirlwind. The book concludes with an Epilogue (42:7–17),
which takes us back to the folk tale of Chapters 1 and 2.

If we read only Chapters 1 and 2 ending with verse 10, and then
Chapter 42 beginning with verse 10 (leaving out the clause "when he
had prayed for his friends"), we have a story that stands entirely by itself, with a meaning quite distinct from that of the Dialogue. This fact
has led scholars to speculate that the author of the Dialogue used the
folk tale as a framework and a starting point for his own discussion of
the problem of justice in a universe that seems indifferent to the
human plight, even to the suffering of a good man. It is difficult if not

impossible to believe that the Dialogue author wanted us to take the restoration of Job recounted in Chapter 42 as his final answer to the profound question raised in the Dialogue.

The Dialogue begins with Job's curse against the day of his birth. His life is so wretched that Sheol, that place which otherwise is so dreadful, looks attractive to him by comparison: "There the wicked cease from troubling, and there the weary are at rest" (3:17). In this first speech Job voices the question that is of first importance throughout the Dialogue: "Why is light given to a man whose way is hid, whom God has hedged in?" In other words, why are we given life and then denied knowledge of its meaning? Even more puzzling is the fact that the Lord of the universe—all-powerful, all-knowing, and presumably good—has himself made this knowledge impossible. *He* has built the hedge around our understanding.

Reacting to Job's dismay, Eliphaz the Temanite tells Job that "from visions of the night" he has heard a voice that asks, "Can mortal man be righteous before (or *more than*) God?" (4:17). He assumes that Job has sinned, since "Man is born to trouble as the sparks fly upward" (5:7), and therefore Job must accept his suffering as "the chastening of the Almighty" (5:17). If Job will seek God, he will be delivered and all will be as before. "Your descendants shall be many . . . you shall come to your grave in ripe old age" (5:25–26)—a cliché that anticipates Job's restoration in the Epilogue.

But Job is not consoled by this piece of traditional advice. His calamity is so great that he wishes for immediate death, lest his pain force him to deny God (Chapter 6). He also wonders why the Lord should be so concerned with him even if he has sinned: "If I sin, what do I do to thee, thou watcher of men? . . . Why dost thou not pardon my transgression and take away my iniquity?" (7:20–21). This rouses Bildad the Shuhite to ask, "Does God pervert justice?" and to assert that if Job is truly blameless, his suffering must be punishment for the sins of his children. If he remains true and upright, God will not reject him but will finally "fill his mouth with laughter" (8:21).

Job's reply is not to Bildad, but to a statement made earlier by Eliphaz (4:17): "Can mortal man be righteous before God?" Presumably Job has been reflecting on this question while Bildad was speaking, and now he asks, "But how can a man be just before God?" (9:2). Chapters 9 and 10 are a powerful statement of the position of Job, a man who is blameless (as we know from the Prologue) but who is nevertheless suffering. When Job considers that wicked men prosper while he, who is blameless, suffers, he wonders why the Creator ever formed him. Was it only to torture him? Why does God not even allow him to live out his short life in a little comfort before he goes to the place of everlasting gloom? "Who does not know such things as these," he says (12:3). These are, after all, the answers of religious orthodoxy stressed in Chapter 28 of Deuteronomy and in the writings of the great prophets. Even the wise men of the Book of Proverbs offer reminders that sin is punished and right action rewarded. The poet of the Dialogue is quite courageous in questioning the conventional conception of God.

Zophar the Naamathite (who, we can guess, must have been waiting impatiently for the opportunity to speak) is angry with Job and accuses him of babbling in a "multitude of words." Certain of his own understanding of God, Zophar asserts that Job is really suffering less than he deserves. God knows which men are worthless, says Zophar, and "when he sees iniquity will he not consider it?" (11:11). So he advises Job to set his heart aright and expunge wickedness from his life, assuring him that then he can expect to be "secure." "You will lie down, and none will make you afraid; many will entreat your favor" (11:19).

Job's answer is a response not only to Zophar but to all his "comforters." He speaks sarcastically: "No doubt you are the people, and wisdom will die with you" (12:2). Who does not know what everyone in his community believes in—or at least gives lip service to? He tells his friends that they "whitewash with lies" and that they are "worthless physicians" (13:4). He cannot believe that they speak for God (verse 8 of Chapter 42 eventually justifies his claim), and he suggests that they will suffer for their arrogant interpretation of God's ways. "Your maxims," he says, "are proverbs of ashes" (13:12). Then Job takes the ultimate stand, which we may consider the climax of the book: "Behold, he will slay me; I have no hope; yet I will defend my ways to his face. This will be my salvation, that a godless man shall not come before him" (13:15–16). Continuing in this courageous vein, Job asks God to take away his suffering and his dread of God. After that, he says, God can ask him to speak, for then the contest will be fair. As it is now, Job has no chance, for his feet are already "in the stocks" (13:27).

In the two remaining cycles of speeches Job and his friends alternate their arguments. These are for the most part repetitious of the first cycle, iterating the conviction that the wicked do not really prosper and that even if they seem to, they will eventually be punished. Eliphaz says that although the wicked may seem to be happy, they actually know "that a day of darkness is ready at hand" (15:23). Zophar adds that "the exulting of the wicked is short, and the joy of the godless but for a moment" (20:5). Job is impatient with Zophar's assurance that if the wicked themselves prosper, at least their children suffer: "You say, 'God stores up their iniquity for their sons.' Let him recompense it to themselves, that they may know it. Let their own eyes see their destruction, and let them drink of the wrath of the Almighty" (21:19–20).

The poem of Chapter 19 is particularly telling. Here we see Job bereft of kinsfolk, friends, guests, servants, even repulsive to his wife.

Engraving by William Blake, "Job Rebuked by His Friends"

Driven to desperation, he calls out, "Have pity on me, have pity on me, O you my friends, for the hand of God has touched me!" (19:21). Yet he cannot believe that he will not at last be vindicated: "For I know that my redeemer lives, and at last he will stand upon the earth; and after my skin has been destroyed, then from (or *without*) my flesh I shall see God, whom I shall see on my side (or *for myself*), and my eyes shall behold, and not another" (19:25–27). Translators consider the meaning of this last verse uncertain, but the thrust of it is that Job, not knowing where to turn, believes that someone (perhaps a close relation, perhaps God himself) will avenge and vindicate him, even after he has died.

Job's words in verses 5–14 of Chapter 26 are an anticipation of what the Lord will later say from the whirlwind. Chapter 28 is a beautiful poem or hymn on wisdom. It may not have been part of the original Dialogue, but it is not entirely out of place. "Where shall wisdom be found? And where is the place of understanding? Man does not know the way to it, and it is not found in the land of the living" (28:12–13). The last verse of this chapter, which says that the fear of the Lord is wisdom and to depart from evil is understanding, offers no new revelation to Job in his predicament, for he has never doubted that God is sovereign. What Job asks is why men suffer even when they fear the Lord and do his will. Indeed, Job's next speech (in Chapter 29) is a long, rhapsodic reflection on the days when the Lord recognized his faithfulness and piety, when Job's "fear of the Lord" was reciprocated by "the friendship of God." Job recites the good deeds he performed and recalls the respect and admiration in which he was held. "Men listened to me, and waited, and kept silence for my counsel" (29:21).

In Chapter 30 Job contrasts his present state with that of his past blessedness. Now disreputable people make sport of him. Although once he helped others, now when he cries out for help he is answered by evil and surrounded by darkness. "My skin turns black and falls from me, and my bones burn with heat" (30:30).

In Chapter 31 Job takes sixteen oaths to verify that he has lived up to the highest ethical standards he knows. He ends with a challenge to God: "Oh, that I had one to hear me! (Here is my signature! let the Almighty answer me!) Oh, that I had the indictment written by my adversary!" (31:35).

Job's words are ended, and the friends have no more to say. Perhaps the original poem ended here. Nevertheless, in the Book of Job as we have it we are still to hear from a young man named Elihu and from the Lord himself. Elihu has evidently been listening to the argument but has refrained from joining in, because he was not invited and because he is much younger than Job's friends. He now breaks in, however, in an effort to accomplish what the friends have failed to do. His words are given in five poems (Chapters 32–37), but although he strives valiantly, he is never answered by any of the four men present. (This is one reason why many critics have concluded that these chapters were interpolated by a later editor.) Elihu argues that Job should not have contended against God, for "God is greater than man," and goes on to say that God communicates with human beings in various ways, even though they do not perceive this—for example, in dreams and visions. God also chastens with pain and may allow a heavenly mediator to instruct the sufferer and bring him to salvation from immediate death. Elihu disregards Job's main argument—that Job's own case makes it obvious that the good suffer while the wicked prosper—and argues that God *does* punish the wicked and that if a good people suffer it is because God wants them to cease their transgressions. "He opens their ears to instruction, and commands that they return from iniquity. If they hearken and serve him, they complete their days in prosperity, and their years in pleasantness" (36:10–11). Elihu's fifth speech (36:26–37:22) is a poem in praise of the wondrous works of God. It serves as a transition to the speeches of God from the whirlwind, which conclude the Dialogue.

In lofty poetry the voice from the whirlwind bombards Job with questions, which finally bring him to his knees: "Where were you when I laid the foundation of the earth? . . . Have you commanded the morning since your days began? . . . Have you entered into the springs of the sea? . . . Where is the way to the dwelling of light? . . . Have you entered the storehouse of the snow? . . . Who has cleft a channel for the torrents of rain? . . . Can you bind the chains of Pleiades, or loose the cords of Orion? . . . Can you hunt the prey for the lion? . . . Who provides for the raven its prey? . . . Do you know when the mountain goats bring forth? . . . Who has let the wild ass go free? . . . Is the wild ox willing to serve you? . . . The wings of the ostrich wave proudly; but are they the pinions and plumage of love?

. . . Do you give the horse his might? . . . Is it by your wisdom that the hawk soars?"

Overwhelmed, Job says, "Behold, I am of small account; what shall I answer thee? I lay my hand on my mouth." But God has still more questions to ask: "Will you even put me in the wrong? Will you condemn me that you may be justified?" He then describes two primeval monsters, Behemoth and Leviathan, and asks whether Job could contend with them. The might of Leviathan is dwelt on in all of Chapter 41. "Upon earth there is not his like, a creature without fear. He beholds everything that is high; he is king over all the sons of pride." Job capitulates again, this time saying, "I know that thou canst do all things, and that no purpose of thine can be thwarted. . . . I had heard of thee by the hearing of the ear, but now my eye sees thee; therefore I despise myself and repent in dust and ashes."

The Epilogue follows, with a return to the prose style and the story of the Prologue. There is a significant statement, however, in verses 7 and 8 of this last chapter. The Lord says to Eliphaz the Temanite: "My wrath is kindled against you and against your friends; for you have not spoken of me what is right, as my servant Job has." They are ordered to offer up for themselves a burnt offering, and Job is told to pray for them, "for I will accept his prayer not to deal with you according to your folly; for you have not spoken of me what is right, as my servant Job has." Is the Lord referring to what the friends have said in a lost portion of the prose story? Or is he referring to the orthodox arguments of the Dialogue? And what has Job said that is "right"? These questions are still unsettled.

After Job prays for his friends, the Lord restores all Job's fortunes. He has ten more children (seven sons and three daughters) and lives for another 140 years.

LITERARY QUALITIES

The Art of the Book
ARTHUR S. PEAKE

There has been much fruitless controversy as to the literary label that should be attached to the book. We cannot force this splen-

THE ART OF THE BOOK   From Arthur S. Peake, ed., *The Book of Job*, New Century Bible Series (London: Marshall, Morgan & Scott Publications, Oliphants; distributed in the United States by Attic Press, P.O. Box 1156, Greenwood, S.C. 29646). Reprinted by permission of Marshall, Morgan & Scott Publications, Ltd.

did fruit of Hebrew wisdom into a Greek scheme, and it is really futile to discuss whether it is a drama or an epic. It is itself. We may more profitably linger on some of its literary qualities. Like Hebrew poetry in general its most striking formal characteristic is its parallelism. Usually the second line repeats the thought of the first, though sometimes it states the contrast to it, or perhaps it completes the thought begun but left unfinished in the first. The parallel structure brings to the ear the same kind of satisfaction as rhyme, but unless very skilfully used it is apt to pall in a long poem. In this book its monotony is largely overcome by the poet's blending of various types of parallelism and by the occasional use of triplets instead of couplets.

The poet is a master of metaphors, taken from many spheres of life. The work of the farm suggests a figure to describe those who sow iniquity and reap trouble, or the comparison of death in a ripe old age to the coming into the barn of the shock of corn in its season. The fate of the wicked is likened to that of the stubble driven by the wind from the threshing-floor or the chaff chased by the storm. Job compares himself in his prosperity to a tree drinking up the water by its roots while its branches were refreshed by the dew. His words were awaited by the assembly as thirstily as the parched clods look up for the rain. In the long life he then anticipated he compared himself to the phoenix. He longs for death as the slave panting under the heat longs for the cool evening which will bring him his rest; or again, death is sought with the eagerness that characterizes those who dig for hid treasures. The wicked is compared to the Nile grass suddenly cut off from the moisture and withering rapidly; his trust can as little support him as a flimsy spider's web. Man's brief life is like the flower opening in beauty and suddenly cut down, the swiftness with which it passes is illustrated by the weaver's shuttle, the courier, the speed of the light skiffs on the river, or of the eagle as it swoops on its prey. The completeness of his disappearance from earth when he passes into Sheol is compared with the vanishing of the cloud. The failure of streams supplies him with several metaphors; thus Job illustrates the disappointment he had experienced from the friends by the caravan that comes to the channel down which the turbid torrent swept in winter, only to find the brawling stream scorched out of existence in the summer heat, and perish in the search for new supplies. The failing waters furnish an apt metaphor for the irretrievable ebbing away of life, while the forgetfulness of past trouble is illustrated by the oblivion into which they run. Military figures are common. More than once Job describes God as an archer with Job for his target. He tortures him with suspense, letting His arrows whistle about him, before He sends them home. Or He is a wrestler of gigantic strength with Job for His antagonist and victim. A third illustration is that of a fortress with a breach made in the walls through which the enemy pours. The fate of the wicked is set forth under the figure of an attack on a den of lions, the old lions have their teeth dashed out and perish for lack of prey, while the whelps are scattered abroad. There are many other metaphors for the evil destiny that awaits the godless. His branch is not green, or it is dried up by the flame, or again his root is withered beneath, and his branch cut off above; he is like the vine that fails to bring to maturity its unripe grape, or the olive shedding its flowers. His path is all beset with snares, the hell-hounds of terror chase him, but which ever way he turns they meet him, closing on him from every side. While he flees from the iron weapon the brass bow pierces him with its arrow. He is driven away as utterly as a dream of the night. While wickedness is a dainty tit-bit in the sinner's mouth, held fast that all its delicious sweetness may be enjoyed, and only reluctantly let go, yet it will turn to the gall of asps within him. Natural phenomena are described by graphic images. Clouds formed the garment and swaddling band for the infant sea, new born from the bowels of the chaotic deep. The clouds as they float in the sky are like bottles filled with water, which when they are tilted spill the rain. The dawn is a woman peeping over the crest of the hills, and the rays of light are her eyelashes. Darkness is a coverlet in which the wicked are shrouded from sight, suddenly the light comes and twitches the covering away so that the wicked are shaken out of it and stand revealed in the glare of day. And under the light the world lies all clear cut like clay freshly stamped by the seal, or like a body clothed with its close-fitting robe. The caracole of the horse is compared to the leaping of a locust.

The book is studded with the most exquisite descriptions. The whole of Yahweh's speech is a sustained effort of the highest genius, unsurpassed in the world's literature. The animal pictures are like instantaneous photographs, catching a characteristic attitude, and fixing it for us in the most vivid words. And with what power and beauty are the marvels of the universe set forth! The laying of its foundation amid the songs of the morning stars and the joyous shouts of the sons of God; the birth of the sea, and the staying of its tumultuous heavenward leap; the punctual dayspring, flooding the world with light; the springs that feed the sea from the nether deep; the gates of Sheol; the dwelling of light and darkness; the stores of hail and snow made ready for God's battles; the sluice cut through the firmament by which the torrential rain descends; the frost that turns the streams to stone; the rain that falls on the waste afar from man; the mighty constellations, obedient to God's behest; the lightning with its purposeful movement; all pass before the mind as God unrolls the panorama of the universe. And fully worthy to be mentioned with this is the wonderful description in Bildad's third speech, closing with the awed confession that we stand but at the outskirts of God's ways, where the deafening thunder of His power is mercifully heard from afar. Less noteworthy than these is the fine description of God's power and wisdom in ix.

5–10. Or take the vision of Eliphaz, where the old terror masters him as he narrates it. How vividly it all passes before us; the preparation in the musings on his night trances; the fear that sets his bones quaking, the cold breath across the face, the hair on end, the vague thing that his straining eyes could resolve into no shape he could name, the dead silence and then the thin voice. Or, for its quiet soothing beauty, the peroration to the same speech. And what a sense of peace steals over the weary as he reads the longing words in which Job describes the untroubled calm of Sheol, where the wicked cease from troubling and the weary are at rest. How full of dismay and yearning is the plaintive assertion of the hopelessness of man's fate (xix. 7–21)! How graphic Bildad's picture of the terrors that surround the sinner and the evil destiny to which he is doomed!

The poet's power of irony is displayed most conspicuously in the speech of Yahweh. But examples may be culled from the debate. Thus Job bitterly asks God what is frail man that He must so narrowly observe him, or whether he is himself a sea or sea-monster that God should set a watch over him. The friends' arguments he satirizes with pungent scorn, their proverbs are proverbs of ashes, their wisdom consists only of platitudes; he tells Bildad that he really must have been inspired to make one of his speeches. One of his most biting and delightful phrases is aimed at them, "How irritating are words of uprightness." Bitter indeed is the question whether he had taxed their friendship by asking them to do anything for him, as if he had thought friendship could stand such a test!

His pathos is deeply moving. Job feels acutely the unkindness of his friends, he even turns to them with the appeal, "Have pity upon me, have pity upon me, O ye my friends!" But it is little that he says to the friends in this strain. It is rather to God that his pathetic pleadings are addressed. "My friends scorn me, But mine eye poureth out tears unto God." With such care had God fashioned him, with such kindness preserved him, why does he wantonly destroy him? Soon he must die under God's stroke, but by and by God's present mood will pass, then He will seek for His servant in love, but alas! too late. Especially the swift movement to death elicits some of Job's most touching words, and the thought of the dreary interminable darkness that awaits him.

The character-drawing of the book is not highly developed. The friends are distinguished to some extent, but they have no clearly-marked individuality, and they take very much the same line. The character-study of Job is more subtle, as the interest of the poem centres about the struggle of his soul caught in the web of mystery and pain. On this, however, it is not necessary to repeat what is said elsewhere.

INTERPRETATIONS

In the article from which the next selection is taken, Richard G. Moulton finds five possible solutions to "the mystery of suffering" in the Book of Job. They may be summarized as follows. (1) Suffering is a test of saintship. (2) All suffering is a judgment upon sin. (3) Suffering is a judgment warning the sinner to escape by repentance from heavier judgment. (4) The whole universe is an unfathomed mystery, and the evil in it is no more mysterious than the good and the great. (5) The bold faith of Job, which could appeal to God against the justice of God's own visitation, was more acceptable than the servile adoration of the friends, who had sought to distort the facts in order to magnify God. In the following passage Moulton considers the fourth and fifth solutions.

from "The Book of Job"
RICHARD G. MOULTON

The Divine Intervention is the finale and climax of the whole drama. But its purport is I believe, commonly misunderstood. It is often supposed to be an indignant denial of Job's right to question the ways of God. That this is not its significance a single consideration is sufficient to show. Such denial of the right to question had been the position of the Friends: Job had resisted, and questioned. Yet in the epilogue God is represented as declaring that the Friends had not said of him the thing that was right, as his servant Job had. Nor can this be met by the suggestion that Job had made submission, whereas the Friends had not, and were therefore under the Divine displeasure because of their misinterpretation of the visitation on Job. The Friends have not been called upon for submission: no part of the Divine Intervention is addressed to them, nor does it bear upon their case. It is impossible to interpret the epilogue except as a pronouncement on the side of Job, however much there may be of rebuke for his wilder utterances. Unless then we are to say that the Divine Intervention pronounces on one side and the Epilogue on the other, it cannot be that the former is a denial of the right to question.

It is a different thing, and nearer the truth, to lay down that the Divine Intervention denies the *possibility* of Job's reading the meaning of God's visitation. Indeed, this is unquestionably part of the significance of this section. But to say this is to say nothing: such inscrutability of providence is a commonplace of the whole poem: the Friends and Elihu proclaim it, Job himself has recognized it in strong language. It would seem that the emphasis upon this topic is a necessity arising from the very character of the literary task here attempted. The poet has undertaken to dramatize God's ways in heaven and earth, God himself being introduced as one of *dramatis personae;* the instinct of reverence makes him seek to counterpoise such bold imagination by making prominent at every point the awful distance between the creature and the Creator. . . .

The Deity of the Divine Intervention is not the God of Judgment but the Soul of External Nature. Job had at one point of the discussion pictured a God beyond the possibilities of human understanding: no two conceptions can be more unlike than the God so conceived by Job and the God here presented by Himself. One note there is in common: the half scornful ease of fathomless energy. But Job's thought was an Infinite Inaccessibility: here we have an Infinite Sympathy. He is the God of Nature, but here revealed in the joyous spontaneities of nature. Omniscience, omnipotence, omnipresence are of course implied; but what is made prominent is an all-pervasive sympathy, embracing the vastnesses that strain the imagination, but penetrating also to the smallest things and things most remote from human interest. Though the Creator of the world, he is not here a creator by fiat, but an earth-builder, rejoicing in his task to secure its foundations and determine its measures, while the corner-stone is laid with the morning stars singing together and all the sons of God shouting for joy. . . .

When such a conception of Deity has been taken in—joyous sympathy with the infinities of great and small through the universe—then we are able to see how this Divine Intervention makes a distinct section of the whole work. For the hopeless suffering in which there is nothing of guilt what treatment can be better than to lose the individual pain in sympathetic wonder over nature in her inexhaustible variety? But the connection can be more logically indicated. The mystery of suffering is not to be solved within the limits of human knowledge; and an imperfect or tentative solution could not be put into the mouth of Deity. But what the Divine Intervention in this drama does is to lift the discussion into a wider sphere. Job and his friends had fastened their attention upon suffering and evil, and had broken down under the weight of the mystery: but the individual experience now seems a small thing in the range of all nature's ways. Hence we have a *Fourth Solution of the Mystery of Suffering: That the whole universe is an unfathomed mystery, and the Evil in it is not more mysterious than the Good and the Great.* The problem of the poem may be insoluble; but there is an advance towards a solution when it can be comprehended in a wider category.

But it may be objected, Job makes submission and repents: of what sin, according to this reading of the Divine Intervention, does he repent? Sin might be found, if necessary, in the wild picturings of providence into which his helplessness under false accusations betrayed him. But surely it lowers the tone of the climax to look for positive transgressions. Job, conscious of innocence of the contention of the Friends, had passionately desired to come into the very presence of his Judge. His desire is granted: but in the purity of that presence the whiteness of innocence abhors itself in dust and ashes.

The drama terminates, and the narrative story is resumed, to introduce a brief Epilogue. The purport of this Epilogue has been already anticipated. God is represented as declaring that his anger is kindled against the Friends of Job, because they had not said of him the thing that was right, as his servant Job had; they are commanded to offer sacrifice, and Job is to intercede for them. We have here a *Fifth Solution to the Mystery of Suffering—the right attitude to this Mystery: that the bold faith of Job, which could appeal to God against the justice of God's own visitation,* was more acceptable to Him than the servile adoration of the Friends, who had sought to distort the facts in order to magnify God.* As Job intercedes for his Friends, God also turns his own captivity; wealth and prosperity are granted him greater than before, and he dies happy and full of years.

In the Introduction and notes to his *Book of Job* in the Soncino Books of the Bible series, Rabbi Dr. Victor E. Reichert offers a *Jewish* commentary, in keeping with the overall aim of the series. "Without neglecting the valuable work of Christian expositors, it takes into account the exegesis of the Talmudical Rabbis as well as the leading Jewish commentators," says general editor A. Cohen in his Foreword to the book (p. ix).

The Meaning of the Book
VICTOR E. REICHERT

The clash between dogma and human experience is the battlefield where the protagonists of these opposing convictions fight for

---

*The suffering that God has allowed Satan to inflict upon him.—Ed.

THE MEANING OF THE BOOK   From *Job with Hebrew Text and English Translation,* by Rabbi Dr. Victor E. Reichert, Soncino Books of the Bible Series (Reverend Dr. A. Cohen, General Editor), Commentary, pp. xviii–xix. London: The Soncino Press, 1960. Reprinted by permission of the publisher.

victory. If we remember that dogma may be only the frozen insight of one generation that cherishes its hard-won truth and will fight with fanatical devotion to maintain its authority, we can understand why the heresies arising from the flux of life will always meet with stormy resistance.

The meanings of the Book of Job emerge from the smoke of this never-ending war for truth. Prophetic Judaism had achieved the faith in an Almighty God Who ruled His universe with absolute justice. Ezekiel had applied this teaching to the individual in his doctrine of individual retribution. The Sages of Israel, speaking in the Book of Proverbs, further stressed the necessary connection between prosperity and piety. The belief had become intrenched that God rewards with material blessings those who live virtuously and punishes the sinner with suffering.

Now experience could not always confirm this comfortable faith. The problem of theodicy thus arose, made more urgent since what befell the individual was regarded as the immediate act of God. Nor had the notion yet taken shape that the scene of retribution and reward could be transferred to another world hereafter. Some such rumours, it is true, were in the air, but Job wistfully speaks of them only to reject them: "If a man die, may he live again?/ All the days of my service would I wait,/ Till my relief should come—" (xiv. 14). "Man that is born of a woman/ Is few of days, and full of trouble./ He cometh forth like a flower, and withereth;/ He fleeth also as a shadow, and continueth not" (xiv. 1–2). "Where then is my hope?/ And as for my hope, who shall see it?/ They shall go down to the bars of the netherworld,/ When we are at rest together in the dust" (xvii. 15–16).

Job, then, is convinced that the fight for meaning and the struggle to reconcile faith with reason must be fought in the only theatre of battle he knows—here on earth. He himself, like the three friends, had accepted the inherited belief of his generation. Bitter human experience now compels him to search for a more adequate ground for spiritual support.

What conclusions does Job reach? To the overarching theme, "What is the moral government by which God orders His universe?" he is finally forced to acknowledge his ignorance. When the Almighty laid the foundations of the earth and the morning stars sang together, he was not present as spectator or partner. Encompassed by the grandeurs of sky and earth, hemmed in by the infinite mysteries of Nature, he bows his head in humble acknowledgment of his human insignificance set against the cosmic majesty. Man cannot attain the absolute wisdom of God. His confidence must be rooted in the perception that: "The fear of the Lord, that is wisdom;/ And to depart from evil is understanding" (xxvii. 28).

The other question, subordinate but more obvious, "Is there retributive justice in the world?" finds positive answer from Job. His own tragic struggle confirmed the paradox that, in appealing from the apparent injustices of God, Job found strength and support in the righteous God Who would one day establish his innocence. Job denies the adequacy of material retribution. Suffering is no sure proof of sin. But there does exist retribution of a higher order: the righteous man is never completely cut off from the fellowship of God. It is to this invincible trust that Job gives immortal utterance when out of the long ordeal of his soul he cries: "But as for me, I know that my Redeemer liveth,/ And that He will witness at the last upon the dust" (xix. 25).

In an essay on the Book of Job in his volume *The Vision of Tragedy*, Richard B. Sewall examines Job as a prototype of the tragic hero that is to develop in Western literature. "More than Prometheus or Oedipus," he says, "Job is the universal symbol for the western imagination of the mystery of undeserved suffering." In their history as it is presented in the Old Testament, the Hebrews "showed a strong critical sense, a tendency to test all their beliefs, even Jehovah Himself, against their individual experience and sense of values."*

According to Professor Sewall, a literature of dissent developed in reaction to the orthodox teaching that God always metes out justice according to one's behavior and merit. Examples of that dissent in the Old Testament are some of the psalms, the story of Jonah, the philosophizing of Koheleth (Ecclesiastes), and the Dialogue of the Book of Job.

The Hebrew tragic vision has "a peculiar depth and poignancy," however, because of the Hebrews' "conception of Jehovah as a person, to be communed with, worshiped, feared, but above all to be loved. . . . The protest embodied in *The Book of Job* came not from fear or hate but from love. Job's disillusionment was deeply personal, as from a cosmic breach of faith."†

The passage that follows is from the conclusion of Professor Sewall's essay.

*Richard B. Sewall, *The Vision of Tragedy* (New Haven: Yale University Press, Yale Paperbound Edition, 1962), p. 9.
†Richard B. Sewall, *The Vision of Tragedy* (New Haven: Yale University Press, Yale Paperbound Edition, 1962), p. 11.

from "The Book of Job"
RICHARD B. SEWALL

It has seemed to many that in the final stages of *Job*—the speech of Elihu, the Voice from the Whirlwind, Job's repentance, and the folk-story ending—tragic meaning, as the Poet has so far defined it, is swallowed up in mystical revelation or orthodox piety. In one sense it is true that the final phase of Job's experience carries him beyond the tragic domain, and the book as a whole is a religious book and not a formal tragedy. The revelation granted Job, and his repentance, would seem to deny the essence of his previous situation—the agony of dilemma, of the opposing compulsions of necessity and guilt. Certainly no such unequivocal Voice speaks to Antigone or Hamlet or Hester Prynne, who conclude the dark voyage in the light of their own unaided convictions, and live out their dilemmas to the end. But in these final scenes the tragic vision of the Poet is still active. Ambiguities remain, and the central question of the book is unanswered. Also, in the treatment of Job's pride, in the final revelation of how Job learned humility, in the irony with which the "happy ending" of the folk story is left to make its own statement, the Poet includes much that is relevant, as we can now see, to the tragic tradition.

At the end of his Oath of Clearance, Job had achieved a state of what Aristotle called catharsis. He had challenged the Almighty, made his case, and purged his spirit. He was in a Hamlet-like state of readiness. In taking him beyond catharsis into abject repentance and self-abhorrence, the Poet makes of him a religious rather than a tragic figure; but the Poem as a whole makes an important statement about pride, which the Greeks were to make repeatedly, though from a different perspective. According to the Poet, and to the Greek tragedians, pride like Job's is justified. It has its ugly and dark side, but it was through pride that Job made his spiritual gains and got a hearing from Jehovah himself. The Lord favored Job's pride and rebuked the safe orthodoxy of the Counselors. The pride that moved Job is the dynamic of a whole line of tragic heroes, from Oedipus to Ahab. It is always ambiguous and often destructive, but it is the very hallmark of the type. . . .

. . . The main movement of Job's experience, from the morbid concern for his own suffering toward membership and partisanship in

THE BOOK OF JOB From Richard B. Sewall, *The Vision of Tragedy* (New Haven: Yale University Press, Yale Paperbound Edition, 1962), pp. 9, 10, 11, 21–24. Reprinted by permission of Yale University Press.

the human family, is extending even farther outward. He must now experience the Infinite or the Absolute. Even though in formal tragedy there is no such apocalypse as Job presently experiences, the direction is the same. Through suffering, as Aeschylus wrote, men learn—not only their littleness and sinfulness but the positive and creative possibilities of themselves and the world they live in. They learn them, in *Job* as in later tragedy, not from Counselors or friends, but directly, on their pulses. As in the long debate with the Counselors Job made many discoveries about himself and the human realm, so now the Voice from the Whirlwind opens up for him the vast economy of the universe. In this new perspective, the question "Why did I suffer?" loses its urgency.

The question loses its urgency—Job never asks it again—but it is never answered. To the Poet, in contrast to the teaching of the Counselors or *The Book of Proverbs* or the first Psalm, the universe was not reasonable and not always just. He did not see it as a sunny and secure place for human beings, where to prosper one has only to be good. Even after the Voice ceased, Job was no nearer an understanding of what justice is than when he began his complaints. Unjustified suffering must be accepted as part of a mystery; it is not for man to reason why. The universe is a realm of infinite complexity and power, in which catastrophe may fall at any time on the just as well as the unjust. There may be enough moral cause-and-effect to satisfy the members of the chorus or the Counselors. But all the hero can do, if he is visited as Job was, is to persevere in the pride of his conviction, to appeal to God against God, and if he is as fortunate as Job, hear his questionings echo into nothingness in the infinite mystery and the glory.

Even the folk-story ending contains a tantalizing ambiguity. Few people go away happy at the end of *Job,* or if they do they miss the point. Of course, the sense of frustration is largely eliminated by Job's rewards. God is good; justice of a sort has been rendered; the universe seems secure. We are inclined to smile at how neatly it works out—the mathematical precision of the twofold restoration of Job's possessions and his perfectly balanced family, seven sons and three daughters—a sign perhaps that we are in the domain of something less elevated than Divine Comedy. But the universe seems secure only to those who do not question too far. Can a new family make up for the one Job lost? What about the faithful servants who fell to the Sabeans and Chaldeans? These questions the folk story ignores, and its reassuring final picture also makes it easy to forget Job's suffering and his unanswered question. Although the irony of the folk conclusion seems unmistakable, it was no doubt this easy piety, like the pious emendations to the bitterness of Ecclesiastes, that made *The Book of Job* acceptable to the orthodox for centuries. Actually, it is a "dangerous book." Although the Hebrews had their recalcitrant figures, capable, like the Poet of Job, of deep penetration into the realm of tragedy, they are rightly regarded as the people of a Covenant, a Code, and a Book. This is one reason, perhaps, why they never developed a tragic theater, where their beliefs and modes of living would be under constant scrutiny. Their public communication was through synagogue and pulpit; their prophets and preachers proclaimed the doctrine of obedience to divine law, and the rabbis endlessly proliferated the rules for daily life. The rebellious Job was not typical. For the most part, their heroes were lonely, God-summoned men whose language was that of witness to the one true light.

SUGGESTED READINGS

Glatzer, Nahum N. *The Dimensions of Job: A Study and Selected Readings.* New York: Schocken Books, 1969.

Pope, Marvin H., ed. *Job*. Rev. ed. The Anchor Bible Series, No. 15. New York: Doubleday & Company, 1973.

Terrien, Samuel. "The Book of Job: Introduction and Exegesis." In *The Interpreter's Bible*, Vol. 3, edited by George A. Buttrick, pp. 877–1198. Nashville, Tenn.: Abingdon Press, 1954.

QUESTIONS FOR DISCUSSION AND WRITING

1. Chapters 1 and 2:1–10 and 42:10–17 are described by some critics as the Prologue and Epilogue to the Book of Job. They are considered a separate story—perhaps a folk tale—used by the author as a framework for his Dialogue. Read these parts of the book together, and consider the message they convey. Would the friends have approved of this version of the story of Job? Why or why not?

2. Compare the poem on wisdom (Job, 28) with the two poems on wisdom in Proverbs (1:20–33 and 8:1–9:6). Would the friends have agreed with the Job view of wisdom, or with the Proverbs version? Why?

3. What do the speeches of the Lord from the whirlwind contribute to the progress of the argument in the Book of Job?

4. Review Arthur S. Peake's essay on the art of the Book of Job. Select about twenty lines from Job that you find especially poetic and moving and "translate" them into your own prose, deliberately stripping them of their poetic effects. When you have arrived at the literal meaning of these lines, what of importance has been lost?

5. In Chapter 13 of the *Poetics*, Aristotle says that a perfect tragedy should imitate actions which excite pity and fear and that therefore, "It follows

plainly, in the first place, that the change of fortune presented must not be the spectacle of a virtuous man brought from prosperity to adversity, for this moves neither pity nor fear; it merely shocks us. Nor again, that of a bad man passing from adversity to prosperity, for nothing can be more alien to the spirit of Tragedy; it possesses no single tragic quality; it neither satisfies the moral sense nor calls forth pity or fear. Nor, again, should the downfall of the utter villain be exhibited. A plot of this kind would doubtless satisfy the moral sense, but it would inspire neither pity nor fear; for pity is aroused by unmerited misfortune, fear by the misfortune of a man like ourselves. Such an event, therefore, will be neither pitiful nor terrible. There remains, then, the character between these two extremes—that of a man who is not eminently good and just, yet whose misfortune is brought about not by vice or depravity, but by some error or frailty. He must be one who is highly renowned and prosperous—a personage like Oedipus, Thyestes, or other illustrious men of such families."

Does Job meet Aristotle's requirements for the ideal tragic hero?

6. In what ways may we consider Job a "Suffering Servant" or a prototype of Jesus?

7. Arthur S. Peake says, "In this book [the monotony of parallel structure] is largely overcome by the poet's blending of various types of parallelism and by the occasional use of triplets instead of couplets." Find an example of a triplet, and an example of a blending of repetition, contrast, and completion of the thought—the usual three types of parallelism.

8. What "spheres of life" has Peake listed as sources from which the author of Job has taken his many metaphors? Can you cite some that Peake has not mentioned?

9. Peake says that "The character-drawing of the book is not highly developed." Nevertheless, write as adequate an analysis as you can of *one* of these characters: Eliphaz, Bildad, Zophar, Elihu, Job—or God.

10. What significance does Richard G. Moulton see in the Deity's intervention? Why does he interpret it as a not entirely unsatisfactory "answer" to Job's questionings?

11. Why does Moulton prefer solution 5 to solution 4? Do you agree with him? Why or why not?

12. According to Rabbi Reichert's interpretation of the Book of Job, although Job cannot completely understand the justice with which God orders the universe, it is nonetheless true that "the righteous man is never completely cut off from the fellowship of God." What evidence do you find in the text for this interpretation?

13. Richard B. Sewall writes that "The pride that moved Job is the dynamic of a whole line of tragic heroes, from Oedipus to Ahab." Compare Job and the Oedipus of Sophocles' *Oedipus the King* as characters whose "dynamic" is pride.

14. Sewall says that "In the long debate with the Counselors Job made many discoveries about himself and the human realm." What were these discoveries?

15. Why does Sewall describe the Book of Job as "dangerous" (p. 361)?

16. Sewall writes that the Book of Job "as a whole is a religious book" but

that the poet of this book is also "capable . . . of deep penetration into the realm of tragedy." Which aspects of the book does he consider primarily religious and which does he see as expressions of the poet's tragic vision?

17. Considering the stand taken by the author of Job against much of the teaching of the Hebrew Scriptures, argue that he himself is heroic.

18. Compare the Book of Job with "The First Job" in Samuel Noah Kramer's book *History Begins at Sumer* (New York: Doubleday Anchor Books, 1959), pp. 114–18.

19. Compare the Book of Job with Aeschylus' *Prometheus Bound*.

ECCLESIASTES

SUMMARY

Accurate dating of the composition of Ecclesiastes is impossible. Some place it around 200 B.C., because its author uses many Aramaic words and because it breathes an atmosphere of Greek rationalism. Others place it earlier, arguing that Greek philosophy had penetrated the Middle East by the fifth century B.C. Most agree, however, that it was written much later than the time of Solomon (tenth century B.C.) and that the sentence "I the Preacher have been king over Israel in Jerusalem" (1:12) describes a literary role, which the author drops after Chapter 2.

Ecclesiastes is a difficult book to present in an organized way, because it often shifts in mood and thought. Perhaps it is basically a wise man's notebook to which were later added the verses asserting that fear of God is necessary regardless of the seeming meaninglessness of the universe. Verses 9–14 of Chapter 12 certainly strike the reader as an editorial addition.

Richard G. Moulton says that "Ecclesiastes is not a book with a continuous argument, but is a miscellany of wisdom: made up of a number of reasoned compositions, such as I designate essays, and also strings of disconnected brevities—maxims, epigrams, unit proverbs. . . . In Ecclesiastes the essays, though each is an independent composition, unite in a common drift of thought; and they are further bound into a unity by a prologue and epilogue."*

Moulton outlines Ecclesiastes as follows.

Prologue (1:1–11)
Essay I, in the Form of a Dramatic Monologue: Solomon's Search for Wisdom (1:12–2:26)
Essay II: the Philosophy of Times and Seasons (Chapter 3)
Essay III: the Vanity of Desire (4:1–7:21)
Essay IV: a Search for Wisdom with Notes by the Way (7:23–11:10)
Essay V: Life As a Joy Shadowed by Vanity (12:1–8)
Epilogue: All is Vanity—Fear God (12:9–14)†

The Revised Standard Version uses the word Preacher (rather than Ecclesiastes, Qoheleth, or Koheleth) for the speaker of the book. All these names refer to one who conducts an assembly or a school.

The Prologue sets the tone of the book and states the thesis: Everything is as ephemeral as a breath of air; nothing is new; we simply do not remember that everything we experience has also happened in ages past. Assuming the vantage point of King Solomon in Jerusalem, the Preacher begins an investigation of life's meaning. As Solomon he not only is in the best position for this but also has the wisdom to make a thorough search.

First he tries pleasure. Searching with his mind for ways to get the most out of everything, he drinks wine and makes for himself houses, vineyards, gardens, parks, pools, and forests. He buys and raises slaves and has herds and flocks of cattle, sheep, and goats. He has silver and gold, with which he obtains singers and concubines. He finds that his work in *seeking* pleasure is rewarding, but then he realizes that it all amounts to nothing: His *heart* finds pleasure, but his *mind* pronounces it vanity (2:10).

Next the Preacher turns to consider "wisdom and madness and folly." He finds that wisdom is superior to folly, but he falls into despair when he reflects that the wise person dies just as the fool does and that the one who inherits the possessions gained by the wise person's toil may well be a fool. (The paragraph consisting of 2:24–26

---

*Richard G. Moulton, ed., *The Modern Reader's Bible* (New York: Macmillan, 1895), p. 1470.
†Ibid., pp. 1634–36.

"The Feast of Tabernacles." Since the sixth century A.D., this feast has been associated with Ecclesiastes. The engraving shows a family celebrating the occasion in an arbor decorated with branches and lanterns. The feast is a reminder of the time when the Israelites lived in the open air during the wanderings in the Sinai Desert.

seems to strike a confusing note. However, as explained in the footnote to 2:26 in the *Oxford Annotated Bible,* this verse is "a note originally made in the margin of the manuscript by a scribe, correcting the view that goodness makes no difference to one's fate.")

The first nine verses of Chapter 3 are a poem on the pattern of existence, whose theme is that there is a time appointed for everything. Yet although God has given us a sense of past and future, he has not revealed the meaning of life. Therefore it is best to enjoy our pleasures when we can. There may be a time appointed for the righteous and the wicked to receive their just rewards, and perhaps God deliberately makes it appear that men are no better than animals, as a test. But since we cannot know whether after this life a human being is any better off than a beast, we might as well enjoy our work. That is all we can count on.

Seeing the suffering of people who are oppressed, the Preacher reflects that it is better never to have been born than to have such a life. And when he sees a miser living alone and piling up wealth, he wonders at the folly of one who will give up warm human relationships for possessions.

The worshiper should speak cautiously when in the house of God. It is best to say very little, and if one makes a vow to God, one should be careful to fulfill it.

367

Those are favored by God who have been given not only wealth and possessions but also the heart to enjoy them. On the other hand, those who lack nothing and yet cannot enjoy anything suffer "a sore affliction," which cannot be remedied even if they live two thousand years.

No amount of argument can tell us what is good for us, because we cannot know our ultimate destiny. In keeping with our human condition, it is more appropriate to associate ourselves with the sadness of things than to spend our lives in mirth: "It is better to go to the house of mourning than to go to the house of feasting" (7:2). It is best to be moderate in all things rather than overrighteous, overwise, overwicked, or overfoolish.

We should not take it too seriously when people curse us, for we should remember how many times we have cursed others.

Despite all his searching, the Preacher finds that he cannot plumb the depths. He does find, however, that although God made them upright, human beings (especially women) are full of devious ways.

Be practical in your relationships with those who govern, says the Preacher. When the king orders you to do something, do it. If you are wise, you will find an appropriate way to carry out his commands.

The inconsistency in 8:10–9:6, where we are told at one time that the wicked will finally be punished and the good rewarded and at another time that "one fate comes to all, to the righteous and the wicked," may no doubt be resolved if we consider 8:11–13 the interpolation of a scribe or editor.

We should make the most of what we have, for "the race is not to the swift nor the battle to the strong" (9:11). After all, wisdom is worthwhile even though it is cherished very little by most people.

Finally, the Preacher recommends that we act: "Cast your bread upon the waters, for you will find it after many days" (11:1). And even if our "days of darkness will be many," he tells us to rejoice. Obviously, he does not believe that human beings would be happier as mindless beasts: They should derive what happiness they can from life even while they are aware that ultimately their happiness will make no difference.

Ecclesiastes ends with a prose-poem advising us to remember our Creator in our youth, before the latter days when it is usual to do so—"before the silver cord is snapped, or the golden bowl is broken . . . and the dust returns to the earth as it was, and the spirit returns to God who gave it" (12:6–7).

Tacked on to the last chapter are some comments by an editor. He assures us that the Preacher wrote words of truth, that we should not go beyond the words of the wise, and that above all we must "fear God, and keep his commandments" (12:13).

LITERARY QUALITIES

from "Qoheleth: The Limits of Wisdom"
EDWIN M. GOOD

There is a certain pious assumption that anything in the Bible must be true; the question easily becomes not whether a book or passage has truth but what its truth is. But it is by no means self-evident that Qoheleth has a stance in truth. To be sure, a follower, who perhaps wanted to reassure readers or even to reverse the book's effect, claimed that he did: "Qoheleth sought to find pleasant words, and he wrote truthful words uprightly" (ch. 12:10). But many of those who have studied Qoheleth most closely are not at all convinced that that judgment is sound. Morris Jastrow titled his book on Qoheleth *A Gentle Cynic*. D. B. Macdonald thinks that Qoheleth inculcates amorality (not, mark well, immorality) on the basis of the divine amorality. Terms like "fatalism," "pessimism," "nihilism" are often used of Qoheleth. And [Aarre] Lauha holds that the only reason to maintain the book in the Biblical canon is that its negativity clarifies Scripture's positive faith, because this book's darkness shows how impossible life is without Scriptural faith.

The major difficulty in understanding Qoheleth is that the book seems not to present a thoroughgoing, well-organized argument. The observation that it contradicts itself raised grave doubts among the early rabbis about retaining the book in the canon. On the one hand,

> The wise man's mind is on the house of mourning,
> But the fool's mind is on the house of rejoicing.
> (Ch. 7:4)

And on the other hand:

> I lauded rejoicing, because there is no good for man beneath the sun except to eat and to drink and to rejoice. (Ch. 8:15)

Again:

> The destiny of men's sons and the destiny of the beasts are the same destiny. As the one dies, so does the other, and all of them have the same

spirit. And the advantage man has over the beast is nil. So the whole of it is vanity. They all go to the same place: all have come out of dust, and all return to dust. Who knows the spirit of man? Will it go upward? And the spirit of beasts: will it descend down into the earth? (Ch. 3:19–21)

But:

> The dust returns to the earth as it did,
> But the spirit returns to God who gave it.
> (Ch. 12:7)

Examples could be set side by side for several more pages. It is a baffling book that exhorts not to be "overly righteous" nor "overly wicked" (ch. 7:16–17) but closes with the injunction to keep the commandments of God (ch. 12:13). Can we ascribe to such a book a "stance in truth"?

Scholars have ordinarily solved the dilemma by postulating an original author and one or more editors and glossators. The most elaborate theory, propounded by Siegfried in 1898, was that the book was written by a philosophical Jew influenced by Greek thought, and comments were added by three other persons: a Sadducean Epicurean, who suggested that we enjoy life while it lasts; a "wise man" (*chākām*), who set forth the advantages of wisdom; and a "pietist" (*chāsîd*), who referred to the divine judgment. Further additions, according to Siegfried, were made by a glossator concerned with wisdom, two redactors, and three contributors to the epilogue (ch. 12:8–14). The flaw in such a theory is that one decides beforehand what the thought and style of the "original" author were and ascribes anything inconsistent with them to an editor or glossator. It is always a circular argument, and one seldom fails to come to the conclusions with which he originally started. . . .

Perhaps we are too certain that we know what a "book" is: a unified, logically argued and constructed whole. When we discover that Qoheleth as it stands does not fit the definition, we are baffled. We are forced to assume, therefore, either that its disunity, lack of construction, and failures of logic are illusions, to be dispelled if we work hard enough, or that somebody has been tampering with the original, which must, *ex hypothesi*, have corresponded to our definition of a "book." So we search out the "original," brush aside all that rings falsely with it, and bask in the warm assurance that once again we have justified our definition of a "book."

The fact is that we have before us a "work." To our minds, trained in certain ways and on certain assumptions, the work appears a scattered, miscellaneous, unstructured, and internally inconsistent congeries of remarks. Perhaps—the hypothesis has been proffered—it was a diary in which the writer set down thoughts without telling us when or why, or a kind of commonplace book in which the writer

mixed ideas of his own with quotations that he fancied, or miscellaneous meditations of the author somewhat on the model of Pascal's
Pensées. Perhaps it is any or none of these. Does it really matter? To
analyze the book's origin is not necessarily to solve its problem. The
issue is to permit it to speak for itself so far as it will, and not to
decide prematurely what it must say. The unity of the book, if unity
there be, must emerge from the book itself, not from the student's
predispositions, little as those predispositions can be totally oblitera-
ted. But we must above all avoid the modernizing error of confusing
the person of an author with the integrity of the work. In Qoheleth we
have to do with the work, not with a hypothetically reconstructible author. If in the pages that follow I use the pronoun "he," I do not mean
by it any securely grasped and analyzed personality. The purpose of
interpretation is at any rate not to reconstruct and analyze a personality but to grapple with truth—or with falsehood.

I believe, as will shortly appear, that there is a basic unity of
thought in the book. If that requires the postulation of a single author,
I am prepared to postulate a single author. But I fail to perceive a clear
formal structure to the book.

SOME BASIC AXIOMS

Qoheleth was no systematician—or, if he tried to be, he failed
spectacularly. But certain axioms seem to hold true for the entire book.
Primary among them is that every man must find the significance of
his life within that life, not beyond it. The references to death point
out that man must make the most of life.

> The wise man's eyes are in his head,
> And the fool walks in darkness.
> But I also know
> That one destiny
> Befalls them all. . . .
> The wise man dies just as the fool does.
> (Ch. 2:14, 16)

This life is all we have. Meaning is to be found here or not at all.
"Who can bring [man] here to see what will come after him?" (ch.
3:22; cf. chs. 6:12; 7:14; 8:7; 9:10; 10:14.) It may be unfortunate that we
cannot look beyond life, that all we do may go over to someone unworthy of our toil (cf. chs. 2:18–21; 4:8; 5:12–16). It may even drive one
to despair and to hatred of life (ch. 2:17, 20). But nothing is to be
gained by brooding over life's limits. What is left is rejoicing at what
one has to rejoice over: eating, drinking, the toil one is given to do,
the wife with whom one lives, youth and vigor (cf. chs. 2:24–26;
3:12–13, 22; 5:17–19; 6:1–6 [negatively]; 9:7–10; 10:19; 11:7–10). It is
useless to look either to the past or to the future. The past is forgotten

(ch. 1:11), and the future cannot be possessed (ch. 3:22). We have the present, and there life makes sense or does not make sense. But it must also make sense in the light of the boundary that death sets to human aspirations. "The living know that they will die, but the dead know nothing" (ch. 9:5). "For if many years a man should live, in all of them he should rejoice. But he should remember the days of darkness—for they too will be many" (ch. 11:8). "Remember your grave in your youthful days, before the unhappy days come, and the years reach you when you will say, 'I have no pleasure in them' " (ch. 12:1).

Secondly, it is axiomatic that distinctions are to be drawn in this life between what is good and what is bad, between righteousness and wickedness, wisdom and folly. To be sure, "what is good" (*tôb*) sometimes means "what is to be enjoyed" (e.g., chs. 2:1; 3:13), and "what is bad" (*ra'*) often means "what is unpleasant, unhappy" (e.g., chs. 1:13; 5:12, 15; 6:1). Likewise Qoheleth enjoins:

> Do not be overly righteous,
> And do not be too terribly wise.
> Why should you cause yourself trouble?
> Do not be overly wicked,
> And do not be a fool.
> Why should you die when your time has not come?
> (Ch. 7:16–17)

Even so, there is a difference between them. Wisdom is preferable to folly (ch. 9:17). There are places where, expecting to find justice and righteousness, we should be shocked to find wickedness (ch. 3:16), though we should not be surprised (ch. 5:7). It is not amusing that the wicked are sometimes praised as if they were righteous, and that men seem bent on doing what is bad (ch. 8:10–12). Qoheleth finds it strange that "there are righteous men who are treated according to the works of the wicked, and there are wicked men who are treated according to the works of the righteous" (v. 14). But he does not draw the conclusion that nothing distinguishes righteousness from wickedness. Moral distinctions are to be drawn; that is so axiomatic that Qoheleth does not even ask or implicitly answer the question, "How do you know?"

Thirdly, it is axiomatic that the circumstances of life come from God. Qoheleth does not argue the point; he states it. "There is nothing better for a man than that he should eat and drink and show himself a good time in his toil. I saw that this too comes from God's hand. For who can eat, and who can have pleasure, apart from him?" (ch. 2:25–26). That is God's "gift" (ch. 3:13). "For any man to whom God gives riches and property and makes him master of it, to eat of it and to take his lot and to have joy in his toil—that is God's gift" (ch. 5:18). "Consider the things God does. For who can straighten out what he has made crooked? In the day of prosperity, be happy. And in the day of unhappiness, consider: God has done both the one and the other, in order that man may not figure out anything after him" (ch. 7:13–14). The work of God has a certain inscrutability. Man cannot "figure it out" (cf. ch. 3:11). . . .

VANITY

In view of this account of Qoheleth's axioms, we must now attend to the difficult saying that we may take as the book's motto:

> Vanity of vanities, says Qoheleth,
> Vanity of vanities, all is vanity.
> (Chs. 1:2; 12:8)

This motto seems to justify the assumption that Qoheleth has no stance in truth, that he looks resignedly on life as useless, as a mere vapor (which may be the etymological basis of the word *hebel*, "vanity"). If etymology were the last word, we could as well translate the motto, "A mere breath." Ginsberg thinks that the word means, in effect, "zero." Macdonald translates it as "transitoriness or transitory." Staples, connecting it with the Israelite view of Canaanite cultic rites, assumes that it refers to "incomprehensibility." Nötscher says, "frail, nothing, without result," Barton, "fruitless, ineffectual, unavailing." Gordis thinks the basic meaning is "unsubstantial."

We must not assume the word's meaning beforehand, but need to see how and where Qoheleth uses it. He uses words with meanings peculiar to himself. The fact that Third Isaiah can use *hebel* to mean a "vapor" (Isa. 57:13) does not mean that Qoheleth must do so.

Let us note what Qoheleth describes by the word *hebel*. "All the deeds that are done beneath the sun" are *hebel* (ch. 1:14). More specifically, "all my deeds which my hands have done and my toil at which I toiled" are *hebel* (ch. 2:11; cf. v. 17). But those deeds and that toil are *hebel* because "I must set it by for the man who will succeed me. And who knows whether he will be a wise man or a fool? Yet he will lord it over all my toil for which I toiled and used my wisdom beneath the sun. This too is *hebel*" (ch. 2:18–19; cf. v. 21). It is also *hebel* that "to the man who is good in [God's] sight he gives wisdom and knowledge and joy. But to the sinner he gives the business of gathering and collecting, only to give it to the one who is good in God's sight" (v. 26). Hence, the whole of toil and its restlessness are *hebel* (v. 23). The man who toils unremittingly without an heir, never asking himself for whom he is working, is *hebel* (ch. 4:7–8), as is the fact that toil and skill derive from a man's jealousy of his fellow (v. 4).

Pleasure too is *hebel* because it accomplishes nothing (ch. 2:1). But it is also *hebel* that a man who has all that heart could desire never has pleasure from it, but someone else does (ch. 6:2). Yet he fails to enjoy it for another reason:

> The lover of money
> Is not satisfied with money,
> Nor is he who is in love with wealth
> Satisfied with profits.
> That too is *hebel*.

(Ch. 5:9)

There is even *hebel* connected with wisdom:

> And I saw that there is an advantage to wisdom over folly just as there is an advantage to light over darkness. The wise man's eyes are in his head, but the fool walks in darkness. But I also know that one destiny befalls them all. And I said to myself, "What befalls the fool will also befall me. So why have I been so extremely wise?" And I told myself that this too is *hebel*. (Ch. 2:13–15)

When death enters the picture, the apparent advantage of wisdom over folly turns out to be an illusion. "For what is the wise man's advantage over the fool? And what the poor man's who knows how to walk in life? Better the eye's sight than the soul's [or desire's] wandering. That too is *hebel* and a regard for wind" (ch. 6:8–9). Yet wisdom is better than folly; the "poor and wise youth" is preferred to the "old and foolish king." "And that too is *hebel* and a regard for wind" (ch. 4:13–16). At the same time, "man's advantage over the beast is nil," for they have "the same spirit" and come to "the same destiny." That too is *hebel*. "All go to the same place. All have come out of dust, and all return to dust" (ch. 3:19–20; cf. Gen. 3:19). We seem to have the same sentiment, referring only to man's destiny, in ch. 9:2, if we read *hebel* for MT's* *hakkôl* "all of it": "*Hebel* it is, that one destiny comes to all, to righteous and wicked alike," etc.

Clearly *hebel* is connected with the question whether man or some group of men have any profit or advantage (*yithrôn* or *yôthēr*). The difficult passage in ch. 6:10–11 suggests this:

> Whatever has been was named long ago, and its destiny was known. Man is not competent to plead a case with him who is mightier than he. For the more words, the more *hebel*, and what advantage [*yôthēr*] is that to man?

In trying to overcome the scheme of things, man multiplies *hebel* and increases words: "For in many dreams there are also *hebels*, and words increase. But you fear God" (ch. 5:7 [Heb., ch. 5:6]). To increase words is to find *hebel*, as the fool does (cf. ch. 5:2). Dreams, then, like the "soul's wandering" (ch. 6:9), come out to *hebel*. "For God is in heaven

---

*Masoretic Text: text of the Old Testament handed down by a group of Jewish scholars piously intent on preserving the text of the Hebrew Bible unchanged. Finished work about 1100 A.D.—Ed.

and you on earth. Therefore make your words few" (ch. 5:2 [Heb., ch. 5:1]).

Qoheleth points also to the *hebel* involved in moral perception:

> There is a *hebel* that occurs on earth, namely, that there are righteous men who are treated according to the works of the wicked, and there are wicked men who are treated according to the works of the righteous. I said that that too is *hebel*. (Ch. 8:14)

One might not expect, and surely would not hope, that that would happen. But it does happen, and it is twice called *hebel*. Similar to it is the difficult passage preceding it:

> And then I considered wicked men buried; they had come in and gone out of the holy place, and were even praised in the city where they had acted so. That too is *hebel*. Because the sentence on evil deeds is not executed quickly, men's sons fill their minds with the doing of such deeds, because a sinner can do evil a hundred times and still prolong his life. (Ch. 8:10–12)

The passage is textually difficult, though some such sense as that can be made of it. The *hebel* seems to point to the incongruity of act and public reaction. Going deeper in the same direction, but more like ch. 8:14, is ch. 7:15:

> I have considered all this in my days of *hebel:* there is a righteous man who perishes because of his righteousness, and there is a wicked man who prolongs his life because of his wickedness.

This is followed by the advice not to indulge in too much wisdom or in too much wickedness (ch. 7:16–17).

In ch. 7:6c, it is difficult to know the referent of *hebel*. It follows a list of pairs in which one is "better than" the other. Perhaps *hebel* refers to the entire list, or perhaps it refers only to the first part of v. 6, or perhaps to the last saying, vs. 5–6. It is possible, on the other hand, that *hebel* refers not to what precedes it but to what follows in v. 7, or in vs. 7–8. In that case, we should have to take *kî* in v. 7 to mean "that," as a relative adjective, rather than "because":

> And this too is *hebel*,
> That oppression makes a wise man mad,
> And a bribe destroys the heart.

Qoheleth refers to *hebel* twice in his advice in ch. 11:

> For if many years
> A man should live,
> In all of them he should rejoice.
> But he should remember the days of darkness,

> For they will be many—
> All that comes is *hebel*.
> Rejoice, young fellow, in your youth,
> And be cheerful of heart in your young manhood.
> And go as your heart directs you
> And with the sight of your eyes.
> But put vexation away from your heart,
> And put away sadness from your flesh,
> Though youth and its black hair alike are *hebel*.
>   (Ch. 11:8–10.)

The youth is to "rejoice" in spite of the *hebel* of what is coming and of youth itself. We meet the same theme elsewhere in the book, for example, in ch. 9:9: "Enjoy life with your wife (if *r$^{e'}$ēh* means "enjoy" and not "consider") whom you love all the days of your life of *hebel*," because that is "your portion." On the other hand,

> Who knows what is good for man in life, the sum of the days of his life of *hebel*, which he accomplishes like a shadow, so that who can tell what will happen next beneath the sun? (Ch. 6:12)

Life can be referred to in general as "a life of *hebel*" (cf. ch. 7:15), and that may be meant by the obscure saying that a premature fetus "comes into *hebel* [or "in *hebel*"] and goes into darkness" (ch. 6:4).

The problem, then, is, what does *hebel* mean? Apart from general remarks like "all that comes is *hebel*," the references to life as *hebel*, and the book's motto, "all is *hebel*," the word is used to point out incongruities. It is incongruous that a man's work may go for the advantage of someone he does not know who has not done the work. It is incongruous that wise and fool, good and bad, pious and impious, come to the same destiny. It is incongruous that the righteous and the wicked are treated as if they were the opposite, that the wicked should be praised for doing badly. It is incongruous that a man toils merely to keep up with the Joneses. It is incongruous that, although rejoicing is the best thing for man to do, it accomplishes nothing. It is incongruous that man should foolishly multiply his dreams and his babblings before God. The whole of life, the motto says, is a tissue of incongruity.

That is, Qoheleth uses the term *hebel* to mean something very close to "irony" and "ironic." Wherever he uses it, the subject is treated ironically. Labor and the acquisition of goods are ironic because no man can know the future, and therefore he cannot know for whose benefit he is toiling. The piling up of wealth is ironic because nobody is ever satisfied with his pile but wants a bigger one. The sinner's toil is ironic because it goes to enrich the pious man. Wisdom is ironic because it lacks the power to alter a man's final fate, even though for the time it may preserve him alive.

That these are "vanities" does not mean that Qoheleth rejects the whole. He is engaged in pointing out the incongruities because only when the incongruities are perceived, only when the ironies of life are felt, can life have any integrity. The significance of life, whatever it may be, must be found in life. But the discovery will be possible only if we look at life without clouds of darkness over our eyes. "Better is the sight of the eyes than the soul's wandering" (ch. 6:9).

BUSINESS AND PLEASURE

Dahood makes the intriguing observation, which he does not work out, that the book's vocabulary is shot through with commercial terminology. Most of the key terms are in the list: "advantage or profit" (*yithrôn, yôthēr,* and *môthār*), "toil" (*'āmāl*), "occupation, business" (*'inyān*), "money" (*keseph*), "portion" (*chēleq*), "success" (*kishrôn*), "riches" (*'ôsher*), "owner" (*ba'al*), "lack, deficit" (*chesrôn*), etc. "The overall picture delineated by Ecclesiastes suggests a distinctly commercial environment."

We have seen that many of the ironic "vanities" to which Qoheleth draws attention are commercial in character. The toil (*'āmāl*) at which men labor produces all kinds of incongruities (chs. 2:11, 17–26; 4:7–8). It is ironic that the capitalist is never satisfied with his capital (ch. 5:9). Vanities are also characteristic of wisdom, for although wisdom would seem to show an advantage (*yithrôn*) over folly, the wise and the fool come to the same end (ch. 2:13–16).

I suggest that Qoheleth is musing upon a society dominated by commerce, an acquisitive society that sees the meaning of man's life in his assertive achievement. But Qoheleth is very dubious about this philosophy. "What profit has man from all his toil at which he toils beneath the sun?" (ch. 1:3) "And then I turned to all the deeds my hands had done and to the toil I had given to do them. And behold, all that was vanity and a regard for wind, and there is no profit beneath the sun" (ch. 2:11). "What profit has the worker in what he toiled over?" (ch. 3:9) "And I looked at all the toil and all the skill of work, but this is a man's jealousy of his fellow. And that too is vanity and a regard for wind" (ch. 4:4). "The lover of money is not satisfied with money; nor is he who is in love with wealth satisfied with profit. That too is vanity" (ch. 5:10). It is not that Qoheleth speaks only of business and commerce. But he takes especial aim at those constellations of commonly held values in a primarily commercial society. And he is, if not thoroughly disillusioned, at least concerned to dispel many illusions about life. . . .

What, then, is the point of being wise? Though Qoheleth claims great wisdom, still using his first-person rhetorical fiction, he comes finally to an ironic conclusion. "What befalls the fool will also befall me. So why have I been so extremely wise? And I told myself that this too is vanity" (ch. 2:15). "For what is the wise man's advantage [yôthēr] over the fool? And what the poor man's who knows how to conduct himself in life?" (ch. 6:8) The answer is ambiguous: "Better is the eye's sight [or perhaps "enjoyment"] than the soul's wandering. That too is vanity and a regard for wind" (v. 9). Whatever the precise meaning of the cryptic remark about eye and soul, the net result seems to be the ironic one that the wise man finally has no noticeable yôthēr over the fool. And wisdom is difficult, if not impossible, of attainment. "I said, 'I will be wise.' But that was far from me. Distant is that which has been, and deep, deep indeed. Who can figure it out?" (ch. 7:23–24)

> When I set my mind on knowledge and wisdom, and on consideration of the buiness that occurs on earth, that neither night nor day do one's eyes see sleep, then I considered all the work of God, that man is not able to figure out the happenings that occur beneath the sun, on account of the fact that man toils to seek, but he cannot figure it out. And even if a wise man says that he knows, he is unable to figure it out. (Ch. 8:16–17)

Life simply does not turn out as man would fashion it. . . .

The irony of wisdom is that it may turn into a means of man's attempted self-assertion. Qoheleth's continual pricking of wisdom's bubble, his ironic tone in laying bare its limitations, can only mean that he is speaking to those who expect wisdom to provide the certainties of life and the means of power. But ignorance is much more pervasive in life, Qoheleth argues, than knowledge. And knowledge, taken seriously, produces still more ignorance.

> I turned my mind to knowledge, to penetrate and seek out wisdom and logic, and to know the wickedness of foolishness and the folly that leads to madness. And I came up with this [gravely limited conclusion]: more bitter than death is the woman whose heart is nets and snares, her hands fetters. He who pleases God escapes from her, but the sinner is caught by her.

"Consider this that I figured out," says Qoheleth, "putting one and one together to figure out the logic which my soul has sought again and again, but I could not figure it out. One man out of a thousand I figured out, but not a single woman among them all could I figure out. Consider this alone, which I did figure out: that God has treated man uprightly, but they have sought out many dodges" (ch. 7:25–29).

In that last verse, frequently analyzed as a gloss, is a central key to Qoheleth's point. For here the basic axioms come together. Every man must find the meaning of his life within that life, not beyond it. Distinctions are to be drawn in life between what is good and bad, what is wise and foolish, what is righteous and wicked. And, keystone of all, the circumstances of life come from God. Those who are not prepared to admit the last point Qoheleth deftly skewers on the point of his irony. For if men refuse the third axiom, if they "seek out many dodges," they are doomed with regard to the first two. In affecting to ignore and escape God's "upright" treatment of them, they bypass the possibility of life's meaning and the perception of the necessary distinctions.

To be sure, Qoheleth confesses ignorance about the quality of the divine sovereignty. No one knows whether it means hate or love (ch. 9:1), though it involves both prosperity and unhappiness (ch. 7:14). The "times and occasions" through which men pass consistently evince this duality (ch. 3:1–8). But this is not merely whimsy or blind destiny. "[God] has done it all as lovely in its time" (v. 11a). God is not blind; man is. "But he has put ignorance into [men's] hearts, so that man cannot figure out the deed which God has done from beginning to end" (v. 11b). Neither man's wisdom nor his toil can overcome the fundamental fact of life, that all depends on God. Qoheleth is well aware of the anguish this can cause (cf. chs. 2:17–18; 4:2–3). Man far prefers to be master of his own destiny, but for Qoheleth death, the ineluctable, makes that ironically impossible.

But his solution is neither resignation nor the descent into fatalism. Relative goods are to be found in wisdom, in keeping the eyes open. But the good that he enjoins on men again and again, in a constant refrain, is to live life as it comes *in joy*. "There is nothing better for man than that he eat and drink and show his soul good in his toil. This too, I saw, for it comes from God's hand. For who can eat, and who can have pleasure, apart from him?" (ch. 2:24–25.) "I know that nothing is good for [man] except to rejoice . . . and to do what is good in his life. And moreover, all of those who eat and drink and see what is good in all their toil—that too is God's gift" (ch. 3:12–13). "Behold, what I myself have seen to be good, that is, lovely, is to eat and drink and see the good in all one's toil at which he toils beneath the sun his whole life long, however much God gives him, for that is his lot. For any man to whom God gives riches and property and makes him master of it, to eat of it and to take his lot and to have joy in his toil—that is God's gift" (ch. 5:17–18; cf. the negative example in ch. 6:1–6). The remark following may, to be sure, sound a mildly ironic note: "For he does not much recall the days of his life, because God occupies him with his heart's joy" (ch. 5:19). That would suggest that God keeps a man sufficiently content not to remember the bad times. The verb "to recall" (*zākar*) might, however, be interpreted to mean "to brood over, to dwell on." Man's "heart's joy," then, is of enough more importance than anything else that he wastes no effort brooding over what he can do nothing about.

This constant harping on joy preserves Qoheleth's injunctions from mere resignation, a mere *carpe diem*. Rather, he urges the potentially positive in a present life that has its boundaries. . . .

A man must, of course, bear in mind that life is not endless.

"The wise man's mind is on the house of mourning, but the fool's mind is on the house of rejoicing" (ch. 7:4; cf. v. 2). That would seem to suggest that the wise man refrains from rejoicing. But Qoheleth is speaking here about the differentiation between wise man and fool, a differentiation that, in the long view of the book, is of a limited value. We have seen above that the joy men are to have is set in the context of the death that puts a stop to it all. Fools do not understand the boundary in their joy. Hence it is "better to go to a house of mourning than to go to a house where they are feasting. For the former has to do with every man's boundary, and the living may take it to heart" (v. 2). The irony, then, is that the joy proper to man, the joy God gives to lend significance to life, must have its ingredient of sorrow.

> And sweet is the light
> And pleasant to the eyes
> To see the sun.
> For if many years
> A man should live,
> In all of them he should rejoice.
> But he should remember the days of darkness,
> For they too will be many—
> All that comes is vanity.
> Rejoice, young fellow, in your youth,
> And be cheerful-hearted in your young manhood.
> And do as your heart directs you
> And with the sight of your eyes.
> But put vexation away from your heart
> And put sadness away from your flesh,
> Though youth and its black hair alike are vanity.
> Remember your grave in your youthful days,
> Before the unhappy days come,
> And the years reach you when you will say,
> "I have no pleasure in them."
> (Chs. 11:7 to 12:1)

There follows the magnificent, moving, and melancholy sketch of the day of death (vs. 3–7), a passage sufficiently obscure to exercise Old Testament exegetes for many decades to come. But the thrust of the whole is clear. The meaning available to man will be found in life, and it must come before the onslaught of death's final victory. Here, perhaps more clearly than in any other passage, Qoheleth suggests wherein life's meaning lies: in rejoicing in the years God gives. Those years are full of vanities, incongruities, ironies. But the incongruities to which Qoheleth so sharply points are not incompatible with the joy that is his constant exhortation.

Within that joy, everything else has its place. The joy "attends you" in toil. It makes relative wisdom useful. It renders the puzzles of life bearable. Since God has given joy, the efforts of man to make his own way are quite useless, vain, incongruous. There is no "profit." Man cannot expect that, nor can he wrest it out of life. Indeed, he can exact nothing of life. What is important, what is alone available, God gives. For that, joy is sufficient. The secrets of the universe may remain hidden. The effort to penetrate the future may be abandoned. No one but God knows either the secrets of the universe or the contents of the future.

It is man's "portion" to accept what God gives him with a joyful heart. God, after all, is not to be trifled with.

> Guard your steps when you go to God's house. And approach him to listen, rather than setting fools to sacrificing. For none of them know they are doing evil. Do not be hasty with your mouth nor in a hurry in your heart to bring out a matter before God. For God is in heaven, and you are on earth. Therefore, make your words few. (Chs. 4:17 to 5:1)

Man's position before God carries that necessary, restraining irony. Only the fool, the man who thinks he can make his own way in life, will hold lengthy discourses with God. He who knows what life is all about is prepared to accept his subordinate status.

The book is not a systematic or complete presentation of a theology, a philosophy, an ethic, a way of life. The large gaps that remain, Qoheleth's sardonic wit might have filled delightfully, but we must leave them blank. He was clearly addressing a society possessed by many of the commercial values that our own has in such abundance, and his reactions perhaps combine some of the best traits of an H. L. Mencken and a Harry Golden. One could wish that he had said more about the religion of his day.

Whatever the shortcomings of his thoughts, Qoheleth stands firmly on a comprehension of truth. Certainly it is not the whole truth; neither is it a rejection of truth. We can too easily be misled by his ironic rejection of his own day's commonplaces into thinking that he saw life very darkly indeed. But he had his eyes in his head. And he saw how useless it is to try to "straighten out what [God] has made crooked" (ch. 7:13).

INTERPRETATIONS

Koheleth and Modern Existentialism
ROBERT GORDIS

In recent years it has been suggested that there are important affinities between Biblical Wisdom and modern existentialism. Some writers have gone further and maintained that the authors of *Job* and *Koheleth* are actually precursors of existentialism. These comparisons are relatively easy to make and correspondingly difficult to evaluate because "existentialism" represents a wide spectrum of differing and even contradictory viewpoints. . . .

From the varying formulations of existentialism extant, its essential features may be set forth as the distrust of reason and the placing of individual existence at the center of its world view. It is, however, not so much its doctrine—or its hostility to doctrine—that has made it influential today. Basically its impact derives from its preoccupation with failure, dread, and death. Hence, existentialism tends to approach life not in joyous anticipation but in "fear and trembling," which is, incidentally, the title of one of Kierkegaard's best-known works.* In existentialism "individuality is not retouched, idealized, or holy; it is wretched and revolting, and yet, for all its misery, the highest good."

It is obvious why existentialism appeals so powerfully to the modern temper. Our age has been marked by massive chaos and mass brutality unexampled in history. As a result, tremendous numbers of sensitive men and women have been persuaded of the meaninglessness of life and the lack of purpose in the universe. Existentialism offers a basis for abandoning all abstract theory, which seems to have been weighed in the scales of experience and found tragically wanting.

It would be misleading to say that the various manifestations of culture we call "modern" are all derivatives of existentialism. It would be more accurate to regard modern art, music, and literature as parallel reflections of the same "modern spirit" that nurtured existentialism.

*"Fear and Trembling" and "The Sickness Unto Death," trans. Walter Lowrie (Princeton, N.J.: Princeton University Press, n.d.).—Ed.

KOHELETH AND MODERN EXISTENTIALISM From Robert Gordis, *Koheleth: The Man and His World* (New York: Schocken Books, 1967). Reprinted by permission of Bloch Publishing Co., Inc.

At least one factor in the development of the various schools of modern painting and sculpture has been the effort to depict the broken, misshapen character of existence, as modern men often encounter it. The atonality of modern music does not arise from a desire to shock the sensibilities of the traditional listener. Undoubtedly the creative desire to explore new, unheard dimensions of sound plays an important role. But avant-garde music in all its stages is also a reflection of the disordered and chaotic pattern of our urbanized, technological lives, disaster-ridden and death-laden. . . .

As existentialism has gained in influence, a natural tendency has arisen to seek its forerunners. The great works of unconventional Biblical Wisdom, like *Job* and *Koheleth*, which found it impossible to accept on faith the teaching of traditional religion concerning God and man, express a position that seems closely akin to that of existentialism. In *Job*, the suffering hero challenges the accepted doctrines of religion with regard to the purpose of life and the meaning of human suffering, not by juxtaposing a theory of his own but by confronting it with his own raw and bleeding experience. Job has therefore seemed to many modern writers to be the "existential hero *par excellence*." Koheleth, too, it is argued, refuses to go beyond the testimony of his own observation and experience and hence he rejects the conventional religious ideas of his day. The conclusion at which he arrives is therefore "vanity of vanities, all is vanity."

It is often maintained in current treatments of the subject that both Koheleth and the existentialists see the world as absurd and incomprehensible, with nothing in life truly significant or worthwhile. As a result, it is argued, both Koheleth and the modern existentialists exhibit a feeling of psychological nausea or dread in the face of reality, a feeling of despair in the face of man's inevitable annihilation.

To question the validity of this comparison between *Job* and *Koheleth* on the one hand, and existentialism on the other, is not to belittle the significance of the movement, both in its own right and as a corrective to older tendencies characteristic of the classic schools of philosophy. Existentialism has made a valuable contribution in reminding men of the limitations of reason, for which too much was claimed on too little evidence. For in the past, philosophy in large measure was cultivated by thinkers who regarded themselves as rational but in truth were merely rationalists.

Another abiding value in existentialism has been its insistence that the heart of ethics—and of wisdom—lies not in the theoretical analysis of the good or in the passive contemplation of the eternal, but in making a concrete decision in each critical hour of existence. When existentialism came upon the scene, philosophy was pursued along one of two lines. The traditional philosophers were engaged in abstract theorizing and the formulation of lifeless systems of thought. Their positivist opponents, who rejected this approach, became immersed in the minutiae of linguistic analysis instead. As against both schools, existentialism has insisted that man must grapple with the abiding issues of human life with which classical philosophy at its greatest and Biblical thought at its deepest are concerned. It may be true that in its attack upon the "beautiful whore," reason, existentialism threw the baby out with the bath. Nonetheless, its contributions are very real and valuable.

It is, however, necessary to point out that there is a fundamental difference between existentialism and Biblical Wisdom, which is far more significant than any superficial similarity. It is true that Koheleth is deeply pained by the realization that man cannot understand the purpose of the universe, a theme to which he returns again and again. But because he is a Hebrew living within the Jewish tradition, a world without God is impossible for him, because the existence of this world testifies to its Creator. Hence Koheleth does not doubt for a moment that there is such a purpose, known to God, though unknown to man:

> I know the concern which God has given men to be afflicted with. Everything He has made proper in its due time, and He has also placed the love of the world (*'olam*) in men's hearts, except that they may not discover the work God has done from beginning to end.

No matter how the difficult word *'olam* is interpreted, Koheleth recognizes that everything in the world is *yapheh b^e 'itto* (lit, "beautiful, proper in its time"). To be sure, the meaning of reality is veiled from man, *but the meaning exists*. This conviction makes it possible for Koheleth to constantly exhort his readers to enjoy the world, because its blessings are willed by God and granted by Him:

> Here is what I have discovered: it is meet and proper for a man to eat, drink and enjoy himself in return for the toil he undergoes under the sun in the scant years God has given him, for that is man's portion, and not long will he remember the days of his life. Indeed, every man to whom God has given wealth and possessions and granted the power to enjoy them, taking his share and rejoicing in his labor, that is the gift of God, for it is God who provides him with the joy in his heart.

Similarly, the author of *Job* is unable to accept the neat theories regarding the problem of suffering expounded by the Friends as the exponents of conventional religion. In the speeches of "The Lord Out of the Whirlwind" (Job 38–41), the poet presents what he regards as man's truest response to the problem of suffering—the realization that man is not the center of the universe around which all else revolves, but that, on the contrary, the universe in its entirety, and therefore its purpose and meaning, are beyond man's grasp. This insight the poet validates in magnificent nature poems that are more than paeans of praise to nature.

384

Can Job comprehend, let alone govern, the universe that he weighs and now finds wanting? Earth and sea, cloud and darkness and dawn, sleet and hail, rain and thunder, snow and ice, and the stars above—all these wonders are beyond Job. The lion and the mountain goat, the wild ass and the buffalo, the ostrich, the wild horse, and the hawk, all testify to the glory of God. Now these creatures glorified by the poet are not chosen at random. For all their variety they have one element in common: they are not under the sway of man, nor are they intended to serve his purpose. The implication is clear: the universe and its Creator cannot be judged solely from the vantage point of man, and surely not from the limited perspective of one human being.

The first speech of the Lord has glorified creatures that were not created for man's use, but nevertheless possess a beauty and grace that man can appreciate. The poet now goes a step further. The hippopotamus and the crocodile can lay no claim to beauty, but on the contrary, are physically repulsive and even dangerous to man. When the poet glorifies these beasts, he is calling upon us to rise completely above the anthropocentric point of view which, however natural for man, distorts his comprehension of the world. Precisely because they are unbeautiful by human standards, these monstrosities, fashioned by God's hand, are a revelation of the limitless range of God's creative thought. Since His ways are not man's ways, how can man's thoughts grasp God's thoughts—and, what is more, pass judgment upon Him?

In these chapters the author of *Job* has not given us a catalogue of natural phenomena, but a vivid and joyous description that underscores one additional and basic truth: nature is not merely a mystery but also a miracle, a cosmos, a thing of beauty. From this flows the poet's basic conclusion: just as there is order and harmony in the natural world, though imperfectly grasped by man, so there is order and meaning in the moral sphere, though often incomprehensible to man. This, the heart and essence of the God-speeches, is made by implication, but nonetheless effectively.

In sum, the Biblical Wisdom teachers find themselves unable to accept the easy answers offered by conventional religion to the perennial issues: the purpose of life, the meaning of suffering, the nature of death. With all their heart and soul the Biblical sages yearn to penetrate to the ultimate truth of reality. But that there *is* a purpose and meaning in the world they do not doubt for a moment. Hence the characteristic stigmata of existentialism are lacking in their writings. There is pain and passion, even resignation, before the Unknown and the Unknowable in *Job* and *Koheleth,* but no nausea or despair, no disgust or dread, no fear of failure. In a moment of bitterness or frustration Koheleth may say, "Therefore I hated life" (2:18), but it is not his dominant mood, which is an affirmation of life. In the depth of his misery, Job may picture his loneliness (19:13ff.), but he never succumbs to a sense of permanent alienation from mankind, whose sorrows he has made his own and in whose name he demands justice from God. The ultimate stance at which both writers arrive is positive acceptance, not permanent rebellion. Koheleth urges the enjoyment of life as the fulfillment of the Divine purpose in the world, to the degree to which that purpose is known to us. The author of *Job* exults in the beauty of the universe and therein finds an anodyne to suffering. . . .

The deep gulf separating Biblical Wisdom from modern existentialism becomes clear in the differing attitudes toward life which each school of thought engenders. Whether a man will approach existence with nausea or dread, or will face life with joy, depends in large measure on whether he regards the world as possessing no meaning, or believes that it does possess a meaning, though known only imperfectly to man. The quietism and the defeatism flowing out of the existentialist's confrontation of life undoubtedly require courage, but it is a courage born of desperation. It is poles apart from the courage of joyous acceptance derived from the Biblical sage's vision of the world. . . .

In sum, Koheleth does not claim to have penetrated to the secret of the meaning of life. Nor, strictly speaking, does the author of *Job* offer a justification for suffering from man's point of view. But they have done far more. They have demonstrated that it is possible for men to bear the shafts of evil that threaten the human condition if they cultivate a sense of reverence for the mystery and miracle of life and strive to discover intimations of meaning in its beauty.

Like modern existentialism, Biblical Wisdom speaks to the modern mind because it rejects the unsubstantiated claims often advanced by conventional religion as well as the lifeless systems to be found in the accepted schools of philosophy. Both Wisdom and existentialism insist instead upon the irrefragable testimony of each man's experience here and now, as an indispensable instrument for understanding man's place in the universe.

But Biblical Wisdom offers modern man a *via tertia*, distinct both from the superficial and comfortable affirmations too often preached in the name of traditional religion and from the shattering negations of life and its meaning propounded by existentialism. Thornton Wilder concludes his haunting novel *The Eighth Day* with a paragraph that sets forth the options open to modern man in contemplating a world he never made:

> There is much talk of a design in the arras. Some are certain they see it. Some see what they have been told to see. Some remember that they saw it once but have lost it. Some are strengthened by seeing a pattern wherein the oppressed and exploited of the earth are gradually emerging from their bondage. Some find strength in the conviction that there is nothing to see. Some

The basic approach of existentialism is spelled out in the last choice given by Wilder: "Some find strength in the conviction that there is nothing to see." There is, however, one attitude missing from his list of options. Perhaps the author hints at it in his final, unfinished and unpunctuated sentence. It is the outlook of the Biblical Wisdom teachers who point the way to a world view that can sustain man's spirit without demanding the abdication of his mind. That man counts in this mysterious universe, that life has meaning and can be endowed with joy—even if the meaning is often veiled from man and the joy must be achieved in the face of frustration and pain—these convictions are possible for the Biblical sages, who look upon the world clear-eyed and unafraid and refuse to accept cant or convention. For they hold fast to the central faith of the Biblical world view: "In the beginning, God . . ." Is there any better way for modern man?

The Right Time
PAUL TILLICH

Everything has its appointed hour,
    there is a time for all things under heaven:
    a time for birth, a time for death,
    a time to plant and a time to uproot,
    a time to kill, a time to heal,
    a time to break down and a time to build,
    a time to cry, a time to laugh,
    a time to mourn, a time to dance,
    a time to scatter and a time to gather,
    a time to embrace, a time to refrain,
    a time to seek, a time to lose,
    a time to keep, a time to throw away,
    a time to tear, a time to sew,
    a time for silence and a time for speech,
    a time for love, a time for hate,
    a time for war, a time for peace.
                       Ecclesiastes 3:1–8

You have read words of a man who lived about 200 years before the birth of Jesus; a man nurtured in Jewish piety and educated in Greek wisdom; a child of his period—a period of catastrophes and despair. He expresses this despair in words of a pessimism that surpasses most pessimistic writings in world literature. Everything is in vain, he repeats many times. It is vanity, even if you were King Solomon who not only controlled the means for any humanly possible satisfaction but who also could use them with wisdom. But even such a man must say: All is in vain! We do not know the name of the writer of this book who is usually called the Preacher, although he is much more a teacher of wisdom, a practical philosopher. Perhaps we wonder how his dark considerations of man's destiny could become a Biblical book. It took indeed a long time and the overcoming of much protest before it was accepted. But finally synagogue and church accepted it; and now this book is in the Bible beside Isaiah and Matthew and Paul and John. The "all is in vain" has received Biblical authority. I believe that this authority is deserved, that it is not an authority produced by a mistake, but that it is the authority of truth. His description of the human situation is truer than any poetry glorifying man and his destiny. His honesty opens our eyes for those things which are overlooked or covered up by optimists of all kinds. So if you meet people who attack Christianity for having too many illusions tell them that their attacks would be much stronger if they allied themselves with the book of the Preacher. The very fact that this book is a part of the Bible shows clearly that the Bible is a most realistic book. And it cannot be otherwise. For only on this background the message of Jesus as the Christ has meaning. Only if we accept an honest view of the human situation, of man's old reality, can we understand the message that in Christ a new reality has appeared. He who never has said about his life "Vanity of vanities, all is vanity" cannot honestly say with Paul, "In all these things we are more than conquerors through him who loved us."

There is a time, an appointed hour, for all things under heaven, says the Preacher. And in fourteen contrasts he embraces the whole of human existence, showing that everything has its time. What does this mean?

When the Preacher says that everything has its time, he does not forget his ever-repeated statement, "This too is vanity and striving for the wind." The fact that everything has its appointed time only confirms his tragic view. Things and actions have their time. Then they pass and other things and actions have *their* time. But nothing new comes out of this circle in which all life moves. Everything is timed by an eternal law which is above time. We are not able to penetrate into the meaning of this timing. For *us*, it is mystery and what *we* see is vanity and frustration. God's timing is hidden to us, and our toiling and timing are of no ultimate use. Any human attempt to change the rhythm of birth and death, of war and peace, of love and hate and all the other contrasts in the rhythm of life is in vain.

This is the first but it is not the whole meaning of the statement that everything has its appointed hour. If the Preacher says that there is a time to plant and a time to uproot, a time to kill, a time to heal, a time to break down and a time to build, a time to mourn and a time to dance, a time to speak and a time to be silent, he asks us to be aware of the right time, the time to do one thing and not to do another thing. After he has emphasized that everything is timed by an unsurmountable destiny, he asks us to follow this timing from above and to do our own timing according to it. As a teacher of wisdom who gives many wise rules for our acting, he requests right timing. He knows that all our timing is dependent on the timing from above, from the hidden ruler of time; but this does not exclude our acting at the right and not at the wrong moment. The whole ancient world was driven by the belief that for everything we do there is an adequate hour: If you want to build a house or to marry, if you want to travel or to begin a war— for any important enterprise—you must ask for the right moment. You must ask somebody who knows—the priest or the astrologer, the seer or the prophet. On the ground of their oracles about the good season you may or may not act. This was a belief of centuries and millennia. It was one of the strongest forces in human history, from generation to generation. The greatest men of the past waited for the oracle announcing the appointed hour. Jesus Himself says that His hour has not yet come and He went to Jerusalem when He felt that His hour *had* come.

The modern man usually does not ask for oracles. But the modern man knows of the need for timing as much as his predecessors. When in my early years in this country I had to discuss a certain project with an influential American business man he said to me, "Don't forget that the first step to a successful action is the right timing." Innumerable times, when reading about political or commercial actions, I was reminded of these words. In many conversations about activities and plans the problem of timing came up. It is one of the most manifest patterns of our culture, of our industrial civilization. How does it compare with the words of the Preacher?

When the business man spoke to me about timing he thought of what *he* had done and what *he* would do. He betrayed the pride of a man who knows the right hour for his actions, who was successful in his timing, who felt as the master of his destiny, as the creator of new things, as the conqueror of situations. This certainly is not the mood of the Preacher. Even if the Preacher points to the need of right timing he does not give up his great "All is vanity." You must do it, you must grasp the right moment, but ultimately it does not matter. The end is the same for the wise and the fool, for him who toils and for him who enjoys himself, the end is even the same for man and for animals.

The Preacher is first of all conscious that he *is* timed; and he points to our timing as a secondary matter. The modern business man is first of all conscious that *he* has to time, and only vaguely realizes that he *is* timed. Of course, he also is aware that he has not produced the right time, that he is dependent on it, that he may miss it in his calculations and actions. He knows that there is a limit to his timing, that there are economic forces stronger than he, that he also is subject to a final destiny which ends all his planning. He is aware of it, but he disregards it when he plans and acts. Quite different is the Preacher. He starts his enumeration of things that are timed with birth and death. They are beyond human timing. They are signposts which cannot be trespassed. We cannot time them and all our timing is limited by them. This is the reason why in the beginning of our modern era death and sin and hell were removed from the public consciousness. While in the Middle Ages every room, every street, and, more important, every heart and every mind were filled with symbols of the end, of death, it has been today a matter of bad taste even to mention death. The modern man feels that the awareness of the end disturbs and weakens his power of timing. He has, instead of the threatening symbols of death, the clock in every room, on every street, and, more important, in his mind and in his nerves. There is something mysterious about the clock. It determines our daily timing. Without it we could not plan for the next hour, we could not time any of our activities. But the clock also reminds us of the fact that we *are* timed. It indicates the rush of our time towards it. The voice of the clock has reminded many people of the fact that they are timed. In an old German night-watchman's street song every hour is announced with a special reminder. Of midnight it says: "Twelve—that is the goal of time, give us, O God, eternity." These two attitudes toward the clock indicate two ways of timing—the one as being timed, the other as timing for the next hour, for today and tomorrow. What does the clock tell you? Does it point to the hour of rising and working and eating and talking and going to sleep? Does it point to the next appointment and the next project? Or does it show that another day, another week have passed, that we have become older, that better timing is needed to use our last years for the fulfillment of our plans, for planting and building and finishing before it is too late? Or does the clock make us anticipate the moment in which its voice does not speak any more for us? Have we, the men of the industrial age, the men who are timing every hour from day to day, the courage and the imagination of the Preacher who looks back at all *his* time and all *his* timing and calls it vanity? And if so, what about our timing? Does it not lose any meaning? Must we not say with the Preacher that it is good for man to enjoy life as it is given to him from hour to hour, but that it is better not to be born at all?

There is another answer to the question of human existence, to the question of timing and being timed. It is summed up in the words of Jesus: "The time is fulfilled and the kingdom of God is at hand." In these words, God's timing breaks into our human timing. Something new appears, answering the question of the Preacher as well as the question of the business man. We ask with all generations of thinking men: What is the meaning of the flux of time and the passing away of everything in it? What is the meaning of our toiling and planning when the end of all of us and our works is the same? Vanity? And this is the answer we get: Within this our time something happens that is not of our time but of our eternity, and this times *our* time! The same power which limits us in time gives eternal significance to our timing. When Jesus says that the right hour has come, that the kingdom of God is at hand, He pronounces the victory over the law of vanity. *This* hour is not subject to the circle of life and death and all the other circles of vanity. When God Himself appears in a moment of time, when He Himself subjects Himself to the flux of time, the flux of time is conquered. And if this happens in one moment of time, then *all* moments of time receive another significance. When the finger of the clock turns around; not one vain moment is replaced by another vain moment, but each moment says to us: The eternal is at hand in *this* moment. This moment passes, the eternal remains. Whatever in this moment, in this hour, on this day and in this short or long-life-time happens has infinite significance. Our timing from moment to moment, our planning today for tomorrow, the toil of our life-time is not lost. Its deepest meaning lies not ahead where vanity swallows it, but it lies above where eternity affirms it. This is the seriousness of time and timing. Through our timing God times the coming of His kingdom; through our timing He elevates the time of vanity into the time of fulfillment. The activist who is timing with shrewdness and intuition what he has to do in his time and for his time, and for our whole activistic civilization cannot give us the answer. And the Preacher, who himself once was a most successful activist, knows that this is not an answer; he knows the vanity of our timing. And let us be honest. The spirit of the Preacher is strong today in our minds. His mood fills our philosophy and poetry. The vanity of human existence is described powerfully by those who call themselves philosophers or poets of existence. They are all the children of the Preacher, this great existentialist of his period. But neither they nor the Preacher know an answer. They know more than the men of mere acting. They know the vanity of acting and timing. They know that we *are* timed. But they do *not* know the answer either. Certainly we must act; we cannot help it. We have to time our lives from day to day. Let us do it as clearly and as successfully as the Preacher when he still followed the example of King Solomon. But let us follow him also when he saw *through* all this and realized its vanity.

Then, and then alone, are we prepared for the message of the eternal appearing in time and elevating time to eternity. Then we see in the movement of the clock not *only* the passing of one moment after the other, but also the eternal at hand, threatening, demanding, promising. Then we are able to say: "In spite!" In spite of the fact that the Preacher and all his pessimistic followers today and everywhere and at all times are right, I say yes to time and to toil and to acting. I know

391

the infinite significance of every moment. But again in saying so we should not relapse into the attitude of the activist, not even of the Christian activist—and there are many of them, men and women, in Christendom. The message of the fulfillment of time is not a green light for a new, an assumedly Christian activism. But it makes us say with Paul: "Though our outer nature is wasting away our inner nature is renewed every day—because we look not to the things which are seen but to the things that are unseen. For the things that are seen are transient, but the things that are unseen are eternal." In these words the message of the Preacher and the message of Jesus are united. All is vanity but through this vanity eternity shines into us, comes near to us, draws us to itself. When eternity calls in time, then activism vanishes. When eternity calls in time, then pessimism vanishes. When eternity times us, then time becomes a vessel of eternity. Then we become vessels of that which is eternal.

SUGGESTED READINGS

Gersh, Harry. *The Sacred Books of the Jews*, pp. 92–95, "Wisdom Literature in the Bible." New York: Stein & Day publishers, 1972.

Hendry, G. S. "Ecclesiastes: Introduction." In *The New Bible Commentary*, edited by D. Guthrie, pp. 570–78. London: Inter-Varsity Press, 1970.

McCasland, S. Vernon. *The Religion of the Bible*, pp. 178–85, "Proverbs and Ecclesiastes." New York: Apollo Editions, n.d.

Rankin, O. S. "Ecclesiastes: Introduction." In *The Interpreter's Bible*, Vol. 5, edited by George A. Buttrick, pp. 3–20. Nashville, Tenn.: Abingdon Press, 1956.

Sandmel, Samuel. *The Enjoyment of Scripture: The Law, the Prophets, and the Writings*, pp. 213–21, "Ecclesiastes." New York: Oxford University Press, 1972.

Scott, R. B. Y., trans. *Proverbs and Ecclesiastes*. The Anchor Bible Series, No. 18. New York: Doubleday & Company, 1965.

QUESTIONS FOR DISCUSSION AND WRITING

1. Argue for or against Ecclesiastes as a part of Holy Scripture.
2. How should one live, according to the Preacher?
3. What is the Preacher's estimation of human beings in general?
4. What portrayal of the Deity is revealed in Ecclesiastes?
5. Write a character analysis of the Preacher.

6. What basic unity of thought does Edwin M. Good discover in the Book of Ecclesiastes?
7. Why don't the contradictions in Ecclesiastes invalidate the book for Edwin M. Good?
8. According to Edwin M. Good, how can the Preacher's views on his own society's values be applied to our own society as well?
9. Analyze the Preacher's message, using the concept of irony as the key to its meaning.
10. What, according to Robert Gordis, do Job and Ecclesiastes have in common with modern existentialism?
11. According to Gordis, what do Job and Ecclesiastes offer us that modern existentialism does not?
12. Compare the character of the Preacher with that of Job.
13. How do you think the Preacher would respond if he were in Job's situation?
14. What advice do you think the Preacher might have given Job if the Preacher had been one of the Friends?
15. Why does Tillich consider Ecclesiastes a valuable asset to the Scriptures?
16. Compare Paul Tillich's interpretation of modern existentialism with that of Gordis.
17. Would Gordis agree with Tillich that the modern "philosophers or poets of existence . . . are all the children of the Preacher, this great existialist of his period"?

ESTHER

SUMMARY

The events of the story of Esther purport to have taken place in Persia during the reign of King Ahasuerus, identified as Xerxes I, who ruled from 485 to 464 B.C. (Xerxes I is well known as the Persian ruler who failed in his attempt to subjugate the Greeks.) The story begins with a royal banquet. On its seventh and last day the king orders his queen, Vashti, to appear before his guests wearing, evidently, only the royal crown, for he wishes to display her beauty. The queen refuses, and the king in his anger deposes her. Then he goes about selecting a new queen from among many beautiful virgins who come to stay in his harem. A Jew named Mordecai sends his niece, Esther, to the harem. She gains the special favor of Hegai, the man in charge, and Ahasuerus chooses her as his new queen. No one at court at this time knows that she is a Jew.

One day when Mordecai is in attendance at court, he overhears a plot against the king. He discloses it to Esther, who in turn tells the king. The plotters are hanged, and the incident is recorded in the royal chronicle.

The king makes Haman, a descendant of King Agag of the Amalekites, second in command, perhaps to tighten security at the royal court. When Haman learns that Mordecai is a Jew and will not do obeisance to him, he seeks to destroy all the Jews in the kingdom. First he orders a casting of lots (Pur) to determine a day for the pogrom, and then he persuades the king to issue an order for the destruction of a people in his kingdom who do not respect his laws. Haman also offers to pay ten thousand talents of silver (an enormous sum) into the treasury. The king gives Haman his signet ring and tells him to do as he wishes. Haman issues a decree that is read in every province of the empire: Every Jew is to be killed on one day, the day before the Jewish Passover.

When Mordecai hears the decree, he puts on sackcloth and ashes. Although in such a condition he may not pass through the palace gate, he manages to communicate with Esther and to inform her of the decree. She must help her people, he says, "for who knows whether you have not come to the kingdom for such a time as this?" (4:14). Esther promises to do what she can, even if she dies in the attempt. She obtains an audience with the king and invites him and Haman to a dinner. When at the dinner the king offers to give her what she wants "even to the half of my kingdom" (5.3), she requests that he and Haman come to another dinner the next night, and then she will make known her request.

Although Haman is delighted to be asked to another dinner with the king and queen, his delight is short-lived, because he sees that Mordecai still will not bow down to him. He orders that a seventy-five-foot gallows be built, intending to ask the king to hang Mordecai on it. But the king has a restless night, and to pass the time he reads the royal chronicle, where he notes that it was Mordecai who had informed on the two plotters. When on inquiry he is told that Mordecai has not been rewarded, he calls Haman to him and asks "What shall be done to the man whom the king delights to honor?" Thinking that it is he the king has in mind, Haman proposes an honor, which the king then has him bestow on Mordecai. The humiliated Haman has little time to grieve before the king's eunuchs arrive to take him to Esther's second banquet.

Again the king asks Esther to tell him what it is she wishes from him. He is astounded when she requests that he spare her life and that of her people. Apparently he has been ignorant of the implications of the terrible decree. And when he asks who is responsible for it and learns it is Haman, he is enraged and orders Haman hanged on the very gallows built for the death of Mordecai.

Now Mordecai is given Haman's place in court, and Esther is given Haman's house. The decree still stands, however, so Esther asks

Ahasuerus Panel, Dura-Europas Synagogue, Mesopotomia, 245 A.D. Illustrates the Esther Scroll. From left: Mordecai in royal robes on a white horse, led by Haman dressed as a stable slave; citizens of Suza. Ahasuerus on his throne receiving a messenger or sending out a message, with Queen Esther in the garb of the city Tyche beside him. Royal scribes behind the king, a female attendant beside the queen.

the king to recall the letters sent out by Haman. That cannot be done, but Mordecai is permitted to send out other orders, which allow Jews everywhere in the kingdom to defend themselves and to exterminate and plunder any people who attack them.

On the very day that the Jews were to be exterminated, they turn on their enemies and slaughter them. They are helped by Persian leaders and officials who fear the power of Mordecai. Although the Jews are permitted to plunder, nowhere do they do so, perhaps remembering that Saul and his men had taken spoil from the Amalekites against the Lord's command.

Verses 20–32 of Chapter 9 (thought to be an addition from another source) record the institution of the feast of Purim, which presumably celebrates this victory of the Jews over their enemy Haman.

The Book of Esther ends with a brief chapter extolling the might of Ahasuerus and the greatness of Mordecai.

LITERARY QUALITIES

Esther
PETER F. ELLIS

God's watchful providence in saving His people from destruction is the theme of the book of Esther. The author wrote some time during the Persian period, or shortly thereafter, to impress upon his readers the care of God for His people and to recount for them the origin of the happy feast of Purim.

Like Tobias, the book of Esther is a midrash.* The author writes to edify and encourage his readers. To do this he seizes upon an otherwise unrecorded event in Israelite history—a massive pogrom against the Jews of the dispersion that failed because of the intervention of a woman—and elaborates it freely and dramatically.

The historian does not know how much objective historical fact can be salvaged from the book of Esther because the author's primary interest was religious edification rather than professional historiography. However, it is assumed from the nature of the midrash, which usually began with an historical nucleus, and from the verisimilitude of the situation and the character of the Persian king, that the book of Esther is historical in substance and perhaps even in many of its particulars. As such the book is of some interest to historians.

The author's purpose, however, is not historical but didactic, and it is in his portrayal of God's care for his people that we find his intended message. To dramatize this consoling truth, the author uses all the techniques of the skilled story-teller: contrasts between the petulant Vasthi and the serene Esther, between the dedicated and humble Mardochai and the ambitious and proud Aman; passing remarks about seemingly insignficant events which at the end of the story are seen in their true significance; the gradual heightening of suspense by means of the apparent success of Aman's plot; the ironic use of the gibbet prepared for Mardochai for the execution of Aman; the destruction of the enemies of the Jews on the very eve of the day determined by Aman for the destruction of the Jewish people. Until

---

*Midrash: the traditional Jewish interpretation of the scriptures. Also, a commentary.—Ed.

ESTHER From Peter F. Ellis, *The Men and the Message of the Old Testament*. Published by The Liturgical Press. Copyrighted by The Order of St. Benedict, Inc., Collegeville, Minnesota.

the telling of the story of the Prodigal Son, no better story-teller arose in Israel.

The Hebrew text of Esther is somewhat shorter than the Greek text. In the Greek there are additions which make the book almost one third longer than the Hebrew. While the Jews and the Protestants reject these additions as uninspired, the Church has accepted them as equally inspired with the rest of the book. No one can determine where precisely the additions came from, whether they belonged to the original book and became detached from it by design or accident, or whether they are, as most Catholic authors consider them, inspired additions to the original text of Esther. The book can be divided into four parts:

I. (Ch.   1–2) The setting of the scene in the court of Assuerus with the deposition of Vasthi and the exaltation of Esther the Jewess.

II. (Ch.   3–7) The development of the plot. Aman, because of Mardochai, plots the destruction of the Jews (ch. 3). Mardochai urges Esther to intercede with Assuerus (ch. 4). While Aman prepares a gibbet for Mardochai, Esther, unknown to him, prepares his downfall (ch. 5). By happy chance Assuerus reads of Mardochai's unrequited service to him in revealing an assassination plot and rewards him (ch. 6). Esther reveals Aman's plot against the Jews and brings about his execution on the gibbet prepared for Mardochai (ch. 7).

III. (Ch. 8–10) Mardochai becomes chancellor and Aman's letters decreeing the destruction of the Jews are reversed (ch. 8). The Jews are allowed to destroy their enemies, and in remembrance of their preservation from Aman's machinations, the feast of Purim is instituted (ch. 9–10).

IV. (Ch. 11–16) Deutero-canonical additions to the book found only in the Greek.

INTERPRETATIONS

The Book of Esther
from *The New Westminster Dictionary of the Bible*

Esther, The Book of, is the last O.T. historical book in the English Bible; it is often regarded as a historical romance to explain the origins of the Jewish Feast of Purim (ch. 9: 19 ff.). In the Hebrew canon it stands among the Hagiographa, and is grouped with 4 other rolls which were used on 5 solemn anniversaries. The last of these anniversaries is Purim; hence Esther is placed among the Five Rolls (Megilloth). Long after the completion of the canon, the right of Esther to its place in that canon was called in question by the Jews—probably, however, not seriously, but to afford opportunity for intellectual display in its defense. The Jews now regard it with special honor. Christians have been more divided on the subject of its merits. Melito of Sardis and Gregory of Nazianzus omitted it from their lists of canonical books; Athanasius classed it with noncanonical books, and Luther denounced it. Opposition to it was based mainly on the fact that the name of God does not occur in it even once. But ch. 4: 14 implies the existence of Providence; ch. 4: 16 recognizes fasting as a religious practice, and ch. 9: 31 not merely·fasting, but a cry or prayer. The great lesson of the book is, in fact, the overruling power of Providence.

Scholars who seek for a possible mythological or legendary origin for certain narratives of the O.T. argue that The Book of Esther springs from such a source; they would make it of Babylonian origin. In its principal form this theory rests its claim for acceptance mainly on the evidence that Esther is a late form of the name of the Babylonian goddess Ishtar; and that Esther's other name Hadassah is the Babylonian word *hadashatu* (bride, originally myrtle), and is used as a title of goddesses. Mordecai is the same as Marduk, the patron deity of Babylon. He is the cousin of Esther, and it is possible thus to relate Marduk to Ishtar. Haman, the adversary of Mordecai, represents Hamman or Humman (Humban), a chief god of the Elamites, in whose

THE BOOK OF ESTHER From *The New Westminster Dictionary of the Bible*, edited by Henry Snyder Gehman. Copyright © MCMLXX, by The Westminster Press. Used by permission.

capital, Susa, the scene is laid; and Zeresh, the wife of Haman, may be the same as Kirisha, an Elamite goddess, presumably the consort of Hamman. Vashti (Washti, Mashti) is also an Elamite deity, presumably a goddess. The successful resistance of Mordecai and Esther to Haman, Zeresh, and Vashti is the conflict of the gods of Babylonia with the gods of Elam; in other words, it is the struggle between Babylonia and Elam for supremacy, which lasted for a thousand years and ended in the victory of Babylonia (Jensen, *Wiener Zeitschrift f. d. Kunde des Morgenlandes* (1892), vi. 47 ff., 209 ff.; Gunkel, *Schöpfung und Chaos*, 310–314, who admits that the basis is lacking so long as the word Pur remains unexplained). If this theory were established, it might show that the Jews of the Dispersion, feeding their hopes on the prophecies of deliverance, instituted a joyous feast and made use of the contest of Marduk and Ishtar with Hamman and Vashti to illustrate or typify the certain victory of the Jews over all their foes.

This theory has serious weaknesses, and many scholars have regarded the book as a historical romance written to glorify the Jews in a period when they were hated and envied by their neighbors, and to explain the origin of Purim. This feast has been variously assigned to a Persian or Babylonian origin.

It is easier and more satisfactory, however, to regard the book as having a historical foundation. The narrative claims to be historical and refers to the chronicles of Persia as containing a record of the events in question (chs. 2: 23; 6: 1; 10: 2). It gives the origin of Purim, which in the time of Josephus was observed in all parts of the world (Jos. *Antiq.* xi. 6, 13); the connection of the book with such an ancient Jewish feast still forms a considerable presumption in favor of its being founded on facts. This book gives a lifelike representation of Persian manners and customs, especially in connection with the palace at Susa (chs. 1: 5, 10, 14; 2: 9, 21, 23; 3: 7, 12–13; 4: 6, 11; 5: 4; 8: 8). Furthermore, the character of Ahasuerus is in harmony with that of Xerxes as he is known in history. It appears that Xerxes held a great council of war in the 3d year of his reign before setting out for Greece and that he returned to Susa in the spring of his 7th year (cf. Herod. vii. 8; ix. 108). This agrees with the dates assigned to the great feast and the choice of a successor to Vashti (chs. 1: 3; 2: 16).

The narrative is minute and circumstantial, containing many names of courtiers and princes (ch. 1: 10, 14). The Book of Esther tells more about Haman than his name. It knows him as the son of Hammedatha and an Agagite (chs. 3: 1, 10; 8: 5; 9: 24), and gives the name of 10 sons of his (ch. 9: 7–10). Concerning the Hebrews who figure in this narrative, Esther is known in the book as the daugher of Abihail and a queen of Ahasuerus. Mordecai either means "belonging to Marduk" or is a diminutive form of Marduk. The form of the name, however, points to a man, not a god. Such names were not wanting among godly Hebrews: cf. Apollos, Henadad, Shenazzar. The name Mordecai itself was borne by another Jew of the exile besides the cousin of Esther (Ezra 2: 2). The narrative takes Mordecai's lineage back through several ancestors to the tribe of Benjamin (Esth. 2: 5).

No substantial ground has been found for regarding Esther, Mordecai, Haman, and Vashti as deities; in the narrative they are human beings. Against the heathen origin of Purim is the acceptance of the event by the Jews as historical. Furthermore, against the theories that assume a heathen festival as the origin of Purim, the grand objection is that no heathen celebration has yet been discovered for the 14th and 15th days of Adar, the 12th month of the year. The present form of the narrative, which can hardly be pure invention, probably goes back to an actual persecution of the Jews, which may have taken place in the Persian period. The book was probably handed down together with the Feast of Purim in the Jewish dispersion of the East and later taken over by the Jews of Palestine. The Feast of Purim is not mentioned in Ecclesiasticus or in I Macc. 7: 49, but II Macc. 15: 36 refers to the day of Mordecai. . . .

The language of The Book of Esther is the Hebrew of the late period, but with many Persian words. From ch. 10: 2 it would seem that Xerxes was dead when it was penned. By some, the date of composition is fixed in the reign of Artaxerxes Longimanus (465–424 B.C.); materials, however, do not exist for definitely dating the book. Generally it is assigned either to the early years of the Greek period (which began 332 B.C.) or to the 3d century B.C. Some favor c. 300 B.C. The book is not quoted in the N.T., nor alluded to. Certain additions to it appear in the LXX.* Jerome separated them and put them at the end of the book, and they now find a place in the Apocrypha.

Esther
JAY G. WILLIAMS

Although conservative scholars through the ages have taken this [the story of Esther] to be a factual account of an historical event, it is clear that this is by no means the case. The story bears too many marks of a highly contrived melodrama to be considered historical. It is true that the author was fairly knowledgeable about the goings-on in a Persian court, but he also makes a good many mistakes. For in-

---

*LXX: *The Septuagint,* the Greek version of the Old Testament, translated by a group of scholars at Alexandria in the third century B.C.—Ed.

ESTHER From Jay G. Williams, *Understanding the Old Testament* (Woodbury, N.Y.: Barron's Educational Series, 1972), pp. 304–306. Reprinted by permission of the publisher.

stance, the Persian Empire never had 127 provinces, as the story claims (1:1). Persian court records do not name either Vashti or Esther as the name of Ahasuerus' queen, nor is there any indication that Purim was ever celebrated in Jewry during the Persian period.

If Esther is not history, one must ask, why was it written? Is it simply the product of an individual's creative imagination or does it have some deeper significance? And if Purim was not founded in this way, how did it come into being? Perhaps the best way to answer these questions is to look at Purim itself. Purim, to say the least, is a most decidedly nationalistic fesival. It is a time when Jews make merry and remember the occasion when the Semites beat the anti-Semites at their own game. Esther, however, is more than just a story about anti-Semitism. It is the prototype of all those melodramatic stories in which the good guys, though hard pressed at the X Bar X corral, finally shoot it out and kill all those rather slick fellows in the black hats. It is, in effect, a myth about good (that's us) triumphing over evil (that's them).

There are some indications that the original story upon which Esther is based was far more mythological and far less "historical" than the present one. Clearly Esther is a variant form of Ishtar, the Babylonian goddess of sexuality and fertility. Mordecai may well have been drived from Marduk, the king of the Babylonian pantheon. Perhaps what happened is this. While in captivity (or perhaps even before) the Jews came into contact with a pagan festival of great merriment. It was a mid-winter festival which celebrated the victory of the good gods over the demonic forces. Although the mythological meaning itself was pagan, the festival was nonetheless attractive.

The author of Esther took the essential myth and retold it as an historical narrative. The good gods become Jewish "patriots"; the demons, the Gentile antagonists. The merriment of the pagan festival is preserved, but the festival now becomes thoroughly Jewish and highly nationalistic. Such a transformation should not surprise any one who knows anything about the history of religion. Halloween, for instance, was originally a Celtic festival marking the end of the reign of the God of life and the beginning of the reign of Samhain, the God of death. The Christian Church did not deny the celebration of the day, but by placing All Saints Day on November 1 converted the original pagan festival into All Hallows Eve. The ghosts and goblins remained, but the theological context was changed.

In this connection, one feature of Esther is particularly striking. Although the author removed nearly all obvious remnants of pagan mythology from the story, he did little or nothing to reclothe it with the theological orthodoxy of Judaism. The word GOD, to say nothing of the name of God, does not even appear in the text. There are some hints that the triumphs of Esther and Mordecai took place providentially, but this idea is thrust very much into the background. Neither of the heroes offers prayers nor do their fellow Jews. Esther, as it has already been said, breaks the Jewish dietary laws and only reveals her Jewishness under duress.

Why? Why should such an obviously Jewish book avoid so consistently any kind of theological affirmation? Perhaps the author decided that it would be just too much to put a pious Jewish prayer in the mouth of a figure who was originally a pagan goddess. Perhaps he realized that Purim was essentially a secular festival and therefore decided to keep theology out of it. Or perhaps he was one of those who had decided that the orthodox faith of Israel was no longer relevant in his age. In any event, Esther is a thoroughly secular book which sees Jewry alone in the world, without God, depending upon its own resourcefulness for survival. God may act providentially, but the Jews no longer recognize his action as such. Lamentations ends with a question-mark; will God return? Esther affirms that whether he returns or not Jews will fight for themselves against all comers. The Shulammite is locked in the harem of Solomon, and she has decided, despite adversity, to make the best of a bad situation. When she wins a little for herself, she will exult and be glad.

The Book of Esther
Julius A. Bewer

[Anti-Semitism] flourished particularly in the Hellenistic capitals of Alexandria and Antioch. In this era* when anti-Semitism was already a factor in the West a book appeared that told of how it had failed in the East. That book was Esther.

The tale is told with remarkable literary ability. [The author's summary is omitted.]

[The book] is seeking to promulgate a nationalistic festival to strengthen Jewry. The studied avoidance of any reference to religion and even of the name of God, where it was naturally called for, is striking. When Mordecai refused to fall down before Haman, we are not told that it was for religious reasons. When he admonished Esther to rescue her people, else help would come "from another source," he meant of course from God, but he did not say so. When Esther fasted three days before her perilous undertaking, prayer is not mentioned, although fasting and prayer inevitably go together in such cases.

*Hellenistic era: Greek culture after 323 B.C.—Ed.

THE BOOK OF ESTHER From Julius A. Bewer, *The Literature of the Old Testament,* third edition, completely revised by E. G. Kraeling (New York: Columbia University Press, 1962), pp. 316–20, by permission of the publisher.

When the people celebrated their deliverance, they rejoiced and feasted, but did not thank God. This purely secular character of the story finds its explanation probably not in the author's lack of religion or opposition to it but in the nonreligious character of the festival of Purim, whose origin it describes.

Purim was not one of the ancient yearly festivals commanded in the law. It had arisen in the East, probably in Susa where the story is placed. It may have been an Elamite or Persian festival which the Jews adopted and interpreted to suit their own purpose, after the Hellenistic conquest had changed the old order of things. Which particular festival Purim was, we do not know, for none of the suggestions thus far made is satisfactory.[1] Some see in the names of the leading personages of the tale, Mordecai, Esther, Vashti, and Haman, the names of gods (the most obvious being the Babylonian deities Marduk and Ishtar). They look for a mythological background in the story. But Babylonian names were long, and the theophorous element is put first in them. The tendency of Jews to abridge them could easily have produced such personal names as the ones here given. The links of this story are with folklore rather than mythology.

It may have been some time before a festival of eastern Jews would find acceptance in Palestine. The author of Ecclesiasticus, who wrote around 190 B.C., does not list Mordecai in his praise of famous men (cf. Eccl. 49:13f.), and hence probably did not know the book of Esther. It may even be that Nicanor day, which was celebrated on the 13th of Adar, one day before Purim, in commemoration of the victory of Judas Maccabaeus over the Seleucid general Nicanor in 161 B.C., was instituted as a rival festival in Palestine (1 Macc. 7:49). In any case the oldest allusion to the festival is the remark of 2 Macc. 15:26 (written about 50 B.C.) that Nicanor day was celebrated on the day before Mordecai's day. The colophon of the Greek translation of Esther was written 78–77 B.C., an indication that the book had been known for some time in Palestine.

During the Maccabean wars for religion and national independence the Book of Esther was bound to become more and more popular, for it expressed the spirit of the people during the latter half of the second century. A strong national self-consciousness and pride had been created in those wars; and the sufferings inflicted by the hated heathen were not forgotten.

Of course the purely secular character of the Book of Esther was to many an evidence that it was not inspired by God, and orthodox scholars fought for a long time against placing it among the sacred

[1]It gets its name from *pūr*, pl. *pūrīm* "lot," as explained in 9:24–26, cf. 3:7. The word is a loanword from the Akkadian (Assyro-Babylonian) language, and is explained with the common Hebrew word for "lot."

writings.[2] The Greek version tried to obviate their objections by inserting a number of religious interpolations, such as prayers of Mordecai and Esther, which, however, breathe the same exclusive, nationalist spirit. Though they were not introduced into the Hebrew text, the book nevertheless overcame all scruples by its great popularity and its intense patriotism, and has ever since been read as the lesson at the yearly festival of Purim.

As mentioned in the selection by Bewer just presented, the Greek version of the Book of Esther contains several religious interpolations. The following excerpts from the Apocryphal Esther,* which contain prayers attributed to Esther and Mordecai, serve to indicate the tone and general nature of that version.

"Then Queen Esther, caught up in this deadly conflict, took refuge in the Lord. She stripped off her splendid attire and put on the garb of mourning and distress. . . . And so she prayed to the Lord God of Israel: '. . . Thou knowest in what straits I am: I loathe that symbol of pride, the headdress that I wear when I show myself abroad, I loathe it as one loathes a filthy rag; in private I refuse to wear it. I, thy servant, have not eaten at Haman's table; I have not graced a banquet of the king or touched the wine of his drink-offerings; I have not known festive joy from the time that I was brought here until now except in thee, Lord God of Abraham. O God who dost prevail against all, give heed to the cry of the despairing: rescue us from the power of the wicked men, and rescue me from what I dread' " (14:1, 2a, 3, 16–19).

"Mardochaeus said, 'All this is God's doing. For I have been reminded of the dream I had about these things; not one of the visions I saw proved meaningless. There was the little spring which became a river, and there was light and sun and water in abundance. The river is Esther, whom the king married and made queen; the two dragons are Haman and myself; the nations are those who gathered to wipe out the Jews; my nation is Israel, which cried aloud to God and was delivered. The Lord has delivered his people, he has rescued us from all these evils. God performed great miracles and signs such as have not occurred among the nations. He . . . remembered his people and gave the verdict for his heritage' " (10:4–9, 12b).

[2]No scroll of Esther has as yet turned up at Qumran. Opposition to it lasted into the second century A.D. among Jews; and Christians too were slow in accepting it.

*Quoted from The New English Bible with the Apocrypha: Oxford Study Edition, ed. Samuel Sandmel et al. (New York: Oxford University Press, 1976).

SUGGESTED READINGS

Anderson, Bernhard W. "Esther: Introduction." In *The Interpreter's Bible*, Vol. 3, edited by George A. Buttrick, pp. 823–32. Nashville, Tenn.: Abingdon Press, 1954.

Chase, Mary Ellen. *The Bible and the Common Reader.* Rev. ed., pp. 240–43, "Esther." New York: Macmillan, 1962.

Gaster, Theodor H. *Myth, Legend, and Custom in the Old Testament,* pp. 829–37, "Esther." New York: Harper & Row, 1969.

Neil, William. *Harper's Bible Commentary,* pp. 218–19, "Esther." New York: Harper & Row, 1975.

QUESTIONS FOR DISCUSSION AND WRITING

1. What elements of good storytelling are present in the Book of Esther? Give examples of how the author uses them to achieve his aims.
2. How does *setting* (the time, the place) affect the *plot* (the action) in the Book of Esther?
3. Esther is not an obviously religious book. Why was it included in Hebrew Scripture?
4. Argue that Esther is a religious book even though God is never mentioned in it.
5. Look up "Purim" in an encyclopedia and in various handbooks and commentaries on the Bible. Then write a short essay about this feast.
6. What opinion of women is implied or expressed in the Book of Esther?
7. Do you agree with Peter Ellis that "the author's primary interest in the Book of Esther was religious edification"? If you do, make a case for that interpretation.
8. Of the three theories about the origin and meaning of the Book of Esther described in the *New Westminster Dictionary of the Bible,* the editors of the *Dictionary* prefer the "historical foundation" theory over the "mythological" and "historical romance" theories. Sum up their argument in your own words.
9. Criticize Jay G. Williams's interpretation of the Book of Esther in the light of the analysis presented in the *New Westminster Dictionary of the Bible.*
10. Which interpretation of the Book of Esther do you prefer—that of the *New Westminster Dictionary of the Bible,* or that of Julius A. Bewer? Defend your preference.
11. Compare the Book of Esther from the Old Testament with the Book of Esther from the Apocrypha. Which is the better story?
12. Try to adapt the story of Esther to modern times—for example, to the plight of the Jews in Nazi Germany.

RUTH

SUMMARY

The events of the story of Ruth occurred approximately sixty years before the birth of David, perhaps in the late twelfth or very early eleventh century B.C. The date of composition is uncertain, however; scholars place it anywhere from the time of Samuel to the third century B.C. Herbert G. May says that "The nature of the theme, the literary style, the numerous Aramaisms in the Hebrew text (although this in itself is not conclusive), and its position in the Hebrew Bible among the Writings—all these when taken together speak strongly for a postexilic origin, and this is the more general view. . . . Many scholars have taken the book as a tract written in opposition [to the reforms of Ezra and Nehemiah]."* Ezra, for example, had said: "You have trespassed and married foreign women, and so increased the

---

*Herbert G. May, "The Book of Ruth," in *The Interpreter's One-Volume Commentary on the Bible*, ed. Charles M. Layman (Nashville, Tenn.: Abingdon Press, 1971), pp. 150–51.

guilt of Israel. Now then make confession to the Lord the God of your fathers, and do his will; separate yourselves from the peoples of the land and from foreign wives" (Ezra 10:10, 11). And Nehemiah had admonished the people in the same vein: "In those days also I saw the Jews who had married women of Ashdod, Ammon, and Moab; and half of their children spoke the language of Ashdod, and they could not speak the language of Judah, but the language of each people. And I contended with them and cursed them and beat some of them and pulled out their hair; and I made them take oath in the name of God, saying, 'You shall not give your daughters to their sons, or take their daughters for your sons or for yourselves' " (Nehemiah 13:23–25).

Scholars who argue that the Book of Ruth is a response to this narrow nationalism place its composition between 450 and 350 B.C. For an argument implying that this book was written many centuries earlier, see the article by Millar Burrows on pages 413–19.

The story can be summarized as follows. "In the days when the judges ruled" (i.e., before Saul was named king), Elimelech and his wife Naomi leave Judah to live in Moab, evidently seeking relief from a famine. They have two sons, Mahlon and Chilion, and when Elimelech dies, Naomi is left to bring them up. Mahlon and Chilion marry Moabite women, Orpah and Ruth. But after some years the two sons also die, and Naomi determines to return to Judah, where "the Lord had visited his people and given them food" (1:6).

Aware that her daughters can probably find homes and husbands with their Moabite families, Naomi wishes them well and kisses them goodbye. After some protest, Orpah agrees to Naomi's wishes. But Ruth insists on going with her mother-in-law to Judah: "Entreat me not to leave you or to return from following after you; for where you go I will go, and where you lodge I will lodge; your people shall be my people, and your God my God; where you die I will die,

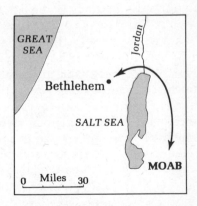

The areas where Ruth lived.

Gustave Doré, "Boaz and Ruth"

and there will I be buried. May the Lord do so to me and more also if even death parts me from you'' (1:16, 17).

Naomi and Ruth return to Judah and arrive at Bethlehem at the beginning of the barley harvest. Ruth goes out to glean in the grain fields, and "she happened to come to the part of the field belonging to Boaz" (2:3), who also happens to be of the family of her late father-in-law, Elimelech. Boaz notices her and sees to it that she is not molested by the young men. He invites her to lunch with him and to dip her morsel in the wine. When they go back to work, Boaz instructs the young men to make things easier for her than for anyone else.

When Ruth returns home that night and tells Naomi of the good fortune that has befallen her, Naomi sees it as doubly good fortune that she has been working for a man who is a close relative, and she encourages her to continue. In fact, Naomi instructs Ruth to go down that evening to the threshing floor where Boaz is at work, but not to make herself known until Boaz has eaten and fallen asleep. Then she is to uncover his feet, lie down, and wait; Boaz "will tell you what to do," says Naomi. Ruth follows her mother-in-law's instructions to the letter, and when Boaz discovers her at his feet he shows no disinclination to "cover her with his skirt," an act which apparently symbolizes the marriage relationship. Happy as he is at Ruth's invitation to fulfill the obligations of next-of-kin, Boaz tells Ruth that he must consult another man who is more closely related to her than he is. If that man refuses to fulfill the obligation, Boaz tells her that he himself will be happy to do so. He gives Ruth six measures of barley to take home, and when Naomi learns of what has happened, she is certain that Boaz will quickly bring about a conclusion.

Naomi is right. Boaz locates the next of kin at the city gate, and with the requisite number of elders standing by he tells this man that he can redeem Elimelech's property, but that in doing so he must also marry Elimelech's daughter-in-law. The man is willing to buy the property but not to marry Ruth, because in doing so he would be putting his own inheritance in jeopardy. He therefore "drew off his sandal" to affirm before the elders and the others present his willingness to let Boaz purchase from Naomi all the land that had belonged to Elimelech and his two sons, and to marry Mahlon's widow, Ruth the Moabitess, as well. The elders and the people at the gate all witness the transaction, and they wish Boaz prosperity and a large family.

The first child born to Boaz and Ruth is a restorer of the family name, so that the women who blessed Naomi can even say, "A son has been born to Naomi" (4:17). This son is named Obed, who, it is said, "was the father of Jesse, the father of David" (4:17).

LITERARY QUALITIES

Ruth
MARY ELLEN CHASE

The book of Ruth is one of the most graceful and charming of short stories not only in ancient literature but of any time and in any

RUTH Reprinted with permission of Macmillan Publishing Co., Inc. from *The Bible and the Common Reader*, rev. ed., by Mary Ellen Chase. Copyright 1944, 1952 by Mary Ellen Chase, renewed 1972 by Mary Ellen Chase.

language, and well deserves the high place accorded it by critics of various countries and ages. Goethe, among many others of its admirers, calls it the most beautiful of all idylls.

The story was written about the year 450 B.C., or some one hundred years after the Return to Jerusalem from Babylon. Its unknown author, however, sets it some seven hundred years earlier, for he begins it well and directly with the words: *Now in the days when the judges ruled, there was a famine in the land.* There has always been a controversy among students and admirers of his story over whether he had a purpose in telling it beyond simply the writing of a pleasant tale, as to whether he was an ancient propagandist or merely an ancient artist. Artist he certainly was, too good a one to append a moral to his tale. But when one considers the date of its composition and the conditions of the time from which it came, it is difficult not to believe that he was a liberal of his day with strong ideas of his own at variance with those dominant ones about him.

If we recall for a moment some of the conditions which met the Jews upon their disillusioning return from Babylon, we shall remember that among the vexatious and anxious problems awaiting and besetting them on all sides was the problem of mixed marriages. Their prophets of the Return had inveighed against this deplorable custom which began to spread even among the former exiles themselves; and Nehemiah had enforced the prohibition of such marriages by ruthless measures. This situation, coupled with the fact that some practical purpose usually lay behind most of the Hebrew writings, leads me, in common with many others, to feel that the author of Ruth had something definite to say in relation to his time and that he used his story as a lovely means to a good and wise end.

Although he places it in the wild, rough times of the judges, around 1100 B.C., the impression we have throughout is one of idyllic, even idealized surroundings. After the generous decision of Ruth, her husband Mahlon having died, to return to Bethlehem with Naomi from her native country of Moab, the scene is largely set in the fields of Boaz, the kinsman of Naomi, at the beginning of the barley harvest. The picture of Ruth, the Moabitess, working with the reapers and receiving her portion of food at noonday from the hospitable hands of Boaz, of the seemly behaviour of his young men toward her, of her gleaning until evening, has a pleasing, pastoral quality which reminds one of other ancient settings of Arcadian simplicity, drawn by Theocritus or by Vergil.

This idyllic atmosphere extends also to the characters. The author has drawn them with no sense of those depths and crosscurrents of human psychology such as the writer of the story of Jonah was to show so brilliantly a century or two later. Not one of them is in the least complex; the natures of all are open and simple. Naomi, it is true, may show shrewdness in her foresight in planning for her daughter-in-law's future happiness at the hands of Boaz; nevertheless, her act is

411

not so much designing on her part as it is in accordance with the Hebrew custom of reminding a kinsman of his duty. The characters are as idealized, in fact, as are the setting and atmosphere. Boaz is the ideal landowner and overseer, friendly and fatherly toward those who work for him. Naomi is as thoughtful of her foreign daughter-in-law as though she were of her own kindred, not failing, for instance, at night, in a homely touch of the author, to save supper for her after her day's work in the fields. Ruth herself, in the words of Boaz, is blessed by God in spite of her Moabitish inheritance in that she has eyes for no young men "whether poor or rich." And even the neighbours are capable of honest rejoicing with Naomi when her grandson is born and of saying that this foreign daughter-in-law of hers has proved better to her than seven sons.

A charming air of courtesy runs throughout the story. Everyone is on his best behaviour from start to finish. Everyone has gentle manners and is extremely gracious and considerate toward everyone else. All address one another in formal, courteous salutations; each appreciates openly the good qualities of each; the young men are chivalrous; even the kinsman, faced by the alternative offered him by Boaz, is frank and friendly.

Tradition and custom add their age and, therefore, their richness of atmosphere. The approach of Ruth to Boaz by night, the redeeming of the inheritance, the "manner in former time in Israel" of plucking off the shoe as a testimony—these add atmosphere and charm. The same values are gained by the blessing of Ruth and Boaz by the people of Bethlehem, who compare her to Rachel and Leah, the two women held in reverence by them all as builders of the house and lineage of Jacob.

Throughout his short, even slight story the style and language of the author heighten the effect which he wishes to gain and hold. His simple and direct prose has from first to last an undertone of poetry. There is even poetic form in Ruth's well-remembered words to Naomi: *Entreat me not to leave thee or to return from following after thee: for whither thou goest, I will go; and where thou lodgest, I will lodge: thy people shall be my people, and thy God my God.* This same poetic effect is easily apparent in Naomi's words: *I went out full, and the Lord hath brought me home again empty,* and in those of Boaz to Ruth when he prays that a full reward may be given her from the God of Israel "under whose wings thou art come to trust." It is apparent, too, in the manner of the narrative itself quite apart from dialogue: *For she had heard in the country of Moab how that the Lord had visited his people in giving them bread. So they two went until they came to Bethlehem.* And in the simple, suggestive description of the earliest dawn: *And she rose up before one could know another.*

As a work of literary art, the story of Ruth cannot be justly called profound in its emotional appeal. When one compares it with

the stronger and far richer story of Jonah, it seems undeniably sentimental, even perhaps a bit "pretty." Yet we must not demand of its
writer that he do something of which he had no intention. Within his
narrowly prescribed limits he has beautifully done what he obviously
set out to do: to suggest by means of a lovely and simple story the
truth of which he was himself convinced, that God is no respecter of
persons, that human love is able to bridge the shallow differences of
nationality, and that true religion is a matter of the heart and not of
race.

Nor is he devoid of humour. He must have taken especial delight in the climax to his story, in the nice touch of Naomi's neighbours deciding upon the baby's name, and finally in his quiet
announcement that this child, born of a marriage between Israel and
Moab, became no other than the grandfather of the exalted David!

INTERPRETATIONS

The Marriage of Boaz and Ruth
MILLAR BURROWS

The whole story of the marriage of Boaz and Ruth, and of the
transactions connected with the marriage, makes a strong impression
of reality, but it does not fit into the picture of Israelite law and custom
presented by the rest of the OT, particularly the laws of the Pentateuch. The same elements appear elsewhere, but in different connections and with different implications. For example, the ceremony of
drawing off the sandal is connected with levirate marriage in Deuteronomy 25:9 f., where the widow removes the sandal of her brother-
in-law, while in Ruth 4:7 the kinsman voluntarily removes his own
sandal in connection with the redemption of a piece of land. Part of
the trouble lies in the fact that we have in Ruth a combination of three
institutions which are not elsewhere found together. Levirate marriage, redemption, and inheritance are all familiar to the reader of the
OT, but only here do we encounter a transaction which involves all
three of them.

The marriage of Boaz and Ruth is represented as having the
same purpose as levirate marriage, "to raise up the name of the dead

THE MARRIAGE OF BOAZ AND RUTH   Article by Millar Burrows from *Journal of Biblical Literature* 69
(1940), 445–54. Reprinted by permission of the author and the Society of Biblical Literature.

upon his inheritance, that the name of the dead be not cut off from among his brethren" (4:5, 10; cp. Deut 25:6 f.). Yet neither Boaz nor the nearer kinsman is Ruth's brother-in-law (*levir*). Each appears rather as a redeemer (2:20, 3:9–13, 4:3–17) though nowhere else is there any indication that the duty of the brother-in-law might devolve upon any other relative. The entirely irregular procedures recounted in Genesis 19:30–38 and 38:13–26 do not indicate that anything of this sort was ever sanctioned by law or custom. It is true that the geneal- ogy at the end of the book of Ruth reckons Obed as the son of Boaz, but critics are agreed that this genealogy is secondary. In 4:14 the women call the child Naomi's redeemer, and in verse 17 they say, "A son is born to Naomi." In short, we have here a combination of two institutions, levirate marriage and redemption.

But this at once introduces complications regarding the third in- stitution, inheritance. In levirate marriage the firstborn son of the union is heir of the deceased husband. In redemption, however, the redeemer buys the property, which therefore becomes, presumably, a part of his own estate. Further difficulty is caused by the fact that Boaz buys Elimelech's land from Naomi, who thus appears as her hus- band's heir, though ancient Hebrew law, so far as our sources in- dicate, did not recognize widows as heirs of their husbands' property. Incidentally we may note that the whole question of the property, indeed its very existence, is not even suggested until the gate-scene in the last chapter.

Amid all this confusion a few points are fairly clear, and they may be stated first as a basis for further discussion. First, Boaz re- ceives the whole estate of Elimelech. The language of 4:3 might in- dicate only a part of it, but the formal statement of verse 9 makes it clear that the transaction is all-inclusive.

In the second place, Boaz receives the property not as heir but as purchaser. Attempts to treat the affair as a case of inheritance by the nearest male relative have only confused the issues. The verb *yrš* and its derivatives are not used. Boaz acts as redeemer, and land was redeemed by purchase (Lev 25:23–34; Jer 32:8). True, the payment of the price is not mentioned, and *qnh* does not necessarily mean "buy" (though it is actually used in that sense in Lev 25, and everywhere else except in poetry); but *mkr* (4:3) means "sell" and cannot mean any- thing else. The possibility that the transaction was only nominally and formally a purchase must be recognized (see below), but it was at least that.

A third point which is clear is that Boaz bought the field di- rectly from Naomi. In Lev 25 redemption comes into play when a man has already sold his property to one outside of the family. The perfect tense of the verb in 4:3 suggests that Naomi "has sold" the land pre- viously, and now a few commentators have adopted this view, but it is definitely disproved by the words "from the hand of Naomi" in verse 9. Accordingly some interpreters read the present participle instead of the perfect in verse 3. This is quite possible but not really necessary, since the perfect tense need not mean more than that the property has been offered for sale or is about to be sold. Furthermore, while Lev 25 attests only the redemption of property which has already been sold, the prevention of such a sale by the redeemer through direct purchase from his impoverished relative would be entirely natural; in fact, it is actually attested by Jer 32:6–12. There is thus no difficulty in the clear indication of the narrative that Boaz purchased Elimelech's land from Naomi, except for the fact already noted, that it is surprising to find Naomi in possession of the property.

That Naomi was the possessor of the estate is indeed puzzling, though clearly indicated. One wonders who had been holding it during all the years of Naomi's absence in Moab. That question, however, is equally difficult on any other interpretation of the affair. Perhaps we may assume that Elimelech's property had been held in pledge by a friend; at any rate our author does not take the trouble to enlighten us on this point. One wonders also why it was necessary for Ruth to glean in order to provide sustenance for herself and Naomi, if the latter had a field of her own. Possible answers to that question too may be imagined;[1] in any case Naomi and Ruth had a house to live in—again the author does not tell us where or how. Gunkel, indeed, reverses the argument, saying that if Naomi had sold the land previously she would have had enough money to make Ruth's gleaning unnecessary.[2] It is fairly safe to suppose that the field in question was not a large one. It may have been only a remnant of the original property of Elimelech and the price Naomi could expect to receive for it may have appeared to her sufficient for her own support if she could find a home for Ruth.

The fact that OT law does not provide for inheritance by widows remains to be considered. To meet this difficulty Jensen ingeniously supposes that Naomi had inherited the property from her father, and that Elimelech had merely administered her inheritance as *errēbu*-husband.[3] But this is refuted by the statements of 4:3, 9 that the property belonged to Elimelech and his sons. Mittelmann holds that Naomi was not the owner of the land but merely regulated the succession of heirs as an executrix, so to speak. The Code of Hammurabi (§171) allows a widow to live in her husband's house and apparently to administer his property if her sons are minors, but does not allow

[1] Gunkel (*op. cit.*, 80) says the author assumes that Naomi has lost possession of the field, but that the occupant can say nothing when a man of Boaz' position comes forward as Naomi's representative, declaring that she owns the field and is offering it for sale.

[2] *Op. cit.*, 81n.

[3] The redeemer, of course, would then have to belong to Naomi's family, but Boaz is said to be a kinsman of Elimelech; hence Jepsen is driven to the inference that Elimelech and Naomi were related.

her to sell any of it. In the book of Ruth the sons are dead and have left no heirs; under such circumstances we might expect that the property would pass to the nearest male relative, but apparently this did not happen. In 2 Kings 8:1–6 a widow appears as the owner of property; to be sure her husband's death is not specifically stated, nor is it said that she had inherited her land from him, but both inferences are reasonable. In any case, we must admit that the book of Ruth assumes the practice of inheritance by widows.[4] In such circumstances, if not in more ordinary cases, it must have been allowed. At any rate our author assumes that his readers will not regard it as strange.

So much, then, is sufficiently clear. Boaz acquires the whole estate of Elimelech and his sons, acquires it by purchase from Naomi, who is therefore the acknowledged owner. But this leaves us with several problems on our hands. What is Ruth's position in the whole complicated transaction? We may say definitely that she is not inherited as a part of the estate, as is supposed by those who regard her marriage as an extension of levirate marriage and consider the latter a form of inheritance. Boaz does not inherit Ruth; he acquires her along with the field, which he purchases as redeemer.

While our sources afford no evidence regarding such cases, redemption must have involved some provision for all destitute members of the family, including widows. In that case Boaz, as $g\bar{o}'\bar{e}l$, was expected not only to buy his dead kinsman's property but also to provide for the support of his dependents. Was he not then responsible for Naomi as well as Ruth? Probably he was, unless the price he paid for the field was sufficient to provide for her support.

Ruth differed from Naomi, however, in being still of marriageable age. For her, therefore, the normal means of support was marriage. The redeemer, obliged to provide for her, would naturally seek a husband to assume the responsibility for her support, or marry her himself. The situation was thus similar to that presupposed by the famous statement of Tabari regarding the remarriage of widows among the pre-Islamic Arabs. The practice he describes, indeed, while treated as a matter of inheritance, should perhaps be regarded rather as redemption, especially in view of the optional character of the arrangement for both widow and heir.

The conclusion to which these considerations lead us is that Ruth's position in the affair is that of a dependent who happens also to be a marriageable woman. Naomi secures a home for Ruth (3:1) by appealing to the $g\bar{o}'\bar{e}l$. Boaz accepts his responsibility for her support by marrying her, after first offering to the nearer kinsman the option of doing this. So far the situation and the transaction growing out of it

---

[4] Gunkel (loc. cit.) sees here a combination of two legal conceptions, an older one by which the field had to remain in the family, and a later one by which the widow inherited it if there were no children; the combination of these required that the redeemer buy the property from the widow.

are clear, and sufficiently explained by the conception and practice of the $g^{e'}ull\bar{a}h$.

From this point of view, however, there is no occasion for the idea of levirate marriage. The purchase of the land and the provision for the widow's support do not involve raising up a son for the dead. A tempting solution for this problem was proposed some years ago by Bewer, namely, that the references to the levirate-idea in 4:5, 10 should be deleted as interpolations. Unquestionably this simplifies the matter. On the other hand, simplification by excision should be practised with great caution, and only as a last resort. In this case it is not acceptable, for it raises as many questions as it answers. Obed is not regarded as the son of Boaz except in the genealogy (4:18–22), which few modern interpreters would regard as a part of the original book. The response of Boaz to Ruth's appeal to him, moreover, is hard to explain on this basis. He invokes the blessing of Yahweh upon her, because the *ḥesed* she now shows is greater than her previous *ḥesed* (3:10). To what does this refer? She has shown no personal kindness to Boaz previously. The former *ḥesed* of which he speaks must be Ruth's loyalty to the family of her husband in leaving her own land and coming to Bethlehem with Naomi (cp. 2:11). Her "latter loyalty" must then mean the further expression of that devotion to her husband and his family in offering herself to Boaz for a union of the levirate type. In that case, the references which Bewer would delete merely prove that Boaz had understood Ruth's intention.

Why the levirate-responsibility should be assigned to such a distant relative as Boaz still remains to be explained. It was not involved in the redemption of the land, for by purchase the land now belonged to Boaz and his heirs. The obligation to raise up a son to the dead must have been a part of the redeemer's responsibility to his clan, like the duty of blood-revenge (Num 35:12, 19 etc.). But the interest of the clan would be satisfied if the *gō'ēl* begot a son in his own name. The requirement of continuing the name of the widow's previous husband presupposes the emergence of the small family as a distinct social unit and the conception of the necessity of continuing the individual's life and name, as in levirate marriage. In Deut 25 and Gen 38 this responsibility is limited to the immediate family. This is logical, for levirate marriage is an affair of the family, whereas redemption is an affair of the clan. Apparently the book of Ruth represents a transitional stage between redemption-marriage as an affair of the clan and levirate-marriage as an affair of the family.

But if Boaz as redeemer was expected to beget a son for his dead kinsman, and if that son would be the heir of the dead man's estate, why should Boaz be required to buy the property? There was no such purchase of the estate in levirate marriage, to say nothing of purchasing the widow. The support of the mother and child would seem to be all that could reasonably be required. Since the child would inherit the estate of his mother's previous husband, one is driven to ask what Boaz got for the money he paid for the land. Doubtless the amount was small, as always in cases of forced sale. Possibly, indeed, as we have already noted in passing, the price was merely nominal and the transaction a sale in form only. Just as in our laws transfer of title in real estate, even though it be actually a gift, requires the mention of some payment to make the deed valid, so here it may be that the transfer of the property to Boaz had to be made in the form of a sale to be legal. Professor Speiser has adduced evidence from the Nuzi tablets to show that the act of drawing off the sandal was a form of legal validation in such transactions, as Ruth 4:7 explicitly states.

Be that as it may, it is clear that here too the emergence of the immediate family as an important social unit and the idea of direct individual succession are presupposed. The refusal of the nearer kinsman to act as gō'ēl implies that to do so would be disadvantageous for him. While the author does not indicate that Boaz would likewise suffer by the transaction, or that he had any family of his own whose interests were at stake, the obvious intention of the author to enhance the virtue of Boaz by contrast with the selfishly calculating spirit of the nearer kinsman gains in force if we assume that the two men were in the same situation. Certainly there is nothing to suggest the contrary.

In view of all this, it seems probable that the redeemer's obligation to buy the property, to assume the support of the widow, and also, when possible, to raise up a son to preserve the name of his dead relative, was a duty imposed by custom and public opinion in the interest of the family, in spite of its conflict with the individual's own interests. If this be so, the restriction of the levirate-duty to the brothers of the dead man would be a natural consequence. The fact that the nearest relative might refuse to undertake this onerous obligation, and that the assumption of it was a proof of extraordinary virtue and family-spirit, supports this view of the matter, indicating a stage of transition, when the anomaly of the triple obligation had come to be realized.

Before this conclusion is adopted, however, other possibilities should be given full consideration. We must face, for example, the possibility that the whole situation portrayed, with all its implications, is unhistorical. It is certainly complicated and confused, and the author leaves many questions unanswered. Yet he shows throughout the story a keen interest in details of popular custom and a considerable acquaintance with them, and he assumes that his readers will regard the story as at least plausible. To be sure, he finds it necessary in one instance to explain that the custom he describes was practised in earlier times (4:7). This may be taken to mean that he feels he has gone too far beyond the bounds of probability and hence must explain to his readers that the custom was an ancient one, now obsolete. But why should he deliberately drag in an improbable item which he does not need? The very fact that what he says is obviously contrary to the custom of his own day is evidence of its authenticity. In the same way, the fact that the picture is confused and complicated may indicate, not that the author has failed to work out a consistent idea, but that he is portraying actual practices instead of an artificial, idealized situation.

The lack of agreement with the laws of the Pentateuch at a number of points is not necessarily a sign of unfaithfulness to real life. Law is often artificial and sometimes idealistic, and it is not uncommonly more consistent than custom. The idealistic character of much of the Deuteronomic legislation is well known. With regard to many laws in the Pentateuch historians have found reason to question whether they were ever enforced. Laws frequently represent attempts to alter prevailing custom. All this may well be true of the laws regarding redemption and levirate marriage, in which case Ruth may give us a more accurate picture of ancient Israelite life than the Pentateuch gives.

It must be remembered also that circumstances alter cases. The situation presented by the story of Ruth is undoubtedly an unusual one. The emigration to Moab, the death of the father and both his sons, and the return of one of the daughters-in-law with the mother to the old family home are all quite credible, but they could hardly have occurred in combination very often. The procedure required by this situation, therefore, may have gone somewhat beyond what was customary in ordinary cases. All that need be supposed is that it was what Israelite public opinion would approve as in accord with accepted custom and the requirements of the particular case.

Another possibility which should be recognized is that local peculiarities may be responsible for some of the details of the picture. All we can say about this, however, is that there is no perceptible evidence of it.

Allowing for the possibility that all these alternative explanations may contain some truth, the most probable view on the whole is that the peculiar features of the story of Ruth represent a particular stage of historical development in the customs connected with marriage, inheritance, and redemption. We conclude therefore that the marriage of Boaz and Ruth corresponds to a stage of folk-custom in Israel earlier than those represented by the Pentateuchal laws regarding inheritance, redemption, and levirate marriage, a transitional stage between redemption-marriage as an affair of the whole clan and levirate marriage as an affair of the immediate family. The bearing of this conclusion on the historical value and the date of the book of Ruth is obvious.

The Book of Ruth
Georg Fohrer

1. TERMINOLOGY AND CONTENT

This small book takes its name from one of the three figures that play the major roles in it. From the very beginning it belonged to the third part of the Hebrew canon, the "Writings," although its canonicity was once in doubt. . . . It was later used as a festival scroll for the Feast of Weeks, i.e., the festival of the wheat harvest. Since it purports to narrate a story from the period of the Judges, the LXX and other translations placed it after the book of Judges. In content, it is a continuous narrative.

1:1–6 Introduction: Emigration to Moab of a Judahite family from Bethlehem; death of the father, Elimelech; marriage of the sons to Moabite women; death of the sons; the mother Naomi's wish to return home.

1:7–22 Return of Naomi with her daughter-in-law Ruth ("where you go, I will go," referring to the mother-in-law); Orpah, the other daughter-in-law, remains behind.

2 Boaz, a wealthy relative of Ruth's husband, is attracted to the diligent and virtuous Ruth as she is reaping grain.

3 Ruth's mother-in-law advises her to go to Boaz at night and lie at his feet, to remind him of his duty as a relative to redeem her by marriage and urge him to perform it.

4:1–17 Another relative relinquishes his claim to Ruth; Boaz marries her; a son, Obed, is born to them.

4:13–22 Genealogy of David.

2. LITERARY TYPE AND HISTORICAL BACKGROUND

The resemblance to popular saga suggests that the narrative is based on such a saga—like the framework narrative of the book of Job. Originally, it may even have had poetic form. . . . In the dress of its present style, however, it conforms to the literary type of the novella, composed by an unknown author. He is responsible for the characterization of the major figures.

In its basic features, the narrative was a single unit from the outset. The suggestion that Naomi was originally the only woman involved or the most important figure . . . cannot be demonstrated and is unlikely. The only doubtful point is whether 4:17b, 18–22 belonged to the original narrative.

The ancient saga had a historical setting, particularly with respect to its date and locale. The formation of the names "Boaz" and "Elimelech" also fits in with the period of the Judges. "Naomi," too, is a common feminine name; but since it means "pleasant," it seems to have been chosen deliberately as a symbolic contrast to the bitter fate of the woman who bore it. Though it cannot be proved conclusively, it seems probable that the names of Naomi's two Moabite daughters-in-law have a certain symbolic significance: "Orpah" may mean "faithless" and "Ruth" may mean "companion." This is absolutely certain with respect to the names of the dead sons: "Mahlon" means "weakness" and "Chilion" means "consumption." Whether all these names occurred already in the popular saga or derive in part from the author of the novella cannot be determined. In any case, they are not related to any fertility cult at Bethlehem, whose myth is represented by the narrative. . . .

3. CONNECTION WITH DAVID

The crucial problem for interpretation of the novella is its relationship to David (4:17b, 18–22). It is recognized almost universally that the genealogy of David, which derives either from I Chron. 2:2–15 or the same tradition, must be considered a later postscript. The genealogy, beginning with Perez (4:18–22), was added because of the nuptial good wishes to Boaz (4:12), which mention Perez, and also because of the appearance of Boaz and Obed among the ancestors of David.

The question remains, however, whether the two clauses of 4:17b ("They named him Obed; he was the father of Jesse, the father of David") originally belonged to the narrative. Eissfeldt has rightly denied their originality on grounds of form and content. Formally, the name of Ruth's child should either occur in 17a, where we now find the statement that "the neighborhood gave him a name," or be introduced in 17b with *therefore*, as in other examples. In terms of content, the explanation of the name, "A son has been born to Naomi [the pleasant one]," bears no relation to the name "Obed" ("servant, worshiper"). As others have accurately observed before, the child should have been named something like "Ibleam" or "Ben Noam". . . . This means that 4:17 is not in its original form, but has at least been expanded by the addition of 17b, apart from possible alterations in 17a. The original name has been removed and the name "Obed" introduced in order to make the child David's grandfather, who, according to tradition, was named Obed. The narrative of the book, therefore, originally had no connection with David. It is out of the question that the book presupposes an ancient tradition of David's Moabite origin, which it attempts to gloss over and neutralize by judaizing David's ancestors and the heritage of his family. . . . Instead, the book was transformed into a narrative concerning David's family after it was finished. This is in line with the interest the late period shows in David, which by no means must always take the form it does in the Chronicler's History. That we are dealing here with a secondary alteration can also be seen from the fact that the narrative does not reckon Elimelech or Boaz among the ancestors of David.

4. INTERPRETATION

The significance of the novella, therefore, cannot be ascribed to its recounting the early family history of the house of David. . . . Neither does it consist in a protest against the ruthless attitude of Ezra and Nehemiah in the question of mixed marriages. . . . Not a single sentence suggests such a purpose. Instead, like the Job legend, the purpose of the narrative from the very outset was edification. Just as Job proves equally faithful in good fortune and ill, so Naomi and Ruth pass the difficult tests to which they are subjected: the former is concerned for the good of her daughter-in-law rather than for her own good, while remaining faithful to the family of her husband; the latter attaches more weight to her obligations toward her mother-in-law than to her previous national and religious ties and her chances for personal happiness. . . . Boaz, however, who fulfills his ancient obligations, opens thereby a new way out of the trials. To fulfill one's traditional obligations when subjected to the trials and tests of life because this course leads to change of fortunes—such was the teaching even of the ancient sage.

The author of the novella gave it a more profound religious significance by connecting it with faith in Yahweh's beneficent providence, which guides history. Ruth's arrival in the proper field is due to Yahweh's guidance; the success of Naomi's plan is due to Yahweh's grace; and the blessing of a son bestowed upon the marriage with Boaz is due to Yahweh's kindness. . . . What Boaz says to Ruth when they first meet expresses the religious content of the book: "Yahweh recompense you for what you have done, and a full reward be given you by Yahweh, the God of Israel, under whose wings you have come to take refuge." At the same time, we hear a similar magnanimity toward those who belong to another nation, like that expressed in the book of Jonah.

5. ORIGIN

In dating the book, we must distinguish between the different stages in its formation. The novella did not originate in the late period of the monarchy . . . and certainly not in the period of the Solomonic enlightenment . . . ; this date is likely, however, for the popular saga. The author of the novella should be dated in the postexilic period; this conclusion is supported by the intellectual content of the book, its linguistic character, and its position in the third division of the canon. We must probably think in terms of the close of the fifth century or, even more likely, the fourth century B.C. The alteration and expansion making the book refer to David must be dated even later.

SUGGESTED READINGS

Bettan, Israel. *The Five Scrolls,* pp. 49–72. Cincinnati: Union of American Hebrew Congregations, 1953.

Crook, Margaret B. "The Book of Ruth—a New Solution." *The Journal of Bible and Religion* **XVI** (1948), pp. 155–60.

Knight, George A. F. *Ruth and Jonah.* New York: Harper & Row (Torchbooks), 1950.

Rowley, H. H. "The Marriage of Ruth." *The Harvard Theological Review* **XL** (1949), 77–99.

Smith, Louise P. "Introduction and Exegesis, the Book of Ruth." In *The Interpreter's Bible,* Vol. 2, edited by George A. Buttrick, pp. 829–52. Nashville, Tenn.: Abingdon Press, 1953. (Includes biblical text.)

QUESTIONS FOR DISCUSSION AND WRITING

1. Analyze the Book of Ruth as a short story, giving consideration to its setting (background), character development, and plot structure (beginning/middle/end, with rising action, climax, and dénouement).
2. Compare the story of Ruth with the story of Isaac's acquisition of Rebekah in Genesis 24.
3. According to Georg Fohrer, what are the three stages in the composition of the Book of Ruth?
4. As noted in the Summary, some scholars claim that the Book of Ruth is a response to the narrow nationalism of such prophets as Ezra and Nehemiah. In contrast, Georg Fohrer asserts that the book is *not* "a protest against the ruthless attitude of Ezra and Nehemiah in the question of mixed marriages. . . . Not a single sentence suggests such a purpose." Argue for or against Fohrer's point of view.
5. Mary Ellen Chase says that "The author [of the story of Ruth] has drawn [the characters] with no sense of those depths and crosscurrents of human psychology such as the writer of Jonah was to show so brilliantly

a century or two later." Do you agree? Write a short paper comparing character treatment in Jonah and in Ruth.

6. Read at least two commentaries on levirate marriage, and then explain the term in your own words.

7. Millar Burrows says, "The bearing of this conclusion on the historical value and date of the book of Ruth is obvious." What is the conclusion to which he refers? What bearing does this conclusion have on the historical value and date of the book?

8. Louise P. Smith (see "Suggested Readings") divides the Book of Ruth into six "scenes": (1) Moab (1:1–18), (2) Bethlehem (1:19–22), (3) The Harvest Field (2:1–23), (4) The Threshing Floor (3:1–18), (5) The Gate (4:1–12), (6) Conclusion (4:13–22).

Using this format, compose a radio script of the story. If possible, record it, using members of your class as actors.

JONAH

SUMMARY

The composition of Jonah is of uncertain date. Those who accept it as the work of the Jonah referred to in 2 Kings 14:25, where he is a prophet who counseled Jeroboam II, place its composition in the eighth century B.C., whereas those who interpret it as a parable depicting the universality of God as opposed to the narrow nationalism of Ezra and Nehemiah place it somewhere in the fourth or third century B.C.

The Lord orders Jonah, the son of Amittai, to go to Nineveh, the Assyrian capital, and "to cry against it" because of its wickedness. But Jonah evidently does not wish to warn Nineveh of the Lord's wrath, perhaps because he does not want an enemy nation to survive and later destroy Israel. So he takes ship at Joppa (modern Jaffa) and sails for Tarshish (probably in southern Spain), intending to go as far as he can in the opposite direction from Nineveh.

When the ship sets out to sea, the Lord sends a storm that

threatens to wreck it. The sailors are so frightened that they call on their various gods and even throw their merchandise overboard to lighten the ship. The captain is angry with Jonah when he finds him sleeping in the hold; he tells Jonah to get up and pray to his God for the salvation of the ship and the men.

The men cast lots to determine who among them might be the cause of their imminent disaster, and "the lot fell upon Jonah" (1:7). Under their angry questioning Jonah admits that he is a Hebrew and that he is in fear of his God. They reprove him for having displeased his God and ask what they should do to him to still the raging of the sea. Jonah tells them to throw him into the sea, but they try to avoid such a drastic measure by rowing harder than ever for the shore. It is useless; the sea becomes even more tempestuous. When they finally throw Jonah into the sea, they do so with trepidation, begging Jonah's God not to hold them guilty of innocent blood. The sea becomes calm, and the men "feared the Lord exceedingly, and they offered a sacrifice to the Lord and made vows" (1:16).

Now the Lord sends "a great fish," which swallows Jonah and holds him in its belly for three days and three nights. In a psalm of thanksgiving that very likely was not composed by the author of the story but was either quoted by him or inserted later by someone else, Jonah is made to say that he cried out to the Lord to save him and that the Lord did so. After this prayer of thanksgiving the Lord speaks to the fish, and Jonah is spewed out upon dry land.

Again the Lord orders Jonah to go to Nineveh. This time he obeys, telling the people that the city will be destroyed in forty days. The people of Nineveh accept his prophecy as the word of God, and they repent: "They proclaimed a fast, and put on sackcloth, from the greatest of them to the least of them" (3:5). Even the "king of Nineveh" (of Assyria?) arises from his throne, dons sackcloth, and sits down in ashes. He publishes a decree throughout the city, proclaiming a fast for man and beast. Man and beast must all wear sackcloth and "cry mightily to God." They must all turn from evil and violence. When they have all done this, says the king, "Who knows, God may yet repent and turn from his fierce anger" (3:9). And God does change his mind and spares Nineveh.

Angered by this contradiction to his prophecy, Jonah tells God that this is why he fled to Tarshish. Knowing the graciousness, mercy, and love of God, he had feared that God would save the city. And so it has come to pass, and now Jonah wants to die. He goes outside the city, builds a lean-to for shade, and sits down to watch what will become of the city.

To provide him more shade, the Lord makes a plant grow up over his head. Jonah is pleased. The next day, however, the Lord sees to it that the plant withers; then he sends a sultry east wind, which along with the heat of the sun brings Jonah near to fainting. When he

426

"Jonah Sheltered by the Vine" (artist unknown)

again expresses his desire to die, the Lord questions him. Is Jonah angry over what has happened to the plant? Yes. But he did not bring about the flourishing or the withering of the plant, and yet he pities it. So why should the Lord not pity the city of Nineveh? There are more than a hundred and twenty thousand simple, ignorant people in that city, says the Lord—"and also much cattle."

LITERARY QUALITIES

Jonah
MARY ELLEN CHASE

Jonah was written perhaps a hundred, perhaps two hundred, years after the book of Ruth and also by an unknown author. It purports to be a story about an ancient prophet named Jonah, who sup-

JONAH Reprinted with permission of Macmillan Publishing Co., Inc. from *The Bible and the Common Reader*, rev. ed., by Mary Ellen Chase. Copyright 1944, 1952 by Mary Ellen Chase, renewed 1972 by Mary Ellen Chase.

posedly lived and prophesied about 750 B.C., but none of whose prophecies has come down to us, and who was the son of an unknown man named Amittai. Its author evidently shared the views of the author of Ruth, for his ironic narrative has obviously the purpose of proving that the compassion of God is not restricted to the Jews but extends even to the heathen. Through it he is clearly protesting against the religious arrogance of his people, against their hope, even expectation, that God will annihilate these heathen for their own benefit and well-being; yet, like the author of Ruth, he is too good an artist to append a moral to his tale. Instead he allows Jonah and God to discuss an uncomfortable situation with sullen fury on Jonah's part and with keen enjoyment over Jonah's predicament on the part of God.

In this story of Jonah we are reminded of the many-sided humour often seen in the old miracle plays. Nor is the parallel, I think, a bad one, for the story itself is dramatically constructed in three clearly defined acts: the disastrous flight of Jonah which ends by his being swallowed by the fish; his final arrival in Nineveh and his bitter humiliation there; and God's triumph over his recalcitrant and still sulky servant. Moreover, as in many of the old plays we find in the story a mingling of all manner of material, credible and incredible, serious and comic.[1]

In spite of the simplicity of the author's narration, perhaps indeed because of it, Jonah emerges from the story as one of the most complex characterizations in the Old Testament. Although he takes at least the name of a prophet, he is, first of all, an egotist, who does not want God interfering with his life. When he hears God telling him to go to Nineveh and cry against its wickedness, he makes up his mind that he will do nothing of the sort. Instead he determines to escape from God by going on a Mediterranean cruise to Tarshish, presumably the ancient name for the port of Cadiz in Spain. He is also something of a braggart or at least a most voluble and indiscreet soul, for we are informed that he has already told the sailors that he is fleeing from God. He has, however, like most romanticists, a strong sense of justice in his nature, for, once the storm becomes disastrous and he is conscious that the lot cast by the sailors has fallen to him as its cause, he begs them a bit dramatically to throw him into the sea lest he be the means of their death. We actually know nothing of him during his three days and three nights in the fish's belly; for the pious psalm accorded to him, in Chapter 2, Verses 2–9, as he languished there was added by a later editor, who may have thought the original author too jocose and lighthearted and, therefore, interpolated the psalm to put a more solemn face on things. From the author himself we know only

---

[1] So far as I have been able to discover from a study of lists of miracle plays, there is no evidence that one was written upon Jonah.

that Jonah in the fish's belly prayed to God and was straightway "vomited out" upon dry land.

Deciding wisely to take no more perilous chances, Jonah proceeds to Nineveh when the second call comes from God, and, again loudly asserting himself, enters the city and informs the people of Nineveh that their days are numbered. He is, of course, entirely unprepared for their immediate repentance and conversion and quite obviously not only incensed but humiliated in that his effectiveness as a terrorizer has been so suddenly pricked and that his mission has proved fruitless. After furiously informing God that His foolish leniency and not the honest repentance of the people of Nineveh has brought Jonah to this embarrassing fix, he begs God to take his life, for he cannot bear the awkward and ridiculous position in which he has been placed. Infuriated further by the taunting question of God, *Doest thou well to be angry?* he escapes from the now triumphant Nineveh and sulks by the roadside under the shadow of a booth which he has made. And so far as we know from the story he emerges from the sulks only to be exceedingly rude to God by a saucy and belligerent answer to God's repeated question.

The author of the story again shows his ironic gift for characterization in his portrait of God. And here again the comparison to certain of the old miracle plays is, I think, an apt one, for God displays many of those distinctive human attributes which the medieval plays often assigned to Him. The God who commands Jonah to go to Nineveh and cry out against that wicked city is a God who is clearly not going to stand any flouting of His commands. Nor is He above using every measure He can conceive in order to humiliate Jonah and to make him a laughingstock. He creates a mighty tempest in the sea; He prepares a great fish to swallow Jonah and to house him for three miserable days and nights; He decides to teach Jonah a lesson even at a sacrifice of His own dignity; and at length He even descends to a kind of practical joking in first preparing a gourd to cover Jonah from the heat, then in creating a worm to eat the gourd, and finally in raising up "a vehement east wind" to cause Jonah at first to faint and then to declare that he is weary of his wretched existence. All of these acts, though they serve as object lessons to Jonah, are too quixotic not to be taken humorously, and it seems to me very evident that the author meant them to be so taken. The almost impertinent sparring between God and Jonah in the last chapter, God's climaxing concern over the 120,000 infants in Nineveh, so young that they cannot tell their right hands from their left, and over the "much cattle" there, and throughout the story both His apparent pleasure in Jonah's discomfiture and His ingenuity in devising means of increasing it must have given delight to the author who conceived them.

I am sure that the scholars and the theologians are right when they see in the story of Jonah an object lesson for the rigid, law-ridden

Jews of the time in which it was written and when they characterize its author as a man of vision and tolerance, impatient before the narrow exclusiveness of many of his race and universal in his conception of the limitless compassion of God. I think, however, that too few of them give him his due as an artist who effectively used his gifts of irony and of imagination in the charming conception and construction of his story. I even think that he may have been daring enough to use the name of a prophet in this same way and to have pictured the distinctly human, even fun-loving attributes of God in the same spirit as a means of making more vivid his protest against the narrow, nationalistic tendencies of his day.

That he enjoyed telling his story is evident in every line of his sharp, eager narrative; and that he loved fiction for itself is shown by his use of the material doubtless current at the beginning of the Greek period in which he probably lived. Big fishes like that of Lucian and of the author of the book of Tobit play a part in many ancient tales; gulling and baiting an embarrassed victim is as old as mankind, though few might have the temerity to make God employ such means; and the odd description of the beasts of Nineveh repenting in sackcloth has an echo in the story of Herodotus, who describes in one of his vivid tales how horses and oxen were shaved of their hair at a season of mourning.

At all events, whether one is uplifted by Jonah's message or delighted by its fun, here is his story. Moreover, uplift and delight do not, I think, need to be mutually exclusive emotions!

INTERPRETATIONS

from "The Last of the Old Testament Prophets"
G. ERNEST WRIGHT AND REGINALD H. FULLER

Jonah is a most eloquent book. It differs from other prophecies in that it is the story about a prophet rather than a collection of the words of the prophet. The prophet chosen for the story is mentioned in II Kings 14:25 as a popular prophet who predicted the great victory for Israel in the reign of Jeroboam II. He was a contemporary of Amos,

THE LAST OF THE OLD TESTAMENT PROPHETS From *The Book of the Acts of God* by G. Ernest Wright and Reginald H. Fuller. Copyright © 1957 by G. Ernest Wright. Reprinted by permission of Doubleday & Company, Inc.

the latter seeing in the same events predicted by Jonah a warning of future doom. The language of the book is much later, however, than the eighth century, and most scholars date the book in the fifth century. It was written at a time when nationalistic exclusivism on the part of the Jerusalem priesthood had become very strong. It sought, therefore, to remind the new community of the restored exiles what Second Isaiah had previously reminded them of, namely that the love of God was broader than they were conceiving it, that he did not choose Israel in order to play favorites among the peoples of the earth, but that he chose her and his prophets to be instruments of his saving power in the earth. The true prophet is, therefore, the author of the book, rather than the man about whom the story is told. The book serves as a kind of parable. Jonah is portrayed as a prophet in Palestine who hears the command of the Lord to become an instrument of mercy to the city which was the worst enemy of his people, Nineveh, the capital of Assyria. Refusing to carry out the Lord's command, he flees in the opposite direction by boat as fast as he can go. But the Lord will not let him get away. He hurls a great storm into the sea, the sailors discover by a means typical of the day that the culprit is Jonah, and they are forced to throw him into the sea. God has him swallowed by a big fish who vomits him up again on the shore of Palestine, where he is once again commanded to go to Nineveh.

Many people, when they read the story of the big fish which swallowed Jonah, never get any further because they bog down in speculation about whether or not such a thing could actually happen. One can be certain that if the author of the book had only known the trouble this fish was to cause the minds of men, he would have been perfectly willing to substitute some other device. His concern is simply to show that one cannot run away from God; the fish is simply a device in the story whereby Jonah is returned and faced again with his duty. This time the prophet obeys, and in a remarkable way his proclamation gets results; the city of Nineveh wholeheartedly repents, so that God does not have to punish it by destruction. Yet this is precisely what disgusts the prophet Jonah exceedingly. He quotes one of the great confessions of God's love in the Old Testament, namely that God is merciful and gracious and slow to anger and full of mercy, and uses that as precisely his excuse for his anger. The mercy of God is a fine thing when it was directed to his own people, but a disgusting thing when directed toward his enemies. Hence the prophet exclaims that he would prefer to die rather than to live. He goes outside the city and builds a booth there in order to see what will happen. A heat wave arrives, but a plant which has grown up over the hut protects it from the sun. During the night the plant withers and dies because of a worm that attacks it, and again Jonah wishes in his heart that he might die. And now gently God asks whether Jonah has a right to be angry, and Jonah in great disgust affirms his right to be angry even unto death. Then God replies even more gently that inasmuch as he, Jonah, has had such great concern for a plant which was simply a child of the night, should not he, God, have concern for a great city wherein there are 120,000 people who cannot tell their right hand from their left? And as though that were not sufficient, he makes a final humorous appeal to the prophet's common sense by suggesting "and also much cattle"—that is, it would be a shame to destroy so many excellent animals!

The Book of Jonah was obviously written by a great spirit who was struggling against the narrowing of the faith within the confines of the tiny province of Judah during the period after the exile. Yet the book stands at the very end of the prophetic movement. From this time forth the community of Judah seems unable longer to listen to prophets. Priests and lawyers in the law are those who are most needed in the developing Judaism, whereas prophets only create embarrassments. The belief that God was about to do the new thing in each succeeding crisis faded, and its place was taken by what was known as apocalypticism. That is a view which interprets current history as being a dark and terrible time which is constantly getting darker and more terrible until it will finally be brought to a halt by the intervention of God and the coming of the Messiah. In this viewpoint the "now" loses a great deal of its dramatic significance; it becomes a time only for watchful waiting and for obedience as one understands obedience to the Lord. The period of excitement and urgency is gone. Indeed, it would seem that those who framed the canon of scripture were quite right in leaving the centuries between Ezra and John the Baptist very largely a blank. Only with the opening of the New Testament is the spirit of Old Testament prophecy again revived and the Lord who is about to do the new thing is again known, this time in Jesus Christ.

The Testing of Jonah
ROBERT NATHAN

Jonah stood leaning upon his staff in the darkness. A few lights gleamed among the trees, whose branches bent above him as though to envelope him in their quiet embrace. The odors of night crept around him; he remembered his youth, spent in this village, and he

THE TESTING OF JONAH From Robert Nathan, *Jonah* (New York: Alfred A. Knopf, 1925, 1934). Quoted in Douglas C. Brown, ed., *The Enduring Legacy* (New York: Charles Scribner's Sons, 1975), pp. 283–93. Reprinted by permission of the author.

felt in his heart a longing for that lonely boy whose only friends had been an old man and his own dreams. So much of life had gone by, yet here he was again, wearier, wiser, still led by hopes, of what he did not know, hurt by memories, but why he could not tell. He heard the voices of Aaron and his friends fading in the distance; he knew that in the shadows young lovers whispered together, although he could not see them. All about him trembled the happy laughter of youth, the peace of age, the quietness of rest after labor. The sky of heaven, shining with stars, bent upon his home a regard of kindness; and the wind, moving through the sycamores, spoke to him in the accents of the past.

Bowing his head upon his breast, he thought, "Jonah, Jonah, what have you done with your youth?"

God was worried about Jonah. Watched by reverent cherubim, whose wings fanned the air all about Him, the Lord of Hosts walked up and down in the sky, and said to Moses, who was accompanying Him,

"I must find something for this young man to do."

Moses looked down at Jonah with an expression of contempt. "He is hardly worth the effort," he declared gloomily. "He seems to me to lack character."

"You are right," said God. "Still, he expects something from Me."

And He added, smiling gently, "Perhaps that is why I am fond of him. He has not your strong and resourceful mind, Moses, nor Noah's faithful heart; but he has suffered. He is simply a man, like anybody."

"What?" cried Noah, hurrying up, "are you talking about me?"

God replied: "I was saying that Jonah did not trust Me as you did, My friend."

"No," said Noah; "but then, what do you expect? There are so many different ideas now in the world. I do not recognize my posterity in these warring nations. Let us have another flood, Lord."

Moses looked sadly down at Jerusalem, where golden idols were being sold in the streets. "You are right, Noah," he said, "but I do not like the idea of a flood. A flood does not teach people how to live. Sometimes I wonder if anything can teach people what they are unwilling to learn."

"Nonsense," said Noah. "A flood is the most sanitary thing. Wait and see; even you could learn something about sewers from a good flood."

God checked the old patriarch with a kindly hand. "Things are not the same as they used to be in the early days," He said. "I cannot drown the world today without drowning My wife, Israel. She is young, and a nuisance, but she has yet to bear Me a son. I foresee that

He will give His mother a great deal of pain, but that cannot be helped.

"Let us not think of Israel now, but of the prophet Jonah. Moses is of the opinion that he is not a first-class prophet, and I am inclined to agree with him. He is a poet; and for that reason I feel warmly inclined toward him. After all, you, Noah, and you, Moses, see only one side of My nature. You try to look upon the Greater Countenance, but what you see is the Lesser Countenance. It is different with a poet. He does not see Hod, or Chesed, the thrones of Glory and Mercy. He looks through Beauty to the Crown itself. Whereas you, Moses, have never seen beyond Knowledge; and you, my good Noah, have seen My face only in Severity."

Moses and Noah bowed their heads. "It is true, Lord," said Noah humbly.

God continued:

"At this moment Jonah does not see Me at all. In the first place, he is unhappy, and he no longer looks toward beauty. He believes that there is no more beauty in the world because his heart is broken. He is mistaken; and after a while his sorrow will sharpen his eyes. Then he will see more than before."

"In that case," said Moses, "why do You bother Yourself?"

The Lord considered a moment before replying. It was obvious that He wished to express Himself in terms intelligible to His hearers.

"The trouble, My friends," He said at last, "is this: our young prophet is a patriot. He is convinced that I am God of Israel alone. I do not mind that point of view in a prophet, but it will not do in a poet. Severity, glory, knowledge, belong to the nations, if you like. But beauty belongs to the world. It is the portion of all mankind in its God.

"I have covered the heavens with beauty, the green spaces of the earth, the cloudy waters, the tall and snowy peaks. These are for all to see, these are for all to love. Shall any one take beauty from another, and say, 'This is mine'?"

"Now He is beginning to talk," said Moses in an undertone to Noah; "this is like old times."

But God grew silent again. Presently he continued wearily,

"It is your fault, Moses, that the Jews believe I belong to them entirely. Well, I do not blame you, for you could not have brought them safely through the desert otherwise. But you did not tell them that I was a bull. I foresee that for a long time yet men will be irresistibly led to worship Me in the form of an animal."

"Well, then," said Noah, "if You foresee so much . . ."

"Be silent," said God, in a voice of thunder which made the wings of angels tremble. He continued more gently, "Actually, at the moment, I am not interested in theology. I am thinking of Jonah."

And He walked quietly up and down in the sky, thinking. The

cherubim, moving all about Him, beat with their snowy wings the air perfumed with frankincense; and the clouds rolled under His feet.

Left to themselves, Moses and Noah regarded each other in an unfriendly manner. At last Moses shrugged his shoulders. He was vexed to think that he did not know everything.

"Well, old man," he said to Noah, "have you nothing to talk about except the flood? You do not understand conditions in the world today."

"I understand this much," replied Noah calmly, "that faith is more important than knowledge. Where would you be, with all your wisdom, if it had not been for me and my ark? You would be a fish, swimming in the sea."

"Do you take credit for saving your own skin?" cried Moses. "Wonderful. I, on the other hand, was comfortable in Egypt. What I did was from the highest motives. I am not even sure that I am a Jew."

"I believed in God," said Noah stoutly, "and I did as He told me."

"So did I," said Moses angrily, "but I also used my wits a little. Faith is nothing; any animal can have faith. You and your faith had to get inside a wooden ark, in order to keep dry. But when I wished to take an entire nation across the sea, I simply parted the waters. I shall not tell you how I did it, because it would be lost on you. It takes a first-rate intelligence to understand such a thing."

Noah replied excitedly, "Please remember that I am your ancestor, and treat me with more respect."

"You are an old drunkard," said Moses.

But at this point God joined them again, and they were silent, to hear what the Holy One had to say.

"This young man," said God, "does not believe in Me any more. How then shall I convince him of Myself?"

Desirous of showing his knowledge, Moses began to quote from the Book of Wisdom: "Infidelity, violence, envy, deceit, extreme avariciousness, a total want of qualities, with impurity, are the innate faults of womankind."

"Nevertheless," said God, "they are also My creations. In My larger aspects I am as impure as I am pure; otherwise there would not be a balance. However, as I have said, we are not concerned with My larger aspects."

Noah broke in at this point. "Send him to sea, Lord," he begged. "There is nothing like a long trip at sea to quiet the mind. It is very peaceful on the water. One forgets one's disappointments."

"You are right," said God; "we need the sea; it will give him peace. But as a matter of fact, I do not care whether he finds peace or not. As I have told you, I simply wish this poet to understand that I am God, and not Baal of Canaan. The attempt to confuse Me with a sun-myth, with the fertility of earth as symbolized by the figure of a bull, or a dove, vexes Me. Increase is man's affair, not God's. Besides, where will all this increase end? I regret the days of Adam and Eve and the Garden of Eden. Already there are more people on earth than I have any use for, socially speaking. Now I could wish there were more beauty in the world. I should like some poet to speak of Me in words other than those of a patriot. Yet if I try to explain Myself, who will understand Me? Not even you, Moses, with all your wisdom. And so I, in turn, must forget My wisdom, in order to explain Myself. I must act as the not-too-wise God of an ignorant people. That this is possible is due to the fact that along with infinite wisdom, I include within Myself an equal amount of ignorance."

He sighed deeply. "I shall send Jonah to Nineveh," he concluded. "The subjects of King Shalmaneser the Third are honest, hardworking men and women. I enjoy, in some of My aspects, their vigorous and spectacular festivals. Nevertheless, repentance will not do them any harm, since for one thing they will not know exactly what it is they are asked to repent of, and for another, they will soon go back to their old ways again.

"Thus I shall convince Jonah of Myself where he least expects to find Me. He shall hear from Me at sea, and again within the walls of Nineveh. It will surprise him. And perhaps the rude beauty of that city will speak to his heart, dreamy with woe."

"I do not doubt that it will surprise him," said Moses, "but will he be convinced?"

God did not answer. Already He was on His way to earth. And Noah, looking after Him, shook his hoary head with regret.

"A flood would have been the better way," he said.

God went down to the water. He stood on the shores of the sea and called; like the voice of the storm a name rolled forth from those august lips across the deep. And the deeps trembled. Presently a commotion took place in the waters; wet and black the huge form of Leviathan rose gleaming from the sea, and floated obediently before its God.

The Lord spoke, and the whale listened. After He had explained the situation, God said:

"I foresee that Jonah will not go to Nineveh as I command. He will attempt to flee from Me, and he will choose the sea as the best means of escape. It will not help him. I shall raise a storm upon the waters, and the ingorant sailors will cast him overboard as a sacrifice to the gods of the storm. That is where you can be of assistance to Me, My old friend. As he sinks through the water, I wish you to advance upon him, and swallow him."

"Ak," said the whale; "O my."

"Well," said God impatiently, "what is the matter?"

The great fish blew a misty spray of water into the air. "It is impossible," he declared; "in the first place, I should choke to death."

"You are an ignorant creature," said God; "you have neither faith, nor science. Let Me tell you a few things about yourself in the light of future exegesis. Know then, that you are a cetacean, or whale-bone type of whale. Such animals obtain their food by swimming on or near the surface of the water, with their jaws open."

"That is true," said the whale, reverent and amazed.

"The screen of whalebone," continued the Lord, "opens inward, and admits solid objects to the animal's mouth. This screen does not allow the egress of any solid matter, only of water. As the gullet is very small, only the smallest objects can pass down it.

"Jonah will therefore be imprisoned in your mouth. You cannot swallow him; and he cannot get out, because of the screen of whalebone."

"Then he will suffocate," said the whale.

"Nonsense," said God. "Remember that you are an air-breathing, warm-blooded animal, and can only dive because of the reservoir of air in your mouth. When this air becomes unfit to breathe, you must rise to the surface for a fresh supply.

"While you have air to breathe, Jonah will have it also.

"So do not hesitate any longer, but do as you are told." ·

The whale heaved a deep sigh; his breath groaned through the ocean, causing many smaller fish, terrified, to flee with trembling fins.

"How horrid for me," he exclaimed.

God replied soothingly, "It will assure you a place in history."

So saying, the Lord blessed Leviathan, who sank sadly back to the depths of the sea; and, turning from the shore, the Light of Israel rolled like thunder across the valleys toward Golan.

The night came to meet Him from the east, pouring down over the hills like smoke. In the cold night air God went to look for Jonah.

Poor Jonah, he had not found peace after all. The lonely desert, so calm and quiet in the past, had given no rest to his thoughts. His mind went back over and over again to those days at home; he felt the wonder of the lovenight, his heart shrank again with sickness for what followed. And he asked himself for the thousandth time how such things could be. Then he cried out against Judith for her cruelty; yet the next moment he forgave her.

And these thoughts, climbing and falling wearily up and down through his head, kept him awake until long after the desert was asleep. In the morning, when he awoke, it was with regret; he tried to sleep a little longer, to keep his eyes closed, to keep from thinking again . . . why wake at all? he wondered. There was nothing to wake to. Only the hot sun over the desert, only his heavy heart, which grew no lighter as the days went by.

Why wake at all?

God found him sitting wearily upon a rock, his head bowed between his hands. The Lord spoke, and the desert was silent.

"Jonah," said God in a voice like a great wave breaking, slowly, and with the peace of the sea, "Jonah, you have wept enough."

Jonah replied simply, "I have been waiting for You a long while, and I am very tired."

"I had not forgotten you," said God; "I have been thinking."

And He added, "Now I have something for you to do."

Jonah remained seated without looking up. He seemed no longer to care what God had for him to do.

"Arise, Jonah," said God, "and go to Nineveh. Cry out against that great city for its sins."

But Jonah looked more dejected than ever. "What have I to do with Nineveh?" he asked. "Am I prophet to the Assyrians? I am a Jew. Do not mock me, Lord."

"I do not mock you," said God gravely. "Go, then, and do My bidding."

And as Jonah did not reply, He added sadly, "Do you still doubt Me?"

Jonah rose slowly to his feet. His eyes blazed, and his hands were tightly clenched. "Oh," he cried bitterly, all the passion in his heart storming out at last in a torrent of despair, "You . . . what are You God of? Were You God of Israel when a Tyrian stole my love? Was I Your Prophet then? Have You Power over Tyre, that You let Your servant suffer such anguish? Or are You God of the desert, where the demons mock me night and day, where the very stones cry out against me, and the whole night is noisy with laughter? Nineveh . . . Nineveh . . . in whose name shall I cry out against Nineveh? Do the gods of Assur visit their wrath upon Jerusalem? What power have you in Nineveh? For my youth which I gave You, what have You given me? How have You returned my love, with what sorrow? What have You done to me, Lord? I stand in the darkness, weary, and with a heavy heart. What are You God of? Answer: what are You God of?

And God answered gently, "I am your God, Jonah, and where you go, there you will find Me."

Jonah sank down upon the rock again. His passion had exhausted him; but he was not convinced. "Well," he said in a whisper, "You are not God in Nineveh, and I will not go."

Then the wrath of the Lord, slow to start, flamed for a moment over the desert, and Jonah cowered to earth while the heavens groaned and the ground shook with fright. And in his hole by the pool in the Land of Tob, the little fox said to himself, "Jonah is talking to God."

But God's anger passed, leaving Him sad and holy.

"Peace unto you, Jonah," He said in tones of divine sweetness; "take up your task, and doubt Me no more."

And He returned to heaven in a cloud. Overcome with weariness, empty of passion, Jonah fell asleep upon the ground.

No jackals laughed that night. Silence brooded over the desert. The stars kept watch without a sound, and Jonah slept with a quiet heart. . . .

Jonah was let out of the whale in the North, near Arvad, and not far from Kadesh as the crow might fly, which is to say, over the coastal hills and then in a straight line across the jungles and the desert. This was the route he took as being the shortest way to Nineveh. He was in a hurry; he was impatient to begin his mission. He was filled with enthusiasm.

How different from his flight to sea, this vigorous return across the land dry with the sun of midsummer. Now he marched with a firm and hurried step, his face darkly radiant with divine purpose, with pious anger. Yes, he would speak; Nineveh would hear him. Let them stone him if they liked, God would amply repay them for it. What glory.

And this was all his, not hers, not for her sake; let her be proud of him if she liked; what did it matter any more? She would hear enough of it in Tyre; Jonah here, and Jonah there . . .

Yes, they would speak of it in Tyre.

As he passed the wayside altars of the baalim with their pillars surmounted by horns of sacrifices, he smiled at them in derision.

"You," he said scornfully, "you . . . what are you gods of, anyway?"

At Kadesh he saw statues of the river deities, Chrysonhoa and Pegai. He spat in the dust before them; fortunately, no one was looking. In the sun of late afternoon their shadows pointed like great spears toward Nineveh.

"Israel will hear my name again," he thought proudly.

The evergreen oaks of the hills gave way to the tamarisks of the Syrian jungles, and the palms and scrub of the desert. He slept the first night in the wilderness between Kadesh and Rehoboth. The jackals were silent, awed by the presence of lions among the rocks. Padding to and fro, the great beasts watched Jonah from afar, with eyes like flames. . . .

In the fresh light of early morning a mother goat divided her milk between the prophet and her ewe. "These are stirring times, Jonah," she said; "angels are abroad in great numbers." Recognizing a minor deity, Jonah blessed her and resumed his journey.

At the end of the second day he began to pass the boundary stones of Assyria, set up to warn trespassers upon private property.

Thinking them altars, Jonah cursed each one as he went by. The next day he passed kilns in which colored bricks were being baked. As far as he could see, the blue, green, and yellow bricks stood in rows on the red earth.

That night he slept outside the gates of Nineveh. The city rose above him in the dark; he heard the sentries challenge on the walls.

In the morning he entered the city with some farmers on their way to the markets. The sun was rising, gleaming upon the great winged bulls before the temples, the green and yellow lions upon the walls. Under the clear upland sky the city shone with color like a fair. The markets opened; the streets filled with men and women in their colored shawls and clashing ornaments. And Jonah, looking and looking, was astonished. "Why," he thought, "this is strange; there is something bright and bold about all this. This is fine, after all." And he felt a gayety of heart take hold of him. How vigorous these mountain people looked with their insolent faces and their swaggering air. There was nothing old or sad in Nineveh. He forgot why he had come; he was excited, and happy. It was not at all what he had expected; and he forgot himself.

But not for long. As the hours passed, he grew weary; and as the brightness wore off, and he began to think of his own life again, he began to hate Nineveh, to hate the bold colors all around him, the youth that carried itself so proudly and carelessly in the streets. "Yes," he thought, "that is all very well for you; but you know nothing about life." And, lifting his arms, he cried aloud with gloomy satisfaction, "Yet forty days, and Nineveh shall be overthrown."

The success of this remark astonished him. Without waiting to find out any more about it, the Assyrians hurried home and put ashes on their heads. Nineveh repented like a child of its sins; in an orgy of humility the city gave up its business, and dressed itself in sackcloth. The king, even, left his throne, and sat down in some ashes.

Jonah was vexed. This, also, was not what he had expected. He had looked for a wind of fury, for stones, and curses, and a final effect of glory. And when he learned that because of its repentance Nineveh was to be spared, his courage gave way in a flood of disappointment.

"I knew it," he said bitterly to God; "I knew You'd never do it."

And with an angry countenance he retired to an open field on the east side of the city, to see what would happen. His heart was very sore.

"Where is my glory now?" he thought.

Then God, who was anxiously watching, spoke to Jonah from the sky. "Why are you angry?" said the Holy One. "Have I done you a wrong?"

Jonah replied, sighing, "Who will ever believe me now, Lord?"

And for the rest of the day he maintained a silence, full of reproach.

Then because the sun was very hot, and because where Jonah was sitting there was no shade of any sort, God made a vine grow up, overnight, to shelter Jonah.

"There," said God, "there is a vine for you. Rest awhile and see."

That day Jonah sat in comfort beneath his shelter. The wind was in the west, full of agreeable odors; at noon a farmer brought him meal, salt, and oil; he ate, was refreshed, and dozed beneath his vine. The sun went down over the desert; and the evening star grew brighter in the sky, which shone with a peaceful light. The dews descended; and Jonah, wrapped in his cloak, dreamed of home.

But in the morning worms had eaten the leaves of the vine; gorged and comfortable, they regarded Jonah from the ground with pious looks. As the day progressed, the sun beat down upon him without pity, a strong wind blew up from the east, out of the desert, and the prophet grew faint with misery. Too hot even to sweat, he nevertheless refused to move.

"No," he said, "I shall sit here."

An obstinate rage kept him out in the sun, although he half expected to die of it. "Well," he said to himself, "what if I do?"

It seemed to him that he had nothing more to live for.

Then God said to Jonah, "Do you do well to be angry, My son?"

Jonah did not wish to reply. But he was sure of one thing: that he had every right to be angry. "Why did You wither my vine, Lord?" he asked bitterly. "Was that also necessary?"

God, looking down on His prophet, smiled sadly. "What is a vine?" He said gently. "Was it your vine, Jonah? You neither planted it nor cared for it. It came up in a night, and it perished in a night. And now you think I should have spared the vine for your sake. Yes . . . but what of Nineveh, that great city, where there are so many people who cannot discern between their right hand and their left hand? Shall I not spare them, too, for My sake, Jonah?"

Jonah rose wearily to his feet. "Well," he said, "I may as well go home again."

And with bowed head he passed through the city, and out of the western gate. In the streets the citizens made way for him with pious murmurs and anxious looks, but Jonah did not notice them. All his courage was gone, his pride, his hope of glory, all gone down in the dust of God's mercy to others, to all but him. To him alone God had been merciless and exacting. One by one the warm hopes of the youth, the ardors of the man, had been denied him; peace, love, pride, everything had been taken from him. What was there left? Only the desert, stony as life itself . . . only the empty heart, the deliberate mind, the bare and patient spirit. Well, Jonah . . . what a fool to think of anything else. Glory . . . yes, but the glory is God's, not yours.

But he had not learned even that. He was not a good prophet. The flowers of his hope, the bitter blossoms of his grief, sprang up everywhere, where there should have been only waste brown earth. No, he was not a prophet; he was a man, like anybody else, whose love had been false, whose God had been unkind.

And as he trudged dejectedly along, his heart, bare now of pride, filled with loneliness and longing. He thought of Judith, of the happiness that would never be his, and he wept.

High among the clouds, God turned sadly to Moses. "You Jews," He said wearily, "you do not understand beauty. With you it is either glory or despair."

And with a sigh He looked westward to the blue Aegean. Warm and gold the sunlight lay over Greece.

SUGGESTED READINGS

Gaster, Theodor H. *Myth, Legend, and Custom in the Old Testament*, pp. 652–56, "Jonah." New York: Harper & Row, 1969.

Herschel, Abraham J. *The Prophets*, Vol. 2. Pp. 59–78, "The Meaning and Mystery of Wrath." New York: Harper & Row, Harper Torchbooks, 1971.

Neil, William. "Jonah, Book of." In *The Interpreter's Dictionary of the Bible*, Vol. 2, edited by George A. Buttrick, pp. 964–67. Nashville, Tenn.: Abingdon Press, 1962.

Murphy, Roland E. "The Book of Jonah." In *The Interpreter's One-Volume Commentary on the Bible*, edited by Charles M. Laymon, pp. 480–82. Nashville, Tenn.: Abingdon Press, 1971.

Robinson, D. W. B., "Jonah: Introduction." In *The New Bible Commentary*, edited by D. Guthrie. London: Inter-Varsity Press, 1970.

Ryken, Leland. *The Literature of the Bible*, pp. 265–68, "Biblical Satire." Grand Rapids, Mich.: Zondervan Corp., 1974.

Smart, James D. "Jonah: Introduction." In *The Interpreter's Bible*, Vol. 6, edited by George A. Buttrick, pp. 871–75. Nashville, Tenn.: Abingdon Press, 1956.

QUESTIONS FOR DISCUSSION AND WRITING

1. Is the story of Jonah at once more sophisticated and more profound than either Esther or Ruth? Explain your answer.
2. Discuss the part played by each character in the story of Jonah. Explain how each contributes to the meaning or theme.
3. According to Mary Ellen Chase, what common purpose can be found in the Books of Ruth and Jonah?
4. Why does Mary Ellen Chase consider Jonah an ironic and somewhat humorous narrative?
5. What elements in the story of Jonah make it difficult to accept the narrative as historically factual?
6. Interpreted allegorically, what can the story mean? (For example: Jonah is Israel, etc.)
7. Compare the "spirit" of this book with that of the Book of Esther.
8. Can you see anything in the poem in Chapter 2 to support the opinion of some critics that it was written about someone who almost drowned and perhaps inserted here by the author or by a later editor?
9. Compare God as he is depicted in the Book of Jonah with God as depicted in the Book of Joshua.
10. Compare the character of Jonah as described in Robert Nathan's "The Testing of Jonah" with the character of Jonah depicted in the biblical book.
11. What picture of God do we get from Nathan? What portrayal of Moses?
12. What light, if any, does Nathan's re-creation of the story of Jonah shed on the Old Testament story of Jonah?
13. Compare the God of Jonah with the God of the prophet Amos.
14. Argue that the Book of Jonah expresses in a nutshell the best of the Old Testament religion.

INDEX

A 7
B 8
C 9
D 0
E 1
F 2
G 3
H 4
I 5
J 6